Multilateralism and
U.S. Foreign Policy

**CENTER ON
INTERNATIONAL
COOPERATION**

Studies in Multilateralism

MULTILATERALISM AND U.S. FOREIGN POLICY

Ambivalent Engagement

edited by
Stewart Patrick
Shepard Forman

LYNNE
RIENNER
PUBLISHERS

BOULDER
LONDON

Published in the United States of America in 2002 by
Lynne Rienner Publishers, Inc.
1800 30th Street, Boulder, Colorado 80301
www.rienner.com

and in the United Kingdom by
Lynne Rienner Publishers, Inc.
3 Henrietta Street, Covent Garden, London WC2E 8LU

Library of Congress Cataloging-in-Publication Data
Multilateralism and U.S. foreign policy : ambivalent engagement /
edited by Stewart Patrick and Shepard Forman.
    (Center on International Cooperation studies in multilateralism)
    Includes bibliographical references and index.
    ISBN 1-58826-042-9 (alk. paper)
    ISBN 1-58826-018-6 (pbk. : alk. paper)
    1. United States—Foreign relations—Philosophy. 2. United States—
Foreign relations—1989–   3. International cooperation. I. Title:
Multilateralism and U.S. foreign policy. II. Patrick, Stewart.
III. Forman, Shepard, 1938–   IV. Series.
E183.7 .M85 2001
327.73—dc21   2001048120

British Cataloguing in Publication Data
A Cataloguing in Publication record for this book
is available from the British Library.

Printed and bound in the United States of America

The paper used in this publication meets the requirements
of the American National Standard for Permanence of
Paper for Printed Library Materials Z39.48-1984.

5 4 3 2 1

Contents

v

Part 4: The Future of Multilateral Cooperation

Acknowledgments

THIS BOOK IS THE OUTCOME OF SUSTAINED COLLABORATION AMONG TWENTY individuals over the course of eighteen months. The volume testifies, in its own way, to the potential rewards of "multilateral" cooperation. As editors, we consider ourselves fortunate to have worked closely with such affable, dedicated, and thoughtful colleagues. Acting as a team, they helped create a final product that exceeds the sum of its parts.

Throughout the project, we benefited from the wisdom and counsel of our policy advisory board, including John Brademas, Colin Campbell, Richard N. Haass, Lee Hamilton, Rita Hauser, Mahnaz Ispahani, Henry Kaufman, Abraham F. Lowenthal, William Luers, Jessica Mathews, Donald F. McHenry, Joseph S. Nye, Anne-Marie Slaughter, Franklin A. Thomas, Paul A. Volcker, and Richard S. Williamson. We are also grateful for the candid and constructive comments offered by participants at our November 2000 conference on multilateralism and U.S. foreign policy.

We owe particular thanks to our colleagues at the Center on International Cooperation: Barnett Rubin, the center's director of studies, who helped us to refine our conceptual framework and offered valuable advice on particular chapters; Linda Long, our administrative assistant, who managed many of the project's logistical and financial components; and Charles Graybow, a graduate assistant, who provided research assistance and editorial skills.

This book would not have been possible without generous support from the Rockefeller Brothers Fund for the center's project on multilateralism and U.S. foreign policy. We thank Colin Campbell, former president of the fund, and his successor, Stephen Heintz, for finding merit in this initiative. We are grateful to Priscilla Lewis, assistant to the president and director of communications at Rockefeller Brothers, for her involvement and advice. In addition, we thank the Ford Foundation and the John D. and Catherine T. MacArthur Foundation for their continuing core support for the activities of the Center on International Cooperation.

Finally, we mourn the loss of our colleague Harold K. (Jake) Jacobson, a pioneer in the study of international cooperation and a warm friend. We will miss him.

—*Stewart Patrick*
—*Shepard Forman*

PART 1

SETTING THE CONTEXT

1

Multilateralism and Its Discontents: The Causes and Consequences of U.S. Ambivalence

Stewart Patrick

THE HORRIFIC TERRORIST ATTACKS ON THE UNITED STATES OF SEPTEMBER 11, 2001, brought home to all Americans the startling capacity of transnational forces to influence U.S. national security. Groping for historical analogies of sufficient magnitude, many commentators invoked the memory of Pearl Harbor. The analogy reflected a widespread belief that—as after December 1941—neither U.S. foreign policy nor American society would ever be the same. It is too early to predict the implications of these terrible events for the country's global role, or to declare with any certainty that they portend a dramatic change in the nature of world politics. But the attacks did make two things abundantly clear: The United States is vulnerable to international threats, and sustained multilateral cooperation will be essential in confronting these dangers.

Both U.S. policymakers and the public understand that the nation is not immune from global developments. It can no more retreat from the world today than it could sixty years ago. But U.S. engagement can take various forms, and the manner in which the United States responds to the challenges and opportunities of global integration will determine its success in shaping a world consistent with U.S. interests and values.

For the past decade, policymakers and pundits have debated the appropriate role of the United States in a single-superpower world and the best means to advance U.S. objectives within it. Setting aside the implausible option of isolationism,[1] battle lines have been drawn between two contending visions of internationalism, divided on the value and wisdom of multilateral cooperation. As generally framed, the debate has been about whether the United States should act "alone or with others."[2]

Advocates of multilateralism have recommended greater reliance on international rules and frameworks of cooperation, perceiving these as essential to address and manage growing transnational problems, to spread the burdens of leadership, and to win global legitimacy for U.S. purposes. They have counseled the United States to eschew the short-term gains of

1

independent action and to pursue its goals with others.[3] Those more skeptical of multilateral cooperation have called on the U.S. government to defend unfettered freedom of action abroad and untrammeled sovereign rights at home. In the latter view the United States should exercise its largely unchallenged power to advance its interests, unencumbered by global rules, institutional entanglements, or foreign partners. In its most missionary guise, this perspective recommends a "benevolent American hegemony" as the basis of world order.[4]

To depict the alternatives before the United States so starkly, however, poses a false choice and obscures the real issue. As this book makes clear, few of today's foreign policy challenges are really amenable to unilateral action—to truly "going it alone." In most instances, cooperating with other countries and with international institutions is less an option than a necessity. Typically, the choice is not between unilateralism and multilateralism but among variants of the latter. The task for U.S. policymakers is to design strategies that maximize the benefits and opportunities of acting with others while minimizing the costs and constraints.

Retreat from Multilateralism?

This book explores the causes and consequences of U.S ambivalence toward multilateral cooperation. It is motivated by a puzzling disjunction between global trends and U.S. foreign policy. Since the end of the Cold War, the principles of democracy and the market have won new adherents worldwide. Meanwhile, the deepening of global interdependence has bred multiple transnational problems that no one country can resolve on its own, from humanitarian catastrophes to financial instability, from environmental degradation to terrorism and weapons of mass destruction. Given the spread of liberal principles and the rise of a new global agenda, multilateralism would seem to offer the obvious way to advance U.S. national interests, pursue common objectives, and exercise U.S leadership. Yet, the United States has been deeply ambivalent about multilateral engagement and highly selective in assuming new international commitments.

One manifestation of this attitude during the 1990s was the country's shrinking budget for international affairs. Despite an economic boom of unprecedented length, by the year 2000 U.S. spending on foreign affairs had shrunk to just over 1 percent of the federal budget—down from 4 percent in 1960 (and one-sixteenth what the country spends today on national defense). Spending on foreign aid, already the lowest per capita among advanced industrialized countries, has fallen to its lowest budgetary percentage in decades. These cuts have weakened the United States' capacity for multilateral diplomacy and may force unpalatable trade-offs in U.S. foreign policy.[5]

The United States' ambivalence, however, has not been expressed purely in fiscal terms. On a number of prominent occasions in recent years, the United States has opted out of multilateral arrangements or insisted on acting alone to address global problems. At times, it has demanded exemptions from proposed international regimes, declined to ratify or implement agreements widely supported by the world community, or retreated from formal multilateral obligations.[6] As the chapters of this book demonstrate, unease with multilateralism has shaped U.S. policy on matters ranging from the use of force to peacekeeping, nonproliferation, arms control, the United Nations, sanctions, the International Criminal Court, human rights, international trade, and the global environment.

To begin with, the United States has occasionally engaged in armed military action without authorization from the Security Council of the United Nations (UN). This pattern departs from the precedent of the Gulf War, when Washington asked the UN to authorize the coalition that ultimately ousted Iraqi forces from Kuwait. By the late 1990s, Washington was sometimes impatient with the constraints of multilateral diplomacy. For example, it did not await Security Council approval prior to bombing Iraq (with Britain) 1998.[7] Nor did Washington seek Security Council authorization for the campaign by the North Atlantic Treaty Organization (NATO) to dislodge Serb forces from the province of Kosovo in spring 1999. Although many justified the latter action, persuasively, as a moral imperative, others feared that it might set a precedent for other, less worthy, great power interventions.

Meanwhile, the United States retreated significantly from its initial post–Cold War willingness to support multidimensional UN peace operations. After failures in Somalia and Bosnia-Herzegovina, Washington placed stringent restrictions on authorizing and participating in these missions.[8] When the United States began to reenter the peacekeeping fray at the turn of the century, it did so hesitantly and selectively, intervening in Europe through NATO (rather than the UN) but declining to devote troops or significant support to UN peace efforts in Africa.[9]

In the field of peace and security more broadly, the past decade provided evidence of U.S. skepticism toward multilateral nonproliferation and arms control efforts, coupled with a determination to address the threat of weapons of mass destruction (WMD) independently, if necessary. During the 1990s, the U.S. Senate stalled, diluted, or defeated several multilateral initiatives aimed at the WMD threat.[10] For example, the Senate ratified the Chemical Weapons Convention (CWC) in 1997, but only after inserting problematic exemptions that experts contended threatened its full implementation.[11] More dramatically, in October 1999 the Senate rejected the Comprehensive Test Ban Treaty (CTBT), overriding warnings from close U.S. allies that this step would grievously weaken global nonproliferation norms.[12] By summer 2001, there were indications that the Bush administration was trying to kill the test ban treaty altogether.[13]

By 1999, meanwhile, both major U.S. political parties had embraced the goal of a functioning national missile defense (NMD) system, despite the concerns of both allies and rivals that it would violate the 1972 Anti-Ballistic Missile (ABM) Treaty, undermine extended deterrence, weaken global strategic stability, and set off a nuclear arms race.[14] In spring 2001, President George W. Bush reaffirmed NMD as a top foreign policy goal and authorized intensive consultations to persuade allies, as well as China and Russia, of U.S. resolve.[15] Although he hoped to secure Moscow's agreement to any modification of the ABM Treaty, Bush described it as a Cold War "relic" and signaled his intent to withdraw from it "within months" in the absence of progress with the Russians.[16]

More fundamentally, the *New York Times* reported that the Bush administration had begun a "far-reaching [internal] debate over whether the United States should simply abandon the business of negotiating strategic arms treaties."[17] This skepticism extended to other unconventional threats. In July 2001, the Bush administration scuttled international efforts to add a long-sought verification protocol to the 1972 Biological Weapon Convention, judging the draft text accepted by all other parties (including Russia, China, and Iran) to be so "fatally flawed" that it could not serve as the basis for further negotiations.[18]

U.S. wariness toward multilateral arms control and nonproliferation efforts has not been limited to WMD threats. In June 1997, the Clinton administration declined to join the vast majority of the world's countries in signing the Ottawa Convention banning the production, trade, and use of antipersonnel land mines.[19] More recently, in July 2001, the Bush administration stood alone in objecting to a proposed draft UN convention to reduce the illicit trafficking in small arms and light weapons, insisting that its provisions be diluted.[20]

U.S. ambivalence toward multilateral engagement was also manifest in the country's declining financial contributions to international institutions during the 1990s. By 1997, the United States was in arrears to most global organizations, most notably the UN.[21] Washington, one commentator wrote, had "willfully marginalized and bankrupted" an organization that "is now more central than ever to America's global interests," making the UN a scapegoat for shortcomings resulting partly from U.S. parsimony.[22]

Meanwhile, many foreign governments have chafed under the U.S. policy of certifying their performance in arenas like human rights, technology transfers, antiterrorism, and narcotics interdiction—and particularly the heavy reliance on unilateral sanctions to punish countries that fail to meet U.S. standards.[23] Most controversial has been the use of extraterritorial sanctions, such as the Iran-Libya Sanctions Act and the Helms-Burton Law regarding Cuba, which penalize foreign companies and individuals doing business with what Washington considers pariah states. "This is bullying,"

Canadian Foreign Minister Lloyd Axworthy declared of Helms-Burton. "But in America you call it 'global leadership.'"[24]

As the world's leading status quo power, the United States presumably has a fundamental interest in the development of the international rule of law. Yet it has often seemed skittish about committing itself to proposed international legal regimes. A case in point has been U.S. policy toward the International Criminal Court (ICC), intended to prosecute war crimes, crimes against humanity, and genocide.[25] Although President Bill Clinton signed the Rome Statute of the ICC shortly before leaving office, prospects for ratification remain dim under George W. Bush. Wariness toward international legal regimes is also apparent in the human rights field. The United States and Somalia, for instance, remain the only countries that have not ratified the Convention on the Rights of the Child (1989). Likewise, the United States is the only advanced industrialized democracy that has not ratified the Convention on the Elimination of Discrimination Against Women (CEDAW).

During the early 1990s Washington guided a series of historic achievements in multilateral trade liberalization: the negotiation of the North American Free Trade Agreement (NAFTA), the completion of the Uruguay Round of the General Agreement on Tariffs and Trade (GATT), the formation of the World Trade Organization (WTO), and the creation of the Asia-Pacific Economic Cooperation (APEC) forum. Yet even during this period, U.S. commitment to open trade coexisted uneasily with the pursuit of "aggressive unilateralism" to secure market concessions. Moreover, in November 1997 Congress declined to renew presidential authority to negotiate multilateral trade agreements on a "fast-track" basis.[26] More broadly, U.S. support for trade liberalization has been challenged by a growing backlash against globalization spearheaded by labor and environmental groups. In November 1999, the Seattle summit of the WTO collapsed amid disagreement between the United States and developing countries about whether to incorporate labor and environmental standards in the global trade regime.[27]

Finally, the United States has sometimes been reluctant to enter regimes and conventions to govern and protect the global commons. Most significantly, the United States has failed to reach agreement with foreign partners on a common approach to the potentially catastrophic challenge of global warming. Although President Clinton signed the Kyoto Protocol on climate change in 1998, the Senate remains staunchly opposed to its ratification. In March 2001, the Bush administration angered allies by announcing that it had "no interest" in proceeding with the protocol and was exploring ways to "unsign" the treaty, while offering no alternative ideas about how to confront climate change.[28] Judging the Kyoto Protocol to be "fatally flawed," the administration stood on the sidelines four months later as 178 signatories hammered out a compromise agreement to reduce greenhouse gases.[29]

Taken together, the preceding examples suggest significant U.S. reluctance to embrace multilateral engagement. Such developments have occasionally led the United States' friends abroad to wonder, in the words of UN Secretary General Kofi Annan: "Is Washington's will to lead diminishing even as many around the world look to it for leadership? Is it no longer convinced of the myriad benefits to be had from multilateral cooperation?"[30]

What accounts for U.S. ambivalence toward multilateral cooperation? What costs or benefits might it have for U.S. national interests and international institutions? Hoping to answer these questions, the Center on International Cooperation at New York University in January 2000 assembled a study group to examine the tensions between multilateralism and unilateralism in U.S. global engagement. We asked participants to analyze ten issue areas in which the United States had recently exhibited ambivalent multilateralism:

- The use of force
- Peacekeeping
- Nuclear weapons
- Chemical weapons
- The UN
- Extraterritorial sanctions
- The ICC
- Human rights
- International trade and monetary relations
- Global warming

In each case we asked the authors to describe U.S. ambivalence, examine the causes of U.S. decisions to opt out or act alone, evaluate the consequences for U.S. national interests and international institutions, and offer concise recommendations for U.S. foreign policy.

Simultaneously, we asked other members of the study group to examine five crosscutting dynamics that might shed light on the United States' selective and ambivalent approach to multilateral cooperation. These included (1) the frequent clash between domestic and international conceptions of political legitimacy; (2) the changing domestic context in which U.S. foreign policy is formulated; (3) patterns of U.S. public opinion on multilateral cooperation; (4) the place of multilateralism in U.S. "grand strategy"; and (5) the reactions of other countries to perceived U.S. "unilateralism." These thematic essays, included as Chapters 2–6 of this book, provide a lens through which to interpret the issue area investigations, which are covered in Chapters 7–16. The final chapter places the book's findings in the context of an emerging "international public sector," arguing that multilateralism is increasingly a matter of necessity for the United States.

This introductory chapter begins by discussing the historical sources of U.S. misgivings about multilateral cooperation. It then describes how several recent developments, at both the international and domestic levels, have brought this latent ambivalence closer to the surface. It subsequently catalogues some of the costs of perceived U.S. unilateralism. It closes by offering a brief overview of the thematic and case study chapters that follow.

The Roots of U.S. Ambivalence

The United States has never been very comfortable with the constraints and obligations of multilateralism. Indeed, a hallmark of U.S. foreign relations is that the nation has been the world's leading champion of multilateral cooperation and, paradoxically, one of the greatest impediments to such cooperation.[31] No other nation has done so much to create international institutions, yet few have been so ambivalent about multilateralism, so well positioned to obstruct it, or so tempted to act unilaterally. This ambivalence reflects three features of the American experience: the nation's singular political culture, its domestic institutional structure, and its global dominance.

Exceptionalism: There's No Place Like Home

American "exceptionalism" refers to a pervasive faith in the uniqueness, immutability, and superiority of the country's founding liberal principles, accompanied by a conviction that the United States has a special destiny among nations. The founders saw the country as a new form of political community, dedicated to the Enlightenment principles of the rule of law, private property, representative government, freedom of speech and religion, and commercial liberty. This creed is so taken for granted that it is now synonymous with "the American way of life."[32]

All countries are to some degree unique. But the American creed also presents the United States as *exemplary*—that is, a beacon for other nations (indeed, the validity of the country's liberal principles derives from their presumed universality).[33] This sense of national mission has long influenced U.S. foreign policy goals and the style of U.S. global engagement.[34] Yet exceptionalism pulls in two directions, encouraging both a desire to "go it with others" and an urge to "go it alone." On the one hand, it inspires a crusading zeal to recast international society in the United States' domestic image. By sponsoring and leading multilateral institutions, the nation might transform an anarchic, conflict-prone world into an open, universal community under law, in which countries could pursue common security, prosperity, and welfare.[35] On the other hand, exceptionalism also arouses a countervailing determination to preserve the unique values and institutions of the United States from corruption or dilution by foreign contact and a vigilance to defend U.S. national interests, sovereignty, and freedom of action against infringement by global rules and supranational bodies.[36] The United States remains a model for humanity in this view, but it must limit its global responsibilities and safeguard its internal and external freedoms.

The predilection to "go it alone" was reinforced by the nation's formative decades, as a young republic distant from major world powers. This fortuitous circumstance permitted it to follow the counsel of George Washington, in his farewell address, to "steer clear of permanent alliances with any part of the foreign world." Nineteenth-century U.S. foreign policy was guided by unilateralism, unconstrained by foreign countries or international institutions.[37]

By 1900 the United States had become a great power. Less preoccupied with protecting liberty at home, U.S. leaders now aspired to export it abroad. As foreign policy became a means to *define,* rather than simply defend, the nation, the United States evolved, as Walter MacDougal writes, from a "promised land" to a "crusader state."[38] But what form would this internationalism take? At pivotal moments, particularly after the two world wars, U.S. policymakers turned to multilateral institutions as a blueprint for world order.[39] At the same time, U.S. multilateralism would be qualified and limited by the country's domestic institutions and overwhelming power.

An Invitation to Struggle: The Separation of Powers

In contrast to parliamentary democracies, in which governing coalitions control the legislature, the U.S. Constitution establishes the executive and legislature as coequal branches of government, jointly controlling foreign policy. This shared mandate makes it harder to assume multilateral obligations. Because the ratification of treaties requires the concurrence of two-thirds of the Senate, for instance, political minorities may block U.S. participation in proposed conventions. The effect is to narrow the scope of agreements acceptable at both domestic and international levels, particularly when different parties control the presidency and Congress. Given U.S. power, major executive-legislative disagreements often reverberate globally.[40]

That this separation of powers could complicate U.S. multilateralism became clear in the fate of the League of Nations. During World War I, President Woodrow Wilson articulated a comprehensive vision of an open postwar world order based on international law, collective security, national self-determination, and free trade.[41] Ultimately, the Republican-controlled Senate refused to support U.S. participation in the League of Nations on Wilson's terms. The fractious domestic debates during 1918–1919 were less between isolationism and internationalism than about how to reconcile the latter with U.S. constitutional traditions, national sovereignty, and freedom of action.

A generation later, World War II gave U.S. liberal internationalists a second chance to win domestic support for multilateral engagement.[42] Haunted by the interwar failures of collective security and the fragmentation of the world economy, the administrations of Franklin D. Roosevelt and Harry S. Truman sponsored an array of international institutions to stabilize global political and economic relations, most notably the United Nations Organization and the Bretton Woods institutions. Multilateral frameworks presumed a coincidence between national and world interests, alleviating any discomfort Americans might feel in exercising their awesome power and assuming global responsibilities. And unlike the situation in 1918–1919, the executive branch was able to forge bipartisan consensus in Congress on behalf of postwar multilateralism.

This commitment to multilateralism was altered—but not abandoned— by the onset of the Cold War during the late 1940s. Indeed, the strategic threat posed by the Soviet Union reinforced bipartisan support for multilateral institutions, since the latter might help forge an anticommunist coalition. As the hoped-for "one world" fractured into two, Washington pursued a policy of enlightened self-interest, consolidating and nurturing a narrower, "free world" community within consensual institutions like NATO and GATT, in which countries could collaborate on common purposes, express national preferences, and obtain satisfaction.[43]

U.S. Hegemony and the Limits of U.S. Multilateralism

Tremendous power, however, also provided the United States with unmatched capacities, incentives, and opportunities to opt out or act alone. Even during the bipolar conflict, it never renounced the freedom to act in its narrow self-interest, and it sometimes yielded to unilateral temptations. Such proclivities were especially apparent during the Reagan administration, which expressed such antipathy toward international treaties like the Law of the Sea and international organizations like the United Nations Educational, Scientific, and Cultural Organization (UNESCO) that observers at the time discerned a "crisis of multilateralism."[44]

On one level, U.S. skepticism about international cooperation is unsurprising. Great powers rarely make great multilateralists.[45] Multilateralism implies a relationship based on rules rather than power, with countries agreeing that behavior in a certain sphere (e.g., trade) should be governed by shared principles, norms, and rules (such as most favored nation treatment), regardless of individual interests, capabilities, or circumstances.[46] Moreover, multilateralism implies costs as well as benefits, and a globally dominant power should be particularly sensitive to these trade-offs. Multilateral principles of nondiscrimination, reciprocity, and self-restraint are particularly attractive to the weak, since such principles provide the latter with diplomatic leverage lacking in conventional bilateral negotiations and serve to "domesticate" the strong.[47]

By contrast, a dominant power like the United States is apt to find multilateral cooperation constraining. Possessing extensive policy options—including unilateralism, bilateral arrangements, or temporary coalitions—it can often afford (at least in the short term) to bypass consultations, enforce its will, or absorb the costs of acting alone. Policymakers in Washington have also been sensitive to the potential pathologies of multilateral institutions, which are vulnerable to "free riding" (on public goods that the United States may provide) and "buck passing" (since responsibility tends to be diffused). Likewise, the premium placed on consensus can slow decisions, dilute objectives, constrain instruments, and culminate in policies of the lowest common denominator. Finally, critics fear that multilateralism may entangle the United States in foreign adventures on behalf of global agendas or subordinate its sovereignty to structures of "global governance."

Critics of multilateralism have tended to focus on its potential costs while overlooking the trade-offs and limitations inherent in acting alone. They often assume that the United States possesses unlimited maneuverability and that unilateralism will necessarily be effective. These assumptions are rarely warranted. Multilateralism often *expands* rather than limits U.S. options,[48] so that the United States can achieve objectives it is unable or disinclined to pursue alone. Global regimes can provide mechanisms to consult, resolve differences, solve problems, share burdens and risks, coordinate action, and monitor and enforce commitments. These functional benefits are critical in addressing today's transnational challenges, such as the spread of weapons of mass destruction and the growth of global terrorist networks like al Qaeda, headed by Osama bin Laden.

Multilateralism can also increase the legitimacy of U.S. leadership, improving prospects for voluntary cooperation by weaker countries, as Washington discovered during the Gulf War.[49] The legitimacy benefits of multilateralism are partly a function of one's timeframe. If the United States fears that acting alone will set dangerous precedents or generate resistance down the road, it may be wiser to accept modest multilateral constraints on maneuvering room or sovereign prerogatives today in order to "lock in" a set of rules that will continue to serve its interests even after its current dominance fades.[50] These long-term benefits help explain why, despite its ambivalence, the United States made a general commitment to multilateralism after 1945.

U.S. Multilateralism Today: Ambivalent—and Selective

If U.S. ambivalence toward multilateral cooperation is nothing new, has it grown in recent years? Here the evidence is mixed. To some degree,

Figure 1.1   Multilateral Treaties in Force for the United States (by decade)

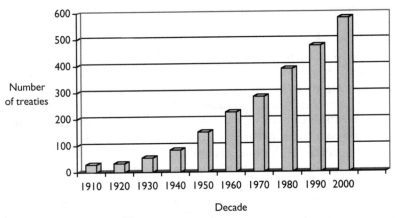

Source: U.S. Department of State
Note: The graph shows the number of multilateral treaties in force for the United States as of December 31 of the year indicated. Note that the State Department Website, *www.state.gov,* provides data only for treaties that are currently in force for the United States. While the notes accompanying each treaty entry in the State Department listing provide some evidence of earlier treaties that are no longer in force, complete data on defunct treaty commitments are not available. Therefore, although the trend toward multilateral commitments remains, the graph likely undercounts the number of treaties in force in earlier decades. Graphic compiled by Charles Graybow.

**Figure 1.2   U.S. Ratification of Multilateral Treaties 1900–2000
(number of treaties ratified, five-year increments)**

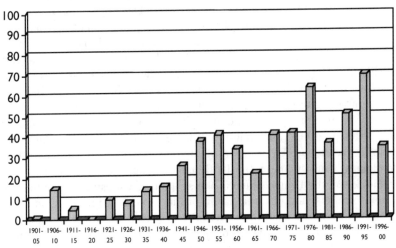

Source: U.S. Department of State
Note: As in Figure 1.1, this figure includes only treaties still in force, and thus may undercount slightly the ratification of multilateral treaties in earlier decades. Graphic compiled by Charles Graybow.

perceptions of "rising" U.S. unilateralism are an artifact of dramatic increases in the number of multilateral regimes, organizations, and treaties. Between 1970 and 1997, the number of international treaties more than tripled, and from 1985-1999 alone, the number of international institutions increased by two-thirds.[51] By 2001, the United States was a member of hundreds of intergovernmental multilateral organizations (both universal and regional) and party to hundreds of treaties. (Figure 1.1 depicts the growing number of multilateral treaties in force for the United States during the twentieth century. Figure 1.2 sorts these treaties according to their ratification date.) This thickening web of multilateral "contracts" provides the United States with more opportunities to express its ambivalence, whether or not its actual propensity to act alone has increased.

It would be unfair, moreover, to suggest that the United States has repudiated multilateralism. Since the end of the Cold War, Washington has adapted, created, and expanded a broad array of international regimes, organizations, and partnerships to address important economic, security, and social objectives. During the 1990s, it showed vigorous support for the World Bank and the IMF and championed the transformation of the GATT into the WTO. At the regional level, it moved to stabilize post-Soviet Europe through overlapping multilateral frameworks like the Organization for Security and Cooperation in Europe, the Partnership for Peace, and an expanding NATO. In the Americas, it helped reinvigorate the Organization of American States, negotiated NAFTA, and proposed a Free Trade Area for the Americas. Likewise, it championed Asia-Pacific trade and financial liberalization through APEC and fostered stability through subregional multilateral entities like the Korean Peninsula Energy Development Organization. In Africa, it offered diplomatic support for the Organization of African Unity and sponsored an African Crisis Response Initiative. Finally, the United States has expressed much of its "multilateralism" not through formal entities like the UN and NATO but periodic gatherings like Group of Eight (G-8) summits or ad hoc coalitions like the Contact Group for the Balkans.

At the same time the U.S. commitment to multilateralism has been *selective*. Washington values multilateral institutions for their burden sharing and legitimating functions, but only if these allow it to exercise significant control over the agenda, preserve its margin of maneuver, safeguard U.S. sovereignty, and increase the likelihood of success.[52] Accordingly, the United States often engages in "forum shopping," choosing among the UN, regional entities, and informal coalitions to expand its influence and limit its obligations. As a rule, the United States prefers narrower collectivities that unite "like-minded" market democracies to diverse bodies with universal membership. It also favors institutions that allow it to bring its leverage to bear through mechanisms like veto power and weighted voting (like the Security Council or the World Bank) over egalitarian, one-state one-vote bodies (like the UN General Assembly).

Since 1990, skepticism has increased in the U.S. foreign policy community about the value of multilateralism in the country's global engagement. Indeed, attitudes have shifted dramatically over little more than a decade. In the initial euphoria accompanying the end of the Cold War (and the U.S.-led victory in the Gulf War), President George Bush enunciated his vision of a "new world order" based on principles of collective security, the rule of law, democratic governance, and expanding trade.[53] The Clinton administration, similarly, took office in 1993 committed (at least rhetorically) to "assertive multilateralism." By working with foreign partners and international institutions, explained UN envoy Madeleine Albright, the U.S. could garner material and diplomatic support for its objectives and legitimate its global leadership. Multilateral institutions would also underpin a new, postcontainment U.S. grand strategy: "the enlargement of the world's free community of market democracies."[54]

The Clinton administration soon discovered that multilateralism could be more complicated in practice than in principle. This was particularly true in peace and security matters, where the requirements of consensus and collective decisionmaking might limit U.S. options and block decisive action.[55] Following fiascos in Bosnia-Herzegovina and Somalia, realist critics like Henry Kissinger accused the White House of "trying to submerge the national interest in multilateral ventures."[56] Faced with congressional and public misgivings, Clinton retreated to a pragmatic internationalism, encapsulated in the mantra of "multilateral when we can, unilateral when we must." But this truism elided difficult questions of when it was possible to do the one rather than the other and, if multilateralism were advisable, what form it should take.[57]

By the mid-1990s, the term "multilateralism" had fallen into disrepute, seeming to imply unacceptable constraints on U.S. power and national sovereignty. Senator Robert Dole (Republican-Kansas), the Senate majority leader, complained in 1995 that "international organizations—whether the United Nations, the World Trade Organization, or any others . . . [t]oo often . . . reflect a consensus that opposes American interests or does not reflect American principles and ideals."[58] The time had come, wrote one analyst, to "reject the global buddy system."[59]

More recently, controversy over multilateralism swirled around the 2000 presidential campaign. Condoleezza Rice, an advisor to George W. Bush, chided the Clinton administration for subordinating U.S. foreign policy to "the interests of an illusory international community" and for clinging to "the belief that the support of many states—or even better, of institutions like the United Nations—is essential to the legitimate exercise of power." Republicans understood, she wrote, that "multilateral agreements and institutions should not be ends in themselves," but *means* to secure U.S. interests. In the words of fellow Bush advisor Robert Zoellick, "Every issue need not be dealt with multilaterally."[60] During its first six months in office, the new Bush administration moved to implement this foreign policy philosophy, walking away from a number of proposed international treaties and commitments. Whereas its predecessor had made a blanket commitment to multilateralism, explained State Department director of policy planning Richard Haass, the Bush administration's approach would be "à la carte." Participation would depend on hard-headed, case-by-case assessments of the implications for U.S. national interests.[61]

The initial reaction of the Bush administration to the September 2001 terrorist attacks on New York and Washington appeared to mark an abrupt departure from its early, often unilateral orientation. Confronting a transnational terrorist network with tentacles in several dozen countries, the administration worked diligently to forge the broadest possible international coalition for what was predicted to be a long and arduous anti-terror campaign. It was not clear at the time of this writing whether the multilateral response would remain a temporary expedient, narrowly targeted to confront a discrete threat, or whether the administration would use its coalition strategy as a springboard to pursue multilateral approaches to other global challenges. Although the latter option has much to recommend it, there remain significant structural obstacles to any general U.S. commitment to multilateral cooperation.

Specifically, four broad trends have reinforced longstanding U.S. misgivings about multilateralism. These include the advent of a unipolar world in which the United States has greater room for maneuver; the emergence of a new global agenda and new international actors; the rise of transnational problems that challenge traditional U.S. conceptions of national sovereignty; and shifts in the balance of power that the president and Congress wield over foreign policy.

Don't Fence Me In: Freedom of Action in a Unipolar World

To begin with, the United States confronts a strategic landscape drastically different from the Cold War. During the bipolar struggle, U.S. officials often regarded their choices as tightly constrained by the imperatives of containment. What is striking today is the relative *absence* of constraints on the United States.

The scope and reach of U.S. power is unprecedented. The simultaneous military, economic, monetary, technological, and cultural dominance the nation now enjoys has led French Foreign Minister Hubert Vedrine to label it the world's first "hyperpower." No longer confronting a major adversary and able to secure most traditional objectives either alone or bilaterally, the country has fewer obvious incentives to rely on international institutions, runs fewer risks in opting out of them, and faces more temptations to act alone. In a unipolar world, multilateral bodies are often viewed less as potential sources of national strength than as foreign schemes to enmesh the country in a thickening web of commitments and obligations.[62]

Simultaneously, the scale of U.S. superiority can provide justifications for acting alone. As the ultimate guarantor of world order, the United States is said to have certain "custodial" obligations; it cannot afford to be constrained by rules and institutions. "Given America's responsibilities in the world," Zoellick writes, "it must retain its freedom to act against serious dangers" when collective action is stymied by clashing values or interests.[63] During the late 1990s, the Clinton administration invoked such arguments in its (ultimately vain) efforts to secure U.S. exemptions from treaties establishing a global ban on antipersonnel land mines and an International Criminal Court (ICC). As David Scheffer, the chief U.S. negotiator on the ICC, explained, "the United States has special responsibilities and special exposure to political controversy over our actions." Because it was "called upon to act, sometimes at great risk, far more than any other nation," it required assurances that the new judicial instrument would not be used as a political weapon.[64] Unfortunately, the U.S. role as guarantor is neither codified in international law nor recognized by all countries. Nor is there any global consensus on what constitutes a threat to "world order," nor any clear criteria to distinguish between disinterested policies and more self-interested U.S. behavior.

My Way or the Highway:
Globalization and the New Multilateralism

The dilemma of reconciling the United States' unilateral instincts with multilateral cooperation has been sharpened by accelerating globalization. Whereas the Soviet threat provided a single (if distorting) lens for strategy, U.S. officials today face an unfamiliar and shifting international landscape shaped by transnational forces, new actors, and unfamiliar threats. As transborder flows of capital, goods, services, information, and people grow in magnitude and accelerate in velocity, the world confronts new challenges— economic integration, environmental degradation, international crime, human rights violations, population growth and migration, weapons proliferation, and global epidemics—that no single country, even one as powerful as the United States, can manage alone.

Globalization has also blurred the boundary between foreign and domestic, challenging traditional conceptions of national interest and stretching the capacities of national governments. What were once national issues, such as economic prosperity, public health, law enforcement, and environmental regulation, increasingly take on characteristics of international public goods that require coordination and harmonization for their provision. Where the issues pertain to technical or functional tasks, multilateral norms, standards and decisionmaking procedures may be relatively uncontroversial. They become increasingly contentious when they appear to collide with (or supersede) U.S. domestic law or to impinge on matters of U.S. national security.

As the nature and scope of multilateral cooperation evolves and power diffuses to nongovernment actors, the United States has found it harder to control the agenda and outcome of international negotiations or to exercise a free hand in global institutions. The spread of conference diplomacy, coupled with the trend toward democratization, has raised expectations that transnational problems ought to be addressed and negotiated in open, egalitarian forums with universal membership. But the United States often feels uneasy in such settings, where its dominance counts for less and where its delegations often find themselves in a minority position. These dynamics were on display at the 1998 conference on the ICC in Rome. According to Ruth Wedgwood, the U.S. failure there "may tell us some disturbing things about America's current position in the world and the state of our multilateral diplomacy." Washington will need to adapt to these new realities, for "the style of diplomacy and conference governance seen in Rome is likely to become more rather than less common."[65]

As countries become more interconnected and permeable, multilateral cooperation increasingly transcends conventional diplomatic negotiations among sovereign countries. One new dimension is the growth of informal networks of public officials from different countries.[66] Even more significant is the surging influence of private actors, including multinational corporations, nongovernmental organizations (NGOs), and issue advocacy networks. Transnational NGOs, in particular, have exploited the Internet and other communications technologies to bypass national gatekeepers and intergovernmental channels, raise the salience of certain global problems, mobilize broad coalitions, shape the agenda of multilateral negotiations, and promote the norms and standards of new international regimes. The Ottawa Convention on banning antipersonnel land mines, perhaps the most celebrated example of NGO influence, has been hailed as a defining moment in the democratization of international law making.[67] To their champions NGOs are organic expressions of "global civil society." But many U.S. critics see them as unelected interest groups encroaching on the prerogatives of national governments by attempting to realize on the global stage what they cannot accomplish domestically.[68]

Don't Tread on Me: U.S. Sovereignty at Bay

Many Americans are understandably anxious that new mechanisms of multilateral cooperation will not be sensitive to U.S. national interests, diplomatic freedom, and constitutional traditions. There is an ironic perceptual gulf on this issue. Abroad, observers often perceive that international organizations are inevitably controlled by the United States or do not matter in the face of overwhelming U.S. power. At home, the dominant sense is that the country rarely gets its way in international institutions and is losing control over the terms of its interdependence with the rest of the world. In addition, many Americans fear that U.S. national sovereignty is beset by international regimes of widening scope and deepening intrusiveness and besieged by unaccountable and undemocratic organs of "global governance."[69]

In most other market democracies, and particularly in Europe, political leaders and publics have come to terms with some gradual erosion of national sovereignty—as well as "pooling" sovereignty for shared benefits. Their counterparts in the United States are more inclined to see sovereignty as a fragile and precious commodity, to insist that it remain inviolate, and to perceive an inverse correlation (or even zero-sum relationship) between its preservation and the capacities of international organizations. These concerns help explain a paradox in U.S. attitudes toward multilateral cooperation: although the United States promotes and conforms to many standards of global behavior (like norms against war crimes), it prefers voluntary participation in flexible arrangements to the binding rules and procedures of formal organizations or conventions (like the ICC), which may be unresponsive to U.S. needs, insufficiently transparent, or incompatible with the country's domestic institutions and laws. These misgivings have some merit. International institutions do suffer from democratic deficits: international bureaucracies take decisions affecting the lives of a nation's citizens without the interposition of national legislatures. Such institutions not only entail binding commitments that narrow policy autonomy but also may open the country to external scrutiny—as in the monitoring and verification provisions of arms control conventions.

Accordingly, the trend toward the gradual "legalization" of multilateral rules is troubling for the United States.[70] Washington has sometimes been surprised by the "bite" of new global entities.[71] In response to perceived incursions on the nation's prerogatives, U.S. officials have sometimes tried to marginalize global agencies or organizations they find hard to control. They generally depict such actions not as a rejection of multilateralism per se but as a "corrective" to alter entities that have gotten off track or assumed inappropriate undertakings.[72]

More broadly, voices from across the U.S. political spectrum have called for a vigorous defense of the country's national sovereignty, constitution, and freedom of action against the encroachments of global norms, multilateral institutions, and international law. In autumn 1999, a largely left-wing coalition of activists took to the streets of Seattle to protest the (allegedly) antidemocratic nature of the WTO, as well as the World Bank and International Monetary Fund (IMF), and the perceived complicity of these organizations in driving down global labor and environmental standards. Some activists sought the abolition of multilateral organizations, others sweeping reform to democratize and incorporate social concerns into global economic regimes.[73]

Many conservatives and libertarians, meanwhile, regard the spread of multilateral regimes into formerly domestic arenas like health, immigration, and the environment as the thin edge of a wider wedge of global govern-ment. These "new sovereigntists" warn the United States not to cede its lawmaking authority to unelected and unaccountable global bureaucrats.[74] According to John Bolton, under-secretary of state for arms control and dis-armament, "the debate over global governance, fought out at the confluence of constitutional theory and foreign policy" is *the* decisive issue facing the United States internationally."[75]

Such sovereignty concerns were at issue when Jesse Helms, then Re-publican chair of the Senate Foreign Relations Committee, spoke before the UN Security Council in January 2000. He cautioned the UN against setting itself up "as the central authority of a new international order of global laws and global governance," warning that "a United Nations that seeks to impose its presumed authority on the American people without their consent begs for confrontation and, I want to be candid, eventual withdrawal."[76]

An alternative view, of course, would be to see U.S. participation in in-ternational organizations and entry into multilateral agreements as an *ex-pression* rather than betrayal of the nation's democratic will. After all, the United States only enters such arrangements after the country's elected rep-resentatives have an opportunity to shape the content of multilateral agree-ments and to decide, after weighing the costs and benefits, whether to sign, ratify, and implement them.

Advice and Consent: The Reassertion of Congressional Power

Finally, U.S. ambivalence toward multilateralism has been strengthened by the post–Cold War activism of Congress in U.S. foreign policy. For several decades after 1945, the White House typically took the lead in shaping U.S. foreign and security policy. Although congressional deference had limits (as the Vietnam War showed), the communist threat constrained legislative ac-tivism. The collapse of the Soviet Union removed a central justification for the "imperial presidency," permitting Congress to reassert its significant prerogatives in foreign affairs and inaugurating a messier pattern of inter-branch leadership in the government. As James Lindsay observes, "The era of undisputed executive preeminence on foreign policy is over."[77]

Today, Congress competes with the White House to control inter-national affairs, exploiting congressional powers of legislation, appropria-tion, confirmation, ratification, oversight, and advocacy to influence the terms of U.S. engagement.[78] This is not inherently a negative development. Indeed, a modicum of healthy tension between government branches can advance the national interest by encouraging open debate about the costs and benefits of multilateral cooperation. The history of the twentieth cen-tury suggests that domestic support for U.S. global commitments can be sustained only if liberal proponents of multilateral engagement are prepared to compromise to win over influential skeptics on Capitol Hill, from Arthur Vandenberg to Jesse Helms.[79]

Still, the deflation of presidential power can complicate U.S. commitment to credible multilateralism. For one thing, it increases the chance that the executive branch will agree to assume international obligations that the legislature either opposes or has no intention of fulfilling. This predicament is likely to be most acute when different parties control the two branches, as was the case for most of the past decade. During the 1990s, Congress used the power of the purse to reduce foreign aid, cut IMF and World Bank funding, withhold UN assessments, and impose budgetary retrenchment and bureaucratic consolidation on the State Department complex. Following the 1994 elections, a prolonged interbranch struggle produced disarray in U.S. foreign policy, including the stalling of a dozen multilateral conventions.[80]

During the Cold War, the United States' foreign partners could take comfort in the bipartisan U.S. consensus on international engagement and the relative orderliness and transparency of policymaking in Washington.[81] Changing strategic and domestic circumstances, however, have cast doubt on the credibility of U.S. commitments to multilateral institutions. To begin with, there is no domestic agreement today about the composition, scope, and ranking of U.S. national interests, the resources needed to pursue them, or the global commitments they warrant. Moreover, the first post–Cold War decade saw a marked erosion of the longstanding bipartisan internationalist consensus in Congress. Many stalwarts of constructive internationalism in both parties were replaced by colleagues preoccupied with domestic concerns or suspicious that global regimes and organizations infringe on U.S. sovereignty, thwart U.S. interests and values, or place unacceptable checks on U.S. options. Foreign policy was increasingly the subject of partisan squabbling and ideological disagreement. In an inversion of the old adage, as Sarah Sewall observes, "partisanship seemed to grow stronger at the water's edge."[82] The politicization of foreign affairs has been reinforced by the growing salience of "inter-mestic" issues, like trade and immigration, which blur the boundary between foreign and domestic policy and tend to divide rather than unite Americans.

Within Congress, moreover, the making of foreign policy has become increasingly decentralized and atomized with the decline in party discipline and the proliferation of committees touching on foreign policy matters.[83] This development allows individual legislators to establish independent foreign policy platforms. This activism is troubling, argues Lee Hamilton, former chair of the House Foreign (now International) Affairs Committee, because members have little incentive and are poorly organized to engage in multilateral diplomacy. It has resulted in "a bias towards unilateralism in foreign policy," making it "harder to manage alliances, institutions, and long-term policies across regions and topics in a highly interconnected and complex world."[84]

During the 1990s, Clinton administation officials often called congressional critics of its multilateral initiatives "isolationists."[85] This was largely a mischaracterization, for internationalists dominate both parties in Congress. Where these internationalists disagree is over how selective U.S. engagement and responsibilities should be and, in particular, whether the United States should rely on and defer to international organizations, accepting some constraints on its sovereignty and freedom of action in return for the benefits of multilateral cooperation. As a broad generalization, Republicans—in Congress, among elites, and in the wider public—tend to be more sensitive to these constraints than Democrats, and thus more prepared to act alone in the national interest.[86] However, attitudes toward multilateralism do not break cleanly along partisan lines. Both parties are often internally divided about its trade-offs. And in certain matters such as trade Republicans are arguably the more "multilateral" party.

Any president hoping to sustain multilateral cooperation must adapt to the new era of congressional assertiveness, seeking to persuade legislators that globalization makes constructive U.S. engagement imperative. He or she will need to articulate a persuasive rationale for multilateralism, be commited to continual consultation with Congress, and mobilize important domestic constituencies behind constructive internationalism. In this vein, broadly speaking, U.S. elites might be divided into four different orientations, according to their support or rejection of multilateralism and unilateralism, as depicted in Figure 1.3. These groups include liberal internationalists, who consistently advocate multilateral approaches; hard-line conservative internationalists, who strongly prefer unilateralism; moderate internationalists, who are open to either strategy depending on the circumstance; and a small minority of isolationists (either conservative or liberal), who reject either form of engagement.

The challenge for proponents of multilateral engagement is to build coalitions across these ideological divides, particularly by uniting liberals and moderates. Prospects for doing so would appear to be good if, as polling data indicate, a solid majority of American elites prefer multilateral responses to global issues and problems.[87]

The Costs of Acting Alone— and the Benefits of Acting with Others

The chapters in this book depict the United States' power position, exceptionalist traditions, and domestic political institutions as important background sources of ambivalence and selectivity toward multilateral engagement. The more proximate causes of specific decisions to act alone or opt out have varied. They have included a U.S. insistence on freedom of action and policy autonomy, particularly in matters of peace and security; a desire

Figure 1.3 Ideology and Elite Attitudes Toward Multilateralism and Unilateralism

Multilateralism?

	Yes	No
Unilateralism? Yes	Moderate Internationalists	Conservative Internationalists
Unilateralism? No	Liberal Internationalists	Isolationists (conservative or liberal)

Source: Drawn from Holsti and Rosenau, "Internationalism: Intact or in Trouble?" pp. 134–137; Holsti, "Public Opinion and U.S. Foreign Policy after the Cold War," pp. 157–159.

to impose U.S. preferences on solutions to global problems; concerns to protect the U.S. role as custodian of global order; fears of losing national sovereignty and subordinating the U.S. constitution to global institutions and international law; misgivings about the effectiveness and reliability of international regimes; and disagreements with foreign partners over burden sharing. Resistance to multilateral engagement has often emanated from Congress, with executive-legislative struggles over global engagement being tinged with partisan politics. Poor presidential leadership has also contributed to hesitant U.S. engagement, with the White House failing to build constituencies on Capitol Hill behind new international commitments, to resolve disagreements among different agencies, or to ensure adequate U.S. preparation for multilateral negotiations.

The geopolitical, cultural, and institutional sources of U.S. ambivalence are unlikely to disappear anytime soon. Nor can we expect the United States to adopt a consistent policy of multilateralism or unilateralism: the former would ignore the occasional need to act alone, while the latter would force the country to confront all global problems on its own. For the foreseeable future, then, U.S. multilateralism will remain both ambivalent and selective. But there is a difference between an ambivalence grounded in a realistic assessment of trade-offs and one based on unwarranted fears and narrow ideologies, and a distinction between informed selectivity on the one hand and capriciousness on the other. The chapters in this book suggest that the United States has sometimes acted alone or opted out of multilateral initiatives to pursue immediate gain or avoid short-term pain, without due consideration of the long-term ramifications for its own national objectives and the sustainability of international institutions.

Uncritical ambivalence and shortsighted selectivity carry costs for U.S. national interests and international cooperation. They may thwart the formulation and pursuit of coherent policies; frustrate the achievement of U.S. objectives in multiple issue areas; sabotage collective responses to transnational problems; undermine the spread of global norms, regimes, and international law; and injure the United States' reputation as an enlightened world leader.

To begin with, a wavering stance toward multilateral engagement can deprive U.S. officials of the ability to formulate coherent, constructive, and effective policies toward particular global challenges. Internally divided about the merits of an ICC, for example, the U.S. government vacillated before ultimately opting out, without proposing a compelling alternative or launching a timely initiative to build support for its preferences. As an outsider, the United States will be unable to ensure the emergence of an accountable and impartial court, while running the risk of a future confrontation with it.

During the 1990s, similarly, the U.S. prodded the UN to take on ambitious peacekeeping mandates while neglecting to provide the world body with adequate political, financial, and military support, ultimately blaming the organization for inevitable failures. Such policies have reinforced domestic skepticism about the capacities of the UN, despite the latter's role in coping with regional threats or internal conflicts that engage U.S. interests and values.

Second, the decision to act alone in one arena may complicate multilateral cooperation in another. During 1998–1999, for example, U.S. air strikes (with Britain) eroded global support for the UN Special Commission for Iraq (UNSCOM), created to inspect and eliminate Iraq's capacity to develop weapons of mass destruction. "The problem," UNSCOM official Scott Ritter explained, "is that we can't demand compliance with Security Council resolutions while simultaneously shunning the Security Council by pursuing a unilateral campaign to remove Saddam from power."[88] Similarly, the unilateral withholding of arrears, with the aim of lowering U.S. assessments and imposing reform on the United Nations, undermined the United States' capacity to exercise leadership and build coalitions within the UN. By dominating U.S.-UN relations, the long financial crisis of the 1990s inhibited constructive cooperation on substantive matters.

Third, given the United States' global dominance, a U.S. decision to stand apart can cripple the ability of a multilateral regime to address urgent challenges. The Kyoto Protocol provides a case in point. Because the U.S. is responsible for more than one-third of greenhouse gas emissions among industrialized countries, its abdication effectively renders that treaty inoperable. The U.S. decision to repudiate the Kyoto treaty (without charting an alternative vision) left the international community adrift and embittered, as foreign partners perceived the United States as shirking its duty to help prevent a looming catastrophe.[89]

Fourth, over the longer term, the decision to opt out of international conventions and regimes like the CTBT, ICC, or CEDAW may slow the spread of robust international norms governing nuclear nonproliferation, prosecution of war crimes, or women's rights. Policymakers have not always borne in mind the real trade-offs inherent in opting out of such agreements. In rejecting the CTBT, for example, the United States may have gained marginal improvements in its ability to ensure the reliability of the U.S. nuclear stockpile, but at the cost of abrogating a long-standing bargain between nuclear and nonnuclear countries that represents the core of the nonproliferation regime. Similarly, by watering down the CWC, the United States may protect military and industrial facilities from unwelcome foreign intrusions. But the cost has been to weaken an inspection regime that serves U.S. security interests, to erode the position of the U.S. on the treaty's governing body, and to weaken prospects for a verification protocol to the Biological Weapons Convention (which will require even more rigorous inspection procedures).[90] U.S. foreign policy and defense officials understandably seek to maximize U.S. national security, but unilateral steps that endanger multilateral cooperation risk undermining it in the long term.

Undercutting Claims of "Benevolent Hegemony"

Finally, perceived unilateralism may undermine the legitimacy of U.S. global leadership and claims to be a benevolent hegemon. During the late 1990s, the Clinton administration referred to the United States as the "indispensable nation," able by virtue of its unmatched power and universal values to "stand taller and see farther" than its partners. This dominance was said to be benign, since it was based not on coercive imposition but on the attraction of U.S. values, commercial products, and popular culture and on the natural congruence between U.S. national interests and the interests of humanity at large.[91]

This vision is understandably beguiling to Americans. But it is a sentiment not universally shared abroad, where some observers regard the United States as too powerful and willing to impose unilateral solutions to suit its narrow national (or internal political) interests.[92] To some degree international resentment of the United States is inevitable, since its tremendous power ensures that it is often seen as coming on too strong, thus alienating its partners, or too weak, thus disappointing them. It is not always evident, however, that foreign critics are prepared to assume the increased burdens that joint management of world order would presumably imply.[93]

But many foreign observers believe that the United States has exacerbated its predicament by claiming the right to define the global interest, pursuing policies without regard to the opinions of those it claims to lead, holding itself above norms and rules binding on other actors, and bypassing relevant regimes or organizations. They question whether it is as prepared to assume the obligations of global leadership as it is to enjoy its privileges. Such criticisms rang out in the voluble global criticism after the U.S. Senate rejected the CTBT in October 1999.[94]

Significantly the nation's allies and partners, not merely its rivals, have sometimes expressed unease with the magnitude of current U.S. domination and the unilateralism they believe it encourages.[95] In the weeks before NATO's 1999 air campaign against Serbia, several European leaders complained about Washington's high-handed tendency "to go it alone." The very "weight [of the Americans] carries them towards hegemonism," French Foreign Minister Vedrine observed, "and the idea they have of their mission is unilateralism. And that is unacceptable."[96] International perceptions of U.S. unilateralism increased after the Bush administration took office in 2001, and appeared to challenge several proposed and existing treaties, institutions, and procedures of international cooperation.[97]

Based on historical precedent, one might expect frustrated countries to try to counterbalance U.S. power. A possible warning sign was the signature in July 2001 of a treaty of cooperation between Russia and China; this strategic partnership is aimed explicitly at creating a "new international order" in which the United States no longer enjoys "unilateral military and security advantages."[98] Nevertheless, the emergence of an enduring, strategic anti-U.S. coalition seems improbable in today's world, which is dominated by a "security community" of advanced industrial democracies, among whom the rules of power politics may no longer apply. Even outside this Organization for Economic Cooperation and Development (OECD) zone of peace, most countries continue to regard the United States as an indispensable (if occasionally troubling) partner. Thus, resistance to U.S. power has remained largely symbolic, merging with a diffuse cultural anti-Americanism and finding expression in ways that meet domestic political needs without threatening a catastrophic rupture with the sole superpower.

However, the temptation to act alone or opt out of multilateral cooperation may carry greater risks in the future. Looking to the year 2015, the Central Intelligence Agency's National Intelligence Council predicts that "some states—adversaries and allies—will at times try to check what they see as American 'hegemony'" through "tactical alignments on specific policies and demands for a greater role in international political and economic institutions."[99] Resentment over perceived exploitation may embolden countries to try to frustrate U.S. foreign policy through various strategies, including tacit noncooperation with U.S. initiatives or insistence on equal rights to act alone, as well as renewed efforts to bind the United States more tightly in institutional webs.

There is modest evidence that some of these potential consequences are already occurring. In several recent instances, countries frustrated with U.S. "unilateralism" have united to deprive the United States of representation on multilateral bodies. Angered by U.S. withholding of dues payments, for example, other UN member states voted the U.S. representative off the UN's Advisory Committee on Administrative and Budgetary Questions from 1996 to 1999. In May 2001, likewise, the United States lost its seat on the UN Human Rights Commission.[100]

One of the central dilemmas confronting the United States today is how to exercise its overwhelming power in ways that neither threaten others nor encourage resistance.[101] This context provides a powerful "realist" rationale for multilateralism. As Michael Mastanduno writes, "Multilateral procedures are more reassuring to other states and may help convince them that their preferences matter, and that they are not simply being coerced or directed to follow the dictates of the dominant state."[102] Unilateralism, in contrast, risks undermining the confidence of allies, being imitated by others, and weakening the legitimacy of U.S. leadership.

Reluctant Sheriff or Lone Ranger? Leadership Versus Unilateralism

What is the appropriate role of multilateral cooperation in pursuing the national interest? The answer to this question depends on how we conceive of the national interest in a global age. A central message of this book is that the U.S. foreign policy agenda is being transformed by global and transnational challenges. Coping with this new agenda will require a broader conception of the national interest, awareness that few of today's problems are amenable to unilateral approaches, and an understanding of multilateralism's role in legitimating U.S. power.

As a sovereign country, the United States has the right to withhold its consent to be bound by proposed treaties or to act alone in addressing transnational issues. In rare cases—when stakes are high, when fundamental interests clash, when institutions are paralyzed, or when U.S. initiative is a prerequisite for mobilizing a coalition—unilateralism may be the only alternative to doing nothing. But in most circumstances it is neither wise nor sustainable.[103]

In the end, the strongest argument for multilateralism is less the costs of acting alone than the benefits of acting with others. It is grounded not in wooly idealism but in sober calculations about the best means to pursue U.S. ends in a globalizing world. The United States has little choice but to collaborate with foreign governments and international institutions to make progress on a wide variety of pressing challenges, such as promoting sustainable development; stabilizing the world's population; managing the global commons; arresting the degradation of the world's environment;

ameliorating humanitarian catastrophes and global health crises; controlling illegal immigration; thwarting and prosecuting organized crime syndicates, terrorists, and narcotics traffickers; protecting U.S. citizens abroad; ensuring the stability and liquidity of global financial markets; enforcing international law; promoting human rights; stemming the proliferation of weapons of mass destruction; regulating small arms trade; and maintaining an open and nondiscriminatory world trading system. Even in the sensitive issue of the use of force, pure unilateralism will be the exception rather than the rule, given the practical dependence of the United States on other countries for concrete assets like "base rights, overflight, intelligence, combat forces, economic help, and political support."[104] In a similar vein, defeating transnational terrorism will require sustained partnership with an array of countries and international institutions that possess political, economic, financial, and military instruments and that can lend legitimacy to U.S. policies.

Given the unwillingness (or inability) of the United States to resolve global problems alone, it must make use of various forms of multilateralism, including issue-specific groupings of concerned states, ad hoc coalitions of the willing, formal alliances, regional organizations, and universal regimes or organizations like the UN.[105] A recurrent challenge will be to design frameworks that expand U.S. policy options while minimizing the dilution of U.S. objectives, infringements on sovereign prerogatives, and constraints on freedom of action.[106]

The United States has been described aptly as a "reluctant sheriff," often called upon to assume international leadership but uneasy about the burdens of being the world's policeman. Any sheriff, and especially a reluctant one, requires reliable deputies. To ensure the support of followers, the United States must broaden its concept of leadership and devote greater attention, energy, and resources to cultivating partners and recruiting followers. It must be willing not simply to take the initiative but also to forge consensus about desirable responses to global challenges. This leadership will be more effective and enduring if the United States reassures partners that it is sensitive to their concerns, is commited to genuine and timely consultations prior to taking firm positions, avoids the temptation to veto proposals on the basis of narrow self-interest, and is prepared to compromise on the objectives and forms of collective action.[107] U.S. officials also need to help incubate new norms and standards, communicating domestic obstacles to foreign governments in a timely manner, and offering alternatives around which the United States might rally.

Constructive multilateral engagement may require some adjustments in U.S. attitudes and expectations, such as the long-standing presumption that multilateral forums exist largely to legitimate existing U.S. positions and the assumption that international regimes should constrain other countries but not the United States.[108] The United States will also need to balance its traditional insistence on diplomatic freedom and sovereign prerogatives with the practical necessity of institutionalizing common international norms and rules.

An Outline of the Book

Dimensions of Multilateralism

Chapters 2 through 6 of this book expand on the sources and consequences of U.S. ambivalence toward multilateral cooperation.

Competing claims of legitimacy. A fundamental source of U.S. unease, Edward Luck contends in Chapter 2, is the frequent clash between domestic and international conceptions of political legitimacy. To be stable, any political order must be legitimate: that is, actors must comply with its institutions not simply out of expediency or under duress but also because they perceive these norms and rules to embody generally accepted principles of right process. But legitimacy is a fragile commodity, particularly at the global level, where it is founded on unstable political compacts among sovereign actors.

More than any other country, Luck explains, the United States has difficulty reconciling the structure and processes of international organizations with its own, domestically generated conception of political legitimacy. Compared with their counterparts abroad, Americans are more likely to demand that the decisions of international organizations be consistent with fairness and justice; to require that global bodies be accountable and transparent; to insist that their nation's exceptional values and power warrant special privileges and exemptions; to take the pragmatic view that results matter more than process; and to defend their national sovereignty at home and freedom of action abroad. Luck, examining four major instances since 1980 in which the United States has used military force, concludes that Americans consistently look to domestic rather than international sources of legitimacy. His chapter raises questions about whether it is possible to construct international organizations that enjoy high legitimacy simultaneously at both levels.

The changing domestic context. In Chapter 3, Princeton Lyman explores the deepening link between domestic and international affairs and the challenge this poses for the executive branch and Congress. He argues that effective responses to today's transnational problems require improved collaboration between traditional foreign policy actors and traditional domestic agencies now involved in global activities. Within the executive branch, policy coherence has been hampered by poor coordination among multiple agencies, each possessing its own institutional budget, culture, mandate, and interests. Meanwhile, Congress may be even less prepared to cope with the global agenda, given the loss of many prominent internationalists from leadership positions, the proliferation of international affairs committees, the atmosphere of budgetary austerity on Capitol Hill, the access afforded to single-issue interest groups, and the tendency of individual members of Congress to behave as foreign policy entrepreneurs.

Complicating U.S. engagement, Lyman notes, is the increase in foreign policy activism by state and local governments, which sometimes run afoul of U.S. treaty commitments by passing sanctions legislation on behalf of human rights concerns. Even more notable has been the rise of NGOs, many based in the United States. Capable of crafting coalitions on behalf of particular causes, NGOs have had a powerful but ambiguous impact on U.S. multilateralism. Lyman closes by offering advice for how political leaders might frame global issues in order to build domestic constituencies in support of multilateral engagement.

A multilateral, but misperceived, public. Significantly, U.S. ambivalence toward multilateral cooperation is not driven by any groundswell of public skepticism. Contrary to conventional wisdom, Steven Kull argues in Chapter 4, Americans have neither turned inward toward isolationism nor embraced unilateralism. Rather, polling data suggest the public appreciates the growing importance of transnational problems, remains steadfastly internationalist, and would prefer to address foreign policy challenges through multilateral institutions and partnerships.[109]

Public support for the UN is robust, with majorities in favor of strengthening the UN's capacities and relying on it to authorize and organize military force. Most Americans do not perceive the world body as a threat to national sovereignty. Indeed, they are comfortable with the idea of placing U.S. troops under UN command—or even creating a UN standing army. This preference for multilateral cooperation extends to other global challenges, with the public supporting stronger international legal institutions like the ICC, binding regimes to protect the world environment, and continued trade liberalization through the WTO (provided the latter incorporates labor and environmental standards).

Yet politicians and policymakers consistently underestimate Americans' willingness to accept international obligations. What accounts for this misperception? Kull suggests that elites too often underrate the public, fail to seek out the real attitudes of citizens, conflate "vocal" minority opposition with majority sentiments, and try to insulate foreign policy from public engagement. And since voters seldom choose candidates on the basis of foreign policy, political elites lack incentives to understand the public's true feelings.

Multilateralism and U.S. grand strategy. Advocates of multilateralism are often criticized for utopianism—that is, for assuming a natural harmony of interests among competing nations and showing undue reverence for global institutions and legal rules. Deference to multilateral principles, in this view, distracts policymakers from the pursuit of the national interest and international stability. In Chapter 5, G. John Ikenberry disputes these claims, arguing that support for multilateralism has been a successful grand strategy for the United States since 1945—and remains a critical foundation for its global leadership today. Besides allowing the United States to realize gains from cooperation, multilateralism promises to prolong a world order hospitable to U.S. power and interests.

As Ikenberry explains, weaker countries are willing to follow the U.S. lead only because they are confident that the United States will neither exploit its powerful position nor retreat from its obligations. Washington's response in the era of U.S. hegemony that began in 1945 has been to adopt a policy of "strategic restraint," embedding itself in multilateral institutions that give the weak opportunities to be heard, safeguards against abandonment, and protections against the arbitrary exercise of U.S. power. In return for ceding some policy autonomy, the United States legitimated its leadership and locked other countries into stable and predictable policy orientations. This has reduced the costs of securing compliance with U.S. preferences and the likelihood that shifts in global power will stimulate challenges to U.S. leadership. Indeed, Ikenberry suggests that multilateral institutions are now more important to U.S. grand strategy than ever, for they help the United States to manage its global primacy in a manner that discourages global backlash or foreign efforts to balance U.S. power.

International perceptions of U.S. "unilateralism." If a commitment to multilateralism underpins the United States' global leadership, then presumably perceived U.S. unilateralism risks undercutting the latter. In Chapter 6, British political scientist William Wallace evaluates European perceptions of U.S. "unilateralism." The United States has multilateral links with numerous foreign countries, but those uniting the Atlantic community may be the broadest and deepest of all. The foundations for transatlantic order were laid in the 1940s, and succeeding architects have buttressed and embellished this edifice with supports and flourishes, both formal and informal.

Notwithstanding this ongoing multilateral dialogue and collaboration, the U.S-European relationship is periodically rocked by controversies over what Europeans consider a U.S. penchant for unilateralism. Many Europeans today regard the United States as a "flawed superpower" and are skeptical of its claims about the superiority of the U.S. social and economic model. Wallace's main point is that transatlantic relations have long been governed by an "implicit bargain"—in effect, European subordination for American protection—that is today outdated, being inconsistent with the economic prosperity and political vigor of a united Europe. He counsels Washington to replace its insistence on U.S. "leadership" with a more mature Atlantic "partnership," based on shared rights and responsibilities.

U.S. Multilateralism Across Issue Areas

The second part of the book analyzes recent U.S. policy in ten different issue areas. To facilitate comparison, the editors posed a common set of questions to each case study author.[110]

- First, we asked the authors to *describe* U.S. policy in their particular case. At what stage did the United States demonstrate ambivalence toward multilateral cooperation? How was this expressed? Did U.S. policy depart from past attitudes in this realm?
- Second, we asked them to examine the *causes* of U.S. ambivalence. Did U.S. policymakers see multilateralism as possessing certain costs and benefits for the pursuit of U.S interests? Did these calculations reflect the particular global challenge,[111] the mechanism proposed to address it,[112] the behavior of other countries, or perceptions of U.S. responsibilities? Was U.S. policy shaped by such domestic factors as political culture, presidential leadership, executive-legislative disagreements, partisan wrangling, bureaucratic competition, interest group activism, or public mobilization?
- Third, we asked participants to explore the *consequences* of U.S. deviations from multilateral cooperation. What short-term costs and benefits have accrued to the United States? How did other countries react? What are likely to be the long-term effects for U.S. national interests, the health of international institutions, and the resolution of transnational problems? Would a more multilateral approach have improved outcomes both for the nation and for the international community?[113]
- Finally, we asked participants to distill practical *recommendations*. What lessons do the authors' findings hold for U.S. foreign policy, both in their particular issue area and for U.S. engagement more broadly? What reforms do they suggest are necessary?

By addressing a common set of questions, the case studies promised to expose patterns and permit generalizations across different arenas of U.S. policy. At the same time, we encouraged the authors to draw out those factors they considered most pertinent or enlightening.

The use of force. The principles of multilateral cooperation are not easy to reconcile with the divergent power and interests of sovereign countries. Nowhere are these tensions more apparent than in the realm of war and peace, where the doctrine of collective security frequently collides with state practice. In Chapter 7, Ruth Wedgwood examines recent instances in which the United States has taken military action without an explicit mandate from the UN Security Council. She argues that U.S. devotion to collective security is complicated by immense disparities between U.S. power and military expenditures and those of other countries. Given its willingness to subsidize world security and run disproportionate risks, she suggests, the U.S. may deserve certain exemptions to act alone or through ad hoc coalitions.

Wedgwood concedes that multilateralism has many advantages: It can improve coordination; permit economies of scale; allow the sharing of burdens, risks, and responsibilities; and legitimate military action. But the drawbacks are considerable, and may include slow decisionmaking, resistance to hard choices, loss of secrecy, cumbersome systems of command and control, and circumscribed freedom of action.

Rejecting rigid dichotomies between multilateralism and unilateralism, Wedgwood argues that nuance and gradation are inevitable in a messy world. Washington has shown ingenuity in adapting the UN Charter to unforeseen contingencies and in clothing U.S.-led interventions in multilateral garb. She uses the case of Kosovo to counsel against a slavish obeisance to the procedural norms of collective security, noting that insistence on an explicit Security Council sanction would have left the United States and its NATO allies unable to protect fundamental human rights that the UN was created to uphold. Given the shortcomings of the UN Charter, the United States must occasionally rely on "creative ambiguity" in legitimating the use of force.

Peacekeeping. Over the past decade, Sarah Sewall recounts in Chapter 8, U.S. policy toward multilateral peace operations has shifted from vigorous support to disillusionment, to retrenchment, and eventually to tentative reengagement. During the early 1990s, she notes, the Bush and Clinton administrations both advocated an enhanced UN role in muscular, "second-generation" peace operations. Following debacles in Somalia and Bosnia-Herzegovina, however, the Clinton administration reversed course, adopting a more sober approach that enumerated factors to consider when contemplating U.S. authorization and involvement in such endeavors.

Sewall attributes the U.S. about-face to a combination of factors. These include the United States' unfamiliarity with such missions; fears about public intolerance for U.S. casualties; Congress's concerns about war powers and sovereign control of U.S. military forces; and intense partisanship between Republicans in Congress and the Clinton administration. Faced with congressional opposition to UN missions and resistance to paying U.S. peacekeeping assessments, President Clinton essentially ceded the field. The United States thus missed a critical opportunity to strengthen the legitimacy and capacity of the UN to handle lesser threats to global security—and to shoulder some of the U.S. burden of promoting world order.

Sewall's tale has an ironic ending. Despite its continued ambivalence, the United States has been drawn back—hesitantly and selectively, but inevitably—to support new UN peace operations to cope with regional and intrastate conflicts that Americans find intolerable but are unwilling to address alone. At such times, only the UN can provide "a collective mechanism for financing the operation, a mantle of political legitimacy, an umbrella for other states to participate and share the burden, and a route toward disengagement for the lead nation." Sewall counsels U.S. officials to break their shortsighted habit of asking the United Nations to take on daunting responsibilities while failing to provide it with the political, military, or financial resources for success—and then making a scapegoat of the world body for failures of U.S. leadership.

Nuclear weapons. In Chapter 9, Thomas Graham and Damien LaVera argue that a unilateral trend in U.S. nuclear weapons policy has dangerous implications for international peace and security. The U.S. Senate's rejection of the CTBT and the renewed commitment to pursue a national missile defense (NMD) threaten to unravel the nuclear nonproliferation regime that has been the cornerstone of strategic stability in the nuclear age.

In Graham and LaVera's view, the defeat of the CTBT was a watershed event that has jeopardized the world's most import multilateral arms control regime, the nuclear Non-Proliferation Treaty (NPT). The NPT rests on a tacit bargain between the nuclear "have-nots," which have agreed to forswear nuclear weapons, and the nuclear "haves," which have committed to eventual nuclear disarmament. Nonnuclear states are likely to consider the Senate's action a repudiation of this commitment and a license to develop their own nuclear forces.

The NPT regime has been dealt a second blow by U.S. determination to construct NMD. For three decades, global strategic stability has been based on the doctrine of mutually assured destruction, embodied in the Anti-Ballistic Missile Treaty of 1972. The U.S. commitment to a functioning NMD system—intended to cope with threats from "states of proliferation concern"—has elicited widespread condemnation from potential adversaries and longtime allies. Moscow has warned Washington that NMD may force it to keep its strategic forces on a hair-trigger setting and jeopardize cooperation on critical arms control agreements. China, which regards NMD as a direct threat to its modest deterrent, has threatened to cease cooperation in bilateral and multilateral arms control forums, to transfer nuclear and other weapons technology, and to expand dramatically its nuclear weapons capability—raising prospects of an Asian nuclear arms race. Finally, NATO allies have expressed anxiety that NMD may undermine the foundations of extended deterrence and portend a "decoupling" of U.S. and European security. The authors conclude that the United States cannot afford to be seen as improving its own security at the expense of others'. Nor can it expect other nations to accept behavioral limitations it refuses to countenance.

Chemical weapons. As Amy Smithson recounts in Chapter 10, U.S. ambivalence has also been expressed in the delayed approval, subsequent dilution, and incomplete implementation of the CWC. The most ambitious and intrusive arms control and nonproliferation treaty ever negotiated, the CWC is the first to outlaw the production, stockpiling, transfer, and use of an entire class of weapons: poison gas. It creates an intrusive inspection regime requiring all parties to open their military installations and private chemical industry facilities to routine international scrutiny and (unannounced) challenge inspections.

The United States showed early leadership in winning international support for a chemical weapons treaty. At home, likewise, a rigorous regime won backing from the U.S. military, both political parties, and the domestic chemical industry, and President Clinton signed the treaty in early 1993. Yet, despite this favorable domestic constellation, the United States took four years to ratify the treaty. Moreover, Congress added conditions to the implementing legislation that threatened to "make a mockery of the CWC's multilateral underpinnings," by implying that the United States "should be able to live by a different set of rules." Subsequently, U.S. officials sometimes shirked their treaty obligations by adopting an obstructionist posture toward international inspectors at U.S. military facilities. Such obstructionism has weakened a treaty with more than 140 signatories, including China, Russia, India, and Pakistan, as well as states of proliferation concern. Other parties have emulated the U.S. example, claiming their own exemptions and refusing full compliance. As has been the case with nuclear weapons, Smithson argues, U.S. policy on the CWC has cast doubt on the country's commitment to cooperative security.

The United States and the UN. Few aspects of U.S. foreign policy since the end of the Cold War have been as frustrating to liberal internationalists as Washington's shortsighted conduct toward the United Nations. In Chapter 11, Margaret Karns and Karen Mingst document the role of the United States in precipitating the UN's financial crisis during the 1990s and evaluate the damage done to the world body and to the nation's global reputation.

Although the United States served as both parent and midwife to the United Nations, the relationship between the country and its offspring has always been ambivalent and complicated. Despite the UN's value in providing essential global public goods, setting new standards for the international community, and offering a venue to legitimate U.S. policies, the United States often finds it difficult to reconcile support for the world body with its own tremendous power, exceptionalist traditions, and separation of powers. An important barometer of U.S.-UN relations, Karns and Mingst write, is Washington's willingness to fulfill its financial obligations to the world organization. During the 1990s, the climate was poor indeed. The Republican-controlled Congress, rejecting the long-established principle that UN dues represent a formal legal obligation, repeatedly withheld annual U.S. assessments in a unilateral effort to impose reform on the UN and limit U.S. obligations to it. At the same time, the United States adopted an a la carte approach to financing UN activities, providing voluntary funding (sometimes at high levels) to favored specialized agencies.

This highhandedness and selectivity carried significant costs. By withholding its assessments, the United States devastated UN finances, encouraged other states to shirk their fiduciary obligations, and (by weakening the UN) strengthened the hands of the institution's critics. Under heavy congressional pressure, the Clinton administration negotiated a partial settlement of the arrears crisis in late 2000, persuading other member states to concede significant reductions in U.S. contributions to the UN's regular and peacekeeping budgets, linked to benchmarks on UN performance. According to the authors, the crisis over arrears typifies a general U.S. reluctance to assume the nonmilitary costs of global engagement. As global interdependence deepens, symbolic battles with the UN will become a luxury the United States can ill afford.

Extraterritorial sanctions. Among the most controversial of U.S. foreign policies has been the extraterritorial extension of U.S. law to punish foreign actors doing business with countries that Washington has labeled rogue states. The two most prominent examples are the Iran-Libya Sanctions Act and the Helms-Burton law regarding Cuba. The former imposes penalties on foreign companies whose investments might assist Iranian or Libyan abilities to develop energy resources. The latter penalizes foreign actors engaged in or profiting from the trafficking in property confiscated or nationalized from U.S. citizens after the Cuban revolution. Given the dubious legality of extraterritorial sanctions and the international fury they elicit, Michael Mastanduno contends in Chapter 12, they earn the epithet "hyperunilateralism."

As Mastanduno observes, extraterritorial sanctions typically draw the executive branch in a delicate two-level game, with the president and State Department caught between pressure from Congress and domestic constituencies to get tough with "rogue states" and fierce objections from allies and trading partners maintaining commercial relations with the target state. If skillful at this two-level game, the president may gain flexibility to waive the harshest sanctions in return for a demonstrable hardening of allied positions toward the target state.

Extraterritorial sanctions have few benefits, most of which are symbolic and flow to narrow domestic groups. Their costs are significant and are borne by the entire nation. Besides damaging short-term cooperation with allies, such sanctions threaten over the longer term to undercut U.S. claims to benevolent leadership of the international community. These measures also carry economic costs, depriving the country of valuable trade and investment opportunities and earning U.S. companies a reputation as unreliable business partners. Assuming that such sanctions will remain part of the political landscape, Congress and the White House face the challenge of designing them in a sophisticated manner to satisfy domestic political constituencies while permitting sufficient flexibility in their application and enforcement.

The International Criminal Court. Whereas extraterritorial sanctions force other countries to conform to U.S. law, resistance at home to the ICC evinces a deep reluctance to submit to the jurisdiction of international legal rules or the scrutiny of global bodies. In summer 1998 Washington tried mightily to block agreement on the Rome Statute of the ICC. It failed, finding itself on the minority of a lopsided 120–7 vote. President Clinton eventually signed the statute in his last days in office, but Senate ratification is unlikely, given the combined opposition of Republicans, the U.S. military, and the administration of George W. Bush. In Chapter 13, Bartram Brown examines the causes and consequences of the United States' reluctance to sign—and later to ratify—the Rome Statute.

Washington has justified resistance to the ICC on the grounds that U.S. soldiers serving in global deployments must be protected from unwarranted indictment. Brown considers U.S. fears unfounded, since the ICC will have jurisdiction over a narrow range of crimes[114] and will prosecute only if the nation of the accused lacks a working judicial system or fails to conduct a legitimate investigation. Moreover, the statute contains safeguards against prosecutorial abuse. In Brown's view, U.S. objections reflect a deeper anxiety: "the prospect that a panel of international judges might sit in judgment of determinations made by the U.S. legal system."

The U.S. failure at Rome underlined the difficulties the White House faces in negotiating simultaneously with foreign governments, an inflexible Congress, and its own agencies. It also revealed deficiencies in U.S. conference diplomacy. Washington failed to respond adequately to the vigorous involvement of international NGOs in the negotiations, and it engaged in clumsy, ineffective efforts to coerce longtime allies. As in the land mines case, the episode revealed the United States' limited capacity to block multilateral initiatives supported by most other governments and significant segments of global civil society. The choice before the United States is whether it will accept the obligations of the proposed legal regime or continue to insist upon special treatment.

Human rights. The United States occupies an ambiguous position with respect to global human rights norms. Since 1945 the promotion of human rights has been an integral component of U.S. foreign policy. Yet the United States has an uneven record of signing and ratifying international human rights treaties, often doing so after long delays, or not at all.[115] In Chapter 14, Andrew Moravcsik attributes this split personality to four features of the United States: its superpower status, stable democratic government, conservative ideology, and political decentralization.

In part, U.S. reluctance reflects the predictable resistance of any great power to binding commitments restricting its freedom of action and internal autonomy. A second factor is the maturity of U.S. democracy: since the United States already respects human rights, it has fewer incentives than transitional democracies to make formal treaty commitments. Yet these explanations alone cannot account for the fervor of the domestic U.S. debates over international human rights conventions. The more fundamental roots of U.S. resistance, Moravcsik believes, are the country's striking conservatism and decentralized political institutions. Specifically, U.S. political culture fits comfortably into the right side of the political spectrum of most advanced industrial democracies. This ideological bias translates into a general preference for civil and political rights over broader conceptions of social, economic, minority, and cultural rights—and explains why domestic disagreements over human rights treaties often take on a partisan hue, dividing Republicans and Democrats. Finally, the Senate supermajority required for treaty ratification offers multiple opportunities for "veto players" to oppose proposed human rights conventions supported by solid legislative majorities. Moravcsik uses this analytical framework to explain why the United States has not ratified the Convention on the Rights of the Child.

Human rights advocates and international lawyers often contend that this reluctance to sign and ratify human rights conventions exposes the United States to charges of hypocrisy, undermines the effectiveness of its human rights promotion efforts, and delays the evolution of human rights norms globally. Moravcsik is skeptical, finding little evidence for these claims. If there are costs of U.S. nonparticipation, these are largely domestic—in depriving U.S. citizens of potential rights and of opportunities to invoke global standards in seeking redress.

Trade and money. Over the past decade, the United States has been largely supportive of multilateralism in trade and monetary relations. Yet, as Kimberly Ann Elliott and Gary Clyde Hufbauer point out in Chapter 15, this commitment has coexisted with a willingness to take unilateral action. Although U.S. unilateralism has sometimes been used to seek narrow national advantage, at other times it has been a form of "leadership" to overcome obstacles to trade liberalization or threats to global financial stability.

The U.S commitment to multilateralism in trade has never been absolute. Perhaps the most notable departure since World War II occurred during the 1980s and early 1990s, when Washington adopted a stance of "aggressive unilateralism," employing so-called Super 301 provisions of the 1988 trade bill to threaten retaliation against countries pursuing "unfair" trade practices. Yet, contrary to dire predictions, aggressive unilateralism actually *strengthened* the multilateral trading system by opening foreign markets, generating momentum for broader and deeper trade rules. The apparent lesson, Elliott and Hufbauer suggest, is that one sometimes needs "to break crockery to move the system forward." Washington's future ability to use unilateral instruments has been constrained, however, by the creation of the WTO, which obliges it to submit any commercial disagreements to a binding dispute settlement mechanism.[116]

Whereas Washington has always insisted on the principle of "equal treatment" in global trade, it has consistently demanded enormous discretion in international financial matters. A case in point is its insistence on weighted voting within the IMF, which gives it effective control over fund activities. At times, U.S. unilateralism has served the interests of the entire global financial system, as when the U.S. Treasury sponsored massive bailout packages for Mexico (1994) and for South Korea during the Asian financial crisis (1997–1998). On other occasions, as when Washington blocked a proposed Asian Monetary Fund in 1998, its actions have been more self-serving. Today, the United States and its major partners confront the challenge of designing a new financial architecture for a global age. Among the critical tasks for U.S. policymakers will be reconsidering the appropriate mandate and scope of the IMF.

Elliott and Hufbauer's chapter suggests that one should distinguish between unilateralism that is constructive—that is, furthering systemic reform and the goal of an open and less discriminatory world in which all may benefit—and that which is destructive, that is, designed to privilege the interests of one nation over others or being corrosive to multilateral regimes. Rather than exclusive alternatives, multilateralism and unilateralism may sometimes be complements.

Global warming. Multilateral frameworks can be especially useful in addressing collective-action problems involving the "global commons." No contemporary environmental problem has the potential to wreak more havoc than global climate change. Unfortunately, the United States has failed to reach agreement with other major emitters of greenhouse gases on a shared approach to the problem. In Chapter 16, Harold Jacobson assesses the causes and consequences of the U.S. failure to ratify the Kyoto Protocol on global warming.

As Jacobson notes, domestic U.S. resistance to the protocol has focused on the questions of whether emissions targets should be binding, whether developing countries should be bound by the same terms as industrialized ones, and whether flexible mechanisms might be used to achieve targets. At Kyoto, the Clinton administration signed a treaty setting ambitious targets for U.S. emissions but none for developing countries, despite unambiguous bipartisan warnings that the Senate would reject any such treaty. Resistance among senators and their business and labor constituents has focused on the burden of adjustment facing the United States and the competitive economic disadvantage it faces vis-à-vis developing countries.

As Jacobson notes, differences in domestic political culture and regulatory philosophies have complicated agreement between the European Union (EU) and the United States. EU member states have advocated a centralized approach, with binding targets to force real emissions reductions on all countries, whereas Washington has pushed for market-based mechanisms like emissions trading and carbon "sinks" to offset high U.S. emissions. Prospects for agreement have also been complicated by the obstacles of Senate ratification and by the U.S. tradition of regarding treaty commitments as legally binding (rather than mere "targets"). Such factors contributed to the collapse of multilateral negotiations in The Hague in November 2000.[117]

In the management of certain global issues, other countries can sometimes afford to leave the United States behind. Climate change is not one of these issues. Because the United States is by far the largest emitter of greenhouse gases, its participation is imperative. Each year of failure to cope with global warming will increase the eventual costs of adjustment for the international community—and the likelihood of disaster.

Multilateral Engagement for a Global Age

In this book's final chapter, Shepard Forman argues that the United States must embrace multilateral engagement to assist the smooth development of an emerging "international public sector." Around the world, nations and peoples increasingly depend on the goods and services provided by a diverse set of international institutions and nonstate actors. Founded upon literally thousands of treaties, conventions, and institutions, the international public sector permits sovereign countries to manage jointly the dilemmas posed and opportunities presented by deepening global interdependence. Although largely unnoticed, this latticework of institutional cooperation is indispensable for advancing U.S. interests in a global age. For the United States, Forman declares, "multilateralism is no longer a choice. It is a matter of necessity, and of fact."

Unfortunately, instead of showing strong and consistent leadership to strengthen this institutional architecture, the United States often takes a shortsighted and overly selective approach to international cooperation, retreating from multilateralism for short-term gain while ignoring the costs of this behavior to its reputation and long-term interests. To make constructive use of its unparalleled power and influence, the United States must accept that acting alone is rarely viable and instead forge multilateral responses to global problems, secure in the knowledge that in most circumstances national and global interests will coincide. Forman calls on official and nongovernmental actors to discuss the proper purpose and scope of the international public sector.

A renewed U.S. commitment to multilateral coopera[tion will require] a new bipartisan dialogue in Congress, institutional reform [in the executive] branch to meet the challenges of globalization, additional financial resources for international activities, and the creation of a public constituency behind global engagement. The United States cannot afford to squander the opportunity to shape the rules and institutions of international life in the twenty-first century.

Notes

I thank Bill Antholis, Shepard Forman, Charles Graybow, Harold Jacobson, Bruce Jentleson, Abraham Lowenthal, and Princeton Lyman for helpful comments on earlier drafts of this chapter.

1. For views recommending sweeping retrenchment from international commitments and an abdication of U.S. global leadership, see Gholz, Press, and Sapolsky, "Come Home America"; Tonelson, "What Is the National Interest?"; and Steel, *Temptations of a Superpower*.

2 Tucker, "Alone or With Others."

3. Gardner, "The Comeback of Liberal Internationalism."

4. Kristol and Kagan, "Toward a Neo-Reaganite Foreign Policy." Kagan, "The Benevolent Empire."

5. By fiscal year 2000, foreign aid had slipped to 0.11 percent of GDP (compared with an OECD average of 0.30 percent), or $29 per capita (compared with an OECD median of $70). Gardner, "The One Percent Solution," pp. 4, 8. Speth, "The Plight of the World's Poor," pp. 13–17. The modest increase in international affairs spending in George W. Bush's first budget is insufficient to rectify years of neglect.

6. Maynes, "America's Fading Commitments." Patrick, "America's Retreat from Multilateral Engagement."

7. Weller, "The US, Iraq, and the Use of Force in a Unipolar World."

8. Blechman, "Emerging from the Intervention Dilemma."

9. Crossette, "UN Chief Faults Reluctance of US to Help in Africa," *New York Times,* May 12, 2000.

10. Crossette, "US Undercuts Arms Control Efforts, Global Panel Finds," *New York Times,* August 3, 1999.

11. Loeb, "Inaction on Chemical Pact Decried," *Washington Post,* September 17, 1998.

12. Schmitt, "Senate Kills Test Ban Treaty in Crushing Loss for Clinton; Evokes Versailles Defeat," *New York Times,* October 14, 1999.

13. Butler, "Nuclear Testing and National Honor, *New York Times,* July 13, 2001.

14. Gordon and Myers, "Risk of Arms Race Seen in US Design of Missile Defense," *New York Times,* May 28, 2000. Andreani, "The Disarray of US Non-Proliferation Policy," p. 59. Ivanov, "The Missile-Defense Mistake."

15. Butler, "Restarting the Nuclear Race," *New York Times,* May 2, 2001. Tyler, "Talks Don't Calm Foes of Antimissile Plan," *New York Times,* May 12, 2001.

16. Sanger, "A Day After Seeing Putin, a Hard-Line Bush Emerges," *New York Times,* July 24, 2001.

17. Gordon, "U.S. Weighing Future of Strategic Arms Pacts," *New York Times,* May 9, 2001.

18. Gordon, "Germ Warfare Talks Open in London; U.S. Is the Pariah," *New York Times,* July 24, 2001.

19. Schneider, "Dozens of Nations, But Not the U.S., Sign Land Mine Treaty," *Washington Post,* December 4, 1997.

20. "America on the Sidelines," *New York Times,* July 29, 2001.

21. Jessica Mathews, "Delinquency Diplomacy," *Washington Post,* March 10, 1997.

22. Hirsh, "The Fall Guy," p. 3. Luers, "Choosing Engagement."

23. Mathews, "Self-Appointed Global Hall Monitor," *Washington Post,* September 17, 1996.

24. Axworthy cited in Sanger, "Talk Multilaterally, Hit Allies with a Stick," *New York Times,* July 21, 1996.

25. Stanley, "US Dissents, but Accord is Reached on War Crime Court," *New York Times,* July 18, 1998.

26. Pearlstein, "On Trade, US Retreating into Globalphobia," *Washington Post,* December 8, 1997.

27. Kahn, "Clinton Shift on Trade: 'Wake-Up Call,'" *New York Times,* January 31, 2000. The incorporation of new labor and environmental standards need not threaten commercial "multilateralism," per se, provided it occurs through a consensual negotiating process, rather than unilateral imposition. In spring 2001, President Bush sought to restore momentum for open trade, requesting fast-track authority from Congress and announcing the goal of a hemispheric-wide Free Trade Area for the Americas.

28. Pianin, "U.S. Aims to Pull Out of Warming Treaty," *Washington Post,* March 28, 2001; Drozdiak and Pianin, "US Angers Allies over Climate Pact," *Washington Post,* March 29, 2001.

29. Revkin, "178 Nations Reach a Climate Accord: U.S. Only Looks On," *New York Times,* July 24, 2001.

30. Cited in Marcus, "Allies, Foes, See Lack of US leadership on Land Mines, Global Warming," *Boston Globe,* December 21, 1997.

31. For an elegant and thoughtful treatment of U.S. ambivalence, see Luck, *Mixed Messages.*

32. The classic work on liberal exceptionalism is Hartz's *The Liberal Tradition in America.*

33. Bell, "The 'Hegelian Secret': Civil Society and American Exceptionalism," pp. 50–51, 63.

34. Dallek, *The American Style of Foreign Policy,* p. xiv. Thorne, "American Political Culture and the End of the Cold War," pp. 314–315.

35. Ruggie, *Winning the Peace,* p. 25. Multilateralism, writes Burley, embodies the "organizing principles of the liberal conception of the polity," projected globally. "Regulating the World," pp. 125–126.

36. Hathaway, "America, Defender of Democratic Legitimacy?" pp. 121–133.

37. MacDougal, *Promised Land, Crusader State,* pp. 36, 71–72.

38. Ibid.

39. G. John Ikenberry, *After Victory.*

40. Zoellick, "Congress and the Making of US Foreign Policy," p. 23. Snidal, "IGOs, Regimes, and Cooperation," p. 326. Evans, Jacobson, and Putnam, *Double-Edged Diplomacy.*

41. These aims were most fully developed in the Fourteen Points of January 1918. Knock, *To End All Wars: Woodrow Wilson and the Quest for a New World Order,* pp. 143–144, 163. Temperley, *A History of the Peace Conference of Paris,* pp. 192–196.

42. Divine, *Second Chance.*

43. Given regional peculiarities, multilateralism dominated Atlantic and Latin American relations, bilateral bargains in East Asia. Moreover, U.S. leadership often rested on a disguised "minilateralism" among key countries. Kahler, "Multilateralism with Small and Large Numbers." Over time, this U.S.-inspired "movement to institutions" began to alter the strategic and normative context in which countries pursued their national interests. Reisman, "Unilateral Action and the Transformations of the World Constitutive Process."

44. Institutions were "now perceived as obstacles—not, as in the past, tools—to the promotion of American foreign policy goals." Thomas Hughes, "The Twilight of Internationalism."

45. Holloway, "US Unilateralism at the UN."

46. Multilateral obligations are reinforced by "diffuse reciprocity," or expectations that the relative benefits from cooperation will eventually balance out, and by "transparency," or the ability to verify that others are complying with their obligations. Caporaso, "International Relations Theory and Multilateralism," pp. 53–54.

47. Williams, "Multilateralism: Critique and Appraisal," pp. 211–213. Reisman, "The United States and Multilateral Institutions," p. 62.

48. Luck, *Mixed Messages,* p. 67.

49. Cooper, Higgott, and Nossal, "Bound to Follow? Leadership and Followership in the Gulf Crisis."

50. Martin, "The Rational State Choice of Multilateralism," pp. 111–113. Ikenberry, "Institutions, Strategic Restraint, and the Persistence of American Postwar Order."

51. National Intelligence Council, *Global Trends 2015,* p. 47.

52. Maynes, "America's Fading Commitments to the World." pp. 88–89.

53. Sloan, "The US Role in a New World Order: Prospects for George Bush's Global Vision."

54. Brinkley, "The Clinton Doctrine."

55. Sterling-Folker, "Between a Rock and a Hard Place."

56. Kissinger, "Foreign Policy Is About the National Interest," *International Herald Tribune,* October 25, 1993.

57. "Our engagement must be selective," the White House explained in February 1995. "We must use the right tools—being willing to act unilaterally when our direct national interests are at stake; in alliance and partnership when our interests are shared by others, and multilaterally when our interests are more general and the problems are best addressed by the international community." White House, *A National Strategy of Engagement and Enlargement.* Rosenfeld, "American Power Plays," *Washington Post,* December 26, 1997.

58. Dole, "Shaping America's Global Future," p. 36.

59. Kagan, "Reject the Global Buddy System."

60. Rice, "Campaign 2000—Promoting the National Interest," p. 47. Zoellick, "A Republican Foreign Policy," p. 69.

61. Shanker, "White House Says the U.S. Is Not a Loner, Just Choosy," *New York Times,* July 31, 2001.

62. Crossette, "Tying Gulliver Down with Those Pesky Treaties," *New York Times,* August 8, 1999.

63. Reisman, "The United States and International Institutions," pp. 71–72. Zoellick, "Campaign 2000—A Republican Foreign Policy," p. 69.

64. Malanczuk, "The International Criminal Court and Landmines: What Are the Consequences of Leaving the U.S. Behind?" p. 5.

65. Wedgwood, "Courting Disaster: The US Takes a Stand," pp. 35, 40.

66. Slaughter, "The Real New World Order."

67. Mathews, "Power Shift."

68. Anderson, "The Ottawa Convention Banning Landmines, the Role of International Non-Governmental Organizations and the Idea of International Civil Society."

69. Thiessen and Leonard, "When Worlds Collide."

70. See the special issue of *International Organization* (Winter 2000).

71. A case in point, discussed in Chapter 15, is the WTO's binding dispute resolution mechanism, which constrains the United States' choice of retaliatory trade measures.

72. Reisman, "The United States and International Institutions," p. 66.

73. Sometimes activists seem unsure about which way to proceed. See Naim, "Lori's War."

74. Peter J. Spiro, "The New Sovereigntists."

75. Bolton, "Should We Take Global Governance Seriously?," p. 12. Bolton regards the ICC, for example, as "a stealth approach to eroding our constitutionalism," motivated by "an unstated agenda . . . the primacy of international institutions over nation-states." "Unsign that Treaty," *Washington Post,* January 4, 2001. Crossette, "US Accord Being Sought on UN Dues and on Court," *New York Times,* December 7, 2000.

76. Crossette, "Helms, in Visit to UN, Offers Harsh Message," *New York Times,* January 21, 2000.

77. Lindsay, "End of an Era: Congress and Foreign Policy after the Cold War," p. 173. See also Rosner, *The New Tug of War.*

78. Carter, "Congress and Post–Cold War US Foreign Policy."

79. Walter Russell Mead, "Why the World is Better for Jesse Helms," April 22, 2001.

80. Hook, "The White House, Congress, and the Paralysis of the US State Department after the Cold War."

81. Cowhey "Elect Locally—Order Globally: Domestic Politics and Multilateral Cooperation."

82. Observation by Sarah B. Sewall, in Chapter 8 of this book.

83. In the House, fifteen committees and thirty-seven subcommittees touch on international affairs; in the Senate, eleven and thirty-four (respectively). Carter, "Congress and Post–Cold War U.S. Foreign Policy."

84. Hamilton comments paraphrased in Zoellick, "Congress and the Making of US Foreign Policy," p. 27.

85. See speech by National Security Advisor Samuel R. Berger before the Council on Foreign Relations, "American Power: Isolation, Hegemony, or Engagement?," October 21, 1999.

86. Holsti, "Public Opinion and U.S. Foreign Policy after the Cold War."

87. Holsti and Rosenau, "Internationalism: Intact or in Trouble?," pp. 134–137.

88. Ritter, "Policies at War," *New York Times,* August 16, 1999.

89. The Intergovernmental Panel on Global Climate Change predicts that the earth's average surface temperature may rise up to 10 degrees Fahrenheit by the year 2100, with calamitous repercussions, including the melting of polar ice caps, extreme weather, and global epidemics.

90. In spring 2001, the Bush administration began reconsidering whether the United States should pursue an optional verification protocol to the BWC. See Gordon and Miller, "U.S. Germ Warfare Review Faults Plan on Enforcement," *New York Times,* May 20, 2001.

91. Rosenfeld, "American Hegemony is a Matter of Style, Not Policy," *Houston Chronicle,* December 30, 1997.

92. Heisbourg, "Perceptions of the US Abroad," pp. 5–15.

93. Whitney, "US and NATO Allies Divided over Defense Needs," *New York Times,* December 3, 1999.

94. According to Michael Sturmer, writing on October 23, 1999, in the German daily *Die Welt,* the CTBT episode revealed a "superpower . . . [that] lacks moral and political responsibility and leadership when it comes to creating an order based on treaties." Brazil's *O Estado de S. Paulo* warned (on October 26, 1999) that such "increasing and unequivocal" demonstrations of "unilateralism may cost the United States [a] superiority . . . that really counts: the leadership of the Western world." "The fact is," concluded Singapore's *Business Times,* October 19, 1999, "Americans are moving away from international agreements and responsibilities; as the world's sole remaining superpower, they see no need to be so encumbered."

95. Marshall and Mann, "Goodwill Toward US is Dwindling Globally," *Los Angeles Times,* March 26, 2000. "Even Allies Resent US Dominance," *International Herald Tribune,* November 5, 1997.

96. To counterbalance such "abusive" tendencies, Vedrine continued, France and other countries must launch multilateral initiatives and strengthen collective forums in which the United States lacked a free hand and might be forced to compromise. German Chancellor Gerhard Schroeder observed that "there is a real danger of unilateralism, not just by anybody but by the United States." See "NATO at 50: With Nations at Odds, Is It a Misalliance?" *New York Times,* February 15, 1999. Whitney, "The French Aren't Alone in Having Gall," *New York Times,* December 6, 1998. Daley, "More than Ever, Europe is Scorning the US," *New York Times,* April 9, 2000.

97. Many Europeans saw the Bush administration as "abrasive toward old enemies, mistrustful of international compromise, America first when it comes to global threats, admonitory toward allies, disdainful rather than constructive in the face of the messy complexities that have replaced the neat old bipolar world." Young, "We've Lost that Allied Feeling," *Washington Post,* April 1, 2001. Hoagland, "The Dangers of Bush's Unilateralism," *Washington Post,* July 29, 2001.

98. Menges, "Russia, China, and What's Really on the Table," *Washington Post,* July 29, 2001. In a visit to New Delhi in 1999, similarly, Russian Prime Minister Vladimir Putin suggested that Russia, China, and India cooperate to create a counterweight to U.S. domination.

99. National Intelligence Council, *Global Trends 2015,* p. 13.

100. "Revolt at the UN," *New York Times,* May 5, 2001. The United States also lost its seat on the UN's international narcotics control board, presumably due to discomfort with its militarized approach to the crisis in Colombia. The United States has since regained its seat on the UN Budget Committee.

101. Clinton officials dubbed this "the hegemon problem." "Strobe Talbott, Anxious Hegemon," *The Economist,* May 30, 1998. Huntington, "The Lonely Superpower." Sanger, "America Finds It's Lonely at the Top," *New York Times,* July 18, 1999.

102. Mastanduno, "Preserving the Unipolar Moment," p. 147.

103. Chinkin, "The State that Acts Alone: Bully, Good Samaritan, or Iconoclast?" pp. 37–38. The status of unilateralism under international law varies. Some unilateral acts are legal and prudent; others illegal but compelled by a higher imperative; and still others both illegal and imprudent.

104. Haass, "Using Force: Lessons and Choices," p. 203.

105. Haass, *The Reluctant Sheriff,* pp. 4, 8, 69.

106. Bruce Jentleson, "Who, Why, What, and How: Debates over Post–Cold War Military Intervention," pp. 63–66.

107. Haass, "What to Do with American Primacy."

108. Snidal, "IGOs, Regimes, and Cooperation," p. 326. Karns and Mingst, "The United States and Multilateral Institutions: A Framework for Analysis," p. 11.

109. For similar findings, see Reilly, "Americans and the World: A Survey at Century's End."

110. This methodology is known formally as a "structured, focused comparison." George and McKeown, "Case Studies and Theories of Organizational Decision-Making."

111. For example, U.S. multilateralism might vary with whether the issue area touched upon security, economic, or social welfare objectives.

112. For instance, Washington might lack faith in the capacity of this machinery to address the given problem, advance U.S. interests, protect U.S. sovereignty, or be held accountable.

113. See Tetlock and Belkin, *Counterfactual Thought Experiments in World Politics,* on the use of such reasoning.

114. These include genocide, crimes against humanity, and war crimes. Pending agreed definition, the court will also have jurisdiction over the crime of "aggression."

115. The United States took until 1986 to ratify the 1948 Genocide Convention; until 1992 to ratify the 1966 covenant on Civil and Political Rights, and until 1994 to ratify the 1984 Torture Convention and the 1965 Racial Discrimination Convention. It has yet to ratify the 1979 Discrimination Against Women Convention or the 1966 Covenant on Economic, Social, and Cultural Rights. Malanzcuk, "The International Criminal Court and Landmines."

116. In 1996, Republican presidential candidate Robert Dole recommended the United States withdraw from the WTO if this panel were to rule against it on three successive occasions.

117. "Nations can only negotiate abroad what they believe they can ratify at home," U.S. delegation head Frank Loy explained. "The United States is not in the business of signing up to agreements it knows it cannot fulfill. We don't make promises we can't keep." Drozdiak, "Global Warming Talks Collapse," *Washington Post,* November 26, 2000.

PART 2

DIMENSIONS OF
U.S. MULTILATERALISM

2

The United States, International Organizations, and the Quest for Legitimacy

Edward C. Luck

IN PUBLIC AND SCHOLARLY DISCOURSE ON U.S. RELATIONS WITH INTER-national institutions, few terms are employed with greater frequency or less precision than "legitimacy." Everyone wants to have it, but there is little agreement on where it comes from, what it looks like, or how more of it can be acquired. Internationalists assert that U.S. interventions abroad are seen, domestically and internationally, as more legitimate if they have been authorized by the UN Security Council or by a well-established regional arrangement. Others, more skeptical of the utility and wisdom of international institutions, stress that legitimacy flows from domestic sources, that is, from the United States' constitutional structures and democratic principles. At times, these two levels of legitimacy work in the same direction and are mutually reinforcing. But what happens when domestic and international notions of legitimacy conflict?

This chapter provides some preliminary answers by looking at how distinctive notions of legitimacy have at times set the United States apart from other countries. The first section reviews scholarship on the meaning and sources of legitimacy as it applies to international institutions. The second part identifies five ways in which U.S. conceptions of legitimacy diverge from those held by most other states. The third section challenges the widely held view that authorization by the UN Security Council or a regional body is needed before the American people will consider the use of force to be legitimate. Drawing on this empirical evidence, the conclusion calls for a greater appreciation of the domestic sources of legitimacy.

Legitimacy Theory

In the disparate literature on the meaning and sources of legitimacy, two characteristics stand out: first, that legitimacy is a subjective condition, a product of one's perceptions; second, that legitimacy matters.[1] As Inis

47

Claude wrote more than three decades ago, "Politics is not merely a struggle for power but also a contest over legitimacy, a competition in which the conferment or denial, the confirmation or revocation, of legitimacy is an important stake."[2] One indicator of its perceived value is the frequency with which the leaders of nations and international organizations assert the legitimacy of their actions and of the processes that produced them. Nowhere has the struggle for legitimacy been more pointed than in debates over U.S. relations with international organizations.

According to David Beetham, power is "rightful or legitimate" when it "is acquired and exercised according to justifiable rules, and with evidence of consent."[3] Legitimacy rests on conformity to rules that are justifiable in terms of shared beliefs and that reflect the expressed consent of subordinates. By this logic a breach of rules will lead to illegitimacy; a discrepancy between rules and beliefs (or the absence of shared beliefs) to a legitimacy deficit; and the withdrawal of consent to delegitimation.[4] As Ian Hurd reminds us, legitimacy "is a subjective quality, relational between actor and institution, and defined by the actor's *perception* of the institution."[5] It is "the normative belief by an actor that a rule or institution ought to be obeyed."

According to Michael Barnett, "All international political orders need some measure of legitimacy if they are to be sustained without the threat or deployment of force."[6] In the most extensive treatment of the concept of legitimacy in world politics, *The Power of Legitimacy Among Nations,* Thomas Franck posits that "legitimacy is a property of a rule or rule-making institution which itself exerts a pull toward compliance on those addressed normatively because those addressed believe that the rule or institution has come into being and operates in accordance with generally accepted principles of right process."[7]

As these definitions suggest, legitimacy has a dynamic and temporal nature. Shaped by the subjective judgments and values of those affected, perceptions of legitimacy may grow or fade as conditions change. They are subject to political manipulation, as various parties seek to place their causes and interests on higher ground. "Power and legitimacy are not antithetical, but complementary," Claude reminds us. "Rulers seek legitimation not only to satisfy their consciences but also to buttress their positions."[8] No doubt this is as true for regional and global hegemons as for national leaders.

At the same time, the pull of legitimacy can also serve as a buffer for the weak and as a means to reinforce and perpetuate community values in the face of raw power. As Beetham has phrased it, "The main way in which the powerful will maintain their legitimacy is by respecting the intrinsic limits set to their power by the rules and the underlying principles on which they are grounded. Legitimate power, that is to say, is limited power; and one of the ways in which it loses legitimacy is when the powerful fail to observe its inherent limits."[9]

Domestically, rules should benefit both rulers and the ruled, helping to define their relations, the appropriate exercise of power, and the way in which change can be peacefully, fairly, and productively managed. Likewise international law and organization, if they are to retain their legitimacy, must be widely perceived as furthering the interests and reflecting the values of a broad cross section of peoples and states, whether weak or strong, over time. Should those interests begin to diverge or should confidence in the equity of the system begin to ebb, then the political foundation on which the international compact was built could also begin to erode, with worrisome implications for international law and order. Likewise, if member state governments fail to represent the interests and values of their citizens in global forums, then the legitimacy of the intergovernmental bodies is also tarnished.

To the extent that it is based on unenforceable agreements among sovereign nation-states, the social and political compact on which international legitimacy is founded is likely to be shallower and weaker than that within individual societies. The rules and procedures of broad-based international organizations, like the UN and WTO, reflect a series of difficult trade-offs among diverse member states. Each prefers some provisions to others, but the resulting compromise is deemed sufficiently worthwhile—and/or the political costs of nonmembership appear so high—that joining is the most attractive alternative, even for the powerful.[10] Yet "the weak are more likely to accept the principles forwarded by the strong," Barnett has noted, "if such principles are convincingly framed as universal rather than particularistic."[11]

Over time, however, the compromises that produce an institution or rule provide fodder for recurring tensions and disputes, as power relationships change or as the ambiguities inherent in the initial package fuel divergent interpretations of what the founders had in mind. Was the legitimacy of the UN, for instance, to derive from the consent of major powers in the Security Council, from the virtual universality of the egalitarian General Assembly, or from the coexistence of the two disparate organs within the same body? The fog of San Francisco, in this case, produced two idealized mythologies and two high and competing standards by which to judge current practice.[12] The perceived legitimacy of international organizations may also be impaired by their tendency, in the words of Barnett and Martha Finnemore, to "exercise power autonomously in ways unintended and unanticipated by states at their creation."[13]

Large powers may come to question the utility of the initial bargain, taking for granted the benefits of systemic stability it has produced, while perceiving the real or imagined restraints it imposes at best as bothersome and at worst as threats to national sovereignty. Other options, such as acting alone or with a few allies, may appear more attractive and less constraining than broad-based multilateral cooperation, tempting powerful states to take a selective approach to their participation in international organizations.

Smaller states, on the other hand, may begin to see the advantages of banding together to counteract the influence and autonomy of the major power(s). Appeals to their own version of legitimacy, defined and backed by their collective voting power, may come to be seen as a powerful political weapon. Over time, there may be less agreement about whether the founding purpose was to constrain powerful actors or to harness their capacities to common goals and more uncertainty about whether global legitimacy can be reconciled with wide disparities in the power capabilities of member states.

These differences matter if, as legal scholars contend, "right process" defines the core of legitimacy. As Franck notes, this emphasis on process reflects "a widely felt desire for order, consistency, and certainty. In an orderly world, rules are made in accordance with prescribed processes, are understood and obeyed, and most violators are punished."[14] Likewise, David Caron concludes that for the Security Council to achieve greater legitimacy "successful outcomes will go far in painting over perceived defects in the process of decision. It is ultimately the process, however, that may allow participants who are somewhat distrustful of one another to believe in and support the organization."[15] The Security Council's "errors are validated so long as they are made in the appropriate way," Lea Brilmayer argues, noting that it is easier to assess whether process is followed than to judge the merits of decisions produced.[16] According to this school, legitimacy depends not on day-to-day outcomes, but rather on whether the rules, procedures, and principles are sufficiently just and fair as to promise equitable and principled results over the long term.

Smaller and medium powers tend to embrace this perspective. A devotion to process and precedent, in their view, acts as a barrier to incursions by the powerful, protecting the former's rights and prerogatives in large international institutions. For intergovernmental bodies with virtually universal memberships—the UN now has 189 member states, and some treaty-based bodies have even more—an emphasis on established rules and procedures does facilitate orderly deliberative and decisionmaking processes.[17] Yet such process-oriented bodies also tend to resist reform of their intergovernmental structures and procedures, unless it is to enlarge the latter to make them more inclusive.[18] So the notion that legitimacy derives largely from "right process" is a particularly comfortable thought for the secretariats and members of global intergovernmental institutions. Yet, as the next section suggests, this cannot be said for their critics in the United States, who usually look elsewhere for the sources of legitimacy.

The United States' Dissenting Voice

As Chapter 4 in this volume documents, U.S. public opinion remains generally supportive of international institutions, activist foreign policy, and cooperation with other countries in multilateral undertakings.[19] There is little pressure for U.S. withdrawal from major international bodies and, despite a series of congressionally mandated withholdings, the United States remains the largest financial contributor to the UN system. Although strains of isolationism persist among those feeling marginalized by the effects of global economic competition, most Americans have grasped the challenges and opportunities posed by globalization with characteristic gusto. Typically, the 2000 presidential election campaign featured its share of unilateralist posturing, yet both major party candidates staked out largely centrist and internationalist foreign policy positions.[20]

None of this, however, should be read as a ringing endorsement of existing international institutions or as an indication that Americans are likely to look first to these bodies to confer legitimacy on U.S. foreign and military policy. Nor, at least in the eyes of the American people, have international bodies succeeded in delegitimating the unilateral exercise of U.S. military power. More than any other major power, the United States has displayed a repeated willingness to stand virtually alone in international forums if its interests, principles, or domestic politics so dictated. As this author has chronicled elsewhere, the roots of U.S. ambivalence toward international organization are centuries deep and the gridlock in Washington on these issues caused by partisanship and executive-congressional differences is not about to disappear.[21] There is every reason to expect that domestic politics will continue, for the foreseeable future, to dictate the course of U.S. relations with international institutions.[22]

U.S. ambivalence toward multilateral rules and organization reflects a distinctive conception of political legitimacy. On five dimensions, the United States judges the legitimacy of international institutions differently than do most of its international partners: (1) whether they are deemed to be fair in their processes and consistent in their values; (2) whether they are considered to be sufficiently accountable and democratic; (3) whether their decisionmaking rules can be squared with U.S. exceptionalism; (4) whether they should be judged on process or results; and (5) whether they preserve or undermine national sovereignty.

Values and Fairness

It is conceivable that a perfectly legitimate international process, one that follows widely accepted and legally established rules, can produce decisions or outcomes that are not deemed to be just in the eyes of many people or fair to the interests of some member states. As Franck observes, "fairness" involves claims to both legitimacy and justice.[23] From the perspective of many Americans, the UN General Assembly has long had a tendency, most pronounced during the 1960s, 1970s, and 1980s, to pass resolutions that are unjust on their merits and unfair to U.S. national interests.[24] More broadly, to many Americans it appeared that the nonaligned movement and the socialist countries had decided to use multilateral forums for a political assault aimed at delegitimating Western values, including private enterprise, free trade, an independent press, and civil and political liberties.

In response, U.S. officials and commentators, including two UN ambassadors, Daniel Patrick Moynihan and Jeanne Kirkpatrick, raised pointed questions about bloc-voting, automatic majorities, and the tyranny of the majority in the General Assembly and other global bodies, claiming that these practices had distorted the functions of these institutions and undermined their claims to legitimacy.[25] Many Americans came to accept Ambassador Moynihan's characterization of the United Nations as an "unfriendly place" or to dismiss the products of the General Assembly as of little consequence or relevance to the real world outside. In short the UN came to be seen as a good idea that had turned sour. Public support for the concept of the UN contrasted with much lower approval ratings for the institution's actual performance, a gap that persists today. The General Assembly's legitimating power, which had been important to the United States when it enjoyed seemingly automatic majorities in the 1940s and 1950s, sagged badly and has been of little consequence to either the U.S. government or the American people since the end of the Cold War.

Accountability and Democratization

Legitimacy, like power, requires accountability. As Ian Hurd has noted, "Any institution that is accepted as legitimate stands in a position of authority over states and thus exercises power."[26] But, he asks, "if international institutions can be authoritative, how do we make them accountable?" Most Americans view accountability through the lens of their own domestic model. In a democratic society, those to whom the citizens delegate power are expected to exercise it in a manner that is as transparent as possible and that permits sufficient oversight by the people and/or their elected representatives. Officials of the executive branch must be able to defend their policies, practices, and use of public monies before Congress and the court of public opinion.[27] Independent and aggressive media, an active civil society, an engaged political opposition, and an inherent public skepticism about the wisdom and efficiency of big government combine to reinforce the constitutional assumption that power and legitimacy flow from the people to the government and not vice versa.

These conditions, of course, cannot be fully replicated in global interstate organizations, where the prime constituents are governments rather than individuals, transparency is limited, a wide spectrum of political cultures is represented, and even parliamentarians lack a formal place at the table. When many agencies and countries are involved in an undertaking, whether it be poverty elimination or peacekeeping, it is unclear who should be held accountable for mistakes, miscalculations, and failures. When everyone is responsible, too often it appears that no one is responsible. Reflecting a common criticism, Jeremy Rabkin charges that UN agencies seek "an authority that is somehow above government, without the accountability that actual governments have toward particular electorates or defined citizen bodies."[28] Therefore, in his view transnational "NGOs—a sort of phantom citizenry—are the perfect partners for the phantom authority exercised by UN agencies."

Those calling for greater accountability and transparency in international institutions are a pluralistic lot. For instance, the anti-institutional agenda of the antiglobalization movement has attracted supporters from both the right and left ends of the political spectrum, leaving the center to defend the legitimacy of multilateral accords and agencies. Patrick Buchanan and Ralph Nader alike have voiced shrill attacks on allegedly anonymous and unaccountable international bureaucratic and intellectual elites, contending that working-class Americans have suffered disproportionately from the machinations of transnational elites and yet have no political avenues open to them for seeking redress or a change in global policymaking.[29]

The developing country majority in the UN has also claimed that greater transparency and democratization would boost the legitimacy of the world body and the Bretton Woods institutions. But their reform agenda focuses on making limited-membership organs like the Security Council more accountable to the membership as a whole and on eliminating unequal decisionmaking procedures like the veto in the Security Council and weighted voting in the Bretton Woods institutions. When these countries speak of democratization, they usually refer to increasing the number of member states around the table, not to giving civil society, the media, or legislators greater access to intergovernment deliberations. A number of influential developing countries, in fact, have successfully opposed any expansion of NGO access to the General Assembly for the past several years. Such steps, of course, merely confirm U.S. skepticism about what the "democratization" of intergovernmental bodies means to countries that do not practice democratic principles at home or to elites that would prefer to insulate foreign affairs from public involvement.

Exceptionalism

Americans have long considered their nation to be special, not only in terms of material measures of economic, military, and political power, but also in the principles and values that it espouses and, most believe, practices.[30] They are unlikely, therefore, to look first to international bodies for an affirmation of the legitimacy of their country's security and foreign policy choices. True, in the UN's formative and adolescent years, U.S. officials regularly invoked the ideal vision of the General Assembly as a sort of global town hall meeting—a place where nations large and small, near and far could air their differences while seeking common ground. This commitment to building multilateral institutions was itself quite exceptional for a nation with the power of the postwar United States. But, as noted above, the United States gradually abandoned this line as the growing and increasingly diverse membership of the United Nations began to challenge U.S. values and interests. Clearly, the rest of the membership was not buying the twin assumptions that U.S. political and economic models have universal validity and that it was the job of international organizations to help codify and disseminate them.

On the other hand, it is striking that U.S. confidence in the supremacy of Western values was not in the least bit shaken by these years of verbal assaults and lopsided resolutions in the General Assembly and other global forums. Most Americans concluded that if anything was amiss, it must have been in the patterns and practices of multilateral diplomacy, not in U.S. positions. From their perspective, the sources of political legitimacy remained domestic, and the postwar system of international agencies was designed to advance, not compromise, core national interests and values. As U.S. administrations changed, so did their tactics at the UN, but fundamental national objectives, values, and strategies remained remarkably consistent throughout the Cold War years and since. At times, when a preexisting domestic constituency would echo or magnify the positions taken by multilateral bodies—on issues such as South Africa, women's rights, or landmines—the resolutions of global forums had an additive, and perhaps legitimating, effect on domestic policy formulation. But even in these cases, Congress in particular was notably resistant to international influences.

A second dimension of U.S. exceptionalism—the country's unsurpassed power—may prove even more problematic in the long run. Some foreign observers, like Coral Bell, have praised the Clinton administration for making extensive use of multilateral institutions and understanding that "the unipolar world should be run as if it were a concert of powers."[31] However, a more common refrain among UN member states, many of which sense that their relative power positions are slipping, is that the United States' position as an unchallenged "hyperpower" (as the French term it) may allow it to dominate world politics, both inside and outside international institutions.

To most Americans, the unparalleled capacities of the United States are not an obstacle to international action but in fact more often a prerequisite for it. An asymmetry in power and even a hierarchy of member states, Brilmayer notes, may sometimes be required to enforce international norms and the decisions of international bodies.[32] As Charles Krauthammer has written, "All the collective goodwill in the world is useless without the power to back it up, and only America has the power. . . . The critics offer collectivism as a substitute for American power. On the contrary, it is a complement to American power and, in the final analysis, its consequence."[33]

Given its singular power, the United States has been more prone than most countries to question the legitimacy and fairness of institutions whose rules and procedures do not take into account the distribution of power in the real world outside. This has not been a serious problem in the Bretton Woods institutions, where voting is weighted by financial contributions; in the WTO and various treaty-based arms control bodies, where voting is not weighted but reciprocity rules on important matters; or in the Security Council, where the United States and two of its allies have veto power. But the one-nation, one-vote rule—which most countries equate with legitimacy and democratization—cannot be reconciled with the growing disparities in national power or with the United States' sense of exceptionalism, especially at a time when some thirty member states are assessed only 1/25,000th as much as the United States. As Franck has underlined, "Equality may be the very expression of fairness, or it may be its nemesis."[34] He suggests that, given the enormous variance in populations represented by UN member states, the voting rule has become the latter.

As its charter makes clear, the UN "is based on the principle of the sovereign equality of all its Members" (Article 2(1)), yet nowhere in the charter's provisions for the General Assembly (Chapter IV) is there any mention of this principle. The founders understood that while sovereign equality was one of the defining legal principles of the nation-state system, it should not be the basis for a voting rule.[35] At San Francisco, a trade-off was agreed: the major powers would be given a veto power in the Security Council, but smaller states would enjoy some say over the running of the world body.[36] Article 18, therefore, stipulates that "each member of the General Assembly shall have one vote" and that a two-thirds majority is required for "important questions." At the founding conference, it was also agreed that the term "sovereign equality" referred not to an equal say in decisionmaking, but to juridical equality, full sovereignty, territorial integrity and political independence, and to a state's readiness to "comply faithfully with its international duties and obligations."[37] For Americans, these legal principles carry far more legitimacy than, and are distinct from, particular voting formulas.

Results, Not Process

Americans are well known not only for their idealism but also for their pragmatism. In international organizations, this translates into a greater emphasis on achieving the right results than on following the right process. Imbued with an economic and political culture that prizes individualism, ingenuity, entrepreneurship, and productivity, Americans often feel confined by the web of rules, procedures, and precedents that provide a sense of security, participation, and order for international bureaucrats and less influential countries. Given their penchant for moral causes in foreign policy, many Americans judge the legitimacy of an international organization primarily by its effectiveness in advancing a particular cause. They are less apt to identify deeply and enthusiastically with general-purpose political forums than with bodies and programs that have a singular focus, produce measurable results, and advance specific norms.[38]

Through the years, U.S. policy has favored a highly decentralized structure for the UN system despite the challenges this has posed for coherent management, interagency coordination, and systemic and financial reform. In American eyes, legitimacy flows from the professional character of the work of the various branches of the system, away from the influence of highly political central organs.[39] At the founding of the UN, the United States placed its greatest hopes on the new body's role in maintaining peace and security, yet (unlike the Soviet Union) it also put substantial stock in its economic, social, and humanitarian potential, as well as in the new financial and trade architecture that was to follow.[40]

Even today, Congress is discriminating in its approach to multilateralism, more willing to provide voluntary funding for specialized agencies and programs than to pay the U.S. share of legally assessed dues to the world organization. A number of prominent skeptics, including Jesse Helms, former chairman of the Senate Foreign Relations Committee, have called for more international activities to be funded through voluntary contributions, so that member states might pick and choose among agencies and causes, rewarding those deemed most efficient and effective.[41] Americans are neither wildly enthusiastic nor well informed about the procedures, or even the operations, of international bodies like the World Health Organization, the WTO, or the World Bank, yet these organizations have gained an aura of legitimacy in Washington because of assumptions about the importance of what they do, not how they decide.[42]

Americans tend to regard an emphasis on form over substance as an invitation to inaction or even paralysis. Writing about Bosnia, Stephen Rosenfeld warned that "multilateralism also can signify a policy of lowest common denominators in which Washington abandons a leadership role and goes with a lackadaisical global flow. Is multilateralism merely a cover for a new isolationism?"[43] Faced in 1999 with an unfolding humanitarian tragedy in Kosovo and a divided Security Council, most U.S. internationalists opted for military action outside the framework of the UN Charter— through NATO—rather than inaction within it. That choice, as documented below, has not been atypical for the American people, however much it may frustrate other member states.

Sovereignty and Control

For a dominant power, the question of how much control to seek over multilateral bodies poses a recurring dilemma that encompasses both style and substance. If a great power aims to draw legitimacy for its initiatives or preferences through the backing or votes of other member states, it may want to employ its influence quietly and subtly.[44] When asked during the presidential debates of 2000 how others should "look at the United States," Governor George W. Bush responded that "if we're an arrogant nation, they'll resent us. . . . Our nation stands alone right now in the world in terms of power. And that's why we've got to be humble and yet project strength in a way that promotes freedom."[45] Adlai Stevenson, who represented the United States at the UN during the Kennedy administration, similarly counseled that the United States can increase the legitimacy of its actions by appearing *not* to be in control and by *not* publicly twisting arms, so that whatever positive results are achieved in international forums would appear to have relatively broad and voluntary support because of the merits of the case.[46] U.S. allies likewise usually urge Washington to adopt a more benign and cooperative profile in global bodies, though when push comes to shove on issues that matter to them, they are relieved to have U.S. power on their side.[47]

The underlying issue, however, is power not style: Who is going to control what and whom? On the one hand, if the United States were not so powerful, then others would be less concerned about its tactics. On the other hand, skeptics here caution that the United States, for all its power in the "real world," could lose control of its own destiny through its participation in, and even more by its reliance on, multilateral institutions. Peter Rodman has charged, for instance, that "one of the main motives for this attempted elevation of the Security Council is to restrain American power"[48] Critics as different as Robert Dole and Ralph Nader have argued that U.S. engagement in multilateral deliberations and negotiations poses the danger that the nation's sources of legitimacy—its values, standards, and institutions (not to mention its interests)—could be compromised through the give-and-take required to reach agreements among large numbers of countries with diverse interests and political cultures.[49]

Americans are divided on these matters, in part, because of differing conceptions of the national interest and the prerequisites of national sovereignty. Most appear to accept, as this author does, that the transnational nature of many policy issues—such as trade, finance, environment, health, terrorism, and weapons proliferation—compels an unprecedented degree of multilateral cooperation. As a matter of national choice, then, the United States should work to strengthen those multilateral agreements that advance both these specific national interests and the nation's generic interest in a relatively stable and predictable international order. Such steps expand national options in some ways and limit them in others, but on balance serve to bolster national sovereignty, not undermine it. From this perspective, there is no need to choose between nationalism and multilateralism when seeking sources of legitimacy, because the two can be mutually reinforcing, not contradictory, means to similar ends.

What sets the United States apart on these matters, however, is the persistence and political clout of a quite different strain of thinking about control, sovereignty, and legitimacy.[50] The rise of transnational challenges has diminished the U.S. capacity to independently control certain functional issue areas, effectively reducing what Stephen Krasner terms the nation's "interdependence sovereignty." As he has aptly pointed out: "While a loss of interdependence sovereignty does not necessarily imply anything about domestic sovereignty understood as the organization of authoritative decision making, it does undermine domestic sovereignty comprehended simply as control."[51]

To those who fret about the United States' decreasing capacity to control external events with domestic consequences, and who see this as a degradation of national sovereignty, international law and multilateral arrangements may well appear as threats to sovereignty, rather than as ways to further national goals and to extend the life of the nation-state system. "Piece by piece," Buchanan declares, "our sovereignty is being surrendered. By accession to NAFTA, GATT, the UN, the WTO, the World Bank, the IMF, America has ensnared itself in a web that restricts its freedom of action, diminishes its liberty, and siphons off its wealth."[52] The more centrist Dole, writing when he was Senate majority leader in 1995, warned that "U.S. sovereignty must be defended, not delegated" and that "even gaining support for an American position can involve deals or tradeoffs that are not in America's long-term interests."[53] By caricaturing international organizations as threats to U.S. interests, values, and sovereignty, this school dismisses them as even potential sources of legitimacy.

The Use of Force

Nowhere are the differences between the perspectives on legitimacy held by the United States and those professed by other countries more pronounced or more consequential than in the use of force. This is ironic, for on one level both the American people and U.S. policymakers do put a high value on gaining the political support and, if possible, the military and financial participation of other countries in military confrontations abroad.[54] This makes sense in at least three ways. First, it allows a sharing of the considerable risks and costs involved, whether measured in human, political, or financial terms. Second, it facilitates the projection of force when the use of forward bases, ports, sea-lanes, and overflight rights matter and when the logistical demands of the operation are high. And third, the backing of other countries offers testimony to the kinds of higher and broader purposes that have long appealed to the American people when the use of force is contemplated, and which U.S. presidents have typically cited when seeking to mobilize public and congressional support for such operations.

Public opinion surveys have shown again and again a strong preference for employing force through the UN rather than unilaterally.[55] Nevertheless, even a cursory review of four cases of the U.S. use of force over the past two decades—the Gulf War, usually cited as the model of multilateral cooperation, Grenada, Panama, and Haiti—suggests that the power of international legitimation to affect U.S. domestic support for the use of force has been decidedly modest.

The Gulf War

Compelling testimony for the potential advantages of using force within a multilateral framework can be found in the memoirs of former President George Bush and his national security adviser, Brent Scowcroft, who saw value in seeking Security Council authorization for expelling Iraqi forces from Kuwait in 1991.

> We also believed that the United States should not go it alone, that a multilateral approach was better. This was, in part, a practical matter. Mounting an effective military counter to Iraq's invasion required the backing and bases of Saudi Arabia and other Arab states. Building an international response led us immediately to the United Nations, which could provide a cloak of acceptability to our efforts and mobilize world opinion behind the principles we wished to project.[56]

They suggest that the multilateral route actually opened additional options to U.S. military planners and increased the likelihood of success on the battlefield, rather than narrowing U.S. choices, as critics typically argued. In addition, their references to "a cloak of acceptability" and the need to "mobilize world opinion" behind U.S. principles would also attest to the power of legitimation, even for a superpower.[57]

Given the public's preference for having allies on board and the perennial concerns in Congress about costs and burden sharing, there is also a strong domestic rationale for choosing a multilateral alternative, when the latter is available and feasible. When diplomatic pressures and economic sanctions failed to budge Saddam Hussein, the Bush administration worked diligently to secure Security Council support for stronger action in the form of Resolution 678, which authorized the use of "all necessary means" to compel Iraq to comply with the Security Council's edicts. This resolution not only "eased some of the problems of coalition maintenance," Bush recalls, "it also changed the debate with Congress, creating a context for the use of force which helped bring it aboard. The Security Council had voted to go to war."[58]

On the surface, then, the Gulf War demonstrates how multilateral legitimation and unilateral power can converge in a decidedly pragmatic and mutually reinforcing manner. The model was so attractive to both the idealistic and pragmatic sides of the U.S. political culture that it spawned talk of a "new world order." But what if Beijing or Moscow had decided to veto Resolution 678, if there had been less support among the nonpermanent members, or if agreement on a sufficiently forceful text had not been achieved? Early on, the White House had prudently decided not to risk putting all its eggs in the UN basket. As Bush and Scowcroft explained, "We would ask the council to act only if we knew in advance we had the backing of most of the Arab bloc and we were fairly certain we had the necessary votes. If at any point it became clear we could not succeed, we would back away from a UN mandate and cobble together an independent multinational effort built on friendly Arab and allied participation."[59]

The White House correctly saw that international legitimation could confer significant political advantages. But it clearly regarded legitimation as a tactical expedient, not as a political prerequisite or a legal necessity. The strategy succeeded: six weeks after the Security Council action, both Houses of Congress also voted to authorize the use of force. Yet President Bush has conceded that he was prepared to act even without legislative authorization. "In truth, even had Congress not passed the resolutions I would have acted and ordered our troops into combat. I know it would have caused an outcry, but it was the right thing to do."[60] Evidently, the sources of legitimacy to which the president looked went much deeper than votes of the Security Council or even of Congress. His personal accounts of the crisis suggest that he chose to act partly on the basis of U.S. strategic interests and the flagrant nature of Iraq's flaunting of core international norms, but even more so on moral and humanitarian grounds.

The Gulf War episode also illustrates how difficult it can be to achieve legality, as well as legitimacy, on the international and national planes simultaneously. Although the parallel movement on the two levels was ultimately reinforcing, the outcome could have been quite different. As General Scowcroft has observed, "The carefully negotiated UN vote also called attention to whether, having asked the United Nations, we were obliged to seek similar authority from Congress."[61] To those on Capitol Hill concerned about war powers and the constitutional prerogatives of Congress, to even pose such a question surely would have seemed odd at best and unconstitutional at worst.[62] The president's comment that it was the Security Council, not Congress, that had declared war framed the issue particularly sharply, if inadvertently.

Beyond the question of constitutionality, U.S. critics of multilateralism began to ask whether the tail was not beginning to wag the dog. According to Jeanne Kirkpatrick,

> Internationalists who favor an active U.S. role in the world worry that Mr. Bush may be leading the U.S. down a slippery slope toward world government. They are concerned that, in seeking U.N. authorization for action

in Kuwait, Somalia, and Bosnia, the Bush administration is creating and reinforcing the idea that the use of force is legitimate only if it is authorized by the U.N. They fear that the U.S. government is delegating sovereignty to the U.N. without having actually decided to do so, undermining the capacity to act on the basis of its own values in pursuit of its own interests, and submitting U.S. foreign policy to the uncertainties of consensus building in the United Nations.[63]

More recently, Krauthammer described the Gulf War model as the exception, not the rule. He acknowledged, ruefully, that the readiness to "take seriously, morally seriously" the decisions of the Security Council is "deeply ingrained" and "runs very deep" in the U.S. political culture. George Bush understood this. "That is why he garnered international cover for the Gulf war—essentially an American operation—through all manner of Security Council resolutions. He did it, however, out of necessity. The Democratic Congress likely would not have approved the Gulf war had it not received the blessing of the U.N."[64]

"The problem with contemporary liberalism is that it believes this nonsense," complained Krauthammer. "It sincerely believes that multilateral action—and, in particular, action blessed by the U.N.—is in and of itself morally superior to, and more justifiable than, the United States unilaterally asserting its own national interest." In his view, the UN is in no position to judge legitimacy, given its "corrupt bureaucracy," a General Assembly that serves as "a playground for the most powerless nations on earth to rant and vent their rage at the powerful," and a Security Council "where the lesser Great Powers are able to deflect, decry, denounce, and often defeat the will of the preeminent superpower." He also questions the devotion of other countries to multilateral ideals. "The French and the Chinese and the Russians must wonder why we put up with this. Certainly none of them would were our positions reversed."

Although most Americans are not this hostile toward multilateral institutions, the basic themes voiced by Krauthammer run as deeply in U.S. history and contemporary political culture as the liberal internationalism he derides. Both strains shape the formulation and execution of U.S. foreign policy, largely accounting for its persistent ambivalence about multilateral engagement.

Likewise, the responsibilities of the United States, as the only power with truly global reach and interests, cut two ways. On the one hand, a dominant power needs to show sufficient respect for multilateral rules, processes, and institutions to ensure that they retain enough integrity to guide the actions of most states most of the time and to be of use in times of crisis, should its interests coincide with those of other member states. On the other hand, such a power also needs to maintain sufficient flexibility and autonomy in the use of force to reassure allies, deter potential aggressors, and rally coalitions in cases where important values and interests are at stake but the Security Council is paralyzed by the opposition of one or more of the other permanent members. Ambassador Princeton Lyman, former assistant secretary of state for international organization affairs, describes the resulting policy well.

> The United States maintains the right to act in defense of its interests, including employing the use of force, whether or not such action has been authorized by the Security Council. That is a sore point with many other countries, including America's European allies, who feel much more comfortable with the political cover of a UN mandate even when they agree that force is merited. . . . The United States values Security Council authorization for the international legitimization and sometimes material support it sometimes brings, but the United States does not feel beholden to it. Yet the United States should not be too cavalier about bypassing the Security Council.[65]

These calculations do not always point in the same direction. Among the variables are the political mix in Congress, the views of the public, the nature of the crisis, the response required, and the extent to which U.S. perspectives are shared by countries in the region and by the other members of the Security Council. In weighing unilateral, coalition, and multilateral options in each case, concerns about effectiveness, costs, and risks take precedence over those about rules and procedures because there is no legitimacy in failure when lives and international security are at stake.

Grenada

In late October 1983, the Reagan administration decided to intervene militarily, with the aim of evacuating American students, restoring stability on the tiny island, and reducing Cuban influence there. From the outset, the U.S. government recognized not only that no UN military option would be available, but also that the action would inevitably spark substantial criticism from the world body at a time of East-West tension. Nor was the Organization of American States (OAS) likely to endorse an essentially unilateral employment of U.S. force in the region. Nevertheless, the administration prepared a legal justification for its actions under the UN and OAS charters. According to former Secretary of State George P. Shultz, it sought to fashion a plan of action that would be "consistent with our national interests and international law."[66] Accordingly, it put great stock in the "signed, formal request" that it received from the little-known Organization of Eastern Caribbean States (OECS) "asking for U.S. assistance in assuring their collective security and in restoring democracy to Grenada."[67] Eugenia Charles, prime minister of Dominica and chair of the OECS, was brought to Washington to act as a media spokesperson and as an interlocutor with the highly skeptical congressional Black Caucus.[68] While U.S. forces did most of the fighting, a contingent of East Caribbean policemen was deployed to give some sense of multilateral participation. As Shultz phrased it, "This early, visible presence showed that it was not just a 'Stars and Stripes' operation."[69]

Despite these precautions, the operation was quickly and roundly criticized by prominent U.S. allies, including Britain, France, and Italy; by most Latin American countries; by congressional Democrats (who controlled the House, but not the Senate); and by a number of legal scholars.[70] The United States had to veto a resolution in the Security Council "deeply deploring" the intervention.[71] The General Assembly then picked up this language, passing overwhelmingly (108 to 9) a resolution that "deeply deplores the armed intervention in Grenada, which constitutes a flagrant violation of international law and of the independence, sovereignty and territorial integrity of that state." Not a single NATO ally voted with the United States.[72]

If international legitimation (or in this case delegitimation) has power, one would expect these condemnatory statements and resolutions to have had some effect on the Reagan administration's stance, or at least on public attitudes. Instead, quite the opposite happened: the administration's position seemed to become more persuasive with its critics over time. In response to the UN votes, U.S. officials pointedly questioned the legitimacy of the world body. Reacting to the General Assembly vote, a senior U.S. official asserted that "the U.N. showed itself to be the irresponsible, rush-to-judgment body that votes at the behest of certain countries."[73] President Reagan's spokesperson described the vote as an indication of the state of affairs at the UN. "We find it sad," he commented, "that the U.N. sees fit to deplore actions" taken to "save innocent lives and protect human rights, in full accord with the principles of the U.N. Charter."[74] When the president was asked how he felt about the General Assembly vote, he dismissively responded that "it didn't upset my breakfast at all."

Apparently the same could be said for (or by) much of the American public. Early public opinion surveys, as is normally the case when U.S. forces are in action, were highly favorable.[75] President Reagan's approval ratings rose "as dividends of his boldness."[76] In light of the favorable public reaction and a House fact-finding report, even House Speaker Thomas P. O'Neill reconsidered his earlier opposition, declaring that the operation was "justified" in seeking to rescue the American students.[77] Apparently, some Western European allies also began to have second thoughts, softening their opposition.[78] According to George Shultz's account, the turning point in U.S. opinion came when the first returning student kissed the tarmac in front of rows of TV cameras upon setting foot back in the United States.[79] When he and his colleagues spoke of their sense of danger on the island, their testimony legitimated the U.S. action for the public and its political leaders, despite the international condemnation.

Panama

Six years after the crisis in Grenada, a new U.S. president, George Bush, faced a deteriorating situation in Panama. Given long-standing U.S. interests there, the administration chose to use force unilaterally, without consulting either the OAS or the Security Council. Although the official rationale cited the United States' security responsibilities in the hemisphere and its right of self-defense under article 51 of the UN Charter, there was no effort to seek either regional or global political cover, as was done in the cases of Grenada and the Persian Gulf. In response, the OAS by a 20-to-1 margin voted for the first time to formally censure the United States.[80] Most Latin American as well as European countries also quickly joined the chorus of protest that came from the UN community. The General Assembly passed a resolution strongly deploring the U.S. action by a large 75-to-20 vote, although 64 member states either abstained or did not vote.[81] The Security Council had earlier voted 10 to 4 to 1 on a draft resolution that would have deplored the U.S. intervention, but the United States was joined by the United Kingdom, France, and Canada in opposing the resolution.[82]

As in the case of Grenada, the barrage of critical comments and resolutions from the UN had no apparent effect on domestic opinion, which was even more favorable this time.[83] Unlike the initial response to the Grenada intervention, however, this time key Democrats (who controlled both houses of Congress) supported the president's initiative from the outset. Their views were shaped by the United States' long history with Panama, their concern about the security of the canal, and their revulsion for Panamanian strongman Manuel Antonio Noriega, as well as by the public's strongly favorable initial reaction to news of the operation.[84] Once again, public views of the legitimacy of the operation stemmed from perceptions of U.S. national interests, the values believed to be at stake, the probability of a successful outcome, and the modest U.S. commitment, rather than from the views of other countries or the resolutions of multilateral institutions.

Just nine months after completely bypassing international institutions in dealing with Panama, the Bush administration turned to the UN as one of the keys to reversing the Iraqi aggression against Kuwait. Both situations were perceived to touch on U.S. national interests, but the United States had exercised a proprietary stance toward crises in the Western Hemisphere since the enunciation of the Monroe Doctrine in the early nineteenth century.[85] In addition, the return of the canal to Panama had proven to be a sensitive domestic issue, and no president would have wanted to have the UN flag planted in the canal zone during his or her tenure. Finally, some elements of the public had been pressing the president to act more decisively against Noriega.

Besides, there was little or no chance of getting either UN or OAS authorization for military intervention in Panama, while Iraq's aggression against Kuwait was so flagrant and so worrisome to developing countries concerned about the integrity of borders that there was unusually substantial, if latent, support for invoking at least multilateral sanctions against Baghdad. Finally, the costs and risks inherent in a military confrontation with Iraq were significantly higher, and the logistics of launching and maintaining an operation were far more demanding. Both factors made it essential to recruit partners for the Persian Gulf operation, thus raising the value of international legitimation.

Haiti

By the time the Clinton administration came into office, it arguably had learned the lessons of the Persian Gulf (that a multilateral blessing has advantages) better than those of Panama and Grenada (that unilateralism is popular when it works). In neither Somalia nor Haiti, however, could any amount of international legitimation compensate for the deep doubts among the public and in Congress about the extent to which important U.S. national interests were involved.[86] Moreover, many in Congress believed that the president's alleged preference for multilateralism had led to a relatively inactive and indecisive approach to the protection of U.S. global interests and values.

Even before the Republicans took control of both Houses of Congress with the November 1994 elections, the administration had gone to great lengths to assure Congress that it would not place U.S. forces under a UN command and would be very cautious about approving or joining new UN operations.[87] At that point, putting an operation under a UN umbrella would have effectively delegitimated it, at least in Washington's eyes, by distancing it from the unvarnished pursuit of U.S. national interests. In essence, Washington politics had turned on its head the scholarly description of the sources of legitimacy outlined at the outset of this chapter.

The Haiti crisis had been simmering since the violent overthrow of elected President Jean-Bertrand Aristide in September 1991. Persistent and often violent oppression in the impoverished nation sparked a series of international monitoring missions, diplomatic efforts, and UN-sponsored sanctions, as well as the exodus of boatloads of refugees seeking a safe haven in Florida. During the 1992 campaign, candidate Bill Clinton was sharply critical of the Bush administration's handling of these issues, but, when he became president, Clinton, too, seemed ambivalent about taking decisive action to reinstall Aristide. In May 1994, the House passed a nonbinding resolution opposing military intervention in Haiti unless there was a "clear and present danger" to U.S. citizens or interests.[88] Some polls in the weeks before the September 1994 U.S.-led international operation showed a two-to-one margin against military intervention.[89] Republicans were particularly unenthusiastic, while African Americans were somewhat more positive and the congressional Black Caucus was widely credited with convincing the initially reluctant White House to go forward.[90] Yet even *after* President Clinton's September 15 speech calling for action and the junta's agreement to give up power, two-thirds of the public declared that the president did not have a clear policy on what to do in Haiti.

Appeals to the legitimacy of the UN apparently did little to relieve public and congressional anxieties about the wisdom of going forward. One August 1994 poll showed a sharp increase in support when the premise shifted from the unilateral use of U.S. force to a "United Nations multinational" operation.[91] But a survey by the same organization the next month found the public almost evenly divided over whether "authorization by the United Nations and the participation of other countries" provided sufficient reason for the intervention.[92] The weak domestic response to a July 31 Security Council resolution (940) authorizing a multinational force to use "all necessary means" was instructive, especially when contrasted to the importance attached to the same wording in the Persian Gulf resolution less than four years before. Even the *New York Times* called the Security Council's attempt to declare the Haitian regime a threat to international peace "a peculiar exercise in circular logic that is hard for anyone to take seriously."[93]

When the operation proceeded smoothly with little resistance, President Clinton received a modest boost in his approval ratings, but nothing close to those received by his predecessors after Grenada and Panama.[94] Over time, public confidence in the success of the mission began to fade, while concerns about getting bogged down surged.[95] In the end, as in the beginning, the public assessed the mission on whether it would forward important U.S. national interests and whether it would succeed and be cost-effective, not on whether other countries or the UN thought that it was the right thing to do.

Lessons and Conclusions

First, these cases suggest that the power of international legitimation as a factor in shaping U.S. public and congressional attitudes toward the use of force is decidedly modest. In general, what others think appears to matter more to Democrats than to Republicans, so presidents may be more prone to seek international legitimation when Democrats control Congress. When the risks involved in the use of force are high and the need for burden sharing is acute, the public and its congressional representatives are more likely to appreciate the advantages of multilateral alternatives. In such situations, as in the Persian Gulf, the backing of the UN or a regional body can serve not only to ease the recruitment of coalition partners, but also to consolidate or reinforce a public predisposition to use force, provided it is skillfully and persistently invoked by the White House.

At least in the cases reviewed here, there is no evidence that the public looks first to international bodies for the legitimation of national decisions to use or not to use force. Exhortations from abroad have done little to assuage doubts about the wisdom of involving U.S. forces in situations where no important national interests were perceived to be at stake. Likewise, the cases outlined above also strongly suggest that efforts to delegitimate popularly supported U.S. military actions through international denunciations have not succeeded. Instead, they usually provoke U.S. opinion leaders to respond with rhetoric designed to delegitimate those international forums that produced or encouraged the international censure.[96]

Second, the theoretical writings on legitimacy discussed in the first part of this chapter do make some useful points: legitimacy does matter as one aspect of power, as attested by the amount of attention that national leaders pay to manipulating perceptions of it; it is a subjective condition that depends on the views and values of disparate political actors; and it cannot be sustained indefinitely if important actors cease to respect the relationships, processes, arrangements, and values that have defined the existing international system. The empirical evidence cited later in the book, however, suggests that some of the basic tenets of the orthodox conception of legitimacy are being seriously challenged by the growing disparities of power among nations, by diverging conceptions of right process, and by U.S. exceptionalism. This challenge is revealed graphically in questions of institutional reform and the use of force.

Third, many international institutions are today facing what David Beetham calls a "legitimacy deficit." That is, there are recurring discrepancies between rules and beliefs or the absence of shared beliefs. This deficit is illustrated by the contradictions that have frustrated efforts to find any widely accepted formulas for restructuring the UN system, or even the Security Council. Likewise, this deficit has long been painfully evident in discussions about the organization of multilateral forces and in the failure of the member states to create anything like the machinery envisioned in chapter VII of the UN Charter for the enforcement of Security Council mandates. Even peacekeeping has become more of a stretch in recent years. While the focus of this volume, and this chapter, is on the United States, a closer examination of the policies and preferences of other major and many lesser powers would also reveal considerable variance from the norms and processes associated with an ideal form of multilateralism.

Fourth, the United States is not alone in looking well beyond the Security Council for sources of legitimacy or in letting domestic political considerations sway its posture on issues before the council. For example, China refused to permit the extension of the UN peacekeeping mission in strategically situated Macedonia, not because of developments in the volatile Balkans, but because of Skopje's dealings with Taiwan. The nineteen nations of NATO went to war with Serbia not only without the Security Council's authorization, but also with a clear understanding that some permanent members of the council would have vetoed any such resolution. Russia has repeatedly told the world that its own handling of civil strife in Chechnya is none of the Security Council's business. Underdeveloped Ethiopia and Eritrea, ignoring the mediation efforts of the UN secretary-general and the appeals of the Security Council, chose instead to fight the bloodiest and most pointless war of the last decade of the twentieth century. A summit of the Organization of African Unity encouraged its members to violate the Security Council's sanctions against Libya, while a growing flood of countries—including permanent members of the council—have decided to flaunt or reinterpret the UN's sanctions against Iraq. And the number of developed countries willing to respond to the secretary-general's entreaties for forces to fill out the peace operations voted by the Security Council has declined markedly in recent years.

None of these member states or regional groups has consciously sought, anymore than the United States has, to undermine the authority of the Security Council, even though that has been the cumulative effect of their actions. Yet, given the unsurpassed power and reach of the United States, the viability and even legitimacy of the system ultimately will be shaped by whether Washington acts and talks as if it values internationally established rules and procedures on the use of force, even as it retains the option to act unilaterally when it feels it must.

Fifth, the evidence cited in this chapter strongly suggests that a disabling flaw of much of the practice and theory of multilateralism has been its insistence on looking at international interactions and processes through the wrong end of the telescope. The search for the sources of legitimacy should begin with an understanding of national values, interests, and political cultures, not with an examination of global treaties, institutions, and processes. For instance, reliance on domestic models of law and order in theories of international legitimacy has led to exaggerated notions of its power over national publics. Surely, if the legitimacy of U.S. policies toward international institutions mattered greatly to the American people beyond affirmative and superficial poll responses, then one of the candidates would have raised U.S. arrears in payments to the UN at some point during the 2000 U.S. presidential campaign.

A top-down perspective is likely to confuse cause and effect and to underestimate the strength of national identities and political processes, even in the face of international censure. To argue that national interests and values should be abandoned when states enter the UN, for example, is to prefer that reality be left outside the building. If our understanding of international politics, norms, and institutions is not based on a sober analysis of national politics, norms, and institutions, then of what is the foundation of our understanding composed? It is the existence of national interests that gives purpose to multilateralism, just as the accumulation of national power provides it with the capacity to act.

Lastly, legitimacy is not a black and white issue. Each action will be seen as legitimate by some domestic and international constituencies and as illegitimate by others. Multilateral cooperation is the product of decisions in dozens of national capitals, shaped both by domestic needs and international conditions, and the lack of cooperation in one matter will not necessarily foreclose it in another. Legitimacy is the product of innumerable interactions between national and global politics on a spectrum of policy issues. These global-national interactions define a two-way street of many lanes, of course, but in the case of a country as powerful and as independently minded as the United States, there tends to be more traffic going up than coming down. It would make sense then, in both theory and practice, to acknowledge that legitimacy is not an all-or-nothing condition, nor is it the sole possession either of international institutions or of national policies. Only through a creative use of shades of gray, then, can the framework for a more durable and sensible relationship between U.S. power and global institutions begin to be crafted. Reassessing notions of legitimacy on both sides would be a good place to start.

Notes

1. Ian Hurd considers legitimacy to be one of the "three currencies of power" and contends that, while this point is widely accepted in domestic affairs, it has been underappreciated in international relations theory. See "Legitimacy and Authority in International Politics."

2. Claude, "Collective Legitimacy as a Political Function of the United Nations," p. 368.

3. Beetham, *The Legitimation of Power*, p. 3.

4. Ibid., pp. 15–20.

5. Hurd, "Legitimacy and Authority in International Politics," p. 381. Emphasis in the original.

6. Barnett, "Bringing in the New World Order," p. 548.

7. Franck, *The Power of Legitimacy Among Nations*, p. 24.

8. Claude, "Collective Legitimacy as a Political Function of the United Nations," p. 368.

9. Beetham, *The Legitimation of Power*, p. 35.

10. For an assessment of why a dominant United States agreed to establish a series of post-war institutions that might have in some way tied its hands, see Ikenberry, *After Victory*, and Ikenberry, "Institutions, Strategic Restraint, and the Persistence of American Postwar Order."

11. Barnett, "Bringing in the New World Order," p. 546.

12. Then and now, the most contentious procedural issue was the granting of veto power to the five permanent members of the Security Council. For an account of the debates at San Francisco over the veto, see Russell, *A History of the United Nations Charter*, pp. 713–749.

13. Barnett and Finnemore, "The Politics, Power, and Pathologies of International Organizations," p. 699.

14. Franck, *Fairness in International Law and Institutions*, p. 477. Such standards are obviously more easily achieved within nations than between them and are subject to reinterpretation as conditions change. Realists, moreover, would be quick to point out the frailty of order in the contemporary world. And political commentators as diverse in their views as Charles Krauthammer and Arthur M. Schlesinger have questioned the utility of international laws and norms that cannot be enforced. According to

Krauthammer, "In any social system, whether of individuals or nation-states, where there is no enforcer, there can be no real law." "A World Imagined," p. 23. Schlesinger has similarly claimed that "law is not law if, in the last resort, it is not enforced." "America and the World: Isolationism Resurgent?," p. 1.

15. Caron, "The Legitimacy of the Collective Authority of the Security Council," p. 562.

16. Brilmayer, *American Hegemony,* p. 157.

17. Some of the most durable contributions of such bodies, therefore, tend to stem from their deliberative and norm-setting functions, from their roles as convenors and forums for broad-based discussion.

18. For instance, of the series of reform proposals announced by UN Secretary-General Kofi Annan in July 1997, those that could be implemented by the secretariat largely have been, while most of those requiring action by intergovernmental bodies have yet to be acted on. Also, all three charter amendments to date have served to enlarge intergovernmental bodies: the Economic and Social Council (ECOSOC) twice and the Security Council once.

19. Also see Kull and Destler, *Misreading the Public,* and Luck, *Mixed Messages,* pp. 34–40 and 260–268.

20. Mallaby, "The Irrelevant Election."

21. Luck, *Mixed Messages.*

22. This does not mean, of course, that all international bodies will be perceived or treated equally. For a discussion of exceptionalism and of the differential congressional attitudes toward the WTO, UN dues, and peacekeeping, see Luck, "American Exceptionalism and International Organization."

23. Franck, *Fairness in International Law and Institutions,* p. 477.

24. The low point came with the passage of the Zionism-racism resolution in November 1975, which sent American public approval ratings for the world body tumbling to some of the lowest levels ever.

25. See, for example, Karns and Mingst, eds., *The United States and Multilateral Institutions,* pp. 7, 12, and Luck and Fromuth, "Anti-Americanism at the United Nations."

26. Hurd, "Legitimacy and Authority in International Politics," p. 403.

27. Congress, unable to exert the kind of oversight of international bodies that it does of domestic agencies, has repeatedly resorted to the power of the purse strings as a direct means of exercising leverage. Contemptuous of the finely tuned decisionmaking processes, legal frameworks, and administrative procedures of multilateral organizations, Congress has mandated that the United States pursue a dual-reform agenda of reducing its costs, burdens, and risks, and of expanding transparency and accountability. Others, of course, have bitterly resented such unilateral tactics.

28. Rabkin, "International Law vs. the American Constitution," p. 37.

29. Whereas Buchanan and most conservative critics usually lump almost all global institutions together as enemies of U.S. values, Nader and the left-wing antiglobalists target the WTO, IMF, and World Bank, which are allegedly doing the dirty work for private global financiers and corporations. In their view, these limited-membership bodies have been both less transparent and more powerful than the generally well-meaning but ineffective UN. For the views of one influential activist, see the interview of Lori Wallach, Director of Public Citizen's Global Trade Watch, in *Foreign Policy* 118 (Spring 2000), and her testimony before the Senate Committee on Commerce, Science, and Transportation, *S.2467, GATT Implementing Legislation,* Hearings, October 17, 1994, 103rd Congress, 2d sess. (U.S. Government Printing Office, 1994).

30. For a historical analysis, see Luck, *Mixed Messages*, pp. 15–40.

31. Bell, "American Ascendancy and the Pretense of Concert," p. 60.

32. Brilmayer, *American Hegemony*, pp. 96–97 and 100–104.

33. Krauthammer, "What's Wrong with the 'Pentagon Paper'?" *Washington Post*, March 13, 1992.

34. Franck, *Fairness in International Law and Institutions*, p. 479. Also see Franck, *The Power of Legitimacy Among Nations*, p. 177. Bruce Russett questions how democratic the UN can be given the enormous asymmetries in power among its members and its lack of "at least some protection for the rights and values of minorities." See Russett, "Ten Balances for Weighing UN Reform Proposals," p. 19.

35. On the notion of sovereign equality, see Kingsbury, "Sovereignty and Inequality," and Smouts, "International Organizations and Inequality Among States." For the handling of these questions in the UN's preparatory meetings, see Russell, *A History of the United Nations Charter*, pp. 111, 120, 349–354, 358–360, and 405, and Hoopes and Brinkley, *FDR and the Creation of the U.N.*, pp. 144–145.

36. According to Ngaire Woods, "a balance had to be struck between 'efficiency' wrought through great-power management and 'legitimacy,' which was necessary to ensure the cooperation of the rest." "Order, Globalization, and Inequality in World Politics," p. 34.

37. Russell, *A History of the United Nations*, p. 672.

38. For instance, the United States has used the International Atomic Energy Agency (IAEA) to further the acceptance of nonproliferation norms central to its security interests, as well as valuing the agency's operational and monitoring activities. See Schiff, "Dominance Without Hegemony," pp. 57–89.

39. This may be one explanation for why Congress has paid much more attention to administrative inadequacies in the central UN than in the specialized agencies.

40. David Mitrany's functionalist theories about how broader international political cooperation could be built on the foundations of piece-by-piece functional cooperation in specific areas were quite influential among Western planners. Mitrany, "The Functional Approach to International Organization," and *The Progress of International Government*.

41. Helms, "Saving the U.N.," pp. 5–7.

42. For a discussion of why Congress accepted the WTO in November 1994, when U.S. support for peacekeeping and for paying assessed dues was at its low ebb, see Luck, "American Exceptionalism and International Organization."

43. Stephen S. Rosenfeld, "Multilateralism Is a Dodge," *Washington Post*, June 18, 1993. Warning against "ritualistic multilateralism," Carl Gershman contended that "multilateralism risks becoming the opiate of the West, a cover for a drift into parochialism and isolationism." Gershman, "The United Nations and the New World Order," p. 15.

44. According to Miles Kahler, in the IMF, "the United States found it valuable to veil its power through conventions that convinced other countries that the rules of the game were reasonably fair or at least better than no rules at all." "The United States and the International Monetary Fund," p. 97.

45. Transcript, *New York Times*, October 12, 2000.

46. Schiffer and Schiffer, eds., *Looking Outward*, pp. 128–129. Beetham makes a similar point, *The Legitimation of Power*, p. 35. When the United States does get its way on highly charged issues in the UN, such as the October 2000 denial of Sudan's bid to win a seat on the Security Council, the losers regularly charge it with "browbeating or paying off" smaller or poorer member states—as if the use of power were somehow illegitimate even in such a highly political body. Crossette,

"Sudan: U.S. Accused in U.N. Role," *New York Times,* October 13, 2000. For a somewhat one-sided and personalized view of the United States as a bully in the UN, see Boutros-Ghali, *Unvanquished.*

47. With the end of the Cold War and with the growing struggle over structure, management, and finance within international institutions, it is striking the extent to which East-West tensions have been replaced by West-West ones.

48. Rodman, "The World's Resentment," p. 34.

49. Senator Dole expressed this concern especially well in his article, "Shaping America's Global Future," pp. 36–37.

50. For a critique of this narrow view of sovereignty, see Spiro, "The New Sovereigntists."

51. Krasner, *Sovereignty: Organized Hypocrisy,* p. 13.

52. Buchanan, *The Great Betrayal,* p. 107.

53. Dole, "Shaping America's Global Future," pp. 36, 37.

54. For a more bullish forecast of the United States' growing deference to international institutions, see Brilmayer, *American Hegemony,* p. 223.

55. Kull and Destler, *Misreading the Public,* pp. 77–80, 100–101, and 293.

56. Bush and Scowcroft, *A World Transformed,* p. 491.

57. As Michael N. Barnett has pointed out, major powers seeking to build coalitions for burden-sharing purposes have often found other states "insisting that the operation be viewed as consistent with the interests and norms of the international community, that is, be blessed by the United Nations." "The Limits of Peace-keeping, Spheres of Influence, and the Future of the United Nations," p. 97.

58. Bush and Scowcroft, *A World Transformed,* p. 415.

59. Ibid., p. 356.

60. Ibid., p. 446.

61. Ibid., p. 416.

62. The historic debates about multilateral military action and its implications for constitutional processes and executive-congressional relations are discussed in Luck, *Mixed Messages,* pp. 163–195.

63. Kirkpatrick, "Secretary-General Needs Lesson in Limits to His Power," *Dallas Morning News,* December 6, 1992.

64. Krauthammer, "A World Imagined," p. 23.

65. Lyman, "Saving the UN Security Council—A Challenge for the United States."

66. Shultz, *Turmoil and Triumph,* p. 326.

67. Ibid., p. 332.

68. Ibid., p. 337.

69. Ibid., p. 333.

70. *New York Times,* October 26–30, 1983.

71. Bernstein, "U.S. Vetoes U.N. Resolution 'Deploring' Grenada Invasion," *New York Times,* October 29, 1983. The vote was eleven in favor, one against, and three abstentions (Britain, Togo, and Zaire).

72. A/RES/38/7 of November 2, 1983. Bernstein, "Behind U.N. Vote: How Much Anti-Americanism?"

73. Bernstein, "Behind U.N. Vote: How Much Anti-Americanism?"

74. Clines, "It Was a Rescue Mission, Reagan Says," *New York Times,* November 4, 1983.

75. A *Merit Report* poll found 64 percent approving and 23 percent disapproving the week following the intervention, while the *Los Angeles Times* found a 59-to-25 percent margin two weeks later, the *New York Times* a 63-to-27 percent difference the following week, and the *Roper Report* a 60-to-26 margin six weeks after the intervention.

76. Smith, "From Beirut to Grenada, the Price of Power Rises," *New York Times,* October 30, 1983.

77. Smith, "O'Neill Now Calls Grenada Invasion 'Justified' Action," *New York Times,* November 9, 1983.

78. Vinocur, "Invasion of Grenada Wins Some Allied Supporters," *New York Times,* November 3, 1983.

79. Shultz, *Turmoil and Triumph,* pp. 339–340.

80. Goshko and Isikoff, "OAS Votes to Censure U.S. for Intervention," *Washington Post,* December 23, 1989.

81. A/RES/44/240 of December 29, 1989, *Washington Post,* December 21 and 22, 1989, and the *New York Times,* January 25, 1990.

82. Schwartz, "U.S. Allies Veto U.N. Council Censure," *Washington Post,* December 24, 1989.

83. In a *Washington Post–*ABC News poll a few weeks after the intervention, eight out of ten respondents expressed support for the U.S. action, an even larger margin called it a success, and 79 percent approved of President Bush's job performance, one of the highest approval ratings of any postwar president. A Gallup Poll that same month gave the president an 80 percent approval rating. Morin, "Poll Shows Rising Support for Bush, Republicans," *Washington Post,* January 18, 1990. Similar results were found in a *New York Times–*CBS News Poll, in which three-quarters of the respondents said that the invasion was justified. Oreskes, "Approval of Bush, Bolstered by Panama, Soars in Poll," *New York Times,* January 19, 1990.

84. Dewar and Kenworthy, "Congress: Decision 'Was Made Necessary By the Reckless Actions of General Noriega'," *Washington Post,* December 21, 1989; and Oberdorfer, "Administration Draws American Support, Denunciation Abroad," *Washington Post,* December 22, 1989.

85. UN involvement in peace processes and in observer, monitoring, and peacekeeping operations in Central America began in earnest as the end of the Cold War lessened East-West factors in these conflicts.

86. For accounts of U.S. policies toward the operation in Somalia, see Senate Armed Services Committee, *U.S. Military Operations in Somalia;* Oakley and Hirsch, *Somalia and Operation Restore Hope;* and Oakley, "Using the United Nations to Advance U.S. Interests."

87. For a discussion of the evolution of administration and congressional attitudes toward peacekeeping in the 1990s, see Luck, "American Exceptionalism and International Organization."

88. *New York Times,* May 29, 1994.

89. Respondents to a June CBS News survey opposed the United States' sending ground troops by a 66-to-25 percent margin. In a September CBS News–*New York Times* poll, interviewees agreed by a 61-to-32 percent margin that sending U.S. troops would not be worth the cost. A poll the same month by the Princeton Survey Research found disapproval of "U.S. participation in a multilateral invasion of Haiti" by a 57-to-34 percent margin.

90. Jehl, "Showdown with Haiti," *New York Times,* September 18, 1994.

91. This survey and one conducted by the University of Maryland are cited in Kull and Destler, *Misreading the Public,* pp. 102–103, 108, and 288.

92. Democrats agreed, 52 to 39 percent, while Republicans disagreed, 50 to 42 percent.

93. Editorial, *New York Times,* September 2, 1994.

94. Kazay, "Mission to Haiti," *New York Times,* September 21, 1994.

95. See polls by the *Los Angeles Times* in October 1994, *Time–*CNN in March 1995 and in April 1995, and Princeton Survey Research in June 1995. In an October 1994 CBS News survey, 85 percent voiced concern that the United States would get

"bogged down in Haiti's domestic turmoil." In November 1994, 64 percent in a *Time*–CNN poll said that "pulling American troops out of Haiti" should be a high priority for the new Congress.

96. It would be reasonable to speculate, however, that if the public is already deeply divided over the use of force, as it was over the Vietnam War, then international protests are more likely to have some domestic resonance. No such cases, however, fell within the scope of this chapter.

3

The Growing Influence of Domestic Factors

Princeton N. Lyman

THE DIVIDING LINE BETWEEN FOREIGN AND DOMESTIC ISSUES IS BECOMING increasingly blurred in the United States. This is an inevitable product of globalization. That process is tying the U.S. economy ever more closely to international markets, raising the salience of cross-border environmental issues, and linking such normally domestic issues as health, education, and crime to international dimensions. Globalization is having a profound effect on governmental organization for foreign affairs, political responses to international issues, and trends in civic society. Older structures for addressing foreign affairs in the United States are not adequate for this situation.

The irony is that this process is occurring as the American public assigns a lower priority to foreign affairs than it did during the Cold War, even though the public is neither unaware of global issues nor immune to U.S. responsibilities. Polls consistently show that a sizeable majority of the citizenry supports an active U.S. role in the world, recognizes the benefits of freer trade, supports integration of human rights and social concerns into foreign policy, believes the United States has a moral responsibility to help poorer nations, and prefers U.S. involvement in peacekeeping or other international military action to be undertaken in conjunction with the UN, an organization to which the public gives high marks.[1] Notably, the public views these issues more from a social and moral perspective than one of purely national interest. But there is considerable ambivalence and division over the right programmatic responses to these issues—for example, just how to integrate concerns about child labor into trade policy or whether foreign aid is effective in helping the poor. World developments appear to the public at large, moreover, as largely episodic, disconnected events, in which the public feels it has little voice and about which it doubts it can be efficacious.[2] This public disengagement opens the door to issue-driven special-interest groups that can command political attention and wield influence perhaps beyond their numerical strength. In the words of one critical observer, the low level of general public emphasis distorts policy choices "to favor the noisy few over the quiet many."[3]

The United States is not alone. These processes are operating in a larger context of globalization everywhere. Globalization, as James Rosenau has pointed out, is moving the world into an era of both integration and fragmentation. On the one hand, a number of factors, both good and bad—such as transformation of economic production and exchange, technological advances, information flows, patterns of migration, and criminal syndicates—are integrating the world. These trends lend support to multilateralism, inasmuch as they seem to demand international collaboration and governance. At the same time, in reaction to this integrative pull is a renewed focus on community, ethnic or religious ties, development of like-minded associations, and resistance to faceless bureaucratic instruments of globalization. These forces of fragmentation can make global cooperation a contentious issue in domestic politics. Given these opposing dynamics, the United States and other countries must increasingly operate across what Rosenau calls the "domestic-foreign frontier."[4] Along this frontier, traditional means of governance and allocations of responsibility are proving inadequate.

The Changing Responsibilities for Foreign Policy

The growing linkage of domestic and foreign affairs poses significant challenges to the management of U.S. foreign policy. The impact of these challenges on U.S. multilateralism is mixed.

Officially, the State Department is charged with the formulation and implementation of foreign policy. Of course, since the end of World War II and the institutionalization of the National Security Council (NSC), it has been clear that foreign policy is more complex, with the Defense Department, the intelligence agencies, and, of course, the White House playing major roles. But these relationships could reasonably be expected to be coordinated in the NSC structure. Today, however, foreign policy is led in many critical areas by other agencies not even part of that structure. The U.S. trade representative (USTR) and the Treasury, Energy, Health and Human Services (HHS), Education, Commerce, Labor, and even Interior departments are playing an increasingly active role abroad. In South Africa alone, twenty-five U.S. government agencies are represented in the U.S. Embassy community. Twenty-four U.S. agencies have become involved in Nigeria since that country's return to democratic government.

Some of this activity is a natural extension of previously established relationships. HHS has long been the official U.S. representative to the World Health Organization (WHO), as Labor has with the International Labour Organization (ILO) and Agriculture to a great extent with the Food and Agriculture Organization (FAO). These relationships have taken on new salience, however, as concern has risen over such international issues as the spread of infectious diseases, biotechnology, workers' rights, and child labor. Some of this activity is also being promoted for traditional foreign policy reasons, out of recognition that the skills and resources needed to deepen bilateral relationships in many cases reside within domestic agencies. This awareness shaped participation in the binational commissions that Vice-President Gore chaired with his counterparts in South Africa, Russia, Egypt, and Ukraine. In each case, cabinet secretaries of several U.S. domestic agencies participated and were directed to develop programs with their counterparts. As a result of this activity, international programs are proliferating within these domestic U.S. agencies.

But, by far, the primary reason for the growth of international activity outside the traditional U.S. foreign policy bureaucracy is the growing interconnectedness of domestic and foreign concerns. In some instances, domestically oriented agencies have come to supersede the authority of the State Department and the NSC. Law enforcement is a prominent example. Not only the Drug Enforcement Agency but also the Federal Bureau of Investigation, U.S. Customs, and the Immigration and Naturalization Service (INS) have expanded their presence abroad. The FBI now has offices in Western Europe, Russia, the Middle East, and all across Africa. U.S. ambassadors overseas are finding that the FBI does not feel bound by the normal rules of ambassadorial oversight—and indeed argues in some cases that such oversight would interfere with the bureau's effectiveness. The FBI's activities can also impinge on other foreign policy objectives such as human rights and democratization.[5]

Economic and trade issues provide another example. Years ago, the State Department conceded responsibility for a large part of international commercial work to the Commerce Department. Today, it has lost ground on what has become a major element of foreign policy, trade negotiations. The USTR has not only filled this role, but has emerged as a major player in foreign policy. Whether in fashioning the lodestone of our relationship with China, the future of the international trading system in the WTO, or, increasingly, the relationship with emerging third-world economies, the USTR is perhaps one of the most powerful foreign policy agencies in this age of globalization. Yet it is not part of the traditional foreign policy structure, nor does it feel bound by the latter.

Trade policy is a good example of the mixed results of globalizing trends on multilateralism. The USTR is both multilateral in its approach and hostile to traditional multilateral institutions. For example, the USTR champions the WTO but fully supports the WTO's demands for independence from the entire UN structure. The USTR representative in Geneva, unlike most other U.S. government representatives there, does not report through the U.S. ambassador to the UN but directly to the USTR in Washington.

As the economic aspects of foreign policy have grown in importance, the Treasury Department has also assumed greater influence in U.S. foreign policy. This became clear in the U.S. response to the Asian financial crisis of 1998. International financial stability was at stake, but so too was the political stability of important countries like Indonesia and South Korea. The U.S. Treasury nevertheless took the lead in fashioning the U.S. response, while the State Department struggled for several weeks to have a seat at the table in order to inject its concerns.[6] But the Treasury Department's influence extends beyond financial matters. Larry Summers, then secretary of the treasury, undertook a ten-day trip to Africa during 2000 to speak about—among other topics—the HIV/AIDS crisis. Health advocates shrugged a bit about this but confessed that he probably had more potential influence on this issue than either the secretary of HHS or the secretary of state.

The Treasury Department's attitude toward multilateral institutions, similar to that of the USTR, is ambivalent. Fiercely defensive of its authority over U.S relations with the World Bank and the IMF, because of their influence on the world economic system, the Treasury Department is at the same time less inclined or perhaps less equipped to advance the development role these agencies play. U.S. policy in these institutions is thus fractured, as the State Department and the U.S. Agency for International Development (USAID) seek to bring their influence with the international financial institutions (IFIs) to bear on precisely these development issues. Like the USTR, the Treasury Department takes a disdainful attitude toward the UN, barely acknowledging that the IFIs are part of the UN system and seeing, if reasonably, no useful role for the UN in international financial policy.

Another agency assuming an increasingly important role internationally is the Department of Energy (DOE). Understandably, it was the secretary of energy who sought to persuade OPEC members to increase oil production during the run-up in oil prices in the fall of 2000. But DOE has been active in U.S. foreign policy on a much broader front. It has undertaken energy-sector studies for African governments, convened meetings of African oil ministers, and provided technical assistance to foreign governments to contain oil spills. In Nigeria, DOE, USAID, and the World Bank are all advising that government on energy policy.

HHS represents perhaps the best example of an agency with traditional multilateral interests seeking to enhance its role substantially on the international scene. HHS has drafted a "global strategy" paper that proposes that the department adopt a more proactive stance toward a slew of international challenges. The document recommends that HHS help improve international capacities to control infectious diseases, prevent noncommunicable diseases (such as those created by tobacco), respond to the threats of biological and chemical terrorism, improve emergency public health and health infrastructure, and spread the benefits of medical research. The rationale in the paper goes directly to the linkages between domestic and foreign policy:

Make no mistake—Americans can no longer think we are isolated and protected from health problems elsewhere in the world. We must think globally now. . . . Infectious diseases have a direct, measurable, and dramatic impact on Americans. A 1999 survey commissioned by the Global Health Council revealed that nearly 50% of the respondents said they know someone with HIV/AIDS, TB, hepatitis or malaria. The outbreak of the West Nile encephalitis on the East Coast has put the infectious disease issue on the front pages, as did earlier outbreaks of plague in India, the avian influenza virus in Hong Kong, and Ebola virus in Africa. With millions crossing borders every day, these diseases are now "only a day away."[7]

The increased salience of international health leads HHS to the conclusion that it must play a greater international role:

While the Department of State is the U.S. Government leader in foreign policy and USAID in development assistance, HHS is the leader and central organization in health. Health will be a vital part of our foreign policy agenda. . . . These issues may demand greater U.S. foreign policy resources, both in terms of money and time of personnel. Only HHS can effectively meet this mandate.[8]

HHS has been a strong advocate of multilateralism. One reason is that effective control of infectious diseases depends on a worldwide surveillance system, which can only be organized through an international institution. As discussed below, HHS's enthusiasm for the WHO outdoes even that of the State Department. A question is whether this will hold true in the Bush administration, especially as the WHO pursues its energetic campaign against tobacco.

The Department of Education is a relatively new actor on this scene and a clear example of the growing recognition that domestic and international interests coincide. On April 19, 2000, President Clinton authorized an International Education Policy, to be jointly administered by the Department of Education and the State Department. Interestingly, USAID was not even informed of the initiative. The president's memorandum is instructive:

To continue to compete successfully in the global economy and to maintain our role as a world leader, the United States needs to ensure that its citizens develop a broad understanding of the world, proficiency in other languages, and knowledge of other cultures. America's leadership also depends on building ties with those who will guide the political, cultural, and economic development of their countries in the future.[9]

The memorandum goes on to recognize just how important foreign students are to U.S. educational institutions. It points out that there are nearly 500,000 international students in the United States today, contributing some $9 billion annually to our economy. Left unsaid, but well understood in the education community, is that many U.S. graduate schools, especially in such areas as engineering and the physical sciences, count heavily on the income from tuition-paying students from abroad. Under the Clinton administration, the secretary of education was out in front in urging U.S reentry into the UN Educational, Scientific, and Cultural Organization (UNESCO). It remains to be seen if the same degree of multilateral interest at the Department of Education continues under the Bush Presidency.

Who's in Charge? Who Pays?

One can welcome this growing internationalism throughout the federal government. Indeed, one could argue that as the line between domestic and foreign policy blurs, both understanding of and support for an active U.S. role in the world should be enhanced. But that is not necessarily the case. Problems of management and funding can impede that process.

So far, the Clinton and Bush administrations have responded to these developments in an ad hoc fashion. During the Clinton administration, the NSC adopted HIV/AIDS as a national security issue and made some progress in coordinating the vast array of government departments and agencies involved in this issue. The relationship between the role of the NSC and that of the special presidential advisor on AIDS was, however, unclear. For the first time the NSC added a health specialist, broadening further its definition of "national security." Meanwhile, the national economic advisor took on the major coordinating role on debt to poorer nations and the recent international education initiative. The Bush administration is experimenting with having international economic issues coordinated jointly by the NSC and the national economic advisor. As of this writing, it was still deciding whether to keep the president's special advisor on AIDS.

These experiments may be instructive, but in the longer run a more fundamental reordering of White House coordination of foreign policy will be required. Certain issues might be designated as "global" or of equal domestic and international concern and coordinating mechanisms established accordingly. Alternatively, a more fundamental restructuring of the NSC, in conjunction with other White House offices, might be required. Equally important, the traditional foreign policy agencies, the State Department and USAID in particular, must adapt to new definitions of "foreign policy" and better ways to tap into the expertise that resides in other "domestic" agencies.

The AIDS crisis is indicative of the complexity of managing foreign policy in a globalizing world. Sandy Thurman, President Clinton's special advisor on AIDS, has said that one of her problems in fashioning an administration response to the epidemic was that over 100 U.S. government agencies and other bodies have a role in AIDS research, policy, or their implementation. It was hard for her even to get all of their representatives into the same room. The AIDS crisis touches not only on public health but also on the issue of patent rights, implying a major role to be played by the USTR; on tax policy relating to public-private partnerships, as proposed by

President Clinton for vaccine research; and on immigration and visa policies that fall within the mandate of the INS. As noted above, the president in declaring AIDS a national security problem gave the NSC a role in herding these entities together, but it is not clear that the NSC is equipped to coordinate fully such a diverse effort. Bureaucratic turf battles arose during 2000, with the State Department and Thurman's office feuding over their relative responsibilities for the designation of a special presidential envoy for AIDS. In the meantime, the opportunity to create an international corps of leaders to address the pandemic—the raison d'être for creation of the envoy position—was lost.[10]

AIDS provides just one example of the difficult challenges the State Department faces in seeking to maintain its historic coordinating role in U.S. foreign policy. It is questionable whether the department is equipped to handle a variety of "global issues" that increasingly dominate the foreign policy agenda, such as health, climate change, and protection of the environment. These are precisely the areas where multilateral cooperation would seem to be increasingly needed. And it is the State Department that has the primary budget (outside of the IFIs) to support multilateral cooperation. Yet, a recent report by the National Academy of Sciences found the State Department seriously deficient in the scientific expertise required to address such technical issues, and it proposed that the department both take on personnel and rely more heavily on the depth of existing expertise in domestic agencies.[11] Budget stringency will surely limit staff increases at the State Department. But as more responsibility in these subject areas is shifted to domestic agencies, where requisite expertise remains concentrated, the responsibility to formulate U.S. policy toward multilateral institutions will become further fractured

This is already true in the area of funding. As noted, domestic agencies like HHS, Labor, and the U.S. Department of Agriculture (USDA) already possess the primary role for maintaining professional and policy relationships with the WHO, ILO, and the FAO, respectively. However, because the budgets for the U.S. contribution to these agencies lie elsewhere—with the State Department and to some extent USAID—there is a constant struggle over U.S. policy. For example, HHS would welcome an expansion of WHO's role and budget, but the State Department, suffering under congressionally imposed ceilings on UN budgets, has fought for zero nominal growth in all UN budgets. Agency interests conflict as well, leading to mixed messages. The USDA's interest in FAO focuses almost exclusively on trade, whereas the State Department and USAID, responsive to the demands of other FAO member states, show more concern with development. Likewise, the Labor Department's interest in the ILO is intermittent at best and reflects largely domestic political pressures.

Just as the State Department is struggling to retain overall control of foreign policy, but is ill equipped to do so, USAID is losing its traditional hold on foreign assistance and is, in fact, caught in a dilemma. Historically, it could control the programs of domestic agencies in developing countries because it was their principal funder. But with its funds declining, USAID can no longer keep up with the international activities of domestic U.S. agencies, such as DOE's growing role in Africa. Nor does USAID have the skills to preempt domestic agencies' burgeoning interest. Recently, for example, the USTR approached USAID to seek funding for trade assistance in Africa. In response, USAID sought not only to maintain the funding for such activities but also to control the recruitment of relevant personnel. Since USAID has neither internal skills nor experience in this area, in contrast to USTR, the latter considered the USAID proposal a nonstarter. There are conflicts, moreover, between USAID's focus on developing country needs and concerns that fall along the domestic-foreign frontier. Domestic agencies often seek USAID funding for their programs in developing countries. USAID typically resists, or tries to resist this importuning, perceiving that such projects do not correspond to its own poverty-focused program. Yet without USAID funds, some of the recent initiatives, such as those implemented through the binational commissions and generally representative of growing mutual interests, may wither and die.

USAID is also generally disdainful of multilateral development programs because it sees funding for these as competing directly with its own bilateral programs. Thus, in 1996, when Congress shifted responsibility for funding the U.S. contribution to the International Fund for Agricultural Development (IFAD) from the State Department to USAID, the latter sought to end such contributions altogether. It took a determined lobbying effort by IFAD and an offer from the State Department to share the funding burden before USAID agreed to maintain U.S. participation, and even then at only a minimal level. In a similar fashion, personnel at the Joint United Nations Program on HIV/AIDS (UNAIDS) note that U.S. attitudes toward their institution shift radically depending on whether HHS or USAID is representing the United States on the governing body.

Clearly, new funding and organizational arrangements are necessary to accommodate the changing nature of the United States' global interests. These arrangements should also help highlight the growing interdependence between U.S. and international developments.

One proposal is that as domestic agencies take on larger international roles, whether bilateral or multilateral, they should assume a larger responsibility for financing them. Under such a principle, for example, U.S. dues for the WHO would be included in the HHS budget and those for the ILO in the Labor Department's budget. Likewise, bilateral projects, such as those undertaken through binational commissions, would not remain dependent on USAID resources but be incorporated in the budget of the sponsoring department. Under such an arrangement, financing for the broad range of the U.S. role in the world would be taken out of the narrow funding limits imposed on "international" activities. At present, the "150 account" of the federal budget, which covers all nonmilitary or intelligence international activities, constitutes less than 1 percent of the total budget—only one-sixteenth of the resources devoted to national defense. In most domestic departments, these international activities would constitute a small percentage of the total budget.

Disaggregating federal spending on international activities would also free such activities from the negative attitudes and cumbersome strictures applied to multilateral agencies by the congressional committees that oversee foreign affairs, such as insistence on zero nominal growth. Presumably, also, domestic constituencies would be activated on behalf of these programs as the interconnectedness between international activities and domestic interests became clearer. Such an approach would also have the benefit of advancing multilateral cooperation. As noted above, for instance, HHS is already a stronger champion of the WHO than either the State Department or USAID.

The argument against shifting federal funding for international activities in this manner is that doing so would further fracture responsibility for coordinating U.S. foreign policy. Domestic agencies would have even less reason to check with the State Department or USAID before launching programs in various countries or multilateral institutions. One could imagine instances in which different U.S. agencies might work at cross-purposes in delicate political situations or duplicate each other's activities. The greater danger, however, is that federal funding for these programs would go down rather than up. Congressional committees that control the budgets of the domestic agencies traditionally have resisted the latter's involvement in activities that appear to divert funds and attention from "domestic" concerns. The budget of the National Institutes of Health (NIH), for example, is strictly limited to research that can be shown to directly affect Americans. Thus, NIH's research on AIDS is overwhelmingly weighted toward those strains of HIV and treatment systems relevant to the United States. Finally, not all domestic agencies with international responsibilities are strong advocates of multilateralism. The Department of Labor, as noted, takes at best a skeptical view of the importance of the ILO. Similarly, the USDA's interest in the FAO is focused primarily on trade matters, being only slightly attuned to concerns about world food security.

Still, one should not dismiss this more radical approach out of hand, nor shrink from exploring wholly new ways to manage problems that cross the domestic-foreign frontier. Clearly the present system of management and funding is obsolete and nowhere near adequate. These obstacles, moreover, lead one quickly to the recognition that the necessary changes in U.S. outlook will have to come from well beyond the innards of the executive branch.

Congress

Georgetown University's Institute of Diplomatic Studies recently published an analysis of the role of Congress in U.S. foreign policy. After examining ten case studies, the authors concluded that "congressional capacity to address foreign policy issues and constructively engage in its formulation continues to deteriorate." The reasons for this include greater turnover in the Congress in recent years and the decline of the seniority system. In the Senate, the chair of every subcommittee of the Senate Foreign Relations Committee during 1999–2000 was a freshman. In the House, the International Relations Committee was considered weak to the point of powerlessness, not having passed a foreign aid authorization bill since 1985. Except for a few key leaders on selected issues, the role of these central committees has declined drastically in historical terms.[12]

In their place, the Banking Committees in both houses have assumed greater prominence, for instance, in increasing the quota for the IMF and responding to financial crises in Mexico and Asia. The Agriculture Committees and the joint Economic Committees played prominent roles in reducing sanctions against India and Pakistan following their conducting of nuclear tests. In the latter case, these committees responded to the special interest of agricultural producers rather than the political implications of the tests. Similarly, abortion opponents on the House International Relations Committee, by attaching an amendment to restrict foreign aid funding for family planning agencies that counsel or perform abortions with their own funds, successfully blocked for two years the administration's—and for that matter the Senate's—efforts to pay U.S. arrears to the UN. Only when President Clinton made significant compromises on this matter was the legislation passed and signed in 1999. Shortly after his inauguration, President George W. Bush signed an executive order putting these funding limits into effect.

However, the Georgetown study concludes that except for a few key special interests, public opinion and even lobbyists played an insignificant role in all ten cases of Congress's role in foreign policy. Instead, the most important factor in success or failure in executive-congressional cooperation was the quality of leadership, primarily in the administration but also in the Congress. For example, the passage of an increased IMF quota stands out as a success story, driven by the Treasury Department's vigorous lead on the issue. Conversely, the failure over several years to resolve the issue of UN arrears was deemed to be in large measure a failure of administration leadership.

A different analysis is offered by Terry Deibel, in a study for the Foreign Policy Association. Deibel suggests that the confrontations between the Clinton administration and Congress over foreign policy were due in part to extreme partisanship, but equally as much to divisions within each party over approaches to the post–Cold War world.[13] He notes that with the end of the Cold War, traditional tendencies in Congress to take more extreme positions than the White House and to inject purely domestic interests into foreign policy became less risky. Moreover, the peculiar structure of power in the Congress after 1994 gave added influence to unilateralists in the Republican Party, to the dismay of both Republican internationalists and Democratic multilateralists. Democrats, meanwhile, have in recent years been divided between idealists who favor a very active multilateral policy and pragmatists who are more circumspect, as well as having differences with the Clinton administration over trade policy. Deibel argues that the history of executive-congressional relations in foreign policy during the Clinton administration reflected as much divisions *within* the two parties as it did the particularly harsh feelings that many Republicans had for Clinton. He cites several foreign policy successes, including the ratification of the Chemical Weapons Convention (CWC), the passage of the North American Free Trade Agreement (NAFTA), the eventual funding of the United Nations, and the deployment of U.S. forces in Bosnia and Kosovo, that resulted from bipartisan cooperation between Republican internationalists and Democratic pragmatists or (in the case of trade) between a Democratic White House and Republican internationalists.

There is certainly a feeling among foreign policy specialists that in recent years Congress has been less responsive to the new global agenda than to narrower special interests—that is, to "the noisy few" mentioned earlier. Former Ambassador Chas Freeman has called this trend the "franchising of foreign policy."[14] Individual members of Congress, whether or not they are on the relevant committees, can drive U.S. foreign policy to support constituent concerns. Their agendas may reflect religious or national origin perspectives, single-issue campaigns, or commercial interests. Examples of the power of special interests abound, influencing U.S. policy on such issues as Israel, Cuba, Armenia, Sudan, India, abortion, or the sale of destroyers to Taiwan. There is something inherently democratic in this process and thus not to be dismissed. But what is often lacking is any consideration of the broader national interest. In the past, one could count on respected leaders in foreign policy, usually from the relevant committees, to keep sight of this larger perspective. "What we have lost in Congress are the statesmen," said a former administration official, "people who tended to look at the bigger picture, who understood the broader range of U.S. interests and how at any given moment one could be more important than another, and who understood that the presidents need flexibility."[15]

In Deibel's view the growing imperatives of a globalizing world, and the lessons of experience, will begin to diminish the strength of unilateralists. A Republican president, he believes, will also be able to contain the more extreme elements among Republicans in Congress, while steering a generally internationalist course.

A factor that may lend credence to Deibel's prediction is the growing international involvement by members of Congress. It was widely reported after the election of 1994 that most of the Republican freshmen did not even have passports, nor saw the need for them. The belief, indeed the common wisdom, has been that Congress continues to be marked by a major indifference to the world around it. But a recent study by the *New York Times* gives the lie to this assumption, showing that 93 percent of members have passports and indeed use them, traveling overseas at least twice a year, on average. Nearly one-third of members have studied or worked abroad, and one in five claims to speak a foreign language.[16] International travel, of course, does not correlate with votes for or against various international undertakings, but it does suggest that global issues are becoming better understood. In the words of one member newly introduced to the world outside his district, "It's hard to legislate something you know nothing about."

Nevertheless, even as Congress becomes more knowledgeable about international issues, there are structural problems that inhibit the type of new funding or organizational arrangements suggested earlier in this chapter. Outside of major crisis situations, it is difficult to transcend the committee system in Congress to address even crosscutting international issues or to overcome institutional blockages. In 1997, the Clinton administration and congressional leaders agreed to a special mechanism for overcoming the impasse on UN arrears. At a meeting of the administration and the leadership from both parties, including the chairs of all the relevant committees, participants developed a plan for joint, across-the-board action, through joint efforts of House and Senate authorization and appropriations committees. It was the last such meeting, however. Committee chairs soon made clear their opposition to what they perceived as an effort to usurp their authority, and they refused to cooperate. Indeed, it proved impossible even to arrange a joint meeting of Senate and House staffs. In the end, the administration painstakingly negotiated the arrears issue with each committee in each chamber.

One reason that Congress is ill equipped to advance multilateral cooperation on global and transnational issues is that its committee structure continues to distinguish between foreign and domestic budgets. This increasingly artificial division often frustrates the interests of actors that these committees represent. Domestic agricultural exporters, for example, recognize the importance of the FAO in setting health and safety standards for agricultural trade. In 1997, an FAO study found no basis for health concerns about hormones in beef, providing scientific basis for the WTO's decision against the ban by the European Union (EU) on U.S. hormone-fed beef, a decision that could mean hundreds of millions of dollars of additional U.S. beef exports. Yet the members of the Agriculture Committee, despite prodding from agriculture interests, made no effort to cooperate with their colleagues on the Foreign Relations Committee in overcoming the problem of U.S. arrears to the FAO, which run close to $100 million.

More importantly, the committees that control the budgets of HHS, the Labor Department, the Environmental Protection Agency (EPA), and the

Interior, Energy, and Transportation departments have from time to time limited the ability of those agencies to conduct international programs. As a result, the domestic departments often bury these activities in other line items, making it difficult to get a handle on exactly how much they do spend on global activities.[17] Sometimes, the situation resembles a ping-pong match. In 1998, Congress stripped the State Department of its budget for sending experts to international meetings, a budget that funded domestic agency experts as well as those from the department, arguing that each agency should fund its own representatives. At the same time, the budgets of domestic agencies were not compensated, creating a serious problem in U.S. representation at the hundreds of expert meetings that now are essential to the functioning of the global economy and our participation in multilateral institutions.

Meanwhile, Congress ordered the State Department to report twice a year on all international travel by executive branch officials to such meetings, an onerous and in many ways intimidating task. It was a good example of how well-placed "unilateralists" in Congress—to use Deibel's characterization—could use a small, almost unnoticeable provision in the law to thwart U.S. participation in the increasingly demanding global system. Stung by this budgetary stringency and criticism of "junkets," the State Department has turned to recruiting outside experts to lead U.S. delegations to multilateral meetings, increasing the potential for serious conflicts of interest and the risk of losing overall foreign policy perspective. A case in point was the U.S. delegation to the International Telecommunications Union in Minneapolis in 1998. Both the U.S.-selected conference chairman and the head of the U.S. government delegation were industry representatives. Serious foreign policy interests were nearly damaged (for instance, through the near seating of a Serb-led "Yugoslavia" delegation and another delegation from Taiwan) when these specialists refused to consider these interests germane to the concerns of industry.

In the past, Congress has sometimes recognized and responded to crosscutting issues by establishing so-called select committees, such as one on hunger chaired by the late Mickey Leland and later by Tony Hall, and on drugs chaired by Charles Rangel. Unfortunately, such committees were abolished in the Gingrich-led Republican "revolution" during the 105th Congress. They would be very useful today in addressing some of the crosscutting issues related to globalization.

These structural problems in Congress will not be easy to fix. In the meantime, leadership will be essential to raising congressional awareness and responsiveness to the demands of an increasingly interdependent world. There are some positive new developments in this regard. During the final weeks of the 106th Congress, Republican Senator Pat Roberts and Democratic Senator Max Cleland led a highly intelligent bipartisan colloquy on foreign policy. Starting out alone, they were joined over the course of the series by several senators of both parties.

Special interests, moreover, are sometimes conducive to supporting broader national interests. Senator Roberts was influenced in this direction by the intense interest of his Kansas constituents in the world grain market. Senator Chuck Hagel (Republican-Nebraska), similarly, has become a champion of international engagement in large part by his understanding of the importance of international commerce to the Midwest. Senator Jesse Helms (Republican-North Carolina) surprised many when he, along with several conservative Republicans in the House, pledged support for debt relief for poor countries, largely out of religious conviction. In late 2000, the Congress passed bipartisan legislation to provide the full presidential request for debt relief and to pay overdue contributions for UN peacekeeping. Prospects for multilateralism may also grow as the freshmen chairs of the last Congress gain increasing experience in the coming one. Moreover, significant changes are taking place in the committees themselves. There is a new chairman of the House International Relations Committee, the seasoned Henry Hyde, and Republican rules require a change in leadership of the Senate Foreign Relations Committee in 2002. The stage could be set for a more civil and (one hopes) more productive executive-congressional relationship on foreign policy than we have seen for many years.

The Role of State and Local Government

Running against the grain of perceptions about public apathy toward foreign affairs, there is in fact a growing foreign policy activism at local levels in the United States. This local involvement, however, complicates the U.S. pursuit of multilateralism.

One example is the rebirth of state and local government sanctions against foreign governments. Such sanctions were an integral part of the antiapartheid movement in the 1980s, being designed to put pressure not only on companies doing business in South Africa but also on the U.S. federal government, at a time when the administration opposed further sanctions against the apartheid regime. Ultimately, more than 100 state and local governments enacted such sanctions against South Africa. Today, that sanctions campaign is considered to have been largely successful in not only raising the spirits and negotiating power of South Africa's liberation movement, but also finally moving Congress to enact sanctions at the federal level over President Reagan's veto.

The contemporary example of such activism relates to Burma. In 2000, the Supreme Court struck down a Massachusetts law that prohibited state contracts to any company doing business in Burma. Massachusetts was not alone, however. By March 2000, four states and twenty-six municipalities had enacted some form of sanctions against foreign governments.[18] The Clinton administration, which boasted of close ties to the antiapartheid movement, nevertheless entered a strong brief in the Supreme Court against the state of Massachusetts in the Burma sanctions case. The administration, which had put in place some sanctions against Burma on its own, argued that federal responsibility for foreign policy preempted the rights of states and local governments in this area.

The Burma case illustrates two opposing views of how foreign policy should be made. On the one hand, the law in Massachusetts represented grassroots mobilization around a key foreign policy issue, human rights, and the right to use the local political system to influence a Congress that did not reflect the public's views. For those who decry public apathy on foreign policy issues, this activism should have been a welcome development. As in the South Africa case, the advocates argued that their actions at the state and local level were pivotal in pressuring the administration to impose its own sanctions on Burma. On the other hand, those who favor more coherence in foreign policy found the Massachusetts case an invitation to foreign policy anarchy.

Especially relevant to the subject of this book, the Massachusetts law and similar ones in other jurisdictions risked placing the United States in violation at the state and local level of international agreements to which the nation is bound—in this case decisions of the WTO. Indeed, the EU had already threatened to put the case into the WTO dispute resolution mechanism. A bipartisan group of senators and congressmen joined in opposing the Massachusetts law, though some in Congress joined the other side.

The degree to which WTO rules bind state and local governments is in fact a very touchy issue in U.S. politics, one the Clinton administration chose to duck in its argument before the Supreme Court. The issue raises questions about whether the rules and regulations of multilateral agreements should be allowed to run counter to democratic, especially grassroots, participation in foreign policy. The Massachusetts case is a classic example of the dilemmas and anxieties that globalization raises. In Rosenau's words:

> However they may articulate their understanding, individuals everywhere have come to expect, to take for granted, that the advance of globalization poses threats to the long-standing ties of local and national communities, and some groups will contest, even violently fight, the intrusion of global norms even as others will seek to obtain goods, larger market shares, or generalized support from beyond their communities.

The Growing Influence of Nongovernmental Organizations

There is no ground swell in the country today over Burma as there once was over South Africa. But as citizens launch grassroots efforts in order to have a greater say in foreign policy, action at the state and local level will likely continue. But it is only one of several ways citizens seek to have an impact. There is a broader growing activism that has yet to find a satisfactory entree to the foreign policy structure. And in not finding its way in, it is prone to crashing the gates. This activism, represented by NGOs, expresses ambivalence toward multilateralism than runs even deeper than that within the federal government.

The growth in the role and influence of international NGOs is remarkable. The number of such organizations has doubled since 1989, to over 40,000.[19] The NGO presence at international meetings is growing rapidly. At the Rio Conference on the Environment in 1992, some 30,000 NGO representatives were present. Today, no longer content to kibbitz at the fringes of multilateral institutions, NGOs have become even more organized to influence governments toward new agreements and institutions. Their most notable achievement to date was the campaign resulting in a treaty to ban landmines. The leaders of this effort won the Nobel Peace Prize in 1997. A second major success was the pressure NGOs placed on governments to sign the treaty to create an International Criminal Court (ICC) in 1998. In both cases the U.S. government found itself unable to interact effectively with these movements, and the United States became isolated in the presence of overwhelming international pressure.

The NGO phenomenon is explained partly by theories of Rosenau and others about the simultaneously integrating and fragmenting impact of globalization. On the one hand, NGO alliances cross borders, connect once disparate communities, and exploit the technology of instant, inexpensive communication—particularly the Internet—to multiply their numbers and coordinate their actions. They move quickly from national to international coalitions. At the same time, they represent a revolt against the institutional interdependence of the globalization era, organizing to get around and often to oppose outright established nation-state policy structures and international organizations. Thus they rely on the fragmentation that has accompanied globalization to mobilize adherents, reaching into local communities, marginalized groups, and disaffected interest groups to build support from the grassroots. This dual strategy was employed to bring about passage of the Burma law in Massachusetts.[20] It has also been evident in mobilization for the demonstrations against the WTO, the World Bank, and the IMF that have been going on since 1999.

It is not enough to say that the controversy over international institutions is solely one about transparency, as many activists and others argue. Running deep through this heterogeneous set of movements is profound unease over the multilateral demands of globalization itself. Nowhere was the contradiction between the NGOs reaching for global norms and yet retreating from international mechanisms more evident than in the protests in Seattle. Lori Wallach, one of the principal organizers of the Seattle protests, confesses to her own ambivalence on this score. On the one hand, she distrusts the WTO as a faceless and nontransparent multilateral institution; she would prefer to see the ILO given greater powers to enforce international labor standards. But in almost the same breath she admits that the ILO has been "useless and toothless," and that accountability in international organizations is a fundamental problem yet to be solved. Others in this growing protest movement would abolish the World Bank and the IMF entirely.[21]

The NGO attitude at the ICC negotiations was similarly ambivalent regarding multilateral institutions. While agitating for a new, independent international institution with authority to prosecute criminal actions, NGO sentiment was decidedly opposed to giving a role to the UN Security Council. The antipathy toward the Security Council was so strong that the Rome Statute for the ICC opens the door to giving the new court a role in what has long been one of the exclusive powers of the Security Council, the determination of an act of aggression. This problematic faith in the "objectivity" of proposed new international institutions—and yet suspicion of those that already exist—runs through much of today's most important activism.

The internationalization of NGOs, however, will not long be solely the province of those supporting new multilateral norms or new more "objective" institutions. As recently reported in the *Washington Post,* the National Rifle Association is developing its own network of international NGOs to thwart UN efforts to control the arms trade.[22] Indeed, one of the ironies of recent antiglobalization activism is the common ground achieved by the right and left wings of the U.S. political spectrum against multilateral institutions, especially the IFIs, WTO, and NAFTA.[23]

Another matter of concern is the decidedly anti-U.S. tone that NGO coalitions often bring to the table. At the ICC negotiations in Rome, the antipathy toward the United States among the NGOs, especially the U.S.-led ones, was so thick that one would have thought that Pol Pot, Stalin, and Idi Amin had all been U.S. officials. The danger here is of a widening split between the most active public participants in foreign affairs and a foreign policy establishment, particularly in government, that is dedicated to greater international engagement. Surely this attitude will complicate any U.S. initiatives on the multilateral front. For example, if the government seeks to give more power to, say, the FAO or WTO on the issue of biotechnology, there is likely to be tremendous outcry. Likewise, if there are new U.S. government initiatives on world poverty, the World Bank will not necessarily appear an attractive partner.

Finally, there is another problematic form of activism that policymakers must acknowledge. It might be called the "privatization of foreign policy." This is the entree into foreign policy of well-heeled individuals from the media or philanthropic community. A significant part of Ted Turner's $1 billion "gift" to the UN was used in its first two years to launch a megamedia campaign to convince Congress to pay the country's UN arrears. As one director of this effort confided, "Despite all our efforts, there was really no significant new public groundswell on this issue. But television can convey that there is. Besides editorials which we promoted, which convey the same thing, a massive TV ad campaign suggested that the issue had galvanized public opinion."[24] Anyone in Washington the week before Congress's vote on the UN arrears legislation would have been hard put to avoid being blitzed by this campaign and getting the same message. Raising even more questions of propriety was Turner's provision of $34 million to the UN in 2000 to cover the first year's costs to other nations from the lowering of U.S. dues from 25 to 22 percent. It was a case of private money paying in effect to achieve a U.S. foreign policy objective.

On a different front Bill Gates, the founder of Microsoft, has changed the focus of international health efforts by his foundation's massive gifts to a program, managed jointly by the Gates Foundation, WHO, and UN Children's Fund (UNICEF), to produce vaccines for HIV/AIDS, tuberculosis, and malaria. Gates's contribution dwarfs previous U.S. contributions to research in this field and makes the Gates Foundation a principal partner of the WHO. The U.S. government is running to catch up, but in effect Gates has gone around it to become an international actor in his own right on the multilateral scene. The Gates Foundation is also now the second largest contributor, among all donors, to health programs in Africa.

These forms of philanthropy may seem all to the good, especially for the cause of multilateralism. But one can think of other more controversial causes, heavily financed, producing private links to multilateral institutions, that would give pause.

The Public Enigma

An underlying conflict runs through the literature on the public's attitude toward international issues. On the one hand some critics decry the public's apathy, while deploring the activism of NGOs and lobby groups as merely special pleading by the "noisy few." Others insist that the public's interest is greater and more consistent than recognized by either political elites or the media, but that it is largely without passion for a wide variety of reasons, leaving such issues in the end "nonvotable" (that is, issues for which their elected representatives will not be held accountable).[25] At the other end of the spectrum some activists argue that the more visible manifestations of public interest, like the demonstration in Seattle, are reflective of the deeply held views of the public, at least of their fears, and should be taken as a sign of public opinion.[26]

In January 2001 the Aspen Institute, under the auspices of its Global Interdependence Initiative, convened a meeting of some of the most prominent pollsters and researchers on the attitudes of the public toward foreign policy. Some general propositions emerged from this meeting. The public maintains a long-standing and fairly consistent interest in international issues, favoring U.S. engagement but stressing the concept of "fair sharing" of the burden. Thus the public by and large feels positively about multilateralism, specifically the UN, because it embodies such sharing as well as providing a mantle of legitimacy to such U.S. actions as military engagements. At the same time, the public has an exaggerated view of the U.S. role, always estimating the U.S. share of foreign aid or of UN peacekeeping to be three or four times the actual amount. This is perhaps the result of media coverage or a reflection of deeper psychological forces. Americans hold strongly to this image of the United States as a generous nation; so much so that providing contrary information about the actual amounts or shares of U.S. aid or other international contributions does not necessarily change original perceptions that the United States is carrying a heavy burden. As one researcher remarked, "If the facts do not fit the frame, then the respondents change the facts not the frame." Perhaps most striking is the public's tendency to frame these issues in social and ethical terms rather than in terms of self-interest or national security.

Beyond these generalities, it is dangerous to attribute to the public solid positions on specific programs. For example, one study reports that the public favors, by a wide margin, introducing labor and environmental standards into trade agreements, but notes that 40 percent do not believe such a policy will be effective.[27] As noted earlier, Americans favor helping the poorer nations, but many believe foreign aid does not work. These ambivalences leave wide room for policy outcomes. Moreover, the general conclusions described above need to be refined and tested. In particular, we need to plumb more deeply the balance in the public's mind between self-interest and broad social and ethical concerns before reaching strict conclusions about the most important motivating factors.

For activists or policy advocates, the question of how to mobilize public opinion on behalf of their issues is constantly being examined. The finding about favorable attitudes toward multilateralism gives hope to those advocating programs and projects along those lines. But the Aspen Institute's initiative also poses some challenges for those advocates, since it suggests that some of the messages on which advocates rely actually reinforce underlying public resistance to taking on these issues more aggressively.

Contrary to conventional wisdom, it is not necessarily the case that issues must be framed to show a direct link between global issues and self-interest (an approach taken in the HHS paper cited above). Indeed, one researcher found that framing the interview in this way, in discussing the risk of disease, actually produced lower levels of approval for many other socially responsible international activities. Nor is guilt a particularly effective way to mobilize the public. Instead, it is far better to capitalize on

Americans' positive self-image, and then introduce reality in that context, than to repeat how niggardly the United States is—as with the slogan "less than 1% for foreign aid!" USAID goes out of its way, both on its Web site and in consultations with Congress, to emphasize that the vast majority of its funds are spent in the United States or on U.S. experts. But while this might appease a few congressional critics, it reinforces the public's view that very little foreign aid actually reaches the people for whom it is intended. Similarly, organizations that seek funding for humanitarian causes need to recognize that the repeated images of starving children and miserable women reinforce the public's image of the developing countries as never being able, or willing, to get on their own feet. They are worthy of charity—indeed quite generous charity—but not respect nor partnership. And it is partnership that will be needed in the coming decades.

U.S. policymakers also need to come to grips with their ambivalence about the public's role in foreign affairs. Activist groups, like NGOs and ethnic lobbies, are single-issue bodies, and sometimes seem impervious to "broader" national interests. But they also arise because they are able to mobilize some portion of the public on a particular issue. The challenge is whether they, and/or their backers, can be encouraged to become supporters of a broader vision, and whether foreign policy leaders can do more to frame such a vision. Doing so would make the activism that already exists an even more consistent source of support for U.S. engagement. In this regard, Congress has to ask whether it is more comfortable having a "free hand" in foreign affairs or actively engaging its constituents on the looming issues of global concern and the requisite need for more, not less, international collaboration and governance.

Seeking New Paradigms

The most challenging developments in foreign affairs in the coming decade will not be the traditional ones of physical peace and security and alliances. These will persist, but they will be handled largely as in the past, by leaders in both the executive branch and the Congress who acquire the expertise and take on the responsibility for addressing them, without significant public participation. Whenever these challenges reach crisis proportions, the machinery will manage to respond in spite of itself.

The issues that will be most difficult to address, but that will become increasingly relevant, are those that cut across domestic and foreign policy interests, including terrorism, trade, regulation of financial instruments, international health, environmental damage, and human rights (including women's rights and labor standards). These are precisely the areas where new international associations and cross-boundary institutions will be most needed. In other words, this is where multilateral governance will be most relevant.

The U.S. government is particularly ill structured to deal with these issues. More and more, traditional "domestic" agencies will play a greater role in these international arenas. More and more, the State Department and the NSC will struggle to cope, keep up, and manage the process. There will be shortages of skills and money, leaving the government more dependent on the private sector at critical junctures. Congress will bring specialized domestic concerns to bear on transnational issues. Sometimes this domestic focus may advance a foreign policy goal—as was the case with the granting of permanent normal trade relations to China, where domestic economic gains were the primary driving force. But without strong congressional structures for addressing foreign policy in a coherent manner, domestic interests could contribute to fragmentation and undermine effective U.S. leadership.

Outside of government, the lack of consensus or clear understanding of how these global issues relate to U.S. needs and values will only add to the difficulties. Local initiatives, NGO coalitions, and special interests will move to fill the vacuum. The underlying, cohesive public values upon which government might build may be lost in this cacophony of confrontation and special pleadings.

None of these dire possibilities are necessary. But there is no way to address these challenges without strong leadership. This must come first from the president, not in a single speech or a single appointment, and surely not simply in an initial focus on reorganization. For whatever structural problems exist, the first step is greater dialogue with the public. Within the framework of U.S. values, the president must seek to foster widespread understanding of the growing interface between domestic and foreign interests, greater appreciation of the dynamism and value of active U.S. engagement in approaching transnational problems, and domestic support for credible proposals to address these. Similar leadership can come from within Congress.

New structures must follow. They can also help instruct. Traditional domestic agencies must be encouraged to broaden their international engagement. For the government to do otherwise would be to deny the very interconnectedness that makes the emerging global issues so important. Moreover, only in this way will the necessary skills be available for effective international engagement. The State Department must train its staff members in new skills and learn new ways of coordination that allow the department to share responsibility rather than dominate it. There will have to be new coordinating mechanisms in the White House, including cross-cutting arrangements on such issues as climate change and infectious diseases that are able to engage both domestic and foreign affairs agencies and to allocate responsibilities effectively.

Finally, the White House should experiment with new budget models, beginning with budgets that adhere to traditional agency allocations but also demonstrate the interconnectedness of efforts among agencies on behalf of global issues of importance to the nation. Such an effort, carried out in consultation with Congress, could lead eventually to new budget allocations themselves. In the interim, this effort will encourage legislators to give higher priority to activities that remain in the "150 account," as well as to give more support to the international budgets of domestic agencies.

Bringing these issues closer to home will of course not end the competition between domestic and international investments. There will always be a tension between the domestic and the international, between the sovereign and the multilateral impulse. The challenge is to find the means to moderate that tension, to act upon it to achieve the best possible outcome. Both domestically and multilaterally, that is what governance is all about in this new age.

Notes

1. See the next chapter in this volume, by Steven Kull, on U.S. public attitudes toward multilateralism. Also Kull, *The Foreign Policy Gap,* pp. 15–23, 172–184.

2. Bales, "Communicating Global Interdependence," pp. 11–12. See also Ethel Klein/EDK Associates, *Becoming Global Citizens,* pp. 29–32.

3. Lindsay, "The New Apathy," p. 2.

4. Rosenau, *Along the Domestic-Foreign Frontier,* pp. 78–117.

5. Vise, "New Global Role Puts FBI in Unsavory Company," *Washington Post,* October 29, 2000, pp. 1, 30.

6. Gopinath, "Who's the Boss?" pp. 89–94.

7. U.S. Department of Health and Human Services, "Global Strategy: A Healthy World and a Healthy America," p. 3.

8. Ibid, p. 12.

9. White House, *International Education Policy.*

10. Gelman, "Turf Battles Slow Appointment of US AIDS Envoy," *Washington Post,* July 19, 2000, p. A16.

11. National Research Council, *The Pervasive Role of Science, Technology, and Health in Foreign Policy.*

12. Sloan, Locke, and Yost, *The Foreign Policy Struggle: Congress and the President in the 1990s and Beyond.*

13. Deibel, *Clinton and Congress,* pp. 3–5, 59–70.

14. Munson, "Local Politics is Global as Hill Turns to Armenia," *Washington Post,* October 9, 2000, p. 8.

15. Ibid., p. 8.

16. Schmitt and Becker, "Insular Congress Appears to Be Myth, *New York Times,* November 4, 2000, p. A9.

17. In 1994, the Office of Management and Budget estimated these expenditures at $1 billion. There has been no official updating since. Lancaster, *Transforming Foreign Aid,* p. 12.

18. Guay, "Local Government and Global Politics: The Implications of Massachusetts' Burma Law," p. 357.

19. Ibid., p. 361.

20. Ibid., p. 363.

21. Naim, "Lori's War," pp. 34-41, 52. See also, Lewis, "No Ideological Po-tion," *International Herald Tribune,* February 1, 2001, p. 8.

22. Austin, "The Second Amendment Going Global," *Washington Post,* March 26, 2000, p. B.1.

23. The same "strange alliance" is sometimes reflected in the Congress. Dei-bold, p. 21.

24. Confidential interview, June 12, 2000.

25. Kull, *The Foreign Policy Gap,* pp. 15–22, 172–184.

26. Klein, *Becoming Global Citizens,* p. 11.

27. Ibid., pp. 29–32.

4

Public Attitudes Toward Multilateralism

Steven Kull

HOW DOES THE AMERICAN PUBLIC FEEL ABOUT THE UNITED STATES PARTICIPATing in multilateral institutions and activities? Since the early 1990s, there has been a widespread perception in U.S. policymaking circles that the public is going through a neo-isolationist phase in the wake of the Cold War. According to this conventional wisdom, U.S. citizens resist participating in multilateral institutions and activities and guard jealously the country's sovereignty and freedom of action.[1]

A comprehensive review of polling data, as well as polling specifically designed to test these assumptions, reveals a quite different picture of the American public.[2] Trend-line questions that have been asked for decades show continued solid support for U.S. international engagement. And on the question of U.S. participation in multilateral institutions, if anything, the American public appears to be somewhat more supportive of such participation than are U.S. policy elites.

This does not mean that the public is entirely comfortable with the nature of U.S. global engagement. In a variety of ways, the public exhibits unease with the hegemonic character of U.S. foreign policy and a desire to pull back from this dominant role. It is this public reaction that the policy community appears to be (mis)interpreting as isolationism.

A closer reading of public opinion reveals that discomfort with the hegemonic character of U.S. foreign policy does not imply a desire to disengage from the world. Rather, a significant majority of Americans would like the United States to give greater support to multilateral efforts for dealing with world problems. Thus the American people express strong backing for the UN, for multilateral forms of military intervention, for international environmental regimes, for international economic institutions, and for international legal institutions.

The U.S. Role in the World

Trend-line questions, asked repeatedly for decades, reveal an American public that is supportive of U.S. engagement in the world, with no sign of decline since the end of the Cold War. For example, by more than a two-to-one margin, Americans consistently say that the United States should "take an active part in world affairs" rather than "stay[ing] out of world affairs."[3] Only small minorities—most recently just 18 percent—agree with the isolationist argument that "this country would be better off if we just stayed home and did not concern ourselves with problems in other parts of the world."[4]

At the same time, Americans are uncomfortable with the idea that the United States should play a dominant or hegemonic role in world affairs. When asked what kind of role the United States should play, only 16 percent said the United States should "take the leading role," while 57 percent said it should "take a major role but not the leading role" (minor role: 21 percent, no role: 4 percent).[5]

Americans consistently reject the notion that the United States should serve as the world's policeman. Indeed, more than two-thirds say that "the U.S. is playing the role of world policeman more than it should be."[6] Even at the height of the Gulf War, in March 1991, 75 percent said no when asked whether the United States should be playing this role.[7]

When politicians seek to justify U.S. military intervention, they frequently invoke the principle of global leadership. However, this does not strike a positive chord with most Americans. For example, when a CBS–New York Times poll of December 1995 asked respondents to choose among four different reasons to send U.S. troops to Bosnia, the lowest scoring reason was "maintaining the United States role as a world leader." Only 29 percent found this rationale "good enough."

The public's rejection of a dominant role for the United States is closely related to the feeling that the country already does more than its fair share in maintaining world order and helping other countries. In some cases, these feelings are based on an overestimation of how much of an effort the United States is making relative to other countries. (This is especially true in the realm of foreign assistance, where the public holds an extremely exaggerated perception of U.S. generosity.)

If the majority of the public does not want the United States to withdraw from the world or to be the dominant world leader, what *does* it want? The answer is actually fairly clear: Americans want the country to participate actively in cooperative international efforts in which it would contribute its fair share.

In a July 2000 poll conducted by the Program on International Policy Attitudes (PIPA), respondents were presented three general options for the United States' role in the world. Just 15 percent chose the option that "the U.S. should withdraw from most efforts to solve international problems." Similarly, only 11 percent embraced the idea that "as the sole remaining superpower, the U.S. should continue to be the preeminent world leader in solving international problems." Instead, an overwhelming 72 percent endorsed the view that "the U.S. should do its share in efforts to solve international problems together with other countries."

In September 1997, the Pew Research Center asked what kind of a leadership role Americans would like to see the United States play in the world. Consistent with PIPA's results, only 11 percent embraced the isolationist position that the country "shouldn't play any leadership role," and only 12 percent favored the United States' being "the single world leader." Again, an overwhelming majority (73 percent) wanted the nation to accept "a shared leadership role."

Americans consistently reject the notion that the United States should act in unilateralist fashion. Over the past decades, the public has rejected by a two-to-one margin the argument that "we should go our own way in international matters, not worrying too much about whether other countries agree with us or not."[8]

Public support for U.S. global engagement can become overwhelming when it is put in the context of cooperative efforts. For example, just days after the deaths of the eighteen U.S. Army Rangers in a firefight in Somalia in October 1993, 88 percent of Americans nevertheless agreed with this statement: "Because the world is so interconnected today, it is important for the U.S. to participate, together with other countries, in efforts to maintain peace and protect human rights." Asked again in October 1999, 89 percent agreed.[9]

Americans respond very positively to the argument that multilateral efforts to address world problems serve U.S. interests. An overwhelming 78 percent agreed with the statement that "the U.S. should participate in efforts to maintain peace, protect human rights, and promote economic development. Such efforts serve U.S. interests because they help to create a more stable world that is less apt to have wars and is better for the growth of trade and other U.S. goals." Only 39 percent agreed with an opposing argument (while 58 percent disagreed): "It is nice to think that joining in international efforts makes a more stable world. But in fact, the world is so big and complex that such efforts only make a minimal difference with little benefit to the U.S. Therefore, it is not really in the U.S. interest to participate in them."[10]

Arguments that international institutions are too slow and bureaucratic to deserve U.S. support do not dissuade most Americans from supporting them. Only 40 percent of respondents agreed with the statement that it is better for the United States to act on its own in confronting problems like terrorism and the environment because "international institutions are slow and bureaucratic, and often used as places for other countries to criticize and block the US," while 56 percent agreed that to solve such problems "it will be increasingly necessary for the US to work through international institutions."[11]

A majority of the public also favors giving aid as part of multilateral efforts. Presented with two arguments, 57 percent chose the one that supported giving aid multilaterally because "this way it is more likely that other countries will do their fair share and that these efforts will be better coordinated." Only 39 percent chose the counterargument: that it is best to give aid bilaterally "because that way the US has more control over how the money is spent and will get more credit and influence in the country receiving the aid."[12]

Majorities of the public also do not shrink from having international institutions intervene in the internal affairs of countries. Asked to choose between two statements, 61 percent of respondents supported the argument, "To deal with global problems such as terrorism and environmental dangers, it will be increasingly necessary for international institutions to get countries to change what they do inside their borders." Only 35 percent endorsed the argument, "What countries do inside their borders is their own business. International institutions should not try to tell countries what they should do."[13]

Support for the UN

In January 2000, Jesse Helms, the powerful chair of the Senate Foreign Relations Committee, delivered a strongly worded speech to the UN Security Council. He portrayed the American public as holding a fundamentally negative view of the UN; as seeing it as a threat to United States sovereignty; as rejecting the view that the United States is obliged to pay its back dues to the organization; as unwilling to "countenance" the UN's effort to create "a new international order of global laws"; and as seriously considering withdrawing from the world body. All these assertions are vividly contradicted by the findings of numerous polling organizations.

When asked their opinion of the UN itself, a solid majority of Americans express positive feelings. In a November 1997 poll by CNN-*USA Today,* 85 percent said that the "United Nations plays a necessary role in the world today." In a Pew Research Center poll of October 1999, 76 percent of respondents said they had a favorable view of the organization. An overwhelming majority of citizens—more than 90 percent—favors U.S. participation in the UN, while only a very small minority would support U.S. withdrawal. Indeed, a higher percentage supports U.S. membership in the UN than in NATO.[14]

If the public expresses general support for the UN and for U.S. participation in the world body, at times Americans have reservations about the organization's actual performance. Public perceptions about whether the UN is doing a good or bad job appear to fluctuate according to recent news events. Around the time of the Gulf War, UN performance ratings were quite high—as they were at the beginning of the Somalia operation. However, in June 1995, when the UN peacekeeping operation in Bosnia was faring badly, CBS and Times Mirror both found just 42 percent saying that the UN was "doing a good job." After the Bosnia Dayton accords on Bosnia were signed in November 1995, a Wirthlin poll found that approval of UN performance recovered a bit, jumping to 54 percent in December 1995. In August 1998, the "good job" rating had risen to 60 percent (Wirthlin), but by May 2000, perhaps in response to the debacle in Sierra Leone, it slipped again to 52 percent (Gallup).

These fluctuations may help explain why policymakers misperceive the public, mistaking its short-term criticisms of performance for more fundamental objections to the UN itself. In fact, in a variety of polls, the public has given the UN a more positive rating than other major public institutions, including the U.S. Congress and the U.S. government. In a June 1999 Pew Center poll, 70 percent rated their feelings about the UN as mostly or very favorable, while only 56 percent gave the U.S. Congress such a rating. The UN has even been rated as having less waste, fraud, and abuse than the U.S. government.[15] These findings suggest that there is a generally low level of public confidence in big regulatory institutions, and that suspicions of inefficiency and corruption are not specific to the UN. A June 1995 poll by the Americans Talk Issues Foundation (ATIF) appears to confirm this thesis: some 64 percent of respondents agreed that "people are distrustful of almost all institutions today; there is no special reason to distrust the UN more than other institutions."

Strengthening the UN

Whatever reservations Americans feel about UN performance, this does not lead the majority to want to pull back from UN activities. In fact, most Americans would like the UN to be stronger, and only a small minority is concerned that a stronger world body might compromise U.S. sovereignty.

In various polls by the Chicago Council on Foreign Relations (CCFR) and the Pew Center, more than 80 percent of respondents said that strengthening the UN should be a foreign policy goal for the United States.[16] In contrast, only 37 percent agreed (and 57 percent disagreed) with the contrary argument presented in a November 1995 PIPA poll: "Strengthening the UN is not a good idea because if the UN were to become stronger, the U.S. could become entangled in a system that would inhibit it from full freedom of action to pursue its interests." Seventy-three percent agreed with the pro argument: "For the U.S. to move away from its role as world policeman and reduce the burden of its large defense budget, the U.S. should invest in efforts to strengthen the UN's ability to deal with potential conflicts in the world." Respondents also gave strong support to four concrete options for strengthening the UN: (1) improving UN communication and command facilities (supported by 83 percent); (2) holding joint military training exercises (supported by 82 percent); (3) having UN members each commit 1,000 troops to a rapid deployment force at the disposal of the Security Council (supported by 79 percent); and (4) allowing the UN to possess permanent stocks of military equipment stored in different locations around the world (supported by 69 percent). In fact, public support for strengthening the UN extends even to bold ideas like giving the UN the power to collect its own taxes, a step advocated by a number of prominent economists and political analysts.[17]

Americans do not seem especially concerned that a strengthened UN might impinge on U.S. sovereignty. In an April 1995 PIPA poll, respondents were asked to choose between two statements about the power of the UN. Only 36 percent chose the statement: "I am afraid that things like UN peacekeeping are getting so big that the U.S. is losing control of its foreign policy to the UN," whereas 58 percent chose "I am not afraid that the UN is becoming too powerful. The U.S. has a veto in the UN Security Council and therefore the UN cannot dictate anything to the U.S." Likewise, only 17 percent of respondents in a June 1995 ATIF poll agreed with the statement, "The UN might become a world government and take away our freedom." In general, the American public continues to support an expansive UN, even though most Americans appear to grossly overestimate the magnitude of UN activities.[18]

Paying UN Dues

A majority of Americans has consistently shown a readiness to have the United States pay its UN dues in full. In December 1998, for instance, a Zogby poll found 62 percent saying that "the United States should pay all its back dues."[19] Furthermore, much of the opposition to paying UN dues that does exist appears to reflect not intrinsic resistance to the world body but rather reservations about its performance.

Responding to a series of pro and con arguments in an April 1998 PIPA poll, respondents found arguments in favor of paying UN dues more convincing. Perhaps most significantly, just 28 percent were persuaded by the unilateralist argument against paying UN dues—specifically, that "the UN is . . . meddling in areas where the U.S., not the UN, should be taking the lead." An identical low percentage found convincing the argument that paying UN dues "is a bad investment" because "the UN is ineffective and wasteful."

Pollsters get a more varied response from the public when they place the issue of U.S. arrears to the UN in the context of U.S. efforts to reform the world body. In some cases, when only the goal of UN reform is mentioned in the poll question, a plurality or even a majority of the public has endorsed the strategy of withholding dues as a mean of exerting pressure.[20] However, when the two values of seeking financial reforms and complying with the norm of paying UN dues were both presented in a single question, the value of paying dues without conditions prevailed by a modest margin.[21] Moreover, when asked their opinion of five of Congress's key conditions for the payment of U.S. dues to the UN, a majority of respondents endorsed none of these.[22]

Although most Americans favor paying UN dues, there is evidence that many feel the United States is contributing more than its fair share. When given correct information about the actual levels of U.S. contributions relative to other countries, however, a solid majority agrees that the level of U.S. dues is fair. [23]

Multilateral Military Action

In the event that it is necessary for the United States to use military force, a strong majority of the public prefers to act multilaterally whenever possible. In an April 1995 PIPA poll, for example, 89 percent agreed that "when there is a problem in the world that requires the use of military force, it is generally best for the U.S. to address the problem together with other nations working through the UN, rather than going it alone." Strikingly, this overwhelming support came at a time when the UN operation in Bosnia was not going well. Moreover, this preference for multilateral military action was sustained even in the face of a strong counterargument that the United States would be more successful acting on its own. Only 29 percent agreed with (while 66 percent rejected) the statement, "When there is a problem in the world that requires the use of military force, it is better for the U.S. to act on its own rather than working through the UN, because the U.S. can move more quickly and probably more successfully." Various other polls have also found a strong preference for working through the UN rather than using force unilaterally.[24]

Moreover, acting through the UN appears to be even more popular than acting through NATO. In July 2000 PIPA asked the public, "As a general rule, when it becomes necessary to use military force, do you think it is best for the U.S. to act on its own, to act as part of a United Nations operation, or to act as part of a NATO operation?" A plurality of 49 percent said the UN, while 26 percent said NATO, and just 17 percent said "on its own."

An overwhelming majority of the public also favors relying on allies to help the United States protect shared interests around the world, rather than depending on the United States to shoulder the entire burden on its own. Although told that "we cannot be fully confident that allies will effectively protect shared interests," 79 percent nevertheless favored the allies "taking over some of these responsibilities so that the U.S. can reduce its presence abroad."[25]

Collective Security

Americans strongly support the principle of collective security that was the cornerstone of the UN and the security order developed in the post–World War II era. In November 1995, PIPA presented the following question:

The UN was established on the principle of collective security, which says that when a UN member is attacked by another country, UN members should help defend the attacked nation. Some say the U.S. should contribute its military forces to such UN efforts, because then potential aggressors will know that aggression will not succeed. Others say the U.S. should not contribute troops to such efforts, because American troops may be put at risk in operations that are not directly related to U.S. interests. Do you think the U.S. should or should not contribute troops to UN efforts to help defend UN members if they are attacked?

Sixty-nine percent said that the United States should contribute troops to such UN efforts, while 23 percent said it should not.

Attitudes about NATO expansion also reflect support for the general principle of collective security and multilateral cooperation. Polls show fairly strong support for expanding NATO to include Eastern European countries.[26] When presented with pro and con arguments, the public found the strongest arguments for NATO expansion to be those based on the broad principles of collective security.[27] Perhaps most significantly, a majority of the public supported including Russia in an expanded NATO, a step that would of course change NATO from being a traditional alliance to being more of a collective security system.[28]

Multilateralizing U.S. Commitments to Defend Countries

Numerous observers have worried that the American public is no longer willing to support the use of the U.S. military to follow through on its commitments to defend allied nations if they are attacked. Indeed, a 1998 poll by the Chicago Council on Foreign Relations found majority support lacking for using U.S. troops to defend Saudi Arabia, Israel, Poland, or South Korea.

However, other polls reveal that Americans are in fact willing to defend allies, but only if the United States does so as a part of a multilateral operation. In a 1998 PIPA poll, 69 percent of respondents said they would support defending Poland if it were attacked by Russia, provided that this was part of a NATO operation in which the United States participated with NATO allies. Another PIPA poll presented scenarios in which Iraq invaded Saudi Arabia and North Korea attacked South Korea. Respondents were first asked about participating in a UN operation to defend these countries: 76 percent favored it for Saudi Arabia and 68 percent favored it for South Korea. The question, "If other countries in the UN declined to participate, would you favor or oppose the US taking action by itself?" produced only 33 percent support in the case of Saudi Arabia and 21 percent for South Korea.

In November 1995, PIPA asked the public to choose among four different options for dealing with U.S. commitments to protect other countries. Only 4 percent expressed a desire to "withdraw" U.S. commitments, while just 5 percent wanted the country to maintain its commitments by acting "primarily on its own." An overwhelming majority (87 percent) favored more multilateral approaches. The largest group (49 percent) favored maintaining U.S. commitments but "whenever possible" acting "together with allies or through the UN," while 38 percent wanted to see the United States "change its commitments to protect countries so that it is only committed to protecting them together with allies or through the UN."

This preference for protecting other countries through multilateral action is reflected in the level of military *capabilities* Americans believe that U.S. defense spending should support. Offered three options, just 10 percent of the public wanted the United States to "only spend enough to protect itself but not to protect other countries." Eighteen percent wanted the United States to "spend enough so that it can protect itself and other countries on its own." A strong majority of 71 percent wanted the United States to "only spend enough to protect itself and to join in efforts to protect countries together with allies or through the UN." Consistent with this view, a majority of respondents in the same poll rejected the Pentagon position that the United States must have the capability to fight two regional wars simultaneously without the help of allies.

To effectively reduce the demands placed on the United States, multilateral enforcement action would ultimately need to draw on the military capabilities of Japan and Germany. Including both countries in international military operations has been controversial because of historical memories, fear of their military potential, and practical concerns about constitutional limitations in both countries. Nevertheless, the majority of the American public clearly favors doing so.[29]

Peacekeeping and Intervention

Strong majorities in the American public favor U.S. participation in multilateral peacekeeping operations, at least in principle. Even shortly after the deaths of the eighteen U.S. Army Rangers in Mogadishu in October 1993, NBC found 71 percent support for contributing U.S. troops to UN peacekeeping operations. Similar percentages have been found in more recent years, including 72 percent in a Roper Starch poll of March 1997 and 68 percent in a PIPA survey of July 2000.

One of the key reasons that Americans support participation in UN peacekeeping is that they see it as a means of burden sharing. In an April 1995 PIPA poll, an overwhelming 86 percent agreed that "the only way for the U.S. to not always be the world policeman is to allow the UN the means to perform some policing functions. UN peacekeeping is a way we can share the burden with other countries."

While the majority has consistently favored contributing U.S. troops to peacekeeping operations in principle, support for contributing to specific operations varies according to a number of factors. Poll questions that specify that the proposed operation would be multilateral and that other countries would be contributing the majority of the troops usually elicit majority support. However, because Americans tend to assume incorrectly that the United States is contributing more than its share of the troops to peacekeeping operations, the majority will often oppose participation unless pollsters clarify that the United States will be contributing a proportionate share of a multilateral operation. Another determinant of public attitudes is whether respondents perceive that the operation is likely to succeed. For example, support for participation in the Bosnia operation has varied according to changing perceptions of its probable success.

Contrary to widespread assumptions, Americans are indeed amenable to putting U.S. troops under UN authority. In a June 1999 CNN-*USA Today* poll, 75 percent said that they "generally approve of American troops participating in peacekeeping forces under the United Nations command."

Americans also show support for going beyond conventional peacekeeping and intervening in the internal affairs of other countries. A 1999 Greenberg Research poll found that a strong majority (59 percent) wanted to see more "intervention from the international community" to deal with civilian hardships during war, such as "being cut off from food, water, medical supplies, or electricity." Here again, however, Americans insisted that such efforts be multilateral. Only 39 percent wanted to see more unilateral intervention by the United States.

Similarly, an overwhelming majority accepts that international military action may be necessary when governments commit atrocities. In an October 1999 PIPA poll, 77 percent agreed that "if a government is committing atrocities against its people so that a significant number of people are being killed, at some point the countries of the world, including the U.S., should intervene, with force if necessary, to stop the killing." When an opposing argument based on the principle of sovereignty was presented in an April 1999 PIPA poll, just 29 percent agreed that "as a general principle, even if atrocities are being committed within a country, the international community should not intervene with military force because this would be a violation of the country's national sovereignty." Sixty-two percent supported the argument in favor of intervention.[30]

Americans are also quite supportive of creating a standing military force for such interventions, as envisioned in the original formation of the UN and discussed more recently by the former UN deputy secretary-general, Sir Brian Urquhart. In a November 1999 Harris Interactive poll, 64 percent of respondents agreed that "we need to have some kind of truly international army, with troops from many countries, that can be used in places like Bosnia, Kosovo, East Timor, or Rwanda where national governments fail to protect the lives, or even encourage the killing, of their own people." Similarly, 65 percent of interviewees in a 2000 Yankelovich Partners poll favored the idea of "a permanent UN force . . . made up of individual volunteers ready to be sent quickly to conflict areas to stop the violence."

International Environmental Regimes

Americans' support for multilateralism is not limited to the fields of peace and security. An overwhelming majority of the public also supports the idea of establishing international regimes to address environmental problems. In an October 1999 PIPA poll, an overwhelming 77 percent (48 percent strongly) favored having more international agreements on environmental standards. When respondents were presented a series of four pro and con arguments on this question, 78 percent found convincing the argument that the global nature of many environmental problems made international approaches most appropriate. A more self-interested argument—that the lack of international environmental standards would threaten U.S. jobs by encouraging companies to relocate to countries with lower standards—was found convincing by 67 percent. The counterargument, that imposing environmental standards would violate national sovereignty, was not popular (persuading only 33 percent), nor was the argument that doing so would be unfair because the costs of compliance would be different for different countries (convincing only 37 percent).

On the specific question of global warming, a majority of the public supports international efforts to address the problem. In a January 1999 Zogby poll, 63 percent of Americans agreed with the statement: "Global warming is a serious threat. We should take all necessary actions to cut down on fossil-fuel emissions and cooperate with other nations to make that happen." In contrast, only 24 percent agreed with the alternative statement: "The U.S. (United States) should avoid any global warming treaties that put the U.S. at a competitive disadvantage. Taking drastic steps to reduce fossil-fuel emissions could be bad for our economy and way of life." Public support for the Kyoto Protocol on global climate change has ranged from 59 to 79 percent in various polls.[31]

International Economic Institutions

When large-scale demonstrations blocked the meeting of the WTO in Seattle in November 1999, many observers wondered whether this indicated general public opposition to the process of globalization and the growth of trade. Opinion polls have shown that the public perceives these developments as mixed, with the benefits of globalization and trade slightly outweighing the costs. The dominant public response is to look to international institutions to help mitigate these costs.

The American public strongly supports the WTO's extending its range of responsibility and competence beyond narrow trade liberalization to address issues related to labor standards and the environment. PIPA asked respondents about this issue in October 1999, posing contrasting arguments: "Some say the WTO should consider these issues because they are closely related to trade, and good decisions can be made only if all these things are taken into account. Others say the WTO should not consider these issues because its job is to deal only with trade, and trying to bring in these other concerns will interfere with the growth of trade." In response, 76 percent said the WTO should consider labor standards and the environment, while only 18 percent said it should not.

Respondents were also presented pro and con arguments on the idea that "countries who are part of this [trade] agreement should be required to maintain certain standards for working conditions, such as minimum health and safety standards and the right to organize into unions." The public overwhelmingly endorsed the pro arguments. The con arguments—including the contention that imposing labor standards would violate other countries' national sovereignty—did poorly. In conclusion, a near-unanimous 93 percent of the public said that countries should be required to maintain core labor standards.

Data from other sources reinforce these results. According to a 1996 poll by Wirthlin Worldwide, 73 percent of Americans favored including workers' protection and considering environmental issues when negotiating trade agreements. Only 21 percent opposed the idea. A 1997 poll by Peter Hart for the American Federation of Labor-Congress of Industrial Organizations likewise found that 72 percent thought it "very important" to include labor and environmental standards in trade agreements. By overwhelming percentages, Americans agreed with the idea of including "workplace health and safety standards" (94 percent); "laws against child labor" (93 percent); "basic human rights, such as the freedom to associate or have meetings, and the freedom to strike or protest" (92 percent); "a minimum wage based on the poverty line of the country" (81 percent); and "the legal right to form unions and bargain collectively" (78 percent).

Strong majorities also support intervention by international organizations to deal with a variety of international economic problems, such as the financial crisis that struck Asia in late 1997. In an October 1999 PIPA poll, respondents were asked to choose between two arguments: "Some people say the world economy will naturally adjust itself, and that it is not necessary and would probably be ineffective to intervene. Others say that instability in the world economy can spiral out of control and cause a lot of harm and it is worth intervening." Nearly two-thirds said it is worthwhile for international organizations to intervene "to try to stabilize troubled areas of the world economy."

This does not mean that Americans have no reservations about some international economic organizations. In the October 1999 PIPA poll, 65 percent of respondents agreed with a statement that the WTO favors the interests of business rather than doing what is best for the world as a whole. Nonetheless, when asked, 60 percent favored strengthening the WTO. Although no comparable recent data exist, polls from 1994 and 1995 show supporters of the General Agreement on Tariffs and Trade (GATT) or WTO outnumbered opponents by about two to one.

The IMF, by contrast, is less popular. In the PIPA poll of October 1999, only 44 percent favored strengthening the fund. In a CCFR poll of November 1998, 51 percent opposed increasing U.S. contributions to the IMF to meet world financial crises. However, it does appear that Americans grow warmer toward the IMF as they get more information about the organization. For example, while a majority of respondents in an April 1998 PIPA poll opposed depositing more funds with the IMF, among the half of the sample that was better informed 52 percent favored doing so. Moreover, 56 percent of the whole sample favored increasing IMF resources after hearing pro and con arguments about the plan.[32]

Significantly, the American public tends to favor U.S. compliance with the rulings of international institutions, regardless of whether specific decisions favor the United States. In October 1999 PIPA asked, "If another country files a complaint with the World Trade Organization and it rules against the U.S., as a general rule, should the U.S. comply with that decision?" Sixty-five percent of respondents said the United States should comply. Events in spring 1998 provided a more concrete test of this attitude, as the EU sought a ruling from the WTO dispute resolution mechanism on the legality of the Helms-Burton Act imposing extraterritorial sanctions on other countries' trade with Cuba. In a poll taken at the time, 63 percent of respondents said that the United States should agree to have the case decided by the WTO.

International Legal Institutions

Although the data are still a bit sketchy, Americans show modest support for international legal institutions, and in particular for the World Court. In the early 1990s, ATIF conducted a series of polls that found strong support for giving strong powers to the World Court. Seventy-six percent thought the World Court would be essential (26 percent) or helpful (50 percent) in order to have "practical law enforcement . . . in such areas as the global environment, international trade and tariffs, and international security." Overwhelming majorities (more than 80 percent) also supported bringing before an international criminal court leaders who invade neighboring countries, seek to acquire nuclear weapons, support terrorism, violate human rights, damage the global environment, or stymie democratic elections. Even when it was suggested that a U.S. president might be brought before such a tribunal, more than 80 percent of those who supported the idea were unmoved.

In March 1992, the Roper polling organization found that 65 percent of Americans thought that the United States should accept the court's decisions if the court found that "actions by the United States have violated international law." Only 14 percent believed the United States should "ignore" the court's decisions if the United States disagreed with the outcome. More recent polls have also shown substantial support. In an October 1999 PIPA poll, 56 percent of respondents favored strengthening the World Court, while just 25 percent opposed the idea. The same study found a modest majority of 53 percent ready to accept the compulsory jurisdiction of the World Court, with 38 percent opposed.[33]

Support for an international criminal court is substantially higher. An October 2000 poll by Yankelovich Partners found 66 percent support for "an International Criminal Court to bring individuals to justice for crimes of genocide, war crimes or other major abuses of human rights if their own country won't try them." A March 1999 Greenberg Research poll found that 78 percent of Americans believed that there are "rules or laws that are so important that, if broken during war, the person who broke them should be punished." These respondents were then asked an open-ended question about "who should be responsible for punishing wrongdoers." A remarkable 40 percent volunteered the answer of an international criminal court.[34] Significantly, a PIPA poll in October found 61 percent support for such a court, despite noting the U.S. government's concern that "trumped up charges may be brought against Americans, for example, U.S. soldiers who use force in the course of a peacekeeping operation."

Is Support for Multilateralism Weaker than Opposition?

In a series of workshops conducted with members of the broad foreign policy community, PIPA presented data demonstrating American public support for multilateral engagement. A widely expressed response was that while a majority of the American people may pay "lip service," in practice support for such a policy is weak and fragile, while opposition is intense and resilient; thus opposition is more relevant politically. Some said that although support may be "a mile wide," it is still "only an inch deep."

Some workshop participants described the intensity of negative feelings against the UN as intimidating to policymakers. One participant recounted his conversation with a senator who was "afraid to mention the word 'UN' at a public gathering anywhere in his state, because it would arouse so much passion, ferocity, opposition, anxiety—all the emotions. . . . And this is a Republican senator who actually thinks that US interventionism is good." Another explained: "Politics is driven enormously by what'll get you in trouble; and members . . . think through 'Where could it go wrong?' and 'What trouble would I be in?' Now, if they don't vote enough for the UN, they're not going to hear [criticism] from anyone. But if they vote for the UN or vote for a peacekeeping operation and it ends up like Somalia, they know how the phones light up. And the phones did light up then, and they were mostly negative."

To test this assumption of strong opposition and weak support for engagement, PIPA evaluated the strength of public opinion on two dimensions: intensity and resilience. Intensity was assessed by asking whether respondents favored or opposed a position "strongly" or "somewhat." If support for engagement is weak and opposition strong, one would expect the following result: (1) that the balance of opinion among those who said they felt "strongly"—in either direction—would be against engagement or, at the very minimum, (2) that those who opposed engagement would hold their views "strongly" more often than those who supported engagement. In fact, neither proposition was borne out.

PIPA was also interested in measuring resilience: that is, how firmly do people hold their opinions when challenged by opposing arguments? Taking respondents who had initially favored contributing U.S. troops to UN peacekeeping, PIPA asked them to evaluate a battery of strongly worded arguments against such a policy, and then retested them on their attitudes using a fine-grained scale. Likewise, opponents of contributing U.S. troops were subjected to a battery of arguments in favor, and then retested. In fact, supporters of contributing to UN peacekeeping were slightly more resilient, and less malleable, than opponents.

Participants in these workshops often claimed that the segment of the public that really "matters" in foreign policy is an attentive, active minority that wants to reduce U.S. involvement in the world and in multilateral institutions. At first glance, there is some evidence for this view: respondents who identified themselves as attentive to international affairs and as politically active were somewhat less enthusiastic about the UN. This appeared to reflect greater awareness of the institutional problems of the UN. (The same group was also more critical of U.S. government performance.) If anything, however, the attentive and politically active groups were slightly more supportive of international engagement than was the general population, and there was no majority sentiment for disengaging from the UN.

The conventional wisdom that support for multilateralism is less intense than opposition to it nurtures another common belief: that congressional supporters of multilateralism are vulnerable to attacks by an electoral challenger, particularly in the context of political attack ads. To test this premise, PIPA developed a pair of attack ads with the help of some political consultants. In the first, a challenger attacked an incumbent for having voted in favor of paying UN dues. In the second, the incumbent attacked the challenger for opposing doing so. Poll respondents were read the ads and asked, based solely on this information, which candidate they would most likely support. The pro-UN incumbent did better by 19 percentage points.

Why Do Policymakers
Assume the Public Is Not Supportive?

Why have U.S. policy practitioners come to believe that Americans do not support an engaged, multilateral foreign policy? Why have they persisted in believing this claim despite substantial survey evidence to the contrary? Obviously, this is a vast topic requiring a complex analysis. But there are a number of possible explanations to be touched on here, based in part on the interviews PIPA has conducted with members of the policy community.

Failure to Seek Information About Public Attitudes

In virtually every case, members of Congress said they did not commission polling on international issues. Nor did they show much interest in it. A congressional staffer, speaking of his boss, said, "I'm trying to think, the last time—I can't remember the last time he's asked for a poll, and I can't remember the last time I've actually seen one." Explaining this low level of interest, another member said that "foreign affairs just doesn't win elections or lose elections."

This pattern of giving little attention to polls was also reflected in a recent Pew study, "Washington Leaders Wary of Public Opinion," that interviewed 81 members of Congress, 98 presidential appointees, and 151 senior civil servants. Asked, "What is your principal source of information about the way the public feels about issues?," only 24 percent of the members of Congress, 21 percent of presidential appointees, and 6 percent of senior civil servants mentioned public opinion polls.[35]

Responding to the Vocal Public as if It Were the Majority

Consistent with their widespread negative attitudes toward polls, most policy practitioners, especially in Congress, explained that their primary means of getting information about public attitudes was through informal contacts with self-selected and outspoken citizens—that is, with the vocal public. This orientation was also reflected in the Pew study mentioned above: when members of Congress were asked about their "principal source of information about how the public feels," by far the most frequently mentioned (by 59 percent) was "personal contacts," while the second most common (cited by 36 percent) was "telephone or mail from citizens."

Based on numerous reports, there seems to be a consensus that the vocal public takes a strongly negative view of multilateral engagement. From a psychological perspective this seems plausible. Those who see the UN as aspiring to be a world government that would threaten U.S. sovereignty and freedoms are more likely to be motivated to communicate their views than those who think it is a mildly helpful institution.

However, it is also possible that this impression arises from a selective attention on the part of policymakers. After all, there is an active constituency in favor of the UN that does lobby Congress. In several interviews, we asked policy practitioners whether they ever heard from constituents who were supportive of the UN. In several cases the answer was something like, "Oh yeah, but those are just your UNA-types [referring to the United Nations Association]." For some reason, these advocates of the UN were discounted as not being truly representative Americans, while their opponents were.

Viewing Congress and the Media as Mirrors of the Public

Numerous comments from policy practitioners suggested that they assume that Congress is an accurate mirror of public opinion, since the public has elected its members. Congressional resistance to multilateralism, especially regarding the UN, is interpreted as reflecting public sentiments.

This view was especially widespread among journalists. A reporter and columnist, explaining why he relied on Congress rather than polls to get his understanding of public attitudes, observed that "Congress is the best reflection of the American public's views. There is a good chemistry of mixing up ideas that goes on."

Making the dynamic more complex, many members of Congress and their staffs—as well as other members of the policy community—say that they get their cues about the public from the media.[36] It is widely assumed that journalists have their finger on the pulse of the public. Obviously, this creates a closed system in which assumptions about the public echo back and forth between Congress and the media, with little opportunity for refutation.

Underestimating the Public

A fourth possible source of policymakers' misperceptions of the public is their tendency to view the public in a more negative light than may be warranted. When policy practitioners characterized the public in interviews, they frequently did so in a disparaging, if not exasperated, tone. Policymakers may assume that the public is unable to support a policy of multilateral engagement because it is too shortsighted, parochial, and unable to think about foreign policy issues in a long-term framework.

Apparently, this view is not uncommon among the U.S. elite. In a 1996 survey of 2,141 U.S. opinion leaders, 71 percent agreed with the statement, "Public opinion is too short-sighted and emotional to provide sound guidance on foreign policy."[37] On a more general note, in a Pew study, when asked, "Do you think the American public knows enough about the issues you face to form wise opinions about what should be done about these issues, or not?," only 31 percent of the members of Congress, 13 percent of the presidential appointees, and 14 percent of the senior civil servants endorsed the public's ability.[38]

Perhaps the dynamic here may be a general human tendency to underestimate the public—a tendency that appears to exist among the public as well as the policymaking elite. Numerous PIPA polls have found that U.S. citizens themselves tend to underestimate public support for international engagement. For example, a February 1994 PIPA poll asked respondents whether they thought they were more or less supportive of spending on UN peacekeeping than the average American. If the sample had perceived the public correctly, the ratio of those who said "more" would have been approximately equal to those who said "less" (since the sample was representative of the general public). But in fact, 70 percent said they thought they were more supportive than average, and only 17 percent less—more than a four-to-one ratio. Thus it appears the public as a whole grossly underestimates the public's support for UN peacekeeping.

This tendency to misperceive the public has been studied in the social sciences for some decades now. Floyd Allport is generally credited with coining the term "pluralistic ignorance" in the 1920s to describe a situation in which individuals make mistaken judgments about themselves relative to the majority.[39] For example, studies have found that people tend to perceive others as more racist, more conservative, more sexist, and less willing to engage in socially desirable behaviors such as donating blood.[40] We might call this the Lake Wobegon effect—people tend to see themselves as above average.

Lack of Political Incentives

Why do the forces of the political market not correct elite misperceptions about Americans' foreign policy preferences? In general terms, the American public does not pay a great deal of attention to foreign policy. When Americans select candidates, foreign policy positions are a low priority. Thus candidates have little incentive to understand the public's foreign policy positions, and they are unlikely to be punished for getting them wrong. So, once a belief about the public becomes established there is no reliable corrective mechanism.

It is not hard to understand how U.S. policymakers might begin to believe that the American public is going through a phase of isolationism. After all, there is reason to believe that the public did so after World War I, and that they might have done so again after World War II had it not been for the Soviet threat. It seems plausible that they might again turn to isolationism with the end of the Cold War. As Richard Neustadt has observed, historical analogies exert a strong influence on the thinking of policymakers.[41] Once such an image of the public is established, media reporting and congressional behavior can then become self-reinforcing. And because of the low public salience of international issues, the political market does not supply a dependable corrective.

Conclusion

In summary, the preponderance of evidence suggests that, contrary to wide-spread assumptions among the U.S. policy elite, the American public is not only amenable to multilateral engagement, but indeed strongly prefers it over other options—including the alternatives of disengagement or U.S. hegemony. Accordingly, the American public shows strong support for the UN, multilateral use of force, international environmental regimes, international economic institutions, and international legal structures. Americans perceive multilateral institutions as possessing legitimacy and as providing a means for the United States to share the burden of maintaining international order.

This still leaves unanswered the question of why U.S. foreign policy does not move in the direction of multilateralism—as the public seems to want. One explanation is that policymakers are simply accommodating their mistaken perception of the public's preferences. In addition, however, there are reasons to believe that policymakers are themselves resistant to multilateralism. This can create a motivation to perceive the public as opposing multilateral engagement and lead policymakers to seek confirming evidence and ignore or discount disconfirming evidence.

There is indeed some evidence that the U.S. elite is less comfortable with multilateralism than the American public. Although the elite is generally more supportive of international engagement per se, several surveys have found that the elite shows less support for strengthening the UN than is found in the general public. In a 1996 survey by Duke University and in a 1998 survey by the CCFR, just 26 percent and 32 percent, respectively, thought that strengthening the UN was a "very important" foreign policy goal. Among the general public in the CCFR poll, 45 percent felt that way.

There may indeed be structural reasons that members of the U.S. policy community are less supportive of strengthening international institutions. It is a truism that institutions naturally seek to enhance their power. Thus government officials who are employed by and identify with national institutions may well be prone to resist increasing the power of international institutions, which might come at the expense of the power of the national institutions. The public, lacking such a bias, may simply ask itself which institution—national or international—is more appropriate to the task in question.

National policymakers may like to think of citizens as identifying with their nation and thus seeing their national representatives as best able to represent them, but this might be a misperception. For example, an October 2000 poll by Yankelovich Partners asked respondents whether they favored a proposal "for a People's Assembly of the United Nations, directly elected by the world's citizens, to hold . . . [the UN, the World Bank and the WTO] democratically accountable to the public." Fifty-seven percent of the respondents said they favored the idea, with just 30 percent opposed. It is unlikely that the U.S. policy elite would favor such a plan for the American public to bypass its authority.

Apparently the pressure the public exerts in favor of greater multilateralism in U.S. foreign policy is somewhat mild. There is evidence that the public is more inclined to favor candidates who support such an approach. However, because the public does not generally vote on the basis of foreign policy positions, this pressure will continue to be slight. In any case, those who wish to promote multilateralism in U.S. foreign policy need not be concerned that they are swimming against the tide of the public. Although it may be difficult for policymakers to detect, the tide is clearly flowing in favor of increasing integration of the United States with the rest of the world.

Notes

1. These characterizations, as well as others discussed in the chapter, are based on in-depth interviews with eighty-three members of the U.S. foreign policy community, as well as a careful reading of public statements by government officials and journalists. For a more comprehensive discussion, see Kull and Destler, *Misreading the Public: The Myth of a New Isolationism.*

2. See *Misreading the Public.* All of the polls conducted by the Program on International Policy Attitudes (PIPA) are nationwide polls conducted with randomly selected samples of the general population. The margin of error is plus or minus 4 percent or less. This is also true of all of the other polls mentioned, with the exception of Harris Interactive polls, which were conducted with an Internet-based panel.

3. Most recently, 69 percent endorsed taking an active part with just 28 percent for staying out. Gallup for CNN–*USA Today,* May 1999.

4. National Election Study, University of Michigan.

5. Gallup, February 2001.

6. Sixty-eight percent in July 2000; 71 percent in November 1995, PIPA.

7. *Los Angeles Times.*

8. In Pew's September 1997 poll, 62 percent rejected this argument.

9. PIPA.

10. PIPA, October 1999.

11. Ibid.

12. PIPA, November 2000.

13. PIPA, October 1999.

14. In an August 1998 Wirthlin Group poll, 93 percent said that it is important for the United States to be "an active member" of the UN (72 percent very important). This number was even a bit higher than for NATO—83 percent said that it was important for the United States to be an active member of NATO. In November 1997, Gallup found that just 9 percent thought the United States "should give up its membership in the United Nations," while 88 percent opposed the idea. This level of support for membership has been steady for decades in Gallup surveys.

15. When PIPA asked respondents in June 1996 to estimate how much of each year's UN budget is lost to waste, fraud, and abuse, the median respondent estimated 30 percent. When another sample was asked to apply this question to the U.S. government, the median respondent estimate was 40 percent.

16. Among the surveys showing more than 80 percent support for making a stronger UN a foreign policy priority were a November 1998 poll by the Chicago Council on Foreign Relations and a September 1997 Pew poll.

17. In a June 1995 ATIF poll, 72 percent agreed that "the United Nations should monitor and tax international arms sales with the money going to famine relief and humanitarian aid." In an April 1996 Wirthlin Group poll, very strong majorities supported "a charge on international oil sales dedicated to programs to . . . protect the world's environment," "a charge on international sales of tobacco dedicated to programs to . . . improve health care," and a "charge on international arms sales dedicated to keeping peace in regional conflicts."

18. This can be inferred from the public's exaggerated notion of the UN budget. In September 1996 PIPA poll 75 percent estimated that the UN budget was more than four times its actual size.

19. In August 1998, the Wirthlin Group found 73 percent support.

20. For poll results, see the October 1998 Chicago Council on Foreign Relations poll. Wirthlin Group, August 1998. November 1997 Gallup *Time*-CNN poll, February 1997.

21. In response to an April 1998 PIPA poll, 53 percent of respondents said that the United States should not hold back its dues as a means of "pressuring the UN to become more efficient," while 40 percent said that it should.

22. The most popular condition, endorsed by 46 percent, was to require the UN to "lower the US share of UN expenses"; nonetheless, 51 percent rejected it. Forty-five percent endorsed requiring the UN to "make ongoing staff and budget cuts," while 50 percent rejected this. Fifty-nine percent said that the United States should not "require the UN to accept partial payment of US back dues," while the same percentage rejected imposing a condition of "prohibit[ing] other countries from offering ground troops on a standby basis." Wirthlin Group, August 1998.

23. PIPA asked in June 1996, "As compared to other countries, do you think that the amount that the US is assessed for UN dues is more than its fair share, less than its fair share, or about right?" Fifty percent thought that it was more than the United States' fair share, while 31 percent thought the amount was "about right" (less than fair share: 4 percent). Respondents were told, "In fact, UN dues are assessed according to a country's share of the world economy or GNP. The U.S. is assessed 25 percent because that is its share of the world economy"; and then were asked, "Does this method seem fair or not fair to you?" Fifty-six percent found the method fair, while just 37 percent found it unfair. To decide that UN dues are assessed fairly, Americans need to know assessments are based on a country's share of the world economy. When Wirthlin (August 1998) added that European countries paid a third of the UN budget, 60 percent said the U.S. share was fair (unfair: 37 percent).

24. PIPA asked in June 1996: "As a general rule, when it is necessary to use military force to deal with trouble spots in the world, do you feel more comfortable having the U.S. contribute to a UN military action or for the U.S. to take military action by itself?" Sixty-nine percent preferred the United States to contribute to a UN action, while only 24 percent preferred the United States to act alone. ATIF asked in June 1995, "When faced with problems involving aggression, who do you think should be 'policeman to the world,' the United States or the UN?" Only 19 percent said the U.S., while 76 percent said the UN.

25. PIPA, November 1995.

26. Pew's September 1997 poll found 63 percent support for expanding NATO to include Poland, Hungary, and the Czech Republic, while PIPA's February–April 1998 poll found 61 percent support.

27. In the September 1996 PIPA poll, ten arguments in favor of NATO expansion were presented, and respondents were asked to rate them. The most popular argument, rated as convincing by 77 percent (with 48 percent feeling that way strongly), was that "it is better to include Eastern European countries rather than to exclude them, because peace is more likely if we all communicate and work

together." The second strongest "pro" argument was based on a core principle of collective security: 69 percent found convincing the argument that "it is important for potential aggressors to know that they cannot get away with conquering countries." Sixty-five percent also found convincing (28 percent strongly) the argument that through expansion "NATO will be in a better position to resolve conflicts between [Eastern European] countries." The least popular arguments in favor of NATO expansion were those that stressed the Russian threat and the geopolitical competition with Russia. Furthermore, the most popular argument against NATO expansion, rated convincing by 62 percent (31 percent strongly), was that NATO is still too much a military alliance and not inclusive enough. It said: "Instead of expanding NATO, something new should be developed that includes Russia rather than treating Russia as an enemy."

28. CNN-*USA Today* found 54 percent support (January 1994) for the idea; the Fletcher School found 62 percent support (April 1996); and PIPA found 52 percent support in 1996 and 51 percent support in 1998. When PIPA asked about including Russia in NATO once Russia has demonstrated that it is a stable democracy, support reached 65 percent (1996).

29. See "Americans on Defense Spending" (PIPA, November 1995)

30. Sixty-two percent agreed with the argument that "while respect for national borders is important, when large-scale atrocities such as genocide are being committed, this justifies military intervention by the international community." A March 1999 Greenberg Research poll also found 62 percent favored trying to stop wars involving atrocities by "using force and sending troops as part of an international force."

31. See "Americans on Global Warming" (PIPA, December 1998).

32. See "Americans on UN Dues and IMF Funding: A Study of U.S. Public Attitudes," (PIPA, April 1998).

33. Ibid.

34. The next most commonly volunteered answers, offered by 21 percent each, was the "governments in the countries at war" and the "military itself."

35. Kohut, "Washington Leaders Wary of Public Opinion."

36. Based on his interviews with State Department and NSC officials, Philip J. Powlick also found news media and elected representatives to be the primary sources of the policymakers' information on public opinion. See Powlick, "The Sources of Public Opinion for American Foreign Policy Officials."

37. Reported in Ole Holsti, Foreign Policy Leadership Project (sponsored by Duke University and George Washington University), March 1996.

38. Pew, April 17, 1998.

39. Gorman, "The Discovery of Pluralistic Ignorance."

40. Fields and Schuman, "Public Beliefs About the Beliefs of the Public"; Shamir and Shamir, "Pluralistic Ignorance Across Issues and Over Time"; Goethals, "Fabricating and Ignoring Social Reality."

41. Neustadt, *Presidential Power,* ch. 5.

5

Multilateralism and U.S. Grand Strategy

G. John Ikenberry

IN TODAY'S DOMESTIC DEBATE ABOUT U.S. FOREIGN POLICY, IT IS POLITICALLY fashionable to disparage international institutions. Cold War threats are gone. The United States faces the most benign strategic environment in a century. The country is so powerful and seemingly invulnerable that entangling alliances and multilateral commitments appear increasingly to be unjustified impositions on U.S. sovereignty and policy autonomy. For those who argue that the United States should become more reliant on multilateral agreements—or, even more ambitiously, lead the way in building a more rule-based international order—the political headwinds are fierce.[1]

Intellectual legacies in U.S. foreign policy from the past fifty years contribute to this situation. During the Cold War era, realism emerged as the dominant way of thinking about international relations.[2] In this tradition, the "national interest" is advanced primarily by mustering military strength and playing the dangerous game of power politics. Containment, deterrence, and the balance of power—core ideas in the realist tradition—became guiding principles of U.S. foreign policy. Multilateralism and institutional cooperation played a small or nonexistent role in this Cold War vision. Alliances were useful, of course, but beyond this, multilateral institutions and commitments were not part of U.S. grand strategy. Instead, they tended to get justified on other grounds—as tools to manage the world economy or as expressions of American idealism.

A closer reading of many Cold War realist thinkers reveals a more sophisticated view of the role of institutions in world politics. Some realist thinkers have boldly asserted that institutions are of little significance in world politics, while others have advanced arguments that concede that institutions may play a role as tools of power politics.[3] But the wider contemporary political debate about institutions—whether focused on the United Nations, IMF, World Bank, or other multilateral institutions—has been largely disconnected from the dominant ways of thinking about the

121

national interest and U.S. grand strategy. It is hard to make a national interest argument about support for multilateral institutions that is anchored in U.S. foreign policy's power-oriented intellectual core.

The actual historical record, however, is more complicated. U.S. policy toward multilateral institutions and commitments shows a remarkable variation in willingness to establish binding ties with other states. But at key historical turning points, U.S. officials have resorted to multilateral institutional agreements that were related to the basic organization of international relations, using these commitments to advance the goals of grand strategy.

Why did the United States at the zenith of its hegemonic power after World War II and again after the Cold War seek to establish or expand multilateral institutions and agree to insert itself into them? Why did it agree to bind itself to Europe in a 1949 security pact, to deepen that commitment in the years that followed, and to seek the expansion of NATO in the 1990s, even after the Soviet threat that initially prompted such security cooperation disappeared? Why did the United States seek to establish order after World War II in Western Europe through multilateral commitments while pursuing a series of bilateral security agreements in Asia?

This chapter makes three arguments. First, despite longstanding and profound ambivalence about agreeing to operate within rule-based, multilateral institutions, the United States has systematically used multilateral agreements as tools of grand strategy and world order building. Indeed, no country has championed multilateral institutions more enthusiastically than the United States or used these frameworks more effectively in the advancement of long-term national interests. Critics who argue that multilateral commitments either are irrelevant or actually detract from the pursuit of the national interest are profoundly wrong. But those who study international institutions or who champion them in the policy arena have not done a particularly good job of establishing the strategic and national interest underpinnings of these frameworks.

Second, U.S. ambivalence about multilateral institutions reflects a basic dilemma that lies at the heart of international institutional agreements.[4] The attraction of institutional agreements for a leading state is that they potentially lock other states into stable and predictable policy orientations, thereby reducing the need to use coercion to secure the dominant state's foreign policy aims. But the price that the leading state must pay for this institutionalized cooperation is a reduction in its own policy autonomy and unfettered ability to exercise power. The central question that U.S. policymakers have confronted in economic and security affairs since 1945 is this: How much reduction in U.S. policy and restraint on U.S. power is the United States willing to accept in return for "locking in" the policies of other states through the institutionalization of various commitments and obligations?

The differential power between the United States and its partners provides the basis for a potential institutional bargain—a bargain that lies at the heart of the United States' multilateral ties to the outside world and helps to explain the U.S. decision to champion an array of multilateral institutions. Such a bargain is most fully available at pivotal historical junctures, when the old order has been destroyed and a newly powerful state must engage weaker states over the organization of the new order. In entering the institutional bargain, the leading state seeks to reduce compliance costs and weaker states want to reduce their costs of security protection—or the costs they would incur if trying to protect their interests against the actions of a dominating lead state. This is what makes the institutional deal attractive: the leading state agrees to restrain its own potential for doing mischief and harm, such as domination and abandonment, in exchange for the long-term institutionalized cooperation of subordinate states. Both sides are better off with an institutionalized relationship than in an order based on the constant threat of the indiscriminate and arbitrary exercise of power. The leading state does not need to expend its power capabilities to coerce other states, and the weak do not need to expend resources seeking to protect themselves from such coercion. It is the mutually rewarding nature of this exchange that makes the institutional deal work.

Policymakers in both powerful and weak states should be able to recognize the win-win nature of multilateral cooperation. The WTO, for example, recently circulated a document stating "ten benefits of the WTO trading system." One of these presumed benefits captures the institutional logic that lies behind the United States' bargain with the rest of the world: in short, "a system based on rules rather than power makes life easier for all." As the document explains: "The WTO cannot claim to make all countries equal. But it does reduce some inequalities, giving smaller countries more voice, and at the same time freeing the major powers from the complexity of having to negotiate trade agreements with each of their numerous trading partners."[5] This logic is also the rationale for a more general rule-based order for world politics—and it explains the possibility of institutional bargains between strong and weak states.

Third, today one of the United States' central foreign policy problems is its own predominance. In the decade since the end of the Cold War, the United States has become a superpower of unprecedented dominance, and this new reality has unsettled world politics. At the extreme, this unipolar power risks provoking a global backlash and counterbalancing strategies. Overcoming the fears and resentments of other countries is central to U.S. grand strategic interests. This is precisely where multilateralism can play a critical role, since it signals strategic restraint and the willingness of the United States to exercise its power within agreed-upon rules and institutions. It is here—in the attempt to stabilize world political order during an era of extraordinary power disparities—that multilateral institutions can be most fully justified in the pursuit of the nation's core strategic interests.

The first section of this chapter develops the logic of the institutional bargain that informed the nation's postwar order-building experience and continues to have relevance in the new century. The following sections explore various aspects of this institutional strategy as it appears in the United States' post-1945 relationships and again after the Cold War. The chapter ends by assessing the relevance of the institutional bargain in an era of U.S. unipolarity.

State Power and Institutions

Why would a leading state surrounded by weaker states want to establish multilateral institutions? The answer is that institutional agreements can lock other countries into a relatively congenial and stable order.[6] The institutions help create a more favorable and certain political environment in which the leading state pursues its interests. This is possible because institutions can operate as mechanisms of political control. When a state agrees to tie itself to the commitments and obligations of an interstate institution, it is agreeing to reduce its policy autonomy. A leading state that has created an institutionalized order that works to its long-term benefit is better off than a leading state operating in a free-floating order in which it must rely on the constant and costly exercise of power to get its way.[7]

Institutions can serve at least two purposes in international relations. First, as "neoliberal institutionalists" argue, institutions can help solve collective action problems by reducing the commitment problems and transaction costs that stand in the way of efficient and mutually beneficial political exchange.[8] But institutions are also instruments of political control. As Terry Moe observes, "Political institutions are also weapons of coercion and redistribution. They are the structural means by which political winners pursue their own interests, often at the expense of political losers."[9] A winning political party in Congress will try to write the committee voting rules to favor its interests. Similarly, in international relations, a powerful state will want to make its advantages as systematic and durable as possible by trying to rope weaker states into favorable institutional arrangements.

Institutions are potentially "sticky" for at least three reasons. First, they can create difficult and demanding legal or political procedures for altering or discontinuing the institutional agreement. Second, an institution can itself over time become an actor, gaining some independence from states and actively promoting institutional compliance and continuity. Third, growing vested interests—or groups with stakes in the success and continuation of an institution—can combine with other positive feedback effects to produce "increasing returns" to institutions, thus raising the costs of ending or replacing those institutions.[10]

The attraction of institutional agreements for the leading state is two-fold. First, if the leading state can get others to tie themselves to a multi-lateral institution that directly or indirectly serves its long-term interests, it will not need to spend its resources to constantly coerce other states. Although the most powerful state would be likely to win many or most of the endless distributive battles in a noninstitutionalized relationship with sub-ordinate states, locking these lesser states into institutional agreements reduces costs of enforcement.[11] Second, if the institutional agreement has some degree of "stickiness"—that is, if it has some independent capacity to create or reinforce order—the institution may continue to provide favorable outcomes for the leading state even after the latter's capacities have declined in relative terms. Institutions can both conserve and prolong the power advantages of the leading country.

But why would weaker states agree to be roped in? After all, rather than locking themselves into an institutional agreement now, they might calculate that it is better to wait until some time later, when power asymmetries no longer favor the leading state quite as much. In fact, weaker states have two potential incentives to buy into an institutional agreement supported by a leading state. First, the institutional agreement may put limits and restraints on the behavior of the leading state. In a noninstitutionalized relationship, lesser powers are subject to the unrestrained and unpredictable domination of the strong. If the weak believe that credible limits can be placed on the arbitrary and indiscriminate actions of the leading state, this might be sufficient attraction to justify an institutional agreement now. Second, when the leading state agrees to circumscribe its behavior, it is giving up some opportunities to gain immediate returns on its power. By agreeing to operate within institutional rules and obligations, it settles for fewer gains than it could achieve now through brute power, in exchange for the prospect of gains in the longer term. Weaker states, in contrast, may have reason to gain more now rather than later. If the discount rates for future gains are different for the leading and lesser states, this makes an institutional bargain potentially more mutually desirable. So the leading state is faced with a calculation: What amount of institutional limitation on its own policy autonomy and exercise of power is worth exchanging for how much policy "lock-in" of weaker states?

Several possibilities follow immediately from this view of state power and institutions. First, a leading state should try to lock other states into institutionalized policy orientations, while trying to minimize limitations on its own policy autonomy and discretionary power. The challenge facing a leading state is analogous to politics in large-scale organizations. As Michael Crozier observes, all individuals in a complex organizational hierarchy are continually engaged in a dual struggle: attempting to tie their colleagues to precise rule-based behavior, thereby creating a more stable and certain environment in which to operate—while also trying to retain as much autonomy and discretion for themselves as possible.[12] Similarly, leading states will try to lock in other states as much as possible, while trying to remain as unencumbered as possible by institutional rules and obligations. In addition, the leading state will limit its own capacity to exercise power in indiscriminate and arbitrary ways, using this self-restraint as a "currency" to "buy" the institutional cooperation of other states.

The availability of the institutional bargain will depend on several circumstances that can also be specified as hypotheses. First, the amount of "currency" available to the leading state to buy institutional cooperation of weaker states is determined by the ability of the leading state to potentially dominate or injure the interests of weaker states and its ability to credibly restrain itself from doing so. A large state might offer to restrain and commit itself in exchange for concessions by other states, but what interests weaker states is its apparent willingness and practical ability actually to do so. The country of Chad, for example, might offer to bind itself to an institutional agreement that lowers its policy autonomy and makes its future policy orientation more predictable, but few other states will care about such an offer from a weak and strategically insignificant state, and they are not likely to offer much in return to get it. By contrast, weaker states will take seriously an offer of self-restraint from a powerful state with the capacity for serious domination and disruption; indeed, they are likely to offer something to get it. But the institutional bargain will work only if the leading state demonstrates both the will and the capacity to actually make good on its pledge of self-restraint and commitment. If a powerful state cannot credibly limit its power, its currency will amount to very little.

Two other factors will determine whether the leading state, if it has the currency to buy institutional cooperation, will in fact choose to do so. One is the strength of the leading state's desire to lock in the policy behavior of other states. This will depend on the extent to which other states' actions actually impinge on the interests of the leading state. In the case of the postwar United States, the security policy of Western European states was extremely important to U.S. officials, but European policies in other arenas—and the policies of minor countries in many areas of the world— would not by themselves have justified an institutional commitment. The second factor is simply the ability of weaker states to be bound by the institutional bargain. The United States may want to lock in the policy behavior of other states, particularly in the security realm, but it may not have enough confidence that it can achieve reliable institutionalized commitments and obligations.

Taken together, these considerations allow us to see how the United States and weaker states might calculate the tradeoffs of binding themselves together in multilateral institutions. The more that the United States is capable of dominating and abandoning weaker states, the more weaker states should desire restraints on U.S. exercise of power—and the more likely they should be to make concessions to get institutional restraint and commitment from the United States. Similarly, the more the United States can credibility restrain and commit itself, the more its weaker partners should be interested in pursuing an institutional bargain. Likewise, the willingness of the United States to accept restraints on its policy autonomy and to seek a lock-in of weaker partners should parallel the perceived importance of the policy behavior of weaker states. The less important this is to the United States, and the less certain it is that a policy lock-in can in fact be accomplished, the lower the prospects that it will offer restraints on its own policy autonomy.

Institution Building and U.S. Grand Strategy

This conceptual framework is useful in making sense of the broad sweep of U.S. institution building in the twentieth century. The major patterns of U.S. policy toward multilateral institutions can be sketched briefly in the following paragraphs. It is not simply that the United States has tended to support the creation of multilateral institutions because it has been able to dominate them, though there is a great deal of evidence to support this straightforward argument. Rather, there is evidence that U.S. support for multilateral frameworks has rested on a slightly more complicated calculation. In short, the United States has tended to compare the costs of reducing its policy autonomy against the gains to be realized by locking other states into enduring policy positions.

Postwar Institution Building

The United States has been most active in seeking institutional agreements after the major wars in the twentieth century: in 1919, after World War I; in 1945, after World War II; and in 1989, after the long Cold War.[13] The reason for this pattern should be clear from the foregoing analysis. There are several distinctive features of postwar moments that make the latter conducive to new institutional initiatives. First, the old institutional order has been cleared away by the war, and therefore in contrast to more "normal" moments in international relations, basic issues of world order are on the table. It is difficult for international actors simply to fall back on the status quo. Second, wars tend to create new winners and losers—and to ratify a new and often heightened asymmetrical distribution of power. A new leading state, which has effectively received a windfall of power, will be faced with the question of how to use these new assets. Should it simply use its new power to win endless postwar distributive struggles, or should it use them to invest in an order that serves its long-term goals? At such junctures, the leading state has incentives to act in a relatively far-sighted way. Institutional agreements offer a potential means to invest in the future—but only if such frameworks are capable of shaping and constraining other actors in the face of shifts in the distribution of power.

Third, because the leading state is newly powerful, secondary states will be particularly eager to gain assurances about its actions. They will seek agreements that reduce its ability to dominate or abandon them. The more powerful and potentially disruptive the new leading state is, the more the weak will fear for their safety and be willing to offer it concessions in exchange for credible restraints and commitments. Fourth, war tends to disrupt the domestic institutions of both new leading states and new secondary states. Often the leading state is actually in a position to occupy or help rebuild the weaker states. Consequently, postwar moments are particularly congenial to the establishment of institutional agreements that bind weaker states into long-term policy orientations.

Finally, if the leading state does want to create an order that is legitimate, it will seek institutional agreements that not only lock weaker states into a desirable order but also render the postwar order mutually acceptable or desirable. Institutional agreements that restrain and commit the power of the leading state will be attractive to the weak, lowering its costs of enforcement.

The trade-offs described above help explain why the United States after 1945 used institutions in such a far-reaching way and why it relied on multilateral agreements again after the Cold War. Institutions are tools of order building. They have helped the United States lock in regional and global order in a way that has advanced its interests over the long haul. By binding other states to multilateral rules and institutions that produce predictable patterns of policy, the United States has been able to conserve its power. The "gains" from this institutional bargain, moreover, promise to last beyond the momentary power advantages that the United States possesses today. The web of consensual multilateral institutions governing world politics means that the United States does not need to use its coercive power in a manner that disrupts world politics or that endangers a stable and legitimate order. The benefits of multilateral institutions make modest restraints on U.S. power worthwhile.

Variations in Postwar Institutional Outcomes

The United States pursued a much more elaborate and wide-ranging institutional agenda after 1945 than it did after 1919. The League of Nations, proposed by President Woodrow Wilson after World War I, was an ambitious and demanding institution that sought to establish a global system of collective security. But Wilson himself believed that the key to collective security would be not international but domestic: it would rest not on the institutional bargain between the United States and other countries but on the democratic revolution that Wilson anticipated.[14] In contrast, the sweeping and detailed U.S. plans for world order after World War II, and the ambition with which the United States sought to remake Europe and Asia, rested heavily on multilateral institutions. Why did the United States pursue a much more far-reaching institutional agenda after 1945?

For one thing, the United States was in a much more asymmetrical power relationship with Europe after 1945 than it had been in 1919. This had a major impact on the ability and willingness of the leading and weaker states to seek an institutional bargain. In 1945, the United States was a fully fledged hegemonic power, with tremendous currency with which to buy the institutional agreement of other states, particularly the Europeans. Likewise, Western Europeans attached a premium to harnessing and restraining this newly powerful state, and they were much more willing to accept institutional agreements in return for a more restrained and committed United States.

Other factors also facilitated the unprecedented post-1945 institutionalism. The United States ended World War II with a much more sophisticated understanding of the causes of the world war and the requirements of a peaceful and stable postwar order. U.S. officials were convinced that the countries of Europe needed to integrate themselves more fully and that Europe as a whole must be locked into an institutionalized order. They also believed that wider social and economic reform would be needed to sustain liberal democratic regimes, and that these reforms would need to be embedded in regional and global multilateral institutions. Just as important, the domestic systems in Japan and Germany would need much more thorough-going reform—made possible by the unprecedented opportunity of the U.S. and Allied occupation.[15] Compared with 1919, in 1945 the United States saw both more lock-in importance and lock-in opportunity in Europe. As a result, it was willing to give more to get it. Likewise, the Europeans were more willing after 1945 to give more concessions to get institutionalized restraints and commitments from the United States.

What about the ability of the leading state to offer credible self-restraint and commitments? The sheer density of Washington's institutional initiatives after World War II provided more "strings" by which to tie the United States to Europe. In 1919, U.S. restraint and commitment to Europe was to be based on the fragile tie of a single treaty, the League Covenant, which the U.S. Senate never ratified. After World War II, it would be based on dozens of intergovernment agreements, the most important of which was NATO. More generally, in the years between 1944 and 1952 the United States took the lead in establishing a wide range of global and regional multilateral institutions—the Bretton Woods group, including the IMF and World Bank; the GATT; and the UNO. Never before had the world witnessed such a frenzy of institution building.

Variations in U.S. Policy Toward Europe and Asia

U.S. institution building after 1945 took different forms in Europe and East Asia.[16] The United States pursued a multilateral strategy in Europe, with

NATO as the anchor, while in East Asia it promoted a series of bilateral security agreements with Japan, Korea, and several Southeast Asian states. This contrast provides an important puzzle, but one that can clarify the logic of U.S. multilateralism.

The first observation to make is that the United States actually did float the idea of a multilateral security institution in Asia in the early 1940s and again during 1950–1951 (when it was depicted as a desirable counterpart to NATO).[17] The second observation is that some of the critical elements that facilitated security multilateralism in Western Europe did not exist in Asia, regardless of U.S. interests or intentions. To begin with, Western Europe had a group of roughly equally sized and closely situated states that were capable of being bound together in a multilateral security institution tied to the United States, whereas in East Asia countries were geographically dispersed. Moreover, Japan was not only geographically isolated but also perceived as a pariah state because of its recent aggression. The third observation is that other countries in East Asia that might have been party to a multilateral security pact—South Korea, South Vietnam, and Taiwan—were all interested in reunification. All three sought to avoid the fate of Germany, whose division the NATO pact seemingly made permanent.[18]

The basic difference between Asia and Europe, however, was that the United States was both more dominant in Asia and wanted less out of Asia. This meant, as a practical matter, that the United States had little need to give up policy autonomy in exchange for institutional cooperation in Asia. In Europe, the United States had an elaborate agenda for uniting the European states, creating an institutional bulwark against communism, and supporting centrist democratic regimes. It had ambitious lock-in goals that it could not realize simply through the brute exercise of power. To get what it wanted it had to bargain with the Europeans, and this meant agreeing to restrain its exercise of power.[19] In Asia, the United States did not have goals that were sufficiently important to purchase by agreeing to restrain its power and policy autonomy; bilateralism was the preferred strategy. In sum, unchallenged hegemonic power meant that the United States had fewer incentives in East Asia to secure its dominant position through international institutions that would have circumscribed its independent decisionmaking. Nor, Peter Katzenstein notes, was it "in the interest of subordinate states to enter institutions in which they would have minimal control while forgoing opportunities for free-riding and dependence reduction." In sum, he writes, "Extreme hegemony thus led to a system of bilateral relations between states rather than a multilateral system that emerged in the North Atlantic area around the North Atlantic Treaty Organization . . . and the European Community."[20]

More recent developments appear to confirm this strategic logic. As U.S. hegemony has declined in relative terms in East Asia and as the United States has developed more specific lock-in goals for the states in the region,

Washington's interest in multilateral institutional building has increased somewhat.[21] U.S. support for the Asia-Pacific Economic Cooperation (APEC) forum, while not an institution that requires much (if any) policy restraint by the United States, is emblematic of this new U.S. multilateralism in Asia.

The Institutional Bargain with Europe

The preceding discussion makes clear that the United States has long used multilateral institutions as a tool of order building. Multilateralism has been at the heart of its grand strategy at critical historical turning points, and particularly after 1945. This logic can be seen most clearly in U.S. policy toward postwar Europe. Across the Atlantic, political order has been built around multilateral institutions that created an elaborate system to restrain power, reinforce commitments, and provide reassurances. The United States and Europe have each attempted to lock the other party into specific institutional commitments. They have accomplished this in part by agreeing, if sometimes reluctantly, to operate within those institutions as well. This institutional bargain remains relevant today.

The institutional bargain between the United States and Europe after World War II was a "rolling" process. The United States saw its goals for Europe expand. It progressively came to realize that stabilizing and reorienting Europe would require active intervention and engineering, including the creation of a variety of new multilateral institutions that would bind the United States to the Continent. It came to value European stabilization even more as tensions with the Soviet Union increased. At the same time the Europeans drove a hard bargain. They actively sought the institutional involvement of the United States in postwar Europe, and their institutional agreement was tightly contingent on specific U.S. commitments and restraints. The order that emerged—the European order, the Atlantic order, and the wider postwar world order—was the result of a complex set of rolling institutional agreements that linked the reorganization of Europe tightly to an expanding U.S. multilateral commitment. Along the way, the United States grudgingly gave up increments of policy autonomy and restraints on its exercise of power, but it did so with the explicit understanding that in so doing it would be buying the institutional lock-in of Europe.

The most elaborate and consequential institutional bargain was the security alliance embodied in NATO. Although established to respond to a growing Soviet threat, the Atlantic pact was also designed to play a wider role in stabilizing relations and reassuring partners *within* the alliance. NATO provided a mechanism to rehabilitate and reintegrate West Germany, serving the purpose of "dual containment." But it also locked in the United States' reluctant security commitment to Europe, tied the European states together, and reinforced movement toward regional integration. In this way, the NATO alliance operated along with other postwar institutions as a multifaceted instrument of "quadruple containment."

The most consistent British and French objective during and after the war was to bind the United States to Europe. The evolution in U.S. policy, from the goal of a European "third force" to acceptance of an ongoing security commitment within NATO, was a story of U.S. reluctance and European persistence.[22]

During and after World War II, Britain and France sought to bind the United States to Europe in order to make U.S. power more predictable, accessible, and usable. The NATO alliance was particularly useful as an institution that made the exercise of U.S. power more certain and less arbitrary. Despite the vast differences in the size and military power of the various alliance partners, NATO enshrined the principles of equality of status, nondiscrimination, and multilateralism.[23] The United States was the clear leader of NATO. But the mutual understandings and institutional mechanisms of the alliance reduced the implications of these asymmetries of power in its actual operation.

The security alliance also reduced European fears of resurgent and unbridled German military power.[24] The idea was to rebuild Germany's economic and military capabilities within European and Atlantic institutions. This binding strategy was widely embraced at the time by U.S. officials. Secretary of State George C. Marshall made the point in early 1948: "Unless Western Germany during the coming years is effectively associated with Western European nations, first through economic arrangements, and ultimately perhaps in some political way, there is a real danger that the whole of Germany will be drawn into the eastern orbit with dire consequences for all of us."[25] When Secretary of State Dean Acheson went to the Senate to answer questions about the NATO treaty, Senator Claude Pepper posed the question: "The Atlantic Treaty has given these Western European nations some confidence against a resurgent Germany as well as Russia?" Acheson replied, "Yes. It works in all directions."[26] As Cold War tensions made West German rearmament increasingly necessary, the elaborateness of alliance restraints on German power also grew, reflected in the complicated negotiations over an integrated military command and the legal agreements accompanying the restoration of German sovereignty.

If NATO bound both West Germany and the United States to Western Europe, it also reinforced British and French commitment to an open and united Europe. The United States was intent not only on rehabilitating and reintegrating Germany, but also on reorienting Europe itself. In an echo of Wilson's critique of the "old politics" of Europe after World War I, U.S. officials after 1945 emphasized the need to reform nationalist and imperialist tendencies. It was generally thought that the best way to do so was to encourage integration. Regional integration would not only make Germany safe for Europe, it would also make Europe safe for the world. The Marshall

Plan reflected this U.S. thinking, as did the Truman administration's support for the Brussels Pact, the European Defense Community, and the Schuman Plan for a European Coal and Steel Community. In the negotiations over the NATO treaty in 1948, U.S. officials made clear to the Europeans that a security commitment hinged on European movement toward integration. One State Department official remarked that the United States would not "rebuild a fire-trap."[27] U.S. congressional support for the Marshall Plan also had its premise, at least in part, not only in transferring U.S. dollars to Europe but also in encouraging integrative political institutions and habits.

Taken together, U.S. power after the war left Europeans more worried about abandonment than domination, and they actively sought U.S. institutionalized commitments to Europe. Multiple layers of multilateral economic, political, and security institutions bound these countries together, reinforcing the credibility of their mutual commitments. The dramatic asymmetries of postwar power were rendered more acceptable as a result. As the post-1945 period unfolded, U.S. lock-in goals for Europe expanded. Stabilizing the European economies, solving the German problem, and reorienting British and French security policies required much more "engineering" than U.S. officials had at first expected. Securing institutional concessions from Europe required the United States to make an institutionalized security commitment and to reduce its policy autonomy.

Post–Cold War Multilateralism

The United States emerged at the end of the Cold War in a newly advantageous position, and during the 1990s the world increasingly moved toward unipolarity. In these circumstances, the United States sought to build and expand regional and global institutions in both security and economic spheres. NATO expansion and the creation of NAFTA, APEC, and the WTO were elements of this agenda. This pattern of policy is consistent with the logic of post–1945 institution building, and it is captured in the model of the institutional bargain. During the 1990s, the United States employed institutions as a mechanism to lock other states into desired policy orientations, and it was willing to exchange some limits on its own autonomy to do so. Other states also seized upon these institutions as ways to restrain and commit the United States.

In the immediate aftermath of the Cold War, the first Bush administration pushed forward a variety of regional institutional initiatives. In relations with Europe, State Department officials articulated a set of institutional steps: the evolution of NATO to include associate relations with countries to the east, the creation of more formal institutional relations with the European Community, and an expanded role for the Conference on Security and Cooperation in Europe.[28] In the Western Hemisphere, the Bush administration pushed for NAFTA and closer economic ties with South

America. In East Asia, APEC offered a way to create more institutional links to the region, demonstrating U.S. commitment to the region and ensuring that Asian regionalism moved in a transpacific direction. The overarching idea was to pursue innovative regional strategies that would result in new institutional frameworks to mediate post–Cold War relations.

These institutional initiatives, Secretary of State James Baker later observed, were the key elements of the Bush administration's post–Cold War order-building strategy. Baker likened these efforts to U.S. strategy after 1945: "Men like Truman and Acheson were above all, though we sometimes forget it, *institution builders*. They created NATO and the other security organizations that eventually won the Cold War. They fostered the economic institutions . . . that brought unparalleled prosperity. . . . At a time of similar opportunity and risk, I believed we should take a leaf from their book."[29] The idea was to "plant institutional seeds"—to create regional institutional frameworks that would extend and enhance U.S. influence in these areas and encourage democracy and open markets.[30]

An institution-building agenda was also articulated by the Clinton administration in its strategy of "enlargement." The idea was to use multilateral institutions to stabilize and integrate the new and emerging market democracies into the Western democratic world. In an early statement of the enlargement doctrine, National Security Advisor Anthony Lake argued that the intention was to "strengthen the community of market democracies" and "foster and consolidate new democracies and market economies where possible." The United States would help "democracy and market economies take root," which would in turn expand and strengthen the wider Western democratic order.[31] The targets were those countries beginning the process of transition to market democracy, particularly in Central and Eastern Europe and the Asia-Pacific region. New trade pacts and security partnerships would encourage—and if possible lock in—promising domestic reforms.

NATO expansion embodied this institutional logic. At the July 1997 NATO summit, Poland, Hungary, and the Czech Republic were formally invited to join the alliance. These invitations followed a decision made at the January 1994 NATO summit in Brussels to enlarge the alliance to include new members from Eastern and Central Europe. Led by the United States, the alliance embarked on the most far-reaching and controversial reworking of institutional architecture in the post–Cold War era.

The Clinton administration offered several basic rationales for NATO expansion, but it consistently emphasized the importance of consolidating democratic and market gains in Eastern and Central Europe and building an expanded Western democratic community. NATO enlargement would provide an institutional framework to lock in the domestic transitions under way in Eastern and Central Europe. The prospect of alliance membership would itself be an "incentive" for these countries to pursue domestic reforms. Subsequent integration into the alliance was predicted to lock in

those institutional reforms. Membership would entail a wide array of organizational adaptations, such as standardization of military procedures, steps
toward interoperability with NATO forces, and joint planning and training.
By enmeshing new members in the wider alliance institutions and participation in its operations, NATO would reduce their ability to revert to old
ways and reinforce the liberalization of transitional governments. As one
NATO official remarked: "We're enmeshing them in the NATO culture,
both politically and militarily so they begin to think like us and—over
time—act like us."[32]

NAFTA and APEC initiatives also embodied this logic, although the
commitments and lock-in mechanisms were less demanding. The Bush administration supported bringing Mexico into the United States-Canada free-
trade area for political reasons as well as for the anticipated economic
gains. Mexico was undergoing a democratic revolution, and U.S. officials
wanted to solidify these watershed reforms. Mexican officials championed
the trade accord for the same reason: it would commit their successors to
new economic policy orientations and discourage political backsliding.
APEC also had at least a trace of this same reasoning. A multilateral economic dialogue had become possible in East Asia because of a long-term
shift in the developmental orientation of the emerging economies of the region. Japan and Australia were the initiators of the APEC process, but the
United States quickly lent its support. At least part of APEC's appeal in the
region was its potential to serve as a counterweight to unilateral U.S. trade
tendencies: the multilateral process would help restrain the worst impulses
of U.S. trade policy—symbolized in the Super-301 authority of the 1988
omnibus trade bill. For the United States, APEC offered a means to encourage an open East Asian economic regionalism and to reinforce the market reforms that were unfolding across Asia and the Western Hemisphere. If
APEC's actual ability to lock in policy orientations in the region was limited,
the restraints on U.S. policy autonomy were also more symbolic than real.

This pattern of institution building can be seen as a continuation of the
logic that underlay the post-1945 world order. The United States has pursued institutional agreements to reinforce domestic governmental and economic changes that, in turn, tended to cement desired policy orientations.
As a leading State Department official in the administration of President
George H. Bush described the institutional strategy, "Our intention was to
create institutions, habits, and inclinations that would bias policy in these
countries in our direction."[33] The United States was able to ensure political and economic access to these countries and regions and to gain some
confidence that these countries would remain committed to political and
market openness. In exchange, its partner countries gained some measure of
assurance that U.S. policy would be steady and predictable. The United
States would remain engaged and do so through institutions that would
leave it open to market and political access by these countries.

After the Cold War, not unlike the earlier postwar junctures, the United States has used multilateral institutions as tools of order building. These institutions have helped to consolidate the political and economic reforms that swept the world in the wake of communist collapse. NATO expansion, NAFTA, and APEC provided institutional arrangements that reinforced the commitments of weak but rising states to both the market and democratic governance. In return, the United States offered its own assurances of restraint and commitment. The institutions also provided mechanisms for weaker states in East Asia, Eastern Europe, and the Americas to gain access to U.S. power. The institutions have provided a brake—modest perhaps but nonetheless real—on U.S. unilateralism and disengagement.

Conclusion

Some conclusions follow from this analysis. First, a general institutional logic has informed U.S. foreign policy since 1945. It is a logic that sees a direct link between multilateralism and the United States' strategy. Institutional bargains are driven by concerns about policy autonomy, legitimacy, the exercise of power, and political certainty. Their motivation is to promote a predictable and favorable international environment. The United States and other countries are self-interested actors who jealously guard their policy autonomy and sovereign authority, but who are also willing to bargain if the price is right. Ironically, it is precisely the asymmetry of power between a strong state and weaker partners that creates the potential for mutually beneficial exchange. The United States has an incentive to take advantage of its dominant position to lock in a favorable set of international relationships—that is, to institutionalize its preeminence. The subordinate states are willing to lock themselves in, at least up to some point, if it means that the leading state will be more manageable as a dominant power.

Second, this perspective on multilateralism assumes that institutions can play a role in muting asymmetries in power. They allow the United States to calculate its interests over a longer time frame, with institutions serving as a mechanism to invest in future gains, and weaker states to be confident in credible restraints on the arbitrary and indiscriminate exercise of hegemonic power. If institutions are unable to play this role, the calculations and trade-offs highlighted in this analysis are unlikely to be of much consequence. But U.S. officials themselves have acted in a way that suggests that at least they think institutions can in fact play such a shaping and restraining role.

Third, the actual costs and benefits of the trade-off between policy autonomy and policy lock-in are difficult to specify in advance. The postwar crisis in Europe and the multiple engineering tasks that the United States saw as absolutely critical were real enough to justify restraints and commitments on the part of the United States. It is more difficult to evaluate whether other potential institutional bargains today—in fields like economic reforms, human rights standards, environmental protection, or war crimes laws—are worth a specific amount of reduced policy autonomy. The institutional perspective is better at identifying dilemmas facing states than at specifying in advance how such trade-offs will be made.

Finally, despite the prevailing political climate, the United States today has reason to assign a greater rather than lesser value to multilateral institutions. Institutions are the most critical tools available to manage the United States' unipolarity problem. After World War II the United States launched history's most ambitious era of institution building. The United Nations, the IMF, World Bank, NATO, GATT, and other institutions provided the most rule-based structure that had ever existed to regulate political and economic relations. The United States was deeply ambivalent about making permanent security commitments to other states or allowing its political and economic policies to be dictated by intergovernment bodies. The Soviet menace was critical in overcoming these doubts. Networks and political relationships were built that simultaneously and paradoxically made U.S. power not only more far-reaching and durable but also more predictable and malleable.

In effect, the United States spun a web of institutions that connected other states to an emerging U.S.-dominated economic and security order. But in doing so, these institutions also bound the United States to other states and reduced, at least to some extent, Washington's ability to engage in the arbitrary and indiscriminate exercise of power. Call it an institutional bargain. The United States got other states to join in a Western political order built around economic openness, multilateral management of trade and monetary relations, and collective security. The price for the United States was a reduction in Washington's policy autonomy. Institutional rules and joint decisionmaking reduced U.S. unilateralist capacities. But what Washington got in return was worth the price. The United States' partners also had their autonomy constrained but in return were able to operate in a world where U.S. power—channeled through institutions—was more restrained and reliable.

The array of postwar multilateral institutions does provide constraints on U.S. actions in the world. But the United States gets something significant in return. Secretary of State Dean Rusk noted this in testimony before the Senate Foreign Relations Committee in 1965. "We are every day, in one sense, accepting limitations upon our complete freedom of action. . . . We have more than 4,300 treaties and international agreements, two-thirds of which have been entered into in the past 25 years. . . . Each one of which at least limits our freedom of action. We exercise our sovereignty going into these agreements." But Rusk argued that these agreements also create a more stable environment in which the United States can pursue its interests.

"Law is a process by which we increase our range of freedom," and "we are constantly enlarging our freedom by being able to predict what others are going to do."[34] The United States gets a more predictable environment and more willing partners.

There have been many moments when Asian and European allies have complained about the heavy-handedness of U.S. foreign policy, but the open and institutionalized character of the U.S. order has minimized the possibilities of hegemonic excess over the long term. The untoward implications of sharp power asymmetries are reduced, cooperation and reciprocity are regularized, and the overall hegemonic order is rendered more legitimate and stable. The bargain—on both sides—remains intact. But to survive as a tool of U.S. foreign policy in the years ahead, the integral role of multilateralism in the country's grand strategy will need to be more fully recognized and advanced.

Notes

1. This chapter builds on Ikenberry, *After Victory: Institutions, Strategic Restraint, and the Rebuilding of Order After Major War;* Ikenberry, "Institutions, Strategic Restraint, and the Persistence of American Postwar Order"; and Ikenberry, "Constitutional Politics in International Relations."

2. For surveys of realist thinking in U.S. foreign policy, see Kahler, "Inventing International Relations: International Relations Theory After 1945"; and Hoffmann, "An American Social Science: International Relations."

3. Kenneth Waltz's classic statement of neorealism assigns little significance to the role of international institutions. See Waltz, *Theory of International Politics.* For recent discussions of institutions in the realist tradition, see Schweller and Priess, "A Tale of Two Realisms: Expanding the Institutions Debate;" and Robert Jervis, "Realism, Neoliberalism, and Cooperation: Understanding the Debate."

4. For other attempts to specify this logic, see Martin, "The Rational State Choice of Multilateralism;" and Lake, *Entangling Relations: American Foreign Policy in its Century.*

5. World Trade Organization, "10 Benefits of the WTO Trading System."

6. This discussion of state power and institutional strategies simplifies enormously the political context in which governments make choices. Domestic politics, cultural traditions, bureaucratic struggles, and many other factors also shape the way states act. The goal in this section is to isolate the international logic of state choice and generate hypotheses that can be explored across historical cases.

7. See Reisman, "The United States and International Institutions."

8. The classic statement is Keohane, *After Hegemony.*

9. Moe, "Political Institutions: The Neglected Side of the Story," p. 213.

10. This view of institutions can be contrasted with two other perspectives. One is a more narrowly drawn rationalist account that see institutions as contracts—agreements that remain in force only so long as the specific interests that gain from the agreement remain in place. It is the interests and not the institution that are sticky. The other view is a constructivist view that sees institutions and the institutionalization of interstate relations as built upon shared ideas and identities.

11. To the extent that the locking in of institutional commitments and obligations is mutual—that is, the leading state also locks itself in, at least to some

extent—makes the asymmetrical relationship more acceptable and legitimate to the weaker and secondary states. This, in turn, reduces the enforcement costs. See Ikenberry and Kupchan, "Socialization and Hegemonic Power;" and Martin, "The Rational State Choice of Multilateralism."

12. Crozier, *The Bureaucratic Phenomenon.*

13. Important explorations of American policy toward multilateral institutions include Ruggie, *Winning the Peace;* and Karns and Mingst, "The United States and Multilateral Institutions: A Framework."

14. See Knock, *To End All Wars: Woodrow Wilson and the Quest for a New World Order.*

15. Smith, *America's Mission: The United States and the Worldwide Struggle for Democracy in the Twentieth Century,* ch. 6.

16. There is a growing literature on variations in regional patterns between Europe and East Asia and on the United States' divergent postwar institutional strategies in the two regions. See Grieco, "Realism and Regionalism;" Grieco, "Systemic Sources of Variation in Regional Institutionalization in Western Europe, East Asia, and the Americas;" Aggarwal, "Comparing Regional Cooperation Efforts in the Asia-Pacific and North America;" Hurrell, "Regionalism in Theoretical Perspective;" and Katzenstein, "Regionalism in Comparative Perspective."

17. See Crone, "Does Hegemony Matter? The Reorganization of the Pacific Political Economy."

18. See Buzan and Segal, "Rethinking East Asian Security;" and Foot, "Pacific Asia: The Development of Regional Dialogue."

19. On the ways in which NATO multilateralism restrained the U.S. exercise of power, see Weber, "Shaping the Postwar Balance of Power."

20. Katzenstein, "The Cultural Foundations of Murakami's Polymorphic Liberalism."

21. See Donald Crone, "Does Hegemony Matter?"

22. The European search for a U.S. security tie was not simply a response to the rise of the Soviet threat. As early as 1943, Winston Churchill proposed a "Supreme World Council" (composed of the United States, Britain, Russia, and perhaps China) and regional councils for Europe, the Western Hemisphere, and the Pacific. In an attempt to institutionalize a U.S. link to Europe, Churchill suggested that the United States would be represented in the European Regional Council, in addition to its role in its own hemisphere. Reflecting U.S. ambivalence about a postwar commitment to Europe, one historian notes, "Roosevelt feared Churchill's council as a device for tying the United States down in Europe." Harper, *American Visions of Europe,* p. 96.

23. See Weber, "Shaping the Postwar Balance of Power."

24. The strategy of tying Germany to Western Europe was consistently championed by George Kennan. "In the long run there can be only three possibilities for the future of western and central Europe. One is German domination. Another is Russian domination. The third is a federated Europe, into which the parts of Germany are absorbed but in which the influence of the other countries is sufficient to hold Germany in her place. If there is no real European federation and if Germany is restored as a strong and independent country, we must expect another attempt at German domination." Two years later, Kennan was again arguing that "without federation there is no adequate framework within which adequately to handle the German problem." "Minutes of the Seventh Meeting of the Policy Planning Staff," January 24, 1950, *Foreign Relations of the United States,* 1950, III, p. 620.

25. Secretary of State George Marshall made the point in early 1948: "Unless Western Germany during coming years is effectively associated with Western European nations, first through economic arrangements, and ultimately perhaps in some

political way, there is a real danger that the whole of Germany will be drawn into the eastern orbit with dire consequences for all of us." "Minutes of the Sixth Meeting of the United States–United Kingdom–Canada Security Conversations, Held at Washington," April 1, 1948, *Foreign Relations of the United States*, 1948, III, p. 71.

26. Quoted in Gardner, *A Covenant with Power*, p. 100.

27. "Minutes of the Fourth Meeting of the Washington Exploratory Talks on Security," July 8, 1948, *Foreign Relations of the United States*, 1948, III, pp. 163–169.

28. See Baker, *The Politics of Diplomacy: Revolution, War and Peace, 1989– 1992*, pp. 172–173.

29. Ibid., pp. 605–606. Emphasis in original.

30. Interview, Robert B. Zoellick, May 28, 1999.

31. Lake, "From Containment to Enlargement" (October 15, 1993).

32. Quoted in Towell, "Aspiring NATO Newcomers Face Long Road to Integration," p. 275.

33. Interview, Robert B. Zoellick, May 28, 1999.

34. Quoted in Luck, *Mixed Messages*, p. 61.

6

U.S. Unilateralism:
A European Perspective

William Wallace

THE UNITED STATES NEEDS PARTNERS. GLOBAL LEADERSHIP IS BEST EXERTED through persuasion and cooperation; without willing partners and followers hegemony deteriorates into domination. The closest and most reliable partners for global U.S. diplomacy for the past fifty years have been the Western European democracies. The foundations for these intimate connections were laid after World War II, when the United States through the Marshall Plan spurred the economic recovery of Western Europe, and through the Atlantic alliance guaranteed its security against Soviet expansion. This was however an unequal partnership, based on U.S. security leadership and European acceptance of that leadership. Sustaining transatlantic partnership in the twenty-first century, as the Cold War fades into the distance, will require the United States to accept a more balanced partnership, including shared leadership and responsibilities. This adjustment will not be easy for Washington, but it is essential to preserve an unprecedented security community.

Western European governments are the most embedded multilateral partners of the United States. They are fellow members of NATO, the institution that more than any other symbolizes U.S. commitment to multilateral security rather than unilateral action. They formally provide four of the eight participants in the Group of Eight (G-8),[1] as well as a majority in the Organization for Economic Cooperation and Development (OECD), the broader forum for economic cooperation among advanced industrial states. The United Kingdom and France sit alongside the United States in the UN Security Council as permanent members, together with another Western European representative on a rotating basis, consulting closely with U.S. representatives and in most cases voting with them as essential components of any U.S.-led group. Within the WTO and at successive UN environmental conferences, the United States and the members of the EU have played more complex roles, on occasion treating each other as the main protagonist to the exclusion of other parties, and attempting to present transatlantic trade-offs as the basis for global deals.

The multilateral regimes and institutions that regulate the global system were, after all, designed and established by the Atlantic allies, under U.S. leadership, in the 1940s and 1950s. The "Western" partnership between the United States and Europe defined not only the former's post-1945 foreign policy, but also the framework for international order its European allies joined to promote. Without the Atlantic relationship, then, there would have been no basis for a multilateral U.S. foreign policy or the world order it helped to promote. Half a century later, this extensive and intensive network of multilateral links remains central to the United States' international commitments. Of course, the United States has recently sought to build tighter links to Asia through the APEC forum and to other Western hemisphere countries through the Organization of American States and the proposed Free Trade Area for the Americas, and some in Washington have promoted these frameworks over the past fifteen years as an alternative to the priority given to transatlantic relations. But these institutions and structures remain relatively underdeveloped, and could not in the foreseeable future offer any comparably broad framework for shared foreign policy. No alternative multilateral framework, moreover, can match the transatlantic linkages forged by a combination of shared values among Western democracies, similar levels of economic development, intense economic interdependence (including rising flows of foreign direct investment in both directions), growing two-way flows of students and tourists, and above all shared membership in an alliance with an integrated military structure. The depth and breadth of this transatlantic interaction is surpassed only by U.S. relations with its immediate Canadian and Mexican neighbors—and is in most respects more balanced than those. Madeleine Albright's comment that the transatlantic relationship is the key to U.S. commitment to a multilateral foreign policy is a statement that ought to be apparent to every member of Congress and newspaper editor in the United States.

For much of the four decades of the Cold War, U.S. global leadership was focused on the European region and was accepted by European allies as necessary to their security. Today, such leadership is more focused on other regions, where U.S. and European interests do not necessarily coincide. In such a context, U.S. attempts to reassert alliance leadership—accompanied by demands that the European allies follow unquestioningly— looks to Europeans like unacceptable unilateralism, a penchant for defining U.S. interests as global interests without a decent respect for the opinions of its most important partners. The rejection by many in Congress of multilateral institutions as vehicles through which to exert U.S. leadership, and the frequent demands by administration officials that allies follow the United States' directions, even when these appear unduly influenced by domestic lobbies, have given impetus to Western European initiatives to increase their autonomy in foreign and defense policy. Western European governments expect the United States to offer them partnership, based on authority and persuasion, not unilateral exercises of power or veto, based on assertions of moral superiority or disregard for non-U.S. interests.

The Clinton administration presented the United States as the "indispensable nation" in global negotiation and crisis management. This chapter argues that Western European states collectively constitute the necessary partner for the United States in any attempt to provide collective leadership, through multilateral cooperation, in world affairs. With the support and cooperation of democratic European governments, the United States carries authority in world politics. Without that support, U.S. foreign policy is necessarily unilateral, resting on power and resistance to international obligations.

Transatlantic relations over the past decade have revolved around attempts to redefine the basis for partnership under post–Cold War conditions. No doubt the new administration of George W. Bush will launch yet another U.S. initiative to redefine the transatlantic relationship, to which the European allies will have to respond. So far, however, neither Washington nor Brussels—nor Paris, London, or Berlin—has succeeded in defining a new rationale for this partnership, or in providing a narrative that can persuade each other's parliaments and publics that fundamental shared interests should override immediate differences. This is not simply a U.S. failure. Since the end of the Cold War, preoccupation with domestic politics, inability to spell out strategic choices either to domestic elites or to foreign partners, and cumbersome and disjointed policymaking processes (which only the most determined outsider can understand) have characterized Western European as much as U.S. politics.

Old Partnership, New Circumstances

The most striking characteristic of transatlantic relations, more than a decade after the end of the Cold War, is continuity rather than change. The gloomy (and remarkably ill-informed) predictions of "realists" in the United States that Europe would fall apart into international anarchy without the two controlling superpowers and their immense military weight have proved entirely mistaken. NATO not only survives but also has developed new tasks and attracted new members. The EU has also expanded both its tasks and its membership, and it is negotiating with an additional twelve applicant states.[2] An extended, institutionalized regional order is slowly emerging across Europe, constructed on the dual foundations of the EU and NATO, with the United States as a key partner and participant.[3]

Transatlantic relations are embedded in a dense network of multilateral links. These include annual G-7–G-8 meetings of heads of government, underpinned by a network of working groups on topics ranging from international economic management to cooperation against organized crime; shared membership in the OECD, a forum for expert dialogue across a very wide range of issue areas (and one largely unreported outside governments or the specialist press); semi-annual U.S.-EU consultations, involving senior commissioners and the president in office of the Council of Ministers meeting with the USTR, senior officials from the Departments of State and Commerce, and (when in Washington) the U.S. president—and with continuity being maintained through the large, multiagency U.S. Mission to the European Union in Brussels and European embassies and the Commission Delegation in Washington; and of course NATO, the preeminent transatlantic organization, including biennial heads of government meetings, frequent ministerial meetings of foreign and defense ministers, and permanent national delegations in Brussels working in the same headquarters alongside a large common secretariat.

Given the density of these institutional linkages, the agenda for transatlantic dialogue is far wider than the occasional disputes that hit the headlines and elicit overheated political rhetoric in Congress and in national parliaments. Largely unnoticed by outsiders, for example, has been the development over the past fifteen years of an extensive network of discussions among U.S. and European law enforcement agencies on the subjects of organized crime, money laundering, and the smuggling of drugs and people, which has evolved alongside the EU's own network of cooperation on "justice and home affairs."[4]

Most of the time this extended multilateral dialogue works well. It is driven by the mutual interest of North American and Western European participants in maintaining free flows of trade in goods, services, and information. The work of the Financial Action Task Force of the OECD during 1999–2000 provided a classic example of convergence of national policies—in this case on the sensitive and highly technical issues of offshore investment and tax havens. U.S. and European officials worked together constructively to agree on criteria for categorizing offshore financial centers. This agreement has had significant impact: without any immediate sanction, such centers have begun to reform their practices to gain better categorization in this ranked list. Such demonstrable progress in transatlantic cooperation has been obscured by the focus of newspapers and, occasionally, members of Congress, both of which have paid far more attention to the U.S.-EU dispute over the use by U.S. companies of offshore export arrangements as a means of reducing tax liabilities. Over the long term, however, the largely unnoticed multilateral process may have achieved much more to limit tax avoidance by companies and individuals than has the divisive and public transatlantic argument over export rebate schemes.

Rapid technological change and increasing flows of foreign direct investment across the Atlantic (in both directions) have placed a range of new issues on the transatlantic agenda, including biotechnology and competition policy. Different U.S. and Western European assumptions—and regulations—about risk, health, and safety loom larger when scientific advances enable companies to modify plant and animal growth through genetic engineering or chemical additives (like beef hormones or stimulants to milk production). Transnational mergers in an increasingly integrated global economy raise issues of competition across national boundaries and invite extraterritorial interventions by antitrust authorities. There have been several public transatlantic disputes over chemical and biological innovations in food production in recent years, fueled (in European eyes) by the influence that U.S. companies can buy in congressional politics. Yet on mergers and competition policy it is remarkable how well U.S. and European authorities have cooperated, even on such sensitive issues as the Boeing takeover of McDonnell Douglas or the market behavior of Microsoft.

Despite the headlines generated by trade disputes, mutual political charges of failure to contribute a "fair" share to common responsibilities, and accusations of "antiamericanism" or "unilateralism," the fact remains that more U.S. officials from more agencies of the U.S. government meet regularly with their European counterparts today than they did ten years ago (to say nothing of twenty or thirty years ago) to discuss shared interests and to agree on common responses. Yet the perception, on both sides of the Atlantic, is of an increasingly fraught relationship, in which those who recognize the overriding imperatives of shared interests in an open world economy and a stable international order struggle against a tide of hostile comment in the media and in national parliaments. How much is this perception (or misperception) related to the public presentation of the stakes involved in transatlantic relations? To what degree do the disputes and threats of the post–Cold War era reflect a gradual loosening of commitment to and understanding of the transatlantic relationship, either in the United States alone or on both sides? This chapter attributes the gap between increasing multilateral cooperation at the working level and increasing mutual irritation at the political and public level to five factors:

1. Divergent U.S. and European understandings of the "implicit bargain" that underpinned the transatlantic partnership from the late 1940s onward, reflected today in distinct perceptions of the meanings of "burden sharing" and "partnership."
2. An overemphasis in the U.S. foreign policy debate on political-military issues, in response to perceived threats and potential enemies, matched by a comparable overemphasis on economic relations in the European foreign policy debate. In brief, perceptions of threat have diverged sharply on the two sides of the Atlantic, and there has been insufficient effort to build a broad multilateral dialogue to help understand and narrow this divergence.
3. An erosion of common values, with European elites criticizing certain aspects of American society and U.S. elites vigorously rejecting such criticism. A particular irritant to European elites is the frequent

assertion by their interlocutors in the United States of "U.S. exceptionalism" and of the superiority of the U.S. economic, social, political and legal models over European ones. Today, the U.S. model no longer carries the prestige it commanded in the postwar years.

4. An unwieldy policymaking structure on both sides of the Atlantic, characterized by divided centers of authority and decision and by multiple veto points, a situation exacerbated by unwillingness to recognize the structural weaknesses in one's own system when criticizing weaknesses on the opposite shore. Washington policymakers repeatedly criticize the incoherence and slow pace of European policymaking processes, while refusing to admit that the identical shortcomings of Washington policymaking do comparable damage to multilateral cooperation.

5. A widening gap between transgovernment cooperation and domestic debate, which has left national parliaments and publics largely uninterested and uninformed about the multilateral bargaining and delicate compromises required for the management of transatlantic relations and the concert of U.S. and European approaches to global governance. Even though the schedules of heads of government and their senior ministers are now filled with multilateral meetings, these leaders and officials survive politically by playing to national audiences that are interested primarily in domestic issues. Since the end of the Cold War, few democratic leaders have seen advantages in educating domestic audiences about the need for multilateral cooperation on international issues, while many opposition politicians have sought political advantage by attacking those in office for devoting too much time to compromising with foreigners. The media on both sides of the Atlantic have followed popular preferences, paying less attention to covering and interpreting international negotiations. The result—on *both* sides of the Atlantic—is a democratic deficit, with publics mistrusting the multilateral deals their governments conclude behind closed doors in foreign countries.

The Legacy of the Implicit Atlantic Bargain

One of the most puzzling features of transatlantic relations for European observers is that the very elite in the United States who throughout the 1990s proclaimed the success and continuing dynamism of the U.S. economy should at the same time complain so bitterly about the costs of world leadership to the nation and the perceived unwillingness of its allies to share the burden. A second source of puzzlement—and not infrequently cynicism—is that each new administration in Washington calls for a redefinition of the Atlantic "partnership," but does so in terms that continue to imply an unequal partnership between the United States as alliance leader and the Europeans as followers. Such a structural imbalance was perhaps acceptable under Cold War conditions, but it lacks justification in the post–Cold War era. This is not simply a matter of obstructive unilateralism by congressional leaders who are holding back administration policymakers from adopting an internationalist approach; it is far more a matter of the assumptions held by successive generations of policymakers in the National Security Council (NSC), the State Department, the Pentagon, and throughout the executive branch that the United States remains the alliance's natural agenda setter and leader and that the Europeans are junior partners that should share unquestioningly the alliance's common burdens and U.S.-defined tasks. Internationalists within the U.S. foreign policy elite, from the Kennedy to the Clinton administration, have called for the reassertion of U.S. leadership. But in post–Cold War circumstances such positive leadership, with limited consultation, often looks to the United States' partners as being as unilateral in its impact as congressional intervention.

Divergent perceptions of the underlying character and structure of the Atlantic community go back to its origins in the Marshall Plan and the Atlantic alliance. The United States intended its generous postwar economic assistance and its large commitment of ground troops to buy time for its Western European allies to rebuild their shattered economies. Once the Europeans were able to shoulder the burden of their own defense, the United States would again withdraw much of its conventional forces. The onset of the second Berlin crisis in the early 1960s, however, reversed the rundown of U.S. forces begun by the Eisenhower administration, so that 300,000 or more U.S. troops in fact remained in Western Europe for another thirty years. The Kennedy administration's "grand design" for an Atlantic partnership rested on the assumption that the European allies would share the U.S. perception of Western objectives and contribute their fair share to pursuing them. It foundered on the refusal by French President Charles de Gaulle to accept that U.S. leadership and Atlantic partnership were compatible.[5]

The underlying tension between leadership and partnership reemerged in the Nixon-Kissinger "Year of Europe" initiative of 1973–1974, in which U.S. Secretary of State Henry Kissinger attempted to rein in a French-led attempt to develop West European consultations on foreign policy. He did so by insisting that Washington should have access to all such consultations, while also reminding the European allies in blunt realist language that they owed the United States more economic cooperation in return for the provision of U.S. military protection.[6]

The U.S. response to the end of the Cold War showed the strengths and weaknesses of this approach to leadership, and the continued power of historical assumptions in shaping U.S. foreign policy. The Bush administration provided decisive and effective leadership, in partnership with the German government, in negotiating the reunification of Germany, while French and

British political leaders hesitated. But Washington made clear that the provision of economic assistance to regimes in transition should be led by the European Community. In other words, the follow-through was to be the responsibility of Western European governments. "Last time we paid for you," was the blunt message; "this time you pay for them."[7]

Each forward step toward European autonomy in defense and foreign policy during and after the Cold War, even when it has appeared as a necessary part of a greater European commitment to common defense, has been accompanied by a U.S. warning. Since the end of the Cold War, these admonitions have included the "Bartholomew telegram" of 1991, Secretary of State Madeleine Albright's "three Ds" warning about the 1998 French-British defense initiative, and Secretary of Defense William Cohen's speech to the NATO defense ministers' meeting in October 2000.[8] The U.S. posture has rested on an underlying presupposition, accepted by successive U.S. administrations: specifically, that the United States is a benign hegemon and that the Western Alliance can work well only on the basis of clear U.S. leadership, rather than by moving toward the balanced partnership for which President Kennedy and so many of his successors have called.

The United States has by now accepted the EU as an economic partner, alongside Japan; but the idea of sharing leadership in political-military matters has yet to gain serious consideration in Washington. U.S. policymakers thus continue to give their partners contradictory signals: calling on the Europeans to shoulder more of the burden of global responsibility and to share more responsibility for regional and world order, but remaining unwilling to trust them to develop an autonomous political-military capacity or to accept that they may have a different set of foreign policy priorities. Peter Rodman's congressional testimony on the European defense initiative in November 1999 summed up this assumption that the world will be safer if the United States maintains its leadership, with the Europeans content to provide loyal support.[9] "Rather than joyfully falling in step behind our global leadership," he noted, European governments "are looking for ways to counter our predominance."[10] This demand that the United States' European allies continue to accept an unequal partnership represents a unilateral approach to multilateral cooperation. It is likely to breed continuing resentment both in the United States and Europe. In the United States, it will breed frustration whenever its partners fail to follow the U.S. lead or press the United States to consider their distinctive interests as well. In Europe it will breed resistance to perceived domineering by the United States, and so weaken NATO.

The idealists and optimists who managed U.S. foreign policy in the decades after 1945 seem not to have anticipated the contradiction between U.S. leadership and Atlantic partnership. There was an implicit assumption that democratic European states would always share U.S. goals, seeing the world from the same rational and benevolent perspective. The bitterness that developed between France and the United States in the course of the Gaullist challenge made it easy to dismiss proposals for greater European autonomy as "antiamerican"; but in fact a more equal transatlantic relationship had been implicit in U.S. policy all along—being embedded in U.S. sponsorship of Western European integration, of a "United States of Europe" alongside the United States of America. Yet U.S. unilateralists continue to dismiss the possibility of equal partnership, insisting that U.S. foreign policy can be defined only in terms of U.S. power and principles, with a degree of "figleaf multilateralism" (as a fellow from the American Enterprise Institute recently told a European audience) to cover the nakedness of U.S. supremacy. U.S. internationalists face a more difficult challenge: they have to make the intellectual leap from advocating U.S. hegemony to supporting a concert of powers as a framework for global order, explaining to their domestic audience that constructive cooperation requires compromise by the United States as well as by others, and that the United States cannot continue to call on others to share burdens without being prepared to share responsibility for taking and implementing decisions.

The Burden-Sharing Debate

Repeated transatlantic disputes over burden sharing should be interpreted within this conceptual framework: U.S. policymakers have assumed that the allies should naturally share U.S. values and objectives and are consequently resentful when the allies fail to contribute fully to these. For example, French-American differences during the 1960s over the role of the dollar as a reserve currency revolved around the U.S. perception that the dollar deficit stemmed largely from the contributions the United States was making to the maintenance of world order and the French assertion that the deficit allowed U.S. companies to buy advantages in Europe. U.S. resentment at the refusal of its European allies to give full support to the U.S. commitment in Vietnam helped to justify the unilateral decoupling of the dollar from gold in August 1971. In the 1980s, when the sense of U.S. overcommitment contributed to a mood of incipient national decline, it was plausible to depict the European allies as "living in luxury behind an American shield," as Flora Lewis of the *International Herald Tribune* memorably put it.[11] But after the Cold War, with U.S. troops in Europe reduced to a third of their previous strength, and with the U.S. economy surging ahead, this sense of grievance should have disappeared.

European and U.S. perceptions diverge most widely on the burden-sharing issue. George W. Bush's demand, in the second televised debate of the 2000 presidential campaign, that European governments should put troops on the ground in Kosovo touched a raw nerve in European elite opinion. This was true not only in France, the European partner that continues to arouse most suspicion of disloyalty inside the Washington Beltway, but also in Britain, traditionally the United States' most loyal European ally.[12] The history of Western involvement in Bosnia and Kosovo since 1991 has alternative European and U.S. narratives. Europeans have contrasted the British and French commitment to put ground troops in harm's way with U.S. determination to use its predominant air power (and to criticize its European allies for their shortcomings in aircraft capabilities). Likewise, U.S. perceptions of European hesitation in the early stages of the conflict are matched by European perceptions of U.S. intervention from the sidelines, most significantly in undermining the Vance-Owen plan, followed by Richard Holbrooke's abrasive and unilateral imposition of the Dayton accords on the European allies eighteen months later.[13]

The U.S. definition of burden sharing remains a narrow one, confined to European contributions to U.S.-led military operations and to economic assistance programs to which the United States has given priority.[14] European governments, meanwhile, can point to their greater contribution to the UN budget (37 percent of the overall UN budget, and 39 percent of the peacekeeping budget, and not in arrears); to their joint and several contributions to the economic reconstruction of Central and Eastern Europe; to their far larger contributions to development assistance in Africa and Asia; and to their substantial assistance to Egypt and the Palestinian Authority in support of an Arab-Israeli peace process defined and controlled by the United States.[15]

The image of the United States as a country that sees itself as the world's lonely superpower, and also as the world's most powerful economy—while demanding that others pay for it to maintain its position—is deeply damaging to European confidence in U.S. foreign policy. This image was set most sharply in the 1991 Gulf War, when the United States demanded that Germany, Japan, and Saudi Arabia defray the costs of the U.S.-led intervention in Kuwait. To Europeans, shared burdens would seem to imply shared responsibilities; a U.S. administration that defines Western strategy in terms of U.S. leadership but is unwilling to pay for the privilege of leadership risks losing the respect and support of its allies.

Global Strategies and Global Threats

"The United States," Henry Kissinger declared baldly in his "Year of Europe" speech of April 1973, "is a global power, while Europe is a regional power." Most of the internationalists in today's U.S. foreign policy elite would still accept this statement, with its implications that the United States carries the lonely burden of maintaining global order and that the United States has the responsibility to define the threats to this order and the appropriate responses to these threats. European observers, however, perceive that the United States has become unhealthily preoccupied with the identification of potential enemies and with primarily military responses, without investing in efforts to encourage political accommodation with or transition within authoritarian regimes believed to pose such threats. To many Europeans, the United States appears too prone to seeing global politics in geopolitical terms, without allowing for the subtleties of local conflicts and instabilities. Over dependent on military force, it risks provoking the very terrorist reactions against which its forces are now deployed.[16]

U.S. expectations that European allies should support Washington's unilateral definition of "Western" strategy are strongest in the Middle East, the region where European governments now have the most doubts about the rationality of U.S. policy. But expectations and assumptions also differ on the definition of foreign policy priorities in Central Asia and the Caucasus, in East Asia, in Africa, and in Latin America—although differences in levels of commitment to these regions (with the United States far more engaged in East Asia and Latin America than European states, and European governments conversely more committed to unavoidable engagement in Africa) limit the space for active disagreement.[17]

In the Middle East, European governments are uneasy about the contradiction between the United States' simultaneous commitments to Israel and to Saudi Arabia, about the U.S. tendency to depict Islam as a fundamentalist and fundamentally hostile force while being allied to the defender of the "holy places" of Islam, and about the long-term risk that maintaining U.S. troops on the ground in Saudi Arabia will undermine the stability of the current regime in Riyadh. Yet Europeans are blocked by Washington's insistence that Middle East diplomacy is a U.S. *chasse gardée* and by the attention that U.S. policymakers pay to domestic audiences in formulating and pursuing Middle East policy.

This U.S. tendency to insist that its allies follow its lead and its interpretation of international crises is not new. During the Vietnam War, first the Johnson administration and then the Nixon Administration brought sustained pressure on their European allies to provide greater support, both financial and military, in the Southeast Asian conflict.[18] In 1979–1980, the Carter administration canvassed its allies to provide public support for its interpretation of crises in Afghanistan, Iran, Poland, and the Horn of Africa. "We don't want to hear about the problems of your domestic politics," one staffer at the NSC told a group in London, "we need you to line up publicly behind the American position—or we will have real problems carrying Congress."[19] The perception among the European allies, however, is that successive administrations, from Ronald Reagan onward, have invested less and less effort in persuading their European partners of the rationality of U.S. priorities outside the European region, while paying more and more attention to the fears and preconceptions of domestic lobbies and power brokers. The post–Cold War concept of "rogue states," for example, was never compelling to Europeans: it conjured up implacable enemies to replace the lost Soviet threat, it exaggerated the military capabilities of several of the states thus listed, and it lumped together into a single category regimes with distinctive internal dynamics and external aims.

European policymakers have followed with increasing skepticism the twists and turns of U.S. policy toward the Middle East and Southwest and Central Asia: from support for prerevolutionary Iran as the Western pillar against communism to support for Iraq in its war against revolutionary Iran, and to investment in Saudi Arabia as the new Western pillar against "rogue states"; and from support and training for Islamic fighters against godless communism to the identification of Islamic fundamentalism as a terrorist threat to the West as a whole. At each twist, the conviction of successive representatives of U.S. policy that their approach was rational and deserved (even demanded) allied support failed to persuade. European governments, of course, needed no convincing of the character of these regimes, nor of the threats they posed to their neighbors; Libya, after all, had fired a missile at the Italian island of Lampedusa, the only direct attack on the territory of a NATO member state during the alliance's existence. European responses to the Iraqi invasion of Kuwait were strongly supportive of the U.S. lead, with the British and French providing both air and ground forces.

More than any other factor, a divergence of attitudes toward the Arab-Israeli conflict and its underlying causes has lain behind European doubts about the rationality of U.S. policy in the Middle East. Even the most internationalist of U.S. policymakers seem to have accepted the projection of domestic perceptions, as conveyed by that strange alliance between Christian fundamentalists and the Israeli lobby, onto the complexities of this deeply embedded dispute. The team from the American Enterprise Institute that traveled around West European capitals in October 2000, presenting Middle East politics as a choice between right and wrong in which "the Israelis are a civilized country and the Arabs are barbarians," put it more crudely than most; but the rhetoric of "Islamic fundamentalism" and "Arab terrorism" that runs through Washington think tanks and congressional reports suggests that the U.S. foreign policy establishment—and not just the neoconservative proponents of unilateralism—have internalized this discourse about the Middle East.[20]

The U.S. approach to oil security and supply routes in the Middle East and Central Asia evinces an overemphasis on the geopolitical and military dimensions of international politics and a failure to link concern with energy security to broader issues of domestic consumption patterns or climate change. European policies on energy conservation and taxation have diverged from those in the United States over the past twenty years. The dominant European perception, conveyed through the European business media, is that the power of the U.S. energy lobby and the increasing dependence of the suburban United States on the automobile have combined to block significant changes in U.S. energy policy. Thirty years after President Nixon's "Project Independence" and more than two decades after President

Carter declared the pursuit of energy independence "the moral equivalent of war," the United States (with a population of 290 million) now accounts for nearly 26 percent of world energy imports, while the 500 million people in Europe west of the former Soviet Union account for less than 24 percent. Energy consumption per head in the United States is now around 6.2 tons of oil equivalent each year, twice the 3.1 tons in Europe.[21]

The U.S. argument that it is protecting the West's oil security in the Middle East, and above all protecting a Western European economy particularly vulnerable to an Arab oil boycott, has thus become less persuasive. Western Europe, it is true, imports a higher proportion of its oil from Middle Eastern sources than does the United States, but this is partly because the United States now depends more heavily on imports from Nigeria and Angola, as well as from Venezuela. European criticism of the U.S. stance on the Kyoto Protocol on global climate change—and particularly the demand that the United States should be able to buy tradable permits from others, rather than take steps to reduce domestic consumption—are strengthened by the perception that U.S. negotiators are projecting their domestic failures onto the global stage instead of seeking an acceptable multilateral compromise.[22]

European anxieties about the U.S. "trend towards increasingly dire threat assessments" have been heightened by the twin U.S. preoccupations with unconventional delivery of weapons of mass destruction (WMD) and National Missile Defense (NMD), both of which seem to "assume the existence of states absolutely opposed to the United States, and totally heedless of the cost of their behavior."[23] European governments do not underestimate the threat of terrorism. They have suffered many incidents of terrorism on their soil over the past thirty years: from Irish Republicans; from left-wing revolutionaries (in Germany and Italy) supported by East Germany; from Kurdish and Algerian militants; and from Basques, Corsicans, Muslim revolutionaries, and Sikhs.[24] But they do not overestimate the WMD threat, and they recognize that a political response must accompany counterterrorism and preventive measures. No European government has initiated technical programs to respond to unconventional weapons and terrorist threats comparable to initiatives that have been undertaken in the United States, because the marginal risks of biological or chemical weapons being deployed in European cities are not seen to justify such a response.

The U.S. commitment to NMD also appears to European elites to be a disproportionate response to a distant potential threat, one driven by domestic psychology and promoted by entrenched economic interests and those whose underlying agenda is confrontation with China rather than with North Korea. The willingness of think tanks and university research centers in the United Statse to accommodate this emerging consensus, accepting research contracts to investigate the potential effect of WMD incidents in

U.S. cities and to examine how the Anti–Ballistic Missile Treaty might be adapted, is of as much concern to European observers as the hard-line unilateralism of "America-firsters" who appear to drive the debate.[25]

No significant participant in the U.S. foreign policy debate has yet suggested that the United States would be better off without NATO. The projection of U.S. power across the world by long-range bombers flying from U.S. home bases depends on the provision of intermediate bases for refueling tankers. Carrier groups benefit from forward bases, and U.S. forces in Europe now serve as the framework for potential deployment across Eurasia and the greater Middle East. Yet the impression given by U.S. commanders and officials—in Somalia, Bosnia, and Kosovo—who say they see no need to listen to the local knowledge of their allies in assessing situations has undermined respect for U.S. political-military leadership among the European allies. The perceived U.S. unwillingness to accept casualties while ordering others (as at Pristina) to take greater risks, preoccupation with media opportunities, and preference for high-level bombing over commitment on the ground have undermined respect further, particularly within the British and French militaries.

In defense policy more generally, Europeans perceive the U.S. preoccupation with the "revolution in military affairs" (that is, with high-technology warfare capabilities) to be motivated more by a domestic agenda, and particularly by the interests of U.S. industrial and defense lobbies, than by any clear external requirement.[26] European governments are following a different agenda, preparing to fight limited wars and to contain disorder and, if necessary, to invest in the "nation-building" activities of the sort George W. Bush decried in the second presidential debate in autumn 2000. Just as the shared experience in Bosnia provided the foundation for the French-British defense initiative, so shared European engagement in Kosovo has pressed the EU toward developing an autonomous capability for military planning and deployment. U.S. officials have not welcomed this initiative, which is a logical consequence of the divergence in strategic assumptions and force requirements. But the United States will have to accommodate the perspectives of its allies to some degree if it wishes to maintain the advantages it gains from this multilateral vehicle for projecting U.S. power.

For the European allies, excessive U.S. preoccupation with the military dimension of international politics hits home most directly with Washington's tendency to give NATO pride of place in the transatlantic relationship, while underplaying the importance of the EU and its contribution to European order and prosperity in the largest sense. U.S. attitudes toward Western European integration, a process that started under U.S. leadership and direction, have swung over the past twenty years from dismissal of "Eurosclerosis" to exaggeration of the European competitive threat, and back to dismissal of European governments as incoherent and of the European economy as sclerotically constrained by social regulation and divergences of national policy.

The Clinton administration sprang the first post–Cold War enlargement of NATO on the European allies, partly in response to lobbying by Polish Americans, partly due to the determination of officials that the future shape of European order should be defined by NATO rather than left to the EU.[27] The unilateralism of U.S. policy on enlargement has been striking throughout the process so far. Within eighteen months, U.S. policy swung from a blunt warning by the secretary of defense to the prime ministers of the Baltic states that they could not hope for NATO membership[28] to President Clinton's announcement at a meeting of Lithuanian Americans that the Baltic states would be included within the foreseeable future. European governments anticipate that the new administration of George W. Bush will similarly be driven as much (or more) by domestic as by foreign policy imperatives, and that Washington will not take into account the parallel (and more complex) process of EU enlargement or the distinctive interests that an extensive common border with Russia gives the EU member states.[29]

Western Values, American Style

In nineteenth-century Europe it was the moral superiority that British visitors and diplomats assumed, as well as their wealth, that irritated their continental colleagues—and fueled the *Schadenfreude* that continental elites enjoyed when Britain became bogged down in the deep moral ambiguities of the Boer War.[30] At the end of the twentieth century, the proponents of U.S. exceptionalism aroused the same sentiments among the European allies for the same reasons. The triumphalism of U.S. self-projection in the late 1990s owed something to confidence about the dynamism of the U.S. economy, surging ahead of the European economies and leaving the Asian "tigers" far behind. But it had deep roots in the American national myth, in the moral rhetoric of U.S. foreign policy, and in attitudes toward U.S. and international law.[31]

Here again Europeans have witnessed a gradation of postures, from the confident assumption of U.S. internationalists that allies would accept the self-evident authority of U.S. leadership to the strident assertions of America-firsters that the United States is inevitably right and its allies must follow. American Enterprise Institute scholar Joshua Muravchik's remark at a conference in Warsaw in early 1998, "Everyone knows that the United States is a righteous nation," rang in the memory of officials and academics in West European capitals who had attended, when they were interviewed two years later.[32] The impression had been conveyed, one senior British official remarked, that the United States was the only country that was entitled to promote democracy, and that the U.S. model was the only valid model of democracy. European *Schadenfreude* at the confused outcome of the year 2000 presidential election, including revelations of the overwhelming importance of campaign finance, of Florida's peculiar arrangements for counting votes, and of its discriminatory rules for excluding citizens with past prison sentences from voting, was increased by this sense that the preacher-man had been caught sinning.[33]

Americans and Europeans *do* share political and social values, to a great extent. The U.S. investment in building (and rebuilding) democracy and market economies across Western Europe after 1945 paid off in deepening a convergence of assumptions about the role of law and of government accountability and about market rules and limited government—much assisted by the immense prestige that attached both to U.S. democracy and to the dynamism of the U.S. market economy in those years. There remained significant transatlantic differences, however, mainly regarding Western European commitments to higher levels of public spending, social welfare, and corporatist patterns of consultations between employers and organized labor. But the contrast with authoritarian socialist regimes provided a solid foundation for the reaffirmation of shared Western values—even while the European allies deplored the sophistry with which successive presidential administrations justified their support for authoritarian regimes in Spain, Greece, Turkey, Central and South America, and Pakistan.

The triumph of liberalism in the 1990s, however, has unavoidably brought into the open transatlantic differences over interpretations of the liberal tradition, as well as the different responses available to governments in the densely populated states of Western Europe compared with those available in the wide open spaces of North America. To some extent, in the United States as in Britain, criticism of "continental corporatism" has been an extension of domestic political debate onto the international plane, with the Anglo-Saxon Right determined to demonstrate the superiority of their preferred market/libertarian model over the corporatist pattern inherent in social democracy. The remarkable success of the U.S. economy during the course of the 1990s and the long European economic slowdown (sparked by the unanticipated costs of German unification) added plausibility to these free-market criticisms. But the stridency of U.S. criticisms of the European social model, together with U.S. unwillingness to accept that mutual criticism might be justified, has provoked a critical response in the European press and from the political elite. Europeans have pointed to their lower crime rates and far lower prison populations, to the smaller gap between high- and low-income groups, and to their safer cities and better protected countryside. The reintroduction of capital punishment in the United States, including its disproportionate use to execute black prisoners, has become for informed Europeans a symbol of the weaknesses of U.S. domestic society and law; while images of violent crime based on the free availability of guns have further fueled Western European disrespect for the U.S. model.[34]

The result has been a growing divergence between the United States' self-perception as the moral and political leader of the West and European perceptions of the United States as a flawed superpower. This loss of U.S. prestige (and consequently authority as alliance leader) has been compounded by the image created by the bitter partisan politics in the United States during the Clinton years. There is now a substantial gap between the moral authority U.S. leaders assume and what European partners are willing to grant them. Unilateralists in the United States may not worry about this loss; but for those who take for granted U.S. leadership supported by figleaf multilateralism, and even more for those who cling to an internationalist concept of hegemonic leadership, declining respect among the United States' allies represents a real cost. The United States needs, at the least, the acquiescence of its allies; and this depends on a degree of sympathy for its leadership and a broader base of support—rather than antagonism—among the publics of European states.[35]

The gap between U.S. self-perceptions and allies' perceptions of the United States has also widened in the area of international law. There is a contradiction between Washington's legalistic pursuit of U.S. objectives through WTO dispute mechanisms and its refusal to accept the supremacy of international law in other fields. This posture extends a long tradition of assertions of extraterritorial jurisdiction and of resistance to rules to which others have agreed. Supreme Court Justice Antonin Scalia's comment, in a 1988 judgment (Thompson v. Oklahoma), that "where there is not first a settled consensus among our own people, the views of other nations, however enlightened the Justices of this Court may think them to be, cannot be imposed on Americans," represented a wholesale rejection of the jurisdiction of international law, underlined by the increasing willingness of federal courts to claim extraterritorial jurisdiction against the actions of foreign governments.[36]

The reputation of the United States regarding international law was damaged during the 1990s by the vigor with which the legal profession, state and city authorities, and Clinton administration officials pursued the cause of Holocaust restitution against European companies and banks—an activism that contrasted markedly with the U.S. refusal to sign and ratify the statute for an international criminal court (ICC). The juxtaposition of congressional leaders insisting that it was right for the United States to hold European public and private authorities accountable for actions taken under different regimes half a century ago, while at the same time insisting that no representatives of the United States could be held accountable by an international tribunal for their actions, presented a claim to exceptional moral and legal status that the United States' allies see no reason to accept.

Yet the U.S. style in foreign policy appears to require continual reaffirmation of the country's identity and mission through moral rhetoric, and also through a continuing process of explanation to European allies in the expectation of allied acquiescence or agreement. In the summer and early autumn of 2000, a succession of teams from Washington think tanks toured

Western Europe, presenting reports and proposals to European audiences.[37] In spring 2001, as in the early months of each previous administration, a new official team will follow, pressing its own worldview on European allies. The impression of U.S. triumphalism, even of arrogance, that has built up in the course of the 1990s will not help them to get their message across.

U.S. Power, Washington Politics

Henry Kissinger is said to have remarked that the problem with "Europe" is that nobody in Washington knew the telephone number to call in event of crisis. The contrast in images he presented was between an efficient, strategically oriented, U.S. government and an incoherent, slow-moving European caucus. This contrast remains a fairly accurate image during immediate security crises in spite of recent improvements in the coordination of European foreign policies in Brussels. But between crises, and with the single exception of the deployment of military forces, the similarities between Washington politics and Brussels politics are arguably greater than the differences. Both suffer from dispersed sources of authority and multiple veto points. Both are sufficiently absorbed in the complexities of domestic trade-offs to disregard the external consequences of the policies they formulate; both tend to impose costs on third parties while distributing benefits among internal negotiating partners. The long and sad history of the EU's Common Agricultural Policy, the hesitant European treatment of post-communist regimes pressing for early entry into the EU, the setbacks faced over ratification of the Maastricht Treaty—all of these have counterparts in the contradictions of U.S. federal politics.[38]

Here again, U.S. self-perceptions and European perspectives diverge. Administration officials propose grand initiatives to their European partners, but they cannot guarantee that they will themselves be able to carry any multilateral outcome through Congress. The alliance leadership asserted in the Clinton administration's drive for NATO enlargement, in 1994–1997, looked less impressive when U.S. negotiators excluded the candidacies of Slovenia and Romania—both supported by the majority of NATO member governments—primarily on the grounds that it would be difficult enough to carry three new candidates through Congress, and impossible to carry five. The congressional imperative, as repeatedly presented to U.S. partners, is an admission of executive weakness, of inability to provide the leadership domestically that U.S. administrations claim abroad. But the dispersed nature of U.S. power is also evident in Brussels, in the meager coordination between two well-staffed extensions of Washington agencies: the U.S. missions to NATO and the EU.

The rise of an explicitly unilateralist rhetoric in Washington made for particular tensions in the late 1990s, but the roots of incoherence in U.S.

foreign policy are far more structural than this. The Comprehensive Test Ban Treaty, rejected in October 1999, is far from the first U.S.-negotiated treaty that the Senate has refused to ratify. Over forty years ago, the Bricker Amendment opposed the intrusion of multilateral organizations like the UN into U.S. domestic politics. During the interwar years, the U.S. Senate resisted acceptance of the jurisdiction of the World Court on the same conditions as other countries, with the same vigor that it has resisted acceptance of the jurisdiction of an ICC at the dawn of the twenty-first century. One long-term obstacle to U.S. acceptance of the rules of multilateralism the U.S. internationalist elite has promoted is the entrenched representation in the Congress of rural areas, the South, and the Mountain States, offsetting the metropolitan centers of population on either coasts.[39]

So far the Brussels policy process has only attracted a limited number of lobbies and think tanks, though there is an extensive traffic between national capitals and Brussels consultations. Washington policy processes, however, present a free market in ideas, a competition for agenda setting and influence in which money and intellect struggle for advantage. Competition among think tanks, whose members pursue the same potential donors and coveted administration positions, breeds exaggeration—of trends and of threats, written up to gain the headline or the op-ed article that attracts wider attention. The overlap between allegedly neutral institutes and lobbies, with companies funding front organizations to support their case, blurs public debate and advocacy. The power of money throughout Washington is evident to European governments in trade disputes, as in the apparent ability of Chiquita, a company trading bananas outside the United States, to buy access in both congressional parties and the administration at the highest level, forcing a minor issue into a transatlantic confrontation. The vigor and multiple access points of the Washington policy debate make for an easy neglect of the interests of outsiders. The United States appears to its partners as often an absent-minded power as a deliberately unilateralist one. Faith in the rationality of U.S. policy, as widespread in academic social sciences as among Washington policymakers, inhibits understanding of the perspectives of outside governments and reflection about whether the United States' allies might justifiably see things from a different angle.

It is not only unilateralists who have difficulty considering the possibility of self-criticism or perceiving that their own actions may replicate the faults of others. The same State Department officials who protested during the multilateral stages of the last Arab-Israeli peace process that allowing the EU to sit in on the negotiations would mean accepting sixteen representatives from fifteen countries demanded that an "observer" delegation of eighteen U.S. senators should be allowed to sit in on the NATO summit in Madrid. Similarly, U.S. officials who have justified the National Security Agency's Echelon intelligence network, which intercepts European commercial and government communications, on the grounds that it enables them to check on the unreformed habits of European companies in offering bribes to foreign governments for contracts, utterly resist the counterargument that the U.S political system is structurally corrupt because of the dependence of politicians at all levels on corporate sources for finance.

At the beginning of the Reagan administration, U.S. officials remarked on the instability and rapid personnel turnover of European governments; they were reminded by their German hosts that they were the third U.S. administrative team in five years to visit a German government that had retained the same governing coalition since 1974. It was a similar inability to consider whether publics (and political and opinion leaders) in other countries might interpret the application of scientific experimentation to the food process differently than those in the United States that led Monsanto into its ill-prepared introduction of genetically modified foods into European markets, compounded by its initial refusal to accept that there might be a case for the resistance it provoked.

Hegemonic powers have a natural tendency to neglect the views of their subordinate partners, to impose their own perspectives, and to insist that their political and moral priorities must define their relations with other states. The stance of the European Union toward its dependent neighbors to the east and south exhibits many of the same hegemonic deformations: for example, in setting stricter conditions than applied throughout the EU on human rights, the status of minorities, and the quality of public administration and border controls. The unilateralist thrust in U.S. foreign policy, seen from a European perspective, is not totally outside this structural tendency; rather, it is an exaggerated version of it, reinforced by an aggressive interpretation of the U.S. tradition of exceptionalism and by a refusal to recognize that the costs of acting alone include others' possibly learning to act alone to the disadvantage of the United States.

The Democratic Deficit

Both the United States and Western Europe need multilateral cooperation to manage the intricate web of transatlantic economic interdependence, which has grown more complex and more intense over the past ten years. Both the U.S. government and its European counterparts *do* cooperate, actively and across a wide range of issue areas. But much of that cooperation is highly technical and invisible to politicians and the public—apparently remote from their domestic concerns, too detailed and too complicated to make good copy for the press or to offer attractive pictures for the TV news. It is only when disputes flare up or failures in coordination make for a breakdown in management that parliaments and press pay attention, voicing cries of betrayal and foreign interference.

The gap between transgovernment cooperation and domestic under-standing of the degree of this engagement is as wide in Europe as it is in the United States. Just as unilateralists in the United States attack the UN and other multilateral institutions for their attempted invasion of U.S. sover-eignty, nationalists in Britain, Denmark, Austria, and other EU member states see the EU as a bureaucratic monstrosity bent on destroying the dis-tinctiveness of national culture and sovereign political institutions. Popu-lar—and populist—revolts against the transfer of authority from nationally accountable institutions to remote intergovernment organizations may take a different shape in Europe than in the United States, but they stem from a similar sense of lost autonomy and uncontrollable change. The predomi-nance of parliamentary government in Europe, which makes governments more secure in their executive authority, limits the ability of opposition par-ties to block the *engrenage* of multilateral engagement. National parlia-ments indeed have in a considerable sense been left to one side in this evolving process of multilateral governance, while their members focus on domestic and constituency politics. One might, however, argue that the role played by the Senate in U.S. politics is played in the EU by governments of peripheral member states, themselves responding to popular anxieties over increasing entanglement in multilateral commitments over which they ap-pear to have no effective control.

Political leaders in Europe and in the United States face difficult choices about how best to pursue the multilateral cooperation they perceive as mutually advantageous while also responding to public anxieties about the disappearance of democratic accountability into a morass of intergov-ernment committees and international secretariats. The temptation to tell one story to the public and parliament and another to colleagues from other governments behind closed doors is hard to resist. So is the temptation to demand that others recognize the imperatives of one's own domestic diffi-culties without pleading their own in return. Neither Western Europe nor the United States was blessed by strong foreign policy leadership during the 1990s; hence the drift on both sides of the Atlantic back to older patterns of nationalist reassertion and fears of international entanglements.

The United States differs from Western Europe in a number of ways, of course. Its size and distance from other continents makes for a deeper re-luctance to accept that global interdependence is unavoidable. Its excep-tionalist tradition in foreign policy has not been broken by foreign occupa-tion or defeat or modified by realization of the limits of national autonomy. The dynamism of its economy and the unchallenged superiority of its armed forces make it easy to deny the necessity of multilateral compromise and to call for the reassertion of a more "American" approach to world pol-itics. But in other ways Western Europe and the United States share the same dilemmas—and suffer from the same structural deformations. Ac-cordingly, a Polish observer could criticize the EU for its unilateralist approach to European international negotiations, and a Moroccan observer could vigorously attack its hegemonic pretensions.[40] To reconcile the demands of democracy with the imperatives of multilateral cooperation is a task that requires a high quality of leadership, not only from governments but also from wider foreign policy elites. That quality has not always been in evidence, on either side of the Atlantic, since the end of the Cold War.

Notes

1. The additional presence of the president of the European Commission and (when held by one of the EU's eleven other member states) the president-in-office of the Council of Ministers gives the Europeans a clear numerical majority in G-8 gatherings.

2. At the Helsinki European Council in December 1999, Turkey was accepted formally as the thirteenth candidate. But the commission's *Regular Report on Turkey's Progress towards Accession,* dated November 2000, makes it clear that Turkey has some way to go before it meets the political criteria for membership.

3. Wallace, "From the Atlantic to the Bug."

4. Den Boer and Wallace, "Justice and Home Affairs"; House of Lords (EU Committee), *Dealing with the Third Pillar.*

5. Grosser, *The Atlantic Alliance;* Cleveland, *The Atlantic Idea and its European Rivals.*

6. Wallace, "Issue Linkage Among Atlantic Governments."

7. This phrase was reportedly used in a number of private exchanges between U.S. officials and their European counterparts; I heard it in a conversation in the National Security Council in early 1991. "Last time" was of course the Marshall Plan.

8. The Bartholomew telegram, setting out U.S. conditions for any autonomous European defense policy, was at last published in full in 1998 in van Eekelen, *Debating European Security.* In December 1998, Albright conditionally welcomed the French-British defense initiative subject to "three D's": that it not *decouple* Europe's security from that of the United States, nor *duplicate* what NATO already provides, nor *discriminate* against European NATO members (such as Turkey) that were not also members of the EU. See Albright, "The Right Balance Will Secure NATO's Future," *Financial Times,* December 7, 1998. Cohen, attending his last NATO ministerial meeting as U.S. Defense Secretary, warned that too great an emphasis on European defense autonomy could make NATO "a relic of the past."

9. Peter Rodman was a White House official in the first Bush administration, and later director, National Security Policy, of the Nixon Center for Peace and Freedom in Washington, D.C.

10. Statement prepared for a Hearing before the Committee on International Relations, U.S. House of Representatives, November 10, 1999; quoted in Sloan, *The United States and European Defense.*

11. In a similar, but less colorful, phrase Richard Perle as Deputy Assistant Secretary for Defense, told the North Atlantic Assembly in 1982 that "the average American is subsidizing the defense of his wealthier European counterpart." Quoted in Chalmers, *Sharing Security.*

12. European states at the time that Bush made this remark were providing 85 percent of forces in Kosovo.

13. Neville-Jones, "Dayton, IFOR and Alliance Relations." See also the robust comment by Lindley-French, "Why America Needs Europe": "If European

performance during air operations of the Kosovo campaign was poor, it simply matched American performance on the ground."

14. Madeleine Albright's public protest, in the context of a NATO foreign ministers' meeting in December 1997, that the United States was providing 90 percent of the funds for a new training program for the Bosnian police, and that "in key areas such as this, other members of the alliance need to do much, much more," was a particularly outrageous example of this. Her brief may have picked out the only program in which the United States was the major contributor; at that time European governments were providing 70 percent of the funds for peacekeeping and civilian reconstruction, and 80 percent of the troops on the ground.

15. Figures on UN contributions are taken from Chalmers, *Sharing Security,* p. 147. OECD Development Assistance Committee statistics indicate that in 1997–1998 the EU and its member governments together provided some $850 million to Egypt, compared with $675 million from the United States; and $235 million to Palestine, compared with $75 million from the United States; *www.oecd.org*

16. See, for example, the response from Olivier Roy to Steven Simon and Daniel Benjamin, "America and the New Terrorism: An Exchange."

17. For a skeptical European view of U.S. African policy under the Clinton administration, noting its preoccupation with domestic presentation, the active involvement of U.S. corporate interests, the absence of any significant financial assistance, and the antagonism toward France, see Alden, "From Neglect to 'Virtual Engagement.'"

18. Treverton, *Dollar Drain and American Forces*, describes the pressures the United States placed on Germany to buy U.S. bonds as an indirect means of support.

19. Personal note taken of conversation.

20. Personal note of American Enterprise Institute presentation in London.

21. These figures are taken from *BP Amoco Review of World Energy,* June 2000, based on consumption and trade patterns for 1999.

22. See, for example, the *Financial Times,* November 7, 2000, "Trading Filth."

23. Andreani, "The Disarray of U.S. Non-Proliferation Policy," pp.44, 47—particularly criticizing a report to Congress from the defense secretary in November 1997 that argued that "American military superiority actually increases the threat of nuclear, biological, and chemical attack against us by creating incentives for adversaries to challenge us asymmetrically."

24. Britain more than any other, mostly from the Irish Republican Army (IRA). British policymakers recall the difficulties they faced in persuading U.S. counterparts that the United States owed its ally support in facing this threat. Even when the Libyan government was supplying guns to the IRA, funds continued to flow from the United States to IRA front organizations.

25. In spring 2000, Daalder, Goldgeier, and Lindsay told European readers ("Deploying NMD: Not Whether, but How") that "critics of missile defence have lost the debate," and came close to arguing that the Russians and the European allies must now accept what had become an imperative of domestic politics.

26. Lindley-French, *Leading Alone or Acting Together?*

27. It should, however, be noted that almost all ex-communist regimes in central and eastern Europe had been pressing for admission to NATO since they took office; Partnership for Peace was a multilateral response devised by NATO to postpone the question of eventual admission.

28. This occurred in the margins of a NATO Council meeting in Bergen, Norway, and without prior consultation with other NATO ministers at that meeting.

29. One of the senior foreign policy advisers to the Bush campaign reported to a conference in the European Parliament on Western relations with Russia, in January 2000, that European and U.S. exposures to developments in Russia were equivalent because both had direct borders with that state. A Finnish member of the European

Parliament responded that the traffic in people and goods across the Bering Straits was rather smaller than across the Baltic. One of the delicate issues in the accession of the Baltic states to the EU, under negotiation in 2000–2001, was that after entry more than a third of Russian exports would be carried through EU ports or through transit to the Kaliningrad enclave.

30. English schoolchildren today learn the history of the concentration camps of Nazi Germany, but not that the term and the principle of a "concentration camp" was invented by the British in the Boer War; in the same way American schoolchildren learn about the Jewish Holocaust at German hands but not about the elimination of much of the American Indian population at the hands of white Americans.

31. Lowi, "Making Democracy Safe for the World," notes the tendency toward moral "oversell" that has characterized U.S. foreign policy since before World War I.

32. This remark was first reported by William Pfaff in the *International Herald Tribune*; though Muravchik queried its exact accuracy when quoted in William Wallace and Jan Zielonka, "Misunderstanding Europe," he (and other participants) accepted that this had been the thrust of his argument.

33. Eastern Europeans similarly see Western European governments adopting a similarly unjustified superiority in the conditions and tests they impose for political and administrative behavior before EU entry. An Austrian official outraged Czech members of the audience, during a lecture I gave at the Institut für Wissenschaft der Menschen in Vienna in June 1999, by asking: "But won't it be difficult for these countries which lack our democratic tradition to adjust to membership?"

34. For one mildly expressed effort to explain this shift to a U.S. audience, see "Common Values and Cultural Differences: Why EU-U.S. Relations are Good but Could Be Better," speech by John Williamson, acting head of the EC Delegation in Washington, to the EU Center in Atlanta, Georgia, November 3, 1999; *www.eurunion.org/news/speeches/991103jbr.htm*

35. Suzanne Daley, "Europe's Dim View of U.S.," warns about the costs to the United States of this developing trend.

36. Harold H. Koh, "Transnational Public Law Litigation."

37. In the course of October 2000, for example, I met successive teams from the United States Commission on National Security in the 21st Century, the U.S. Institute of Peace, and the American Enterprise Institute; and there had been other invitations. The U.S. Institute of Peace team was led by Stephen Hadley, and the American Enterprise Institute team by John Bolton, both of whom were later appointed to senior positions in the administration of George W. Bush.

38. Stein, *Thoughts from a Bridge,* develops this comparative theme on "the scope and modalities of foreign-affairs powers in two divided power systems," p. 195.

39. These long-term comparisons are taken from Dunne, "US Foreign Policy in the Twentieth Century."

40. The Polish government's EU negotiator once publicly described the EU's "structured dialogue" with the candidate countries as a structured monologue.

PART 3

POLICY IN PRACTICE

7

Unilateral Action in
a Multilateral World

Ruth Wedgwood

IN THE PAST FIFTY YEARS, THE UNITED STATES HAS CREATED AND SUPPORTED a host of multilateral institutions and treaty organizations to deal with common international problems. Areas of mutual interest have included social matters, such as protection of the environment, the promotion of human rights, the welfare of children, and the control of disease, as well as economic matters concerning trade, agriculture, development, intellectual property, the electromagnetic spectrum, and maritime commerce. Postwar institutions have, over time, enmeshed national actors in a web of intersecting obligations, with deep linkages. Aberrant behavior in one context can have consequences in another, so that the sum of international institutions and multilateral obligations may be greater than its parts. For many nations, international integration can help to stabilize internal democracy by cautioning local actors that disruption may carry wide consequences. The global institutions that produce this gyroscopic, stabilizing effect do not have to be formal or public: perhaps the most powerful is in fact the international capital market. Participation in market processes rewards transparency and sensitivity to investors' expectations in ways that can discipline many other aspects of national behavior. And since economic growth is often key to domestic political success, continued access to capital and trade can be an extraordinarily powerful lever to shape the behavior of national leaders. Economic integration and the reciprocal obligations of free trade may have a profound effect on international political cooperation, as we have learned in Europe and beyond.

But the catastrophe of World War II demanded attention to other centers of global institutional order, beyond the market and civil society. Accordingly, in the past fifty years, there has been a concerted attempt to create effective standing structures for the conduct of diplomacy and security cooperation. The United States has ventured beyond the bilateral tools of embassies and telephones to support international meeting places such as the UN General Assembly, the North Atlantic Council, the Organization for

Security and Cooperation in Europe (OSCE), and the Organization of American States (OAS). In the attempt to address civil conflicts, including ethnic and nationalist disputes, these standing structures have been supplemented by new ad hoc consultative groups for particular crises, marshaling the countries that have influence or interest in a particular matter—including the Contadora Group in the Central American conflict, "contact groups" (a moniker first used in the decolonization of Namibia, then extended to Yugoslavia), "Friends of the Secretary General," or "Friends" of a crisis state.

Consultative institutions have been both formal and informal. Indeed sometimes informality is key to their success. Countries may be more willing to take part in cooperative ventures without any binding legal obligation. Examples include the informal arrangements of the Coordinating Committee for Multilateral Export Controls during the Cold War, and the standard setting of the Australia Group and nuclear suppliers group to control the proliferation of weapons of mass destruction. Multilateral institutions have addressed sensitive aspects of international security, including monitoring pledges of nuclear nonproliferation through the International Atomic Energy Agency and attempting to persuade North Korea to cease and desist from the development of nuclear weapons, with the inducement of energy assistance pledged by members of the Korean Peninsula Energy Development Organization.

In most of these cases, the United States has had evident reasons to use the processes of multilateral institutions and, indeed, to support the long-term stability of their architecture. Acting multilaterally permits coordination, and can commit powerful states that might prefer to spoil a strategy, destabilize a situation, or travel on an inconsistent course. Acting multilaterally can save money by exploiting economies of scale. It can prevent free-riding by countries that might otherwise calculate that a powerful trading nation such as the United States would be willing to absorb the entire cost of international action. Multilateralism can strengthen the perceived legitimacy of an action by demonstrating that the values at stake are commonly held and that no single country's interest is the cause for intervention. A multilateral undertaking can also deter aberrant behavior by making clear that the credibility of a regulatory regime is at stake.

The possible debility of multilateral structures should not mask these advantages. To be sure, multilateral institutions face a host of problems. They can be slow in reaching decisions, sometimes being unable to act at all. Decisions are often made at a level of generality that masks persistent national differences, and unacknowledged national rivalries can corrosively undermine common action. There are monitoring problems, since the pretense of agreement may mask backsliding in implementation or wholesale defection. Coalitions may not endure over time as circumstances change and individual opportunity becomes more alluring. A complicated mixture of independent and common interests may make countries reluctant to share sensitive information or national tactics, impeding sound decisions and effective action. The bureaucracies available to execute multilateral decisions vary in quality and may lack incentives for optimal performance. Cultural misunderstanding, inability to understand allies' political constraints, and technological obstacles to interoperability add to the problems.

In the bipolar architecture of the Cold War, and even in the unipolar epilogue of the past ten years, the most sensitive question in international politics has remained the place of military force. The intense interests at stake arguably make this the most difficult test for the efficacy and viability of multilateral structures.

Military action is a singular case for testing the advantages of multilateral and unilateral decisionmaking. There is no topic more sensitive in Washington political debate, as shown in the mid-1990s congressional controversy over command and control of UN operations. There have been masterful occasions in the past when multilateral engagement has made a world of difference, indeed beginning with the original alliance of self-proclaimed "United Nations" fighting against the Axis in World War II. To understand why the United States has chosen since that time to act unilaterally or multilaterally in the employment of military force, one needs to appreciate a number of unique circumstances related to the nature of modern warfare.

The Asymmetry of Power

First, modern military power arguably differs from other goods handled by international institutions because of the absence of equal exchange. There is an astonishing asymmetry in effective military power in the world. An unbiased observer might expect a general correlation between national military power and the size of national economies—with due allowance for differing perceptions of threat and international ambition. The crucial role of a developed industrial base in sustaining protracted conventional warfare, and the importance of technological innovation, might support this view. But any potential equality of exchange has been muted by three central circumstances of the post-war period—the Cold War, nuclear weapons, and the de facto disqualification of the former fascist powers. To begin with, U.S. nuclear deterrence stood as the ultimate stanchion of Western security in the confrontation with the Soviet bloc. France and Great Britain contributed to the breadth of the West's nuclear force, but the size of the U.S. stockpile and the transcontinental air power developed for its delivery dwarfed the allies' contribution, and the disproportion persists to this day. The French and British economies are today each a quarter the size of the U.S. economy, limiting the allied contribution to conventional forces as well. In economic terms, the other Western security giants should be Germany and Japan, but the memory of wartime depredations has set effective limits to the military capacity and security role of each. The United States currently creates approximately 28 percent of the world's wealth, while Japan produces 19 percent and Germany approximately 9 percent.[1] The size of the military budgets is in far greater disproportion. The U.S. defense budget was $271 billion in 1998 (3.2 percent of U.S. gross domestic product, or GDP), with a roster of 1.37 million active-duty personnel and 1.3 million reservists. Japan had a military budget in 1998 of $37.7 billion (1 percent of Japan's GDP) and 236,000 active-duty personnel under arms, with 50,000 reservists. Germany had military expenditures of $33 billion (1.6 percent of Germany's GDP) and active military personnel numbering 332,800, with 344,700 reserve personnel. The important reserves of Germany and Japan do not mask the disproportionate U.S. spending on military hardware and manpower. Inhibitions springing from World War II, as well as the transformation of domestic political cultures, have also meant that German and Japanese defense capabilities are not designed for the transcontinental projection of military force. For example, Japan lacks any capacity for air-to-air refueling, sharply limiting the range of its fighter aircraft, and Japan has no significant bomber force. Germany has designed its force to fight in Europe, and, despite the talk of a rapid reaction force to be mustered together with the British, it has little capability to project forces outside the continent. In sum, neither Germany nor Japan has been capable of participating in the forward deployment of troops abroad and the prepositioning of equipment in areas such as the Middle East and East Asia.

The economies of other potential allies are substantially smaller. There are no other countries within range of U.S. economic power, and the prominent activity of French, British, Dutch, and other European troops in recent robust peacekeeping operations ought not disguise either the small size of their economies or the even greater modesty of their defense budgets.

Such an asymmetry in power has two obvious effects. A more powerful actor has the capacity to act alone, whereas other countries may be unable to solo effectively.[2] And the more powerful actor may conclude that acting multilaterally does not allow it to gain a proportionate return from its efforts.

Of course many other factors contribute to military effectiveness. One is geography, and as a continental power far removed from areas of interest the United States has a strong impetus to seek structures of cooperation to permit its operations in pertinent theaters. The United States remains in Europe by the permission of its allies, which could abide such a presence largely because of the voice given to them in structures such as the North Atlantic Council. In areas such as East Asia, where there is no overall security organization, perhaps it is not surprising that individual allies have encountered domestic political problems in maintaining a "regional" home for U.S. forces after an individual perception of threat has abated. Host geography and basing alternatives still matter acutely in the attempt to project power in distant theaters.[3]

The extraordinary financial cost of sustained military operations may also be substantially underwritten by other countries, even where their military participation is limited. In the Gulf War, Germany and Japan contributed over $15 billion, and the Gulf states contributed $37 billion. Likewise, host governments have funded the long-term U.S. presence in South Korea and Japan in proportions of approximately 45 and 35 percent, respectively. More generally, the deterrent value of an alliance depends not only on the latter's capability to respond to short-term crises, but also on its capability during conflicts over the longer term. Thus the economic size of U.S. allies does matter, even if their military sector is small, because production lines and assets can be redeployed in the event of a protracted conflict. This is a familiar story from the history of U.S. demobilization after World War I—and remobilization as Hitler advanced. The United States was able to turn to a war economy relatively quickly to sustain military operations in the European and Pacific theaters. The value of an ally includes its potential for mobilization in dire circumstances.

Growing Sensitivity to Casualties

But there is a second factor that may inhibit multilateralism in decisions for the use of military force. If international cooperation is seen as a multiround game, war's threat to the lives and welfare of military personnel and citizens may have a "last-round" quality. The death of citizens and soldiers can be seen as an incommensurable harm, not to be "traded" for any other benefit from international commerce, technology exchange, cultural influence, reputation, honor, promise keeping, or goodwill. Certainly, during the Cold War and the nuclear confrontation with the Soviet Union, doubt about the United States' ultimate willingness to sacrifice large numbers of its citizens for another state's safety was voiced by European allies, who hoped for "linkage." (Washington had to be willing, when push came to shove, to risk a nuclear attack against the continental United States in order to defend Europe. The doctrine of "flexible response," developed in the 1960s, was intended as a partial answer to European skepticism, but the anxiety about "last-round" sacrifice persisted.)

In the post–Cold War era the choices seem less momentous, at least as they concern the civil conflicts and ethnic disputes that have been a major part of the recent multilateral agenda. But democratic tolerance even for modest losses of military personnel and civilians is limited as well. The U.S. experience is shaped by the war in Vietnam. European countries that have given up colonies also show a reluctance to incur large casualties in overseas expeditions.[4] The recklessness of civil war belligerents and the problems of terrorism contribute to this wariness. Intervention in civil conflicts and international disputes involving fundamentalist ideologies has also highlighted the vulnerability of civilian targets in the West, even including sites in the continental United States. For some, the threat of such backlash justifies limiting engagements abroad.

The Impact of Technology

A third factor that may tend to limit multilateralism is the changing technological nature of warfare. In the immediate postwar period, the countries confronting Soviet power attempted to achieve some degree of interoperability, in order to permit flexible joint operations with limited problems of friendly fire and insufficient coordination. In practice, even within NATO, the actual degree of interoperability was modest—procurement was still conducted at the national level, and joint training took place only at the company level. This general problem has been exacerbated by the increasing role of high technology in modern air and ground warfare, including such recent ideas as fluid, multiplatform targeting based on real-time views of an integrated battle space. Compatible communications and integrated data collection are difficult to obtain even among the U.S. military services, and this obstacle is multiplied geometrically in international operations. (The overseas sale of military equipment helps to limit this, but only in part.) The choreography of modern warfare also makes it impractical to allocate rigid sectors of operation. Many national militaries may conclude that to operate safely one needs to operate alone. The close relationship between intensive training and safety in warfare makes it all the more difficult to jerry-rig cooperative field arrangements. Even within the smaller scale of peacekeeping operations, there has been concern among commanders about the safety of joint operations.[5]

Of course, one must distinguish (as we will below) between multilateral operations and multilateral authorization. One can imagine unilateral implementation of a multilateral mandate. But the usual connection between contributions and permission may be hard to break: it requires a strong political culture to constrain a unilateral capability within multilateral halters, especially when there is no reciprocal threat of losing effective cooperation. The legitimating effect of multilateral authorization may also be limited, at least in the eyes of local actors, if enforcement is left to one country alone. In sum, multilateral authority may have an important link to multilateral capabilities.

The Advantages—and Disadvantages—
of Using Force Multilaterally

Nonetheless, there are other central factors that support multilateral engagement in the use of military force. First, pledging joint operations may be necessary to inhibit the competitive growth of national militaries in potentially unstable theaters. The construction of a new Western Europe after World War II depended as much on NATO as on the Common Market. Traditional rivalries on the continent were put aside in the face of a common

Soviet threat, without any concern that national military capability might be misused for other purposes. The U.S. presence within a multilateral framework was key to this. Indeed, even now, any U.S. disengagement from Europe could compel Germany to acquire nuclear weapons as a protection from a resurgent Russia, a radical turn that would concern Germany's European neighbors. In Northeast Asia U.S. troops in South Korea and Japan, as well as patrols by the U.S. Seventh Fleet, have reassured other regional neighbors that they need not engage in a regional arms race to counter Chinese or North Korean power. A unified Korea would change the situation in interesting ways, for if U.S. troops withdrew, other local rivalries might reassert themselves, including reviving the traditional suspicions between Korea and Japan. There are a number of countries in the region that are "virtually" nuclear—possessing the technology and capability of manufacturing nuclear weapons, but forgoing actual production in light of U.S. engagement.

Second, multilateral procedures of authorization may increase the perception of legitimacy, which can be crucial in gaining local political support for military operations. Traditionally, the most powerful international legitimation has proceeded from the authority of the UN Security Council, acting under chapter VII of the UN Charter, or from doctrines of collective self-defense under article 51. The voice of a "universal" organization can help to mobilize the support of democratic citizens and political leaders, especially in countries that are skeptical of military power, thus permitting financial contributions, the broad exercise of basing rights, and the employment of diplomatic and economic levers to terminate a conflict.[6] Multilateral authorization can be seen as impartial certification that an adversary does indeed pose a threat to international peace and security, and that the use of force is not intended to serve the narrow interests of a single country. If multilateral authorization is viewed as a continuing warrant that must be renewed throughout a conflict, some countries may also welcome its authority as a way to police the conduct of a war—including limiting collateral damage, economic effects on third party countries, and the pursuit of additional military objectives. In Operation Desert Storm, for example, allied troops agreed to a cease-fire before reaching Baghdad, reportedly to maintain the coalition supporting the war.[7]

The operational deference shown in Desert Storm may be the exception, however. In Security Council multilateralism, the UN has never operated quite as its founders envisioned. The UN Charter draftsmen in 1945 had rather romantically contemplated that member states would consign national troops to UN command on a permanent basis under article 43 agreements. The U.S. Congress, remarkably enough, also acted in 1945 to authorize President Truman to enter into an article 43 agreement with the UN.[8] But the onset of the Cold War and the growth of NATO, SEATO, and other regional alliances restored a grainy realism to such decisionmaking—leaving the UN to serve as a legal umbrella and political sounding board rather than an operational alliance. The Security Council has been limited to "recommending" or "authorizing" courses of action by member states, rather than deploying UN forces as such. The troops deployed in the Korean War in 1950 and in Desert Storm in 1991 were authorized by Security Council resolution, but they remained under U.S. command.

International alliance building can also be a way of subtly influencing the domestic balance of power during foreign engagements. In modern democracies, decisions to use military force may be unpopular. Individual legislators may prefer to avoid responsibility for initiating or terminating a deployment lest things go badly.[9] Even in parliamentary democracies, where the prime minister enjoys a legislative majority, political coalitions may unravel over disputed steps to authorize force. In the case of the U.S. government, the problems arising from differences in presidential and congressional views are notorious. Part of the repertory of a president seeking to commit the country to multilateral military action is the claim that the country's reputation for reliability and promise keeping is at stake. In the Gulf War, President George Bush also intimated to the Congress that Security Council resolution 678 (which authorized the allies to use "all necessary means" to gain Iraqi withdrawal from Kuwait, and to "restore international peace and security in the area")[10] might be sufficient legal authority for presidential action, whether or not Congress voted to authorize U.S. participation in the impending war.

The concern that participation in multilateral structures may change the domestic distribution of powers is a recurrent theme in U.S. constitutional history. In the debate over joining the League of Nations, preserving Congress's right to authorize or refuse the use of armed force was one of Senator Henry Cabot Lodge's central reservations.[11] The issue was all the more heated because the League Covenant guaranteed, at least on paper, the safety of any country victimized by aggression. The UN Charter steps back from this constitutional brink, since the Security Council may choose not to act and the United States can veto any action it disagrees with. Nevertheless, the separation of powers within the U.S. government may still be seen as vulnerable in the face of international engagements. The U.S. president is constitutionally charged with the conduct of diplomacy,[12] and this responsibility arguably includes casting votes in the Security Council, the decisions of which under chapter VII are binding on member states as mandatory obligations.[13] During the mid-1990s, congressional Republicans led by House Speaker Newt Gingrich expressed the fear that Security Council votes could be used as a way to compel U.S. military participation, and insisted that the use of U.S. armed forces had to be approved by the Congress, even in execution of a Security Council mandate. Although the Democratic White House disputed this as a constitutional claim, it agreed to brief the Congress at least two weeks in advance of any Security Council

vote, which often had the practical effect of delaying Security Council action on matters of peace and security. The same constitutional scruple about
the binding force of international engagements can be seen in the language
of the North Atlantic Treaty. The political guarantee of collective security
in article 5 is, technically, only a promise that each individual NATO member will take such action "as it deems necessary."[14] The guarantees of the
Rio Treaty are similarly confined.[15]

The Several Meanings of Multilateralism

In judging the place of "multilateralism" in recent decisions to use military
force in U.S. foreign policy, we should also bear in mind several more dis-
tinctions before analyzing particular cases.

First, there is a potential difference between operations and authorization. The military execution of multilateral mandates may have a single
country at its center, and thus act as a mixture of the two models. There may
be an unspoken rivalry for control of such matters as scope of operations,
the duration of the conflict, and the conditions for conflict termination.

Second, there is a difference between prohibitory and mandatory multilateralism. The UN has never asserted the right to require a country to go to
war, even in defense of international peace and security. The UN Charter
may have abolished neutrality regarding UN operations, for all states are
obliged to obey chapter VII mandates,[16] but there is no textual suggestion
that any state is legally obliged to muster its military forces in execution
of a mandate. Just as the Security Council retains discretion about whether
to act, so do member states. Rather, the asserted multilateral role of the
council has been prohibitory—involving a "double-key" arrangement *limiting* resort to force and providing authorization (by council action) to countries embarking on military operations that extend beyond the limits of self-
defense. This makes military multilateralism quite different from other
areas of international concern, where an international body may have authority (under a treaty arrangement or otherwise) to order a national government to take action. The use of force is a "negative" multilateralism, at
least in the Security Council's architecture.

Third, we should recognize that international institutions too have political cultures, as well as legal charters that must be read against state practice. This means that the characterization of a decision as unilateral or multilateral may not be so simple. How should one characterize a vote of
multilateral authorization when the initiating country implies that it might
go forward with the military strike in any event?[17] How should one classify
a national security action taken without the formal authority of any immediate vote by a standing international institution, yet preceded by extensive
informal consultation with treaty partners and other interested states?[18]

What characterization is appropriate where limited opposition to the act is expressed in a half-hearted voice, amounting to a grudging acquiescence? And what of private assurances—where one or more states oppose an action on the record, but privately say that they do not care?

Even characterizing the formal action of multilateral institutions may not be simple. What label applies to the use of force when multilateral approval is given after the fact?[19] Does the failure of a draft resolution to condemn unilateral action imply authorization? And what of multilateral action that builds upon the results of a unilateral use of force? The accepted principles of state responsibility forbid the recognition of territorial gains made through illegal means or aggression; does multilateral action thus amount to a "cure" of any prior violation, or serve as evidence of earlier implied permission? What of unilateral decisions to take enforcement action in support of prior standing UN Security Council resolutions? In such a case, the instant decision to resort to force may be unilateral, but the gravamen of the action is multilateral. As a matter of law and politics, the choice between unilateralism and multilateralism is not all or nothing. There is no quantum space, with singular alternatives.

Fourth, there are indeed many different multilateral forums, where approval or disapproval of an action may be expressed. The Security Council is charged with responsibility for responding to threats to international peace and security and acts of aggression, under chapter VII of the U.N. Charter. But the Pan American Union existed before the United Nations, and chapter VIII of the UN Charter was careful to preserve room for regional action. Some legal scholars have interpreted Chapter VIII as requiring *prior* Security Council authorization for any regional act of enforcement.[20] But other scholars read chapter VIII with more latitude,[21] and in real-life enforcement actions the distinction has been offered that a regional organization "recommending" action, rather than requiring it, is exempted from chapter VIII restrictions.[22] Does the moniker of multilateralism belong only to the Security Council, or is the use of an alternative forum of disputed authority to be counted in the same camp?

And finally, under the UN Charter national military force avowedly can be used in self-defense against armed aggression.[23] In some sense, then, even unilateral action enjoys a "multilateral" umbrella, for it is recognized by the UN Charter as a necessary first line of resistance until the Security Council may later take action to preserve international peace and security. (One might also argue that instances of "collective self-defense" under article 51 qualify as a form of multilateralism by virtue of their broader participation.) Although there are disputes over the permitted range of self-defense—for example, whether force can be used in anticipation of an attack, and how countries may respond to cross-border guerrilla activity—the category of self-defense can be seen as a necessary limitation and implicit delegation of multilateral authority as well.

Postwar Incidents of State Practice

In judging the place of multilateralism in post-1945 U.S. practice, one must begin with the Korean War. When North Korean troops barreled south in 1950 across the armistice lines established at the end of World War II, Secretary of State Dean Acheson chose to resort to the Security Council for a resolution authorizing the allied defense.[24] There were a number of plausible reasons for this, both legal and political. A Security Council resolution avoided any accusation of improper intervention in a civil war. (Article 51's right of collective self-defense has been taken to apply only to interstate conflict.)[25] A council vote served to condemn the North Korean action with the strongest form of public obloquy. And it permitted the argument that the military response was a UN "police action" rather than a war, seemingly excusing Truman from resorting to the U.S. Congress for legislative authorization. The Soviet delegate was boycotting the Security Council at the time to protest the seating of a Taiwanese representative in China's Security Council seat, and only this serendipitous circumstance avoided a Soviet veto.

Subsequently, after that delegate resumed his council seat, Secretary Acheson chose the alternative precaution of seeking a General Assembly resolution to back up allied action. The famous "Uniting for Peace Resolution"[26] was hardly contemplated by the drafters of the UN Charter—indeed, that document explicitly forbids the General Assembly from making recommendations on a security matter when the Security Council is seized of the problem.[27] Acheson's gambit thus amounted to two-tier multilateralism, but its second portion was legally innovative. It may count as the first proof that procedural perfectionism was not held to be a more important value than the realization of the underlying purposes of the UN Charter.[28] The defense of South Korea involved more than fifteen countries, variously contributing ground, naval, and air forces.

A decade later, the Cuban missile crisis also brought Washington to seek multilateral authorization, albeit in a surrogate form. U.S. concerns about Cuba's acquisition of intermediate-range missiles centered on the problem of self-defense, but mere development of a weapons system was not necessarily to be equated with an armed attack under article 51. The United States famously sought to avoid escalatory rhetoric, styling its operation to intercept the missiles at sea as a "defensive quarantine" rather than a blockade. Washington also resorted to the UN Security Council to make plain the provocation, showing surveillance photographs of Soviet missile construction in Cuba, though without seeking any council resolution to authorize military action in light of the inevitable Soviet veto. Rather, to bolster its action the United States resorted to the OAS, a regional organization in which its voice was dominant. The subsequent vote by the OAS "recommended" that member states take any necessary action to prevent the installation of Soviet missiles.[29] In practice, the military operations of air surveillance and maritime interception were conducted solely by U.S. craft, and the right of regional organizations to act without Security Council approval was—and remains—contentious.[30] But the successful outcome of an extraordinarily dangerous bipolar confrontation muted any more abstract questions about legal authority or *ultra vires* multilateralism.

The U.S. intervention in the Dominican Republic in 1965 followed from concern about the example of a communist Cuba. Countering a coup backed by the Dominican Revolutionary Party, the action was styled as humanitarian intervention to protect U.S. nationals. Washington sought to bolster its warrant by obtaining an OAS resolution of authorization.[31] An OAS Inter-American Peace Force also was fielded. By resorting to the OAS, the United States avoided a Soviet veto in the Security Council and reaffirmed its traditional reluctance to submit Western Hemisphere disputes to council scrutiny. This was technical multilateralism, where Washington resorted to the most adaptable multilateral structure. Grudging hemispheric acceptance of the U.S. action was determined more by suspicion of Cuba than by procedural niceties. A U.S. Army study of the intervention argues that "the United States lost trust among Latin American nations" concerning "adhere[nce] to the norm of non-intervention in international law."[32] Another commentator observed, however, that the fact that the OAS was "forced into action by the U.S. unilateral military intervention or that the peace force was predominantly American is of little consequence. The perception of OAS action existed, and in international politics, perceptions often carry as much weight as fact."[33]

But as political scientists, we may wish to note the existence of a sliding scale of authority: that is, multilateral authorization may enhance political acceptance of the use of force to a greater extent where the organization is one in which opposition has been voiced in the past. Of course, in the case of Central America, the exercise of power fell within a traditional U.S. sphere, recognized and expected (if not universally condoned) as international practice during the Cold War.[34] Other countries familiar with the exercise of U.S. power were willing to accede to the intervention under the polite umbrella of consultation.

So, too, the intervention in Grenada in 1983 by the United States was draped with the authorization of a little-used multilateral body, the Organization of Eastern Caribbean States. Suspicion of the left-oriented "New Jewel" movement, and fear that the Soviet Union might gain an operational airbase nearer to Latin America, impelled Washington's opposition to a change of regime in Grenada. But more traditional justifications were mustered as well, including the need to insure the safety of American medical students studying abroad (leading to *bons mots* about the imperial power of the junior year abroad), and a cited invitation by the former governor-general of the island (whose constitutional capacity to invite intervention was disputed by some observers). The thin multilateralism of a subregional

Caribbean organization was testament, perhaps, to a shared anticommunism and the extent of North American influence, though it did serve as quiet acknowledgment that intervention at will in the Caribbean Basin was no longer politically congenial. Questions about the legal capacity of the minimultilateral group to authorize intervention were muted, as in the Dominican Republic incident.

In the Panama intervention in 1989, multilateralism played a more significant part. Observers from the OAS called attention to ongoing human rights violations by the government of General Manuel Noriega, and to repressive tactics in the 1989 campaign for the Panamanian presidency (including the public beating of an opposition candidate for the vice-presidency). The electoral victory of opposition coalition candidate Guillermo Endara was certified by OAS observers, and an OAS delegation visited in summer 1989 to attempt to persuade General Noriega to respect the results of the election. When Noriega clung to office, there was a coup attempt in October 1989. In December 1989 the United States sent an intervention force, claiming as *casus belli* the shooting death of a U.S. soldier in Panama City, and arrested General Noriega under an outstanding federal indictment for narcotics smuggling into the United States.

The invasion, which caused 300 civilian deaths, was criticized by the UN General Assembly, the OAS Commission of Jurists, and the Ibero-American Summit meeting. The Panamanian representative to the UN also argued that the United States had failed to bring its complaints about Noriega's abuse of U.S. soldiers to the attention of the Security Council. However, the lack of more serious diplomatic repercussions for the United States from the 1989 use of force has generally been ascribed to the central role of regional observers in denouncing Noriega's undemocratic rule. Even though Latin America has clung to an ethos of nonintervention, the inconsistency of Noriega's regime with regional standards of democratic government powerfully served to limit public criticism of the invasion. The public embrace of democracy as a regional norm in the 1991 OAS Santiago Declaration and in OAS resolution 1080 has also affected the historical view of the U.S. intervention.

In the 1990s, the end of the Cold War promised to permit a more consistent resort to the Security Council to justify the international use of force. The early UN Protection Force (UNPROFOR) peacekeeping intervention in Bosnia, following the collapse of European Community efforts at a negotiated solution to the Yugoslav conflict, was diplomatically supported by the United States as a chapter VII operation with a limited mandate. Intervention in Somalia in 1993 to provide famine relief and security for food distribution was framed as a chapter VII operation as well. But the three-phase effort in Somalia—involving a UN force, followed by a U.S. force, then handing off again to a UN force—was punctuated by the murders of Pakistani and U.S. peacekeepers in downtown Mogadishu. It gave rise to a perception that peacekeeping missions could be too ambitious in their mandate, as well as to criticism (well founded or not) that multilateral operations were unworkable in hazardous environments. In the aftermath of Somalia, the warnings of interethnic conflict in Rwanda did not inspire any members of the Security Council to volunteer a robust military force, and the United States made plain its opposition to any combat mission under the UN flag. In a sense, the passivity in Rwanda shows the hazard of multilateralism, for an effective response may be captive to the views of one or more major members. The only timely action was France's Operation Turquoise, an intervention in southwestern Rwanda. This was undertaken unilaterally, though it obtained later Security Council blessing, and was characterized by critics as an attempt to shelter escaping Hutu Interahamwe militia.

The U.S. intervention in Haiti initially promised happier results. The threatened use of force came after repeated attempts by the OAS to persuade General Raoul Cedras to step down and to respect the 1991 election of Jean-Bertrand Aristide to the presidency. The modality of multilateral efforts in Haiti was particularly interesting, for negotiators such as Argentine diplomat Dante Caputo carried the credentials of both the OAS and the UN. The studied attempt by the Cedras regime to rebuff mediation, including the riotous attempt to prevent the USS *Harlan County* from landing in Port-au-Prince, bolstered support for intervention under chapter VII to force the Cedras regime from power. Like Somalia and Bosnia before it, this was an adaptive use of chapter VII's aegis of meeting threats to "international peace and security," but the evident need for some solution to flotillas of refugees adrift in the Caribbean won Security Council support for the multilateral flagging of a "forced entry" in October 1994 to force Cedras to step down.[35] The episode also demonstrated how multilateral military operations may be held hostage to extraneous concerns: the People's Republic of China threatened to veto any extension of the mission because Haiti had diplomatic relations with the government of Taiwan. Still, multilateral authorization served as a curative to regional skepticism about intervention in internal regimes—especially by the United States, which had occupied Haiti from 1909 to 1934. A sense of modesty about the accomplishments of armed intervention, whether under multilateral or unilateral aegis, also has followed: the Aristide regime was unwilling to privatize the economy, failing to meet the conditions for release of $1.2 billion in foreign aid pledged by international donors, and did not always act liberally toward political opponents.

The major military action of the 1990s was the Persian Gulf action, following Iraq's invasion of Kuwait. The deployment of troops to defend Saudi Arabia and to push Iraq out of Kuwait would have been amply justified as an instance of collective self-defense under article 51 of the UN Charter, without further action by the Security Council. However, the coincidence of interests in stabilizing this oil-rich region allowed the United States to obtain Security Council authorization for the imposition of mandatory sanctions in August 1990, and three months later, in November 1990, for the use of armed force to eject Iraq from Kuwaiti territory. Any lingering differences of strategy and sympathy were overcome by the blatant nature of Iraq's violation of Kuwaiti sovereignty and by the need of countries as diverse as Russia and Japan for secure access to oil and natural gas from the region. This multilateral support, in the UN and Gulf Cooperation Council, prevented Iraq from garnering sympathy in the Arab world or from interweaving the crisis with strands from the Israeli–Palestinian conflict. The time needed for the staged deployment of a major military ground operation also allowed a long interval for diplomatic efforts to build the coalition and to attempt (futilely) to persuade Iraq to withdraw. Substantially, after the air and land campaign was concluded in March 1991, the UN Special Commission on Iraq (UNSCOM) discovered a chilling lesson about diplomatic delay and its potential costs: Saddam Hussein had used the interval between November 1990 and the beginning of the allied air campaign in February 1991 to newly "weaponize" offensive biological reagents, loading aerial bombs and warheads for front-line deployment against the allied force.[36]

The aftermath of the Iraqi conflict, however, made plain the tensions between multilateralism and unilateralism. Under the terms of the ceasefire to the Gulf War, embodied in Security Council resolution 687,[37] Iraq was obliged to dismantle all production and stockpiles of weapons of mass destruction, including nuclear, chemical, and biological reagents, and ballistic missile systems with a range of over 150 kilometers. The innocent expectation that Iraq would cooperate in this endeavor was soon put to rest, and UN monitoring of Iraqi compliance broke down into a multilateral game of cat and mouse. In 1993, Baghdad's threat against the safety of UNSCOM air traffic provoked three permanent members of the Security Council to undertake a limited set of air strikes to enforce the mandate of resolution 687. This action followed the council's conclusion that Iraq was in "flagrant violation" of the conditions of the cease-fire resolution, but there was no new Security Council authorization for the use of force. Following the revelation of Iraq's biological weapons program in 1995, matters continued to deteriorate, and in autumn 1997 Iraq declined to allow U.S. inspectors to continue taking part in on-site inspections within Iraq. This led to a British-U.S. threat to use force in early 1998 and a four-day bombing campaign in December 1998 by U.S. and British aircraft. There was, and there remains to this day, an open dispute between the United States and some other members of the UN about whether a multilateral mandate can be enforced by unilateral action without specific, renewed approval by the Security Council.[38] This dispute about efficacy in enforcement was overtaken in the case of Iraq by other political circumstances, reflecting the difficulty in sustaining credible deterrence through multilateral means. Support for continued economic sanctions against Iraq to gain compliance with the UN weapons inspections began to dwindle based on both humanitarian and commercial grounds. The object lesson one might take away is that there is a limited half-life for multilateral projects. One cannot expect a consensus to last indefinitely, and traditional differences in national interest, sympathy, and ambition will almost inevitably reemerge. (The United States might also take away the lesson that using a multilateral vehicle for alleged national intelligence operations carries evident costs, and that attaching such unilateral foreign policy objectives as the removal of Saddam Hussein to multilateral sanctions may begin to erode support.)

Multilateral authorization in the Persian Gulf War served the significant purpose of burden sharing (funding the allied effort with contributions totaling $52 billion from Japan, Germany, and the Gulf states), as well as preventing political caricature of the reasons for the use of force. And for a limited postwar period, it also permitted weapons monitoring and a program of forced disarmament of a sort otherwise impossible absent an adversary's unconditional surrender. However, the postwar confrontation also showed that multilateral alliances are prone to fracture, and that even the United States may overtax its structure in adding additional political objectives to the latticework.

The U.S. air strikes in Sudan and Afghanistan on August 20, 1998, directed against assets of the terrorist Osama bin Laden, were perhaps the most controverted unilateral actions of recent U.S. policy. Here, too, the action is embedded in a multilateral background of measures against terrorism. The embassies in Nairobi and Dar-es-Salaam were bombed by terrorist action in August 1998, with 224 people killed and 4,600 wounded. The United States has supported the negotiation of multilateral criminal justice treaties through the UN, with "universal jurisdiction" requirements to extradite or prosecute offenders who have engaged in attacks on diplomats, aircraft, and most recently, UN peacekeepers. The multilateral treaty declaring attacks on diplomats to be an international crime undergirds the extradition of suspects in the East African bombings,[39] though at least one defendant was sent to the United States by irregular means. Criminal indictments accuse twenty-two suspects, including Osama bin Laden, of conspiring to stage the embassy bombings out of opposition to the U.S. presence in the Persian Gulf and support for Israel. The gravamen of bin Laden's complaint about U.S. policy in fact stems from the Security Council–authorized defense of Kuwait and Saudi Arabia against Iraqi threats in the Gulf War.

Sudan and Afghanistan both have been the subject of multilateral sanctions. The Security Council voted sanctions against Sudan in 1996 for shielding suspects wanted for the attempted assassination of President Mubarak of Egypt.[40] The Security Council also has voted sanctions against

Afghanistan for sheltering bin Laden, with the remarkable concurrence of permanent members China and Russia.[41]

The air strikes in August 1998 (aimed against bin Laden's headquarters in Afghanistan and against a pharmaceutical plant in Sudan allegedly associated with the transfer or manufacture of chemical weapons) were mounted unilaterally in the asserted exercise of the right of self-defense under article 51 of the UN Charter. There was no real doubt that bin Laden had engaged in an armed attack on U.S. nationals and U.S. embassy installations, also killing and wounding thousands of Africans in doing so. Much of the proof was later made public in the federal trial of four members of Al Qaeda in New York City from February to May 2001, with 92 witnesses and over 1,300 trial exhibits. The U.S. counterattack caused few civilian casualties, and (despite its dramatic use of stand-off technology) fulfilled the *jus in bello* requirement of proportionality. Still, there was unease in the international community for two primary reasons: the sites of the attacks in third-party territory and the question of the evidence supporting the Sudan targeting choice. Afghanistan and Sudan could argue that in a system of sovereign states, the primary responsibility for controlling the actions of a resident belongs to the local state, precluding direct foreign action even in self-defense until all other steps are exhausted. (The United States would rejoin that both Afghanistan and Sudan had already shown a concerted failure to control terrorist activities organized on their soil.) The cruise missiles directed against bin Laden's camp in Afghanistan also had to overfly Pakistani territory at a time of great tension with India in the nuclear arms race. While Pakistan has supported the fundamentalist Taliban regime in Afghanistan that shelters bin Laden, Pakistan was not implicated in the embassy bombings. The consultation with Pakistan consisted of a contemporaneous dinner conversation between General Joseph Ralston (then deputy chairman of the Joint Chiefs of Staff) and the Pakistani general in charge of missile forces.

The second dispute concerns the evidence underlying the choice of the Al Shifa pharmaceutical plant in Khartoum as a target. The initial U.S. explanation was the discovery of Empta, a precursor of VX chemical weapons, in the soil outside the plant. This became tangled in a debate over whether taking only one sample was reliable and whether the Empta residue might reflect a different product. (Interestingly, much of the press criticism of the U.S. sampling methodology came in after-hours statements by high-level staff members of the UN Organization for the Prohibition of Chemical Weapons [OPCW] in The Hague. Whether this was within OPCW's mandate is debatable, but the political dynamic reflected OPCW's desire to distance its own inspection regime from any unilateral use of force.) At press briefings, some senior U.S. officials also were not cognizant that the Al Shifa plant was manufacturing pharmaceuticals for Iraq as part of a UN contract under the sanctions regime. (This is not itself inconsistent with other uses of the plant.) Electronic intercepts apparently linking Al Shifa plant officials to the head of the Iraqi chemical weapons program were not publicly mentioned until after most of the U.S. press derided the targeting decision.

Following the air strikes, there was an earnest suggestion that the United States should submit its targeting information to the scrutiny of the Security Council as part of its article 51 letter invoking the right of self-defense. However, this proposal shows the grave difficulty in squaring multilateral authorization or justification with the closely held nature of ongoing military and intelligence operations. Monitoring bin Laden remains crucial even now, as one can see in the aftermath of the more recent attack on the USS *Cole* in Yemen. Transparency of decisionmaking may help to gain political support from other countries, and provide a way to show that standards on the use of force have been met, but it may carry an undue cost in current security crises. Ironically, there was a species of surrogate multilateralism, for a number of other countries' intelligence services were equally persuaded that bin Laden posed a palpable and continuing threat (the British publicly confirmed this), and few countries pressed for any action in the Security Council.[42]

The most remarkable use of force in recent years (albeit again without direct Security Council authorization) was the NATO air campaign in the former Yugoslavia during spring 1999. This action was designed to force Serbia to withdraw its police and military forces from Kosovo and to protect Kosovo's Albanian population against ethnic cleansing. Although there was no council action directly authorizing the use of force, the NATO decision was embedded before and after in multilateral diplomacy. The Security Council acted on several occasions in 1998 to warn Slobodan Milosevic that his assaults on civilian populations in Kosovo amounted to a threat to international peace and security. The council also required him to cooperate with NATO and OSCE in order to verify Serb military and police withdrawals from Kosovo. In February 1999 negotiations were convened at Rambouillet, France, by the "contact group" (the United States, United Kingdom, France, Germany, Italy, and Russia), with the Serbs and Kosovar Albanians, in the open understanding that a Serb refusal to negotiate would be followed by military action. Finally, it must be noted that NATO itself is a multilateral defense organization uniting nineteen countries. Some legal analysts may dispute its ability to act without prior authorization from the Security Council except in self-defense, but its breadth of view at least ensured that the decision to use force would not reflect U.S. solipsism.

International reaction during the campaign reflected the world of ambivalent multilateralism. In one sense, the campaign was designed to uphold the highest values of the UN in opposition to ethnic cleansing. The refusal to use effective force to stem ethnic violence in the former Yugoslavia and genocide in Rwanda was a heavy moral burden on the UN, and the world body was hard put to argue that it could take NATO's place in the case of Kosovo. But in another sense, the air campaign seemed to disregard the primacy of the Security Council in authorizing the use of force outside of self-defense. The United States did not try to obtain an authorizing council resolution because of an anticipated Russian veto. Yet a draft resolution to condemn the NATO campaign, sponsored by Russia, India, and Belarus, precipitously failed in the Security Council by a vote of three to twelve, defeated without any exercise of a veto.

After a protracted bombing campaign, Belgrade finally did agree to withdraw most of its forces from Kosovo. The UN immediately built upon the results of the military action in resolution 1244, acting under chapter VII to establish an "international security presence" and an "international civil presence" in Kosovo. The operation was tasked to "[p]romot[e] the establishment, pending a final settlement, of substantial autonomy and self-government in Kosovo," while "taking full account . . . of the Rambouillet accords." Under the principles of state responsibility, such acceptance of the war's results would have been unthinkable if the military action were deemed aggression.[43] The ultimately successful inclusion of Russian troops in the peacekeeping operation, as well as Russia's prominent role in negotiating an end to the war, helped to cure any slight to Russia in the earlier Rambouillet process, thus serving one of multilateralism's premier purposes: avoiding great power provocation. The postconflict statements of the UN secretary-general have also recognized that the authority of the Security Council may depend on its ability to respond to urgent occasions of humanitarian intervention.[44]

Conclusion

The willingness of the United States to act multilaterally in the employment of force is a complicated matter, as the case studies above may make clear. The slow timing and procedural obstacles to obtaining multilateral authorization through the Security Council have often led Washington to embrace "substitute" forms of multilateralism—through regional and subregional organizations and ad hoc coalitions. Consulting with interested parties, making a case in the court of public and diplomatic opinion, preventing unnecessary surprise, and attempting to avoid military tactics that will strain foreign partners can go a long way to filling the gap when UN machinery is unavailable. This substitute multilateralism may cause sleepless nights for some international lawyers, but has often seemed to salve the concerns felt by other countries at the singular career of a country with formidable military power. At the same time, the unwillingness of the United States to declare that it will permit its military power to be governed by multilateral machinery may reflect an equally grave concern: that the credibility of deterrence depends on an adversary's conviction that a response will be forthcoming. If adversaries (including rogue regimes) were able to rely opportunistically on the blocking mechanisms of multilateral machinery, the global regime for governing the use of force could end up causing international conflict rather than quelling it. Hence the state of creative ambiguity is likely to continue.

Notes

1. See International Institute of Strategic Studies, *The Military Balance* (1999).

2. Of course, this depends on the scale of operation. France has, for example, intervened alone on several occasions in West Africa, and most recently, conducted Operation Turquoise in Rwanda in the aftermath of the Hutu genocide.

3. A recent example of geographical leverage can be seen in the prelude to the intervention of international peacekeeping forces in East Timor in 1999. Reportedly, the United States was at first reluctant to take any active role in the military operation. But Washington changed its position at the urging of both Australia and Portugal, supplying transport and materiel. Among the persuasive techniques used by Portugal, as a member of NATO and former administering power of East Timor, was to deny the United States the right to land and refuel its planes in the Azores on thirteen separate occasions.

4. To be sure, in the UNPROFOR mission in Bosnia-Herzegovina, French, British, and other European troops suffered significant casualties, but these losses were gradual. In Rwanda, the deliberate murder of ten Belgian peacekeepers by the Hutu militia led Belgium to order the rest of its troops to withdraw immediately.

5. At times, this misgiving is exacerbated by concerns about intelligence and operational security in a multinational force. For example, in the UNOSOM military operation in Somalia (originally designed to distribute famine relief), Pakistani and Malaysian armored units available to support U.S. Army Rangers were not informed in advance about a planned operation to arrest clan leader Mohammed Aideed, because of U.S. doubts about intelligence security in some international units. See Allard, *Somalia: Lessons Learned.* Recent mishaps in the UN peacekeeping mission in Sierra Leone may reinforce the point. Within days of their arrival in the country, 240 Zambian peacekeepers were taken prisoner by Foday Sankoh's Revolutionary United Front. A UN investigation showed that the Zambians operated without appropriate briefings on the changing nature of the local threat.

6. The centrality of Security Council authorization is supported by most countries, but some capitals have questioned the council's limited membership and its expanding authority in civil conflicts. In addition, a number of countries have proposed allowing the International Criminal Court to charge the crime of aggression even where the Security Council has not given a supporting opinion. See Discussion paper proposed by the Coordinator, Consolidated text of proposals on the crime of aggression, Preparatory Commission for the International Criminal Court, Working Group on the Crime of Aggression, U.N. Doc. PCNICC/1999/WGCA/RT.1 (December 9, 1999), at 3-5 (conditions for the exercise of jurisdiction); Proceedings of the Preparatory Commission at its sixth session (November 27–December 8, 2000), U.N. Doc. PCNICC/2000/L.4/Rev.1 (Dec. 14, 2000), Annex V (Crimes of Aggression).

7. See Baker, *The Politics of Diplomacy,* and Bush and Scowcroft, *A World Transformed.*

8. United Nations Participation Act, Pub. L. No. 79-264, ch. 583, 59 Stat. 619 (1945), 22 U.S.C. §§ 287-287e (2001). See Stromseth, "Rethinking War Powers."

9. In the Vietnam War, John Hart Ely has argued, the U.S. Congress initially supported the war through budget resolutions as well as the Gulf of Tonkin resolution—disowning the conflict only later. See Ely, *War and Responsibility.*

10. S.C. Res. 678 (November 29, 1990).

11. See Lodge Reservations to United States Ratification of the Treaty of Versailles, 58 Congressional Record, 66th Congress, 1st Session, pp. 8777ff, numbered para. 2, also reprinted in Hartmann, *Basic Documents of International Relations* (doc. 11), pp. 63–64. This reservation to the League of Nations Covenant, voted by the Senate, made clear that "the United States assumes no obligation to preserve the territorial integrity or political independence of any other country or to interfere in controversies between nations—whether members of the league or not—under the provisions of article 10 [of the League Covenant], or to employ the military or naval forces of the United States under any article of the treaty for any purpose, unless in any particular case the Congress, which, under the Constitution, has the sole power to declare war or authorize the employment of the military or naval forces of the United States, shall by act or joint resolution so provide."

12. See U.S. Constitution, Article II, paragraph 7 ("the President shall have the power to receive Ambassadors"). See also Hamilton, *Pacificus No. I.*

13. See UN Charter, article 25 ("The Members of the United Nations agree to accept and carry out the decisions of the Security Council in accordance with the present Charter.")

14. Under article 5 of the North Atlantic Treaty, the parties "agree that an armed attack against one or more of them in Europe or North America shall be considered an attack against them all and consequently they agree that, if such an armed attack occurs, each of them, in exercise of the right of individual or collective self-defence recognized by article 51 of the Charter of the United Nations, will assist the Party or Parties so attacked by taking forthwith, individually and in concert with the other Parties, such action as it deems necessary, including the use of armed force, to restore and maintain the security of the North Atlantic area." North Atlantic Treaty, 4 April 1949, 63 Stat. 2241, TIAS No. 1964, 34 U.N.T.S. 243, reprinted in British Command Paper, Cmd. 7789.

15. See, e.g., Article 20 of the Inter-American Treaty of Reciprocal Assistance (Rio Treaty), 62 Stat. 1681, T.I.A.S. No. 1838 (September 2, 1947) ("no State shall be required to use armed force without its consent.").

16. UN Charter, article 25.

17. This was the case in the Gulf War.

18. In March 1998, the United States threatened to use armed force in support of UN weapons inspections in Iraq. Secretary-General Kofi Annan journeyed to Baghdad, where he obtained renewed assurances of cooperation from Iraq, temporarily stemming the crisis. Afterward, he was asked whether the United States needed a new Security Council resolution in support of its threatened use of force. Mr. Annan gave a careful reply: the United States had consulted broadly throughout the crisis, and would undoubtedly continue to do so, he noted. "If the U.S. had to strike," Mr. Annan said, "I think some sort of consultations with other members would be required." See "This Week: Remarks of Secretary-General Kofi Annan" (ABC television broadcast, March 8, 1998), in Federal Document Clearing House, Transcript 98030802-j12, available in LEXIS, Nexis Library, News File. The interviewers asked on another occasion, "Do you believe, though, that the strike is already sanctioned . . . by U.N. resolutions to date?" The secretary-general again gave a studied reply: "I think it will require consultations."

19. Enforcement actions by Nigeria and Ghana in West Africa (in Sierra Leone and Liberia) were undertaken without prior Security Council authorization, through the vehicle of the Economic Community of West African States. The Security Council noted its approval of the regional action only after the fact. See S.C. Res. 788 (November 19, 1992) (Liberia); S.C. Res. 1132 (October 8, 1997) (Sierra Leone).

20. See Simma, *The Charter of the United Nations: A Commentary,* p. 734 (Bruno Simma, ed., 1994) (commentary on article 53 by Prof. Georg Ress of Saarbrücken, stating that ex post authorization "cannot be reconciled with the requirement of effective SC control over regional enforcement action. Such control is only generated by clear and prior authorization"); and Dinstein, *War, Aggression, and Self-Defence,* pp. 286–287.

21. See generally Murphy, "Force and Arms," pp. 247, 300: "Neither the political organs of the United Nations nor the International Court of Justice has issued authoritative statements regarding the scope of the authority of regional organizations or agencies to threaten or use armed force to maintain international peace and security"; Wippman, "Enforcing the Peace," pp. 157, 182 ("danger of discouraging regional interventions that genuinely merit, and eventually receive, Council approbation, but that would be rendered ineffective or unduly costly if forced to await prior authorization."); Levitt, "Humanitarian Intervention by Regional Actors in International Conflicts," pp. 333, 347; Olonisakin, *Reinventing Peacekeeping in Africa,* p. 112.

22. See note 30.

23. The UN Charter recognizes an "inherent right" of self-defense, although the treaty speaks only of responding to an armed attack or "aggression armée" (in the French translation of the Charter). See UN Charter, article 51: "Nothing in the present Charter shall impair the inherent right of individual or collective self-defence if an armed attack occurs against a Member of the United Nations, until the Security Council has taken measures necessary to maintain international peace and security."

24. See S.C. Res. 83 (June 27, 1950) (Council "Recommends that the Members of the United Nations furnish such assistance to the Republic of Korea as may be necessary to repel the armed attack and to restore international peace and security in the area."); and S.C. Res. 84 (Jul. 7, 1950) (recommending that forces be made "available to a unified command under the United States").

25. But see Wedgwood, "NATO's Campaign in Yugoslavia," p. 828.

26. General Assembly Resolution 337A, B, and C (November 3, 1950), 5 U.N. GAOR Supp. (No. 20) at 10-12, U.N. Doc. A/1775 (1951) ("Resolves that if the Security Council, because of lack of unanimity of permanent members, fails to exercise its primary responsibility for the maintenance of international peace and security . . . the General Assembly shall consider the matter immediately with a view to making appropriate recommendations to Members for collective measures, including . . . the use of armed force when necessary."). See also Petersen, "The Uses of the Uniting for Peace Resolution since 1950," p. 219.

27. UN Charter, article 12(1): "While the Security Council is exercising in respect of any dispute or situation the functions assigned to it in the present Charter, the General Assembly shall not make any recommendation with regard to that dispute or situation unless the Security Council so requests."

28. See generally Goodrich, *Korea.*

29. OAS Resolution (October 23, 1962), U.S. Department of State Bulletin 47 (1962), p. 723.

30. Abram Chayes, serving as legal adviser of the U.S. State Department, argued that a "recommendation" by a regional organization was distinct from "enforcement

action" under article 53 of the UN Charter. See draft memorandum of the legal adviser dated 9/29/62 on Legal Issues Involved in OAS Surveillance Overflights of Cuba, reprinted in Chayes, *The Cuban Missile Crisis*, pp. 135, 146–148. However, the distinction reopens the question of self-defense, for it is not evident why a regional "recommendation" should permit a member country to act beyond article 51, unless one subscribes to a broad view of regional enforcement power.

31. See Lecce, "International Law Regarding Pro-Democratic Intervention, p. 247; Yates, *Power Pack;* Lowenthal, *The Dominican Intervention.*

32. Ibid., p. 254.

33. Greenburg, *Unilateral and Coalition Operations in the 1965 Dominican Republic Intervention,* p. 93.

34. See Memorandum for the Attorney General Re: Legality under International Law of Remedial Action Against Use of Cuba as a Missile Base by the Soviet Union, in Abram Chayes, note 30, pp. 109, 113 (quoting April 12, 1961, memorandum of Assistant Attorney General Nicholas Katzenbach).

35. S.C. Res. 940 (July 31, 1994).

36. Report of the secretary-general on the status of the implementation of the Special Commission's plan for ongoing monitoring and verification of Iraq's compliance with relevant parts of section C of Security Council resolution 687 (1991), U.N. Doc. S/1995/854, at 29, para. 75(w).

37. S.C. Res. 687 (April 3, 1992).

38. See Wedgwood, "The Enforcement of Security Council Resolution 687," p. 724. But see Lobel and Ratner, "Bypassing the Security Council," p. 124.

39. Convention on the Prevention and Punishment of Crimes Against Internationally Protected Persons, including Diplomatic Agents, Dec. 14, 1973, 28 U.S.T. 1975, TIAS No. 8532, 1035 U.N.T.S. 167 (entered into force on February 20, 1977), *reprinted in* 13 I.L.M. 43 (1973).

40. S.C. Res. 1054 (April 26, 1996).

41. S.C. Res. 1267 (October 15, 1999).

42. See generally Wedgwood, "Responding to Terrorism: The Strikes Against bin Laden," p. 559.

43. See generally Wedgwood, "NATO's Campaign in Yugoslavia."

44. The secretary-general noted in his opening address to the 54th General Assembly that "the imperative of effectively halting gross and systematic violations of human rights with grave humanitarian consequences" is an interest "equally compelling" as the protection of Security Council authority.

8

Multilateral Peace Operations

Sarah B. Sewall

THIS CHAPTER DESCRIBES AND SEEKS TO EXPLAIN THE CYCLE THROUGH which U.S. policy toward multilateral peace operations has traveled over the past decade.[1] After presidents George Bush and Bill Clinton articulated policies of strong support for UN peacekeeping in 1992 and 1993, Congress forced the White House to back away from providing such support, and the Clinton administration increasingly relied on regional organizations to conduct peace operations. Clinton's policies, while leaving the nation better prepared to support NATO peace operations, helped weaken the UN politically and economically and did not significantly strengthen UN military peacekeeping capabilities. This chapter identifies some of the key factors that shaped U.S. policy and argues that the U.S. failure to strengthen UN peace operations has undermined other stated U.S. foreign policy objectives.

Three main ironies characterize the Clinton administration's approach to peace operations. While the administration conceived of support for UN peacekeeping as a way to limit U.S. military involvement overseas, influential members of Congress feared UN peacekeeping as a potential expansion of U.S. military commitments. As Ivo Daalder points out, Clinton's promotion of multilateralism and UN peacekeeping was borne of a desire to free his energies for domestic politics, yet the effort foundered on domestic politics.[2] Finally, while U.S. policy was premised on the need to strengthen UN capabilities, the United States (along with other nations) simultaneously pushed the UN far beyond its operational and conceptual reach.

The harsh realities of the difficulty of conducting peace operations, congressional-executive tensions, partisan politics, administration miscalculations and competing priorities, and an underlying ambivalence within the broader body politic about the United States' global role all contributed to a reshaping of U.S. peace operations policy as it had originally been conceived by the Clinton administration. These dynamics produced an outcome that neither President Clinton nor peacekeeping foes had intended: the United States increasingly took the lead in organizing and conducting the most nettlesome humanitarian interventions.

While the benefits of UN peacekeeping have been uneven, operations in places such as Macedonia, Mozambique, El Salvador, and Eastern Slavonia demonstrate the contributions that UN missions can make to international peace and security. Nonetheless, by the mid 1990s, the United States had pushed to curtail UN operations and fallen further behind in paying its assessments for UN peacekeeping. The administration began expanding the use of American troops for peace operations largely through the North Atlantic Treaty Organization (NATO). It is not surprising, nor necessarily problematic, that the globe's leading power prefers to run the humanitarian interventions to which it contributes heavily. After all, NATO remains the only institution truly capable of undertaking complex and militarily challenging operations. The problematic aspect of this trend was the neglect of UN peacekeeping.

Toward the end of the decade, the administration found its own calculations of interest dictating renewed support for ambitious UN operations. International instability and international politics inevitably drew the UN back into challenging peace operations. Since June 1999, the United States has supported five new UN operations and a doubling of UN forces in the field to almost 40,000 troops,[3] even as Congress has kept the country deeply in arrears to the world body.

This neglect of UN peacekeeping has had significant costs. The United States lost an opportunity to help the UN expand its legitimacy and effectiveness in promoting international security, a goal espoused first by the Bush and then by the Clinton administrations during the 1990s. As a result, the United States has been unable to accomplish the often stated objectives of increasing international burden sharing and reducing demands upon U.S. military forces. U.S. policies helped prevent UN action in some instances that deserved a response, most notably the 1994 genocide in Rwanda—for which President Clinton subsequently expressed regret.[4] In underpaying its bills and using the UN as a political scapegoat, Washington weakened both the UN's reputation and its capacity relative to its expanded peacekeeping responsibilities. These policies increasingly were mirrored by other militarily and financially powerful industrialized nations, further diminishing the legitimacy and capabilities of UN peacekeeping. To the extent that the UN broadly, and UN peacekeeping specifically, advances U.S. interests, U.S. policy has undermined both. It has undoubtedly reinforced international concerns that the world's leading power focuses on narrowly defined interests at the expense of broader international security goals.

President George W. Bush confronts a world filled with demands for military intervention. Not all of these demands can be met by U.S. (or NATO) forces. Nor can all crises be ignored without jeopardizing other U.S. policy objectives. The new president will inevitably find himself asking the UN to address international security problems of lesser order to satisfy international political demands, to help keep chaos from spreading, and to limit the exposure of U.S. troops. Unfortunately, U.S. policies since the mid-1990s have made it less likely that the UN will be able to accomplish these objectives.

U.S. Multinational Peace Operations Policy and Practice

Evolution of UN Operations

During the Cold War, the UN undertook a relatively small number of peace-keeping operations, most of which involved "classical" peacekeeping: the stationing of unarmed monitoring forces with the consent of the local parties.[5] These UN interventions often aimed to stabilize areas of Cold War competition. Accordingly, the Security Council's five permanent members generally refrained from contributing peacekeeping troops, while providing significant financial, and occasionally logistical, support. Peacekeeping was a tool of finite value, useful once the parties had reached an agreement and needed a neutral, watchful eye.

But by the late 1980s requests for UN intervention had surged. The goals of peace operations began to change from observing cease-fires to facilitating political transitions. In 1989 the UN monitored Namibia's first free election and the withdrawal of external forces, an effort heralded as a great success. The UN also enjoyed enhanced credibility both within the United States and worldwide, through its association with the Persian Gulf War. The end of superpower ideological conflict further encouraged faith in the UN's potential to enhance international security.

By the early 1990s, UN peace operations had been transformed both in number and purpose. Increasingly, UN forces were sent to provide humanitarian relief, to usher in new political arrangements after long wars, or to facilitate the cessation of hostilities. The UN sought to distinguish between lightly armed neutral monitoring forces—dispatched pursuant to chapter VI—and troops deployed to "enforce" a settlement under chapter VII.[6] U.S. doctrine similarly came to draw a line between peacekeeping ("military or paramilitary operations that are undertaken with the consent of all major belligerent parties . . . designed to monitor and facilitate implementation of an existing truce agreement and support diplomatic efforts to reach a long-term political settlement") and peace enforcement ("the application of military force or the threat of its use, normally pursuant to international authorization, to compel compliance with generally accepted resolutions or sanctions").[7] In practice, the lines often blurred. Blue helmets—often woefully incapable or unprepared—increasingly encountered hostile host governments, uncontrolled armed insurgent groups, unclear lines of demarcation, and civilians who viewed the UN as the enemy. As UN Secretary-General Boutros Boutros-Ghali said in 1994, "Peace-keeping has to be re-invented every day. There are as many types of peacekeeping as there are confrontations. Every major operation provokes a new question."[8] Policy-makers failed to understand or accept the difficulties inherent in the ever-expanding tasks they assigned to the UN and the inherent limits of the world body's capabilities.

Bush Administration Policy

As the Cold War and the Gulf War drew to a close, President George Bush began focusing on ways to help the UN assume a greater role in international security, an approach designed to advance U.S. foreign policy objectives in a new era. He made a pragmatic case to expand and improve peacekeeping capabilities to help shape a world consistent with U.S. values and interests. "As conflicts are resolved and violence subsides," he declared, "then the institutions of free societies can take hold. And as they do, they become our strongest safeguards against aggression and tyranny."[9] Bush's concept of a "new world order" governed by the rule of law required an effective UN peacekeeping capability.[10] So, in January 1992 he urged the new UN secretary-general to examine ways to strengthen UN peacekeeping, pledging full U.S. support.[11]

That summer, President Bush ordered a policy review that culminated in National Security Directive (NSD) 74 of November 1992. This directive, the first U.S. policy statement since the Truman administration to advocate active U.S. support for UN peacekeeping, recommended a variety of U.S. and UN initiatives. Ivo Daalder reports that in deference to the view of the Department of Defense (DOD) that the United States should contribute only "unique" military capabilities necessary for the success of a UN mission, the policy did not call for expanding participation of U.S. forces.[12] The final Bush administration national security strategy committed the United States only to helping plan and support UN operations.[13] Nevertheless, given subsequent Republican hostility toward UN peace operations, the administration's enthusiasm for both the UN and blue-helmet peace operations seems virtually heretical.[14]

President Bush summarized his new policy in a September 1992 address to the UN General Assembly, in which he urged delegates to "think differently about how we ensure and pay for our security in this new era."[15] He called on nations to develop and train military units for possible peacekeeping duty and to make them available on short notice, and he advocated multinational planning, training, and field exercises to better prepare UN peacekeeping forces. He said he had directed his defense secretary "to place a new emphasis on peacekeeping," particularly on the "training of combat, engineering, and logistical units for the full range of peacekeeping and humanitarian activities." He pledged that the United States would "work with the United Nations to best employ our considerable lift, logistics, communications and intelligence capabilities" and would "offer our capabilities for joint simulations and peacekeeping exercises to strengthen our ability to undertake joint peacekeeping operations."[16]

Bush also called for the development of UN planning, crisis management, and intelligence capabilities for peacekeeping. He offered to provide U.S. military expertise to the UN and to broaden U.S. support for monitoring, verification, reconnaissance, and other UN peacekeeping requirements.[17] He further noted the need for "adequate, equitable" financing for UN peacekeeping, and promised to explore new ways to ensure adequate American financial support for UN peacekeeping.[18]

Reactions to his address ranged widely. Some diplomats and observers were surprised at this "hijacking" of the recommendations contained in Boutros-Ghali's 1992 document, *An Agenda for Peace,* which responded to President Bush's initial challenge to strengthen UN peacekeeping. Officials in the Pentagon were reportedly startled by the implications for their work.[19] One newspaper concluded: "If fully implemented, the President's proposals would profoundly change Washington's relationship with U.N. peacekeeping forces."[20] Some diplomats probably assumed that the United States was throwing its weight behind UN peacekeeping. Others remained skeptical, given U.S. arrears in payments to the UN and Bush's failure to propose a solution to this funding problem.[21]

Bush of course never implemented his policy. It would appear, given his decision to enhance UN peacekeeping generally and his commitment of U.S. forces to a UN-authorized relief operation in Somalia, that he was headed for many of the same challenges that the Clinton team would face. Indeed, Congress was reluctant to authorize the Somalia relief operation and rejected Bush's request for a UN peacekeeping assessment contingency fund,[22] signaling major challenges ahead.

Development of the Clinton Administration Peacekeeping Policy

During the 1992 presidential campaign, candidate Bill Clinton had expressed support for UN peacekeeping primarily as a way to reduce the costs of U.S. security.[23] While stating that he would never turn the nation's security over to the UN or any other international organization,[24] he simultaneously called for a UN rapid-deployment force to be used for purposes beyond traditional peacekeeping.[25] The expansive internationalist rhetoric of the incoming president and his officials seemed to adumbrate a deeper commitment to peace operations and the UN.

In the spring of 1993, NSC staff members drafted Policy Review Document (PRD) 13, which had the stated aim of improving UN peacekeeping. The Pentagon created a new position of assistant secretary for democracy and peacekeeping and requested defense dollars from Congress to pay for U.S. participation in peace operations, to improve the UN's peacekeeping headquarters, and to train foreign peacekeeping troops. The administration pressed the UN to launch an operation to relieve the bulk of U.S. forces in Somalia and began discussing potential UN operations in Haiti and Bosnia. The president said the United States would express its "leadership through multilateral means, such as the United Nations, which spread the costs and express the unified will of the international community."[26] That June the U.S. ambassador to the United Nations, Madeleine Albright, outlined a policy of "assertive multilateralism" in testimony before Congress.[27]

PDD 25

The Clinton administration PRD 13 review took Bush's NSD 74 as a starting point, adopting its emphasis on improving UN planning and intelligence capabilities and ensuring adequate UN financing. The review differed, however, in its willingness to consider direct U.S. troop participation in all aspects of UN operations. Clinton's draft policy would consider deploying regular combat units, not just providing "unique" capabilities such as logistics, intelligence, or transportation. Early in the policy review process there apparently was a proposal to create a standing UN army or its "light" version, an on-call brigade-sized unit for rapid reaction. This proposal was killed by the Pentagon before interagency representatives met to review the initial draft document.[28]

Otherwise, the content of the policy changed relatively little during its year-long gestation, retaining the following core elements: a list of factors for the United States to consider when contemplating support for multilateral peace operations; proposals to improve UN peacekeeping; conditional support for the conduct of peace operations by regional organizations; a call for reductions in the cost and U.S. share of financial support for UN peace operations; and a policy on command and control of U.S. forces participating in UN peacekeeping operations.

The biggest substantive changes in the document concerned a proposal to pay for peace operations ("shared responsibility" between the State Department and DOD, with the latter picking up part of the costs)[29] and a section on consultations with Congress added late in the process. Policy regarding U.S. forces under foreign command[30] and the list of factors to consider in U.S. decisions concerning peace operations changed slightly. By its final draft, the policy document also painstakingly spelled out many of its underlying assumptions in order to dispel myths that had grown up during the year of virtual administration silence about PRD 13. Thus, the document ultimately stressed that peace operations did not define the national security strategy of the United States and that operations likely to involve combat would be evaluated according to traditional war-fighting criteria.[31]

The final policy, Presidential Decision Directive (PDD) 25, established a generally sound and workable framework for U.S. peace operations policy.

Taken at face value, it should not have become the lightening rod for a host of real, imagined, and unrelated congressional concerns. Nor can the document fully explain the specific actions and missteps of the Clinton administration. It was largely a pragmatic policy. It was criticized both by those who feared its implied activism and those who feared it would justify U.S. inaction.

Some critics, largely in the press and NGOs, and from foreign countries, objected to the policy's "factors for consideration" in making decisions about specific peace operations. They argued that the "factors" had become so demanding that the United States would never support or participate in UN operations. In reality the factors had not changed dramatically during the policy's development.[32] More important, they remained highly subjective and were written explicitly to serve as a checklist for consideration, not to impose a policy straitjacket.[33] Thus, from the outset PDD 25 necessarily begged critical questions related to U.S. support for specific UN operations. Interagency debates about prospective missions amply demonstrated that each factor (e.g., whether the United States had sufficient interests at stake or whether international support for an operation existed) was open to interpretation. One perceptive analyst concluded, "PDD 25 is designed to provide the Clinton administration with the greatest possible flexibility in addressing international crises."[34]

One of PDD 25's most important contributions, in the eyes of a seasoned Clinton administration official, was promoting the limited application of force as an "antidote to the Powell/Weinberger doctrine of overwhelming force."[35] This was of course something that worried many in Congress and the U.S. military: the United States' becoming simultaneously more active and less effective in its application of military force. And their objections later were transformed into concerns about the effects of participation in peace operations (albeit not necessarily UN operations) upon the readiness of the U.S. armed forces to fight and win the nation's wars.

By the time PDD 25 was unveiled, its tone and pitch had changed significantly. PDD 25 concluded that

> properly constituted, peace operations can be one useful tool to advance American national interests and pursue our national security objectives. The U.S. cannot be the world's policeman. Nor can we ignore the increase in armed ethnic conflicts, civil wars and the collapse of governmental authority in some states—crises that individually and cumulatively may affect U.S. interests. This policy is designed to impose discipline on both the UN and the U.S. to make peace operations a more effective instrument of collective security.[36]

The rhetorical change reflected progressive developments in administration thinking, the result of real world experience, and, most significantly, mounting congressional criticism. In September 1993, National Security

Advisor Lake had stressed in a major policy address that specific peace operations in Somalia and Bosnia did not define the United States' broader strategy in the world. Days later, President Clinton lectured the UN that it would have to ask "harder questions" about proposed peacekeeping missions,[37] warning that if the United States was to say yes to peacekeeping, "the United Nations must know how to say no."[38] The press, Michael Mackinnon observed, "began to speak of a policy in 'retreat.'"[39] Lake explained at the policy's unveiling in May 1994 that the administration some nine months earlier "began to ask harder questions at the United Nations and to try to work more closely with the Congress." The policy, he concluded, expressed a more coherent version of the administration's philosophy.[40]

The administration launched an unprecedented (for a PPD) series of briefings on Capitol Hill. They emphasized that PDD 25 was not a blank check for peace operations, did not support a "foreign legion," promoted caution in decisionmaking, and required that NATO or another capable force do the difficult interventions. By stressing the constraints, the administration hoped to regain congressional support for "more effective and selective" peace operations.

Unfortunately, critics in Congress remained unmoved by the "new" policy, even as the wider world worried that the United States had signaled its disengagement from peace operations.[41] While PDD 25 as a policy still called for strengthening UN peacekeeping, the administration encountered increasingly less political room to maneuver.

Congress Balks

Congressional antipathy toward peace operations congealed during the first year of the Clinton administration. By late October 1993 Somalia had become the poster child for the failure of UN peacekeeping. Many members of Congress, and particularly Republicans, feared that the administration's peacekeeping policy was too proactive, overly supportive of the UN, and divorced from U.S. national interests. The Pentagon's proposed assistant secretary position was abolished following congressional objections to the nominee. Congress rejected the Defense Department's peace operations budget requests. The United States fell further behind in its peacekeeping payments to the UN, and Congress developed legislation designed to hamper U.S. involvement in UN operations. The administration expended significant time parrying legislative restrictions and succeeded in blocking the most pernicious initiatives. But the strategy became one of seeking to minimize political costs, accommodating Congress wherever possible. Unwilling to elevate the stakes, the executive branch increasingly lost control of the issue.

Democratic Senator Robert Byrd was an early leading opponent of Clinton policies, questioning both the wisdom and presidential prerogative of committing U.S. troops to "nation building" in Somalia.[42] When President Clinton announced a plan to pull out U.S. troops after October 3, 1993, Byrd nonetheless pushed through legislation mandating the withdrawal of U.S. forces.

During 1994, Republican leaders Robert Dole and Newt Gingrich elevated opposition to UN peace operations to a major party issue. Dole made his anti–UN peacekeeping "Peace Powers Act" a top priority for Senate action, and Gingrich included similar provisions in the "Contract with America," the Republican election platform for regaining control of the House of Representatives. After the GOP triumph the document provided a legislative blueprint for Congress.

The victorious Republicans quickly pushed measures to prohibit U.S. forces from serving under UN command; to require a further reduction in the U.S. share of UN peace operations assessments; and to require reimbursement for U.S. military actions taken "in support of" UN Security Council authorizations. The net effect of such provisions would have been to end U.S. support for UN peace operations.[43] To assert control over U.S. peace operations policy, Congress increasingly turned voluntary offers from the executive branch (e.g., to provide regular briefings, advance notifications, additional documentation) into legislative requirements and transformed even minor issues (such as providing limited equipment to UN forces) into matters of principle.[44] Congressional requirements complicated and often delayed actions ranging in importance from the provision of U.S. logistical support to formal UN Security Council decisions about peace operations.

While some attempts to legislate restrictions either dissipated or were defeated,[45] two issues continued to dominate the debate during the 1990s: the payment of UN assessments and specific U.S. troop deployments. Congress's most damaging actions concerned the payment of past and current UN bills, including those for peacekeeping.[46] As UN peace operations surged, so did U.S. assessments for these activities. Historically, peacekeeping costs had been relatively predictable, around $50 million annually through the mid-1980s. But between fiscal year (FY) 1988 and FY 1989, the country's peacekeeping assessment more than quadrupled, from $43 million to $195 million.

By FY 1992 the costs had nearly tripled again to about $565 million.[47] By the summer of 1993, the administration faced the prospect of becoming nearly $1 billion in arrears for peacekeeping by the end of FY 1994. Some members of Congress sympathetic to UN peacekeeping urged the president to treat it as a higher priority, making a personal appeal for more funding.[48] In 1994, Congress did agree to pay past UN dues. This was due in part, Jeremy Rosner argues, to legislators' perception of the issue as one of past debts rather than future obligations. But the victory was short-lived. U.S. peacekeeping arrears quickly surged again (see Figure 8.1), as Congress failed to approve the administration's initial funding requests or supplemental

Figure 8.1   U.S. Funding for Peace Operations, FY 1981–2000 (in FY 01 dollars)

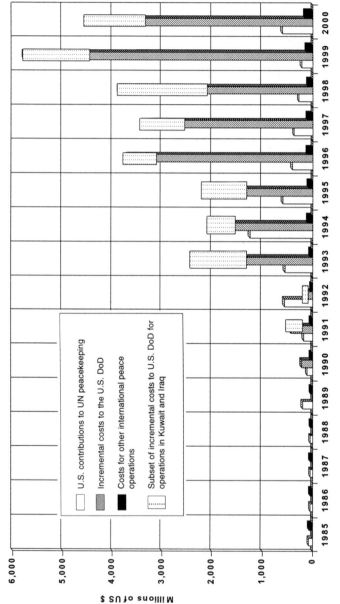

Legend:
- U.S. contributions to UN peacekeeping
- Incremental costs to the U.S. DoD
- Costs for other international peace operations
- Subset of incremental costs to U.S. DoD for operations in Kuwait and Iraq

Sources: Marjorie Ann Brown, *United Nations Peacekeeping: Issues for Congress,* CRS Issue Brief IB90103 (Congressional Research Service, January 12, 2001); Nina Serafino, *Peacekeeping: Issues of U.S. Military Involvement,* CRS Issue Brief IB94040 (Congressional Research Service, January 17, 2001); Laurinda Zeman, *Making Peace while Staying Ready for War: The Challenges of U.S. Military Participation in Peace Operations,* CBO Paper (Congressional Budget Office, December 19, 1999); Budget of the United States Government: Fiscal Year 2001 (Washington: U.S. Government Printing Office, 2000), pp. 990–991; Congressional Budget Office National Security Division, *Costs of Operations,* January 24, 2001, N.p., n.d.

appropriations for UN peacekeeping assessments. (Administration requests for supplemental funding for the deployment of U.S. forces had greater success.) In October 1995, Congress capped U.S. payments at 25 percent instead of the UN assessment rate of 30.4 percent, guaranteeing that future bills would be underpaid.

Facing mounting international criticism as the world's biggest UN deadbeat, the administration ultimately decided to back Senator Joseph Biden of Delaware, the ranking Democrat on the Senate Foreign Relations Committee, as he negotiated a funding deal with the committee's chairman, Republican Jesse Helms. Because Helms was a longstanding opponent of both the UN and its peace operations, it was no great surprise that the eventual deal contained onerous conditions.

The 1997 "grand bargain" allowed for the phased payment of the majority of U.S. arrears,[49] but only if UN member states agreed to make significant changes in the institution and its procedures. Had any other nation made these demands—including for a reduction of just one nation's peacekeeping assessment and limits on UN budgets—the United States would have found them laughable. Instead, Congress sought to impose them unilaterally upon the world body. To make matters worse, Helms could not deliver on his end of the bargain: antiabortion activists in the House initially killed the State Department authorization bill containing the "grand bargain."

Over the next couple of years, the White House sought to make the substance of the deal less objectionable and more politically achievable, while struggling to unlink the issue of UN dues from family planning. Clinton administration officials also attempted to improve "understanding" between the UN and Congress, bringing UN Secretary General Kofi Annan to Capitol Hill and shepherding U.S. legislators to the UN headquarters in New York.[50] This process culminated at the outset of 2000, when Jesse Helms used an unusual audience before the UN Security Council to lecture the United Nations about its proper place in global affairs.[51]

NATO Assumes Center Stage

As the 1990s progressed, Washington gradually moved away from participating in UN operations, and even from politically supporting UN operations in cases that were not deemed to be of sufficiently direct interest to the United States. In explaining why PDD 25 mattered, Ambassador Albright implied that it had been instrumental in blocking overambitious UN operations in Burundi, Georgia, and Angola.[52] Instead of relying so heavily on the UN, the United States began promoting regional organizations and coalitions of the willing as the solution to international crises, even when such entities were clearly ineffective or biased.[53]

The administration did manage to preserve its freedom to deploy U.S. forces for peace operations when the president deemed it important. In

Haiti, the United States deployed a large independent force that was authorized by the UN, and only later blue-helmeted (under a U.S. commander). In transforming the operation into a UN peace operation, the United States obtained political legitimacy, financial support, and a graceful way out of what was essentially a U.S. occupation. In Macedonia, the United States placed a company of soldiers under UN command to help deter the spread of conflict in the Balkans. But, increasingly, participation in a UN force was perceived to be politically and practically untenable. With the political heat turned up, it was more feasible to defend action in the context of NATO than the baggage-laden UN. Therefore if the United States were to commit significant forces, NATO would need to be in charge of military operations, even if the UN ultimately ran other aspects of the overall effort. Accordingly, it was through NATO that U.S. forces came to participate in peace operations in Bosnia and later Kosovo[54] (see Table 8.1).

Each large U.S.-led peace operation met with popular skepticism and strong congressional opposition. Historically, legislators had demanded consultation prior to U.S. military deployments and had criticized particular operations. During the Cold War, Congress had usually avoided straight up or down votes on the commitment of forces, considering these too risky and unpatriotic. But, with those historical constraints eroded, votes to oppose peace operations became common. These were usually nonbinding and often inconsistent, seemingly demonstrating disarray in U.S. foreign policy. Congress typically was reluctant to dictate withdrawal or to impose a completely rigid deadline for an operation, and legislators generally provided much of the requested supplemental funding. Thus the president preserved what he considered his essential prerogatives as commander in chief. Congressional action appeared designed to put the president on notice that any deployment would be his failure and that any nominal successes could be his, too.

In retrospect, it is remarkable that the administration was able to keep U.S. troops so highly engaged in peace operations. But there were changed terms: no U.S. forces would be placed under UN command; the United States would have to run the show. The UN ultimately paid the price for the underlying political accommodations that preserved the administration's freedom of action.

Full Circle by the Decade's End

It was not until late in 1999 that President Clinton compromised on the abortion issue that had tied up the grand bargain to pay UN debts. The legislation provided some relief in the near term and many of its terms have been met, but it appears certain that the United States cannot meet 100 percent of the conditions—specifically the reduction of the U.S. peacekeeping assessment share to 25 percent.

Table 8.1 Contributions of Troops in Formed Military Units[a] to UN and Non-UN Peace Operations, Including Contributions of Permanent Members of the Security Council (illustrative example during May–June 2000)

Top Ten UN Troop Contributors	Troops Provided to UN-led Operations	As Percentage of 27,466 UN Troops Deployed	Five Permanent Security Council Members and Other Top Contributors to Non-UN Operations	Troops Provided in Formations to UN-led Operations	Troops Provided in Formations to SFOR and KFOR	As Percentage of 67,100 Troops in SFOR and KFOR
India	3,957	14%	United States	0	10,400	16%
Nigeria	3,231	12	France	253	8,100	12
Jordan	2,217	8	United Kingdom	310	6,100	9
Australia	1,842	7	Russian Federation	0	4,300	6
Bangladesh	1,509	6	China	0	0	0
Ghana	1,438	5	Italy	46	8,000	12
Kenya	1,124	4	Germany	14	7,600	11
Poland	992	4	Spain	0	2,600	4
Thailand	908	3	Canada	187	2,350	4
Philippines	825	3	Poland	992	2,220	3
Total	18,043	66	Total	1,802	51,670	77

Sources: United Nations Department of Peacekeeping Operations; U.S. Department of Defense, Office of the Assistant Secretary for Peacekeeping and Humanitarian Affairs. © 2000, The Henry Stimson Center.

Note: a. Not individual observers or police.

Richard Holbrooke, appointed U.S. ambassador to the UN in 1999, made reducing U.S. assessment rates his top priority. On December 22, 2000, he astonished observers by negotiating an agreement in principle to reduce the U.S. share of the UN regular budget from 25 to 22 percent and the share of the UN peacekeeping budget from 30 to 27 percent.[55] Senator Helms concluded that he would support changing the law to permit an additional $585 million to be released, despite the fact that, in his view, the "U.N. missed the [assessment reduction] target."[56] Even if Congress were to act swiftly on this score, it would still have to resolve the outstanding issue of "disputed arrears," which has resulted in arrears of over $400 million.[57] Congress has continued to resist funding *specific* UN peace operations, such as those in Western Sahara and the Central African Republic. Recent newspaper leads have mirrored those from the early days of the Clinton administration: "UN peacekeeping in question; GOP, opposed to growing mission, wants to cut funds."[58] Unless the new administration of George W. Bush addresses these issues and finds a way to ensure full future payments, arrears will continue to climb.

Since 1999, the UN has authorized ambitious operations in Kosovo and East Timor and a mission to monitor the Ethiopian-Eritrean cease-fire. The UN also has expanded or changed operations in Sierra Leone, Democratic Republic of Congo, and Lebanon. Clinton administration officials argued that they had promoted better diplomatic agreements, required greater responsibility of the parties on the ground, and otherwise improved the shape and mandate of these operations. The scale of planned UN operations is not likely to return to the 1993 high of almost 80,000 fielded forces, but the costs of UN peacekeeping are predicted to climb near the record levels that originally fueled congressional revolt.[59] The requirements of several missions, including administering territories and recreating devastated state structures, are reminiscent of the very "nation-building" objectives that damaged the UN's reputation only a few years ago. The UN remains little better prepared operationally for these challenges than it was a decade ago, when President Bush stressed the need to improve its capacities.

Factors Shaping U.S. Policy

A host of factors combined to move the United States away from its espoused goal of enhancing UN peacekeeping. These include administration political priorities and calculations, congressional opposition politics, the structural tensions between Congress and the White House, and the lack of national consensus about the U.S. role in the world. These factors help explain why the Clinton administration's policy galvanized such vehement opposition in Congress (including among some Democrats) and why the executive branch chose not to fight with the vigor reserved for other issues.

Clinton Administration Actions

While the Clinton administration initially wanted the UN to play a more assertive security role, Washington fundamentally underestimated the difficulty of the new "peace enforcement" operations.[60] This was perhaps predictable and inevitable. The United States had little experience in traditional peacekeeping and did not understand the more challenging operations that lay on the horizon.

Somalia. On December 9, 1992, President Bush sent U.S. forces to provide humanitarian relief in the middle of an ongoing conflict. The UN was to provide the follow-on force, although Bush officials had discussed placing a significant number of U.S. logistics forces under UN command.[61] The UN took over in the spring.

The UN Security Council's subsequent decision to call for the capture of General Aideed, a local Somali warlord, flowed from a legitimate desire to respond to his killing of Pakistani troops and to protect the UN's reputation. But the end result of that decision left the UN more vulnerable than before, in no small part because of the U.S. reaction to its military role in the effort.

The Clinton administration had strongly backed the call to arrest Aideed and provided special U.S. forces (under separate U.S. command) for this purpose. On October 3, 1993, eighteen U.S. soldiers were killed in a firefight with Aideed's forces. As television broadcast Somalis dragging a U.S. soldier's body through the street, domestic political criticism rained down upon Clinton policies, permanently tarring the UN and peacekeeping.

It is tempting to speculate about what might have happened had Aideed been captured or had the Somalia peace operation simply ended without tragedy. But while Somalia certainly fueled congressional opposition to— and administration distancing from—UN peacekeeping, it caused neither. Prior to October 3, the Clinton administration already had begun to adapt its policy in response to ongoing operational experience and challenges from Congress. Congressional opposition would, in all probability, have continued to grow along with the pace and scope of UN operations. There were many events that contributed to or might have crystallized concerns about UN peacekeeping: The about-face of the USS *Harlan County* when it encountered angry mobs on Haitian shores, the ineffectiveness of UNPROFOR in stopping the carnage in Bosnia, the murder of Belgian soldiers sent to monitor a peace agreement in Rwanda, and, later, the shame of Srebinica, where blue helmets stood by as thousands of Bosnian Muslim noncombatants were summarily executed. Strong political leadership to acknowledge mistakes, learn from them, and move on would be required in each case.

President Clinton's response to these early events in Somalia was critical, then. He ended the U.S. commitment to the operation, sought compromise in Congress, and wrongly implied that the UN was to blame.[62] The administration already had become uneasy about the Somalia commitment, and the October 3 event provided impetus for an exit. But instead of underscoring the value of the Somalia intervention, and placing the soldiers' deaths in the context of a nobler purpose—saving thousands of lives—the president's actions made it appear that the UN mission had not been worthwhile. Moreover, he seemed to blame the UN for the deaths of the U.S. servicemen, when the latter had actually operated under an independent U.S. chain of command.[63]

Overreaching at home and abroad. Peacekeeping policy offers another cautionary tale of the early days of the Clinton presidency. Like the issue of gays in the military or health care policy, the administration plunged ahead on peacekeeping without having a firm sense of the political terrain. In terms of both crafting U.S. policy and pushing the UN into peace operations, the administration's initial approach to promoting change actually harmed the underlying policy objectives.

The administration began by looking at peacekeeping policy in a curiously technical way. First, it appeared to assume that Bush administration policy had provided a solid foundation on which to build. Second, it barely considered the policy's political ramifications[64] or the impact upon Congress, where the issues were considered central to congressional prerogatives.[65]

Because it had not yet resolved the issue of how to pay for peacekeeping, the Clinton administration failed to brief, let alone consult with, legislators on the development of peacekeeping policy. "As funding issues dragged out," one official recalls, "suspicions grew on the Hill about what was in the presidential directive, and people were able to plant rumors—that it was going to call for sending U.S. troops into more peacekeeping operations, etc. Suspicions and fears grew because they weren't being talked to about it."[66] The bloodless issue of financing U.S. assessments procedurally held the administration's broader policy hostage, even though Congress ultimately never implemented the proposed "shared responsibility" arrangement between State and DOD.[67]

The most politically controversial aspect of PDD 25—the participation of regular U.S. units in UN peace operations—was infrequently implemented under Clinton. Yet preserving the possibility that U.S. service members would be placed under UN command, even though the armed forces agreed with the administration on this narrow point, helped to doom politically other efforts to strengthen UN peacekeeping.

Early in the Clinton administration, U.S. officials frequently looked to satisfy short-term policy goals via the UN, sometimes regardless of the consequences for the organization or for other U.S. objectives of the longer term. For example, Washington was so eager to bring home U.S. forces from the initial Somalia operation that it pushed the UN to take over operations before New York had recruited necessary forces or staffed the administrative structure of the UN Operation in Somalia (UNOSOM) II. Likewise, an administration desire to "do something" about atrocities in the former Yugoslavia led the United States to back UN Security Council resolutions that stood little chance of implementation, eventually at great cost to civilians on the ground. In an effort to make the UN appear to address unwieldy political or security challenges, Washington often pushed the UN beyond any reasonable expectations, and then stepped away when the UN failed.

Administration priorities. Bill Clinton was elected to focus on domestic politics using the campaign mantra: "It's the economy, stupid." The president rarely threw his political weight behind a foreign policy initiative. Advancing U.S. support for UN peacekeeping necessarily required strong support from the top, but there were few bureaucratic impulses to change the president's calculations. Although specific peace operations consumed many senior officials' days, the issue as a matter of overarching policy was not anyone's single highest priority. The biggest push to promote the administration's overall foreign policy occurred in September 1993,[68] but the Somalia debacle followed shortly thereafter, and debate about peace operations became more deeply partisan.

The administration's retrenchment on peacekeeping, one senator observed, was "a recognition of the political reality of the moment. Congress believes the American public doesn't want to get bogged down in military adventures whose benefits don't seem to justify the casualties and costs. To ignore that would be to squander political capital and good will that the president needs for his top domestic agenda."[69]

The fate of the administration's proposal to have DOD assume payment for some UN peace operations reveals Clinton's domestic priorities. As Jeremy Rosner reports, the 1994 meeting between the president and defense legislators to discuss "shared responsibility" was delayed—and ultimately canceled—while the White House focused on health care reform. In the words of one Pentagon official, "The president never touched it. The involvement from the top levels of DOD was half-hearted, sporadic and late. So the legislative people completely didn't push it because it was in the 'too hard' category—it undermined their efforts on their other priorities."[70]

Shortly after the U.S. deaths in Somalia, Madeleine Albright, then U.S. Ambassador to the UN, told Congress that it was essential to reestablish a politically sustainable consensus on peacekeeping policy. The administration's strategy increasingly seemed to consist of agreeing with critics of the UN wherever possible while fighting tactical battles for specific peace operations. Eventually, the White House compromised on the principle that the United States owed its UN dues unconditionally. Clinton drew the line only around his prerogative as commander in chief to deploy U.S. forces.

Many officials rationalized this accommodation as unavoidable; after all, Congress controlled the purse strings. One official who had worked on PDD 25 later justified its constraints on U.S. support for multilateral military action, saying that "the document is essential if Congressional support is to be sustained for any UN peacekeeping operations at all."[71] Yet it is not clear what support executive branch concessions bought.

At the same time, it is difficult to know whether a more combative administration approach might have succeeded. The president could have decided that enhancing UN peace operations capabilities was as important to national security as NAFTA or NATO expansion, launching a public offensive, deploying agency "principals," and courting key members of Congress. While even the most forceful campaign might not have changed congressional calculations about certain issues (particularly placing U.S. forces under UN command),[72] it might have yielded payment for UN dues or greater acceptance of a UN role in peacekeeping. But it would have been costly.

Instead, a tacit bargain emerged during the mid-1990s. The administration purchased from Congress the freedom for the United States to conduct important operations abroad, at the price of the former's giving up its support for new UN peace operations. This bargain certainly was better than refusing both to support the UN *and* to lead independent peace operations.[73] At the same time, the net effect was to undermine—in practice, if not by administration design—the UN role in promoting international peace and security.

Congress

Congressional prerogatives. Institutional interests played an important role in galvanizing congressional opposition to peace operations, particularly among Democrats who might otherwise have supported their president. The decisionmaking process for peace operations—that is, decisions cleared within the executive branch, negotiated in New York, and presented to Congress as a fait accompli—were abhorrent to defenders of legislative prerogatives. There had been little controversy when UN peace operations had been fairly few, uneventful, and inexpensive—and when they had rarely involved U.S. forces.[74] But changes in the pace, character, and cost of peace operations vastly increased the stakes for Congress.

Now, a presidential commitment of U.S. troops to peace operations threatened to destroy any pretense of a congressional role in placing U.S. forces in harm's way. Democrats, who had traditionally asserted congressional warmaking prerogatives to restrain the executive branch, were now in the awkward position of looking the other way as Republicans began invoking the Vietnam-era War Powers Resolution to limit the president's power.

Diplomacy in New York had begun to feel like executive branch imperialism, since U.S. votes at the UN would generate an assessment bill, which the administration would present to Congress as a supplemental budget request. There was nothing new about this process, but, again, the scope and import of decisions had changed dramatically. It was not surprising that Congress refused the administration's requests to provide advance funds for future UN assessments. Legislators already had a virtual rubber stamp role.

The parochial congressional committee structure complicated the funding challenge. Assessments for UN peacekeeping are incorporated into the State Department budget, falling under the jurisdiction of the Commerce-Justice-State Subcommittee, where they compete with regular State Department funding. Besides putting the secretary of state in an awkward position,[75] this means that peacekeeping funding also is weighed against Justice and Commerce department priorities like new courthouses or seizing illegal aliens. It was obvious to congressional appropriators which sets of issues were more important back home.

Partisans. The UN remains a lightning rod for many concerns that, while they cross party lines, resonate most strongly among Republican members of Congress. In some circles, the world body is virtually synonymous with potential world government, global taxation, and unelected bureaucrats and illegitimate rules impinging upon U.S. citizens and sovereignty. These fears, symbolized by the UN, combined with other predominantly Republican priorities (in particular, protecting U.S. military readiness) to make opposition to UN peacekeeping resonate broadly among GOP members of Congress. These substantive objections fused seamlessly with partisan politics. UN peacekeeping, as espoused by a Democratic president with weak military credentials, became a unifying target for Republicans and a prominent GOP theme during the 1994 elections.

After regaining control over the House and the Senate, the GOP sought to use peacekeeping as a foreign policy sword to slay President Clinton. As Rosner notes, congressional Republicans "used attacks on peacekeeping to support a larger critique of President Clinton's stewardship of U.S. national security."[76] It became almost reflexive. During the Clinton presidency partisanship seemed to grow stronger at the water's edge.

Public opinion, Congress, and the vocal minority. Robert Johansen concludes that during the 1990s, two-thirds of the U.S. public "quite consistently" endorsed UN peacekeeping and that U.S. participation in such missions enjoyed, on average, the "fairly consistent" support of 58 percent of Americans.[77] Not surprisingly, public support for U.S. participation in specific operations often decreased depending on the nature of the mission, the role of U.S. forces, the likelihood of success, and other factors. Even before the death of the U.S. Army Rangers, for example, support for U.S. forces in Somalia had declined from 84 percent to 43 percent, presumably due to perceptions that the original mission (humanitarian relief) had been achieved and to misgivings about seeking to end the civil war.[78] Yet, in the days following the incident, 58 percent still favored U.S. participation in UN operations.[79] Months after the Somalia debacle 84 percent of the U.S. public said they supported UN peacekeeping.[80] Steven Kull in Chapter 4 discusses further this consistent and durable majority of U.S. support for UN peacekeeping and U.S. participation.

Perhaps more surprisingly, polling indicates that a majority of Americans support placing U.S. troops under UN command and creating a standing UN army—two of the most controversial issues on Capitol Hill. Yet legislators continue to cite "public concerns" about U.S. involvement in peacekeeping to justify their opposition. What might explain this apparent disconnection?

First, peace operations are hardly a burning issue for the electorate, and the breadth of support for such missions is not matched by its depth. Accordingly, members of Congress face few incentives from constituents to support peace operations either generally or in specific instances. No strong peace operations lobby or constituency exists to promote or educate members about U.S. involvement.

Given thin public support on an issue, a vocal minority of opponents can wield disproportionate influence in the political process. A member of Congress is more likely to get mail opposing than supporting a UN peace operation, and critics are more likely to get press coverage than proponents. The same principle is mirrored in the House and Senate. If a handful of members feels very strongly about opposing U.S. participation in peace operations, it can greatly increase the costs of supporting a U.S. role. There are virtually no negative electoral or other political ramifications for failing to support the UN or peace operations; indeed, opposition to such missions can provide inexpensive "protection" against critics on the right, buying political space for other objectives. Thus support for peace operations appears to carry few benefits, but offers significant risks, especially if the operation turns sour.

Ambivalence About America's Global Role

As Mats Berdal has written, peace operations policy engages "a central dilemma of U.S. foreign policy after the Cold War: how to articulate interests and maintain a moral foundation for policy in the absence of direct threats to U.S. strategic interests."[81] During the Cold War interests and values often coincided nicely. Today their congruence is less apparent, particularly when the U.S. policy community continues to define interests narrowly.

Rather than challenging a distinction between values and interests—or broadening the conception of "national interests"—the Clinton administration stated the case for peace operations in the language of traditional interests. Many remained unconvinced by these arguments. In the summer and early autumn of 1993 prominent Republicans launched an onslaught of criticism. Henry Kissinger, for example, charged the administration with abandoning U.S. interests altogether in pursuing peace operations, warning: "The implication that the absence of any definable national interest is a viable criterion for risking American lives could erode the willingness of the American people to support any use of military power for any purpose."[82] Likewise, Jeanne Kirkpatrick described Clinton's policy as one "from which national self-interest is purged."[83] Until the country achieves a broader consensus about the nature of U.S. global leadership and its responsibilities, peace operations will continue to be a lightening rod for the nation's underlying ambivalence.

The debate about ends has been mirrored by ambivalence about means. Congress does not object to "multilateralism" per se. It supports NATO, where commonality of interests is assumed and U.S. control is significant. But critics tend to see the UN, despite the U.S. veto on the Security Council, very differently. Multilateralism as embodied by the UN remains suspect. Jeanne Kirkpatrick argued that the pursuit of multilateral means implied the pursuit of multilateral (rather than national) goals. She also charged that the "reason the Clinton administration's foreign policy seems indecisive is that multilateral decision-making is characteristically complicated and inconclusive. The reason Clinton policy seems ineffective is that UN operations—in Bosnia or Somalia or wherever—are characteristically ineffective."[84]

The debate about national interests and the means to pursue them is far from resolved, and multilateral peace operations remain a contentious issue. Republican presidential candidate George W. Bush vowed never to put Americans under UN command.[85] He rejected President Clinton's retrospective view that the United States should have acted to prevent the 1994 genocide in Rwanda,[86] and he said that he would stop deploying U.S. forces to conflicts that did not affect U.S. strategic interests.[87]

Interests and Consequences

U.S. Interests in UN Peacekeeping

In the new millennium two underlying realities persist. The first is that the United States remains more heavily engaged in multinational—if not UN—peace operations than anyone would have predicted in 1994. Peace operations offices remain ensconced throughout the bureaucracy, including the Pentagon. Congress eventually saw the wisdom of helping foreign countries improve their peacekeeping capabilities so that the United States would not have to respond to all crises alone.[88] The U.S. military slowly kicked into gear, developing training and doctrine and processing lessons from peace operations.[89] Launching peace operations became a formal role for NATO, in official documents and on the ground. Even as official U.S. strategy continued to downplay the importance of peace operations, they remained the primary activity of the U.S. armed forces. This is a major accomplishment of the Clinton administration.

The second reality is that after a significant hiatus, international security and political demands have pushed the UN back into the peace operations limelight, and the United States has found it in its interests to support this expansion of the UN's role. "Coalitions of the willing" have been unwilling or unable to address continuing civil strife and regional wars, particularly in African nations of no strategic or economic interest to stronger nations. Even when a coalition or nation has agreed initially to take the lead (e.g., NATO in Kosovo, Australia in East Timor), UN involvement has been attractive for a variety of reasons. The UN can provide a collective mechanism for financing the operation, a mantle of political legitimacy, an umbrella for other states to participate and share the burden, and a route toward disengagement for the lead nation.

As Jeffrey Laurenti writes about the recent surge in UN peace operations, "Washington had resisted U.N. intervention in all these troubled spots, but ultimately concluded that there was no alternative to a United Nations mission."[90] It turned out that even if a UN operation were not of great importance to the United States, it might well be a priority for close allies or whole regions of the world whose support in other contexts might be critically important to the United States. Washington could not block the UN from serving broader international security interests without paying different types of costs in bilateral relations and U.S. international standing generally. While U.S. political leaders rarely discuss the degree to which political horse trading and compromise are integral to policymaking, support for UN peace operations is necessary to satisfy certain nations and communities so that they can help advance U.S. interests in other arenas.

Even where the United States has decided it has strategic interests, as, for example, in Kosovo, the UN proved critical. For example, Jeffrey Laurenti concludes, "Only by accepting U.N. administration of Kosovo could Washington get Russian support and extricate NATO from a lengthy air war."[91] And of course the UN is indispensable for a wide range of U.S. foreign policy objectives ranging from the containment of Iraq to the regulation of air traffic. For all of these reasons, a policy that undermines the institution's most visible public role—peace operations—is costly.

The Clinton administration by the middle of the decade had sought to avoid reliance on the UN, but this approach proved inconsistent with broader U.S. interests. So by 1999, the president acknowledged before the General Assembly that the UN remained the world's "indispensable" institution.[92] His administration once more advanced an agenda of expanded and strengthened UN peace operations, describing these as essential to both the United States and to the entire world community. "The most important thing for the United States is to recognize that, flaws and all, the U.N. serves our national interests because it deals with problems that we do not wish to take on unilaterally," Ambassador Holbrooke declared. "In my personal view, the U.N. has a significant role to play in certain parts of the world which are beyond the immediate reach of American strategic interests, but are nonetheless part of our interests."[93]

Missing the Post–Cold War Moment

Institutional change in world politics often requires an unusual confluence of events. The early 1990s provided a significant opening for enhancing UN peacekeeping. In 1992, Secretary of State James Baker had described UN peacekeeping as a "national security priority" and a "pretty good buy."[94] The world's leading power was committed to enhancing the UN's capacity for peace operations, seeking to help the organization fulfill its promise of enhancing international peace and security.

The United States subsequently failed politically, militarily, and financially to keep this pledge. The UN foundered repeatedly in Somalia, Bosnia, Rwanda, and more recently in Sierra Leone. In the eyes of the world, including our closest allies, the United States played an important role in these failures, weakening an institution that should have assumed a more prominent role in the post–Cold War world.[95] U.S. reluctance to strongly support the UN has cascaded into hesitation on the part of other Western powers and bitterness from nonaligned and developing nations. There are serious questions about whether the squandered opportunity to enhance UN peacekeeping can be recaptured.

Weakening UN Peacekeeping Capabilities

During the 1990s, the UN improved the Department of Peacekeeping Operations (DPKO). The latter has created a situation room and information-gathering capabilities, and has improved its recruitment, training, and equipping of forces. The UN has sought to learn from its mistakes, issuing clear-eyed reports detailing its failures in Rwanda and Srebrenica. Yet the organization today, while marginally better prepared to execute the peace operations it is assigned, is still woefully inadequate.

Strengthening DPKO remains the serious challenge it was a decade ago. As U.S. Ambassador to the UN Richard Holbrooke complained, "They're running worldwide operations and they're stretched to the bone. They work around the clock. They don't have sufficient technical expertise. No serious military force would have been sent out with the command and control and communications structures that the U.N. has sent into some areas."[96]

The May 2000 rebel killing and capture of UN peacekeepers in Sierra Leone underscored the continuing problems in both the tasking and execution of UN peace operations.[97] These chronic problems prompted Secretary-General Kofi Annan to appoint an independent panel led by Undersecretary-General Lakhdar Brahimi to reassess UN peacekeeping. The Brahimi Report, released in August 2000, included recommendations to improve the UN's (not so) rapid deployment capabilities; the design, management, and financing of peacekeeping missions; the capacities and performance of DPKO; and—not least—the support that member states give UN peacekeeping operations.[98] While the report contains many excellent recommendations, many of them variations on longstanding proposals, there is, unfortunately, little evidence to suggest that they suddenly will be heeded.

The UN's weaknesses stem, first and foremost, from the divergent views and policies of its diverse member states. These include not only powerful members focused on advancing their own agendas, but also less developed or repressive states that for different reasons fear foreign intervention with a UN imprimatur. The latter have blocked legislative reform of DPKO and helped end the Western practice of supplying "gratis" military officers to DPKO; resentment of disproportionate Western influence in the department apparently was greater than concern about the severe staffing shortage caused by this policy change. The UN also suffers from institutional weaknesses, including its bureaucratic staleness, culture of "peace," conceptions of peace operations, and personnel practices.[99]

The UN's ineffectiveness is not principally Washington's fault or responsibility, and the United States has helped in some modest ways to overcome specific weaknesses (for example, by seconding military personnel and providing an architecture for computer upgrades). But by the most important measures discussed below, the world's leading nation has fallen short.

U.S. funding. As Margaret Karns and Karen Mingst detail in Chapter 11, congressional actions, such as insistence upon zero UN budget growth and refusal to pay assessments, posed great challenges for the UN just as it assumed a larger role in international security. As early as 1993, Richard Thornburgh, then U.N. undersecretary-general for administration and management, reported that the UN's ongoing finances were in crisis and that "peacekeeping funding is still much like a financial 'bungee jump,' often undertaken strictly in blind faith that timely appropriations will be forthcoming."[100]

At the end of 1998, the UN owed over $1 billion to member states for their participation in peacekeeping,[101] while the United States accounted for over 60 percent of the almost $1.6 billion that nations owed for peacekeeping assessments.[102] U.S. arrears contributed to delays in UN reimbursements to nations that contributed peacekeeping troops.[103] These delays have frustrated U.S. allies and provided a disincentive for poorer nations to participate in peace operations. Budget crises have also resulted in freezes on certain types of activities, including hiring personnel to administer peace operations. This has resulted in further delays in peacekeeping operations purchases and deployments.

U.S. positions on UN financing have had other operational implications. Less developed nations have argued that DPKO staff slots formerly filled by "gratis" officers should be funded through the regular budget, but the United States objects to increased costs. In fact, while the Clinton administration was supportive of the Brahimi Report, it was concerned about the report's request for additional resources in light of the U.S. policy of zero nominal UN budget growth. The impact of Congress's fiscal straitjacket cannot be underestimated.

U.S. military support. If U.S. political support is a prerequisite for UN approval of a peace operation, almost any type of U.S. military support can help encourage or enable other nations to participate.[104] This is particularly salient because even many of the more militarily powerful UN members can no longer perform brigade-level missions, cannot deploy themselves over significant distances, and often lack necessary equipment. As we have seen, however, congressional opposition meant that the United States largely stopped sending combat forces to participate in blue-helmet operations. The United States even failed to provide sufficient logistical support or equipment to certain UN missions. By charging standard "leasing" rates on its airlift and other equipment, the United States has effectively discouraged the UN from calling upon a reliable, fast, and most capable transport option. Internal U.S. government procedures sometimes have made it difficult for UN forces to obtain necessary equipment.[105] It would cost relatively little to ease the restrictions on such provision of goods and services, strengthening the UN and earning the United States considerable goodwill. But Congress requires reimbursement for, and imposes other conditions on, all DOD contributions to UN peace operations.[106]

Blocking Efforts to Protect International Peace and Security

The Clinton administration occasionally blocked the UN from undertaking peace operations. Some objections reflected valid concerns, such as the lack of a clear mission or an overly ambitious UN role. But because the United States did so little to enhance UN capabilities or otherwise support UN peace operations, U.S. caution on substantive grounds was viewed with skepticism by other nations. As one critical foreign paper reported, "The opportunity to create a genuinely global system of peace-keeping and peace-making has been lost, largely because the U.S. decided that it could not sustain any commitments that were not clearly in American interests, and were not wholly under its control."[107] Washington did not appear to understand that the UN was intended to protect *international* peace and security.

The most forceful example is the case of Rwanda in 1994. Washington became a vocal advocate for pulling the small UN peacekeeping contingent out as the genocide began sweeping the country. There were legitimate concerns about the deteriorating situation and its implications for the impartial, chapter VI mandate to which troop-contributing nations had committed themselves. But the United States appeared uninterested in shaping an appropriate response; the administration had just promised congressional leaders in briefings on PDD 25 that the new policy was to be "selective."

When the genocide unfolded, the United States could have pushed for a new or augmented UN force, lobbying Belgium, Canada, and other nations with troops on the ground to accept a different mission.[108] At a minimum, it could have agreed to provide willing nations with the lift, equipment, and logistical support necessary to respond. Even after the world body finally authorized an expanded UN force (after the bulk of the killing had subsided), the DOD refused to waive the costs of transporting foreign troops to Rwanda.[109]

At a more subtle level, weaknesses in UN peacekeeping operations capabilities have restricted the options for less powerful countries or parties in conflict. The UN often cannot be counted on either as a counterweight or as a protecting force; it can only confirm and help implement whatever deal a weak party might be offered. If the UN offered a more capable military force, Security Council member states might be better able to shape diplomacy in meaningful ways. Take the example of Sierra Leone. The UN's inability to protect the government contributed to pressures to sign a reprehensible peace agreement that brought a war criminal into government, assigning him de facto control over the nation's resources. The UN was then powerless even to enforce this bad deal, resulting in yet another humiliation involving the murder and taking hostage of UN peacekeepers. There is considerable scope for the UN to expand its capabilities while still eschewing the more difficult peace operations that should be conducted by NATO or a coalition of the willing.

The United States' Image

Few nations expect (or perhaps, at bottom, want) the United States to conduct peace operations only under UN command. In fact, other leading nations increasingly are uneasy about committing troops to UN operations. But it would be a mistake to equate the issue of U.S. soldiers' donning blue helmets with that of U.S. support for UN peacekeeping. The fundamental problem, from the perspective of other nations, is not that the United States wants to do its own thing, but that it has failed to take significant financial, political, logistical, or other steps to strengthen the collective option of UN peacekeeping operations.[110]

This inaction by the United States is doubly frustrating for foreign observers who understand both that UN peacekeeping often serves direct U.S. interests (e.g., in the Middle East, Haiti, Bosnia, Kosovo) and that the UN has a mandate to promote international, not just American, peace and security. Foreign editorials and news reports chronicle the wider world's disillusionment with U.S. views of its global security role.[111] "Everywhere in Europe you bump into the thesis that America is the 'rogue superpower,'" bemoans one commentator.[112] There are many sources of this attitude, but U.S. reluctance to support UN peace operations contributes to perceptions that the United States is unwilling to assume its share of common international responsibilities.

President Clinton understood that the U.S. failure to pay UN dues created a political problem for him in diplomatic circles.[113] It makes it more difficult to explain other aspects of U.S. international security policy that are necessarily unilateral or controversial. And as one respected journalist reported: "Diplomats, including Americans, say that anger toward the United States [regarding UN arrears] is beginning to erode support on issues vital to Washington."[114] Apparent U.S. unwillingness to support UN peacekeeping may also undermine what Joseph Nye terms the United States' "soft power," the invisible strength a nation can derive from the values and beliefs it embodies. To those who believe that U.S. dominance is a largely preferable state of world affairs, the implications are troubling.

Conclusion

U.S. policy toward multinational peace operations has come full circle during the past decade for reasons that are unlikely to change. The demand for intervention will continue to outpace the desire or capacity of regional organizations or key states to respond. In many instances, the UN will remain the vehicle to which other nations—even the United States—look to address crises. By failing to strengthen UN peacekeeping, Washington finds itself in a curious place: increasingly reliant on a tool it has weakened.

The United States will continue to approve or to encourage UN intervention in a variety of circumstances. Washington may be unable to ignore a crisis but not wish to send U.S. forces and see no other option. Alternatively, key allies may seek UN involvement in an area of special interest. Washington may at times need to support a UN peacekeeping operation for instrumental reasons having to do with Security Council politics or bilateral relations. Or it may find a UN operation critically important for political legitimacy, for burden sharing in postconflict reconstruction, or for allowing U.S. disengagement (as in Somalia, Bosnia, and Kosovo).

If the United States chooses not to strengthen UN peace operations capabilities, it should assume the responsibility for, and costs of, limiting the demands member states place on the organization. Otherwise, the cycle of disillusionment will continue—states will set the UN up to fail, undermine its international standing, and confirm its critics' predictions. Eventually, the United States might find itself with a choice between assuming the UN's responsibilities or allowing entire regions of the world to become consumed by conflict.

This dilemma—a choice between ignoring spreading violence and becoming the world's policeman—is precisely what President Bush and President Clinton had hoped to avoid by strengthening UN peacekeeping capabilities.

Appendix

Ongoing UN Peace Operations

Begun Prior to 1990

Middle East	UNTSO	June 1948–
India-Pakistan	UNMOGIP	January 1949–
Cyprus	UNFICYP	March 1964–
Golan Heights	UNDOF	June 1974–
Lebanon	UNIFIL	March 1978–

Begun After 1990

Western Sahara	MINURSO	April 1991–
Iraq/Kuwait	UNIKOM	April 1991–
Georgia	UNOMIG	August 1993–
Bosnia & Herzegovina	UNMIBH	December 1995–
Croatia	UNMOP	January 1996–
Kosovo	UNMIK	June 1999–
Sierra Leone	UNAMSIL	October 1999–
East Timor	UNTAET	October 1999–
Democratic Republic of the Congo	MONUC	December 1999–
Ethiopia and Eritrea	UNMEE	July 2000–

Completed UN Peace Operations

Begun Prior to 1990

Middle East	UNEF I	November 1956 to June 1967
Lebanon	UNOGIL	June 1958 to December 1958
Congo	ONUC	July 1960 to June 1964
West New Guinea	UNSF	October 1962 to April 1963
Yemen	UNYOM	July 1963 to September 1964
Dominican Republic	DOMREP	May 1965 to October 1966
India/Pakistan	UNIPOM	September 1965 to March 1966
Middle East	UNEF II	October 1973 to July 1979
Afghanistan/Pakistan	UNGOMAP	May 1988 to March 1990
Iran/Iraq	UNIIMOG	August 1988 to February 1991
Angola	UNAVEM I	December 1988 to May 1991
Namibia	UNTAG	April 1989 to March 1990
Central America	ONUCA	November 1989 to January 1992

Begun After 1990

Angola	UNAVEM II	May 1991 to February 1995
El Salvador	ONUSAL	July 1991 to April 1995

(continued)

Cambodia	UNAMIC	October 199
Former Yugoslavia	UNPROFOR	February 19
Somalia	UNOSOM I	April 1992 to March 1993
Cambodia	UNTAC	March 1992 to September 1993
Mozambique	ONUMOZ	December 1992 to December 1994
Somalia	UNOSOM II	March 1993 to March 1995
Rwanda/Uganda	UNOMUR	June 1993 to September 1994
Haiti	UNMIH	September 1993 to June 1996
Liberia	UNOMIL	September 1993 to September 1997
Rwanda	UNAMIR	October 1993 to March 1996
Chad/Libya	UNASOG	May 1994 to June 1994
Tajikistan	UNMOT	December 1994 to May 2000
Angola	UNAVEM III	February 1995 to June 1997
Croatia	UNCRO	March 1995 to January 1996
Former Yugoslav Republic of Macedonia	UNPREDEP	March 1995 to February 1999
Croatia	UNTAES	January 1996 to January 1998
Haiti	UNSMIH	July 1996 to July 1997
Guatemala	MINUGUA	January 1997 to May 1997
Angola	MONUA	June 1997 to February 1999
Haiti	UNTMIH	August 1997 to November 1997
Haiti	MIPONUH	December 1997 to March 2000
Croatia	UNPSG	January 1998 to October 1998
Central Africa Republic	MINURCA	April 1998 to February 2000
Sierra Leone	UNOMSIL	July 1998 to October 1999

Notes

With many thanks to Drew Lewis for his research assistance, and William Durch, Lee Feinstein, Michael Ignatieff, Len Hawley, Ivo Daalder, Michael MacKinnon, Victoria Holt, Charles Arnold, and Stewart Patrick for their comments on earlier drafts of this chapter.

1. While "peacekeeping" is not the equivalent of "peace operations," for variety in this chapter the terms are used interchangeably. Peace operations include both traditional peacekeeping taken pursuant to Chapter VI of the UN Charter and peace enforcement operations authorized under Chapter VII. For more on differing definitions, see the United Nations, *An Agenda for Peace*, p. 4 (where peacemaking and peacekeeping are distinguished) and the Department of Defense, *Dictionary of Military and Associated Terms*, pp. 346–347. The U.S. military defines peace enforcement as including sanctions enforcement and other uses of force that may not be primarily humanitarian. See also note 106 below.

2. Daalder, "Knowing When to Say No," p. 40.

3. See UN peacekeeping Web site *http://www.un.org/Depts/dpko/dpko/ops.htm*

4. "Clinton in Africa," *New York Times*, March 26, 1998, p. A12.

5. Durch, ed., *The Evolution of UN Peacekeeping*, pp. 7–9.

6. Although peacekeeping is not mentioned specifically in Chapter VI.

7. These are definitions contained in the first U.S. military manual devoted exclusively to peace operations: the army's *FM 100-23 Peace Operations*, issued December 30, 1994 (Headquarters Department of the Army, *FM 100-23*, pp. 4–7). They are substantially the same definitions contained in 1999 Joint Publication 3-07.3 (Department of Defense, *Joint Publication 3-07.3*, pp. 16–17).

8. Boutros-Ghali, "School for Advanced International Studies Commencement Address," Federal News Service, May 26, 1994.

9. Bush, *Remarks to the United Nations Security Council*, January 31, 1992.

10. Bush, *The President's News Conference on the Persian Gulf Conflict,* January 18, 1991.

11. Bush, *Remarks to the United Nations Security Council.*

12. Daalder, "Knowing When to Say No," p. 38.

13. Ibid., p. 62.

14. This was roughly the same time period in which former President Ronald Reagan called for a standing UN army in a speech at the Oxford Union. Merriweather, "Reagan Calls for Military Action in World's Hot Spots," UPI, December 4, 1992.

15. Bush, *Address to the United Nations General Assembly in New York City,* September 21, 1992.

16. Ibid.

17. This pledge was realized in the form of U.S. military officers seconded to the UN Department of Peacekeeping Operations.

18. Bush, *Address to the United Nations General Assembly in New York City.* Secretary of State James Baker reportedly proposed looking at DOD as a possible source of UN peacekeeping funding. See Rosner, *The New Tug of War,* p. 75.

19. The Defense Department did not have any troops earmarked for peace-keeping missions and, until the Bush speech, had no plans to train any. "The Joint Chiefs of Staff does not have a single planner responsible for peacekeeping operations, the officials said." Kempster, "Improve Forces, Bush Urges UN," *Los Angeles Times,* September 22, 1992, p. A1. See also, Scherer, "Bush Casts Eye on Election," *Christian Science Monitor,* September 23, 1992, p. 1.

20. Kempster, "Improve Forces, Bush Urges UN."

21. Scherer, "Bush Casts Eye on Election."

22. Holt, *Briefing Book on Peacekeeping,* pp. 14–15.

23. Rosner, *The New Tug-of-War,* p. 68

24. Ibid., p. 68

25. Daalder, "Knowing When to Say No," p. 40.

26. Vita, "U.S. Military Training for New Mission," *Atlanta Journal and Constitution,* June 19, 1993, p. A16.

27. International Security, International Organizations and Human Rights Subcommittee of the House Foreign Affairs Committee, *U.S. Participation in UN Peacekeeping Missions,* 24 June 1993. Ambassador Albright's comment is found on p. 3 of Lexis-Nexis version.

28. Daalder, "Knowing When to Say No," pp. 43–44. Thus, candidate Clinton's endorsement of a UN rapid deployment force appears to have been abandoned prior to the formal first policy review draft. NSC officials later inserted language that could be said to satisfy the president's campaign commitment; PDD 25 supported a rapidly deployable UN *headquarters unit* as well as the UN's standby forces arrangements. See Clinton, "Major Foreign Policy Speech, Foreign Policy Association," Federal News Service, April 1, 1992. Comment on UN rapid deployment force found on p. 7 of Lexis-Nexis version.

29. The Clinton Administration's Policy on Reforming Multilateral Peace Operations (referred to as PDD 25 in following instances) proposed "shared responsibility" between the State and Defense departments, a division of responsibility between the agencies for funding obligations for and primary policy control of certain types of operations. The innovation was proposed primarily in hopes of solving the peace operations funding crisis. Department of State, PDD 25, p. 2.

30. The Joint Chiefs of Staff, which had the lead on the command and control aspect of peace operations policy, removed an earlier condition that U.S. troops could disregard a foreigner's command if it were militarily unsound. Such a loophole would not only have jeopardized the integrity of UN operations; it would have

created a precedent that would have haunted U.S. command of multinational operations. Department of State, PDD 25, pp. 9–11.

31. Department of State, PDD 25, p. 5.

32. Additional Powell-Weinberger criteria were added as factors for consideration for U.S. participation "when there is the possibility of significant U.S. participation in Chapter VII operations that are likely to involve combat" (Department of State, PDD 25, p. 5), but these were implicit in any commitment of U.S. forces to possible conflict. Factors that "lowered the bar" for participation or support (e.g., that consideration of the cost of *not* acting be weighed) were also added to the list following consultations with Congress, despite the fact that most members of Congress urged more stringent criteria.

33. Department of State, PDD 25, p. 4. President Bush's January 1993 farewell address also seemed to reject the application of "rigid criteria" to decisions about the use of force. See MacKinnon, *The Evolution of US Peacekeeping Policy*, p. 19.

34. Sokolsky, "Great Ideals and Uneasy Compromises," p. 286.

35. Interview with Lee Feinstein, who served as deputy director of the State Department Office of Policy Planning and in the peacekeeping office in the Office of the Secretary of Defense, author's notes, January 30, 2001.

36. Department of State, PDD 25, p. 15.

37. The United States succeeded in having the Security Council adopt decisionmaking guidelines modeled on PDD 25's criteria. They had little, if any, demonstrable effect on decisionmaking. See "Peace-keeping Guidelines Set Out by Security Council," *UN Chronicle*, p. 54.

38. White House, "Remarks of President Clinton," p. 1901.

39. MacKinnon, *The Evolution of US Peacekeeping Policy*, p. 24.

40. White House Office of the Press Secretary, "Press Briefing by National Security Advisor Tony Lake," May 5, 1994.

41. "[I]t has taken him less than a year to retreat from the bold multi-lateralist approach to the world's post–Cold War troubles that he called for during his campaign," Fletcher, "US Retreats from Role as World's Policeman," *The Times of London*, January 31, 1994.

42. "Americans by the dozens are paying with their lives and limbs for a misplaced policy on the altar of some fuzzy multilateralism." Senator Robert Byrd (Democrat-West Virginia), "Carnage in Somalia," October 4, 1993.

43. For a discussion of congressional restrictions and reasoning see Johansen, "U.S. Policy Toward U.N.," pp. 13–19.

44. For example, the administration in 1994 began regular consultations on peace operations on Capitol Hill. Congress soon demanded extensive reporting requirements in advance of administration actions.

45. These included legislative proposals regarding command and control and reimbursement for costs "in support of" UN resolutions.

46. For a thorough introduction to the issues and survey of early 1990s policies, see Rosner, *The New Tug of War*, pp. 74–91.

47. See Figure 8.1. Note that FY 1994 saw the historic high for U.S. assessments for UN peacekeeping of about $1.26 billion.

48. Rosner quotes letter to Clinton from Representative Lee Hamilton on August 5, 1993. Rosner, *The New Tug of War*, p. 83.

49. Not the "disputed arrears" stemming from the 25 percent cap on UN peacekeeping assessments.

50. Ambassador Holbrooke would later say, "We have also changed congressional attitudes to some degree . . . by the most intense exchange of visits between the U.N. and the Congress. . . . I think we've had somewhere in the neighborhood

of 60 to 70 members of Congress here. . . . I won't say there's been a sea change, but there's been a significant improvement in congressional relations." Kitfield and Hirsch, "In Holbrooke's View, 'We Have a Stake'," p. 2730.

51. Helms, "Address to Security Council," January 20, 2000.

52. Sciolino, "New US Peacekeeping Policy," *New York Times,* May 6, 1994, p. A1.

53. For example, neither ECOMOG troops in Liberia nor Commonwealth of Independent States forces deployed throughout the former Soviet Union were successful or acted in a manner consistent with minimum standards of military responsibility.

54. It is noteworthy that President Clinton stated as early as September 1993 that he would only deploy U.S. forces to Bosnia under NATO command. See Friedman, "Clinton Rebuffs Bosnian Leader," *New York Times,* September 9, 1993, p. A1.

55. Crossette, "After Long Fight," *New York Times,* December 23, 2000, p. A6.

56. Senate Committee on Foreign Relations, *United Nations Reforms,* January 9, 2001. Senator Helms' comments may be found on p. 3 of the Lexis-Nexis version.

57. Congress's 25 percent cap on peacekeeping assessments was incorporated into the Helms-Biden "grand bargain" and will likely remain a contentious issue.

58. "UN Peacekeeping in Question," *Boston Globe,* October 5, 2000.

59. U.S. General Accounting Office, *Costs of Peacekeeping Is Likely to Exceed Current Estimates,* p. 4.

60. I say this as a former Clinton administration official who initially argued that the UN should be able to assume a peace enforcement role. Today it is obvious that operations in which significant combat can be anticipated are beyond the UN's reach and likely to remain so.

61. Hirsch and Oakley, *Somalia & Operation Restore Hope,* p. 46.

62. See Bowden, *Black Hawk Down,* for an account of the UN force's rescue of the Rangers.

63. Clinton: "My experiences in Somalia would make me more cautious about having any Americans in a peacekeeping role where there was any ambiguity at all about what the range of decisions were which could be made by a command other than an American command with direct accountability to the United States here." White House "The President's News Conference," p. 2068.

64. Rosner, *The New Tug of War,* p. 70.

65. The administration believed that war powers issues could be separately addressed through an alternative policy review.

66. Rosner, *The New Tug of War,* p. 84.

67. Ibid., pp. 84–85.

68. See Daalder, "Knowing When to Say No," pp. 55–56.

69. Goshko, "Clinton Seen Calming Hill on Peacekeeping," *Washington Post,* October 2, 1993, p. A16.

70. Rosner, *The New Tug of War,* p. 87.

71. Scheffer, *Atrocities Prevention: Lessons from Rwanda,* 29 October 1999.

72. Even today, this remains a hot button issue, the focus of proposed legislative restrictions, and the campaign pledge of President George W. Bush.

73. Berdal, "Fateful Encounter," p. 37.

74. U.S. participation in small numbers is also governed by the UN Participation Act (22 USCS § 287d-1). Once U.S. participation became significant, however, there was no legislative framework for addressing the commitment of U.S. forces to a UN operation.

75. Rosner, *The New Tug of War,* pp. 76–77. See especially the discussion of a memo to Secretary of State Christopher regarding cuts that might be needed in the Department of State's operating budget to meet peacekeeping needs.

76. Rosner, *The New Tug of War,* p. 68.

77. Johansen, "U.S. Policy Toward U.N.," pp. 20, 22.

78. Daalder, "Knowing When to Say No," p. 65.

79. Johansen, "U.S. Policy Toward U.N.," p. 21.

80. Ibid., p. 19.

81. Berdal, "Fateful Encounter," p. 35.

82. Kissinger, "Cooking Up a Recipe for New World Chaos," *Houston Chronicle,* September 5, 1993, p. 1.

83. Kirkpatrick, "Where Is Our Foreign Policy?," *Washington Post,* September 5, 1993, p. A19.

84. Ibid.

85. Bush, "Speech by Govenor George W. Bush," November 19, 1999.

86. Bush, "Interview with George W. Bush," Federal News Service, January 23, 2000.

87. Ibid.

88. There are two ongoing programs to enhance foreign peacekeeping: the African Crisis Response Initiative (ACRI) and the more modest FMF program, Enhancing International Peacekeeping Capabilities. See Rupert, "U.S. Troops Teach Peacekeeping to Africans," *Washington Post,* September 26, 1997, p. A16, and Department of State, *Congressional Budget Justification for Foreign Operations,* pp. 5–7 of version found at *http://www.state.gov/www/budget/fy2001/fn150/forops_full/150fy01_fo_global-prog.html*

89. The U.S. Army is even becoming more mobile, buying light armored vehicles to replace tanks in order to "respond quickly to small conflicts and peacekeeping missions." See Shenon, "An Army Contract Signals a Shift," *New York Times,* November 17, 2000, p. A21.

90. Laurenti, "The United Nations and International Security," pp. 3–4.

91. Ibid., p. 3.

92. Clinton, "Remarks to the UN General Assembly," September 21, 1999.

93. Kitfield and Hirsch, "In Holbrooke's View, 'We Have a Stake'," p. 2730.

94. Commerce, Justice, State, and Judiciary Subcommittee of the House Appropriations Committee, *State Department Fiscal Year 1993 Funding Proposal.* Secretary Baker's comments may be found on p. 6 of the Lexis-Nexis version.

95. Europeans were frustrated for years by the U.S. desire to control policy toward Bosnia while refusing to contribute troops to UNPROFOR. Many observers blame the United States for the UN's failure in Rwanda, including the French parliament, which issued a report accusing the United States of opposing a sizable UN response "for both political and budgetary reasons," throwing down numerous "administrative obstacles" that blocked reinforcements to the UN Mission in Rwanda (UNAMIR), and playing a "primarily negative" role in the crisis ("French Parliament Blasts US over Rwanda Genocide," *Agence France-Presse,* December 15, 1998). The same criticisms can be heard with regard to Sierra Leone: "European officials have . . . privately complained that an international response has been curbed by the Clinton administration's embrace of a military doctrine of no casualties." Fitchett, "West Exasperated by a Failed Intervention."

96. Crossette, "U.S. Ambassador to U.N. Calls for Changes," *New York Times,* June 14, 2000, p. A8.

97. "Badly Trained, Ill-defined and Under-funded UN Peacekeepers Endure Humiliations," *The Guardian,* May 11, 2000, p.4.

98. United Nations, "Report of the Panel on United Nations Peace Operations," p. 54.

99. Laurenti, "The United Nations and International Security," p. 4.

100. Holt, *Briefing Book on Peacekeeping*, p. 10.

101. U.S. General Accounting Office, *Status of US Contributions and Arrears*, p. 12.

102. GAO, *Status of US Contributions and Arrears*, p. 15.

103. Crossette, "Darkest Hour at U.N.," *New York Times*, p. A6.

104. Laurenti, "The United Nations and International Security," p. 5

105. Crossette, "U.S. Ambassador to U.N. Calls for Changes."

106. This helps explain why the Clinton administration differentiated between DOD voluntary support for UN peace operations and other UN-authorized operations. The Clinton administration did not regard the Iraq no-fly operations as peace operations, despite the fact that many government budget guardians and DOD terminology would seem to indicate otherwise. The distinction therefore has been incorporated into the budgetary chart (Figure 8.1).

107. Woollacott, "Peace in Your Own Back Yard," *The Guardian*, September 16, 1994, p. 22.

108. A larger, more capable force with a Chapter VII enforcement mandate would have been required.

109. The United States will not waive or reduce costs on airlift. See Crossette, "U.S. Ambassador to U.N. Calls for Changes." This rigidity originally stemmed from Department of State–DOD battles on the provision of "in-kind" U.S. support for peace operations, and later was legislated by Congress. The United States ultimately spent hundreds of millions of dollars providing relief to refugees who both fueled and fled the Rwanda crises. But they were not DOD dollars.

110. See *The Economist*'s coverage of U.S. peacekeeping policy. The magazine was particularly critical of Congress's "brattish conditions" for payment of international dues obligations. See "Pay up and Play the Game."

111. Brock, "Faltering White House," *Times of London*, September 28, 1994, quotes an "embittered NATO official" as calling Clinton a "flake who has lost control of his legislature." "'PDD 25' therefore marks a retreat from America's old superpower role."

112. Gedmin, "Our European Problem."

113. Rosner, *The New Tug of War*, p. 83.

114. Crossette, "Darkest Hour at U.N.," *New York Times*, September 21, 1998, p. A6.

9

Nuclear Weapons:
The Comprehensive Test Ban Treaty
and National Missile Defense

Thomas Graham Jr. and Damien J. LaVera

THE U.S. SENATE'S VOTE IN OCTOBER 1999 AGAINST THE COMPREHENSIVE
Test Ban Treaty (CTBT) and the renewed drive in recent years toward the
deployment of a U.S. National Missile Defense (NMD) system have caused
analysts in the United States and abroad to express concern about the apparent U.S. trend toward a unilateral approach to security. In a speech given
shortly after the CTBT vote, for example, U.S. National Security Advisor
Samuel Berger registered his concern, noting that "the internationalist consensus that has prevailed in this country for more than 50 years increasingly
is being challenged by a new isolationism. . . . The new isolationists are
convinced that treaties—pretty much all treaties—are a threat to our sovereignty and continued superiority."[1] The CTBT vote, the push for NMD, and
other developments addressed elsewhere in this book in fields like peacekeeping and the Chemical Weapons Convention (CWC) have kindled concerns that the United States no longer finds it necessary to work with other
nations to maintain cooperative security, and that this unilateral trend in
U.S policy may undermine international peace and stability.

In the United States, opponents of the CTBT and proponents of NMD
assert that their views are driven not by isolationism or unilateralism, but
rather by their belief that post–Cold War threats demand new approaches to
U.S security. But the perceived resurgence in U.S. unilateralism nevertheless has grave consequences for both U.S. and international security. A particularly troubling aspect of recent U.S. behavior has been the overt dismissal of the views of allies on the issues of CTBT ratification and NMD.
Responding to an opinion piece by British Prime Minister Tony Blair,
French President Jacques Chirac, and German Chancellor Gerhard Schroeder
urging U.S. ratification of the CTBT, Senator Jesse Helms (Republican-
North Carolina), chair of the Senate Foreign Relations Committee, noted
that he would rather rely on the views of the treaty's U.S. critics than on
"three overseas people who don't know anything about our country."[2] Similarly, when Senator Joseph Biden (Democrat-Delaware) expressed concerns

about the impact CTBT rejection might have on U.S. allies, Senator James Inhofe (Republican-Oklahoma) remarked, "Frankly, I am not concerned about our allies. I am concerned about our adversaries."[3] Such statements can only cause alarm among allies already concerned about U.S. attitudes toward global approaches to security.

This chapter uses the ongoing debates on the CTBT and missile defense to explore the costs of U.S. unilateralism—whether real or perceived—for global nonproliferation efforts. It addresses the historic development and contemporary relevance of each issue, examines the underlying tensions between unilateralism and engagement inherent in each sphere, and describes the impact of recent U.S. behavior in both cases for the nuclear nonproliferation regime.

Cause for Concern

Like no other time in history, the principal threats to U.S. security center today not on risks posed by nations, but on transnational concerns such as the proliferation of weapons of mass destruction, terrorism, economic instability, and environmental degradation. The most important of these threats are the litany of dangers associated with the spread of nuclear weapons. As Chirac, Blair, and Schroeder noted in their October 1999 opinion piece, "As we look to the next century, our greatest concern is proliferation of weapons of mass destruction, and chiefly nuclear proliferation. We have to face the stark truth that nuclear proliferation remains the major threat to world safety."[4] It is also the gravest danger to U.S. national security, since the acquisition and subsequent use of nuclear weapons is the only means by which an adversary could offset the overwhelming advantage that the United States currently enjoys in political, military, and economic might, and thereby fundamentally challenge or undermine U.S. interests abroad.

But, while security analysts on both sides of the engagement-unilateralism divide agree that the spread of nuclear weapons must be prevented, they differ sharply on the means of achieving this goal and on the ways the United States should protect itself from the dangers of proliferation. Those on the engagement side favor promoting and strengthening international restraint regimes to counter this threat, arguing that the inherent dangers of nuclear proliferation are such that anything that undermines global nonproliferation regimes represents a net detriment to both U.S. and global security. Unilateralist critics of this view, however, maintain that the unequaled strengths of the United States give it broader interests and unparalleled responsibilities to act alone, if need be, to preserve international security and world order. Senator Jon Kyl (Republican-Arizona), for example, contends that "the United States cannot be held hostage to world opinion. We have obligations they don't have, and if they don't care about building a defense for their people, we need to because we can be a target of rogue nations whereas other countries may not be. They are not making the decisions and actions in the world that may cause these terrorists or rogue states to retaliate against them."[5]

The NMD and CTBT controversies reveal the tensions that exist between the need to promote (and subsequently strengthen) global nonproliferation regimes and the United States' unique interests and obligations. They also demonstrate the potential for global and national security objectives to overlap and, depending on one's perspective, to compete. The CTBT and NMD issues affect national security as well as global stability, and in both cases—at least from the unilateralist perspective—the immediate security requirements for the United States may be inconsistent with those of the international community. In the case of NMD, the United States is perhaps the only country that has a chance of being able to develop and someday deploy an effective missile shield. But such a shield would run a significant risk of exacerbating global nuclear proliferation problems. Likewise, while bringing the CTBT into force would unquestionably benefit the nonproliferation regime, opponents in the United States worry that it could have a negative impact on the effectiveness of the U.S. nuclear deterrent. A central element of both issues is disagreement over the role that global restraint regimes such as the nuclear Non-Proliferation Treaty (NPT) and the CTBT can, and should, play in U.S. national security. The recent U.S. shift toward NMD deployment and away from the CTBT promises to have a significant impact on the effectiveness of the nuclear nonproliferation regime, with negative consequences for U.S. and global security.

U.S. Secretary of State Albright referred to the NPT, in an opinion piece in March 2000, as "the most important multilateral arms control agreement in history."[6] As a result of the NPT, which opened for signature on July 1, 1968, the international community has been largely successful in preventing the spread of nuclear weapons. While the number of nations that possess the technological capabilities to produce nuclear weapons has grown to more than seventy, according to a recent International Atomic Energy Agency (IAEA) report, only a handful of states have crossed the nuclear threshold.[7] The success of the NPT is rooted in the treaty's core bargain. In exchange for a commitment from the nonnuclear weapon states (today numbering 182 nations) never to develop or otherwise to acquire nuclear weapons and to submit to international safeguards intended to verify compliance with this commitment, the nuclear weapon states (the United States, Russia, United Kingdom, France, and China) promised in NPT article IV unfettered access to peaceful nuclear technologies and pledged (article VI) to engage in disarmament negotiations aimed at the ultimate elimination of their nuclear arsenals.

Nonproliferation and the Test Ban

This central bargain—nonproliferation in exchange for eventual nuclear disarmament—is the foundation upon which the NPT regime rests, and the CTBT has long been considered a litmus test of nuclear weapon states' commitment to their end of the bargain. The linkage between the CTBT and the nonproliferation regime is enshrined in the preamble to the NPT. It was further emphasized in 1995, when the states parties met to decide the future of the NPT. When initially signed, the NPT had been given a twenty-five-year lifespan. In 1995, after this initial period had ended, the international community faced the choice of either extending it indefinitely or extending it for a fixed period (or periods), which could have led to its eventual termination.

Despite the treaty's success in stemming proliferation, in 1995 a significant number of key nonnuclear weapon states were dissatisfied with the progress made by the nuclear weapon states in fulfilling their article VI side of the bargain. As a result, many were reluctant to accept a permanent NPT that would lock them into what they saw as an inherently discriminatory regime. The NPT explicitly does not legitimize the arsenals of the nuclear weapon states, but many non-Western states were concerned that a permanent NPT would remove the incentive for the nuclear powers to reduce their arsenals. To ameliorate this concern, the NPT states parties at the 1995 Review and Extension Conference negotiated an associated consensus agreement, called the Statement of Principles and Objectives for Nuclear Non-Proliferation and Disarmament, intended to strengthen the regime and, politically if not legally, condition the extension of the treaty. The statement pledged the NPT states parties to work toward a number of objectives, including universalization of NPT membership, a reaffirmation of the article VI commitments, and the completion of the CTBT by the end of 1996. The latter was the only objective given a timeline for achievement, demonstrating the importance of the test ban to the health of the NPT regime. Indeed, the CTBT was the price the nuclear weapons states, including the United States, paid for an NPT of indefinite duration.

History of the Test Ban Treaty Debate

Tensions between unilateralism and engagement have been a feature of nuclear arms control and nonproliferation discourse almost since the beginning of the nuclear age, and no single issue demonstrates this better than the nearly half-century-old debate on banning nuclear tests. On the one hand, a comprehensive test ban treaty has long been considered a crucial element of nuclear nonproliferation efforts. Even in the early 1950s, nonnuclear weapon states saw a CTBT as an essential restraint on the development of more advanced weapons, while the nuclear powers viewed it as a means of preventing the nonnuclear weapon states from developing advanced weapons of their own. The first steps toward a comprehensive test ban were taken in 1954. But, even at this early stage, there were concerns in the United States about whether a test ban could be verified and about what effect an unverifiable ban could have on national security (principal concerns of unilateralist opponents of the CTBT today). These misgivings prevented the negotiation of such an agreement throughout the 1950s and early 1960s.[8] It was not until after the Cuban missile crisis in October 1962, which had a sobering effect on the superpowers, that the United States, Britain, and the Soviet Union finally agreed to a test ban—although even this was not a comprehensive one. The Limited Test Ban Treaty of August 1963 prohibited only nuclear test explosions conducted in the atmosphere, underwater, and in outer space. At that time, a complete ban on underground nuclear tests was considered by some to be unverifiable.

It would be another decade, during which other arms control initiatives were given priority, before additional agreement on banning testing could be reached. In July 1974, President Richard Nixon and Soviet General Secretary Leonid Brezhnev signed the Threshold Test Ban Treaty (TTBT), which proscribed all underground tests with yield above 150 kilotons (more than ten times the explosive yield of the Hiroshima bomb). In 1976, Brezhnev and President Gerald Ford signed a companion treaty banning peaceful nuclear explosions (PNET) of the same yield. But a CTBT remained elusive, especially after the Reagan administration took office in 1980 and pronounced that while a test ban was something that would ultimately be in the nation's interest, first the United States would pursue the completion of verification protocols to the TTBT and the PNET.

The balance between unilateralist and engagement forces began to shift with the changing geostrategic climate of the late 1980s and early 1990s, which culminated in the fall of the Berlin Wall and the end of the Cold War. As the U.S.-Soviet nuclear relationship changed dramatically, both sides unilaterally undertook significant cuts in nuclear weapons beyond those negotiated in the Strategic Arms Reduction Treaty (START I). In the context of these changing conditions, President George Bush announced in July 1992 that the United States would no longer conduct nuclear tests for the purpose of verifying new warhead designs. Unilateralist-leaning participants in the test ban debate had long regarded the ability to design and test new warheads to be a central reason for opposing a CTBT. But by 1992, a bipartisan congressional coalition led by Senator Mark Hatfield (Republican-Oregon) and Representative Michael Kopetski (Democrat-Oregon) had already introduced legislation calling for a U.S. testing moratorium. Senators George Mitchell (Democrat-Maine) and James Exon (Democrat-Nebraska) vigorously supported the measure, which became known as the Hatfield, Mitchell, Exon Amendment and passed in the Senate on September 13, 1992, by a vote of 68–32. It was attached to the Energy and Water Development

Appropriations Act, considered veto-proof legislation with the election not far away. It subsequently passed in the House of Representatives by a margin of 224–151 on September 24, and President Bush signed it into law on October 2, 1992. The amendment legislated a nine-month U.S. testing moratorium, placed strict conditions on any further U.S. testing, and required test ban negotiations to be completed before September 30, 1996.[9]

In July 1993, President Clinton announced that the United States would extend its testing moratorium and seek to negotiate a CTBT. The balance had firmly shifted in favor of the pro-CTBT and proengagement forces, albeit aided by significant advances in test ban monitoring capabilities.[10] Thus, in August, with U.S. support, the Geneva Conference on Disarmament (CD) established an Ad Hoc Committee on a Nuclear Test Ban with a mandate to negotiate the CTBT. Formal negotiations for a CTBT, which began in January 1994, were significantly aided by the U.S. decision, announced in January 1995, to extend once again its testing moratorium and to drop its insistence on the right to suspend the treaty temporarily after ten years in order to conduct a few tests, and by Washington's August 1995 decision to support a true zero-yield test ban. On June 28, 1996, at the end of the 1996 CD session, the chairman of the Ad Hoc Committee, Ambassador Jaap Ramaker of the Netherlands, tabled a compromise draft treaty text. President Clinton hailed this occasion as bringing "us one step closer to the day when no nuclear weapons are detonated anywhere on earth."[11] In early August, after consultations with the Ad Hoc Committee members, Ramaker asserted his belief that further negotiations on the draft treaty as a whole were unlikely to break an impasse that had developed. On August 16 the committee sent a report on the draft treaty to the CD, stating that no consensus could be reached either on the text of the treaty or on its formal conveyance to the CD due to irreconcilable differences among some of the parties to the negotiation. India, which wanted any treaty to include a time-bound framework for global nuclear disarmament, and Iran blocked consensus approval of the treaty within the CD. To overcome this obstacle, Australian Foreign Minister Alexander Downer on August 22 proposed a resolution seeking endorsement of the CTBT from the UN General Assembly and its opening for signature on the earliest possible date, a maneuver which India could not veto.

The UN General Assembly adopted the CTBT text on September 10, 1996, by a vote of 158 in favor, with 3 opposed (India, Bhutan, and Libya) and 5 abstentions (Cuba, Lebanon, Syria, Mauritius, and Tanzania). On September 24 President Clinton became the first world leader to sign the treaty, calling it the "the longest-sought, hardest-fought prize in the history of arms control."[12] The treaty requires each state party not to "carry out any nuclear weapon test explosion or any other nuclear explosion," thus prohibiting tests—including peaceful nuclear explosions—in any element (e.g., underground, underwater, in the atmosphere). The treaty establishes an extensive verification regime intended to ensure compliance by the states parties. The regime is designed to monitor seismic and other events worldwide, in order to detect nuclear explosions anywhere in the world and thus deter possible efforts to evade the ban on testing. The verification regime established by the treaty consists of an international monitoring system, with global networks of seismological, radionuclide, hydroacoustic, and infrasound sensors; on-site inspections; consultation and clarification provisions; and confidence-building measures involving voluntary data exchanges.

The CTBT is a treaty of indefinite duration, but its entry into force is conditioned upon ratification by all forty-four states listed in an annex as those states that were members of the CD at the conclusion of the negotiations and listed by the IAEA as states that possess nuclear reactors or other nuclear facilities, including such nations as North Korea, India, Pakistan, Israel, and the United States. This formula was agreed upon to ensure that the treaty could not enter into force until it was ratified by the five nuclear weapon states, the threshold states (India, Pakistan, and Israel), and states of proliferation concern (e.g., North Korea, Iran, Iraq). To date, 160 nations have signed the CTBT and 69 have ratified it, but only 41 of the required 44 have signed it (with India, Pakistan, and North Korea as the three holdouts), and only 30 of the 44 have ratified it.

Engagement Versus Unilateralism in the CTBT Context

The optimism that reigned immediately following the end of the Cold War had shifted the balance in favor of engagement strategies, making the negotiation of the CTBT possible in the early 1990s. By the end of the decade, however, the glow had begun to fade and a unilateralist streak had begun to emerge in the United States, similar in some respects to post–World War I isolationism. This development was exacerbated by the election results in 1994, which changed the ideologies as well as the political balance in both houses of Congress, and the rise of several avowed unilateralists to key Senate leadership positions. When it finally came time for the Senate to consider the CTBT in 1999, opponents cited a variety of issues. These included, among others, alleged difficulties in verifying compliance with a zero-yield test ban (particularly on the part of China, Russia, and the states of proliferation concern) and uncertainty about whether the United States could effectively maintain its nuclear deterrent without testing.

In short, the traditional unilateralist concerns about a test ban had reemerged. While such misgivings are serious issues that should be considered when addressing the merits of the test ban, the United States has accommodated these concerns in signing previous arms control agreements, including the LTBT, the Intermediate-Range Nuclear Forces (INF) Treaty, START I and II, and the CWC. Most of these concerns, moreover, could likely have been addressed by including carefully crafted conditions in the resolution of ratification, such as occurred in the case of the CWC. In fact, for many Senate opponents, the problems with the CTBT had less to do with any specific treaty provisions than with animosity toward the Clinton administration, partisan politics, and, most important, a preference for unilateralism rather than multilateral engagement in U.S. foreign policy.

The CTBT debate revealed the incompatibility of efforts to provide U.S. security exclusively through military and economic might, on the one hand, and efforts to preserve U.S. security through regimes based on mutual restraint, on the other. Some senators feared that the CTBT would someday "allow" states such as China and Russia to erase the U.S. advantage in nuclear weapons technology by hindering efforts to modernize and maintain the current stockpile and inhibiting the development of new nuclear weapons designed to meet new post–Cold War threats. This view ignores the fact that the United States is better prepared than any other nation to maintain its arsenal without testing and that the United States has already successfully modified one existing warhead package, the W-61, to provide it with earth-penetrating capabilities without conducting explosive nuclear tests. Nevertheless, unilateralist critics of the treaty have contended that the United States would be at a disadvantage under the CTBT since, as an open society, it could never cheat on a test ban, whereas other, less reputable treaty partners could and would. They were unconvinced by those who argued that U.S. security requires that it maintain a global nuclear test monitoring capability regardless of whether the CTBT ever enters into force and that the CTBT's verification regime significantly contributes to the United States' already impressive verification capabilities. Moreover, critics suggested, the benefits to the nonproliferation regime of bringing the test ban into force would be ephemeral and largely artificial, given the treaty's alleged lack of effective verification elements and enforcement provisions and the fact that nonnuclear weapons states are already prohibited under the NPT from acquiring (and by extension testing) such weapons.

In any case, some argued, the NPT would be better maintained by U.S. conventional and nuclear weapon threats than by a fuzzy "bargain" about disarmament. Supporters of this view contend that the U.S. policy of ambiguity with respect to the conditions under which the United States would use nuclear weapons deters potential adversaries from pursuing nuclear weapons and other weapons of mass destruction. They argue that this policy of "calculated ambiguity" undermines the utility of weapons of mass destruction by evoking fears of a massive U.S. retaliation with nuclear weapons in response to an attack with chemical or biological weapons (CBW) on the United States or one of its allies and thus provides a disincentive to proliferation. Unilateralists suggest that veiled threats to use nuclear weapons in response to a chemical weapon attack deterred the use of chemical weapons by Saddam Hussein during the Gulf War. We will likely never know if this is true, but revelations in memoirs by senior policymakers that the United States was bluffing and never had any intention of using nuclear weapons, even in response to a CBW attack, have ensured that "calculated ambiguity" probably will not be effective in the future. Rather, it is likely that such a bluff would be called, thereby placing pressure on the United States to actually use nuclear weapons, a potentially disastrous outcome.

Treaty critics also argued that the United States should not ratify the CTBT because of its indefinite duration. They argued that the Clinton administration, in light of the opinions of some scientists that the effectiveness of the science-based Stockpile Stewardship Program (which has been charged with maintaining the safety and reliability of the U.S. nuclear deterrent without testing) cannot be determined with certainty for at least ten years, should have negotiated a treaty of limited duration or should seek to amend the treaty to so limit its duration. This ignores two key factors, however. First, the CTBT as negotiated is the best the United States could have hoped to negotiate, and opening negotiations for amendments would certainly open the door to proposals that would pose problems for the United States. Indeed, as former Chairman of the Joint Chiefs of Staff General John Shalikashvili notes, "No U.S. opening position [at the treaty's negotiation] drew more fire from all directions than its 'ten-year, easy out' proposal. This would have allowed Parties to leave the Treaty after ten years without providing any justification."[13] If the United States sought to revisit the question of the treaty's duration, China would likely press again for an exemption for "peaceful nuclear explosions," India would likely seek to link the treaty to a time-bound framework for global nuclear disarmament, some countries would likely seek to weaken the treaty's on-site inspection (OSI) provisions, and others would probably try to eliminate data gathered through national technical means of verification as justification for an OSI request. None of these changes to the treaty would be in the U.S. interest.

Second, the CTBT, as with most contemporary arms control treaties, has a "supreme national interest clause" that would allow the United States to withdraw from the treaty should being party to it at some point no longer be in the interest of national security. And when the Clinton administration submitted the CTBT to the Senate for consideration, it included a list of safeguards under which U.S. adherence to a zero yield test ban would be conditioned. These included a requirement that the safety and reliability of the weapons in the nuclear stockpile be certified annually and that, if such certification cannot be made the president would be prepared to consider withdrawal from the treaty.[14]

Proponents of "security-through-engagement" strategies, on the other hand, argued that failure to bring the CTBT into force, coupled with renewed efforts by nuclear weapon states to modernize their arsenals, would reinforce in the minds of potential proliferators the value of nuclear weapons. In other words, as a former Indian defense minister noted, any country seeking to challenge the United States, or even simply to get a seat at the table, had "better get nuclear weapons." Advocates of the CTBT warned that rejecting the treaty could lead to the eventual disintegration of the NPT regime and the spread of nuclear weapons around the globe, an utterly nightmarish scenario for U.S. security interests. Such a development would render the conventional superiority of the United States irrelevant and impotent, with every conflict, no matter how small, running the risk of going nuclear. Moreover, with nuclear weapons so widespread, it would be nearly impossible to keep them out of the hands of terrorists.

International Reaction and the Cost to the NPT Regime

After a truncated debate, which included compressed versions of the aforementioned arguments, the composition of the Senate and the partisan nature of its debate conspired to ensure the success of the unilateralist camp in October 1999. As with any treaty ratification debate, there were varying degrees of opposition, opponents who had limited and addressable concerns, and members of the Senate who broke ranks with party leaders. A normal treaty ratification process involves lengthy preparations by proponents and consultation with opponents to determine ways to develop a proratification consensus, but with the CTBT this was not the case. In fact, immediately before the debate, sixty-two senators signed a letter to the majority and minority leaders requesting that the vote be put off to allow further consideration. The agreement scheduling a ratification vote stipulated that consensus would be required to delay a vote, but hard-core opponents refused to accept a delay. In the end fifty-one senators, many of whom would have rather seen further consideration of the treaty, voted against ratification in a largely party-line vote.

What have been the consequences of this momentous vote, and what is the likely impact of a prolonged inability by the United States to ratify the treaty? First and foremost, the CTBT cannot enter into force for any nation until the United States, as one of the required forty-four states, ratifies the treaty. Some nonnuclear weapon states might reasonably see U.S. rejection as an attempt to circumvent the U.S. commitment to conclude a CTBT by 1996 in return for the indefinite extension of the NPT. If, after a significant period, the CTBT is still not in force, some of the states that were reluctant to accept a permanent NPT—including countries not necessarily friendly to the United States—may decide to reconsider their commitment to the nonproliferation regime. After India and Pakistan conducted nuclear tests in May 1998, experts in Japan and other countries, for example, asserted that their own governments' commitments to the NPT had presumed a world with five nuclear weapon states, not seven, and that the treaty had also presupposed eventual global nuclear disarmament. Some experts suggested that if North Korea were to become the eighth nuclear power, Japan likely would very soon become the ninth, South Korea the tenth, Indonesia the eleventh, and so on. A chain reaction of withdrawals from the NPT would almost certainly cause the treaty to collapse. Should this occur, and should several additional states acquire nuclear weapons, Israel might see little reason to continue avoiding declaring itself a nuclear power. Such a step would, of course, eliminate any hope for successful nonproliferation efforts in the Middle East. In other words, failure to bring the CTBT into force would hasten precisely the nightmarish scenario the United States has long sought to avoid.

The tendency toward unilateralism will likely undermine U.S. ability to draw such nations as India, Pakistan, and Israel into the nuclear nonproliferation regime. Bringing the CTBT into force would, at the very least, hinder nations such as Iran, Iraq, and North Korea from developing all but the least sophisticated nuclear weapons, and it would prevent India, Pakistan, and Israel from further developing their arsenals. But until the United States itself has ratified the treaty, it will be very difficult to persuade these countries to do likewise. After all, how can Washington ask these nations to accept limitations on their actions if the United States is not prepared to accept those same limitations? As President Clinton noted on his return from India and Pakistan in early 2000, the United States has "lost all leverage" to persuade these countries to sign the CTBT as a result of the Senate's vote.[15] Unilateralists respond by noting that the decisions by India and Pakistan to test nuclear weapons had nothing to do with the United States and its policies, but rather on their specific security requirements. While this is in part true, bringing the CTBT into force would benefit these countries by limiting further development of advanced nuclear weapons by their rivals (be they China, India, Pakistan, or others). But the ability of the United States to argue the merits of the CTBT along these and other lines is significantly undermined by the fact that Washington's own refusal to ratify the treaty prevents its entry into force. And even though U.S. policies in some cases cannot directly convince a nation to act in a desired way, strengthening multilateral regimes such as the NPT and the CTBT can adjust that nation's security requirements and thus help convince it to subscribe to those regimes.

The U.S. rejection of the CTBT has also hindered international efforts to implement the strengthened safeguards associated with the NPT. By the terms of the 1995 Statement of Principles and Objectives, states parties agreed to strengthen the capacity of the IAEA to verify that nonnuclear weapons states are not diverting materials and resources from peaceful nuclear programs to nuclear weapons programs. The importance of enhancing the IAEA's verification capabilities had been underscored by revelations after the Gulf War that Iraq, despite its membership in the NPT regime, had advanced further than previously thought in its efforts to develop nuclear weapons, as well as by recurring problems involving North Korea. In response to these concerns, the IAEA developed an enhanced safeguards protocol, enabling the agency to use (among other things) environmental monitoring techniques to detect trace amounts of residue left behind during the enrichment of uranium and the manufacture of plutonium. For these safeguards to be implemented, states are required to sign and subsequently ratify an additional protocol to their IAEA safeguards agreements with the agency. To date, fewer than sixty nations have signed such a Protocol, and only eighteen such agreements have entered into force, thanks in part to the U.S. rejection of the CTBT. As the IAEA's director-general, Mohamed El Baradei, noted in June 2000, "The Senate vote against the ban on nuclear tests was a devastating blow to our efforts to gain acceptance of more intrusive inspections of nuclear facilities around the world."[16] Said another senior IAEA official, "Innovations like this require diplomatic momentum, and without the U.S. in the lead, momentum disappears."[17] In sum, U.S. unilateralism has eroded nations' confidence in Washington's leadership of the nuclear nonproliferation regime and, as a result, their confidence in the NPT regime itself.

National Missile Defense and the NPT Regime

Just as the consequences of the Senate's rejection of the CTBT demonstrate the cost of U.S. unilateralism to the nuclear nonproliferation regime, so too does the U.S. drive toward deployment of a national missile defense system. As with the CTBT, the debate surrounding whether the United States should deploy missile defenses is essentially a debate about whether or not the country can and should rely on international restraint regimes to protect its security. Proponents of NMD believe strongly that in the new post–Cold War era, the United States has the ability and responsibility to defend itself against newly emerging missile threats, even if at the expense of existing international commitments. Diplomatic considerations should not prevent the United States from utilizing its strength and technological capacity to defend itself. Opponents of NMD, in contrast, believe that the only truly effective defense against missile attack is a strong international nonproliferation regime, accompanied by an unquestioned will to retaliate if attacked. They contend that the linchpin of this regime is the international network of arms control treaties, a crucial element of which is the Antiballistic Missile (ABM) Treaty of 1972. Take away the ABM Treaty and deploy missile defenses, they argue, and the nonproliferation regime will begin to unravel.

Signed in 1972 during the first Strategic Arms Limitation Talks (SALT I), the ABM Treaty prohibits the deployment of national missile defenses by either the United States or the Soviet Union (now Russia) and limits each side to one ABM deployment site. The treaty was intended to stabilize nuclear deterrence between the superpowers, which was based on the doctrine of "mutually assured destruction" or MAD. The MAD concept depended upon the ability of each nation to respond to a first strike with a massive nuclear retaliation. This meant that both sides had to have so many deliverable nuclear warheads that enough would survive the enemy's initial attack to be able to retaliate in a manner that would incapacitate the enemy. Were one nation able to build a significantly larger arsenal than the other, gaining the capacity to destroy the opponent's retaliatory forces, such an attack would presumably become more likely.

Likewise, if both nations could build defenses against missile attacks, each would naturally attempt to build arsenals large enough to overwhelm the opponent's defense. This would lead to an unlimited arms race—an inherently unstable condition. Even worse, if only one nation could deploy an effective nationwide defense against a missile attack while the other could not, the defenseless state would be forced to build larger and larger arsenals to be assured a retaliatory capacity to overwhelm the defenses—again, an inherently unstable condition. Moreover, if one nation had an effective nationwide defense, it might be perceived as more inclined to initiate a first strike, with the expectation that the undefended opponent's remaining arsenal would be insufficient to penetrate the defensive shield—once again, a highly unstable situation. Both the United States and the Soviet Union determined that the absence of defenses was safer than any of these possible scenarios. In this manner, the ABM Treaty enhanced the national security of both countries. And by preserving U.S.-Soviet deterrence while allowing both sides the freedom to pursue reductions, it became the cornerstone of strategic arms limitation. Even after the Soviet Union disappeared the United States and Russia determined that, friendlier relations aside, the interests of mutual security demanded that the ABM Treaty be preserved.

The consensus in the United States on the need to maintain the ABM Treaty, while always shaky, began to erode seriously with the release in July 1998 of the Rumsfeld Report, which argued that "rogue" states such as Iran, Iraq, and North Korea might be able to threaten the United States with intercontinental ballistic missiles as early as 2005. Some unilateralists intensified arguments that the ABM Treaty is a Cold War relic that prevents the United States from defending itself against this new missile threat. They recommend that the United States withdraw from the treaty and deploy a missile shield—described as "limited"—to protect against such attack from states of proliferation concern. As Secretary of Defense–designate Donald Rumsfeld noted in his confirmation before the Senate Armed Services committee in January 2001, "The old deterrence of the Cold War era is imperfect for dissuading the threats of the 21st century." He went on to say, "Effective missile defense—not only homeland defense but also the ability to defend U.S. allies abroad and our friends—must be achieved in the most cost-effective manner that modern technology offers."[18] This sentiment—not to mention electoral considerations—was the motivation for Congress's overwhelming approval of the National Missile Defense Act of 1999, which declared it U.S. policy "to deploy as soon as is technologically possible an effective national missile defense system capable of defending the territory of the United States against limited ballistic missile attack."[19] This legislation, the so-called Cochran Bill, was a long-sought prize for congressional unilateralists.

International Reaction and Consequences for the NPT Regime

But the ABM Treaty has not lost its importance for strategic stability, and the consequences of NMD deployment are no less dangerous then they would have been during the Cold War. The former Soviet Union did pose a unique threat to the United States, but its dissolution did not eliminate the potential for a strategic situation that the ABM Treaty was designed to avoid. The danger of strategic instability, stemming from concern that a potential opponent with a massive nuclear arsenal might acquire a first-strike capability by building a nationwide NMD system, remains a valid concern today. As long as Russia continues to possess thousands of nuclear weapons and strategic delivery vehicles, it remains a unique partner in maintaining strategic stability. The mutual deterrence of the two superpower strategic arsenals, both of which still exist nearly ten years after the end of the Cold War, remains the essential object and purpose of the ABM Treaty.

For this reason, the willingness of the United States to consider, and the apparent growing consensus in some quarters to support, NMD deployment has prompted widespread and harsh criticism from both potential adversaries and longtime U.S. allies. A survey of statements from international leaders suggests that unilateral NMD deployment by the United States would have a dire impact on the nuclear nonproliferation regime. Perhaps even more than continued U.S. rejection of the CTBT, NMD deployment would threaten the disintegration of the international nuclear nonproliferation regime.

Russian Response

The Clinton administration's missile defense proposal and the more ambitious proposal put forth by the administration of George W. Bush in 2001 are inconsistent with the ABM Treaty as currently written. Absent Russian agreement on amendments to the treaty—which have made little headway in bilateral discussions—a U.S. decision to deploy the system would require abrogation or violation of the ABM Treaty, with deleterious effects on the nonproliferation regime. As Russian Foreign Minister Igor Ivanov noted in a recent *Foreign Affairs* article:

> With the ABM Treaty as its root, a system of international accords on arms control and disarmament sprang up in the past decades. . . . Inseparable

> from this process is the creation of global and regional regimes of nuclear nonproliferation. . . . These agreements, comprising the modern architecture of international security, rest on the ABM Treaty. If the foundation is destroyed, this interconnected system will collapse nullifying 30 years of efforts by the world community.[20]

This is an alarming sentiment. Russian concerns about NMD deployment are likely to have the greatest impact on the NPT regime, since the continued reduction of the U.S. and Russian nuclear arsenals is crucial to the long-term viability of nuclear nonproliferation efforts.

As noted above, the global nonproliferation regime rests on a central bargain: the commitment by the nuclear weapon states to eventually eliminate their nuclear arsenals in exchange for a pledge by the nonnuclear weapon states to foreswear the nuclear weapon option. Without demonstrable short-term progress toward reducing global nuclear arsenals, it will be difficult to maintain the NPT regime over the long term. By freezing—if not reversing—the significant progress made in reducing strategic nuclear arms since the end of the Cold War, NMD deployment could do irreparable harm to the NPT regime. If the ABM Treaty is abrogated or violated, Russia is likely to reevaluate its other arms control treaty obligations. As Ivanov notes, "In accordance with the statement made when START I was signed, Russia will regard the withdrawal of the United States from the ABM Treaty or the Treaty's substantial violation as an exceptional circumstance giving Russia the right to withdraw from START I."[21] As one of the conditions for passing START II in 2000, the Russian Duma added a provision to the resolution of ratification mandating that Russia will withdraw from this agreement if the United States withdraws from the ABM Treaty. Colonel General Vladimir Yakovlev, commander of Russian Strategic Missile Forces, has also noted that Russia might consider withdrawing from the INF Treaty: "Such a step is possible as [an element of] Moscow's asymmetrical answer to Washington's exit from the 1972 Anti-Ballistic Missile Treaty."[22]

Moscow's principal motivation for withdrawing from these treaties would not be to damage the nonproliferation regime—even though this would be an inevitable consequence—but rather to allow Russia to deploy multiple warheads on its missiles (currently prohibited under START II) to be able to overwhelm the U.S. NMD system if necessary. Russia would similarly be compelled to keep its forces on higher alert, a potentially disastrous scenario and the last thing the United States should want. One need only look at the high number of "near-misses" during and after the Cold War—including a much publicized incident in 1995 when Boris Yeltsin was minutes from launching a nuclear retaliation in response to a sounding rocket launched from Norway—for evidence of the danger of Russia keeping its forces on high alert.

Foreign Minister Ivanov further recognized the impact that U.S. NMD deployment and the Russian reaction would have on the NPT regime. "At the [2000 NPT Review Conference] held in New York this past spring," he noted, "many countries called for vigorous measures to cut nuclear weapons stockpiles as a necessary condition for strengthening the Treaty. Further nuclear arms reductions will not happen without the ABM Treaty, and thus the viability of the NPT itself would be threatened."[23] The United States, by seeking to provide for its security through the unilateral deployment of an NMD system, would be setting in motion a sequence of events that would likely wreck the nonproliferation regime. As with the fallout from the CTBT debacle, the prospect of unilateral U.S. NMD deployment can only cause the international community to question further U.S. leadership of the NPT regime. As Ambassador Gérard Errera, a senior French diplomat, noted in March 2000, "A combination of the continuing rejection of CTBT ratification and a unilateral abrogation of the ABM treaty would seriously put in jeopardy the whole edifice of non-proliferation and arms control. . . . Those who defend this logic [that the ABM Treaty is outdated and irrelevant] must also be prepared to hear some countries apply the same logic to all of international law, including, in the first place, for example the NPT."[24]

China and the South Asian Chain Reaction

The potential damage to the NPT regime that would result from NMD deployment is also doubly worrisome when one considers the likely Chinese response. On this issue China has taken a harder line than Russia. While Russia's strategic deterrent is not directly affected by the proposed NMD system, China's strategic deterrent, particularly vis-à-vis the United States, could be rendered impotent if a deployed NMD system functioned effectively. The proposed, "limited" NMD system is intended to offset an attack with as few as one or two dozen missiles by such "problem states" as North Korea, Iran, or Iraq. While Russia has thousands of intercontinental ballistic missiles (ICBMs) capable of reaching the United States, China reportedly has only twenty to twenty-four such missiles, just what the proposed NMD system is designed to counter. As a result, efforts to reassure China that the proposed NMD system is not intended to offset Beijing's deterrent have met with little success. U.S. intentions notwithstanding, China believes that it cannot ignore the practical impact of the proposed system.

Consequently, China is likely to take measures in response to a U.S. deployment of NMD that could have a significant, negative impact on the NPT regime. First, international security experts and some Chinese officials predict that Beijing may expand its arsenal of nuclear weapons and ICBMs capable of reaching the United States by a factor of ten, so as to overwhelm the proposed NMD system.[25] Thus, while China currently has fewer than 500 total nuclear weapons, and fewer than two dozen ICBMs capable of reaching the United States, NMD deployment could provoke China into deploying an additional 200 weapons capable of attacking the United States by 2015. As Ambassador Sha Zukang, director of the Chinese Foreign Ministry's

Department of Arms Control and Disarmament, noted in May 2000, "To defeat [U.S.] defenses we'll have to spend a lot of money, and we don't want to do this. But otherwise, the United States will feel it can attack anyone at any time, and that isn't tolerable. . . . We hope [the United States] will give this up. If not, we'll be ready."[26] Any increase in the Chinese nuclear arsenal would, of course, have a dangerous impact on the nuclear balance in South Asia. India, whose own nuclear weapon program is in part a response to China's, would undoubtedly feel compelled to respond to such a Chinese escalation by resuming nuclear testing and increasing its own arsenal, with predictable results in Pakistan.

In addition, to ensure a capacity to saturate any U.S. defensive system, China would likely accelerate its efforts to miniaturize its nuclear warheads in order to employ multiple warheads on its missiles or to utilize decoys and other countermeasures. This step may require a resumption of nuclear testing by China, especially if the United States has not ratified the CTBT, with serious implications for the NPT regime. Moreover, statements by Chinese officials make clear that if the United States proceeds with NMD, Beijing will be uncooperative in multi- and bilateral arms control forums, including NPT-related forums, which could mean such measures as the resumption of nuclear assistance to Pakistan and the provision of such assistance to Iran. China could also respond to NMD by aiding other states with their weapons programs by such steps as selling missile technology, which China has done in the past. China has also pointedly warned that the full array of space-based commercial and military support activities has no explicitly established legal foundation and that these activities would be highly objectionable in the context of the projected U.S. NMD program. Who can say where this might lead? Thus, as in the Russian case, the likely Chinese responses to unilateral U.S. deployment of a missile defense system could have a significant destabilizing effect on the international community and the global nonproliferation regime and severely damage U.S. security.

The Allies

Close U.S. allies, too, are concerned about the impact of NMD deployment, fearing that it could ultimately contribute to a breakdown of the nonproliferation regime in Europe and Asia. In both Europe and Asia, allies who rely on the U.S. nuclear umbrella could begin to worry about "decoupling" if they perceive that the United States has begun to separate its security from their own. Confidence in U.S. willingness to come to their defense in case of attack will be eroded. NMD deployment might be seen as placing European and Asian cities at greater risk of missile attack than cities in the United States.

While some NMD proponents suggest that this "decoupling" concern can be addressed by protecting U.S. allies with missile defense shields, some NATO allies, who view the ABM Treaty as a cornerstone of the NPT regime, are concerned that abrogating or violating the ABM Treaty would undermine nuclear nonproliferation and disarmament efforts. As one senior British official asked in the *Financial Times,* "What would [scrapping the ABM Treaty] do to missile control regimes, and what would its effect be on the third world?" He worried that deployment might disrupt efforts to get India and Pakistan into the NPT and the CTBT. Similarly, allies worry that NMD deployment could prompt renewed arms races involving the United States, Russia, and China, prompting Russia and China to build more nuclear weapons and ICBMs. Should this occur, the already small British and French nuclear deterrents would be seen as even smaller, forcing Britain and, particularly, France to seek larger nuclear deterrents as a hedge against U.S. unilateralism. This would also have a negative effect on the nonproliferation regime.

Conclusions and Implications

These concerns may not be enough for U.S. unilateralists, who tend to see a coalition of forces aligned against the United States and to view NMD and an ever-changing, modernized nuclear deterrent as critical to U.S. security. Those who advocate NMD and reject the CTBT are focused on current or imminent threats from a set of states that may seek to undermine U.S. global interests, including states of concern like Iran, Iraq, North Korea, and Libya but also longtime nuclear powers like China and Russia. For NMD proponents and CTBT critics, who regard the interests of such countries as inherently incompatible with those of the United States, multilateral arms control agreements (including the nonproliferation regime), bilateral undertakings to ease tensions, and similar engagement strategies are of limited utility, because they rely on (allegedly) untrustworthy totalitarian regimes to keep their word. For unilateralists the dangers of trusting miscreant states outweigh the benefits of engagement. Moreover, these threats make essential both NMD and new nuclear weapon designs, regardless of their impact on the NPT regime.

But, in the age of globalization and interdependence, no state is or can be made immune from international dangers. There is no such thing as absolute security, no matter how strong a nation's military or economy. Countries must be mindful of ripple affects resulting from their actions and of the possible unforeseen or unintended consequences of their behavior, particularly in the national security realm. After all, as French President Chirac noted in December 1999, "If you look at world history, ever since men began waging war, you will see that there's a permanent race between sword and shield. The sword always wins. The more improvements that are made to the shield, the more improvements are made to the sword. . . . [Missile defenses] are just going to spur sword makers to intensify their efforts."[27] The nuclear nonproliferation regime is intended in large part to encourage nations to forswear permanently the most dangerous sword imaginable, nuclear weapons. U.S. leadership will be crucial to the long-term success of international efforts to contain the spread of nuclear weapons. But the perception abroad that the United States is pursuing unilateral approaches to preserving its security at the expense of the nonproliferation regime likely could lead to the erosion of that regime over time.

The United States must at all times be attentive to the impact of domestic unilateralist trends and the resultant undermining of U.S. global leadership. Today, as a result of U.S. actions with respect to NMD and the CTBT, the path to strengthening international constraints on the spread of nuclear weapons has been diverted from the core mission of constraining proliferators to reinvigorating the traditional leadership of the United States in these efforts. Rather than leading the congregation, the preachers have been forced to reconvert the bishops. As Senator Byron Dorgan (Democrat-North Dakota) observed during the CTBT debate in the Senate, "This country ought to be a leader on this issue. Now we are being asked by our allies to please lead. We ought not have to be asked to provide leadership to stop the spread of nuclear weapons."[28] If other nations lose confidence in U.S. leadership, they probably will lose confidence in the nonproliferation regime. The ultimate costs of U.S. unilateralist approaches to national security, especially regarding the CTBT and NMD, may be the loss of the NPT regime, widespread nuclear proliferation, and a devastating degradation in U.S. security. Ironically, while some in the United States seek to exploit the nation's unprecedented and unparalleled strength to attain absolute U.S. invulnerability, the triumph of such efforts could drastically undermine national and global security.

Notes

1. Berger, "American Power: Hegemony, Isolationism or Engagement."

2. Kamen, "To Helms, Treaty Debate Comes Down to Monica," *Washington Post,* October 15, 1999.

3. Remarks by Senator James Inhofe, "Executive Session—Comprehensive Test Ban Treaty," *Congressional Record—Senate* (145 Cong. Rec. S 12257), vol. 145, no. 138, Friday, October 8, 1999.

4. On October 8, 1999, the *New York Times* printed as an op-ed the letter on CTBT ratification sent by Jacques Chirac, Tony Blair, and Gerhard Schroeder. Chirac, Blair and Schroeder, "A Treaty We All Need."

5. Remarks by Senator Jon Kyl on the CTBT, *Congressional Record—106th Congress,* p. S12284, October 8, 1999.

6. Albright, "Time to Renew Faith in the Nuclear Nonproliferation Treaty," *International Herald Tribune,* March 7, 2000.

7. The International Atomic Energy Agency in 1999 listed the "total number of States with significant nuclear activities" as seventy-one. See *International*

Atomic Energy Agency Annual Report, "Number of States Having Significant Nuclear Activities at the End of 1997, 1998 and 1999," Table A13.

8. In August 1957, motivated in part by public reaction to reports of the negative health effects of radioactive fallout from atmospheric nuclear tests, President Dwight Eisenhower proposed a two-year suspension of testing under certain conditions. These included a permanent cessation of fissionable material production and agreement to an inspection system to ensure compliance. The Soviet Union rejected the conditions, but announced instead the first unilateral moratorium on testing. President Eisenhower responded by proposing a meeting of technical experts to discuss issues related to verifying a test ban. A Conference of Experts met in July and August 1958, and issued a report indicating that adherence to a CTBT could be verified with a network of some 160–170 land-based monitoring stations. That fall, trilateral test ban negotiations began among the United States, the Soviet Union, and Great Britain, but concerns about the effectiveness of verification emerged, as studies were released by test ban opponents in the United States suggesting that countries could hide nuclear test explosions by testing in large caverns or otherwise masking their signal. The negotiations soon stalled. For a more detailed account of this, see Mendelsohn, *Arms Control and Disarmament: The U.S. Commitment,* pp. 45–52, and the Committee on International Security and Arms Control of the National Academy of Sciences, *Nuclear Arms Control Background and Issues,* pp. 187–223.

9. The Hatfield, Mitchell, Exon Amendment allowed for the conduct of five tests per year for three years for strictly limited purposes, after which the United States would be prohibited from testing pending the completion of a CTBT unless another nation tested.

10. Further evidence that the United States had adopted more engagement-oriented nonproliferation strategies can be found in the actions taken by the Clinton administration with regard to North Korea. These included the 1994 agreed framework whereby North Korea consented to freeze its nuclear weapon program in exchange for two proliferation resistant light water reactors and 500,000 tons of heavy fuel oil per year (pending completion of the two power reactors).

11. Clinton, Statement by the president on the Comprehensive Test Ban Treaty, June 28, 1996.

12. Clinton, Remarks by the president in address to the 51st General Assembly of the United Nations, September 24, 1996.

13. Shalikashvili, *Findings and Recommendations Concerning the Comprehensive Nuclear Test Ban Treaty,* p. 25.

14. LaVera, "History and Summary of the CTBT," p. 11.

15. Howard, "News Review," p. 61.

16. Drozdiak, "Missile Shield Eroding U.S. Arms Control Goals," *Washington Post,* June 15, 2000, p. A24.

17. Ibid.

18. Ferullo, "Rumsfeld Urges Missile Defense System During Confirmation Hearing," *CNN On-line,* January 11, 2001.

19. National Missile Defense Act of 1999, H.R.4, 106th Congress of the United States of America, 1st Session.

20. Ivanov, "The Missile-Defense Mistake: Undermining Strategic Stability and the ABM Treaty," p. 15.

21. Ibid., p. 16.

22. Reuters, "Russia May Retaliate on ABM."

23. Ivanov, "The Missile-Defense Mistake," p. 18.

24. Address of Ambassador Gérard Errera, political director, French Ministry of Foreign Affairs Carnegie International Non-Proliferation Conference, March 17, 2000, available on-line at *http://www.ceip.org/files/events/ErreraRemarks2000.asp?p=8*

25. Myers, "U.S. Missile Plan Could Reportedly Provoke China," *New York Times,* August 10, 2000.

26. *New York Times,* May 11, 2000, "China Says U.S. Missile Shield Could Force an Arms Buildup."

27. Whitney, "Chirac Tries to Reassure Annoyed Americans," *International Herald Tribune,* December 18, 1999, p. 5.

28. Remark by Senator Byron Dorgan on the Comprehensive Test Ban Treaty, *Congressional Record—Senate* (Cong. Rec. S 12329), vol. 145, no. 137, p. S12329.

10

The Chemical Weapons Convention

Amy E. Smithson

ON APRIL 29, 1997, THE MAJORITY OF THE WORLD'S NATIONS ACTIVATED AN arms control and nonproliferation accord that aims to compel the gradual elimination of one of the most abhorred classes of weapons. The Chemical Weapons Convention (CWC) outlaws the development, acquisition, production, transfer, and stockpiling of poison gas. The culmination of over two decades of multilateral negotiations, the CWC is generally regarded as the most significant agreement to stem the proliferation of weapons of mass destruction since the 1970 Nuclear Non-Proliferation Treaty (NPT). Moreover, the CWC's path-breaking monitoring provisions are considered to be a model for a proposed verification protocol to an accord banning another category of weapons of mass destruction, the 1972 Biological and Toxin Weapons Convention (BWC).

The long-awaited CWC, alongside the NPT and the BWC, was the final jewel in the triple crown of treaties banning weapons of mass destruction. Unlike the NPT, which bestows upon a small group of nuclear powers the right to possess the very weapon banned elsewhere, the CWC requires all joiners to rid themselves of any chemical weapons and any facilities dedicated to their production.[1] The principle of equality and nondiscrimination among all CWC members encouraged fairly widespread adherence to the CWC in its infancy. Whereas the NPT had seventy members within eighteen months of its activation, the CWC had slightly fewer than 120 members at the same one-and-a-half-year mark.[2]

Although the CWC resembles the BWC in establishing identical guidelines for all participating nations, the CWC contains far more rigorous verification provisions, including a panoply of monitoring tools. Crafted at a time when treaty monitoring was accomplished by satellite instead of onsite inspection, the BWC lacks inspection requirements.[3] Although more than 140 nations have joined the BWC, in part because the treaty places no taxing verification requirements upon them, the absence of monitoring provisions has made the BWC easy prey for violators. Indeed, the Soviet

Union and Iraq flagrantly violated the accord,[4] prompting ongoing negotiations begun in 1995 to strengthen that convention.

Because the CWC contains attractive features wanting in its two sister accords, it is ostensibly well positioned for long-term success in the international arena. Nevertheless, the CWC's launch did not proceed as smoothly as many observers had expected. As this chapter argues, the principal source of weakness in the convention regime has been the shortsighted behavior of the U.S. government.

This chapter begins by providing some background to the treaty. The discussion then moves to how the United States, after signing the CWC in mid-January 1993, left the treaty virtually untended for several years, escaping national embarrassment only through a last-minute ratification just four days before the treaty's entry into force at the end of April 1997. Moreover, the United States took steps to dilute the convention by including in both the ratification and implementing legislation certain exemptions that excluded U.S. sites from the very verification rules that U.S. negotiators had proposed and demanded be included in the treaty.

As this chapter will reveal, Washington's treatment of the CWC has had much less to do with a particular conception of U.S. national interests than with political expediency and the absence of high-level U.S. government oversight of implementation of the treaty. The U.S. government has gone farther off course by failing to meet a major CWC obligation for three years, an error compounded by misguided U.S. conduct during inspections of U.S. military facilities. The chapter concludes with observations about the consequences of U.S. behavior and the lessons that might be learned from the CWC experience regarding the United States and multilateral arrangements generally.

The Main Tenets of the Chemical Weapons Convention

The CWC requires the destruction of chemical weapons production facilities and arsenals over a ten-year period running from 1997 to 2007.[5] The implementation of this treaty is a monumentally difficult undertaking because of the vast number of facilities worldwide where chemical weapons might be manufactured covertly. The commercial chemical industry produces, processes, and consumes enormous quantities of chemicals for countless legitimate products, ranging from fertilizers and pesticides to pharmaceuticals and ballpoint pen ink. These very chemicals could conceivably be diverted to poison gas factories, which made it necessary for the CWC's architects to arm the treaty's inspectorate with strong monitoring tools.

Throughout the treaty's negotiation, the United States was one of the strongest champions of a ban on chemical weapons. In 1984, vice-president

George Bush traveled to the Geneva Conference on Disarmament (CD) to table a draft treaty text that stunned the international community with its scope and intrusiveness. Not only did the United States support a monitoring approach that would routinely reach into the private sector in a breadth and depth not previously attempted for arms control purposes, but Washington also proposed that any treaty member that suspected another participating state of violating the ban could launch a challenge inspection at any time, at any place.[6] In the years after Bush's proposal, U.S. officials consistently extolled the CWC as the centerpiece of international efforts to reduce the chemical weapons threat, prodding and cajoling other countries to conclude an agreement.

Doing so was no small feat, since the CD is a consensus negotiating forum fraught with the conflicting agendas embraced by major powers and alliances. For most of the twenty-four-year talks, the Warsaw Pact countries faced off against the industrialized nations of Western Europe, Australia, Japan, and North America. The other main negotiating bloc was the Group of 21 neutral and nonaligned developing nations (with such members as Iran, Pakistan, Mexico, Brazil), which pushed for the dissolution of export controls on chemicals. Two major global events in the early 1990s spurred the negotiating endgame, namely the collapse of the Soviet Union and the Gulf War. The animosities that had handicapped the negotiations dissolved with the former, and the determination of Western nations to clinch a deal was reinvigorated with the latter. A compromise text tabled early in 1992 deftly set the stage for a final text that eventually met with the approval of states from every corner of the globe.[7]

During the talks, U.S. negotiators succeeded in equipping the inspectors with certain rights that would enable them to conduct their duties without undue interference from displeased government officials or facility managers. Thus, inspectors have the right to review documentation related to the industrial and military facilities and activities that states are to declare, to observe declared areas of the facility, to interview facility personnel, and to request that photographs be taken. Should the inspectors find factual evidence inconsistent with the activities and capabilities that states declare, or should host officials be unable to clarify sufficiently other ambiguities uncovered during the inspection, the inspectors have the right of "unimpeded access" and can use more intrusive tools, such as sampling, to determine whether chemical agents are being produced on site and whether controlled chemicals are being diverted elsewhere. Host officials may object to any request that the inspectors make but are required to allow inspectors to monitor alternative records, facility areas, or activities to demonstrate treaty compliance.[8] While facilities and governments have the right to protect information not related to treaty compliance, they are obligated to cooperate with the inspectors, who have diplomatic status. The inspectors' notebooks and approved inspection equipment are considered inviolable.[9]

That the U.S. chemical industry supported such an intrusive approach, which would require companies to declare above-threshold production, consumption, or processing of specified chemicals at risk of proliferation and to open their doors to international inspectors, took many by surprise. Never before had an industry volunteered for such regulation, but in this instance the private sector took a proactive stance. The Chemical Manufacturers Association,[10] then the leading trade organization for the U.S. chemical industry, teamed with its counterparts in Europe, Japan, Canada, and Australia to help the negotiators figure out how to create an international watchdog against chemical weapons production without placing sensitive business information at undue risk. The U.S. industry even proffered facilities so that proposed inspection procedures could be tested, and pitched in to help the negotiators fine-tune the format for declaration of industry activities. Through participation in the treaty's negotiation and implementation, the industry sought to distinguish its own legitimate commercial activities from the odious business of making poison gas.[11]

By instituting routine inspections that occur with some frequency in participating states, the CWC has the potential over the long term to redefine how states ensure their national security. In return for declaring and submitting to inspection certain activities that were previously considered state secrets or private business endeavors, nations can get data from the CWC's inspectorate that helps to assure them that other participating states do not harbor stockpiles of this type of weaponry. So, the CWC gives governments reason to be confident that managed transparency—a limited waiver of state sovereignty—can enhance national and international security. Throughout the marathon negotiations the U.S. government was one of many espousing this approach.

By the end of the year 2000, the CWC had just over 140 members, including nine states that declared and opened chemical weapons programs to international inspection. The treaty enjoys fairly solid support in all geographical areas of the globe, and it includes Russia, Iran, and China as well as odd bedfellows like India and Pakistan. The number of countries of proliferation concern that have refused to join is relatively small, namely Egypt, Iraq, Israel, Libya, North Korea, Syria, Taiwan, and Vietnam. In accordance with the CWC's automatic trade sanctions, these holdouts are being pressed to accede to the treaty by being denied access to key industrial chemicals that can foster offensive weapons programs.[12]

As of November 15, 2000, the CWC's inspection agency, the Technical Secretariat (based in The Hague), had completed 868 inspections at 416 sites in 44 countries. More than 60 former chemical weapons production facilities had been mothballed and were being destroyed, and inspectors had inventoried the chemical munitions at 34 storage sites in preparation for their destruction. The United States, India, and South Korea have destruction programs under way, but Russia, the world's largest chemical weapons possessor, has been unable to launch a destruction program because of its financial difficulties. In all, more than 230 inspections have taken place at commercial industry facilities, notably without incident.[13] By these yardsticks, the CWC would appear to be well on its way to the strong disarmament and nonproliferation regime that was the articulated goal of U.S. negotiators. Yet, as the year 2000 ended, the treaty had yet to come close to its potential and, indeed, teetered on the brink of becoming a hollow exercise largely because of the poor behavior of the United States.

Missed Opportunities for Leadership

President Bill Clinton had ample opportunity to address the chemical weapons threat and to animate support for the CWC during his first term. Even though Clinton's interest in foreign policy was known to be modest and sporadic, several factors contributed to the presumption that the president would be able to secure with relative ease the Senate's advice and consent to ratification of the CWC. First, Congress had mandated in 1985 that the U.S. chemical arsenal be unilaterally destroyed, and the army began to do so in 1991. The CWC would prompt other chemical weapons possessors to follow suit, reducing the likelihood that U.S. troops would encounter chemical weapons in the future. Second, the Senate had always made the verifiability of an arms control treaty a crucial litmus test for ratifying it. On these grounds the CWC's prospects seemed good, since most of the CWC's rigorous verification measures had been crafted by officials of the Reagan administration, perceived as notorious sticklers for tough verification. Last, the CWC carried the strong endorsement of four important constituencies: the intelligence community, the U.S. chemical industry, the general public, and the Pentagon, including the Joint Chiefs of Staff.[14]

Instead of mobilizing his cabinet to lead this powerful coalition in a concerted push for treaty ratification, however, President Clinton rarely spoke about the CWC in his first years in office. Rather, the White House appeared to take it for granted that the Senate would appreciate the CWC's attributes.[15] This oversight became costly during the waning moments of the 1996 presidential election campaign, when contenders Clinton and former Senate Majority Leader Robert Dole chose to play politics with the CWC. On September 11, 1996, Dole penned a letter to his former legislative colleagues advising them to beware of "illusory" arms control deals. Dole's letter was trumpeted by treaty opponents. Therein he argued that the CWC was not "effectively verifiable and genuinely global" and pledged that, if elected, he would secure a treaty that "really does the job instead of making promises of enhanced security which will not be achieved."[16] Already, Senate Majority Leader Trent Lott (Republican-Mississippi) had begun to question publicly the treaty's lack of universality. On September 9, 1996,

Lott told reporters that he was concerned that Iraq, Libya, North Korea, and Syria had not joined the CWC.[17] Aware that the election would be won on domestic issues and enjoying a comfortable lead in the polls, Clinton chose not to wage an all-out fight on behalf of a little-known arms control treaty. The White House quietly retreated and withdrew the CWC from legislative consideration.[18]

Early in his second term, Clinton had no choice but to mount an eleventh-hour ratification campaign to secure Senate approval of the CWC, lest the treaty enter into force without the United States. The clock had begun ticking on October 31, 1996, with the deposit of the sixty-fifth instrument of ratification (by Hungary); the CWC would enter into force automatically 180 days later, or on April 29, 1997.[19] Even at this late date, however, Clinton's effort seemed little more than an exercise in damage control, an effort to avert a significant blemish on his administration's reputation, both domestically and internationally. Having allowed the treaty's opponents to set the terms of the debate, however, the White House had to fight an uphill battle to secure CWC ratification.

The treaty's opponents were a small but extremely vocal band of anti–arms control stalwarts, catalyzed by a Washington-based organization called the Center for Security Policy. Beginning in 1996, this conservative think tank started papering the Hill with policy briefs blasting tirades against the treaty, which it characterized as "fatally flawed."[20] The center's director, former Reagan Pentagon official Frank Gaffney, recruited a number of prominent CWC critics, who were headlined by former secretaries of defense Caspar Weinberger, James Schlesinger, and Donald Rumsfeld.[21] The opponents argued that the CWC would not be universal, was not verifiable, would impose an intolerable burden upon U.S. businesses, would require the United States to relinquish defense secrets, would lull the nation into a false sense of security, and would infringe upon the rights enshrined in the Fourth and Fifth Amendments to the Constitution (respectively, guarantees against unlawful searches and seizures and against self-incrimination). By harping on the fact that several key suspected proliferators had not signed the accord, and by interpreting select passages of the treaty in a negative light (and in isolation from the rest of the text), the CWC's critics made it seem as though the treaty had dangerous, gaping loopholes.[22] Some of those who spoke out against the treaty were apparently unfamiliar with the treaty's specifics and may merely have been propounding a conservative party line.[23]

One by one, the critics' arguments were all refuted by the chemical industry and by an array of individuals advocating ratification, including former Secretary of State James Baker, former Director of Central Intelligence John Deutch, Gulf War commander General Norman Schwarzkopf, and an impressive list of distinguished military commanders headed by former Chairman of the Joint Chiefs of Staff General Colin Powell.[24] Beyond Washington's Beltway, public opinion and editorials ran heavily in favor of

CWC ratification. Scientific, veterans, and religious groups also rallied around the treaty. An independent poll of 1,000 adults by Wirthlin Worldwide and the Mellman Group, Inc., showed that 84 percent of Americans supported the CWC.[25] Up on Capitol Hill, Senator Richard Lugar (Republican-Indiana), the Senate's leading arms control expert, led a vote-by-vote battle for the treaty's approval.

Among the most powerful arguments negating the critics' case were strong statements by the chemical industry's declaring its willingness to accept the treaty's "reasonable" monitoring burdens. In addition to testifying in favor of the treaty, a coalition of chemical industry organizations placed a pro-CWC advertisement in the Hill newspaper *Roll Call* on April 14, 1997. Sporting buttons that said "Stand by the Ban!" and "It's the Right Thing to Do," chemical industry lobbyists and representatives from member companies met frequently with senators and staffers. The Chemical Manufacturers Association also carried out letter writing and telephone campaigns and issued press releases.[26]

Moreover, advocates reassured legislators that the treaty would not compromise U.S. defense capabilities or alliance commitments, pointing out that the CWC granted the U.S. government the flexibility to provide any treaty member threatened by chemical weapons attack with whatever type of assistance the United States desired. In addition, treaty proponents underscored that the CWC mandated that inspections be conducted in accordance with constitutional provisions.[27] Even though the traditional Republican constituencies of industry, the military, and the intelligence community supported the CWC, protreaty votes were still very difficult to secure.

Within the Republican Party, consideration of the CWC fostered something of an "identity crisis." Although President Ronald Reagan and President George Bush were the CWC's principal U.S. designers, a significant wing of the party repudiated the treaty in the 1990s. Therefore, the CWC was tinder for a confrontation between two groups of Republicans seeking to define the party's post–Cold War approach to defense and foreign policy, a struggle pitting conservative isolationists and unilateralists against more moderate internationalists. One school of Republican thought held that the CWC created a misleading sense of security and that stronger defense, not multilateral arms control accords, was the best way to safeguard the country. Proengagement Republicans, by contrast, believed that U.S. security interests would be best served by activating the CWC, even with its imperfections. According to this second viewpoint, vigilant implementation of the CWC would reduce chemical weapons arsenals, retard the proliferation of these weapons, and reinforce international standards of civilized behavior. Given these dynamics and the rhetoric employed by the isolationist wing of the party, the CWC debate was in important respects more of an ideological struggle about Republican foreign policy than a real referendum on the treaty itself.

During the weeks before the final vote, many Senate Republicans appeared to be looking for a way out of their quandary. Majority Leader Lott and a group of ten to fifteen Republican colleagues remained noncommittal as the floor debate on the treaty began on April 23, 1997. During the second hour of the proceedings, Senator John McCain (Republican-Arizona) interrupted his colleagues to inform them that their standard bearer of the previous year, Bob Dole, was about to execute an about-face on the CWC, throwing his support behind ratification.[28] Dole's reversal altered the political landscape and set the stage for final concessions that both the Clinton administration and Senate conservatives could support. The Senate approved the CWC by a final vote of seventy-four to twenty-six on April 24, 1997—just five days before the activation deadline.[29]

Undercutting Full and Proper Implementation of the CWC

Unfortunately, in drafting the very laws that would ratify and implement the treaty, Congress and the Clinton administration began to make a mockery of the CWC's multilateral underpinnings, establishing a different set of rules for the United States. Hidden in the fine print of these laws were exemptions to the CWC's landmark monitoring regime. The most damaging of these directly contradicts the explicit obligations that Washington undertook in ratifying the CWC by allowing a U.S. president to refuse a challenge inspection on the grounds that it "may pose a threat" to U.S. security interests. A second exemption specifies that no samples collected during an inspection be permitted to leave U.S. territory for analysis. A third exemption narrows the number of industry facilities that are obliged to declare activities involving mixtures or solutions that contain chemicals that pose a proliferation risk.[30]

Such exemptions, if emulated by other nations, would effectively allow potential violators to block challenge inspections, deny inspectors permission to send chemical samples abroad for detailed analysis at independent laboratories, and decrease considerably the number of industry facilities worldwide that are declared and subsequently opened to routine inspection. Even as evidence materialized that these exemptions were damaging the treaty's viability, the Clinton administration downplayed their possible negative consequences.

For example, administration officials claimed that the national security exemption was simply boilerplate language that would protect U.S. interests in the event that frivolous challenges were requested. Alternatively, administration officials contended that this exemption was harmless because it would never be activated. Both were weak justifications, however. The CWC already directs nations not to abuse the privilege of challenge inspections and lays out the penalties for any state launching a frivolous inspection.[31] Likewise, even if this "boilerplate" exemption is never used to deny a challenge, it invites replication and therefore could severely handicap the ability of the inspectorate to catch cheaters.

As for the sampling exemption, the Clinton administration proposed that the U.S. government purchase one or more Pentagon-designed mobile laboratories and donate these to the CWC's inspectorate for use in sample analysis in the United States and in other countries. Such a laboratory, however, is not on the inspectorate's currently approved list of equipment, nor is a mobile laboratory ever likely to be approved for use—even if one were donated.[32] Moreover, the analysis of U.S. samples from such a laboratory would not be recognized internationally because the Pentagon's mobile laboratory would not have accreditation from the CWC's inspectorate. Other governments would be likely to question the impartiality of U.S. analytical results of a U.S. sample, just as U.S. authorities would surely question test results in the event that a suspected cheater conducted sample analysis in its own laboratories. Conversely, if the mobile laboratory were flown overseas, CWC members could justifiably refuse the use of unapproved inspection equipment. Given these circumstances, the Clinton administration's proposed solution for mitigating the effects of the laboratory sampling exemption was no solution at all.

With regard to the U.S. exemption narrowing the scope of industry declarations, it should be recalled that both Russia and Iraq masked their weapons programs within chemical industry sites. Although some observers suspected that the U.S. chemical industry was behind this exemption, this was certainly not the case.[33] As with each of the other exemptions, this one unfortunately received the nod from the White House. If duplicated, this exemption also threatens to undermine U.S. national security because it will shrink the pool of industry facilities to which inspectors have routine access overseas.

As if these exemptions were not bad enough, the U.S. government also dallied for more than three years before submitting a required declaration of its industry facilities, shirking a central treaty obligation. All members were to submit initial declarations of industry activity by the end of May 1997, but it was not until December 1999 that the U.S. government issued regulations outlining U.S. industry responsibilities under the CWC. This gaffe was due partly to failure to pass the treaty's implementing legislation and partly to an interagency squabble about which executive branch agency would oversee the treaty's activities. This neglect set an example that other countries were content to follow. As of September 8, 1998, twenty-nine of the CWC's members had yet to provide the CWC's inspectorate with an initial declaration. Some eighty-two members had filed declarations, although many of these were incomplete or inaccurate.[34] Since the United States has such a huge chemical industry, Italy, China, France, and Germany were among the governments that threatened to suspend industry inspections on their territory until the United States was fully compliant. This pressure-cooker atmosphere was eased when the United States finally submitted its declaration in early May 2000.

When the CWC's international inspector corps made its initial forays into the field in June and July of 1997, among their first stops were chemical weapons storage and production facilities in the United States.[35] Given the experience that the U.S. government had amassed in a variety of bilateral and multilateral inspection activities since the 1980s, the inspectorate's personnel expected their U.S. counterparts to be tough and meticulous, but professional, in their observance of inspection procedures. For their part, U.S. officials appeared to assume they would be able to teach the rookie CWC inspectors a lesson or two. As in other countries, the inspectors and their hosts engaged in a certain amount of mutual testing. The mood hovering over the U.S. inspections, however, was more intense and combative than it was elsewhere. In a telltale sign of this mindset, some officials at the On-Site Inspection Agency apparently referred to their procedures for escorting the Technical Secretariat's inspectors during the first inspections as "rules of engagement," a term of art normally used for encounters with the enemy on the battlefield.[36] In hindsight, both the inspectors and their U.S. hosts conceded that they made some mistakes, and the United States exhibited more cooperative behavior on some subsequent inspections.[37]

Nonetheless, a few more significant and recurring disputes overshadowed early inspections of U.S. military facilities. One disagreement involved the tagging of munitions.[38] From a verification perspective, the CWC recognizes multiple purposes for tagging. First, CWC inspectors have the right to tag munitions to denote ones that are to be sampled to confirm their contents—for example, to see whether a bomb is filled with mustard or sarin gas. Samples of actual munition contents need to be taken randomly because the outside markings on a munition, while a reasonably reliable indicator of munition fill, could be easily altered should a country attempt to cheat by substituting munitions with identical markings and benign contents and hiding some of its real weapons.[39] Second, the CWC inspectors have the right to tag items for other important verification purposes, namely to assist them with the monitoring of weapons inventories over time and through the end point of destruction.[40] Hence, the inspectors sought to tag a sufficient number of items to reliably confirm the U.S. stockpile declaration and the subsequent destruction process, some of which they may opt to sample. The United States, however, argued that the number of rounds to be tagged should be kept to a minimum due to the cost implications of sampling.[41]

The CWC inspectorate and U.S. officials subsequently reached a gentleman's compromise,[42] but the United States essentially held to a position of "trust Uncle Sam, the green-striped ones are mustard gas." Ironically,

U.S. officials asked the CWC inspectors to abandon the philosophy that has guided U.S. inspection activities since the 1980s, former President Ronald Reagan's dictum of "trust, but verify."[43] According to this verification philosophy, U.S. officials adamantly declined to accept a color stripe or other exterior markings on the outside of Soviet munitions as proof of identification during the inspections under the INF Treaty. Instead, U.S. officials insisted on the use of specialized measurement equipment to certify the exact dimensions of missile stages as the standard of verification.[44]

In the case of the CWC, U.S. officials also refused to allow the inspectors to weigh 1-ton containers filled with chemical agent, even though the army weighs these modified commercial containers during its routine stockpile surety checks.[45] Privately, U.S. officials conceded that the real problem was that not all of these containers were filled to the same level and that some evaporation had occurred over time as a result of routine maintenance activities. Weighing the 1-ton containers would therefore reveal inaccuracies in the U.S. declaration, which was based on the nominal, not the actual, fill of these containers. By arguing that the actual weight should not be a key point of verification, however, U.S. officials again deserted their trust-but-verify philosophy and left the Technical Secretariat to try to verify the amount of agent in the containers by ultrasonic measurement and calculation. For verification purposes this approach is insufficient.[46] Given the hard line that the United States has traditionally taken when assessing other countries' arms control compliance,[47] it is hard to believe that U.S. policymakers would find it acceptable if other nations were to insist that inspectors retire after obtaining only a rough estimate of the amount of chemical agent in their bulk containers.

Although the frequency and intensity of disagreements between the inspectors and their U.S. escorts declined, the atmosphere surrounding the inspections in the United States remained tense. Said one individual extremely familiar with the situation, "Every single request that the inspectors make is questioned, disputed. It is as though [U.S. officials] are treating every inspection like it was a challenge inspection."[48] A foreign diplomat described U.S. officials as having "mind sets that are clouded with a confrontational approach, perhaps a legacy of the early bilateral inspections with the USSR, wherein every inspection is treated as a zero-sum game."[49] In other words, the U.S. government has yet to adapt to a multilateral inspection regime and to the transparency and reciprocity that such a regime implies.

In some regards, the U.S. behavior is baffling to those unfamiliar with inside-the-Beltway politics. After all, U.S. military and civilian leaders have forsworn future use of chemical weapons, including for retaliatory purposes.[50] Whether or not the United States participates in the CWC, the U.S. Army is required by law to destroy the U.S. chemical arsenal. Outsiders would therefore tend to think that the United States has nothing to hide, but its behavior has led some countries to question U.S. intentions.

The origins of the uncooperative U.S. behavior during inspections appear to stem from two primary sources. Individuals in the Pentagon with policy oversight of CWC implementation, including key civilian staffers who garnered reputations as fierce anti–arms controllers during the Reagan years, constitute the first source of trouble. The second source of problems was the Clinton White House, which ignored the CWC from the outset and could not be bothered to police how well or how poorly the Pentagon was implementing its obligations. When these two dynamics are taken together, U.S. behavior is less baffling than it is disappointing. Relatively low-level Pentagon officials were able to sabotage the CWC's implementation without any personal consequences or corrective action being taken because neither the cabinet nor the NSC was paying much attention.

The Consequences of U.S. Neglect
and the Lessons to Be Learned from It

At the time that the CWC came into force, the United States had the only operational chemical weapons destruction program and possessed numerous military facilities to be inspected. Accordingly, other nations had an opportunity to observe the way that the U.S. government treated the inspectors before inspection teams arrived on their soil. Whether intentionally or not, the United States initiated a domino effect of uncooperative behavior during CWC inspections. Two other chemical weapons possessors, Russia and South Korea, recited virtually word for word the U.S. reasons for curtailing tagging, sampling, and analysis of their munitions. Similarly, India balked at the use of weighing equipment.[51] If this trend is not reversed, it will degrade verification effectiveness over the long term.

More fundamentally, other CWC members will simply not allow the United States to create for itself a separate and less rigorous verification regime. Foreign governments took note of all three U.S. exemptions, and some countries initiated steps to duplicate them. India, for example, inserted a provision in its implementing legislation that prohibits samples from being taken out of the country. Russian lawmakers have similar legislation on the shelf. When the subject of the U.S. exemptions is broached with Chinese and Japanese diplomats, they strain to hide their grins and state that if their countries are challenged, they will surely follow the U.S. example.[52] Unless the United States moves promptly to preserve the integrity of the CWC's verification regime, it will be largely responsible for sabotaging the international community's principal chemical weapons threat reduction mechanism. To date, therefore, the U.S. experience with the CWC speaks volumes about Washington's proclivity for snubbing the rule of international law when some policymakers deem it desirable or convenient to do so.

Washington's behavior has had several other drawbacks. To wit, the treaty's governing bodies have approved policies detrimental to the CWC's long-term vitality, in part because of the diminished status of the U.S. delegation in these forums. U.S. representatives were ill positioned to protect the CWC's integrity throughout the late 1990s, when the United States was in violation of the accord for not declaring its chemical industry. Moreover, Washington has been paralyzed in the CWC context, unable to demand full treaty compliance from other countries given the U.S. exemption from challenge inspections. No challenge inspections have been conducted under the CWC partly because other governments are waiting for U.S. leadership in confronting and punishing possible cheaters.

Washington's unilateral behavior under the CWC is inconsistent with past U.S. willingness to confront serious international security problems through concerted international action. For instance, Washington led the effort to build the coalition that fought the Gulf War and subsequently gave vigorous support to the efforts of the UN Special Commission to oversee the elimination of Iraq's capabilities to build weapons of mass destruction. The United States cannot by itself stamp out chemical weapons proliferation abroad, nor can it be the sole enforcer of the CWC's prohibitions.

The not so benign U.S. neglect of the CWC has also undermined other important U.S. foreign, defense, and nonproliferation policy objectives. For example, there has been a noticeable spillover into the negotiations to add a verification protocol to the BWC. Monitoring the BWC will be a wildly demanding task, one that makes the CWC's intricate verification provisions look simple by comparison. Without U.S. leadership in the Ad Hoc Group of the Conference on Disarmament in Geneva, the negotiations on the BWC protocol have fallen behind schedule. Countries participating in these negotiations have observed the difficulties hampering the CWC and have begun quietly questioning the merits of establishing another verification regime of that intrusiveness and complexity. In a broader context, the frequent statements of U.S. officials celebrating the United States as the principal global champion of nonproliferation are viewed increasingly as empty rhetoric, since the behavior to back up such statements has been absent.

Despite its multilateralist rhetoric, the Clinton administration never threw its full weight behind the CWC, launching a tardy campaign to get the CWC ratified and implementing the accord in lackluster fashion. Instead of attempting to persuade Congress and the public of the wisdom of proactive engagement in multilateral nonproliferation efforts, the administration allowed a serious foreign policy and international security accord to become fodder for political gamesmanship between the United States' two major political parties and the victim of lip service by an incumbent administration. The CWC underscores the desirability of isolating such treaties from presidential politics and other Washington in-fighting. Otherwise, the United States runs the twin risks of continuing to alienate its allies, on the one hand, and, on the other, of enticing proliferators to build arsenals in the face of inconsistent U.S. support for treaty regimes.

Long before the United States emerged from the Cold War as the sole superpower, the international community perceived it to have special stewardship responsibilities toward the CWC because the United States was home to the world's second largest chemical weapons stockpile and the largest commercial chemical industry. Friends of the CWC hope that the United States will regain its prior form as a steadfast advocate of the treaty in both word and deed. Foes of the CWC stand ready to contribute to the treaty's downfall should Washington not redeem itself as a full and equal partner in this multilateral endeavor.

Notes

1. The nations that joined the NPT as nuclear weapons possessors were the Soviet Union, the United States, China, Britain, and France. For the negotiating history and text of the NPT, see *Arms Control and Disarmament Agreements,* pp. 65–87.

2. The eighteen-month benchmark for the NPT is September 5, 1971. A running tally of the CWC's membership can be found at *http://www.stimson.org* or at *http://www.opcw.org*

3. See *Arms Control and Disarmament Agreements,* pp. 95–104.

4. Just after signing the BWC, the Soviet Union embarked upon a massive biological weapons research, development, testing, and production program that is described in detail in Alibek with Handelman, *Biohazard,* or (more briefly) in Rimmington, "From Military to Industrial Complex?" Iraq's violation of the BWC was uncovered by inspectors of the UN Special Commission, which diligently pursued the matter in the aftermath of the Gulf War. Descriptions of the Iraqi program are contained in Smith, "Iraq's Drive for a Biological Arsenal"; Zilinskas, "Iraq's Biological Weapons: The Past as Future?" See also UN Security Council, *Report by the Secretary-General on the Activities of the Special Commission.*

5. Article IV and article V, Convention on the Prohibition of the Development, Production, Stockpiling and Use of Chemical Weapons and Their Destruction.

6. See Conference on Disarmament, Document 500. At the last minute, the Bush administration got cold feet and tabled less stringent language, only to be held to their original proposal by other nations that wanted a strong accord. On the vacillation, see Smithson, "Chemical Inspectors."

7. For more detail, including a momentary weakening of the U.S. negotiating position on challenge inspections, see Smithson, "Chemical Inspectors," pp. 22–25; "Tottering Toward a Treaty," pp. 9–11, and "Chemical Weapons: The End of the Beginning," pp. 36–40.

8. Chemical Weapons Convention, Verification Annex, Part II, paragraph 27, 40, 45–58.

9. Ibid., paragraphs 11(d), 23, and 62, and Confidentiality Annex, paragraph 17. The inspectorate keeps all inspectors' notebooks securely for a year after an inspection, at which point they are destroyed.

10. In mid-2000, the Chemical Manufacturers Association changed its name to the American Chemistry Council.

11. See Carpenter, "How Industry Came to Support the CWC," and Perroy, "The Contribution of the Chemical Industry," pp. 48–50 and 38–39, respectively; Olson, "Disarmament and the Chemical Industry," pp. 97–106.

12. As of May 2000, CWC members were prohibited from trading in what are known as schedule 2 chemicals with states that had not joined the CWC. Schedule 2 chemicals are a step or two removed from being chemical warfare agents and are not that widely traded. Schedule 3 chemicals, which are used much more frequently within the industry, are expected to be added to the automatic export control list after the CWC's fifth anniversary. Chemical Weapons Convention, Verification Annex, Part VII, paragraph 31-2 and Part VII, paragraph 26-7.

13. Data on the number and type of inspections provided by the Technical Secretariat of the Organization for the Prohibition of Chemical Weapons, November 15, 2000. More complete statistics can be found in *OPCW Annual Report 1999* (The Hague: Organization for the Prohibition of Chemical Weapons, 2000). For more on the difficulties of Russia's destruction program, see Chemical Weapon Destruction in Russia. The progress of the U.S. destruction program, which has eliminated over 21 percent of the original tonnage of its chemical stockpile, can be tracked at *http:// www-pmcd.apgea.army.mil/*

14. On the congressional mandate to destroy the U.S. arsenal, see Public Law 99-145, Title XIV, Part B, Section 1412 (50 USC 1521), November 8, 1985 (Department of Defense Authorization Act, 1986), which mandated the destruction of all unitary weapons in the U.S. stockpile of lethal chemical agents and munitions by September 1994. The United States began full-scale operations at its first destruction facility, on Johnston Atoll, in August 1993, and its second, at Tooele, Utah, in August 1996. On the setting for a successful treaty ratification campaign, with case studies, see Krepon and Caldwell, eds., *The Politics of Treaty Ratification.*

15. For the tale of how the Clinton administration allowed the treaty to languish, see Smithson, "Dateline Washington: Clinton Fumbles the CWC," pp. 169–182.

16. Bob Dole, Letter to Trent Lott, September 11, 1996.

17. "Secret Senate Session Likely on Chemical Arms Pact," Reuters, September 10, 1996.

18. Secretary of State Warren Christopher called Lott to ask that the CWC be withdrawn. See Lott's remarks, April 24, 1997, *Congressional Record,* 105th Congress, 1st sess. S3601. Also, Lippman, "Senate Foes Force Delay," *Washington Post,* September 13, 1996.

19. See article XXI, Chemical Weapons Convention.

20. See, for example, the Center for Security Policy decision briefs "Why the Senate Must *Not* Approve the Chemical Weapons Convention;" "How Can the 'World's Greatest Deliberative Body' Deliberate on the C.W.C. Unless the Administration Answers the Mail?" "What the World Does *Not* Need Is Any More of Clinton's Non-Proliferation *Non*-Achievements;" "Republicans' Senate Leadership Offers Constructive Alternative to Fatally Flawed Chemical Weapons Convention." The Heritage Foundation also opposed the CWC. See Spring, "The Chemical Weapons Convention: A Bad Deal for America," Committee Brief no. 25 (April 15, 1996) and "Ratifying the Chemical Weapons Convention: American Business Will Pay the Price."

21. This trio, Weinberger, Schlesinger, and Rumsfeld, made their views known in "No to the Chemical Arms Treaty," *Washington Post,* March 5, 1997.

22. Among other places, these arguments are presented in Senate testimony and documents. See, for example, *Chemical Weapons Convention,* Hearings before the Committee on Foreign Relations, U.S. Senate; *Military Implications of the Chemical Weapons Convention (CWC),* Hearings Before the Committee on Armed Services, US Senate; *The Chemical Weapons Convention,* U.S. Senate.

23. For example, when Weinberger presented a letter listing over fifty former Reagan and Bush administration officials who opposed the CWC to the Senate Arms Control Observer Group on September 9, 1996, he admonished the group,

chaired by Ted Stevens (Republican-Alaska) to pay heed the advice of the Pentagon and refuse to ratify the CWC. Senator Carl Levin (Democrat-Michigan) rejoined that indeed the senators were listening to the Defense Department, which had counseled in favor of ratification. Eyewitnesses to this exchange noted that Weinberger appeared to be caught totally off guard by the fact that the Pentagon had advocated ratification. Personal conversations with Senate staffers (September 9, 1996; September 10, 1996).

24. See "Lugar Criticizes Anti-Chemical Weapons Treaty Campaign;" Zumwalt, Jr., "A Needless Risk for US Troops," *Washington Post,* January 6, 1997; Scowcroft and Deutch, "End the Chemical Weapons Business," *Washington Post,* February 11, 1997; Baker III, "Our Best Defense," *New York Times,* February 16, 1997; Lippman, "White House Has Rally for Weapons Ban," *Washington Post,* April 5, 1997; Admiral Stanley R. Arthur (USN, Ret.) et al., letter to William J. Clinton, April 3, 1997.

25. Burns, "Poll Backs Chemical Weapons Ban," *Associated Press,* February 28, 1997. For a list of the organizations supporting and opposing the CWC, see *http://www.stimson.org/cwc/supportr/htm*

26. For example, Frederick L. Webber, letter to Trent Lot, June 24, 1996; Frederick L. Webber et al., letter to Trent Lott, August 26, 1996; Frederick L. Webber et al., letter to Trent Lott, April 15, 1997; Frederick L. Webber, Letter to Trent Lott, April 18, 1997. See also Chemical Manufacturers Association and the Business Executives for National Security, "Making Americans Safer," (pamphlet). Webber, "To Stop Poison Gas Attacks," *Washington Post,* April 14, 1995.

27. "The CWC Critics' Case Against Articles X and XI: Nonsense" (issue brief) and "The Chemical Weapons Convention, Constitutionality, and Unwarranted Fears" (issue brief).

28. Statement of Bob Dole on the Chemical Weapons Convention, April 23, 1997. See also, Clines, "Dole No Senator, but Might as Well Be," *New York Times,* April 24, 1997; Horowitz et al., "Winners & Losers."

29. April 24, 1997, *Congressional Record,* 105th Congress, 1st session, S3651. See also S3603, S3616, S3623, S3626, and S3596-3606 for votes on key amendments. See Dewar, "Senate Approves Chemical Arms Pact," *Washington Post,* April 25, 1997; Bill Clinton, Letter to Trent Lott, April 24, 1997. Earlier, to get a vote on the treaty scheduled, the Clinton administration acceded to a long-standing demand of Senator Jesse Helms to reshape the State Department, abolishing or consolidating three of its semi-autonomous agencies. Friedman, "The Big Deal of The Day," *New York Times,* March 27, 1997; Lippman and Baker, "Bipartisanship, but at a Price," *Washington Post,* April 25, 1997.

30. In the Senate's draft of the CWC's implementing legislation, these exemptions were contained in sections 307, 304(f)(1), and 402(a)(2). Almost identical language was in the bill drafted by the House of Representatives, H.R. 2709 in sections 237, 234(f), and 252(a)(2). The origins of the exemption prohibiting the sample analysis outside U.S. territory are in condition number 18 of the Senate's Resolution of Ratification, S.Exec.Res. 75, which the Senate passed on April 24, 1997. On October 20, 1998, the U.S. House of Representatives voted 333-95 in favor of passage of the omnibus spending bill that included the CWC implementation provisions, referred to by the short title "The Chemical Weapons Convention Implementation Act of 1998." The next day, the Senate also passed H.R. 4328 by a margin of 65–29. President Clinton signed the bill into law on October 21, 1998. See Public Law 105-277.

31. Chemical Weapons Convention, article XI, paragraphs 9, 22, and 23.

32. The CWC is governed on a day-to-day basis by a forty-one-member executive council, which would have to give initial approval to the addition of a major

new piece of analytical equipment, such as a mobile laboratory. Final decisions would be taken by the CWC's entire membership, the Conference of State Parties. Numerous countries were ill at ease about having the inspectors carry modern analytical equipment and insisted on "dumbing down" such equipment. These countries are likely to object strenuously to a proposal that the Technical Secretariat field a sophisticated, U.S.-equipped mobile laboratory.

33. The author spent a considerable amount of time in the company of industry representatives during the period when the Senate was considering the CWC and the treaty's implementing legislation was being drafted. She never heard such a request made, nor could she find any industry representative who knew of such a request being made. This exemption originated within the staffs of Senators Jesse Helms and Jon Kyl.

34. Among those holding back declarations at that point was Iran. "Major Breakthroughs at Eleventh Session" (press release).

35. The inspectors had five months of training under their belts, but little real-world experience in the conduct of inspections. The inspectors' training incorporated two-and-a-half weeks of on-site training at chemical facilities. China, Finland, France, Germany, India, Italy, The Netherlands, Rumania, Russia, the Slovak Republic, and Britain hosted training courses. Gee, "Implementing the CWC," p. 6. U.S. chemical weapons storage facilities are at eight different locations in the continental United States. For locations and quantities and types of weapons stored there, see *http://www-pmcd.apgea.army.mil*

36. For instance, during one early inspection, the inspectors found themselves unable to operate some electronic equipment because they brought the wrong adapter instead of the standard one for U.S. electric currents. So captious were the U.S. personnel that they refused to lend the inspectors an adapter or allow them to purchase one at a nearby store, stating that borrowed or newly purchased adapters was not equipment officially approved for CWC inspections. In another display of determination to adhere to the exact letter of the inspection procedures, U.S. officials turned back equipment at the outset of an inspection, the point of entry, because they had received advance notice of a name change for an item. The article in question was the tape used to seal the inspectors' equipment to prevent unauthorized access to it. In the inspection mandate that U.S. officials were sent, the Technical Secretariat listed this item as frangible, fractural, adhesive seals, as it is described on the approved equipment list. On the inspection equipment sealed with this tape, however, the Technical Secretariat marked the seals simply as tamperproof. This technicality—the difference in names—became the U.S. justification for rejecting the equipment sealed with this tape.

37. The United States has lent inspection teams equipment that it had pledged to allow the Technical Secretariat to purchase, but now refuses to provide.

38. Tags are tamperproof markers that allow for the undisputed identification of items of military equipment controlled by an arms control treaty. For more information, see Fetter and Garwin, "Tags," pp. 139–154.

39. Chemical Weapons Convention, Verification Annex, part IV (A), paragraphs 49 and 67. The United States has requested that the inspectors take samples just prior to the destruction of weapons, not in the storage bunker or magazine.

40. The inspectors "shall employ, as appropriate, agreed seals, markers, or other inventory control procedures to facilitate an accurate inventory of chemical weapons prior to destruction." Convention Weapons Convention, Verification Annex, part IV (A), paragraph 62. See also, paragraphs 66-7 of part IV (A).

41. Note that sampling and analysis is an expensive and time-consuming process that requires safety precautions and could delay destruction schedules. Evidently

disregarding the inventory control function of tags and assuming that every munition tagged will be sampled, U.S. officials suggested that the inspectors tag only two munitions per storage magazine.

42. The agreement was that three munitions per magazine would be tagged if U.S. officials stated that the magazine holds munitions filled with only one chemical agent. However, in storage magazines that contained rounds with two different agent fills, U.S. officials still insisted that only three munitions be tagged even though the circumstances instead merit tagging of at least six.

43. At the signing of the Intermediate-Range Nuclear Forces (INF) Treaty on December 8, 1987, President Reagan made the following statement: "But the importance of [the INF Treaty] transcends numbers. We have listened to the wisdom in an old Russian maxim. And I'm sure you're familiar with it, Mr. General Secretary, though my pronunciation may give you difficulty. The maxim is: *Dovorey no provorey*—trust, but verify." From "Remarks on Signing the Treaty," p. 1458. Interestingly enough, "trust, but verify" was the On-Site Inspection Agency's motto until 1993, when it was changed to "trust and verify."

44. At the Votkinsk missile production facility, the United States installed a large machine to X-ray two tiny perimeter slices of exiting railcar canisters to ascertain that they did not contain an SS-20 missile first stage either directly or within the shell of an SS-25 missile stage. Rueckert, *Global Double Zero*, p. 157. See also, "Votkinsk Portal Monitoring System: System Description," Sandia National Laboratories; Harahan, *On-Site Inspections Under the INF Treaty*, pp. 74–78, 83–87; "Bechtel's Cargoscan to Support INF Verification," p. 35. In addition, the United States had the right under the treaty to request periodically that missile canisters be opened, whereupon a piece of equipment called the stage-measuring device was maneuvered into the canister to measure the circumference of the missile stage. The United States insisted that this device have measurement capabilities because exterior markings were not reliable identifiers of an SS-20 missile stage. While visiting Sandia National Laboratories in 1988, the author personally handled this unwieldy piece of equipment, which Sandia personnel were evaluating.

45. When interacting with CWC inspectors, U.S. officials claimed to be wary of health and safety concerns stemming from a possible accident during the weighing process. However, according to an army spokesperson, the ton containers employed at U.S. chemical weapons storage facilities are the same as those used to transport and store a variety of commercially available chemicals (e.g., chlorine). Although this official stated that the U.S. Army does not weigh its ton containers as part of its routine maintenance procedures, U.S. storage facilities do maintain specialized equipment on site, such as cranes and scales, to accommodate requests for weight measurements, should such a need arise. Information provided on September 1, 1998, by Cathy DeWeese, U.S. Army, Edgewood Chemical Activity. Other former U.S. officials familiar with the Chemical Corps' handling of ton containers have been present when these containers were weighed during the 1990s. Interviews with the author, August 13, 1998, August 31, 1998; and September 1, 1998.

46. The ultrasonic sensor may give incorrect readings if the agent inside the container has thickened or crystallized, or has air pockets. A nation attempting to cheat on the CWC could spoof such indirect monitoring methods by removing some of the agents inside bulk containers and diluting the remaining agent with water. In this scenario, a photon-induced neutron spectrometer would still detect the presence of agent inside the container but would be unable to discern whether the agent is concentrated or diluted. Ideally, the Technical Secretariat can employ several monitoring tools in conjunction with each other to safeguard against diversion of agent from bulk containers. Therefore, it is important that the inspectors be able to weigh ton containers at a storage facility at least randomly, if not comprehensively.

47. A prime example where U.S. allegations of noncompliance were adamant was the 1979 outbreak of anthrax in the Soviet city of Sverdlovsk (present-day Yekaterinburg). The U.S. government asserted that the epidemic was caused by a leak from a covert biological weapons production facility, but the Soviets attributed the sixty-four deaths to contaminated meat. Few other nations took issue with the Soviet cover story, which was proved false in 1992 when Russian President Boris Yeltsin conceded that the Soviet Union and Russia had maintained an active biological weapons program in violation of the Biological and Toxin Weapons Convention. Yeltsin's admission was originally given to the Russian newspaper *Komsomolskaya Pravda* and subsequently reported by R. Jeffrey Smith. Smith, "Yeltsin Blames '79 Anthrax on Germ Warfare Efforts," *Washington Post,* June 16, 1992, p. A1. The U.S. charges of noncompliance can be found in the annual arms control compliance reports, which the government began to send to Congress in 1984. For an epidemiological study that concurs with the U.S. government's conclusions about the military origins of this disease outbreak, see Meselson et al., "The Sverdlovsk Anthrax Outbreak," pp. 1202–1208.

48. Interview with author, August 12, 1998.

49. Author's interview with a foreign diplomat, August 27, 1998. Another individual summarized the circumstances with a bit of humor: "The U.S. escorts are so inflexible that they have to call Washington to get permission to put a different topping on the pizza." Interview with the author, August 14, 1998.

50. In the aftermath of the Gulf War, President George Bush revised U.S. policy in May 1991 to state that the United States would "formally [forswear] the use of chemical weapons for any reason, including retaliation against any state, effective when the [Chemical Weapons] Convention enters into force." General John Shalikashvili, then chairman of the Joint Chiefs of Staff, testified that the U.S. military's ability to deter chemical attacks on U.S. troops would be rooted not in a chemical retaliatory capability, but in "robust chemical weapons defense and the ability to rapidly bring to bear superior and overwhelming military force." U.S. Senate Committee on Armed Services, *Military Implications;* U.S. Senate Committee on Foreign Relations, *Chemical Weapons Convention Hearings.*

51. Although one cannot rule out the possibility that India learned of the U.S. behavior by some other means, India was on the executive council and Indian officials therefore saw the U.S. facility agreement, which states that only boxes of munitions (not ton containers) can be weighed.

52. Chowdhury, "Bill to Restrict Arms Inspection," *The Statesman,* May 8, 2000, Internet download. Officials from other countries have told the author in personal conversations that they would copy the U.S. exemptions as the needs arose, but not necessarily put them in writing.

11

The United States as "Deadbeat"? U.S. Policy and the UN Financial Crisis

Margaret P. Karns and Karen A. Mingst

THE ESTABLISHMENT OF THE UNITED NATIONS IN THE CLOSING DAYS OF World War II was an expression of the desire of war-weary nations, led by the United States, for a new global organization that might promote international security and foster the social and economic conditions necessary for peace. More than half a century later, following decolonization, a tripling in the number of member states, the end of the Cold War, and the transformation of the global economy, the UN endures as the world community's central institution. The UN provides member states with essential global public goods, a universal forum to address transnational problems, and a venue to set international norms and standards.

Since the end of the Cold War, the international community has relied more than ever on the UN to deal with ethnic conflicts, failing states, complex humanitarian disasters, human rights concerns, and democratic transitions. The complex UN system is actively engaged in efforts to address a wide range of transnational problems—such as economic inequality, environmental degradation, drug trafficking, AIDS, population growth, and terrorism—that mark a world of accelerating globalization and rising interdependence. Global conferences, convened to address many of these issues, have helped to spur the development of global civil society by facilitating the growth and networking of international NGOs. Yet, the UN has been marginalized in the governance of global economic relations, taking a backseat to the IMF, the World Bank, the G-8, and other actors.

As a set of institutions that has grown up over more than fifty years, the UN has suffered from chronic shortages of resources and is in need of substantial reform. Today, both the Security Council and the Economic and Social Council need to be changed to reflect the enlarged membership. Many of the UN's programs and agencies need systematic review, elimination, or restructuring to reduce redundancy, politicization, and waste. The reform agenda also includes the need for greater transparency of operations, enhanced coordination (especially among specialized agencies), and overhaul of staffing and management practices. Finally, the UN's chronic funding problems need to be addressed. The last reform of the UN Charter took place in 1971, more than three decades ago. In 1997, Secretary-General Kofi Annan launched a series of well-regarded management reforms. But, much remains to be done to improve the use of scarce resources, the professionalism of UN staff members, and coordination among multiple departments, agencies, and programs with overlapping mandates.

Despite the critical role the UN plays in addressing issues of interdependence and threats to peace and security, the U.S. commitment to the world body has fluctuated significantly. Washington has shown little vision in strengthening the UN or U.S. leadership within the institution. The United States has tried periodically to use its power as the UN's leading financial contributor to secure reforms that enhance U.S. control over the organization, but it has seldom advocated reforms that would strengthen the UN's capacity or the legitimacy of its key organs. Indeed, U.S. actions over the past decade have weakened the UN even as the world body has become increasingly indispensable. This failure of leadership is most apparent in the realm of UN financing. By withholding contributions since the 1980s, continually escalating demands for UN administrative and budgetary reform, and attempting unilaterally to reduce assessed U.S. contributions, Washington has exacerbated the UN's financial crisis and eroded its own credibility.

We begin this chapter with a brief overview of the fluctuating relationship between the United States and the UN. We note that although the United States has often used the UN as a valuable tool of U.S. foreign policy, Washington has sometimes regarded the UN as a hostile place where others push issues antithetical to U.S. interests. We then turn to the fractious issue of UN financing, which has become a bellwether for the overall U.S.-UN relationship and is central both to the UN's own future and the effectiveness of U.S. leadership within the organization. We trace the erosion of the U.S. treatment of UN dues as a legal obligation and examine the increasing tendency of Congress to use financing issues to micromanage UN reform efforts. Seeking to account for this behavior, we argue that although strong liberal and idealist traditions have drawn the United States to support the UN, the nation's power, domestic politics, and "exceptionalist" traditions—as well as politics within the UN itself—have encouraged U.S. ambivalence and skepticism about the UN's value. Assessing the consequences of U.S. unilateralism, we conclude that Washington's policy has undermined both U.S. national interests and the health of the world body. We close by calling for a new vision to guide U.S. leadership and interests in multilateralism through the UN in the twenty-first century.

Evolution of the U.S.-UN Relationship

The UN is in many respects a U.S. creation. In 1945, the United States, supported by the Allied powers and a number of smaller states, provided both vision and resources for the UN's development. The U.S. vision was rooted in the country's tradition of idealism and historic sense of its own exceptionalism. The idea of a universal organization for peace and security was first articulated by President Woodrow Wilson at the end of World War I, in the proposal for the League of Nations. Franklin D. Roosevelt subsequently adapted Wilson's ideas in his design for a new system of international security to follow World War II. The blueprints for a United Nations Organization that emerged from negotiations at Dumbarton Oaks and San Francisco in 1944–1945 bore the stamp of U.S. postwar planners.

During the Cold War, the UN was marginalized from dealing with most threats to international peace and security. Yet, whenever possible, the United States sought to use the UN and its agencies as instruments of its national policies. The UN proved particularly useful in providing collective legitimation for the U.S.-led response to North Korea's invasion of South Korea in 1950 and for the censure of Soviet aggression against Hungary (in 1956) and Afghanistan (in 1979). Likewise, the invention of "peacekeeping" provided a useful means to deal with certain regional conflicts. The United States also valued the activities of UN specialized agencies such as the IMF, the World Bank, WHO, and IAEA.

The membership increases that accompanied decolonization, however, made it more difficult for the United States to use the UN as an instrument of U.S. policy and, consequently, made Washington less interested in strengthening the capacities of the world body. Developing countries' interests frequently diverged from those of the United States. As shown in Figure 11.1, the frequency with which the United States voted with the majority of states in the General Assembly dropped steadily over time. In the 1970s, third-world demands for a new international economic order (NIEO) and the politicization of issues like apartheid in South Africa, Palestinian rights, and the Arab-Israeli conflict put the United States in a defensive and often isolated position. These acrimonious conflicts led the U.S. ambassador to the UN, Daniel Patrick Moynihan, to label the UN a "hostile place."

U.S. support for the UN eroded further in response to efforts to promote international regulation of transnational corporations; attacks on market capitalism; statist approaches to economic development; the creation of new UN organs; and mounting evidence of bloated, biased, and inefficient secretariats in such agencies as the WHO, the Food and Agriculture Organization (FAO), and the United Nations Educational, Scientific and Cultural Organization (UNESCO). The United States withdrew from the International Labor Organization (ILO) in 1978 and from UNESCO in 1983. Washington opposed many UN-sponsored development programs and committed resources only selectively and intermittently to others. This growing U.S. skepticism reached its apogee in the early 1980s, when the Reagan administration's antipathy toward multilateral institutions helped create a sense of crisis for the UN system. Washington's alienation from the UN is borne out in the further steep drop in 1981 in U.S. voting with the majorities in the General Assembly (see Figure 11.1). The same trend was evident in the Security Council, where the United States, having vetoed no resolutions from 1946 to 1965, vetoed forty-six between 1966 and 1985, with thirty-four of these vetoes cast between 1976 and 1985.

U.S. antipathy to the United Nations moderated somewhat during the second term of the Reagan administration—even as Congress began unilaterally cutting U.S. financial contributions to the organization. Changes in Soviet policy under Mikhail Gorbachev created new opportunities for UN peacekeepers to help settle regional conflicts in Namibia, Central America, Afghanistan, and the Iran-Iraq war. Subsequently, the Persian Gulf crisis in 1990–1991 appeared to mark "a turning point in the U.S.-UN relationship."[1] The UN's successes in handling new peacekeeping challenges and the enforcement action in the Persian Gulf, made possible by the post-Cold War cooperation of the five permanent members of the Security Council, generated widespread optimism about an expanding UN role in the new post–Cold War era. Indicative of this trend was the fact that between 1991 and 1998, the five members cast only six vetoes (three by the United States).

Figure 11.1   United States Voting Trends in the UN General Assembly

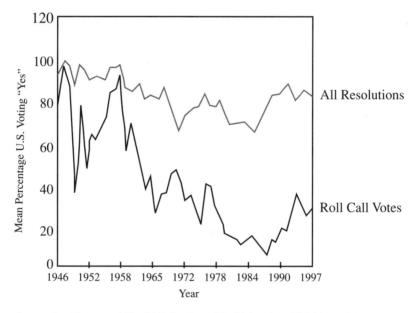

Source: Jon Monger and Harold K. Jacobson, The University of Michigan; data courtesy of the Inter-University Consortium for Political and Social Research, Ann Arbor, Michigan.

The 1990s found the UN in greater demand than ever to deal with international peace and security—as well as with issues like environmental protection, sustainable development, population growth, humanitarian disasters, human rights, and a seemingly ever-widening array of other transnational problems. The number of UN peacekeeping operations soon doubled, and a series of UN-organized global conferences generated ambitious plans of action for addressing issues generated by growing interdependence. At the request of the Security Council, Secretary-General Boutros Boutros-Ghali drafted a document, *An Agenda for Peace*, setting forth an ambitious blueprint for an enlarged UN role in the post–Cold War World. The Bush administration applauded this expansive vision, terming it an "extremely valuable contribution to the consideration—and actual construction—of the United Nations' future role in international security."[2] In 1993 the Clinton Administration articulated a foreign policy of "assertive multilateralism," designed to share responsibilities for global peace with other countries by working through an invigorated UN.

On closer examination, however, the U.S.-UN relationship was much more complex and fragile than the reassuring public rhetoric suggested. U.S. voting with the majority on roll call votes in the General Assembly reached its lowest point ever in 1990 (10 percent) and improved only modestly in succeeding years (Figure 11.1). The record on all resolutions, reflecting the large number approved by consensus, is much more positive, but still shows a downward trend through 1990, followed by an upward one. In contrast to its rhetoric about a "new world order" based on a stronger UN, the Bush administration demonstrated its own willingness to "go it alone" on a number of issues, for instance by refusing to become a party to the Convention on the Rights of the Child.

By 1995, moreover, the early post–Cold War optimism in the United States about the UN had waned substantially, as the problems of peacekeeping operations in Somalia, Rwanda, and Bosnia overshadowed successes elsewhere. In May 1994, PDD 25 outlined a more circumspect view of UN peacekeeping and U.S. participation.[3] For the United States, the benefits of peacekeeping now seemed lower and the costs and risks higher than they had been during the Cold War. This shift coincided directly with the first use of U.S troops in UN operations. Washington's willingness to "go it alone" was also evident in other U.S. actions during the 1990s, such as the unilateral effort to deny Boutros-Ghali a second term as UN Secretary-General in 1996, Washington's refusal to sign the Land Mines Treaty in 1997 and the Statute of the International Criminal Court (ICC) in 1998, the Senate's rejection of the Comprehensive Test Ban Treaty in 1999, and the country's growing reliance on unilateral sanctions to deal with a broad array of foreign policy problems.[4] The ambivalent multilateralism of the 1990s seems especially curious in retrospect, since the United States' own principles of democracy, human rights, and free markets had become widely accepted norms incorporated into UN agendas and programs.

U.S. ambivalence toward the UN was nowhere more visible than in the deepening U.S. financial debt to the world organization. The pattern of U.S. withholding of UN dues, which had begun in the mid-1980s, was never fully resolved. Indeed, Congress became increasingly resistant to meeting U.S. financial obligations, especially after the 1994 elections, when a Republican majority in the Congress faced off against a Democratic president. As partisanship joined with ambivalence, multilateralism became, in the words of one commentator, a "dirty word" in Washington policy circles.[5] At the UN's fiftieth anniversary in 1995, the organization faced a deep financial crisis, triggered by the failure of many members (above all the United States) to pay their assessed contributions and by the absence of political will among all the members to enact reforms in UN administration, financing, and structure needed to adapt the organization to the dramatically different world of the late 1990s.

During the 1990s, the UN was no longer the "hostile place" that it had been in the 1970s and early 1980s—except as U.S. unilateralist actions triggered anti-U.S. reactions and antagonized even close allies. The difficulty for the United States, as Edward Luck has written, is one of "reconciling America's exceptional power and the politics of multilateral bodies."[6] The U.S. insistence on exceptionalism often collides with the U.S. interest in relying on multilateral institutions to address problems of global interdependence and share the burdens of resolving these. The U.S. attitude toward meeting financial obligations to the UN, which reveals these contradictions, has weakened the world body and dominated the UN-U.S. relationship over the past decade.

Financing as a Bellwether Issue

Since the mid-1980s, U.S.-UN relations have been dominated by conflicts over how much money should be spent on UN activities, what countries should pay what share, and the cost effectiveness of UN programs. In return for paying its dues, the United States has sought a de facto veto over UN activities and organizational reform and a reduction in its assessed share of expenses.

Financing the UN

Negotiators at the wartime conferences at Dumbarton Oaks and San Francisco addressed issues of UN financing only late in the negotiations, through two provisions of the UN Charter. Article 17 grants the General Assembly responsibility for UN budgeting and financing, while article 19 provides that states in excessive arrears will lose their vote in the General Assembly unless it is determined that failure to pay is due to conditions beyond the member's control.[7] At San Francisco, the United States agreed to pay almost 40 percent of the UN's budget, a figure that was gradually lowered to 25 percent in 1973. The specific percentage was based roughly on a state's national income, per capita income, and foreign currency reserves, and adjusted for any economic dislocations. In 1963, the UN General Assembly established a separate scale of assessments for peacekeeping operations, although this continued to be controversial for several years thereafter. The permanent members of the UN Security Council and the wealthier countries were to pay proportionately more, given their special responsibilities for peace and security and their economic means, respectively. When this scale was reevaluated in 1973 the United States' figure was set at 31 percent.

Between 1946 and 1960, financing took a backseat to the critical issues of the Cold War. Incremental administrative reforms were made to satisfy different constituencies—a process that Luck labels as "muddling through: reform as a way of life."[8] There were occasional grumblings from members of Congress, warning against the dangers of the United States being "Santa Claus for the rest of the world."[9]

The first of the UN's three major financial crises occurred in the early 1960s as a result of controversies over UN peacekeeping operations in the Congo and the Middle East. Since both operations had been authorized by the General Assembly, after the Security Council had vetoed proposed action, two permanent members—France and the Soviet Union—argued that such actions should not be subject to compulsory financing. As UN debts mounted, the General Assembly in 1961 requested an advisory opinion from the World Court on the interpretation of article 17. Were peacekeeping expenses to be considered "expenses" of the organization under article 17? Should such expenses be "borne by the Members as apportioned by the General Assembly?" If certain states were deemed in arrears, could article 19 be enforced?

The United States led efforts to reinforce the legal basis of states' obligation to pay their assessed shares of UN expenses, including peacekeeping. It supported the World Court's decision in the *Certain Expenses* case, which held that peacekeeping was an ordinary expense of the organization, one that should be borne by all members.[10] Both the UN and the United States worked diligently toward a political compromise that would not jeopardize the UN's viability. Bonds were sold to finance the peace operations and to make up for the budgetary shortfall, and consensus decision-making was instituted for the nineteenth General Assembly session in 1964 to avoid a showdown with the Soviet Union and France. In August 1965, faced with consensus that article 19 should not be invoked and that the General Assembly should return to normal voting procedures, the U.S. ambassador to the UN, Arthur Goldberg, articulated the U.S. view that "the concept of collective financial responsibility . . . is a sound principle." Article 17 was "impeccably clear" and article 19 "clear beyond question." But he demurred, saying, "We must make it crystal clear that if any Member can insist on making an exception to the principle of collective financial responsibility with respect to certain activities of the Organization, the United States reserves the same option to make exception if, in our view, strong and compelling reasons exist for doing so."[11] This principle established the framework for later U.S. action.

Given the hostile environment confronting the United States in the UN throughout the 1970s, it should hardly be surprising that Congress debated various measures to withhold U.S. contributions. In 1978, the legal adviser of the State Department confirmed in a memorandum that article 17 "impose[s] a legal obligation on members to pay the amount assessed."[12] Yet, it became increasingly difficult to make the case for fully unconditional payments on the basis of a legal obligation.

The UN's second financial crisis arose in the 1980s, when the United States began withholding parts of its dues.[13] Congress and the Reagan administration were unhappy with specific UN policies and with the politicization of many specialized agencies and General Assembly procedures, which gave the United States too little influence over budget decisions, UN administration and management, and the size of the U.S. assessment. In 1985, Congress passed three pieces of legislation designed to cut U.S. contributions and secure changes. The Kassebaum Amendment proposed a reduction in the U.S. contribution to the UN budget from 25 percent to 20 percent unless the General Assembly approved a system of weighted voting for decisionmaking on financial matters. The Sundquist Amendment denied, for ideological reasons, U.S. contributions to the salaries of UN staff members from the Soviet bloc. Simultaneously, the Gramm-Rudman Act (The Balanced Budget and Emergency Deficit Control Act) cut funds from federal programs that went to various UN specialized programs, as well as payments to the regular budget of the UN and forty-three other international organizations. These three measures amounted to a 50 percent reduction in U.S. contributions to the United Nations in 1986. The Reagan administration failed to assert the legal obligation for payment, and the assistant secretary of state for international organization affairs, Alan Keyes, even praised the congressional actions.

The UN's second financial crisis was not solely the fault of the United States. Eighteen other member states, including four of the five permanent members of the Security Council, also withheld payments for political reasons. In addition, many other states were late paying their bills for a variety of nonpolitical reasons. The combination of late payments and arrears left the UN unable to fund programs or to reimburse states for peacekeeping expenses.

The General Assembly responded to the 1985 crisis by establishing the Group of Eighteen High-Level Intergovernmental Experts. Along with recommendations to cut the UN staff and simplify procedures to save money, the Group of Eighteen formulated a compromise that gave the major donors increased power to review programs and establish priorities for the use of financial resources. The Committee for Program and Coordination (CPC) would review budgetary expenditures and send them first to the Advisory Committee on Administration and Budgetary Questions (ACABQ), then to the Fifth (Financial) Committee, and finally to the General Assembly itself. Consensus voting in the CPC gave the United States and other major donors a virtual veto over budgetary questions, without technically altering the one-state, one-vote decision system. In other words, UN members were able to make critical procedural changes without amending the Charter. For the United States, this meant a greater ability to influence key UN decisions. The change also met one of Congress's key conditions for resuming payment.

Although these procedural changes ended the immediate financial crisis, they neither alleviated the structural problem of UN financing nor ended the U.S. practice of holding the UN hostage. They did, however, weaken the anti-UN coalition in Congress. Some legislators continued to have concerns beyond the budget, while others felt significant progress had been made. In 1987, a new legislative formula permitted the president to release 40 percent of the U.S. annual assessment but held another 40 percent hostage to UN progress on reform. The final 20 percent was to be released only after congressional evaluation of the reforms. Contrary to expectations, however, Congress never appropriated funds to cover the full assessment, and U.S. arrears mounted.[14]

The third financial crisis arose in 1995, in the aftermath of UN peace operations in a number of countries, including Iraq, Somalia, Cambodia, Haiti, and the former Yugoslavia. The newly elected, Republican-controlled Congress led an all-out assault on the UN. Although the United States had paid its assessment in 1992 and 1993, arrears from the 1980s had never been cleared. In the 1996 budget, Congress mandated (with President Clinton's acquiescence) that the United States not pay its full peacekeeping assessment (31 percent of total peacekeeping cost), and contributions to the regular UN budget dipped below the assessed 25 percent. These actions occurred despite the UN's efforts to meet U.S. demands for consensus-based budgeting and zero–nominal budget growth. In 1997 and 1998, the United States lost its ACABQ seat because of its arrears. Only urgent late payments in 1998 and 1999 prevented the United States from losing its General Assembly vote under article 19.[15]

Disputes over the amount owed complicated the problem of U.S. arrears. Although the UN estimated U.S. arrears at around $1.7 billion, Washington put the amount closer to $1 billion. Regardless of the precise figure, the United States was clearly and deliberately in arrears to the UN, thanks to congressional actions that were intended to embarrass the Clinton administration and to force reform within the UN. Simultaneously, the United

States' pattern of negative voting continued to reflect its ambivalence toward multilateralism. These actions increasingly isolated the United States from both its allies and the majority of UN member states on a broad range of issues, many of which are discussed in separate chapters of this book.

Legal and Political Issues of Financing

Did the United States have a legal obligation to pay its UN assessments, as the State Department's legal adviser and many legal scholars claimed? Or did the United Nations lose its rights to be paid because of actions it had taken? Can political considerations justify the abrogation of legal obligations, as Ambassador Goldberg forewarned in 1965? During the 1980s and 1990s the political justification for withholding prevailed, but it was buttressed by assorted legal arguments.

Three legal justifications have been given for the U.S. withholding under the 1985 Kassebaum Amendment. One suggested that a radical change of circumstances, or *rebus sic stantibus,* had occurred as the UN was transformed by the admission of large numbers of new members whose assessments were minuscule. In the words of two members of Congress, the amendment was intended to "assure a more proportionate influence on the part of the major donors with respect to budgetary matters."[16] This rationale has never been widely accepted. Should there be such a fundamental change in circumstances, members would have only two legal options: to accept the new circumstances or to withdraw from the world organization.[17] The United States did withdraw from UNESCO and the ILO, but withdrawal from the UN was never seriously considered—although conservative politicians did suggest it.

The second legal justification specifies that the minority in an organization enjoy certain rights. Equating the legal right of reservation to withholding, Elizabeth Zoller concludes that the latter prevents "the Organization from turning into 'a Super-State.' Absent an impartial third body to give conclusive rulings on such possible deviations, the power to withhold payment is a necessary and proper power of each member state."[18] Lacking a group of vocal adherents, this argument has not proven persuasive.

The legal justification heard most often centers on the relationship between international law and U.S. domestic law. John Bolton, a former assistant secretary of state for international organizations affairs, has stated that "treaties are simply 'political' obligations . . . treaty obligations can be unilaterally modified or terminated by congressional action, [and] America's constitutional requirements override 'international law.'"[19] Senator Jesse Helms reiterated this interpretation when he spoke before the UN Security Council on January 20, 2000. "Under our system," said Helms, "when international treaties are ratified they simply become domestic U.S. law. As such, they carry no greater or lesser weight than any other domestic U.S.

law. Treaty obligations can be superseded by a simple act of Congress."[20] This is a highly controversial interpretation. Although it is accepted in some conservative U.S. legal circles, it is widely repudiated by foreign legal scholars. Thus, despite the absence of consensus on a legal justification for withholding, the practice itself has continued and is certainly not limited to the United States.

Given the political nature of these arguments, one might have expected U.S. withholding during the mid-1970s, when the United States faced the most hostile atmosphere in the UN. Instead, during that period the United States expressed its disapproval by turning away from the General Assembly, where the one-state, one-vote formula undermined its interests, and focusing its energies on the Security Council and (in the case of economic issues) the IMF and World Bank, where weighted voting protected U.S. influence. By the time of the third financial crisis in the mid-1990s, however, there was significant disapproval on Capitol Hill for both the Security Council's peacekeeping initiatives and the secretary-general's management. Congress thus used conditional withholding of funds to micromanage the United Nations.

A key question is why the Congress chose to focus so much attention on the UN and its procedures (and why, correspondingly, successive presidents have failed to exercise stronger leadership on behalf of the UN). Luck suggests that because most UN activities, including peacekeeping, are not directly linked to U.S. national interests or to the interests of influential segments of the American public, they are vulnerable to rhetorical assaults, cavalier treatment, or disregard.[21] For the same reason, President Bush and President Clinton chose not to spend large amounts of precious political capital to insist that the United States meet its obligations to the UN.[22] The congressional effort to micromanage UN finance and administration may also be linked to the practice of assigning U.S. congressional delegates to the annual General Assembly sessions, particularly to the Fifth (Budgetary) Committee. As a result, members of Congress are better informed "about what the UN spends than about what it does."[23] Likewise, Congress, as Senator Rod Grams (Republican-Miinnesota) noted in 1996, "has often been unhappy with the lack of emphasis that past and present administrations have placed on specific reform proposals."[24] Finally, of course, control over budgets and spending is the major tool that Congress has at its disposal for shaping U.S. domestic and foreign policies and the actions of the executive branch. All other congressional powers, including the power to investigate, pale by comparison to the power of the purse.

Giving or withholding funds is also an issue that resonates with the American public, which, of course, elects members to Congress. There has always been an underlying public discontent with the perception that the United States is "paying more than [its] share" and "not getting enough out of the organization," although polls have also shown public support for meeting current obligations. The General Accounting Office (GAO), which conducts periodic studies for Congress, has usually been critical of organizational inefficiencies in the UN—although in May 2000, the GAO found that reforms had strengthened UN management and that other congressional objectives were difficult to achieve given the complexities of the UN's structure.[25] In the absence of a strong domestic constituency actively supporting the UN, reducing U.S. contributions has always been an "easy" and "safe" congressional choice to make. Senator Helms mirrored the views of many others in Congress when he reminded the UN Security Council in early 2000 that "under the U.S. Constitution, we in Congress are the sole guardians of the American taxpayers' money. It is our solemn duty to see that it is wisely invested."[26] In the absence of strong presidential leadership and with partisanship running strong, Congress has determined U.S. policy toward the UN through its control of contributions.

The Helms-Biden Act: A Solution?

The UN's third financial crisis not only pitted the United States against the UN over mounting U.S. arrears and escalating unilateral demands for UN reform, but also President Clinton, a supporter of fulfilling U.S. financial obligations, against Senator Helms and the Republican majority in Congress. Yet, even Helms had become aware by 1996 that the tactic of unilateral, conditional withholding of contributions had been used too much and was not working. He told a Senate hearing that "withholding contributions has not worked. We have tried that."[27] Hence, the challenge was to find a compromise solution linking UN reforms to substantial arrears payments. This came in the form of bipartisan legislation sponsored by the two senior members of the Senate Foreign Relations Committee: Senators Helms and Joseph Biden (Democrat-Delaware). Still, their effort was complicated by the ability of other legislators to attach unrelated amendments, a strategy used by Representative Chris Smith (Republican-New Jersey) in 1997 and 1998 to link an antiabortion measure to the UN reform and funding bill. Smith's amendment prohibited the administration from financing any international organization that used funds to lobby foreign governments to ease policies on abortions. As a result, President Clinton vetoed the Helms-Biden Act in October 1998, making clear that abortion had a higher priority on his agenda than U.S. international commitments and debt to the UN.

Nonetheless, in his state of the union address of January 1998 President Clinton had, for the first time, made payment of the UN arrears a legislative goal. The October 1998 veto, therefore, did not stop the efforts to find a compromise linking UN reform and payment of arrears. In August 1999, President Clinton instructed the UN ambassador-designate, Richard Holbrooke, to "play a key role in working with the Congress to meet our obligations and to secure needed reforms in the United Nations."[28] Holbrooke's task became more compelling when a GAO report suggested that the United States could lose its vote in the General Assembly beginning on January 1, 2000, unless it paid a portion of its dues by the end of the year. Holbrooke's challenge was to get his foreign colleagues at the UN to make concessions, pending the outcome of congressional negotiations designed to cover the dues and begin to pay the arrears. Holbrooke also met frequently with individual members of Congress.

In November 1999, a compromise on the funding issue was reached in the form of the Helms-Biden UN Reform Act of 1999 (Title IX Public Law 106-113).[29] The compromise gave the president some flexibility to void the antiabortion amendment's provisions for U.S. overseas family-planning programs. President Clinton signed the legislation as the best available deal to get U.S. arrears paid, despite criticism from pro-choice groups, the tough conditions the bill contained for release of U.S. funds, and lingering questions about whether this would solve the longstanding problem of congressional withholding.

Under the Helms-Biden plan, U.S. payments to the UN will be released in three installments. Conditions or benchmarks have to be reached before each tranche of funds can be released. Before the first payment of $100 million could be authorized, Congress had to receive certification from the executive branch that the UN and its related agencies had not taken any of seven types of actions. Three of the certifications related to U.S. sovereignty: (1) the UN and its agencies had taken no actions that would require the United States to violate the Constitution or any U.S. laws; (2) the UN and its agencies had taken no actions that exercised sovereignty over the United States; and (3) no UN agency had exerted authority or control over U.S. property rights. Four other conditions were designed to limit the UN's power: (1) the organization could impose no tax on U.S. nationals; (2) no UN agency had attached interest charges on U.S. arrears; (3) no UN agency had attempted to acquire authority to borrow from external sources; and (4) no steps had been taken to create or develop a standing army under article 43 of the Charter.

Anticipating these provisions to Helms-Biden, the State Department had been working on the necessary certifications; fortunately, these were relatively easy. Once they were complete, the first installment of $100 million was released on December 16, 1999, ensuring that the United States retained its General Assembly vote after January 1, 2000.

The Helms-Biden conditions for the second year, because they affected the operations of the UN and the budgets of other member states, were much more difficult to meet. These focused on reforming the scales of assessments used by the UN for both its regular and peacekeeping budgets. Hence they required the concurrence of a majority of UN members—no easy task in an atmosphere poisoned by resentment at the United States' "deadbeat" status, unilateral withholding, and demands for reform before payment of arrearages. The requisite three conditions were these: (1) no member's assessed share of the UN regular budget should exceed 22 percent, which would mean a 3 percent drop in the U.S. assessment; (2) the U.S. share of the peacekeeping budget should not exceed 25 percent, implying a 6 percent reduction; and (3) the UN should establish a "contested arrearages account" for U.S. arrears not covered by the legislation, and failure to pay contested amounts should not affect application of article 19. In short, the Helms-Biden plan sought to ensure that the United States could continue to vote. These conditions were central to the Helms-Biden initiative, since a primary congressional goal was to force members of the UN to establish a new scale of assessments in which the U.S. share would be reduced *before* arrears were cleared.

Although most countries acknowledged the benefit of having the U.S. share drop, they wanted equity, and they wanted the negotiations over the payment shares to occur *after* the U.S. arrears had been paid. The United States' closest allies, including the EU and Japan, made it clear that they saw an inequity in the new scale of assessments. Based on shares of world gross national product (GNP), they noted the United States should pay 27 percent, in contrast to the proposed 20 to 22 percent. By contrast, the EU countries currently paid 36.6 percent, but their share of world GNP was about 29 percent, and Japan paid 20.6 percent, whereas its share of world GNP was below 15 percent.[30] Japan's UN representative, Yukio Satoh, reported "brewing resentment over Japan's bill" when he met with Diet members. The Japanese legislators asked why "we have to pay this much," especially since Japan was unable to obtain a seat on the Security Council.[31] The resentment became stronger as the U.S. unilaterally sought to reduce its own payments with no guarantee that U.S. arrears would be cleared, given other Helms-Biden conditions. As China's ambassador, Wang Yingfang, diplomatically stated, "Certainly, we regret very much that a big power with great ability to contribute more is not quite constructive in this field."[32] Many UN members commented on how petty the U.S. actions looked in view of the buoyancy of the U.S. economy at that time.

In December 2000, after months of negotiations, UN members agreed to reduce the U.S. assessment to 22 percent and to realign other members' dues, thereby meeting the major second year condition of Helms-Biden. The General Assembly also voted to reduce the U.S. share of peacekeeping expenses from 30 percent to 27 percent, 2 percent short of the 25 percent level mandated in Helms-Biden. The General Assembly did not include a tougher and more confrontational provision supported by many European states that would have made the U.S. reduction conditional on payment of all arrears by 2003. It did, however, include language that left open the possibility of overturning the arrangement if something went wrong. To make up for the reduction in U.S. contributions (and a 1 percent reduction of Japan's contribution), eighteen other countries—including

Thailand, Singapore, South Korea, Brazil, Chile, the Czech Republic, Argentina, and several Persian Gulf oil states—agreed to increase their own contributions. (Russia and China also volunteered to increase their contributions, though marginally.) Critical to acceptance of these changes was a one-time-only grant of $34 million to the U.S. State Department by a private citizen, Ted Turner, to make up for the interim funding shortfall between approval of the new assessments and the countries' next budgetary cycles.[33]

The compromise drew favorable comments in all quarters. Key members of Congress were very positive. Senator Helms praised Ambassador Holbrooke's accomplishment, saying, "I consider it a real leap forward," while noting that all the issues were not resolved.[34] Senator John Kerry (Democrat-Massachusetts) noted that the measure would provide time "to change attitudes in Congress toward the U.N."[35] British Ambassador Sir Jeremy Greenstock echoed the positive sentiments, calling the deal a "huge breakthrough." Holbrooke himself termed it "a tremendous achievement for the United Nations." He had devoted most of his sixteen months as chief U.S. representative to the tough diplomatic work of securing agreement. Few had thought he would succeed, given the poisoned relationship between the United States and even its closest allies on the issue of linking arrears payment to a deal on a new assessment scale.[36]

Ambassador Holbrooke and his colleagues had negotiated endlessly with UN member delegations and the Secretariat, visited national capitals, and arranged the January 2000 visit of Jesse Helms to the Security Council, as well as for the return visit of UN ambassadors to Capitol Hill. Over 800 telegrams were sent on behalf of the U.S. position.[37] In a key move, Holbrooke had framed the issue in terms of changing an outdated allocation system to a flatter and more equitable scale of assessments, a view that others eventually accepted.

The achievement of the Helms-Biden Act's second-year conditions enabled the payment in December 2000 of another $475 million (and a $107 million credit against amounts owed by the UN to the United States for peacekeeping support). That left the still tougher third-year conditions, centering on budget and personnel concerns for the UN and specialized agencies. Ten conditions were outlined. They included a further drop in the U.S. assessment to 20 percent and extended this condition to all specialized agencies—a particular problem, since the latter have separate charters, memberships, and budgets. Another condition called for a guarantee that the United States and the five largest contributors to the UN budget would have seats on the ACABQ. Further stipulations were for the WHO, FAO, and ILO to appoint inspectors general and to achieve zero nominal growth in their budgets. New budget procedures in these agencies and the UN itself were also expected to ensure that any increases in spending would have to be approved by consensus. The U.S. GAO was to be provided with access to all UN financial data in order to review UN operations. Finally, Helms-Biden called for UN staff positions to be filled on the basis of merit and a code of conduct to be established to govern staff behavior.

Under the terms of the Helms-Biden compromise, the president was given some ability to waive specific conditions, namely the contested arrears account and the requirement for lowering the U.S. assessment for the UN's regular budget to 20 percent. Other miscellaneous provisions included a required report on Israel's participation in the organization, a prohibition on payment of any arrears to the UN Industrial Development Organization, from which the United States had withdrawn in 1997, an assessment of costs being borne by the United States for support of all Security Council resolutions, and monthly updates on all current and potential peacekeeping missions. Clearly, one aim of the legislation was to make it more difficult for the president to exercise discretionary power in managing the U.S.-UN relationship.

Although the Helms-Biden Act provided a means of resolving the crisis over U.S. participation in the UN, a number of issues remain unanswered. Is the arrears crisis actually resolved or will the issue arise again in the future? Was the congressional strategy of unilateral withholding of funds a strategy for pushing UN reform or was it undertaken largely for symbolic domestic purposes? If the former, will the steps mandated by the legislation strengthen or weaken the UN? If the latter, what guarantees are there that the strategy of unilateral withholding will not be used again? Can the United States continue to exert power and influence in the UN, having used confrontational strategies that antagonized even its closest allies? Or has the strategy of withholding contributions and demanding changes before payment of arrears permanently weakened U.S. leverage? To begin to answer at least some of these questions, we need to examine the reasons why financing has become a bellwether for the overall U.S.-UN relationship.

Analyzing the Dynamics of the U.S.-UN Relationship

Previous studies of U.S. policies toward international organizations have explained the dynamics of these relationships in terms of the changing nature of issues, specific characteristics of international organizations, and domestic political factors.[38] Several more recent studies have focused on specific country characteristics, such as a preference for multilateralism or an insistence on exceptionalism. Here, we concentrate on the nature of the issues, domestic political factors, the unique characteristics of U.S. political culture, and the current position of the United States as the sole superpower.

Nature of the issues. Resistance to meeting UN financial contributions has occurred most often where significant policy differences on controversial issues have existed between the United States and other member states, and when the United States has found itself isolated and in opposition to large

UN majorities. This has led to perceptions that the UN is a hostile place, encouraging U.S. efforts to pull back from multilateralism and to use U.S. financial contributions as a tool of influence. At other times, Washington has regarded the UN as the desirable place for dealing with certain pressing issues, sharing burdens, and promoting U.S. interests and values. These latter types of issues reinforce U.S. support for paying assessed contributions and, most important, for making voluntary contributions.

Differences between the United States and the majority of UN member states were striking during the 1970s, when the General Assembly debated the proposed NIEO, how to deal with apartheid in South Africa, and other North-South issues. Such matters divided not only the North and South, but also frequently divided the United States and its allies, many of which were more accommodating to developing countries' interests. These differences have persisted in issues relating to Israel and Middle East politics. During the 1970s, such differences led the United States to try to cut its budgetary contributions to the UN and to withdraw from heavily politicized specialized agencies. This trend accelerated in the 1980s and persisted into the 1990s, because the United States saw little reason to finance activities it did not support.

These differences over particular issues became somewhat less apparent in the 1990s, when the General Assembly adopted consensus decision-making procedures for more than 80 percent of its resolutions (Figure 11.1). But differences over Middle East–related issues persist—and account for most of the instances in which the U.S. delegation has voted against General Assembly majorities.[39] Financial contributions have been a key instrument used to express U.S. displeasure with political trends in the UN.

A countervailing pattern can best be seen in those UN issue areas that have drawn consistent U.S. (including congressional) support over the years, and which are funded in large part by voluntary contributions, often amounting to well in excess of 25 percent of a program's budget. These issue areas include global challenges like AIDS, refugees, children's welfare, famine, drugs, and development. Until the late 1990s the United States voluntarily provided logistics support for all peacekeeping operations, moving troops and equipment of other countries to the locations where they were needed. Table 11.1 summarizes total U.S. contributions to the UN, assessed and voluntary, for 1998–2000. The unmistakable conclusion is that the congressional tactic of unilateral fund withholding has applied almost exclusively to the general UN budget and peacekeeping. The United States has actually increased its voluntary contributions to programs and agencies dealing with issues perceived to reflect shared interests.

The biggest puzzle is why Congress has resisted since 1993 paying the full U.S. share of UN peacekeeping costs. Arguably, peacekeeping operations represent burden sharing at its best, especially where other countries provide the manpower. Yet, members of Congress have not only sought to

Table 11.1   U.S. Assessed and Voluntary Contributions, FY 1996–2000

	FY 1996	FY 1997	FY 1998	FY 1999	FY 2000
Total assessed contributions	665.2	618.2	586.5	269.7[a]	355.6[b]
Total assessed peacekeeping contributions	359.0	257.1	194.7	—	—
Total voluntary peacekeeping contributions	52.8	58.5	43.4	—	—
Total voluntary contributions	556.9	807.9	740.1	1,571	1,555

Source: U.S. Department of State, Bureau of International Organization Affairs, "United States Contributions to International Organizations: Report to the Congress for Fiscal Year 1998," available at www.state.gov/www/issues/us_contribs_io/fy98_index.html. See also United Nations document A/55/525 for data on assessed and voluntary contributions received from members states. Available at www.un.org

Notes: a. Includes no payment toward the regular UN budget assessment for that year of $297.7 million. Does not include payment of $355.3 against prior years' assessments.

b. Includes payment of $136.5 million toward the regular UN budget assessment of $304.4 million for that year. Does not include payment of $315.7 against prior years' assessments.

hamstring the executive branch in providing U.S. troops, but they have also used the unilateral withholding tactic to cut U.S. contributions and block the UN from creating a standby capacity for peacekeeping, policing, and administration in such troubled areas as Kosovo, East Timor, and Sierra Leone. Finding an explanation for this behavior requires a deeper search into U.S. domestic politics.

Domestic politics. The dynamics of U.S. domestic politics—and particularly presidential leadership, executive-legislative relations, and public opinion— have historically had a significant influence on the U.S.-UN relationship, especially on financing matters. The constitutional separation of powers creates a dynamic tension between the president and Congress and permits multiple voices to speak for the United States at any given time. Whereas bipartisanship and consensus on foreign policy marked executive-legislative relations during the height of the Cold War, since the aftermath of the Vietnam War and Watergate in the mid-1970s, Congress has been much more assertive in international affairs and has come to define the terms of U.S. participation in the UN. Yet, as Edward Luck notes, Congress "is not organized, equipped, or legally competent to conduct multilateral diplomacy."[40]

The changing dynamic of executive-legislative relations on foreign policy issues has been especially marked in the 1990s. With the end of the Cold War, partisan politics has been more divisive, as Stephen Walt comments, "because using foreign policy to bash one's rivals doesn't place the nation in immediate danger."[41] The differences between the two parties have become sharper and more ideological, with Republicans generally more inclined to unilateralism and Democrats leaning toward multilateralism. The Republican "Contract with America" was sharply critical of UN peacekeeping, among other things. Furthermore, deference to the president has declined, making it harder for presidents to lead. As James Lindsay has noted, "With no major threat to U.S. security on the horizon and with public interest [in foreign policy] waning, the costs of challenging the president plummeted."[42] This was further underscored after 1994 by the overt hostility of the Republican majorities in the Senate and House to President Clinton, their determination to thwart his leadership, and their use of unilateral withholding of U.S. dues both to embarrass the president and to impose reforms on (and limit obligations to) the UN.

Similarly, in the congressional context, absent a consensus on national security threats and in a climate of what Lindsay terms "apathetic internationalism," interest groups and individual members that care deeply about particular issues may be empowered because there is little impetus to block "the noisy few."[43] This explains Representative Chris Smith's success in attaching the antiabortion amendment to the Helms-Biden bill and effectively blocking settlement of the dues issue for two years. Likewise, it explains the success of a variety of human rights, labor, and environmental groups on the issue of "fast-track" negotiating authority on trade and of the extreme right in largely blocking U.S. participation in UN peacekeeping missions. During the Clinton administration the Republican-led Congress rarely missed an opportunity to micromanage foreign policy, including U.S. contributions to the UN.

Yet it is important to note that voluntary contributions did not suffer the same fate. Whereas the annual assessments were perceived as a "rathole" and took on symbolic value in domestic politics, the "good works" of many UN agencies and programs, such as the UN Children's Fund (UNICEF) and the UN High Commission for Refugees (UNHCR), left their funding untouched, if not increased.

The degree of presidential leadership (or its absence) has been another important factor explaining U.S. engagement with the UN. President Reagan's general opposition to international institutions effectively delegitimated multilateralism among many Republicans and resulted in an era of strained and sometimes hostile relations between the United States and the UN. Likewise, President Clinton was slow to appoint a UN ambassador and an assistant secretary of state for international organization affairs, sending a signal to both Congress and the UN that the latter was not high on his foreign policy agenda. Clinton adopted the rhetoric of assertive multilateralism but neglected to make a sustained effort to build consensus in Congress and among the public for UN peacekeeping and for meeting U.S. financial obligations, let alone for serious reform of the UN. In effect, he ceded the field to congressional critics and the Republican majority.

Clinton's foreign policy record was checkered, with episodic periods of intense engagement followed by long periods of inattention and even neglect. He successfully used the powers of the presidency to secure congressional approval of NAFTA, WTO, CWC, and permanent normal trade relations with China. When Clinton's primary focus was on domestic policy, or when he chose not to use political capital in support of a specific vision of the U.S. role in the world, then the administration suffered major defeats—as over the CTBT and the issue of UN arrears. When he failed to use the powers of the presidency effectively, Clinton's assertive multilateralism proved to be empty rhetoric.[44]

In confrontations with Congress, the Clinton administration often framed issues as a simple dichotomy or an epic struggle between the forces of good and evil. Following the defeat of the CTBT, for example, National Security Adviser Sandy Berger declared that "the internationalist consensus that has prevailed in this country for more than 50 years increasingly is being challenged by a new isolationism heard and felt particularly in the Congress."[45] In the debate over UN contributions the question seemed to be, "Are you a John Bircher or do you believe that we should pay our lawfully assessed dues?"[46] This strategy backfired because branding Republicans as isolationists antagonized congressional supporters and critics alike, making it even more difficult for the president to win support from Congress. The failure of presidential leadership in arrears payments contributed to a standoff between Congress and the executive branch and eroded the UN-U.S. relationship.

Throughout these vicissitudes, the American public has remained strikingly supportive of both the UN and meeting the United States' obligations to pay its arrears. U.S. support for the UN has historically ranged between 60 and 75 percent. In June 1999, a Pew Research Council poll found that 70 percent of respondents had a favorable view of the UN. As Steven Kull notes in Chapter 4 of this book, polling data suggest that although the public has some reservations about UN performance and administrative waste, a majority of Americans support full payment of dues, citing the country's obligations. At the same time, the "apathetic" nature of public internationalism has contributed to politicians' neglect of foreign policy, empowered "squeaky wheels" like Representative Smith, and reduced the incentives for Congress to defer to the president on foreign policy.[47] Public opinion has apparently not affected the behavior of Congress on the UN issue, perhaps because members of Congress listen only to the skeptics, who seem "much more passionate and ideological in their rejection of the UN than do the larger numbers of their countrymen who vaguely value the organization and its work."[48]

U.S. political culture. Exceptionalism has a long history in the national political culture. "For most Americans," notes Edward Luck, "the sense of exceptionalism has been so much a part of their outlook, values, and national character that it has received only occasional question or critical comment."[49] The United States is not unique in this regard. Other great powers, such as the Soviet Union, China, and France, have also been "less willing than others to compromise in multilateral fora for the sake of approval or to maintain consensus. . . . Each combined a distinct political culture with an allergy to certain issues on the UN agenda . . . and each has disputed the amount of money it has been assessed by the UN."[50] Today, the cultural roots of U.S. exceptionalism are complemented and reinforced by the exceptional nature of the United States' standing as the sole superpower in the post–Cold War world and, underlying that, the exceptional size and strength of its military capability and economy.

Sole superpower status. From the perspective of many other countries, and from the standpoint of many Americans, the exceptional power the United States currently enjoys explains much of its unilateralist tendencies. The Wilsonian vision may have fostered a world of laws and institutions in the United State's own image, but as the sole superpower, the United States is far from comfortable behaving like just another state in that system. We aver, however, that the explanations for unilateralist behavior derive not merely from the country's structural position in the international system (as many "realists" would contend), but are deeply embedded in U.S. domestic politics and political culture.

At the same time, the rise of global interdependence issues and U.S. devotion to democracy continue to draw the United States toward the UN and toward multilateralism more generally. As John Ikenberry has noted, "The U.S. is not a nineteenth century imperial power and because America's power is derived in part from its values, it must work to strengthen the institutions of world order for the betterment of others rather than hoarding power."[51] Therein lies the dilemma.

Having probed these alternative sources of explanation for the U.S.-UN relationship and how financing became a bellwether issue, we turn now to examine some of the consequences of U.S. failure to meet its financial obligations to the UN.

The Consequences of U.S. Manipulation of UN Finances

There are four distinct consequences of the U.S. tendency to use a financial "carrot-and-stick" approach with the UN. First, the UN has long-standing financial problems because it has no independent source of financing and depends solely on its members for assessed and voluntary contributions. Chronic budget crisis is thus the norm, not the exception. The crisis of the 1990s not only magnified the perennial struggle for resources but also undermined the UN's ability to undertake new operations and support existing ones, particularly in the peacekeeping area. The UN Department of Peace-keeping Operations is estimated to be short at least 100 staffers, leaving it unprepared and unable to meet the current obligations—much less to expand by approximately 250 new personnel, as proposed in the UN's own Brahimi Report, produced in summer 2000 at the request of the secretary-general to offer recommendations for improving UN peacekeeping operations.[52] The financial crisis has affected multiple areas of UN activity. Cutbacks in humanitarian and human rights programs have reduced the UN's ability to provide for the safety of refugees and internally displaced persons. Similarly, allegations of genocide and human rights violations are not pursued. The specialized agencies, such as the WHO and ILO, will be particularly affected when the third-year conditions of Helms-Biden impose zero nominal growth budgets. Have members of Congress calculated the costs of a weakened UN system to the U.S. ability to share the burdens of addressing the wide range of global interdependence issues that concern it? As William Luers notes, "The United States has a vital interest in strengthening the U.N. system. Acting alone is not a sustainable option."[53]

Second, the use of arrears as a financial instrument has had a detrimental effect on U.S. relations with allies who have expressed exasperation with U.S. arrogance. They have heard the U.S. complaints before in NATO or in the U.S.-Japanese alliance, where neither side believes that the other is bearing its fair share of the burden. In the UN, the division between the United States and its NATO allies has never been greater, and the gap in their voting patterns has steadily widened. Whether this "New York effect" has permanently damaged key relationships remains to be seen, but it is one factor contributing to shifts under way in Europe as the EU develops its security and defense policy, enhancing its capability as an independent actor and altering its relationship with the United States.[54]

Third, by using its power of the purse too much and too often, the United States has undercut its leadership in the UN itself. In the view of British UN Ambassador Sir Jeremy Greenstock, the arrears problem has hindered the UN reform effort, and the United States must be prepared to compromise with other states. Former Dutch UN Ambassador Piter van Waisum similarly stated that member states may not attach conditions to paying their assessments. Likewise, Canadian UN Ambassador Robert Fowler stated that the U.S. unilateral approach to crucial UN funding and reform would not lead to useful results.[55] Responding to Senator Helms on the occasion of his January 2000 visit to the Security Council, Ambassador Greenstock said, "The United Nations is not a separate organ, like a fire service. It is the member states, and the United States owns 25 percent of the power and the resources of the United Nations. What it does well, the U.S. get credit for. What it does badly, the U.S. must bear some responsibility."[56] If U.S. behavior persists, foreign delegations may come to regard U.S. commitments as no longer credible. Some countries have already begun to imitate the U.S. "bad habit of delaying payments" until the end of the year, notes Luers.[57]

U.S. decisionmakers are also aware that the ability of the United States to exercise leadership may be jeopardized as a result of its behavior on UN financing. Prominent U.S. foreign policy experts are worried about the effects of U.S. withholding. Princeton Lyman, former assistant secretary of state for international organization affairs, reported in comments appended to the GAO report of May 2000 on *United Nations Financial Issues and U.S. Arrears,* "At every possible opportunity, other member states use the arrears to skewer U.S. negotiating positions, whether the topic is related to arrears or not. The arrears situation has seriously eroded our influence on reform."[58] Secretary of State Madeleine Albright herself acknowledged that if the United States were to renege on its commitment to UN peacekeeping, "our ability to lead at the UN will be damaged seriously. Our influence would surely diminish over decisions ranging from maintaining sanctions against rogue states to UN reform to ensuring greater balance within the General Assembly on resolutions affecting the Middle East." She added, "Our ability to argue that other nations should meet their obligations to the UN and to international law would be undermined."[59] Congressman Chris Shays (Republican-Connecticut), a co-sponsor of the UN Arrears Payment Act, H.R. 1355, captured the concern of many members who recognize the risks to U.S. leadership of the failure to pay up, saying, "Each day that we do not pay our debts to the U.N. we lose our ability to shape world events. This loss of leadership is a national disgrace."[60]

Fourth, the financing issue is not only a bellwether for the U.S.-UN relationship, but also symptomatic of a declining willingness to pay for nonmilitary costs of U.S. engagement in international affairs more generally. For more than four decades, the portion of the U.S. budget designated to nonmilitary international affairs has been steadily declining. Richard Gardner, a former U.S. ambassador and former deputy assistant secretary of state for international organization affairs, has warned against the "'one percent' solution—the fallacy that a successful U.S. foreign policy can be carried out with barely one percent of the federal budget." Gardner notes that an "effective foreign policy will simply be impossible without more money."[61] The executive branch needs the capacity to deal with multiple global issues and to make trade-offs not only at the UN but in other foreign policy arenas as well. Current budget allocations to nonmilitary foreign affairs are clearly inadequate, and UN contributions are but one part of this broader problem.

Is the Past a Prologue for the Future?

The end of the Cold War, and the widespread acceptance of market economics, democratic governance, and human rights, appeared to return the

UN to the center of world politics and to mark the achievement of Woodrow Wilson's vision of open diplomacy, collective security, reduced trade barriers, self-determination, and a general association of nations. As Robert Pastor notes in his essay on the United States in the twentieth century, "The United States was farsighted in internationalizing these tasks and in sharing the burden of financing and responsibility, although another part of the U.S. mind distrusted its international institutional offspring."[62] Thus, ironically, the United States seems increasingly uncomfortable with the institution and rules its earlier vision helped to create. Whereas U.S. exceptionalism and idealism once inspired the United States to engage in constructive internationalism and to foster the development of multilateral institutions and international law, exceptionalism and attachment to sovereignty today drive U.S. opposition to multilateral initiatives to promote human rights, reduce economic inequalities, foster the further growth of global civil society, and arrest environmental degradation.

In the twenty-first century, will the United States find the UN a useful venue in which to pursue U.S. interests? Will it therefore choose to honor its financial commitments? Will it continue to press for legitimate reform without undermining the institution through unilateral withholding of funds? Will it renew its commitment to the liberal internationalist vision of a world marked by the development of international law and institutions, expanded human rights, multilateralism, and democracy? Or will U.S. behavior more closely resemble that of a status quo power, protecting its prerogatives and opposing change? In other words, which past pattern will be the prologue to the future?

The U.S. responses to several recent international trends have been ambiguous. The United States may have fostered the growth of many international institutions including the UN, but there is growing ambivalence, if not outright fear, of emerging pieces of global governance, even if the United States was an initial supporter. The United States has supported some UN reforms, but stifled others, increasing its voluntary contributions to UN agencies and programs in several key areas but seeking reductions in its budget and peacekeeping assessments. It has flouted its legal obligations to pay UN dues because of vague charges of the UN's lack of accountability. It has advocated greater respect for human rights, used the UN's human rights machinery to criticize prominent violators, and threatened sanctions, but it has often refused to enter into several human rights conventions itself and has rejected the jurisdiction of an ICC over U.S. peacekeepers and any suggestion that rights violations in the United States are legitimate subjects of international investigation. To some, these assertions of sovereignty are grounded in the U.S. Constitution. To others, they are grounded in the arrogance of a sole superpower.[63]

Will UN reforms help? Incremental reforms have occurred periodically throughout the UN's history. The types of reforms pushed by the United

States have hardly been radical; indeed, they reflect the conservative interests of a status quo power, for the most part. Congressional micromanagement of UN reform through the withholding of arrears has complicated the picture: Congress has repeatedly moved the "goalposts" just as the UN satisfies earlier demands, a stance that has made other member states less willing to push for reforms under the threat of financial blackmail. The challenge is to identify reforms that both strengthen the UN and secure U.S. support. Secretary-General Annan has instituted widespread qualitative and quantitative reforms and won positive reviews from many quarters, including the normally critical GAO.[64] By his own admission, however, more reforms are needed. The challenge is not unlike that faced in creating the UN in the first place: how to design a world body that will both meet the interests and needs of many countries and ensure continuing U.S. participation.

Innovative steps are taking place far beyond any issues of UN Charter revision. Ted Turner's billion-dollar donation to the UN could be a harbinger for lessening the UN's dependence on member state contributions. A private financing alternative, along with Secretary-General Annan's corporate partnership initiatives, may alleviate some of the financial strains. Greater reliance on NGOs to deliver humanitarian relief, development assistance, and other functions may provide decentralized alternatives to the UN as a centerpiece of global governance. President Clinton, in his address to the General Assembly on September 22, 1997, hailed these initiatives, declaring: "Innovative partnerships with the private sector [NGOs], and the international financial institutions can leverage its effectiveness many times over."[65] Such innovations are not apt to "resolve" the UN's financial crisis, however. Private contributions cannot fund UN programs, since expenses must, according to the Charter, be paid by member states. Perhaps more important, these innovations augur an even greater loss of control by the very same member states that seek enhanced control—and thus would certainly not ensure U.S. commitment to the UN.

The approach the United States has used to secure administrative and managerial reforms and changes in its assessments—namely withholding dues and linking arrears payments to reform—threatens to diminish the United States' leverage and capacity to lead in the future. This approach has reeked of the arrogance of the world's superpower. As former National Security Adviser Samuel Berger warned, "Our authority is built on qualities very different from our power: on the attractiveness of our values, on the force of our example, on the credibility of our commitments, and on our willingness to listen to and stand by others. There may be no real threat to our power today. But if we use power in a way that antagonizes our friends and dishonors our commitments, we will lose our authority—and our power will mean very little."[66]

What the United States needs is a new international vision to guide the use of its unique position in the international system. Almost sixty years ago, such a vision led to the establishment of the UN and a set of other liberal international institutions. If the United States is going to play a leadership role in supporting and strengthening the UN as a central institution for dealing with the challenges of a globalizing and interdependent world, the new Bush administration will need to articulate that vision and forge domestic consensus behind it. The U.S.-UN relationship was a critical foundation for the liberal world the United States sought to create in the twentieth century. Renewing that relationship and restoring the credibility of U.S. commitments to UN financing will be crucial for U.S. leadership and interests in the twenty-first century.

Notes

1. Gregg, *About Face?* p. 94.
2. Quoted in Aita, "U.S. Supports Stronger UN Peacekeeping Operations," October 10, 1992.
3. See Chapter 7 for a thorough discussion of trends in U.S. peacekeeping policy.
4. Haass, "Sanctioning Madness."
5. Jentleson, "Who, Why, What, and How: Debates over Post–Cold War Military Intervention," p. 63.
6. Luck, "American Exceptionalism," p. 30.
7. "Excessive" is defined as the amount of arrears equal to or exceeding the amount of the contribution due from a member state for the preceding two full years.
8. Luck, *Mixed Messages,* p. 210.
9. Smith, *Congressional Record,* 79th Congress, 1st session July 27, 1945, pt. 6, p. 8033.
10. *Certain Expenses of the United Nations* 1962 I.C.J. 151.
11. UN General Assembly, Special Committee on Peacekeeping Operations, August 16, 1965, pp. 6, 7, 8–10, 12.
12. Zoller, "The 'Corporate Will' of the United Nations," p. 610.
13. Mingst and Karns, *The United Nations in the Post–Cold War Era,* pp. 209–210.
14. Karns and Mingst, "The Past as Prologue: The United States and the Future of the UN System," pp. 428–430.
15. Smith, "The United States in the United Nations," p. 9.
16. U.S. House of Representatives, *U.S. Policy in the United Nations,* p. 101.
17. Zoller, "The 'Corporate Will' of the United Nations," p. 629.
18. Ibid., p. 631.
19. Bolton, "U.S. Isn't Legally Obligated," *Wall Street Journal,* November 17, 1997.
20. Quoted in Murphy, "Contemporary Practice" (online version).
21. Luck, "American Exceptionalism," pp. 21–22.
22. Until the middle of Reagan's presidency the United States had met its funding obligations, so that this had not been an issue for previous presidents.
23. Luck, *Mixed Messages,* p. 227.
24. Quoted in Luck, *Mixed Messages,* p. 251.

25. See U.S. General Accounting Office, *United Nations Reform Initiatives*. For an example of earlier, more critical GAO reports see *United Nations Financial Issues and U.S. Arrears*.

26. Quoted in Murphy, "Contemporary Practice" (online version).

27. Quoted in Luck, *Mixed Messages*, p. 245.

28. Quoted in Dimoff, "Congress and President," p. 6.

29. For the online version of the Helms-Biden Amendment see *www.unausa. org/de/info/dc02lOOO.htm*

30. Crossette, "Europeans Reject," *New York Times*, October 3, 2000, p. A8.

31. Quoted in Crossette, "U.S. Begins Lonely Fight," *New York Times*, March 12, 2000.

32. Quoted in Winfield, "U.S. Wins Cut in UN Payments," *San Diego Union-Tribune*, December 23, 2000, p. A24.

33. Crossette, "U.N. Agrees to Cut Dues Paid by U.S.," *New York Times*, December 23, 2000, pp. A. 1, 6.

34. Ibid., p. A.6

35. Schmitt, "Senator Helms's Journey," *New York Times*, December 23, 2000, p. A.6

36. Quoted in Crossette, "U.N. Agrees to Cut Dues Paid by U.S.," p. A.6.

37. Traub, "Holbrooke's Campaign," *New York Times*, March 26, 2000.

38. Kams and Mingst, eds., *The United States and Multilateral Institutions*. See especially Chapter 11.

39. It is important to note that we have used the data in Figure 11.1 on both roll call and consensus votes as indicative of broad patterns in the U.S. relationship with the UN at different points in time. This is not meant to attach great weight to the voting data. Nonetheless, Figure 11.1 is particularly interesting because it charts all resolutions, those approved by consensus (which constitute about 80 percent of the total in recent years), and those on which roll call votes were taken. The perspective this provides is evident if compared with the voting analysis in Holloway, "U.S. Unilateralism at the UN." We are grateful to Harold K. Jacobson at the University of Michigan and especially to Jon Monger, his student assistant, for compiling the data for this figure.

40. Luck, *Mixed* Messages, p. 221.

41. Walt, "Two Cheers for Clinton's Legacy."

42. Lindsay, "The New Apathy," p. 5.

43. Ibid., p. 5.

44. For evaluations of President Clinton's foreign policy record, see Rieff, "A New Hierarchy of Values and Interests"; Kitfield, "Episodic Interest"; Berger, "American Foreign Policy for the Global Age"; and *Foreign Policy*, "Think Again: Clinton's Foreign Policy."

45. Quoted in *Foreign Policy*, "Think Again: Clinton's Foreign Policy," p. 24.

46. Hillen, "Forced Isolation."

47. Lindsay, "The New Apathy," pp. 4–5.

48. Luck, *Mixed Messages*, p. 38.

49. Ibid., p. 16.

50. Luck, "American Exceptionalism," p. 3.

51. Quoted in Campbell, "The Last Superpower Ponders Its Next Move," *New York Times*, February 19, 2001, p. Al5.

52. The *Brahimi Report* is officially known as the *Report of the Panel on United Nations Peace Operations* (A/55/305-S/2000/809) and can be found on the UN Website *(www.un.ore)* under "Peace and Security."

53. Luers, "Choosing Engagement," p. 14.

54. On shifts in Europe, see, for example, Cohen, "Europe's Shifting Role Poses Challenge to U.S.," *New York Times,* February 11, 2001, pp. 1, 4.

55. Both are paraphrased in Murphy, "Contemporary Practice," pp. 353–354.

56. Quoted in Crossette, "Helms, in Visit to U.N.," *New York Times,* January 21, 2000, pp. Al, 8.

57. Luers, "Choosing Engagement," p. 13.

58. Quoted in U.S. General Accounting Office, *United Nations Financial Issues and U.S. Arrears,* appendix 4.

59. Albright, "The United States and the United Nations."

60. Quoted in Dimoff, "U.N. Arrears," pp. 9–10.

61. Gardner, "The One Percent Solution," pp. 2 and 4.

62. Pastor, *A Century's Journey,* p. 235.

63. For a discussion of different views, see Spiro, "The New Sovereigntists."

64. U.S. General Accounting Office, *United Nations Reform Initiatives.*

65. Quoted in Williams, "Billion Dollar Donations."

66. Berger, "American Foreign Policy for the Global Age," p. 39.

12

Extraterritorial Sanctions: Managing "Hyper-Unilateralism" in U.S. Foreign Policy

Michael Mastanduno

EXTRATERRITORIAL SANCTIONS PROVOKE GREATER OUTRAGE AMONG U.S. trade and alliance partners than arguably any other U.S. foreign policy initiative. They motivate otherwise friendly governments to accuse the United States of technological imperialism, diplomatic arrogance, and the flagrant violation of international law. They prompt otherwise friendly populations to harass U.S. diplomats and take to the streets to protest U.S. foreign policy. The use of extraterritorial sanctions deflects attention away from the objectionable behavior of an appropriate target—a Soviet Union that invades its neighbors, an Iran that exports terrorism, a Cuba that abuses its population—and turns attention to the unacceptable behavior of the United States. As Canadian Trade Minister Arthur Eggleton put it in the middle of a recent extraterritorial dispute, "Washington takes aim at its foe and shoots its friend."[1]

Extraterritoriality may be defined generally as "the problem of conflicting claims by nation-states to apply their laws and implement their policies to affect conduct outside their territory in a way that may undermine and conflict with the laws and policies of a foreign government."[2] Extraterritorial economic sanctions typically involve efforts by U.S. officials to apply U.S. sanction laws and policies beyond the borders of the United States. These efforts seek to pressure foreign actors—governments, corporations, even individuals—to abide by sanctions that have been adopted by the United States but not by other governments.

The U.S. government occasionally adopts economic sanctions with no intention of enlisting multilateral support. In most cases, however, U.S. officials face three choices once they are commited to employing economic sanctions for foreign policy purposes. First, they can foster and then abide by a multilateral consensus, and if necessary adjust U.S. national sanctions to whatever is agreed upon multilaterally. Second, they can "agree to disagree" with other sanctioning governments and implement national sanctions above and beyond the multilateral consensus, but without disrupting that consensus. Third, they can refuse to accept any divergence in sanctions strategy and try to force other governments to accept and abide by the U.S. preference for (typically) more comprehensive economic sanctions. The extraterritorial extension of U.S. sanctions is one way, and generally the most controversial way, to carry out this third option. Extraterritorial sanctions clearly reflect the unilateralist impulse in U.S. foreign policy. But this aggressive posture arguably warrants the even stronger label of "hyper-unilateralism"—or the coercive effort to extract the compliance of other actors with the unilateral preferences of the United States.

Proponents of unilateralism in U.S. foreign policy usually are seeking to protect U.S. sovereignty from what they perceive to be the intrusions of, or constraints imposed by, international institutions or agreements. Economic sanctions, however, pose a somewhat different problem. The United States is generally supportive of a multilateral approach to economic sanctions. Its concern in this policy area is not that multilateral cooperation goes "too far," but rather that it does not go far enough in punishing the targets of sanctions, whether they be the Soviet Union, Cuba, and China during the Cold War or Cuba, Iran, and Libya today. Rather than an attempt to protect U.S. sovereignty, extraterritorial sanctions seek to intrude upon the sovereignty of others so that the United States can accomplish its own foreign policy objectives more effectively.

The temptation to extend sanctions extraterritorially emerges whenever the United States employs unilateral sanctions—that is, sanctions that are more comprehensive than those preferred and employed by other sanctioning governments. This temptation is ever present because the United States resorts routinely, and with increasing frequency, to unilateral economic sanctions. The United States is the world's undisputed leader in unilateral sanctions for both political and economic reasons. As the world's dominant military, diplomatic, and economic actor, the United States has foreign policy interests in every corner of the world, in contrast to regionally focused major powers in Europe and Asia. And, even though the United States has strong trade interests, its national economy is relatively more insulated and self-sufficient than those of its major trade-dependent allies. The states of Western Europe and Japan typically have been far more reluctant than the United States to bear the economic costs and disruptions of using economic sanctions as routine instruments of statecraft.

In many cases, the United States grudgingly tolerates the differential between its comprehensive economic sanctions and the relatively limited sanctions of its major trading partners and allies. U.S. officials, in the words of George Ball thirty years ago, often seem content to limit U.S. trade unilaterally "for the momentary moral glow we may derive from an act of self-denial."[3] In certain circumstances, however, U.S. officials prove unwilling to tolerate the limited sanctions of other industrialized states. Instead, they have launched sustained and aggressive diplomatic efforts to secure an expansion of multilateral commitments. At the extreme, they have raised the stakes politically by asserting that the more comprehensive sanctions adopted by the United States apply extraterritorially to other countries. "Classic cases" of extraterritorial conflict include the Siberian gas pipeline dispute of 1982 and a series of conflicts with Canada and Western Europe over trade with China and Cuba during the 1950s and 1960s.[4] More recent cases include the Helms-Burton extraterritorial sanctions (or Libertad Act) of 1996 and the Iran-Libya Sanctions Act (ILSA) of that same year. These two cases will be discussed in detail later in this chapter.

Extraterritorial sanctions offer the United States both benefits and drawbacks. The benefits include the potential for successful coercion if extraterritorial measures convince foreign actors to comply with the demands of the United States and tighten their sanctions against the common target. Even if coercion is not fully successful, certain "signaling" benefits may accrue to the United States. By raising the stakes on any given foreign policy issue, the imposition of extraterritorial sanctions signals to both allies and adversaries that the issue is a U.S. foreign policy priority.[5] Finally, there are potential benefits in the domestic political arena. Extraterritorial sanctions suggest that U.S. officials are taking seriously, or "doing something about," a foreign policy problem; they are getting tough with allies or trading partners who are "trading with the enemy." Extraterritorial sanctions may also be a means to buy off, or perhaps enlist the political support of, particular interest groups and/or their representatives in Congress.

The drawbacks of using extraterritorial sanctions are political as well as economic. The potential diplomatic costs are profound. Extraterritorial sanctions, because they are perceived as posing a direct challenge to sovereign authority, typically elicit reactions of indignation, outrage, and defiance on the part of their targets that in most cases are U.S. allies and trading partners. Stuart Eizenstat, the U.S. policy official assigned to explain the Helms-Burton Act to U.S. partners, was pelted with eggs in Mexico and subjected behind closed doors in Europe to what one State Department official described as "the most undiplomatic language I've ever seen."[6] It is common to observe a "rally around the flag" effect among the targets of extraterritorial sanctions. During the Siberian pipeline dispute, U.S. sanctions did more to unify diverse constituencies in Western Europe than did any actions taken by the ostensible enemy, the Soviet Union. Britain's Margaret Thatcher, France's François Mitterrand, and Germany's Helmut Schmidt generally agreed on very little but did come together decisively in defiance of U.S. extraterritorial sanctions.[7] These sanctions also carry economic costs to the United States. Their imposition tags U.S. domestic firms with reputations as unreliable suppliers, not only in trade with rogue states— the ultimate targets of the sanctions—but even in the more important trade with other industrialized states (the proximate targets of the extraterritorial sanctions).

Do extraterritorial sanctions "work"? This question is necessarily wrapped up in the more general debate over the effectiveness of economic sanctions. Some scholars and policy analysts are convinced that sanctions never work, while others are prepared to grant a qualified endorsement to economic measures as alternatives to other means of statecraft.[8] The answer one gives depends in no small part on the objectives one expects sanctions to achieve.[9] Sanctions pessimists typically focus on the inability of economic statecraft to satisfy ambitious goals such as the overthrow of a target government or the transformation of its foreign policy in some major way. Sanctions optimists stress the complex and multiple objectives of any attempt at influence. But even sanctions optimists do not expect economic measures to be effective most of the time, and they do not expect that sanctions by themselves will be decisive when major foreign policy stakes are involved.[10]

Both pessimists and optimists are likely to agree that however difficult it is to get economic sanctions in general to work effectively, it is all the more difficult to get extraterritorial sanctions to do so. These sanctions are, by necessity, usually aimed at powerful industrial states rather than smaller or weaker targets. Moreover, by imposing U.S. laws on foreign-based subjects, these sanctions challenge not only policy autonomy but also sovereign authority, increasing the political costs to the target government of backing down. Sanctions have a greater chance of success when carried out quietly—that is, when they do not force the target government to defend its sovereignty publicly.[11] But, it is difficult to keep extraterritorial sanctions quiet. Target governments usually have political incentives to publicize their outrage, while initiators or supporters of such measures have political incentives to publicize their attempt.

This last point is particularly relevant in the case of the United States. The central foreign policy decisionmakers of the United States—the president and the State Department—generally have been reluctant to employ extraterritorial sanctions. This is not surprising in light of the expected high costs and modest likelihood of success. Left to their own devices, central decisionmakers would forgo the opportunity to use extraterritorial sanctions. But, in the U.S. political system they do not enjoy that luxury. The U.S. foreign policy process is complex, and decisionmaking authority is shared and decentralized within the executive branch and between the executive branch and Congress. Interest groups have multiple access points to government officials, and the latter are necessarily sensitive both to particularistic interests and to broader public sentiment.

In this context, the use of extraterritorial sanctions has proven to be more a political act, entangled in domestic politics and ideology, than a rational instrument of statecraft. Their use, moreover, dates back many decades. During the Korean War, amid accusations that the United States' closest allies were providing the enemy with the material means to kill U.S.

soldiers, Congress initiated the Battle Act, an effort to force the U.S. allies receiving Marshall Plan aid to abide by the U.S. comprehensive embargoes of China and the Soviet Union. More recently, Congress passed the Helms-Burton bill in response to intense political pressure from Cuban Americans living in Florida, and shortly after three U.S. civilians were killed by Cuban warplanes in international airspace in February 1996. Likewise, ILSA was used against two "rogue" states in the Middle East suspected of aiding and abetting international terrorism, including terrorist acts that directly affected the United States.

In the typical pattern, extraterritorial sanctions are initiated by members of Congress who feel that the United States is not being sufficiently tough with trading partners that refuse to comply with the full measure of U.S. sanctions against some primary target. Congressional action is usually taken in response to public pressure and with the tacit support of allies in the executive branch.[12] The State Department typically opposes the resort to extraterritorial measures. The president, meanwhile, often finds himself in a no-win situation: he is under domestic political pressure to impose or extend sanctions extraterritorially, yet he is reluctant to do so in light of the expected costs—in particular, the diplomatic costs of provoking the ire of other sovereign states.

The solution to what is essentially a political problem lies in the management, or attempted damage limitation, of extraterritorial sanctions. In cases where the president has been unable to withstand pressure to impose sanctions, he (and the State Department) have sought to minimize the subsequent negative effects through a variety of expedients. These tactics have included legislative initiatives, such as the drafting of escape clauses or waivers that give U.S. officials some breathing room in the implementation of sanctions against violators of U.S. law. The executive branch has also relied on diplomatic tactics, including face-saving solutions that enable target governments to cooperate in some way without either giving in or feeling the full force of extraterritorial sanctions. At the same time, U.S. officials have been forced to sell these arrangements domestically, hoping to convince domestic proponents that the threat, if not the actual imposition, of extraterritorial sanctions has brought meaningful results.

In short, extraterritorial sanctions are played out in the context of a "two-level" diplomatic game. We can conceive of the president and State Department officials as being at the center of this game, seeking simultaneously to satisfy the political demands of domestic proponents of sanctions and to minimize the political alienation of foreign partners who are targets of sanctions. The more effectively central decisionmakers can play this game, the more likely they will be to extract some benefits and minimize the costs and risks of this hyper-unilateral tool of statecraft.

In the next section of this chapter, I briefly examine historical episodes involving the management of hyper-unilateral initiatives by U.S. officials.

The purpose is not to provide a comprehensive analysis, but to establish the basic pattern in the initiation and resolution of these sanctions cases. This section offers brief summaries of earlier extraterritorial sanctions cases, followed by more detailed case studies of the two major, post–Cold War efforts to employ extraterritorial sanctions. The final section provides lessons and policy recommendations.

Hyper-Unilateralism and the Two-Level Game: Historical Illustrations

The Battle Act, 1950–1953

This is a classic case of effective executive management.[13] Early in the Cold War, the United States maintained economic sanctions against communist states that were far more comprehensive than those maintained by the United States' more trade dependent and war-ravaged European allies. Executive branch officials were satisfied that cooperation among the members of CoCom (the Coordinating Committee for Multilateral Export Controls, formed by the United States and its Western European allies in 1949) was sufficient, even though it did not reach the level of U.S. controls. Members of Congress were not satisfied, however, and passed legislation requiring the U.S. government to cut off economic and military aid to any U.S. ally unwilling to replicate in full the comprehensive sanctions of the United States. Congressional proponents of the Battle Act accused Western European states of trading with the enemy during the Korean War. These European governments greatly resented the Battle Act, and many warned that if the United States applied the full force of this law, their own internal politics would force them to abandon their economic discrimination against the Soviet Union altogether. U.S. executive branch officials, who had worked hard to forge the multilateral consensus underlying CoCom, feared that the Battle Act risked destroying the nascent Western alliance in order to save it.

The State Department devised a solution that was quietly endorsed by allied governments. In short, these governments agreed to expand their formal restrictions on trade with the communist world, bringing their control lists into closer conformity with the comprehensive list preferred by the United States. In exchange, the United States introduced an exceptions procedure into CoCom that enabled allied countries to trade with the East on a case-by-case basis. This was a win-win arrangement: Members of Congress could point to the expansion of Western European restrictions; Western European nations knew that they would be able in "hardship cases" to export to (or import needed items from) the East. Each year the executive reported to Congress that allied governments were in compliance with the terms of the legislation and explained why the exceptions granted were appropriate.

Effective management enabled the executive branch to minimize the diplomatic damage of employing these second-order sanctions, while at the same time increasing the allied controls. It is worth noting that the U.S. solution was facilitated by the prior existence of a multilateral institution, CoCom. The fact that the executive branch already controlled sanctions coordination within an existing multilateral institution increased that branch's room to maneuver in devising a creative solution to its two-level problem.

The Siberian Pipeline, 1981–1982

The pipeline episode represents an instance of executive branch management that was somewhat less effective. The United States intensified the Cold War during the Reagan administration, and the Defense Department in particular saw an opportunity to cripple the Soviet economy through the coordinated denial of trade. Western European governments, however, viewed U.S. economic warfare as economically costly and unnecessarily provocative politically. They were determined to continue economic relations with the Soviet Union, the cornerstone of which was a massive, long-term exchange of European energy technology and equipment in return for Soviet natural gas. U.S. officials sought to dissuade their allies from this project, but to no avail. Secretary of State Alexander Haig resolved that the United States and its partners should agree to disagree rather than escalate the conflict through extraterritorial sanctions. Influential members of Congress, the Defense Department, and the NSC saw it differently, and in June 1982 they convinced President Reagan to coerce the allies by imposing sanctions against Western European firms, including U.S. subsidiaries based in Western Europe, that participated in the project. These firms were barred from exporting to or receiving supplies from the United States.

Most Western European firms, forced to choose between trade with the United States or the Soviet Union, would have chosen the former. But Western European governments did not allow them to choose, passing legislation forcing the firms to honor their Soviet pipeline contracts. The United States responded with sanctions against the firms. The Western European counterresponse was to reopen dormant disputes in GATT, threaten to withdraw from CoCom, and reconsider the decision by NATO to deploy new intermediate-range missiles. Western European governments were already under pressure from their publics on the missile issue, and the extraterritorial sanctions reinforced the widespread public view of the United States as a domineering, and ultimately dangerous, alliance partner. Placards at peace demonstrations in West Germany captured this sentiment: "Better to have gas from the East than rockets from the West."[14]

The Soviet Union became the beneficiary of the most intense intra-alliance dispute since the Suez crisis of 1956. A face-saving solution came only after several months of confrontation and stalemate. The United States essentially backed down, agreeing to remove its sanctions in exchange for a commitment from allied governments to undertake a series of studies on the risks of East-West trade for alliance security.

The pipeline dispute carried high short-term costs for the United States. Diplomatic resentment increased, and Atlantic trade and security cooperation were set back. U.S.-based firms lost contracts with European affiliates and were tagged as unreliable suppliers. Some European firms in the energy sector reduced reliance on U.S. firms as a source of supply. These costs were avoidable, because the reaction of other NATO governments was predictable. But U.S. officials proceeded with sanctions anyway, in part out of frustration with the failure to get other Western states to see the East-West contest as Washington did, and in part to "wake up" the allies to the dangers of liberalized trade with a potential military adversary. The United States and its NATO allies started down a dangerous road that might have ended in a full alliance rupture. But U.S. officials ultimately resorted to damage limitation, finding a face-saving way to back down before the conflict escalated out of control.

Reexport Controls During the Cold War

Throughout the Cold War, U.S. officials tried to control the movement of particular U.S.-origin goods and services, even after these had left the shores of the United States.[15] According to a system of "reexport" licensing rules, foreign-based firms that imported certain U.S.-origin goods or services were required to ask permission from the U.S. government before reexporting those items to any other location. The United States claimed the extraterritorial right to control, for example, the ability of a German company to resell a piece of machinery to Austria, even after five or ten years, if that piece had originated in the United States.

Reexport controls arguably qualify as a successful exercise of extraterritorial sanctions. Firms in CoCom member countries generally complied with U.S. controls, affording additional protection to exports restricted by the United States and enabling U.S. officials to track patterns in high-technology trade between West and East. More important, these controls allowed U.S. officials to exact the compliance by non-CoCom members with CoCom controls. Faced with the prospect of extensive licensing requirements in trade with the United States, countries such as Austria, Switzerland, Finland, South Korea, and Singapore chose instead to cooperate quietly with CoCom restrictions on trade with the East.

The success of reexport controls resulted from the combination of two exceptional circumstances. First, the firms of other countries were heavily dependent on the United States as a source of the most sophisticated technologies, particularly electronics and computers. This extreme dependence prompted firms, and their governments, to tolerate what were otherwise distasteful extraterritorial measures. Second, reexport controls were "quiet" sanctions, administered without political fanfare through a licensing system controlled by the State and Commerce departments. Neither the United States nor allied governments had strong political incentives to publicize these controls.

This success was not unqualified. On occasion, disgruntled foreign firms forced their governments to protest what they considered to be outrageous U.S. behavior. In one such instance, IBM (prompted by the Defense Department) sent a letter to its customers in Britain reminding them that they needed U.S. government permission even to move computers from one location to another within Britain. U.S. officials sought to mollify their British counterparts after the latter hurled public accusations of "technological imperialism" at the United States.[16] There is also some evidence that other CoCom governments retaliated quietly against the United States by relaxing their own enforcement of export controls. The extent to which this occurred is difficult to ascertain. The same holds true for the (very plausible) claim that reexport controls, like the extraterritorial pipeline sanctions, created economic incentives for foreign firms to limit their dependence on U.S. sources of supply.

Extraterritorial Sanctions After the Cold War

We now turn to post–Cold War examples of the U.S. use of extraterritorial sanctions. The two most salient cases involve measures directed against the foreign trading partners of Cuba, on the one hand, and those of Iran and Libya, on the other. These case studies demonstrate the continued relevance of the basic two-level dynamic that is the central argument of this chapter. In these two cases the impetus for extraterritorial sanctions came from Congress, while strong resistance came from close allies and trading partners of the United States. Executive officials were forced to conduct a delicate balancing act between these internal and external political pressures.

Extending the U.S. Cuba Embargo: Helms-Burton

U.S. sanctions against Castro's Cuba began during the Eisenhower administration and have endured through the terms of eight successive U.S. presidents. A comprehensive economic embargo of Cuba was in effect by 1962. The goals of this long-standing policy have been multiple and complex. They have included (most ambitiously) to undermine Castro and remove him from power; to constrain his ability to export revolution; to isolate

Cuba regionally and globally; and to signal to other states, in the Western Hemisphere and elsewhere, U.S. intolerance for Castro's domestic politics and foreign policy.[17]

At the outset of the embargo, Cuba's economy depended overwhelmingly on that of the United States. Nevertheless, U.S. officials sought to enlist multilateral support both for reasons of political solidarity and to maximize the economic pain imposed on Castro's regime. The Organization of American States (OAS) joined the embargo in 1964. U.S. allies in Western Europe and Japan proved willing to restrict trade selectively, agreeing not to export weapons or civilian goods with military potential. But they were unwilling to impose broad restrictions on the Cuban economy and would not agree to add Cuba to the list of countries targeted by CoCom.[18] Throughout the 1960s, U.S. officials sought, through the Treasury's Foreign Asset Control Regulations, to control extraterritorially the trade with Cuba of U.S. subsidiaries based in Canada and Western Europe. These efforts were a source of continued diplomatic conflict between the United States and its allies, particularly as it became apparent that the Castro regime, supported economically and politically by the Soviet Union, was not going to collapse.

Whatever initial multilateral support the United States managed to obtain had clearly unraveled by the 1970s. In 1975, the OAS voted to lift its embargo of Cuba and to allow each member state to determine its own level and extent of trade with Cuba. At the same time, U.S. officials recognized the reality of expanding trade between Western Europe and Cuba and the futility of trying to prevent it. Accordingly, the Ford administration revoked the regulation denying U.S. aid to countries that permitted ships to deliver goods to Cuba, relaxed restrictions on the trade of U.S. subsidiaries with Cuba, and applied a more liberal interpretation of U.S. reexport controls. These practices continued during the Carter years, when the Treasury Department coordinated a program of voluntary compliance, requesting U.S.-based firms to discourage their overseas subsidiaries from trading with Cuba.[19]

During the 1980s, as Central America and the Caribbean became areas of strategic concern for the United States, the Reagan administration tightened the Cuban embargo. Reagan officials severely restricted the ability of U.S. citizens to travel to the island and redoubled efforts to prevent U.S. exports to Cuba and Cuban-origin goods from reaching the United States. Still, U.S. officials continued to recognize that multilateral support for the U.S.-style embargo of Cuba would not be forthcoming. The United States, in effect, agreed to disagree with its allies and trading partners and pursued its comprehensive embargo unilaterally.

This pattern changed significantly during the 1990s. Cuba lost its principal source of trade and economic aid following the end of the Cold War and the collapse of the Soviet Union. Cuba's new vulnerability presented the United States with an opportunity to squeeze the Cuban economy and to force Fidel Castro either to undertake radical reform or to surrender his grip on power. Since U.S. trade was already closed off, applying additional pressure on Cuba meant restricting the island's access to its main non–Soviet bloc trading partners, most important, Canada, Mexico, and the states of the EU. The Cuba Democracy Act of 1992 took an initial extraterritorial step by reasserting restrictions on trade between Cuba and overseas subsidiaries of U.S.-based firms. Approximately $700 million in trade was affected, including that involving subsidiaries of major U.S. companies such as Dow Chemical, Union Carbide, and United Technologies. The bulk of Cuba's trade, however, valued at some $5 billion annually, was conducted with foreign firms that were not subsidiaries of U.S. firms.[20] For sanctions to have the economic effect desired by U.S. officials, the United States would need to further extend its extraterritorial reach.

The 1992 act was followed four years later by the far more controversial Cuba Liberty and Democratic Solidarity Act (Libertad Act, Public Law 104-114), which entered into effect in August 1996. The Helms-Burton Act, as it is more commonly known, asserts that any individuals or firms that participate in or profit from trafficking in property confiscated or nationalized from U.S. citizens in Cuba after 1959 are in violation of U.S. law.[21] Title III of the act enables U.S. claimants (individuals or firms) to sue the "traffickers" in U.S. courts for damages up to the fair market value of the property. Title IV of the act prohibits traffickers, including the corporate executives of foreign firms and their families, from entering the United States. The Helms-Burton Act, in short, directs U.S. executive officials to impose extraterritorial sanctions on noncooperating foreign firms and individuals, and even allows U.S. citizens to punish them as well.

Helms-Burton: Causes. From at least the middle of the 1970s to the end of the Cold War, U.S. officials were resigned to pursuing the Cuba embargo unilaterally. Why did they escalate the effort during the 1990s with a provocative, extraterritorial extension? A strategic rationale was suggested above. The collapse of Cuba's Soviet patron left the island and regime more vulnerable to economic sanctions than it had been for thirty years. To some U.S. policymakers, this strategic opportunity was too tempting to pass up, even though it necessitated reopening the sensitive extraterritorial issue. Ideology reinforced strategy. The Clinton administration centered its foreign policy, at least rhetorically, on the promotion of democracy, and it had felt compelled to respond with pressure when Haiti's elected leader was overthrown in 1990. Cuba, like Haiti, was located in the United States' immediate neighborhood, and to supporters of democratic engagement it seemed natural to ratchet up the economic pressure on one of the last bastions of Communist rule.

However, domestic politics, in the form of interest group and electoral considerations, had an even more decisive effect. The impetus for extraterritorial sanctions came from Congress rather than from the foreign policy officials of the executive branch. Anti-Castro forces, organized under the auspices of the Cuban American Federation and the Cuban American National Foundation, helped to persuade the majority in Congress to pass the 1992 Act. The inclination of President George Bush, as the Cold War ended, had been to pursue a less restrictive policy toward Cuba. But electoral pressures during 1992 made this politically risky, especially since Bush's Democratic opponent, Bill Clinton, aggressively courted the Cuban-American vote in pivotal states such as Florida and New Jersey. Bush's ultimate endorsement of the 1992 Cuba Democracy Act was a means to disarm Clinton's campaign weapon.

By the mid-1990s, U.S. corporations began to provide a counterweight to the so-called Cuba lobby. U.S.-based firms viewed the end of the Cold War as an opportunity to break into markets previously subject to a variety of political restrictions. China was clearly the biggest prize and received the majority of attention. But corporate officials devoted lobbying efforts to Cuba and Vietnam as well. These markets had considerable growth potential, and U.S. firms were forced by what they perceived as anachronistic Cold War restrictions to sit on the sidelines while their counterparts in other advanced industrial states consolidated and expanded their economic presence.

Late in 1995, members of Congress steered between these crosscutting interest group pressures by passing the Libertad Act—but without including the controversial Title III and IV initiatives. The intent was to support democratic reform in Cuba, which the Cuba lobby favored, but to do so through the incremental and conditional opening of economic relations, which business favored. This delicate balance shifted decisively early in 1996, after Cuban forces shot down two aircraft belonging to U.S. citizens. Congress moved to punish Cuba and strengthened the Libertad Act with the inclusion of Titles III and IV. Foreign policy officials within the executive branch, including the president, clearly held reservations about the prudence of extraterritorial sanctions. But 1996, like 1992, was an election year, and President Clinton responded to the political incentives. He signed the Libertad Act into law in March 1996 and stated:

> This Act is a justified response to the Cuban government's unjustified, unlawful attack on two unarmed U.S. civilian aircraft that left three citizens and one U.S. resident dead. . . . Immediately after Cuba's brutal act, I urged that differences on the bill be set aside so that the United States could speak in a single, strong voice. By acting swiftly—just seventeen days after the attack—we are sending a powerful message to the Cuban regime that we do not and will not tolerate such conduct.[22]

Helms-Burton: Consequences. Any assessment of this extraterritorial initiative must consider its benefits as well as costs. For the Clinton administration, much of the benefits accrued in the domestic political arena. The president's endorsement of Helms-Burton was a dramatic way to signal to the U.S. Congress and public that the administration would not tolerate acts of aggression and was committed to promoting political change in Cuba by depriving the Castro regime of access to hard currency and other economic necessities. The escalation of sanctions—admittedly a costly step—also sent these messages to U.S. allies in the Americas and Europe.[23] For the administration to forgo some type of decisive action in these circumstances would be to risk signaling political weakness at home and abroad.

Extraterritorial sanctions brought additional benefits, in that some foreign firms responded to the threat of U.S. sanctions by reevaluating their existing economic relations with Cuba. The Clinton administration's initial step was to send a letter in July 1996 to selected foreign firms, warning them that their activities in Cuba made them liable under the terms of the new U.S. legislation. Cemex, a Mexican cement firm, reacted by suspending its operations in Cuba. STET, an Italian telecommunications company, struck a deal with a potential claimant, agreeing to pay ITT $25 million for the right to continue using the latter's confiscated property in Cuba. Two Spanish hotel firms withdrew from Cuba after their stock values dropped sharply in anticipation of possible U.S. sanctions against them.[24] As in the case of the Siberian pipeline, some firms, left to their own devices, calculated that it was better to sacrifice their trade with the target country than to incur the wrath of the United States. The reaction of sovereign governments, however, was rather different.

The most immediate costs faced by the United States were in the diplomatic arena. Helms-Burton provoked outrage almost uniformly from governments otherwise friendly to the United States. Twenty-three members of the OAS (with ten abstentions) voted for a resolution condemning the U.S. legislation as a blatant example of unjustified intervention in the internal affairs of sovereign states. Canadian diplomats termed the United States a "bully," and Mexico's President Ernesto Zedillo asserted that Helms-Burton was "simply a violation of international law."[25] The Canadian and Mexican governments introduced retaliatory legislation to protect firms in their countries targeted by Helms-Burton.[26] A powerful coalition of U.S. companies, including Exxon, General Electric, and IBM, sided with foreign governments and launched a lobbying campaign in 1997 in opposition to Helms-Burton in particular and to the unilateral use of economic sanctions more generally.[27]

An even larger problem for U.S. officials involved the risks of escalation. The Helms-Burton initiative had the potential to trigger an action-reaction sequence that would carry costs for the United States that were far disproportionate to any possible benefits. The passage of the act itself provoked a sense of diplomatic outrage and the threat of countermeasures. If U.S. officials decided to enforce Title III and allow U.S. firms and citizens to sue foreign firms and individuals, these countermeasures would most likely be implemented. In addition to "blocking orders" that would make the U.S. legislation unenforceable in their countries, Canada and members of the EU also prepared new "right to recovery" laws that would enable local firms and individuals to countersue U.S. firms in Canadian or European courts to recover damages.[28]

More important, the EU threatened to take the Helms-Burton matter to the newly fortified WTO dispute settlement mechanism. While Washington could deflect such a maneuver by invoking a national security exemption in the WTO, the United States had a strong stake in the success of the new WTO dispute mechanism. For the system's most powerful member to claim a national security exemption in one of the mechanism's first test cases would damage the credibility of the WTO at its infancy. It would make it politically plausible for other states to claim similar exemptions for their own particular "national security" reasons. In short, the implementation of Helms-Burton sanctions risked compromising the effectiveness of the new multilateral trade regime—a regime in which U.S. foreign policy officials were deeply invested. The United States' trading partners, of course, presumably would suffer as well from an escalation of the conflict. But the fact that they perceived Helms-Burton as a blatant and public infringement on their sovereign authority made them reluctant to back down in the face of U.S. pressure.

Managing the risks of escalation by playing the two-level game. Having signed Helms-Burton into law, President Clinton forced his administration into a delicate balancing act. On the one hand, administration officials needed to soften the impact of the legislation to placate their foreign partners and avoid the risks of escalation. On the other hand, they needed to satisfy the domestic constituents whose expectations of a decisive confrontation between the forces of right and wrong were now raised. Between 1996 and 2000 the administration proved fairly effective at striking this balance.

The initial step of executive branch officials was to demonstrate both that they took the legislation seriously and that they were willing to negotiate a compromise. In July 1996 the State Department sent formal notices to selected foreign firms, warning them that they would face punitive measures if they continued to do business in Cuba—including having their top executives and their families barred from entering the United States. A prominent target was Sherritt International, the largest Canadian company involved in Cuba. Sherritt operated, jointly with the Cuban government, a mine that had been expropriated from a U.S. company in 1959. When Sherritt made clear its refusal to yield to U.S. pressure, U.S. officials followed through with sanctions against Sherritt's top executives. The Canadian government promptly responded by introducing legislation to amend its Foreign Extraterritorial Measures Act to give Canadian firms the legal tools to defend themselves against U.S. claims under the Libertad Act.[29]

At precisely the time it sanctioned selected foreign firms, the administration also announced its decision to forbid U.S. firms and individuals, for an initial period of six months, from filing lawsuits against foreign firms using expropriated property. This decision postponed a great deal of potential legal action under Helms-Burton, because as of 1996 almost six thousand U.S. firms and individuals with prior investments in Cuba had filed claims worth almost $2 billion with the U.S. Foreign Claims Settlement Commission.[30]

The administration's strategy was to pursue limited punitive measures under Title IV, while holding off private claims for broader measures under Title III. The message to U.S. trading partners was, in effect, that "we will enforce this, but we'd like to negotiate so that we do not have to." The message to domestic proponents of Helms-Burton was "we are taking the legislation seriously and will not let traffickers get away with it." It is revealing that President Clinton dispatched his chosen envoy, Stuart Eizenstat, in the summer of 1996 not only to twelve foreign capitals, but also to Florida, New Jersey, and to the relevant committees of Congress as well.[31]

The initial six-month waiver of Title III provisions gave U.S. and EU officials some room to negotiate, even as the public posturing accelerated on both sides of the Atlantic. The EU wanted the legislation revoked; short of that, they wanted the president to continue to prevent private claims from going forward under Title III and to forgo state sanctions against foreign executives under Title IV. U.S. negotiators, ideally, wanted compliance with the U.S. embargo of Cuba. Short of that, they wanted their allies and trading partners to take some steps that demonstrated an appreciation of and commitment to the broad U.S. policy objectives in relations with Cuba.

The two sides struck a preliminary deal near the end of 1996. After protracted negotiations with each other and with the United States, EU member governments agreed to a "common position" on Cuba. The common position links improvements in EU relations with Cuba, including economic relations, to fundamental changes in Cuba with regard to human rights and fundamental freedoms.[32] U.S. officials depicted this statement as a major breakthrough, claiming that European countries now recognized and shared the primary U.S. objective of forcing democratic change in Cuba. In return, in January 1997, President Clinton again used his waiver authority under Title III to prevent private claims against foreign expropriators from moving forward. EU officials subsequently agreed to hold off bringing their complaint against Helms-Burton to the WTO dispute settlement mechanism—as long as the president continued to exercise his Title III waiver authority. U.S. officials made clear that the suspension of Title III claims did not remove the right of U.S. individuals and firms to sue at some point in the future. EU officials made clear they were only suspending, and not abandoning, their WTO complaint. Each side compromised, while signaling its determination to keep the other's feet to the fire.

The Clinton administration continued to use its authority to suspend claims under Title III, every six months between January 1997 and July

2000.[33] The end of each six-month interval offered U.S. officials the opportunity to review the performance of other governments in linking their relations with Cuba to that nation's progress toward democratic reform, and to place additional pressure on those governments to do so. For their part, EU governments used the occasions of U.S. review to reassess their common position on Cuba, and, in the face of inadequate progress toward Cuban democracy, to reaffirm their policy. They also committed themselves to assisting the United States in prodding other governments to become involved in the diplomatic effort to promote change in Cuba. Official U.S. statements duly noted these EU efforts.[34] U.S. officials consistently pointed out publicly that what began as a shrill dispute between the United States and its allies had evolved into a collective diplomatic effort, involving governments, NGOs, and the private sector, to promote the changes in Cuba favored by the United States. Eizenstat continually reminded members of Congress of the tacit deal: "This multilateral effort would not be strengthened by the initiation of lawsuits under Title III. To make additional progress, we must continue to have the cooperation of our allies by definition."[35]

The punitive measures initially adopted under Title IV afforded additional diplomatic leverage to U.S. officials. EU members, alarmed at the prospect of their corporate officials being denied entry into the United States, pushed U.S. negotiators to seek an amendment to the Libertad Act that would grant the president permanent waiver authority over Title IV sanctions. The Clinton team agreed to seek this waiver authority, but only if the EU took steps to accommodate U.S. concerns over the use of illegally expropriated property in Cuba. In May 1998, the United States and the EU reached an understanding on expropriated property.[36] The key to the compromise was for the agreement not to focus explicitly on Cuba, but instead on the more general problem of the illegal use of expropriated property. The understanding calls on the United States and EU to recognize illegal expropriation as a global concern; to prohibit government loans, grants, or subsidies to investors currently using illegally expropriated property anywhere in the world; and to enforce an outright ban on future investments of illegally expropriated property. The two sides agreed to establish a registry of claims and commercial assistance for firms and individuals victimized by this illegal activity. In announcing the agreement, U.S. officials proclaimed triumphantly, "Europeans now acknowledge that one of the primary tools the Castro regime used to expropriate property from U.S. citizens appears to have been contrary to international law."[37] European officials made clear that the understanding on appropriated property would not go into effect without an amendment to Helms-Burton granting presidential waiver authority over Title IV sanctions.

The administration's two-level strategy subsequently shifted to the domestic front, but as of the end of the Clinton administration the executive branch was still unable to secure the preferred amendment. The administration labored to convince Congress that considerable progress had been made, and that Castro's lobbying against the U.S.-EU understanding on appropriated property indicated that he recognized that the tide had turned against him and that the understanding would have a chilling effect on investments in Cuba. The strongest proponents of Helms-Burton in Congress, however, expressed skepticism about the EU commitment to enforce the provisions of the understanding, particularly against Cuba.[38]

Despite the stalemate over Title IV, the overall compromise between the United States and the EU held up through the end of the Clinton era. In December 2000 the EU reaffirmed its common position on Cuba. In January 2001 President Clinton returned the favor by suspending once again claims under Title III.[39]

Isolating "Rogue" States: The Iran-Libya Sanctions Act of 1996

The postwar transformation of Iran from an ally into an adversary of the United States has been profound. The shah of Iran proved to be a strong anticommunist (and domestically repressive) partner of the United States from the middle of the 1950s until the collapse of his regime in the late 1970s, which was followed by the fundamentalist revolution and the seizing of the U.S. Embassy in Teheran. Iran and the United States became bitter enemies, and U.S. officials, viewing Iran as the greater of two evils, tilted toward Iraq during the Iran-Iraq war of the 1980s. The relationship continued to sour during the 1990s, even after the United States organized and fought a war against Iran's enemy, Iraq. In 1993, the Clinton administration announced a policy of "dual containment" that equated Iran with Iraq as a threat to U.S. national security.[40] U.S. officials took to depicting Iran, along with Libya and Iraq, as "rogue" states, unfit under their current regimes to be legitimate members of the international community. In April 1995, the Clinton administration banned all U.S. trade with and investment in Iran in response to what it perceived as Iran's support for international terrorism, its efforts to frustrate the Arab-Israeli peace process, and its ongoing programs to develop weapons of mass destruction (WMD).

The United States sought the support of its alliance partners in Europe for the economic containment of Iran, but this was not forthcoming. Germany, with the support of other EU countries, instead chose to pursue a "critical dialogue" with Iran in the hope that political and economic engagement would work better than confrontation to moderate Iranian policy. As German Foreign Minister Klaus Kinkel put it, "It is wrong to isolate a nation of 60 million people which plays a key role in the world and put it into a corner."[41]

This transatlantic disagreement over foreign policy strategy was obviously a disagreement over economic strategy as well. As the U.S. government imposed a comprehensive embargo and sought to discourage investment in Iran, European governments were doing the opposite. They facilitated the rescheduling of some $12 billion of Iran's private debt in 1994–1995, and overrode U.S. vetoes to allow World Bank loans to Iran. Some of the largest German firms, including Mannesmann and Siemens, conducted substantial business in Iran, and the German government subsidized their activities with export credit guarantees. France, Italy, and other EU countries engaged Iran in much the same way. European firms had a particular interest in Iran's energy sector, both because of opportunities for profit on the export side and, for some, their reliance on Iran as an energy source.[42]

This is not to imply the complete absence of multilateral restrictions on Iran. The United States and European governments cooperated in maintaining controls on the export of sensitive technologies through control regimes for WMD, such as the Nuclear Suppliers Group, the Australia Group, and the Missile Technology Control Regime. They also agreed in 1994 to form the Wassenaar Arrangement—a follow-on to CoCom that targets the export of conventional weapons and dual-use technologies to states that demonstrate dangerous or destabilizing behavior. But European governments refused, despite U.S. pressure, to single out Iran (or any other state) as an explicit target of this new regime.

The problem for the United States was familiar. European governments were willing to restrict trade selectively with Iran, in areas with clear military implications, but were unwilling to join the United States in a comprehensive embargo designed to isolate Iran from the normal workings of the world economy. By mid-1995, U.S. officials faced the choice of whether to accept a disparity in economic sanctions or seek to compel other states to abide by the more comprehensive U.S. approach.

The Clinton administration chose the latter option in 1996. The purpose of the Iran-Libya Sanctions Act (ILSA) was to deter foreign firms from contributing to Iranian or Libyan economic development through participation in sizable energy projects. The act targeted foreign firms investing over $40 million in either of the two countries' energy sectors in a given year. It directed the president to impose sanctions against firms whose investments would enhance Iran or Libya's ability to explore, extract, refine, or transport energy resources. ILSA gave the president a menu of possible sanctions: he could deny target firms access to the U.S. market, to Export-Import Bank loans, or to U.S. government procurement contracts, as well as the ability to be a primary dealer in U.S. government bonds or to borrow more than $10 million annually from U.S. banks.

ILSA: Causes. There is a plausible strategic rationale for the extraterritorial extension of U.S. sanctions. Iran's programs to support terrorism and develop WMD require economic resources, and the energy sector is Iran's principal source of revenue. To the extent that multilateral sanctions can constrain Iran's energy sector, especially its hard currency earnings, they make it more difficult for Iran to fund and execute these programs. U.S. unilateral sanctions have had a dampening effect on Iran's energy development, because the National Iranian Oil Company traditionally has made extensive use of U.S.-origin equipment, which it considered superior to the alternatives.[43] Over time, however, Iran could substitute European and even Russian equipment and technology for that of the United States. The successful extension of U.S. sanctions, by closing off access to substitutes, could raise economic costs to the point that Iran might be forced to reassess its domestic and foreign policy priorities.

The Clinton administration tried in 1994 to convince its European counterparts not to reschedule Iran's hard-currency debt, as a way to squeeze the Iranian economy. European governments countered that the United States was hypocritical because it sought European economic sacrifices while U.S. firms continued to supply Iran's energy sector. U.S. officials responded to this challenge in 1995, first by banning a major, already scheduled investment by the U.S. firm Conoco, and then by imposing unilaterally the full economic embargo against Iran. The United States thus signaled its willingness to bear significant costs. But this was still not sufficient to persuade European governments to join the embargo.

As was the case for Helms-Burton, the impetus for the extraterritorial extension of sanctions came from Congress rather than from the executive branch and was driven more by domestic political concerns than by foreign policy strategy. A Republican victory in the 1994 congressional elections gave political initiative to Senator Alphonse D'Amato (Republican-New York), long an advocate of a tougher U.S. approach toward Iran. D'Amato worked to craft the eventual ILSA with the American Israel Public Affairs Committee (AIPAC), which was greatly concerned by Iran's meddling in the Arab-Israeli peace process and its potential to develop and use nuclear weapons against Israel.[44] Representative Benjamin Gilman (Republican-New York) joined D'Amato to sponsor the act, arguing that it was intended to "force foreign companies to choose between investing in our market and those of Iran and Libya."[45]

The Clinton administration initially opposed ILSA, despite its own interest in securing multilateral compliance with U.S. sanctions. It objected to what it viewed as a heavy-handed tactic by Congress, particularly since Washington was already taking political criticism from U.S. allies and trading partners over Helms-Burton. Once again, however, external events in the context of election year politics forced the administration's hand. TWA flight 800 crashed in July 1996, and it was widely suspected that terrorist groups supported by Iran had played some role in the tragedy. The House quickly passed the Senate version of ILSA, and Clinton, reluctant to appear soft on terrorism, signed it into law.

The manner in which Libya became an additional target of this extraterritorial effort reinforces the primacy of domestic political factors.[46]

Libyan complicity in the destruction of Pan Am flight 103 over Lockerbie, Scotland, in December 1998 led the United States, Great Britain, and France to push successfully for UN sanctions against Libya. These sanctions, though not as comprehensive as existing U.S. measures, included a ban on air links with and arms sales to Libya and called for reductions in the number of Libyans stationed in overseas embassies. Senator Edward Kennedy (Democrat-Massachusetts), who had family members of Lockerbie victims among his constituents, had worked in Congress from the early 1990s to tighten and expand the UN sanctions against Libya. When D'Amato's bill for sanctions against Iran reached the Senate floor in 1994, Kennedy inserted Libya as an additional target. This political gesture to Lockerbie families came on the seventh anniversary of the bombing and gained broad congressional support. The Iran bill became the Iran-Libya Sanctions bill, and the TWA explosion of 1996 only served to reinforce the political salience of the terrorism issue. President Clinton, not to be outdone by Congress in symbolic politics, invited family members of the Lockerbie victims to the ceremony in which he signed ILSA into law.[47]

ILSA: Consequences. The most obvious benefits to the U.S. government of extending the Iran-Libya sanctions came in the domestic political arena. Both the administration and members of Congress used the sanctions to convey support for the patient families of terrorist victims and to signal that combating terrorism was a national priority. Extraterritorial sanctions suggested that the U.S. government was determined to pressure not only the suspected hosts of terrorism but also the firms that continued to do business with them.

The supporters of ILSA seemed to believe that their legislation supported U.S. business interests as well. Since U.S. energy firms were denied access to these markets, why should their competitors be allowed to step in, without cost, and reap the benefits? Senator D'Amato took it upon himself to send a letter to the French firm Total, warning that if it took over the project abandoned by Conoco, this would threaten Total's ability to conduct its business in the United States.[48] From the perspective of U.S. firms, however, the extraterritorial extension was probably the least attractive of available options. The ideal outcome for U.S. firms was for the United States to lift its unilateral sanctions. A second-best option was for U.S. officials to persuade other governments to constrain their energy firms. By contrast, any effort to coerce other foreign firms was likely to be counterproductive, because if the United States followed through with secondary sanctions, this would jeopardize cross-border dealings between U.S. and foreign firms. Not surprisingly, the U.S. corporate sector opposed ILSA as it had Helms-Burton. General Electric, a victim of the extraterritorial pipeline sanctions a decade earlier, joined with Siemens of Germany and other U.S. and European firms to lobby against the D'Amato bill. For business, ILSA,

Helms-Burton, and the increasingly routine U.S. resort to unilateral sanctions signaled a troubling expansion of the government interference with trade and investment for foreign policy purposes.[49]

On the foreign policy side of the ledger, the costs and risks of ILSA clearly outweighed the potential benefits. Washington confronted two major problems in an effort to extract compliance. First, there was more at stake for European governments and firms in Iran and Libya than there was in Cuba. This was true in terms of both export markets for machinery and equipment and imports of vital energy supplies. Europe's geographic proximity to the Middle East and vulnerability as a possible target for terrorism meant the political stakes were higher as well. Second, U.S. officials had to contend with the cumulative effect of ILSA sanctions following on the heels of Helms-Burton. European governments and firms, now mobilized, were even more likely to resist than they had been in the Cuban context.

The European response to ILSA was predictable. Officials speaking for national governments and the EU termed the legislation "unacceptable" and warned that Europe would defend its interests vigorously. European officials threatened to defy U.S. sanctions, to implement countermeasures against U.S. firms, and if necessary to escalate the dispute by taking it to the WTO.[50] Robert Litwak is surely correct in noting that the passage of ILSA changed the political dynamic from "the United States and the world versus Iran," to "Iran and the world versus the United States."[51]

ILSA: Playing the two-level Game. The passage of ILSA and the European reaction forced the Clinton administration to adopt a strategy of damage limitation. Even before the bill's passage, President Clinton informed Congress that he would support the legislation only if it covered investment, but not trade. This reduced the potential for conflicts with U.S. obligations under international trade commitments and helped to deflect potential European moves to take the conflict to the WTO. Administration officials also lobbied Congress to ensure that the president would have great flexibility in implementing sanctions. According to the eventual act, sanctions would be aimed only at specific firms, not all the firms of a country. The president was given the authority to waive the imposition of sanctions and, if he decided to impose them, was required to select only two from a set of six possible types of sanctions. Some of these measures were significant, such as denying foreign firms access to the U.S. market, but others were fairly innocuous, such as denying energy firms the ability to be primary dealers in U.S. government bonds.[52]

Once ILSA became law, the best outcome for the administration would have been not to face cases of sanctionable activity. The fact that the bar was set high—a $40 million investment—meant that test cases would probably be infrequent. In the summer of 1997, the administration announced that it would not sanction Turkish firms for building a pipeline to existing pipelines in Iran. U.S. officials interpreted ILSA narrowly, stating that the Turkish activity did not represent investment in Iran and thus was not covered by ILSA.

However, given the allure of the Iranian market and the temptation of foreign firms to exploit abandoned U.S. investments in Iran, it was only a matter of time before the administration faced a serious test. This came in September 1997, when a consortium of French, Malaysian, and Russian firms announced a $2 billion investment in the development of the South Pars gas field in Iran. The three firms involved—Total of France, Gazprom of Russia, and Petronas of Malaysia—had the explicit support of their respective governments. Total signaled its determination to defy U.S. sanctions by finalizing the sale of all its assets in the United States just prior to the announcement of the Iranian deal.[53]

U.S. officials sought unsuccessfully to head off the South Pars deal. Its size and the publicity surrounding it made it necessarily a test case of the U.S. willingness to impose sanctions. On May 18, 1998, Secretary of State Madeleine Albright confirmed that the United States considered the South Pars investment sanctionable activity under ILSA. She also announced that the president, using his authority under Section 9C of that act, would waive sanctions against the three firms on the grounds that to impose sanctions would result in undue harm to the national security interests of the United States.[54]

Albright and other executive branch officials subsequently elaborated the specific rationale for waiving sanctions.[55] They argued that the three firms targeted were insulated from the effect of sanctions and would complete the South Pars deal even if penalties were imposed. Moreover, to impose sanctions would jeopardize U.S. cooperation with the governments involved on an array of such important issues, such as collaboration with EU members on the problems of terrorism and nonproliferation—key concerns in the Iran context. They also noted the delicate state of relations with Russia in the arms control and nonproliferation area. And they argued it would be counterproductive to impose sanctions against a Malaysian firm when Malaysia was struggling to cope with the Asian financial crisis, which U.S. officials were making major efforts to resolve.

The administration was also quick to point out that in the process of trying to thwart the investment, it had extracted certain concessions from the governments involved that served broader U.S. foreign policy goals: The EU had agreed to a set of common objectives in the area of counterterrorism, including the sharing of intelligence and the tightening of export controls on equipment and technology related to WMD capabilities. Russia had similarly promised to implement a set of initiatives to strengthen its export control procedures and to supervise enterprises dealing with nuclear or missile technologies. In Albright's words, the decision *not* to impose retaliatory sanctions was "by far the most effective way to serve overall U.S. interests, and to advance the fundamental objectives of ILSA."[56]

U.S. officials warned that the waiver in the South Pars case should not be taken to mean the United States would ignore subsequent investments in Iran and Libya. But their behavior suggested otherwise. In March 1999 French, Italian, and Iranian companies signed a $1 billion deal to develop oil fields in Iran. Shortly thereafter Albright announced that sanctions would not affect this investment in Iran, either, because it was more important to preserve U.S.-EU cooperation on Iraqi sanctions, the Asian financial crisis, and the settlement in Yugoslavia.[57]

Policy Lessons and Recommendations

The preceding case studies demonstrate that the initiation of extraterritorial sanctions does provide some benefits to the United States. It is important to note, however, that the most significant benefits flow to particular political actors rather than to the nation as a whole. Resort to extraterritorial sanctions placates the demands of interest or lobby groups. The politicians who support these measures score political points in their dealings with these groups. Precisely because these sanctions are dramatic and controversial, they send a strong signal to domestic actors that government officials take their problem seriously and are willing to take action to address it. This is especially so in what are perceived as crisis circumstances: that is, when interest groups or other segments of the public perceive U.S. soldiers, citizens, or values to be under attack and fully expect their government agents to "do something" in response.

Extraterritorial sanctions do bring foreign policy benefits, albeit relatively modest ones, to the nation as a whole. These second-order sanctions frequently increase foreign compliance with U.S.-initiated sanctions. Foreign firms are more likely to cooperate with the United States under the threat of extraterritorial sanctions than are foreign governments. Firms have profit concerns rather than sovereignty concerns, and their reaction to sanctions is typically more pragmatic than principled. That does not mean that firms will always comply; the size and stakes of the particular investments in question clearly matter. In the Cuban case, several firms with modest stakes were willing to "go along in order to get along" with the United States and abandoned their investments. Where the stakes were larger or where government resistance reinforced the backbones of firms (e.g., Total in the Iranian context or Sherritt in the Cuban context), firms joined their home governments in defying the sanctions.

Other foreign policy benefits flow from the fact that executive branch officials can make a virtue of necessity when they are forced by Congress to use this coercive weapon. Even though foreign governments typically find these measures "unacceptable," they generally come to recognize the delicate, two-level position of the executive branch and to accept, however reluctantly, that they can help by making some concessions. U.S. officials do not generally achieve their maximum objectives, but the sanctions do provide a point of entry to get foreign governments to focus more closely on an issue of importance to the United States. European governments did not change their basic position on trade with Cuba as a result of Helms-Burton. But they do seem more sensitive to—and willing to cooperate with—the broader U.S. political agenda regarding Cuba than they did before the sanctions dispute.

The case studies suggest that for the United States as a whole, the costs of resorting to extraterritorial sanctions outweigh the benefits. The short-term diplomatic costs are glaring because few foreign policy measures seem to inspire the outrage of extraterritorial sanctions. Foreign governments perceive them as a public affront to sovereignty and a heavy-handed, unilateral form of coercion that violates the norms of conflict resolution among allies and trading partners. Extraterritorial sanctions are the proverbial 800-pound gorilla. While they are on the table, absent a waiver or other type of compromise worked out by the executive branch, foreign governments have great incentives to defy the United States, or, more often, simply to refuse to make any progress in other areas of mutual concern.

The risks of escalation are more profound than the short-term diplomatic costs. Extraterritorial sanctions provoke a visceral negative reaction that makes target governments less sensitive to rational assessments of costs and benefits. Put differently, these sanctions inspire "chicken" games in which each side, playing to a domestic audience, has incentives to show it is willing to bear costs—even to rupture long-standing positive relationships—rather than back down in humiliation. Cooler heads tend to prevail and compromises tend to be worked out in extraterritorial chicken games, but it would be imprudent to count on this as a foregone conclusion. Policymakers should appreciate that resorting to extraterritorial sanctions is a risky rather than prudent foreign policy.

The costs to reputation are hard to measure, but likely are very significant. The fact that the U.S. government resorts routinely to unilateral and extraterritorial sanctions means that U.S.-based firms are, through no fault of their own, less reliable suppliers and customers than their counterparts in other advanced industrial states. The pipeline episode of 1982 prompted some European firms to "design out" U.S. components from their industrial systems.[58] Whether the ILSA sanctions will inspire similar behavior in the energy sector remains to be seen.

For the U.S. government, extraterritorial sanctions bring significant costs in terms of diplomatic reputation. These sanctions create or reinforce an image of the United States as arbitrary, imperial, and arrogant, and as more prone to dictate to other states unilaterally than to cooperate multilaterally. This problem is magnified by the contemporary structure of international politics. The United States is the dominant power in a unipolar setting, and that fact alone makes many other states uneasy about the country's disproportionate influence. U.S. officials have recognized what the State

Department calls the "hegemony problem" and the general need to reassure other states by projecting an image of the United States as a benign superpower. The resort to extraterritorial sanctions works at cross-purposes to this grand strategic objective. Other governments are alarmed rather than reassured, and they naturally respond by seeking ways to constrain the "hyperpower" of the United States.[59]

The case studies demonstrate that because the costs and risks of extraterritorial measures tend to be profound, it is crucial for the executive branch to practice the two-level politics of damage limitation. Extraterritorial sanctions trap the executive branch between domestic interests and foreign relations. It can neither ignore, nor fully accommodate, either set of political pressures. Because they perceive sovereignty to be at stake, foreign governments would be more likely to escalate than to capitulate if executive branch officials simply relayed to them the full demands of Congress. Similarly, members of Congress would be inclined to take matters into their own hands—and they do have the constitutional power to regulate commerce—if they perceived that executive branch officials treated casually the concerns the legislators expressed through extraterritorial initiatives. The typical challenge in these cases is for executive branch officials to take the demand for sanctions seriously enough to negotiate with foreign partners, yet to find a way to gain concessions without actually having to implement the sanctions. The Helms-Burton and ILSA experiences suggest that the Clinton administration was fairly effective at the politics of damage limitation.

The necessity of damage limitation suggests the most important policy recommendation: the need for flexibility in the design and implementation of extraterritorial sanctions. Since Congress typically initiates the sanctions, executive branch officials can only limit damage if the legislation gives the president the authority to waive sanctions and discretion in how to apply them. As the ILSA case demonstrated, executive branch officials need to focus their efforts both on ensuring flexibility before the legislation is passed and on using the discretion granted once negotiations with trading partners begin. When Congress legislates mandatory, inflexible sanctions (as in the area of nuclear nonproliferation), the potential for damage limitation is significantly reduced. Congressional advocates of extraterritorial sanctions appear to recognize the need to provide some discretion; in exchange, they expect executive branch officials to extract diplomatic concessions in the event they choose to forgo sanctions.

Since unilateral sanctions are generally the facilitator or trigger of extraterritorial measures, a U.S. commitment to strive for and abide by multilateral sanctions would help to reduce the political opportunities for the exercise of extraterritorial measures. Executive branch officials would benefit from the continued mobilization of corporate interests as a counterweight to the kinds of particularistic interests that have typically led to unilateral and then extraterritorial sanctions.

But even with continued corporate pressure, it is unlikely that the U.S. government will abandon unilateral measures entirely. U.S. officials have become accustomed to the "sanctions habit" as a means to signal disapproval or administer punishment in response to what they perceive as objectionable foreign behavior. The fact that the United States defines its national interests in global rather than regional terms means that U.S. officials perceive more situations in which sanctions are warranted than do other states. The fact that the United States is large and relatively self-sufficient economically means that U.S. officials are willing to employ sanctions even without multilateral support.

The end of the Cold War arguably has increased the incentives for unilateral sanctions. As the dominant state in the international structure, the United States finds the unilateralist temptation to be a powerful one. It can act in defiance of international norms without experiencing the punishment or retaliation that weaker members of the international community would face. On the domestic front, the prevailing belief that the United States will remain secure and prosperous, almost regardless of what happens in the wider world, has made it easier for interest groups and members of Congress to use foreign policy as an instrument of partisan politics. As the Senate rejection in 1999 of the CTBT demonstrated, partisan debates are less likely than ever to stop at the water's edge. The absence of a strategic threat or central foreign policy concern has made it possible for interest groups to capture significant parts of the foreign policy process.

Finally, the political culture of the United States also reinforces the sanctions habit. Political actors across the U.S. state and society are more likely than in most countries to view the world in terms of the stark contrast between good and evil, and in particular between virtuous states and evil states. This tendency is apparent in U.S. relations with primary targets—Iran, Cuba, Libya, and, in earlier eras, Nazi Germany or the "evil empire" of the Soviet Union. But moralism is also evident in U.S. relations with allies, perhaps even more so. If the United States perceives evil so plainly, how could other democracies ignore it? One politically plausible answer is that crass material interests prevent U.S. allies from "doing the right thing" in the face of evil. To their proponents, unilateral sanctions signal the moral commitment and superiority of the United States. Extraterritorial sanctions force others to decide whether they are on the side of good or of evil. Against this distinctive domestic backdrop, the challenge for U.S. executive branch officials is to find creative ways to fight the good fight without compromising the broader economic and security interests of the United States.

Notes

1. Shambaugh, *States, Firms, and Power*, p. 1.
2. Rosenthal and Knighton, *National Laws and International Commerce*, p. vii.

3. Ball is quoted in Mastanduno, *Economic Containment,* p. 140.

4. Berman and Garson, "U.S. Export Controls—Past, Present, and Future"; Jentleson, *Pipeline Politics;* Mastanduno, *Economic Containment;* and Shambaugh, *States, Firms, and Power.*

5. The "signaling" benefits of economic sanctions are explored in Baldwin, *Economic Statecraft.*

6. Myers, "Clinton Troubleshooter Discovers Big Trouble from Allies on Cuba," p. A1.

7. See Jentleson, *Pipeline Politics.*

8. For a statement of the former position, see Pape, "Why Economic Sanctions Do Not Work." For the latter, see Baldwin, *Economic Statecraft* and "Evaluating Economic Sanctions"; and Elliott, "The Sanctions Glass: Half-Full or Completely Empty?"

9. It may depend as well on nature of target. Recent work by Shambaugh suggests more effective against private actors (firms) than public actors (governments). Shambaugh, *States, Firms, and Power.*

10. For discussion and analysis, see Haass, ed., *Economic Sanctions and American Diplomacy,* and Mastanduno, "Economic Statecraft, Interdependence, and National Security: Agendas for Research."

11. A classic statement is Galtung, "On the Effects of International Economic Sanctions."

12. In the Siberian pipeline case, executive branch officials in the Defense Department and office of the national security advisor were principal initiators of extraterritorial sanctions.

13. Mastanduno, "Trade as a Strategic Weapon."

14. Mastanduno, *Economic Containment,* p. 260.

15. Shambaugh, *States, Firms, and Power,* ch. 4, and Mastanduno, *Economic Containment,* chs. 4 and 8.

16. A good popular account is Cahill, *Trade Wars.*

17. Good discussions include Baldwin, *Economic Statecraft,* pp. 174–189; Losman, *International Economic Sanctions;* and Purcell, "Cuba," pp. 37–40.

18. Mastanduno, *Economic Containment,* pp. 123–124.

19. Purcell, "Cuba," p. 41.

20. Shambaugh, *States, Firms, and Power,* p. 178.

21. Libertad Act.

22. White House, Statement by the President, Office of the Press Secretary, March 12, 1996.

23. Baldwin, *Economic Statecraft,* and Martin, *Coercive Cooperation,* stress the importance of self-imposed costs to establish the credibility of signals.

24. Shambaugh, *States, Firms, and Power,* pp. 186–187.

25. Myers, "Clinton Troubleshooter," *New York Times,* October 23, 1996.

26. Canada, Department of Foreign Affairs and International Trade, "Government Introduces Legislation to Counter U.S. Helms-Burton Act."

27. Gramna International, "U.S. Companies Launch Campaign Against Helms-Burton Act," April 29, 1997.

28. Shambaugh, *States, Firms, and Power,* p. 197.

29. Canada, Department of Foreign Affairs and International Trade, "Government Introduces Legislation to Counter U.S. Helms-Burton Act."

30. Shambaugh, *States, Firms, and Power,* pp. 180–181.

31. Myers, "Clinton Troubleshooter."

32. Testimony, Stuart E. Eizenstat, undersecretary of state, before Senate Foreign Relations Committee, July 1, 1999.

33. See, for example, U.S. Department of State, Suspension of Title 3 Lawsuit Provisions of the Cuba Liberty and Democratic Solidarity Act, January 16, 1999, July 15, 1999, and January 15, 2000.

34. Spain, for example, was singled out approvingly in a special Helms-Burton press briefing in 1997 for taking the unprecedented step of downgrading the Cuban National Assembly from full participant to observer status in meetings of the Ibero-American Inter-parliamentary Conference. U.S. Department of State, Special Press Briefing on the Helms-Burton Act, July 16, 1997.

35. U.S. Department of State, Special Press Briefing on the Helms-Burton Act, July 16, 1997.

36. Madeleine Albright, Statement on U.S.-EU Understanding on Expropriated Property, London, May 18, 1998.

37. Ibid.

38. Testimony, Stuart E. Eizenstat, Undersecretary of State, House Committee on International Relations, June 3, 1998, and Senate Foreign Relations Committee, July 1, 1999.

39. U.S. Department of State, press statement, President Clinton's Title III Decision—January 2001, Fact Sheet, January 17, 2001.

40. Lake, "Confronting Backlash States."

41. Lane, "Changing Iran: Germany's New Ostpolitik," quotation at p. 84.

42. Iran and Libya accounted for 20 percent of France's energy imports and 44 percent of Italy's during the 1990s. Shambaugh, *States, Firms, and Power*, p. 190.

43. Clawson, "Iran," p. 94.

44. Ibid., pp. 86–87.

45. Shambaugh, *States, Firms, and Power*, p. 185.

46. Rose, "Libya," pp. 137, 142-43.

47. Ibid., p. 147.

48. Shambaugh, *States, Firms, and Power*, p. 185.

49. "U.S. Companies Launch Campaign Against Helms-Burton."

50. Clawson, "Iran," and Shambaugh, *States, Firms, and Power*.

51. Litwak, *Rogue States and U.S. Foreign Policy*, pp. 243–244.

52. Clawson, "Iran," p. 88.

53. Ibid., p. 92.

54. Testimony, Eizenstat, July 1, 1999.

55. In addition to Total's move, Gazprom canceled its possible transactions of up to $750 million under an agreement with the U.S. Export-Import Bank. Petronas had limited connections to the United States. Eizentat, June 3, 1998.

56. See the testimony of Stuart Eizenstat in U.S. Congress, House, Committee on International Relations, "Economic Sanctions," Washington, D.C., June 3, 1998, p. 10.

57. Shambaugh, *States, Firms, and Power*, p. 202.

58. Jentleson, *Pipeline Politics*.

59. Marshall and Mann, "Goodwill Toward US Is Dwindling Globally," *Los Angeles Times*, March 26, 2000.

13

Unilateralism, Multilateralism, and the International Criminal Court

Bartram S. Brown

IN 1992 THE U.S. GOVERNMENT TOOK THE INITIATIVE IN PROPOSING THE establishment of an International Criminal Tribunal for the former Yugoslavia and triggered an intensive decade of progress in building institutions for international justice.[1] These developments created a special challenge for the United States, which, as the world's hegemonic power, sought to maximize its influence and exert global leadership just as the norms and institutions of international criminal justice were undergoing rapid evolution.

A broad coalition of civil society actors and "like-minded" states soon coalesced around the idea of a permanent, independent, and effective International Criminal Court (ICC). Their efforts culminated in the adoption of the Rome Statute,[2] a treaty that, when ratified by sixty countries, will create a permanent ICC. After years of rejecting the statute, the U.S. government signed it on December 31, 2000, which, by the statute's own terms, was the last day that states could sign without ratifying it first.[3] President Clinton stated that signing was "the right action to take at this point," but he noted that "we are not abandoning our concerns about significant flaws in the treaty."[4] Even upon signing Clinton declined to recommend the treaty to the Senate for its approval, signaling that the United States remained unwilling to accept the perceived cost of institutionalized multilateralism in the form of the ICC. Meanwhile, the rest of the international community has hailed the ICC statute as an important achievement and a milestone in the development of international law and multilateral institutions.

U.S. concerns center on the potential exposure of the U.S. military to the jurisdiction of the ICC. The United States has attempted to reduce this potential exposure to zero, but doing so might deprive the ICC of any significant jurisdiction. So, there is little incentive for other states to agree to the U.S. posture. It will be difficult to find a solution that would resolve all U.S. concerns and still be acceptable to the growing number of states that have already signed and/or ratified the statute.

As the world's only remaining superpower, the United States has an exceptional position in the international system. On occasion, it may stand as the only force willing and able to act against aggression and similar threats. Noting this fact, some observers argue that the United States must be exempt from the jurisdiction of the ICC. But it is hard to argue for special treatment on fundamental issues of criminal justice, and even our closest allies consider our opposition to the statute unjustified.[5]

This controversy need not have pitted the United States against the rest of the world. After all, this country shares with the signatories of the Rome Statute the goal of bringing war criminals to justice. Heard in the U.S. government's failed policy toward the ICC are the reverberations of a reflexive hostility to multilateral institutions.

The first part of this chapter considers the historical attitudes of the United States toward multilateral institutions of justice. The subsequent section outlines U.S. policy toward the ICC, considering the merits of the principal U.S. objections to the Rome Statute. Part three identifies the major influences that shaped official conceptions of U.S. national interests as U.S. policymakers formulated a policy toward the ICC. The fourth section considers the causes of U.S. behavior, asking why the United States, the world's only superpower, adopted the policy it did. The fifth section evaluates the costs of extreme U.S. unilateralism with regard to the ICC. Finally, the conclusion offers a few policy prescriptions for the United States, a power seeking to maximize its interests in a world where multilateral institutions are growing in importance.

Historical U.S. Attitudes Toward International Tribunals

The United States has historically supported international mechanisms to enhance accountability for war crimes, crimes against humanity, genocide, and other violations of international humanitarian law. A tradition of U.S. leadership in this field began in the nineteenth century, when this country adopted the Lieber Code,[6] the world's first attempt to craft a comprehensive set of instructions on how to respect the standards of civilized behavior in war.

The United States, as the only true world power to emerge from World War II, led the multilateral coalition that established two international military tribunals after that conflict. The Nuremberg Charter,[7] a multilateral agreement among the United States, the United Kingdom, the Soviet Union, and France, created the Nuremberg Tribunal and provided the legal basis for the prosecution of high-ranking German officials for war crimes, crimes against humanity, and crimes against peace (that is, planning and waging an aggressive war). The allies established a separate Tokyo War Crimes Tribunal to try Japanese nationals accused of similar crimes.

There have been many questions about the procedural fairness of the Nuremberg process, and even more concerning the Tokyo Tribunal, but each was in its time a very forward-looking endorsement of international law and institutions. The very existence of these tribunals broke new ground and fueled expectations of further progress.

The Nuremburg Tribunal established for the world and for history that German leaders had violated fundamental rules of international law. Still, as an institution established by the victorious powers, it was neither a permanent court nor a part of the UN system. When the UN General Assembly passed a resolution endorsing the principles of the Nuremburg Tribunal,[8] the creation of a permanent ICC under UN auspices seemed almost inevitable. Proposals for such an institution were soon drafted, but the advent of the Cold War prevented progress on an ICC for the next four decades.

The idea of a permanent ICC gained renewed life in the early 1990s, following the success of the ad hoc international criminal tribunals established for the former Yugoslavia (the ICTY)[9] and for Rwanda (the ICTR).[10] These bodies were established by the UN Security Council and, like the Nuremburg Tribunal almost fifty years earlier, were created pursuant to a U.S. initiative. The practice of these tribunals demonstrated convincingly that an international court could investigate and prosecute international crimes with a high degree of credibility.

Nevertheless, the political process of creating ad hoc tribunals raises troubling questions of fairness and political privilege. The UN Security Council has created these tribunals selectively, and their narrow geographic focus has resulted in unequal treatment.[11] Indeed, one of the most compelling arguments for a permanent ICC is that it would improve upon the practice of the ad hoc tribunals by holding individuals worldwide to the same standard of international justice. The proposed creation of a strong, independent, and effective ICC, portrayed as the next logical step, challenged the United States and other countries to strike the proper balance between unilateralism and multilateralism. For Washington the task was to exercise leadership in the shaping of this multilateral institution, while at the same time maintaining an appropriate degree of unilateral freedom of action.

Despite its history of support for international humanitarian law, the U.S. government was guarded about a permanent ICC from the start. In 1995, President Bill Clinton announced his support in principle for the idea of an ICC, but only in the final moments of his administration did he support the ICC statute ultimately embraced by the rest of the international community. That statute was adopted in July 1998, at the end of a five-week diplomatic conference in Rome. A total of 120 states voted to approve the text of that treaty, while the United States government was isolated as one of only seven voting against. As of February 2001, 139 countries have signed the Rome Statute, and 27 of them have ratified it. The United States signed on December 31, 2000, only 3 weeks before the inauguration of a new president. The United States is unlikely to ratify anytime soon, but when the number of ratifications reaches 60, the ICC will officially come into being. It is now apparent that this will eventually happen with or without the support of the U.S. government.

U.S. Policy Toward an ICC

It has not been the policy of the U.S. government to commit war crimes, crimes against humanity, or genocide, but it has been U.S. policy to avoid establishing international courts authorized to investigate or prosecute U.S. personnel for these crimes. Because of the limited territorial scope of their jurisdiction, neither the ICTY nor the ICTR was ever expected to investigate or try U.S. military personnel.[12] Accordingly, U.S. policy toward these narrowly crafted institutions has been proactive and strongly supportive. In contrast, U.S. policy toward an ICC with global jurisdiction has been reactive and fundamentally obstructionist.

The United States has favored ad hoc tribunals because these have been created by the UN Security Council, in which the U.S. possesses a veto. The cost of multilateralism to the United States is quite low in these tribunals because the veto ensures that the Security Council will not create or maintain an institution threatening to U.S. interests.

Although it has not ratified the ICC statute, the United States continues to worry that it may not escape the court's jurisdiction. This fear appears unwarranted, because under the statute the court will try only individuals, not states. Moreover, the treaty requires that before any individuals can be prosecuted, either their government (the state of nationality) or the government of the country where the alleged crime took place (the territorial state) must be a party to the treaty, or otherwise consent to such a prosecution.[13]

At the Rome Conference, the United States pushed for a statute that would require consent from the state of nationality in every case, but other governments rejected this provision as too restrictive. They reasoned, with justification, that the requirement of state consent Washington favored would permit corrupt and abusive governments to opt out of ICC jurisdiction. Had this approach been accepted, the ICC would be able to act effectively against nonparty nationals only on the basis of a decision by the UN Security Council. In effect, the ICC would be reduced to administering the same type of ad hoc justice provided by the ICTY and the ICTR.

International law recognizes the universal jurisdiction of all states to prosecute those believed to be responsible for certain special crimes of concern to the entire international community. This extraordinary jurisdiction was first applied to pirates who were recognized as *hostes humani generis*, or enemies of all humankind,[14] and was extended in the nineteenth century to slave traders when international law forbade that commerce. A key issue in the ICC negotiations was whether this universal jurisdiction should apply to the crimes defined in the ICC statute.[15] The U.S. government and other ICC critics argued during and immediately after the Rome Conference that the statute violated international law by extending the principle of universal jurisdiction to the prosecution of nonparty nationals for crimes other than genocide.[16]

In actual fact, the jurisdiction of the ICC is not based on the principle of universal jurisdiction. Instead, as noted above, it builds upon state consent—alternatively, the consent of the territorial state (where the crime is alleged to have been committed) or the state of nationality of the accused. This approach represents a compromise between the very strict state consent requirement favored by the United States and the idea of universal jurisdiction regardless of state consent favored by many other countries.

The United States also objects to the fact that the crimes within the jurisdiction of the ICC include not only genocide, crimes against humanity, and war crimes, but also "aggression." The definitions of the first three of these crimes, to be applied by the ICC, have been carefully refined during long and difficult negotiations. The definition of aggression will be formulated by the parties to the ICC statute at a later date. Some U.S. critics of the statute have argued that its provision on aggression is somehow inconsistent with the prerogatives of the Security Council.

In fact, the ICC statute mentions aggression only in article 5, which first lists it as a crime within the jurisdiction of the ICC but then bars the court from exercising jurisdiction over this crime until an amendment can be adopted defining it. The statute specifically requires that any conditions and definitions applicable to ICC jurisdiction over aggression "shall be consistent with the relevant provisions of the Charter of the United Nations."[17] It is difficult to see how this language could undermine the prerogatives of the Security Council under the UN Charter.

Some critics have argued that the ICC, as formulated by the Rome Conference, will be too weak to be effective, because its jurisdiction will depend upon the consent of either the territorial state or the state of nationality of the accused. Except in cases where the Security Council steps in to authorize extraordinary jurisdiction, critics contend, this consent requirement will leave the ICC unable to assert jurisdiction over someone like Pol Pot who orchestrates genocide against his own people inside his own nonparty country.[18] This criticism of the ICC statute is a valid one, but it is hardly a reason for Washington to oppose it. In fact, the U.S. proposal, to require in all cases the consent of the state of nationality of the accused, would have left the ICC substantially weaker.

In Rome, the U.S. delegation strenuously opposed the right of the ICC prosecutor to initiate investigations or prosecutions on his or her own authority, fearing this power might be used against U.S. nationals or interests. To mollify these concerns, a U.S. proposal was incorporated into the statute requiring the prosecutor to obtain the authorization of ICC judges to continue any investigation he or she initiates.

In addition, the principle of complementary jurisdiction, as incorporated into the Rome Statute, allows any interested state to assert a prior and preemptive right to investigate and prosecute. The ICC will have jurisdiction only if no state is willing and able to investigate and prosecute the case in good faith.[19] The ICC prosecutor can challenge the good faith of a state suspected of conducting a sham investigation or prosecution. Thus, if Iraq said it had investigated Saddam Hussein for war crimes, crimes against humanity, or the use of poison gas (a prohibited weapon), the ICC could nonetheless pursue the case if its judges did not believe that the charges had been legitimately pursued. The United States has not objected to the principle of complementarity itself, but it has balked at the prospect that a panel of international judges might sit in judgment of determinations made by the U.S. legal system.

More than anything else, U.S. opposition to the Rome Statute has focused on concerns that the ICC might investigate or prosecute U.S. military personnel involved in military activity abroad. From the beginning of the ICC negotiations, the U.S. government sought to preclude this possibility by insisting that ICC jurisdiction should be subject to the requirement of strict state consent discussed above. In other words, the United States proposed that either a decision of the UN Security Council or the consent of the state of nationality of the accused should be required in every case. The United States has never objected to ICC jurisdiction when based on a decision of the Security Council because, as a permanent member, it can veto any decision of the Security Council and eliminate that possible route to jurisdiction over U.S. nationals. Requiring U.S. consent for any ICC trial of U.S. nationals would have reduced the potential U.S. exposure to zero.

In Rome, the U.S. delegation complained that the statute might create a powerful international prosecutor not subject to adequate checks and balances, suggesting that he might become an international Kenneth Starr. There are a number of reasons why that is unlikely to happen. First, the ICC statute contains many safeguards against prosecutorial abuse. It specifies, for example, that the court is to prosecute only the most serious crimes of international concern, which are defined in the treaty.[20] Even when there is clear evidence of a technical violation, the ICC is not to pursue a case unless it is "of sufficient gravity to justify further action."[21]

There is little reason to fear that U.S. troops serving abroad, perhaps even on humanitarian missions, might be charged by the ICC prosecutor for a single questionable act. The terms of the ICC treaty make this impossible, since genocide, crimes against humanity, and war crimes are the only crimes presently within the court's jurisdiction. Moreover, the Rome Statute sets out narrow definitions of these crimes that focus on acts committed on a widespread basis or in pursuit of a government policy to commit atrocities. The treaty's high thresholds of scale and proof will preclude the frivolous international prosecution of unwary U.S. soldiers and their civilian leaders.

Perhaps the best safeguard against any hypothetical excesses of the ICC or its prosecutor lies in the secondary nature of ICC jurisdiction. The United States will retain the first right to investigate and deal with any case directed against a U.S. citizen, whether or not it decides to accept the ICC treaty. If the U.S. judicial system steps in and investigates the case, this will divest the ICC of jurisdiction.

Finally, there is the practical limitation of enforceability. Like other international courts, the ICC will depend, de facto, on the support of the Security Council to enforce its decisions. Consequently, it will be in no position to indulge in politicized vendettas against the United States. The veto privilege the United States enjoys as a permanent member of the Security Council is not diminished by the ICC treaty and provides major safeguards for U.S. interests.

The safeguards described above go a long way toward satisfying the principal U.S. objections to the ICC statute. Unfortunately, they were not fully taken into account in the formulation of U.S. interests.

The Formulation of US Interests

A few key factors have shaped the formulation of U.S. interests with regard to the ICC. NGOs have done a remarkable job of mobilizing support for the ICC in capitals around the world, propelling the issue forward on the agenda of the UN. Meanwhile, conservative U.S. legislators have intervened to harden the U.S. negotiating position on ICC jurisdiction. Most critical, however, has been concern about exposing U.S. military personnel, and perhaps their civilian leaders, to the judgment of an international court. Opponents of the ICC fear that this would invite frivolous cases against the United States and compromise its freedom of action in the international arena. Skepticism about the UN also contributed to the unilateralist tilt in U.S. policy toward the proposed court.

The push to create a permanent ICC came not from the U.S. government but from NGOs and the UN General Assembly. Nonetheless, President Clinton endorsed the general idea of a permanent ICC, and his administration repeatedly stressed that the United States could support a court configured along the proper lines. Lengthy multilateral negotiations produced mixed results. During periodic negotiations within the ICC Preparatory Committee held over three years, and later at the Rome Conference where the details of the statute were finalized, U.S. delegates labored tirelessly to influence, and in many cases to improve, the language of the statute. They achieved many U.S. goals, such as ensuring that the statute would incorporate essential fair trial guarantees. Despite these successes, the U.S.

government has consistently objected to specific aspects of the ICC statute that are acceptable to other countries.

Conservative legislators in Congress, led by former Senate Foreign Relations Committee Chair Jesse Helms, have been staunch opponents of the ICC. Four months before the Rome Conference, Senator Helms sent a letter to Secretary of State Madeleine Albright stating that any treaty establishing a permanent UN International Criminal Court "[w]ithout a clear US veto . . . will be dead-on-arrival at the Senate Foreign Relations Committee." He stated flatly that the U.S. negotiators in Rome "do not have any flexibility" on this issue.[22] This threat placed the U.S. delegation in a very difficult position, setting them up for failure at the conference.

For weeks, the U.S. delegation in Rome showed no flexibility on the key jurisdictional issue of U.S. consent as categorically framed by Senator Helms. U.S. negotiators did not offer a compromise proposal on this issue until the last few days of the five-week conference. At that point, however, virtually no time remained for negotiations. Compromise was instead achieved through the intervention of the chairman of the Committee of the Whole, acting on behalf of the "bureau" (the officers of the conference) seeking to break the impasse. Acting on the basis of comments by the delegations concerning two earlier partial draft proposals for compromise, the bureau proposed a single yea or nay vote on a complete compromise version of the statute.

The United States did all it could to convince other delegations to vote against adoption of the proposed Rome Statute. The intense U.S. lobbying effort was sometimes accompanied by thinly veiled threats. Washington warned some countries that their vote on the statute could affect bilateral relations with the United States, including foreign aid. U.S. officials even told Germany that adoption of the statute would require the United States to reconsider its security commitments in Europe. These tactics were all for naught; the Rome Conference adopted the statute by an overwhelming majority vote of 120 to 7 (the United States in the minority), with 21 abstentions.

Citizens groups, organized under the umbrella of the NGO Coalition for an International Criminal Court (CICC), played a major part in mobilizing international support for a strong, independent, and effective ICC. The CICC is a broad-based international network, including more than 1,000 participating organizations, which supports the creation of a just, independent, and effective ICC. Years before the 1998 Rome Conference, the coalition began convening working groups on key issues, arranging meetings between the ICC and representatives of the governments involved in the ICC negotiations, and promoting awareness of ICC proposals and negotiations through newsletters, a Web page, and other media. Since Rome, the CICC has continued to promote ratification of the ICC statute.[23] The surprising success of these efforts left the United States in an uncomfortable, reactive position at the Rome Conference, as more and more U.S. allies joined the "like-minded" group of states dedicated to a strong ICC.

In formulating its ICC policies, the United States was responding to NGO initiatives as much as to the policies and positions of other countries. The U.S. government's relations with the CICC have been simultaneously cordial because the United States is accustomed to working with NGOs in multilateral human rights negotiations and has always kept the door open to discussion and the exchange of views—and strained because of continuing opposition to the statute in Washington. Through educational programs and public-relations efforts, NGOs have stressed that international justice can best be guaranteed by establishing an independent and effective ICC. Their lobbying, so effective with the other liberal democracies, did eventually move President Clinton to sign the statute, but such lobbying has done relatively little to counteract the influence of ICC opponents in the United States. On the issue of the ICC the U.S. government has shown exceptional resistance to NGO influence.

The major stumbling block to U.S. support for the ICC has been the opposition of the Pentagon, which has strongly insisted that it cannot accept any exposure to ICC jurisdiction. Congress has been extremely deferential to this view, as was the Clinton administration, perhaps in part because U.S. civilian leaders, such as the president and the secretary of defense, share the same potential exposure.

The real issue here involves the use of force by the world's last remaining superpower. The U.S. government would like to avoid any risk of its personnel being held accountable abroad for the use of force on behalf of the U.S. government. Critics of the ICC argue that exposure to its jurisdiction is inconsistent with the expanded global role the U.S. military has been encouraged to assume in recent years. These functions include participation in peacekeeping operations in multiple countries, as well as special military operations such as the Gulf War in 1991 and the NATO bombing to drive Serb forces from Kosovo in 1999. By successfully linking the two issues of the ICC and the use of force, the Pentagon strengthened its hand considerably in Clinton administration policy debates. President Clinton's wish to improve relations with the U.S. military may also have contributed to the unusually high deference shown to Pentagon sensibilities.

The Pentagon's concerns about its exposure to international jurisdiction are related to a more general contention: that it is vital for the United States to maintain its freedom of action in international affairs. Many analysts, noting that the United States is often the only power willing and able to act against aggression and similar threats, portray the ICC as inconsistent with the country's global role in preserving international peace and security. These critics are misguided, however, because they overlook the narrow range of jurisdiction granted by the Rome Statute, which will prevent the court from impinging upon U.S. prerogatives. In brief, the ICC will have jurisdiction to try individuals only for genocide, crimes against humanity, war crimes, and, eventually, aggression. Although these terrible crimes are generally committed through the use of force, the use of force itself would not constitute a crime punishable by the ICC.

Moreover, U.S. military personnel and civilian officials are unlikely to face investigation or prosecution by the ICC because of the principle of "complementary" jurisdiction set out in the statute. Under this principle, the court possesses only that minimal level of jurisdiction necessary to establish an international judicial "safety net." The ICC will be able to act only when no national court system is willing and able to investigate allegations of serious international crimes.[24] Any state, whether a party to the statute or not, can deprive the ICC of jurisdiction over a case simply by investigating and/or prosecuting it. The ICC must defer to these national proceedings even if they have concluded that no prosecution is warranted.[25] The only exception arises if the state concerned "is unwilling or unable genuinely to carry out the investigation or prosecution."[26] The possibility that an investigation conducted under U.S. law could be found wanting is indeed remote. Provided that the legal system in the United States has not totally collapsed, there is no possibility that the United States could be considered unable to prosecute. [27] Likewise, the United States could be found "unwilling" to prosecute only if its court proceedings were found to be a complete sham by a first panel of judges,[28] and if that finding were confirmed on appeal.[29]

Under different circumstances, the Clinton administration might well have accepted the ICC statute from the beginning. But that administration attached a much higher priority to continuing U.S. support for multilateral military missions, and it needed at least grudging support from both the Pentagon and Congress to keep the door open to future U.S. participation in such operations. Together, the Pentagon and Senator Helms exercised a decisive influence on the U.S. position on the ICC before, during, and after the Rome Conference.

Only a few days after the Rome Conference ended, Senator Helms called hearings on the ICC to which he invited many of the court's opponents and only one lukewarm supporter. Even the few liberal senators in attendance, when faced with a barrage of negative arguments on the ICC, distanced themselves from the ICC. To this day the court has little support in Congress.

All in all, the ICC was characterized primarily as a threat to U.S. interests rather than as an opportunity for the United States to exert positive leadership in shaping a multilateral institution for the future. This pattern of disproportionate military influence, leading to U.S. isolation and defeat in a major multilateral negotiation, paralleled the U.S. experience with the 1997 Ottawa Convention banning antipersonnel landmines.

Another factor that complicated efforts to mobilize U.S. government support for the ICC was the poor image of the UN, which is widely assumed in Washington to be an inefficient and unreliable organization that cannot be trusted to respect legitimate U.S. interests. For the past twenty years, this negative image has contributed to Congress's failure to authorize full payment of the assessed U.S. share of the UN budget. Legislators who already assume the worst about international organizations have naturally been disinclined to create new ones and to endow these with authority over the lives and interests of Americans.

Finally, some opponents of the ICC have seen it as a Trojan horse for a world government that would gradually eliminate unilateral state prerogatives and erode national sovereignty. Such extreme attitudes have made it difficult if not impossible for the United States to negotiate solutions to the potential problems said to be lurking in the ICC statute. The many safeguards incorporated into its text have not satisfied those who assume that the UN is a hostile force likely to target U.S. interests unfairly.

Causes of U.S. Behavior

Why did the United States formulate its interests and behave as it did in determining its ICC policy? Among the most important causal influences were a long tradition of reflexive opposition to international jurisdiction over U.S. interests; a magnification of sovereignty concerns generated by exceptionalist rhetoric about U.S. "indispensability"; and a difficult two-level game that forced the Clinton administration to negotiate simultaneously with international partners intent on building an effective multilateral institution and with domestic constituencies opposed to any such development.

The origins of U.S. opposition to ICC jurisdiction can be traced, at least in part, to political disputes of the 1950s. At that time, opponents of federal civil rights legislation wanted to prevent treaties from dealing with matters, including civil rights, that they believed were a purely U.S. domestic concern. They proposed a constitutional amendment, known as the Bricker Amendment,[30] specifying that no treaty could authorize or permit any foreign power or any international organization to supervise, control, or adjudicate the rights of U.S. citizens inside the United States.[31] The Senate narrowly defeated the bill only after intervention by Secretary of State John Foster Dulles, who promised that the Eisenhower administration did not intend for the United States to become a party to any international human rights treaties. The resulting policy inertia against human rights treaties was not broken until 1986, when the Senate ratified the Genocide Convention.

Over the past fifteen years, the United States has also become a party to the Torture Convention, the International Covenant on Civil and Political Rights, and the Convention on the Elimination of All Forms of Racial Discrimination. Under none of these treaties, however, has the United States accepted the jurisdiction of a court or other international body. Where these treaties provide for the International Court of Justice (World Court) to decide related disputes, the United States has ratified them with a reservation rejecting that court's mandatory jurisdiction. In contrast, the Rome Statute on the ICC specifically provides that "[n]o reservations may be made to this Statute."[32] The exclusion of all reservations is intended to serve the ideal of equal justice, by ensuring that no country can reserve for itself a special regime under the statute. But the exclusion also precludes the United States from using a favored device for escaping the jurisdiction of international courts.

Although the Bricker Amendment itself is no more than an historical footnote, a failed legislative proposal inspired by the Cold War fears of the 1950s, its influence on U.S. foreign policy lives on in a lingering reflexive opposition to international jurisdiction over U.S. interests.

Misgivings over the ICC's implications for national sovereignty are hardly unique to the United States, since that institution raises essentially the same concerns for all states. These concerns have been magnified in the United States, however, by the exceptionalist rhetoric of U.S. "indispensability." In former Secretary of State Madeleine Albright's now classic statement, the United States is an "indispensable"[33] global power because its economy is overwhelmingly dominant, because no comparable military power exists in the world, and because U.S. capacities are often essential for the success of UN peacekeeping and the use of force by the UN or NATO.

For some, the logic of U.S. indispensability justifies U.S. exceptionalism: the idea that the United States should get special treatment and remain free from the legal restraints applied to other states. According to this view it should retain absolute freedom of action, not only for its own sake but also for the sake of the international community, because in many cases only the United States has the power and the will to act when necessary. This idea of exceptionalism has been invoked, directly or indirectly, as a justification for U.S. objections to the ICC statute.[34]

The notion of U.S. exceptionalism is also attractive to those who are inherently suspicious of all international organizations and who hold exaggerated fears that the ICC represents an unwelcome step toward the creation of a world government. In actual fact, the ICC will not be part of a world government. (Indeed, given its lack of enforcement powers and its narrow jurisdiction, it is unlikely even to become an effective criminal court.) The Rome Statute will permit the exercise of international jurisdiction only to the extent necessary to prevent impunity for the most serious international crimes, and the ICC will be barred from investigating or prosecuting cases that have been pursued in good faith by any state.

An important determinant of Washington's ICC policy has been the "two-level game" that has forced the executive branch to negotiate simultaneously with international partners, including allies who strongly favor an independent court, and with domestic constituencies, represented by Senator Helms, who insist upon some type of U.S. veto over ICC prosecutions. The Clinton administration found it difficult to make the transition from "uncompromising negotiator" in Rome to "impartial assessor" of the ICC's potential impact on U.S. interests. A few days after the Rome Conference,

Ambassador David Scheffer, head of the U.S. delegation, was greeted with a hero's welcome in hearings before the Senate Foreign Relations Committee, where Senator Helms lauded him for having resisted all international pressure to compromise on the demand for a U.S. veto.[35] It would be two-and-a-half years later before the Clinton administration, in its closing moments, was to articulate a more balanced assessment of the ICC statute.

Why is it that the United States failed to garner international support in Rome for its position on ICC jurisdiction? Some reports have suggested that anti-U.S. sentiment made the other countries in Rome ready, even eager, to move forward without the United States.[36] This is a serious oversimplification. It would be more accurate to say that overindulgence in the logic and rhetoric of U.S. "indispensability" led the United States to attempt negotiation without compromise in Rome, apparently assuming that no agreement on an ICC would be possible without U.S. approval. Foreign reaction to this same rhetoric may indeed have contributed to the willingness of other countries to reach agreement without the United States. But after five weeks of hard work at the Rome Conference, most countries in attendance were ready to move forward. The fact that U.S. opposition did not prevent them from doing so should not be taken as evidence of an anti-U.S. bias.

The U.S. delegation was seriously hamstrung by its instructions. Insofar as U.S. proposals tended to anchor the jurisdiction of the ICC upon the authority of the Security Council, they seemed to offer only a regressive move back toward ad hoc international justice rather than progress toward equal international justice.

A U.S. veto over any ICC prosecution of U.S. nationals could be achieved only in one of two ways, neither of which was acceptable to the vast majority of the other negotiating states. One was to require prior authorization from the UN Security Council for all ICC prosecutions. This approach would have allowed the United States, as a permanent member of the council, to veto any proposed prosecution of U.S. citizens or personnel. But the veto privilege, so cherished by Washington, is generally resented by developing countries.[37] Eventually, even the United Kingdom and France, U.S. allies that also hold the veto, agreed that it would be inappropriate to extend that privilege to ICC investigations and prosecutions.

Alternatively, the desired result could have been achieved by bestowing upon every state the right to veto the prosecution of its nationals by withholding ratification. Such an approach would have left the ICC powerless to pursue most of the worst violators, forcing reliance on Security Council authorization for any effective jurisdiction.

The very nature of the issues concerned reduced the influence of the United States on other states, including its allies. The principles of equal justice and accountability for serious international crimes may not be particularly susceptible to compromise.

Consequences of Unilateralism in U.S. ICC Policy

Even for a superpower like the United States, veering too far in the direction of unilateralism can have its costs. One of the most important consequences of Washington's uncompromising unilateralism in the ICC negotiations was that the United States missed an important window of opportunity. The United States went into the last week of the Rome Conference without having shown flexibility or considered compromise on the key jurisdictional issues in dispute. Consequently, the United States never got a chance to explore and pursue its interests through full, positive, and cooperative engagement in the Rome negotiations.

Another consequence of this unilateralism is that the shape of the ICC will be less subject to U.S. influence when it does eventually come into existence. Over the next decade or so, the court's members will make important decisions about its financing and governance. As a state party, the United States would be well positioned to ensure that those decisions are the right ones. It would also have another right that could be used to protect U.S. interests in the future, that is, the right to block any new crimes added by later amendments from providing a basis for the prosecution of U.S. nationals.[38]

U.S. obstructionism with regard to the ICC has no doubt damaged the reputation of the United States as a leader in the field of international justice. In addition, some of the arguments advanced against the ICC statute may have compromised both U.S. credibility and international law. One of the most basic aspects of the law of treaties is the rule that "[a] treaty does not create either obligations or rights for a third State without its consent."[39] In the aftermath of the Rome Conference, the U.S. government argued that the statute violated this rule[40] because, in some cases, it could allow the ICC to try individuals for serious international crimes without the consent of their national governments.[41] The United States appeared to contend that if the ICC tries an individual for a crime, the state of that individual's nationality is in some extended sense being subjected to obligations under the statute.[42]

More recently, the U.S. government has quietly abandoned this novel and unpersuasive argument. The effort to equate potential ICC jurisdiction over individuals with the idea that states are being inappropriately "bound" may work as a rhetorical device, but it is completely false as legal reasoning. Like any treaty, the Rome Statute creates obligations for party states. These include obligations to comply with requests for the surrender and transfer of suspects to the court;[43] to provide requested evidence;[44] to give effect to fines or forfeitures ordered by the Court;[45] and to pay assessments for the regular budget of the Court.[46] None of these obligations applies to any nonparty state, nor does the exercise of criminal jurisdiction against an accused individual bind the accused state of nationality.

The United States was well within its rights in deciding not to become a party state to the ICC treaty, but it risked undermining both U.S. credibility and international law by insisting upon a specious legal argument in its attempt to exempt all U.S. nationals from the entire ICC treaty regime. Every state has certain legal rights with regard to its nationals, but no state, whether a party to the statute or not, has a legitimate interest in shielding its nationals from criminal responsibility for genocide, crimes against humanity, or serious war crimes.

The vote taken at the end of the Rome Conference may come to symbolize declining U.S. leadership in multilateral affairs. Caught on the short end of a 120-to-7 vote in favor of the ICC statute, the United States was also one of only two democracies to vote against it. This result was all the more embarrassing because the United States had raised the diplomatic stakes by warning other states that their relations with the United States could suffer if they failed to support U.S. proposals on the language of the statute.[47] The lopsided result of that vote seemed to confirm the limits of U.S. power and to establish that U.S. threats of retaliation lacked credibility.

In all likelihood, policy inertia will complicate any effort by the United States to reexamine the merits of its ICC policy. It may be that the country has backed itself so far into a corner that no rational ICC policy can emerge from Washington for many years. Indeed, the tone of the language used by the United States has often been harsh, including threats to go to the unilateralist extreme by actively opposing the ICC.[48] More recently, members of Congress hostile to the ICC have introduced legislation that if adopted would prohibit any U.S. cooperation with the ICC; prevent U.S. military cooperation with any countries, other than important U.S. allies, that ratify the statute; and even authorize the president to use force abroad if necessary to free U.S. military personnel incarcerated by the ICC.[49] Ambassador David Scheffer found himself caught between the extremely unilateralist perspectives of domestic ICC opponents and the practical need to pursue some kind of rational ICC policy through multilateral negotiations. He observed that the draconian bill described above would "achieve exactly the opposite of the result intended and would seriously harm our own national security and foreign-policy interests," in addition to depriving the United States of all negotiating leverage regarding the ICC.[50] It is difficult to imagine how such a policy could lead to any positive result for the United States.

Conclusion

If the United States is to maintain its position of global leadership, it must work to play a positive and constructive role in shaping multilateral institutions, using them wisely as an aspect of its exceptional power and influence. Unfortunately, U.S. policy toward the ICC has not followed this model. Instead the U.S. policy process has been fear-driven, reactive, and ineffective, thus raising questions about the future of U.S. global leadership.[51]

When the ICC moved onto the U.S. agenda, those who framed the issue, such as Senator Jesse Helms, had internalized a strong anti-UN bias. As a result, the domestic dialogue on the ICC was focused disproportionately on the fears of skeptics who beat the drum of sovereignty. These sovereignty concerns are shared by all states, but in the U.S. case they were magnified by direct and emotional appeals to U.S. exceptionalism. In the face of these powerful domestic forces, the Clinton administration failed to moderate the ICC debate, for example, by putting sovereignty concerns in perspective and stressing the potential positive value of the institution being created.[52] The president has primary responsibility for balancing the various interests of the United States, and he or she should not allow the distorted perspective offered by one narrow constituency to go unchallenged. This is especially true in the formulation of U.S. foreign policy.

The United States must reduce the risk that domestic political sensitivities will lead to high-profile policy rifts that sabotage U.S. multilateral conference diplomacy. U.S. diplomats lost much of their negotiating leverage on the Rome Statute because a key congressional opponent, acting with the support of the Pentagon and other domestic constituencies, indirectly precluded them from exploring jurisdictional compromise. The Clinton administration, which took domestic risks to support strong international institutions in other fields such as trade, did not show the same dedication and courage on this issue.

A dysfunctional policy process deprived the U.S. delegation in Rome of the chance to achieve an optimal negotiated result, but the ICC statute is nonetheless a compromise document. It incorporates countless U.S. proposals and is, on balance, a very reasonable document. Sometime in the next few years, when sixty countries have ratified the statute, the ICC will become part of the international institutional landscape. The United States will then have a unique opportunity to build a positive relationship with the new institution. But to do so it must avoid the mistakes of the past. There is no need for Washington to draw a "line in the sand" over the creation of the ICC, nor any reason to treat the jurisdiction of the ICC as a provocation.

The United States has already sent a rather alarming message of defiance to the ICC, making it clear that the United States would consider any indictment of U.S. military personnel or civilian leaders to be an unacceptable provocation. The United States should now be able to reach a *modus vivendi* with the ICC that will allow it to be a good neighbor to that institution, even if it does not become a party to the statute. Ultimately, the United States can do more to help the ICC than the ICC can do to help, or to hurt, the United States. U.S. assets will be invaluable to the ICC as it attempts to locate and arrest war criminals. It is inevitable that U.S. support in the Security Council will often be critical to establishing ICC jurisdiction over international crimes.

Negotiations to determine the future of the ICC have continued, and will be a feature of the international landscape for years to come. Even though the means for addressing U.S. concerns at this stage are limited, Washington has been creative in using post-Rome negotiations (focused on the elements of the crimes, and on the rules of procedure and evidence) as final opportunities for making the ICC more palatable. Before leaving office, the Clinton administration offered one last proposal intended to prevent the ICC from trying nationals of nonparty states (like the United States) for acts taken "within the overall direction of" such a state.[53] While unlikely to be accepted, this proposal did at least represent a positive attempt to reach an accommodation with the institution that is soon to be established. By signing the statute on December 31, 2000, the United States placed itself in a better position to influence the evolution of the ICC. The statute provides for periodic meetings of the ICC's Assembly of States Parties, in which the United States, as a signatory, can now participate as a nonparty observer.[54]

U.S. ratification of the statute (which will require the approval of the Senate) remains a remote prospect, but during the next few years the ICC will be born. It will take a while for the new institution to establish itself and to earn the confidence of the international community. The Bush administration should calm the waters of our ICC policy by taking a wait-and-see attitude toward the developing institution. When the United States is prepared to take a fresh look at the ICC, it will find a multilateral institution that, on the whole, can be expected to serve the interests of both this country and the international community.

Notes

1. See Sciolino, "U.S. Names Figures It Wants Charged With War Crimes," *New York Times,* December 17, 1992.

2. See Rome Statute of the International Criminal Court, U.N. Doc. A/CONF. 183/9 (reissued for technical reasons) July 17, 1998 (hereafter "ICC Statute").

3. Rome Statute, article 125(1).

4. "Clinton's Words: 'The Right Action.'"

5. Great Britain, perhaps the closest U.S. ally of all, is enthusiastic about the ICC and has called upon all states to ratify the ICC Statute: "We want to send a clear signal to the perpetrators of the world's most heinous crimes that they will not go unpunished. For that reason we have lobbied other governments to join us in our support for the ICC. I repeat that call here. All States should sign and ratify the Rome Treaty of the International Criminal Court." Robin Cook, U.K. Secretary of State for Foreign and Commonwealth Affairs, "Message from the Foreign Secretary," available online at http://www.fco.gov.uk/news/keythemepage.asp?158 (accessed November 1, 2000).

6. See *Instructions for the Government of Armies of the United States in the Field.*

7. Agreement by the Government of the United States of America, the Provisional Government of the French Republic, the Government of the United Kingdom of Great Britain and Northern Ireland, and the Government of the Union of Soviet Socialist Republics for the Prosecution and Punishment of the Major War Criminals of the European Axis, August 8, 1945, 82 U.N.T.S. 279.

8. G.A. Res. 95, U.N. GAOR 6th Com., 1st Sess., pt. 1, 55th plen. mtg., U.N. Doc. A/64/Add.1 (1946) ("Affirmation of the Principles of International Law Recognized by the Charter of the Nuremberg Tribunal" confirming the status of the Nuremberg Charter).

9. See Statute of the International Criminal Tribunal for the Former Yugoslavia, art. 1, annexed to *Report of the Secretary-General Pursuant to Paragraph 2 of U.N. Security Council Resolution 808,* U.N. GAOR, May 19, 1993, U.N. Doc. S/2-5704 (hereinafter ICTY Statute).

10. Statute of the International Tribunal for Rwanda, annex to resolution 955 (1994), adopted by the Security Council at its 3453rd meeting on November 8, 1994, S/RES/955, November 8, 1994, reprinted in 33 I.L.M. 1598 (1994) (hereinafter ICTR Statute).

11. "Because they only try certain offenders in certain conflicts, these tribunals and their laws and penalties raise fundamental questions about compliance with the principles of legality and about general considerations of fairness . . . ad hoc tribunals generally do not provide equal treatment to individuals in similar circumstances who commit similar violations. Thus, such tribunals create the appearance of uneven or unfair justice, even when the accused are properly deserving of prosecution." (See Bassiouni, "From Versailles to Rwanda in Seventy-Five Years," pp. 60–61.)

12. The 1999 NATO bombing mission for Kosovo did ultimately expose U.S. flyers to the jurisdiction of the ICTY, but it is safe to say that the United States did not anticipate this possibility when it pushed for the creation of that tribunal. In any case, the ICTY has decided that there are no grounds for further investigation or prosecution of the NATO forces involved. See International Criminal Tribunal for the Former Yugoslavia: *Final Report to the Prosecutor by the Committee Established to Review the NATO Bombing Campaign Against the Federal Republic of Yugoslavia.*

13. See Rome Statute, Article 12.

14. See Brierly, *The Law of Nations,* p. 311.

15. The U.S. Restatement endorses a very long list of crimes subject to universal jurisdiction. "A state has jurisdiction to define and prescribe punishment for certain offenses recognized by the community of nations as of universal concern, such as piracy, slave trade, attacks on or hijacking of aircraft, genocide, war crimes, and perhaps certain acts of terrorism" Restatement of the Foreign Relations Law of the United States, §404. Brownlie distinguishes the generally accepted right of any state to try to punish war criminals from the principle of universality that in his view is still disputed. He notes that "in so far as the invocation of the principle of universality in cases apart from war crimes and crimes against humanity creates misgivings, it may be important to maintain the distinction." Brownlie, *Principles of Public International Law,* p. 305.

16. "The delegates in Rome included a form of 'universal jurisdiction' in the Court statute. This means that, even if the U.S. never signs the treaty, and even if the U.S. Senate refuses to ratify it, the countries participating in this Court will regard American soldiers and citizens to be within the jurisdiction of the International Criminal Court. That, Mr. Chairman, is nonsense." *Statement of Senator Jesse Helms Hearing on the United Nations International Criminal Court,* July 23, 1998.

17. Rome Statute, article 5(2).

18. "By providing that the court is to have jurisdiction only when it is accepted by the state where the crimes have been committed or by the national state of the accused, the treaty effectively lets off future Saddam Husseins or Pol Pots, who kill their own people on their own territory. This provision makes the court largely ineffective in dealing with rogue regimes, except when the Security Council exercises its Chapter VII authority to extend jurisdiction to them." Meron, "The Court We Want," *Washington Post,* October 13, 1998, p. A15.

19. Rome Statute, article 17(1).

20. "The jurisdiction of the Court shall be limited to the most serious crimes of concern to the international community as a whole. " Rome Statute, article 5(1).

21. The ICC Prosecutor may decline to investigate a case if he or she determines that "taking into account the gravity of the crime and the interests of victims, there are nonetheless substantial reasons to believe that an investigation would not serve the interests of justice." Rome Statute, article 53(1)(c).

The Prosecutor may also, after an investigation, decide not to prosecute on similar grounds. Statute Article 53(2)(c).

22. "Helms Declares U.N. Criminal Court 'Dead-on-Arrival' in Senate Without U.S. Veto."

23. CICC home page, *http://www.igc.apc.org/icc/html/coalition.htm,* accessed October 14, 2000.

24. Rome Statute, article 17(1).

25. Ibid., articles 18(2) and 19(2)(b).

26. Ibid., article 17(1)(a) and (b).

27. "In order to determine inability in a particular case, the Court shall consider whether, due to a total or substantial collapse or unavailability of its national judicial system, the State is unable to obtain the accused or the necessary evidence and testimony or otherwise unable to carry out its proceedings." Rome Statute, article 17(3).

28. Article 17(2) of the statute provides as follows:

2. In order to determine unwillingness in a particular case, the Court shall consider, having regard to the principles of due process recognized by international law, whether one or more of the following exist, as applicable:

(a) The proceedings were or are being undertaken or the national decision was made for the purpose of shielding the person concerned from criminal responsibility for crimes within the jurisdiction of the Court referred to in article 5;

(b) There has been an unjustified delay in the proceedings which in the circumstances is inconsistent with an intent to bring the person concerned to justice;

(c) The proceedings were not or are not being conducted independently or impartially, and they were or are being conducted in a manner which, in the circumstances, is inconsistent with an intent to bring the person concerned to justice.

29. Rome Statute, article 19(6).

30. See Kaufman and Whiteman, "Opposition to Human Rights Treaties in the United States Senate."

31. "No treaty shall authorize or permit any foreign power or any international organization to supervise, control, or adjudicate rights of citizens of the United States within the United States enumerated in this constitution or any other matter

essentially within the domestic jurisdiction of the United States." Bricker Amendment, section 2.

32. Rome Statute, article 120.

33. Secretary of State Madeleine Albright described the indispensable U.S. role as follows: "But if we have to use force, it is because we are America. We are the indispensable nation. We stand tall, and we see further than other countries into the future, and we see the danger here to all of us. And I know that the American men and women in uniform are always prepared to sacrifice for freedom, democracy, and the American way of life." "Secretary of State Madeleine Albright Discusses Her Visit to Ohio to Get Support from American People for Military Action Against Iraq," NBC News Transcripts, *The Today Show,* February 19, 1998.

34. These concerns were summed up in the following terms by David Scheffer, the Clinton administrations special envoy dealing with war crimes:

> [T]he reality is that the United States is a global military power and presence. . . . Our military forces are often called upon to engage overseas in conflict situations, for purposes of humanitarian intervention, to rescue hostages, to bring out American citizens from threatening environments, to deal with terrorists. We have to be extremely careful that this proposal does not limit the capacity of our armed forces to legitimately operate internationally . . . that it does not open up opportunities for endless frivolous complaints to be lodged against the United States as a global military power.
>
> Crossette, "World Criminal Court Having a Painful Birth," *New York Times,* August 13, 1997, Section A, p. 10.

35. Senator Helms warmly congratulated Ambassador Scheffer for taking such a hard line in Rome. "I am aware that the Clinton Administration was eager to sign that treaty, so the very fact that you, Ambassador Scheffer, declined to do so speaks volumes about just how unwise the treaty adopted in Rome really is. . . . Mr. Ambassador, I commend you for voting 'no' on this fatally flawed treaty." Federal Document Clearing House Congressional Testimony, July 23, 1998. Jesse Helms, Senator, Senate Foreign Relations, International Operations U.N., International Criminal Court.

36. According to one report, "the Rome delegates voted down American compromises and amendments amid scenes of anti-American cheering and jeering reminiscent, according to witnesses, of the worst U.N. excesses of the 1970s." Frum, "The International Criminal Court Must Die," p. 27.

37. "Political tensions between North and South at the United Nations also complicated the bargaining. Developing countries feel a new jealousy of the Security Council's exclusive authority over international security matters. The recent, failed attempt of middle-rank powers to expand the Council has exacerbated the mood. Together, these factors made it impossible for the United States to preserve an American veto over prosecution decisions by using the requirement of Council approval." Ruth Wedgwood, "Fiddling in Rome," p. 20.

38. Rome Statute, article 121(5).

39. Vienna Convention on the Law of Treaties, U.N. Doc. A/CONF.39/27, (1969), 8 I.L.M. 679 (1969), Article 34.

40. "I can tell you that it would be bizarre, utterly bizarre consequence for governments to think that this treaty can be adopted and brought into force with the presumption that it will cover governments that have not joined the treaty regime. That is bizarre. That's weird. That is unheard of in treaty law." "Ambassador-at-Large for War Crimes Issues Holds News Conference at National Press Club," Federal Document Clearing House Political Transcripts, July 31, 1998.

41. "[A] form of jurisdiction over non-party states was adopted by the conference despite our strenuous objections. . . . Our position is clear: Official actions of a non-party state should not be subject to the court's jurisdiction if that country does not join the treaty, except by means of Security Council action under the UN Charter. Otherwise, the ratification procedure would be meaningless for governments." David J. Scheffer, "Developments at the Rome Treaty Conference," p. 19.

42. Prof. Theodore Meron, who served as a public (private citizen) member of the U.S. delegation in Rome, argues that "the Statute overreaches in extending the court's sway over states that choose not to ratify the Statute." Meron, "The Court We Want."

43. Rome Statute, article 89(1).

44. Ibid., article 93.

45. Ibid., article 109(1).

46. Ibid., article 117.

47. According to the *New York Times,* the United States pulled out all the stops trying to stop the ICC:

> The United States has been putting pressure on some of its closest European allies to limit the scope of a future permanent international war crimes court. Talking points said to have been prepared for Defense Secretary William S. Cohen, for example, suggested that if Germany succeeded in lobbying for "universal jurisdiction" for the court, the United States might retaliate by removing its overseas troops, including those in Europe. . . . The Pentagon denied today that Mr. Cohen had threatened to withdraw troops from Europe. But the Pentagon spokesman, Kenneth H. Bacon, said Mr. Cohen had argued publicly and privately against sweeping powers for the court.
>
> Stanley, "U.S. Presses Allies to Rein In Proposed War Crimes Court," *New York Times,* July 15, 1998.

48. As one U.S. delegate wrote a few months after the Rome Conference, "[t]here is a real possibility that the United States may become actively hostile to the treaty." Meron, "The Court We Want."

49. See H.R. 4654, the American Service Members Protection Act of 2000.

50. Hearing of the House International Relations Committee, witnesses: David Scheffer, ambassador-at-large for war crimes issues, U.S. Department of State; Walter Slocombe, undersecretary for policy, U.S. Department of Defense, Federal News Service, July 26, 2000.

51. As David Bosco states:

> To the court's opponents, America's stance at Rome was one of principled defiance. But it really demonstrated how much the United States has lost confidence in its ability to lead and shape international institutions. Fear, not reason, accounts for the U.S. position. . . . The court's critics argue that the ICC will undermine the pursuit of international justice by making the United States more reluctant to undertake humanitarian interventions. But it is a far greater danger to American global engagement for the U.S. to believe that a court punishing crimes against humanity is a menace to its interests.
>
> Bosco, "Sovereign Myopia," p. 24,

52. "The United States clearly has the power to undermine this nascent institution. But it would be unfortunate if we did so, because this country has a clear

long-range national interest in deterring atrocities and bringing offenders to justice."
Meron, "The Court We Want."

53. That proposal consists of the Proposed Text of Rule to Article 98 of the
Rome Treaty accompanied by the Proposed Text to a Supplemental Document to the
Rome Treaty (which would be a legal agreement between the UN and the ICC.) The
proposal is reproduced at *http://www.igc.apc.org/icc/html/us2000.html*

54. Rome Statute, article 112(1) and (6).

14

Why Is U.S. Human Rights Policy So Unilateralist?

Andrew Moravcsik

THE STORY OF U.S. "EXCEPTIONALISM" IN HUMAN RIGHTS POLICY—THE aversion of the United States to domestic application of international human rights treaties—has often been told. The apparent paradox is clear. The United States has a long tradition of unilateral action to promote domestic constitutional rights and international human rights.[1] The United States has helped establish and enforce global human rights standards through rhetorical disapproval, foreign aid, sanctions, military intervention, and even multilateral negotiations. It does so even in some areas—most recently humanitarian intervention in Kosovo—where the costs are potentially high. At the same time, however, the United States remains extremely cautious about committing itself to the domestic application of binding international legal standards for human rights. In particular, it has been hesitant to ratify multilateral human rights treaties, despite their acceptance among nearly all advanced industrial democracies, many developing democracies, and, in many cases, nondemocratic governments. When the United States does ratify such treaties, it typically imposes so many reservations that ratification has no domestic effect.[2]

The ambivalence of U.S. human rights policy is widely criticized by human rights advocates. Human Rights Watch and the American Civil Liberties Union (ACLU), for example, immediately denounced U.S. ratification in 1992 of the UN International Covenant on Civil and Political Rights (ICCPR) because they viewed reservations to restrict domestic application as a "half-step" based on "the cynical view of international human rights law as a source of protection only for those outside U.S. borders."[3] The Lawyer's Committee on Human Rights decried the implication that "one set of rules belongs to the U.S. and another to the rest of the world" and accused the U.S. government of outright hypocrisy.[4] Government officials and representatives of NGOs consistently maintain, in the words of Assistant Secretary of State Patricia Derian in 1979, that "failure . . . to ratify has a significant negative impact on the conduct of our human rights policy," undermining its "credibility and effectiveness."[5]

What underlies this mixture of international activism and domestic obstruction? Why are international human rights issues so particularly controversial in the United States, while nearly all our closest allies—many with political ideologies and institutions as distinctive and cherished as our own—are far more likely to accept them?

Perhaps the most common explanation attributes U.S. unilateralism in human rights to a distinctive culture of "exceptionalism"—that is, a pervasive sense of cultural relativism, ethnocentrism, or nationalism. J. D. van der Vyer maintains that "the American approach to international human rights is as much a manifestation of cultural relativism as any other sectional approach to international human rights founded on national ethnic, cultural or religious particularities. American relativism, furthermore, also serves to obstruct the United Nations' resolve to promote *universal* respect for human rights and fundamental freedoms for all without distinction as to race, sex, language, or religion."[6]

David Forsythe points to "American nationalism . . . intellectual isolationism and unilateralism."[7] Natalie Kaufman, a leading historian of postwar Senate deliberations, characterizes consistent concern among U.S. politicians to protect the sanctity of U.S. political institutions in a diverse world as evidence of "an ethnocentric world view, a perspective suspicious or disdainful of things foreign" dating back at least to the early 1950s.[8] Such charges make for powerful political rhetoric among global elites. In the international legal community, in particular, labeling a policy as an instance of "cultural relativism" is a sure means of delegitimating it. For classical international lawyers, a nation either accepts, at least in principle, uniform application of all international human rights norms or it is "culturally relativistic."[9]

Yet as an explanation for U.S. behavior, "cultural relativism" is both incomplete and implausible. Labeling the United States "ethnocentric" or "culturally relativist," even if it were correct in a narrow sense, does not tell us precisely *why* the United States is opposed to universal human rights norms. Any effort to understand U.S. human rights policy, or to transform it, must rest on a precise empirical understanding of the "national ethnic, cultural and religious particularities" that, according to van der Vyver, underlie U.S. exceptionalism. (Anything less borders on the legalistic tautology, hinted at in the quotation above, whereby any government that resists the formal application of UN norms has by definition succumbed to cultural relativism.) Yet there exists, to my knowledge, no such empirical analysis. It has yet to be demonstrated that the fundamental political culture of the United States—its universalist civil rights tradition and polyglot culture—is significantly more "ethnocentric" in such matters than those of other major countries. Is the U.S. conception of domestic political values really more "exceptional" than that of Britain, France, Russia, Japan, Germany, or China? Of all the particularities of postwar U.S. foreign policy—its distinctive geopolitical imperatives, national interests, and domestic political institutions, for example—why should we believe that it is cultural values that account for U.S. policy? And if so, what sustains these cultural values as against the spread of universal human rights norms? Are there not enduring political interests and institutions that promote "exceptionalist" beliefs? One reason to believe that "exceptionalist" culture offers only a superficial explanation for U.S. policy is that Americans manifestly do not share a common cultural predisposition toward international human rights norms. As we shall see in more detail, such norms trigger intense and partisan ideological conflict among domestic political interests. At best the charge of "cultural relativism" raises these essential causal questions; at worst it may be leading us in the wrong direction.

This chapter takes a different approach. The exceptional ambivalence and unilateralism of the U.S. human rights policy, I argue in the first section, is a function of four general characteristics, none of which invokes the "ethnocentrism" of U.S. culture. The United States is skeptical of domestic implementation of international norms because it is geopolitically powerful, stably democratic, ideologically conservative, and politically decentralized. To restate the claim in general terms, support for multilateral institutions is less likely to the extent that a nation possesses strong unilateral bargaining power, stable domestic institutions, preferences about substantive rights that diverge from the international consensus, and decentralized political institutions that empower small veto groups. Any of these four general characteristics render governments less likely to accept binding multilateral norms.

I argue in the second section that the United States, alone in the modern world, exhibits all four of these characteristics. A historical overview of domestic cleavages and debates uncovers direct evidence of the importance of these four factors in postwar U.S. human rights policy. Further empirical support is provided by close examination of the contemporary debate over ratification of the Convention on the Rights of the Child, as we shall see in the second section of this chapter.

Yet, I conclude in the third section, little currently available evidence supports the claim of human rights activists that U.S. ambivalence undermines U.S. foreign policy, U.S. human rights policy, or the global enforcement of human rights. The primary influence of U.S. unilateralism appears instead to be restricted to U.S. citizens, who might otherwise be able to plead a broader range of rights before U.S. courts.

Four Determinants of U.S. Human Rights Policy

The United States has been, almost since its founding, a liberal democracy with a history of intense concern about domestic civil rights and a sense of solidarity with other liberal democracies. Yet four general factors constrain the willingness of U.S. leaders to adhere fully to multilateral human rights treaties: geopolitical power, stable democratic governance, ideological conservatism, and political decentralization. Let us consider each in turn.

The Ambivalent Superpower

The first general factor influencing U.S. multilateral human rights policy is its superpower status in world affairs.

A straightforward "realist" argument links great-power status to unilateralism. Multilateral commitments tie governments down to common rules and procedures designed to promote reciprocal policy adjustment. In deciding whether to enter into a multilateral arrangement of this kind, rational governments must make a cost-benefit calculation as compared with unilateral or bilateral alternatives. For any given state, the costs of multilateralism lie in the necessity for each participant to sacrifice a measure of unilateral or bilateral policy autonomy or legal sovereignty in order to impose a uniform policy. All other things being equal, the more isolated and powerful a state—that is, the more efficiently it can achieve its objectives by unilateral or bilateral means—the less it gains from multilateral cooperation.[10] Powerful governments are therefore more likely to be skeptical of procedural equality than their smaller neighbors. This is not to say that, on balance, great powers will always oppose multilateralism, for the benefits of intense cooperation may outweigh the costs. Yet, all other things equal, there is reason to expect great powers to feel greater ambivalence toward multilateralism than their less powerful neighbors.[11]

Great power ambivalence toward multilateralism seems to pervade many areas of U.S. foreign policy, including trade, monetary, financial, and security policies. In postwar international trade policy, to be sure, the United States emerged as a strong and consistent supporter of liberalization under GATT and the WTO. Yet it was the United States that in 1947 rejected the stronger enforcement capabilities of the International Trade Organization (ITO) and subsequently developed highly controversial capacity (mostly under Section 301) for "aggressive unilateralism"—a capability not yet matched by other major trading partners. Similarly in international financial and monetary relations, the United States has remained engaged yet acted unilaterally between 1971 and 1973 to undermine the system of pegged exchange rates established under the postwar Bretton Woods system. It continues to jealously defend its disproportionate voting power, and the de facto veto this confers, in the IMF. The United States helped create the UN yet maintains its Security Council veto and finds itself in a continually antagonistic financial relationship with it. Finally, in NATO, the United States retains a de jure veto (as do others) and a recognized position of primus inter pares.

We might expect the ambivalence of powerful countries to be particularly pronounced in the area of human rights because the typical model of multilateral human rights enforcement is judicial rather than legislative. Whereas the international organizations we just examined provide forums for interstate bargaining—a mode of interaction in which the powerful tend to retain disproportionate influence—human rights norms are typically enforced through formal legal adjudication at the domestic or international level. To participate fully in such arrangements, in contrast to most legislative institutions, powerful countries sacrifice much of their bargaining power. It has long been argued that there is a general tendency for great and regional powers—the United States, Soviet Union, Britain, China, Brazil, Mexico, and India, for example—to remain aloof from formal international human rights enforcement.[12]

Three salient characteristics of postwar U.S. human rights policy, beyond its general skepticism toward multilateral commitments, appear to confirm the importance of these realist considerations:

- *Consistent U.S. support for treaty reservations.* The United States, often backed by Britain, France, China, and Russia, has consistently opposed efforts by smaller states, backed by international tribunals, to restrict the scope of permissible reservations to human rights treaties.[13] Recent treaties on the ICC and landmines, for example, permit no reservations, and the United States has stayed aloof.[14]

- *Concern for U.S. military forces abroad.* Two international agreements, the Genocide Convention and the ICC, have raised the possibility (albeit remote) that U.S. soldiers might be prosecuted. Is it just coincidence that other governments with significant foreign military involvements (i.e., Israel, China, Russia, France, and initially Britain) were among the initial skeptics of a strong ICC?

- *Concern about allied noncommunist dictators.* As part of its Cold War alliance strategy, the United States long sought to defend nondemocratic leaders of South Vietnam, Pakistan, Iran, the Philippines, Nicaragua, Chile, Taiwan, South Korea, Saudi Arabia, and even the People's Republic of China. Through the realist lens, by which "the enemy of my enemy is my friend," these were viewed as essential "second-best" tactics in the Cold War. Even the Carter administration, though ideologically inclined toward the enforcement of human rights, was selective about human rights enforcement—a policy perhaps best symbolized by the image of Zbigniew Brzezinski waving an M16 rifle at the Khyber Pass in support of Islamic fundamentalists fighting against the Soviet invasion of Afghanistan. This may help explain why the United States seems slightly more willing to ratify multilateral human rights treaties now that the Cold War is over. The Senate ratified no legally binding treaty in the 1950s and one each in the 1960s, 1970s, and 1980s, but four during the early 1990s.

While the desire to maintain the discretion and influence of the United States in world affairs surely contributes to U.S. ambivalence toward formal human rights treaties, it does not tell the whole story. It fails to account in particular for the extraordinary virulence of general domestic opposition to treaty ratification and the specific arguments opponents advance. After all, if geopolitical flexibility were the goal, the United States could have its cake and eat it too by ratifying multilateral treaties and maintaining a parallel unilateral human rights policy. And it could aggressively employ specific reservations to cordon off areas of concern. Such a combination might indeed be viewed as more legitimate, and might thereby prove more effective in world affairs, than strictly unilateral policies. Presidents of both parties—whom one would expect to have had the superpower interests of the United States in mind, as they often did in pressing the country to accept other postwar multilateral commitments—rarely, if ever, held the United States back from full participation in multilateral human rights regimes. Since the controversy over the Bricker Amendment during the 1950s, the locus of opposition has lain in the Senate.[15] Congressional skepticism has persisted even though both parties have generally been internationalist and staunchly anticommunist in foreign policy, which has led them to overcome great-power skepticism to enter into more significant (although not unbounded) treaty commitments, such as NATO and other Cold War military alliances, trade institutions (GATT/WTO), and financial arrangements (IMF). In sum, U.S. views on human rights issues do not simply track the conventional geopolitical concerns of a superpower. To understand why U.S. legislators are so hesitant to cede sovereignty, we must therefore turn to the domestic determinants of U.S. human rights policy.

The Stable Democracy

A second factor contributing to U.S. ambivalence toward multilateral human rights commitments is the exceptional stability of democratic governance inside its borders.

This assertion may seem puzzling at first glance. It is widely believed that well-established democracies are the strongest supporters of international human rights enforcement. Most interpretations of international human rights regimes stress the spread of democratic ideas outward from liberal societies through the actions of NGOs and public opinion, as well as the direct exercise of state power by established democracies.[16] In the broad sweep of history, to be sure, enforcement of human rights is closely linked to the spread of liberal democracy. Publics and politicians in established democracies have long encouraged and assisted democracy abroad, and even fought bitter wars to uphold that very institution, both for idealistic reasons and because they tend to view democracy—correctly so, it now appears—as integrally linked to world peace.[17]

Yet the relationship between stable democratic governance and international human rights regimes is more ambivalent than this simple account suggests. Established democracies are often skeptical of effective enforcement of international human rights norms. This underlying ambivalence, I have argued elsewhere, was particularly evident at the founding moment of the major postwar international human rights regimes under the European Convention on Human Rights, the American Convention on Human Rights, and the UN system. In each case, the most stable and established democracies consistently opposed effective enforcement of international norms, a position that led them into alliances with their most repressive neighbors.

A simple theoretical insight drawn from "liberal" theories of international relations, and from well-established theories of domestic delegation to courts and administrative agencies, explains the ambivalence of established democracies.[18] No national government likes to see its discretion limited through external constraints imposed by a judicial tribunal, whether international or domestic. (The same logic holds for central banks, independent agencies, prosecutors, and other nonmajoritarian institutions.) In this case, why would a self-interested government, democratic or not, ever risk the unpleasant possibility that actions of the government would be challenged or nullified when individual citizens bring complaints before a supranational body?

The most important reason to nonetheless delegate authority to such an international institution is to "lock in" particular domestic institutions against short-term or particularistic political pressures. How would this logic apply to international human rights regimes?[19] Support for domestic application of international human rights is—at least in early phases of the development of a human rights system—an act of calculated national self-interest designed to serve an overriding purpose, namely to stabilize and secure democratic governance at home against threats from the extreme right and left. Governments defend international commitments that promote the enforcement of rights their constituencies favor against their domestic political enemies. Who benefits most from such an arrangement in the area of international human rights? Certainly not nondemocracies, which bear the brunt of enforcement. But also not well-established democracies, which are already confident in the stability of democratic governance at home and gain no additional stability from international delegation. They see only disadvantages. The major supporters are instead the governments of newly established and transitional democracies, which accept such international constraints because they serve to stabilize the democratic political system as a whole, even at the cost of potential short-term inconvenience. At the founding of the European Convention on Human Rights, the most effective system of international human rights enforcement in the world today, the governments of the most established democracies of Europe (Britain, the Netherlands, Sweden, Denmark, Norway, and Luxembourg) sided with Greece, Turkey, Spain, and Portugal against mandatory enforcement.[20]

From this perspective, the reluctance of the United States—an unusually stable democracy—to enter into international human rights commitments is not the exception but the rule. In strictly self-interested terms, the

United States gains relatively little from the domestic enforcement of international human rights norms. In contrast to Europe in the 1950s or Latin America in the past few decades, there is no overarching sense of the need to protect U.S. political institutions against a slow slide into right- or left-wing authoritarianism. This helps to explain why large coalitions of supporters for some human rights treaties—for example, the Genocide Convention—were consistently outmaneuvered by smaller and passionate groups of critics. This may also help explain why the rhetoric of opponents to human rights treaties in the United States tends to be replete with praise of the strong U.S. domestic constitutional tradition, the possibility that international treaties might dilute domestic enforcement of individual rights, and skepticism toward the legitimacy and effectiveness of newly created international institutions.

Yet the stability of U.S. democracy does not provide a fully satisfactory explanation for U.S. reluctance to ratify multilateral human rights commitments. While the opposition of strong democracies to binding human rights treaties may have been the norm in the 1950s and 1960s, it no longer is. In opposing recent treaties, such as the Convention on the Rights of the Child or the ICC, the United States finds itself today in the company of a handful of rogue and failed states. Why has the United States failed to evolve as far in the same direction? From the start, moreover, attitudes toward human rights treaties have not been characterized by apathy and ignorance, as one might expect if the problem were simply the lack of clear benefits. Instead, domestic debate over human rights has been bitterly partisan and intensely ideological, led by those who feel that international human rights norms posed a fundamental threat to the integrity of U.S. political institutions. Any explanation of U.S. policy must account, therefore, for the significantly greater intensity of opposition in the United States than within any other advanced industrial democracy, even as the latter become stably democratic. We must investigate the values and interests underlying domestic cleavages on this issue.

The Conservative Nation

The third general factor helping to shape U.S. international human rights policy is the general conservatism of U.S. politics.

Increasingly, international relations theorists link varying fundamental social purposes of societies to the varying foreign policies of their governments.[21] Particularly important are national ideas concerning the proper provision of public goods—national identity, political institutions, socioeconomic redistribution—that underlie fundamental policy goals. This perspective highlights the partisan and ideological identities of those who support or oppose full participation in human rights regimes. At the crudest level, one would predict that those countries most committed to human rights at home would also be most committed to multilateral policies to promote human rights abroad. Yet the central political problem of human rights enforcement does not lie only in the level of support for universal human rights in theory, but in the tensions among distinctive national conceptions of how to define and enforce those rights in practice. At the heart of most international cooperative ventures are one or more interstate bargains that set the common substantive standards to which states will be held, in this case the precise definitions of human rights. One would expect those countries whose views about the definition of human rights are supported by a majority in the organization (the "median country" in the international system) to be least inconvenienced by the imposition of multilateral norms, and therefore most supportive of them. Governments whose views are furthest from the global norm have sound reasons to be skeptical of the domestic application of binding international norms they do not share.

There is reason to believe that the United States finds itself in this extreme position more often than many other advanced industrial democracies. In comparative perspective, the bundle of constitutional rights generated over more than 200 years by the U.S. political and legal system is distinctive, even idiosyncratic. The United States guarantees exceptionally broad constitutional protections for expression, property, freedom from improper search and seizure, and the right to bear arms, but exceptionally weak protection for welfare rights, labor rights, rights against cruel and unusual punishment, and some cultural rights. In the latter areas U.S. policy varies greatly across states and localities. In the twentieth century federal jurisprudence created a stronger and more uniform set of rights, but much variation remains. Current conservative criticism of international human rights treaties focuses on the possibility that international treaties would override understandings of rights that have evolved organically over a long period through domestic democratic discussion and judicial interpretation.[22] As a result, Lincoln Bloomfield has observed, "For many non-Americans, the most important human rights are not those that Americans regard as paramount."[23]

Yet the idiosyncratic nature of the U.S. conception of specific rights cannot by itself explain the virulence of domestic opposition to unilateral human rights treaties in general. Many other political systems are based on idiosyncratic understandings of particular rights. Concerns about the death penalty, the First Amendment, and so on could in any case be handled through specific U.S. reservations. What explains the depth of political mobilization around binding international human rights treaties?

One important factor is that the entire U.S. political spectrum lies to the right of those found in most other advanced industrial democracies, with the result that the enforcement of international human rights norms triggers central political cleavages different from those in other advanced democracies. These cleavages help explain the intensity and bitterness of ideological and partisan debates over human rights—controversies peculiar to the United States. Two of the most important cleavages lie in U.S. attitudes toward racial discrimination and socioeconomic rights.[24] In both cases, conservatives viewed international human rights treaties as part of a broader movement to impose liberal federal standards—in particular, provisions banning race discrimination and imposing labor standards—on the practices of certain states, notably those in the South.

Since the nation's founding U.S. politics have been deeply influenced by race, and senatorial skepticism toward formal human rights obligations reflects this. When the issue of human rights treaties first emerged, in the immediate post–World War II period, human rights enforcement was inextricably linked to the U.S. civil rights movement. Civil rights remained among the most salient issues in domestic politics from 1945 through the present, generating exceptionally strong domestic opposition and eventually triggering an epochal partisan realignment. International human rights proved bitterly controversial at home. Those who supported or opposed aggressive federal enforcement of civil rights tended, respectively, to support or oppose full adherence to international human rights norms.

The link between race and human rights was quite evident in Senate hearings on the Genocide Convention in 1949, a series of hearings about which one commentator observed that "the major arguments enunciated against *all* human rights treaties were first articulated."[25] Opponents of the convention, who succeeded in capturing the American Bar Association (ABA) and using its resources and prestige to block ratification, stressed the tendency of international human rights treaties to limit U.S. rights. The most persuasive cases involved racial discrimination.[26] In the 1950s, concerns about race were linked to the fear that other minorities, notably Communists, would mobilize around the race issue.[27] One supporter conceded: "You have to face that . . . in getting down to realities . . . the practical objection, the thing that is behind a lot of people's minds on this convention is—is it aimed at lynching in the South? You have to face that."[28]

Such statements may seem somewhat anachronistic today, but the underlying issue is still relevant. The aggressive enforcement of civil rights in the United States remains controversial, albeit in a more subtle form, thereby calling international human rights treaties into question. International human rights advocates critical of U.S. policy focus on the potential of international human rights norms to suppress racial, gender, and linguistic discrimination, as well as to ameliorate U.S. policy on closely related issues like prison conditions, police brutality, and the death penalty—each an area of strong partisan conflict in the United States.[29]

Perhaps an even more striking divergence between the U.S. and other democratic governments lies in the status of socioeconomic rights. In comparative perspective, the United States has a relatively informal and underdeveloped (i.e., nonsolidaristic) conception of economic rights, particularly in the areas of labor and social welfare policy.[30] There has long been opposition, not least in the South and West, to aggressive centralized enforcement of labor and socioeconomic rights.[31] The tendency of the United States not to recognize socioeconomic rights finds few parallels in the former communist world, the developing world, or even among most other advanced industrial democracies. On socioeconomic issues, the central contemporary cleavage in the United States between left and right fits into the conservative half of the political spectrum found in most advanced industrial democracies. Europe and Canada are far more committed to the recognition of economic redistribution and social spending as basic rights. In postwar continental Europe, political alignments were generally reconfigured to create at least one socialist bloc and one center-right bloc, each of which was committed to these rights. For them, the international promulgation of political and economic rights simply acknowledged what had already been conceded at home. Accordingly, as we shall see in more detail below, international treaties were viewed as means to ward off, rather than encourage, radical change at home.

This was a central source of conflict in the early years of postwar international human rights diplomacy. During the Cold War, the topic of socioeconomic rights was a critical point of contention between the developing world, backed by the Soviet bloc, and the United States. The New Deal—itself a modest program by postwar European standards—was just two decades old when the president of the ABA, a prominent conservative lawyer (and admirer of Senator Joseph McCarthy) named Frank Holman, mobilized that organization to oppose ratification of international human rights treaties without reservations, rendering them non-self-executing and inapplicable to state law. As Holman wrote in 1953: "Internationalists . . . propose to use the United Nations . . . to change the domestic laws and even the Government of the United States and to establish a World Government along socialistic lines. . . . They would give the super-government absolute control of business, industry, prices, wages, and every detail of American social and economic life."[32] The Universal Declaration and covenants constituted a program, in Holman's opinion, that would "promote state socialism, if not communism, throughout the world"—a charge that was often repeated in subsequent debates over the UN covenants.[33]

For a half-century these two salient elements of conservatism in the United States, racial discrimination and economic libertarianism, placed the nation distinctly outside the mainstream of the global consensus on the definition of human rights. The result has been intense partisan conflict. The conservatism of the ideological spectrum in the United States means that firm adherence to international human rights norms does not command support from a broad centrist coalition, as is generally true in Europe, but instead creates a deep left-right split between liberals and conservatives. Competing views are represented, respectively, by the Democratic and

Republican parties. Support for adherence to international human rights treaties comes disproportionately from Democratic presidents and members of Congress, while opposition comes disproportionately from Republican presidents and members of Congress. Although there are of course numerous individual exceptions to this rule, it holds up well as a generalization.[34] During the 1950s, partisan opposition was led by Southern Democrats opposed to federal civil rights policy; today it is led by Republican senators due to their (globally idiosyncratic) stand on socioeconomic and racial rights, and also on religious, educational, and cultural issues.

One indicator of the partisan nature of international human rights is the nature of the criticism by international human rights groups of U.S. policy. In 1993, as a response to U.S. ratification of the ICCPR the previous year, Human Rights Watch and the ACLU jointly issued a report entitled *Human Rights Violations in the United States*. The list of violations focused, as it happened, almost exclusively on issues championed by the Democratic Party: discrimination against racial minorities, women, linguistic minorities, and immigrants, as well as on prison conditions, police brutality, the death penalty, freedom of information, and religious liberty.[35] Clearly the domestic application of international standards would favor one party over the other.

Another indicator of the decisive importance of partisan cleavages over human rights is the record of executive submission of and Senate consent to major legally binding human rights treaties. The twelve major human rights treaties found in Table 14.1 are arguably the most important such documents of the postwar period. What patterns do we observe in U.S. human rights policy?

The policies of the two parties diverge.[36] Democratic senators tend to support the enforcement of international human rights norms; Republican senators tend to oppose such enforcement. Accordingly, strong Democratic control of the Senate appears to be a necessary condition for the ratification of international human rights treaties. The Senate has never ratified a binding international human rights treaty when the Democrats held fewer than 55 seats. At least nine of eleven submissions to the Senate for advice and consent were made by Democratic presidents. Eight of twelve postwar agreements have been signed by Democratic presidents.[37]

The rhetoric of congressional and public debates, along with public opinion data, lends further support to this interpretation of U.S. policy. To judge from Senate hearings and speeches, as well as interest group activities, domestic debates have been concerned almost exclusively with the domestic implications of adherence to human rights treaties.[38] Senators and presidents have debated the detailed implications of human rights treaties for U.S. constitutional law in general and for legislation and judicial decisions in sensitive areas like race, education, gender policy, children's policy, labor relations, and the provision of social welfare. Polling reveals that the strongest supporters of human rights enforcement (as well as for the UN

Table 14.1 The United States and Multilateral Human Rights Treaties, 1945–2000 Executive Action and Congressional Consent

	Negotiated (U.S. Vote)	Submitted to the Senate	Senate Consent (Seats/Majority)
Genocide Convention	Truman (Y)	Truman	1986 (55 Dem.)
Convention on the Political Rights of Women	Truman (Y)	Kennedy	1974 (56 Dem)
Supplemental Slavery Convention	*Eisenhower* (Y)	Kennedy	1967 (68 Dem.)
ILO Convention on Forced Labor	*Eisenhower* (Y)	Kennedy	1991 (56 Dem.)
Convention on Racial Discrimination	Johnson (Y)	Carter	1994 (57 Dem.)
Covenant on Civil and Political Rights	Johnson (Y)	Carter/*Bush*	1992 (56 Dem.)[a]
Optional Protocol to the ICCPR	Johnson	NO	NO
Covenant on Economic and Social Rights	Johnson	Carter	NO
American Convention on Human Rights	Carter (Y)	Carter	NO
Convention to Eliminate Discrimination Against Women (CEDAW)	Carter (Y)	Clinton	NO
Torture Convention	*Reagan* (Y)	*Reagan*	1990 and 1994[b] (55 and 57 Dem.)
Convention on the Rights of the Child	*Bush* (Y)	Clinton	NO

Notes: Republican presidents are shown in italics.

a. No implementing legislation has been passed. b. The Senate consented in 1990 subject to subsequent passage of implementing legislation, which became law in 1994.

itself) include Democrats, blacks, and the Jewish community. Among its strongest opponents are Republicans, evangelical Christians, non-Hispanic whites, male veterans, and regular talk radio listeners.[39]

Yet, in order to explain U.S. human rights policy fully we need to go beyond the power of conservative ideology in the United States. Even taken together with the two factors of superpower status and stable democratic institutions discussed above, this explanation leaves critical questions about support for U.S. human rights policy unanswered. Most important, why have consistent legislative, electoral, and public opinion majorities in favor of stricter adherence to international human rights norms failed to achieve reform? As we are about to see in more detail, ratification of human rights treaties has at times been supported by a coalition of interest groups claiming to represent over half the U.S. public, as well as by over half of incumbent senators. Presidents, even Republican presidents, have been at times relatively supportive.[40] To explain the consistent victories of minorities that oppose such treaties, we must consider the structure of the U.S. political system. This system is almost unique in that not merely a simple majority of a unicameral legislature, but rather a two-thirds majority in an elite upper chamber, is required to secure ratification. An exceptionally large and diverse coalition of elites is therefore required to ratify human rights treaties, which is a rare occurrence in any political system.[41]

The Decentralized Political System

The fourth and final determinant of U.S. human rights policy is the decentralized and divided nature of political institutions.

In comparative perspective the U.S. political system is exceptionally decentralized, with the consequence that a large number of domestic political actors often must approve many major decisions. All other things being equal, the greater the number of "veto players," as political scientists refer to those who can impede or block a particular government action, the more difficult it is for a national government to accept international obligations.[42] Two decentralizing elements of the U.S. political system are of particular importance in limiting U.S. support for domestic enforcement of international human rights norms. One is the existence of supermajoritarian Senate voting rules on treaty ratification; the other is the strong separation of powers among the three branches and between federal and state government.

The most obvious veto group, namely recalcitrant senators, is created because the U.S. Constitution requires a two-thirds supermajority vote by the Senate to advise on and consent to an international treaty—higher than in nearly all other advanced industrial democracies, which ratify by unicameral majority or even executive action. It is not surprising, therefore, that the primary barrier to the ratification of human rights treaties has been the inability to gain the necessary senatorial majority. The decentralized U.S. electoral system rarely generates a result decisive enough to give one party (in this case, as we have seen, the Democratic Party) such a Senate majority. Accordingly, the set of domestic veto players almost always includes marginal conservative senators from the majority party, as well as some from the minority party. Senate rules impose, in addition, a supermajority requirement to override the decision of a committee chairman to block consideration of a treaty on the floor. The need to secure the support of the Foreign Relations Committee chair may render ratification difficult if that position is held by, as in the recent case of Republican Senator Jesse Helms of North Carolina, a politician with extremely conservative views.

The resulting history of senatorial opposition to liberal multilateralism spans the twentieth century—from the debate over Woodrow Wilson's proposal for a League of Nations in 1919–1920 to the present. The importance of political institutions is illustrated by the lack of ratification in many cases where there existed (simple) majority support in the Senate. This was true of the League of Nations, which was blocked by a Senate minority. The Genocide Convention was backed by groups claiming a combined membership of 100 million voters, including veterans, racial minorities, religionists, workers, and ethnic Americans. The opposing side contained, by way of organized groups, little more than the ABA. Yet what mattered most were the attitudes of the senators themselves, who disproportionately represent Southern and rural Midwestern and Western states.[43] More recently, more than fifty Senators have publicly declared their support for the Convention on the Elimination of All Forms of Discrimination Against Women (CEDAW), yet this treaty has remained bottled up in committee by Senator Helms and most probably lacks the requisite two-thirds majority support needed to pass on the Senate floor.[44] The specific constitutional role of the Senate helps explain why U.S. government action to support international human rights norms, whether unilateral or multilateral, has tended to come either from the executive branch or the House of Representatives. Presidents have employed executive foreign policy instruments to promote human rights, while members of Congress have employed their control over foreign policy appropriations.[45]

Constitutional separation of powers also grants the U.S. judiciary a strong independent role and establishes important prerogatives for the states vis-à-vis the federal government, which in turn has generated a suspicion of such delegation on the part of conservatives. The nexus of states' rights and federal judicial power was at the center of opposition to international human rights treaties. In the early 1950s, many senators opposed to the application of international human rights norms were concerned about the quite real threat of judicial challenges to the policies of the states, notably those having to do with race. Some of these critics voiced fears that a ban on discrimination might be imposed by an international organization ("world government") in which the United States possessed a "distinctly minority vote."[46] Yet even if adjudication had remained domestic, opponents were concerned that documents like the Genocide Convention and the UN covenants would strengthen the federal judiciary at the expense of the states. States' rights was the salient constitutional principle around which conservative defenses against federal civil rights legislation and international human rights treaties were constructed.[47] In the 1950s ABA spokesmen argued that "minority groups in this country are not vigorously seeking to have . . . discrimination abolished by Federal legislation. Can there be any reasonable doubt that if Congress fails to enact the civil rights laws now being urged upon it and if this convention is ratified as submitted, members of the affected groups will be in a position to seek legal relief on the ground that this so-called Genocide Convention has superceded all obnoxious state legislation?"[48]

This is why "the main opposition to the treaty was rooted in states' rights."[49] In most advanced industrial democracies, the constitution can be amended far more easily than in the United States, and such concerns would more easily have been overcome.

Contemporary U.S. Debates: The Rights of the Child

We have seen so far that the structural conditions under which U.S. human rights policy is made have blocked full adherence to multilateral norms. No other nation is characterized by the same combination of geopolitical power, democratic stability, conservative ideology, and institutional decentralization. The result is an ambivalent policy: the United States maintains unilateral options for promoting global human rights, but remains less committed to membership in multilateral human rights institutions than any other advanced industrial democracy.

These structural constraints continue to influence the most recent of debates, including those surrounding the Convention on the Rights of the Child (CRC), a document adopted unanimously by the UN General Assembly in 1989.[50] The CRC recognizes four underlying principles applying to children: the right to life, the right to be heard in matters affecting them, the right not to suffer discrimination, and the right to have their best interests furthered. It enumerates specific rights that follow. Original drafts focused primarily on social, economic, and cultural rights, as befits a document initially advanced by Soviet bloc countries during the Cold War. To monitor compliance, the CRC established a Committee on the Rights of the Child. This group of elected officials from ten states party reviews reports submitted every five years by member nations and makes recommendations for improvement, though neither the committee nor any other body can investigate or punish states party or individuals.

The U.S. government became involved in the negotiations after some delay and played an active role. It strongly insisted upon the inclusion of civil and political rights, resulting in the drafting of articles 12–17, which promulgate freedom of opinion, expression, religion, and association, as well as the right to privacy and access to appropriate information. The first Bush administration voted for the final agreement. Since then, however, the United States has reverted to its typical ambivalence about domestic application of international norms. More countries have subsequently ratified the CRC than any human rights treaty in history, and they have done so with unprecedented speed and enthusiasm. Within three years the CRC had gained 127 adherents, and, to date, 191 nations have ratified it, including all but two UN member states—the United States and Somalia.

The classic pattern of domestic contestation over human rights dating back to the Bricker Amendment has resurfaced. The ongoing political battle pits liberals against conservatives, each with a differing assessment and evaluation of the domestic consequences, material and symbolic, of ratification. Predictably, Democratic politicians have tended to support ratification, while Republican politicians oppose it. Continuously divided government since 1994 created a stalemate between the executive and legislative branches. With a Republican colleague, Indiana Senator Richard Lugar, Democratic Senator Bill Bradley of New Jersey drafted and secured passage of Senate Resolution 231, which urged the president to forward the CRC to the Senate for its consent. Bradley claimed bipartisan support for ratification, and the Democrats controlled both houses, but President Bush refused to sign it or submit the treaty. In testimony before the Senate, New

Jersey Representative Christopher Smith conceded that many compromises had to be made for the differing cultural, legal, and religious views of the countries involved, but nonetheless maintained that "because we recognize the importance and desirability of adopting the convention without further delay, we do not wish to reopen negotiation on any part of the text."[51] President Clinton did not take advantage of the period from 1992 through 1994 to submit the CRC. The issue of ratification arose again in 1995, but executive-legislative relations were reversed. President Clinton signed and submitted the convention despite a Senate resolution sponsored by Senators Jesse Helms, Trent Lott, and fellow Republicans, who controlled the Senate, urging him not to do so.

Why does the United States remain such a skeptical observer? Neither rhetoric nor domestic cleavages suggest that the issue has much geopolitical relevance. The convention's enforcement provisions are weak, and the United States would sacrifice none of its unilateral bargaining power in the (highly unlikely) event that it sought to deploy it to promote the rights of children. Neither advocates nor opponents lay particular weight on substantive international goals, that is, the traditional "national interest" in foreign policy. Both sides tend to raise generic, often second-order procedural concerns. Advocates point out that by ratifying the convention, the United States would be able to participate in the CRC monitoring committee, the Committee on the Rights of the Child, and assert that the United States would thereby exert greater influence on future decisions concerning the application of international norms. Advocates also maintain that ratification of the CRC is incumbent on the United States as a world leader—the closest thing to a major foreign policy argument for ratification. Yet none of these "national-interest" concerns mobilizes widespread and passionate support or opposition among U.S. citizens and interest groups. One senses that such arguments are tactical. Even where national-interest arguments do play a prominent and apparently sincere role, the real underlying concern is most often the alleged ideological bias of the institution in U.S. domestic politics (for most domestic opponents, a "liberal" or "socialist" bias), rather than the concrete international policy consequences of pursuing it.

Consistent with the argument of this chapter, most domestic debate (particularly domestic criticism) focuses instead on the substantive consequences of the treaty provisions in the United States.[52] This is paradoxical, since the convention would seem to have relatively few domestic implications for a country where children's rights are already strongly embedded in national law. Still, the issue triggers deep domestic ideological cleavages.

Supporters are led by human rights and child welfare activists, who maintain that governments should do more to combat the abuse and exploitation of children. Prominent supporters of the CRC have included Democratic politicians and political liberals, as well as human rights groups like Amnesty International, Human Rights Watch, and the ABA; child welfare groups such as the Children's Defense Fund; general humanitarian groups such as the American Red Cross; and over 300 other organizations.

Behind Republican Senators stand numerous conservative groups, of which the best organized, best funded, most vocal, and most influential are linked to religious groups. These include the Christian Coalition, Concerned Women for America, Eagle Forum, Family Research Council, National Center for Home Education, John Birch Society, and numerous conservative think tanks. Such groups maintain that the CRC is unnecessary and, moreover, threatens the right of parents to care for their families. It usurps their primary role and supplants them with the state—an assessment supported by some legal academics. Opponents defend the opposing concept of "parental rights." They maintain that it is the duty of parents to make decisions regarding the upbringing of their children, and that the UN and its U.S. supporters are attempting to supplant this traditional role with state intervention in the form of social policies dictated by an international organization. These critics reject the supporters' view that children should be considered autonomous human beings, which creates, in the view of one critic, "a vacuum that deprives children of an affirmative source of support and guidance." The CRC, they argue, removes rights that parents should have to protect their children and gives them to minors, who do not necessarily have the information, maturity, or rational capacity to use them appropriately. According to one prominent opponent, who served as deputy assistant to the secretary of health and human services under the first Bush administration, if the UN truly wanted to help children, it should work to reinforce the role of families and parents rather than eroding their authority.

Supporters of the CRC, critics charge, are pursuing a "far-left radical feminist agenda" to degrade the family, eliminate the importance of marriage, and place women at the center of society—a form of "cultural Marxism" in which the family is seen as an obstacle to the state and therefore must be destroyed. Legal scholars point out also that the CRC might have a major influence on domestic law.[53] It may require the provision of some health care, education, and other services not now universally provided. It is significant that the 1995 Senate resolution urging Clinton not to submit the CRC states that if ratified, the CRC would take precedence over state and federal laws pertaining to family life and usurp traditional parental prerogatives, as well as surrendering U.S. sovereignty. Conservatives link these substantive concerns, as they have since the Bricker Amendment, to the power of the domestic judiciary to interpret federal and state law.[54]

Supporters respond that the United States is generally already in compliance with the convention, in the sense that it has established social programs addressing the issues raised in the CRC, and that the language of the convention would be unenforceable without domestic law detailing more precise terms. They add that the CRC establishes standards for national policy to improve the condition of children all over the world, but creates few, if any, enforceable rights. The convention is in fact vague or neutral on many issues, such as abortion and parent's rights, on which conservatives stake their case. In any case reservations can be taken to particular points. This has been common U.S. practice, as we have seen, though the status of such reservations is increasingly disputed. If the United States were to ratify the CRC, even supporters accept that it would probably take reservations to (1) the ban on juvenile execution, as the United States already did in ratifying the ICCPR; (2) article 29, which demands a curriculum teaching values even for private schools, in order to avoid both violating the First Amendment and antagonizing home-schoolers, who fear the CRC will dictate the curriculum taught at home and in school; and (3) the self-executing nature of the treaty, which would all but eliminate the threat of domestic litigation on the basis of the convention (given the CRC monitoring committee's lack of power to investigate or prosecute individuals).

Whatever the substantive merits, the domestic debate over ratification of the CRC has been dominated by its opponents. The CRC has triggered visceral opposition among religious conservatives mobilized by any hint of a threat to their agenda on family issues. These opponents appear to be better organized, better funded, and more motivated than supporters. Senate staffers report that they receive 100 opposition letters for every letter in support of the CRC. While the general human rights community remains convinced of the importance of participating in the international promulgation of the rights of the child, the bulk of liberal public and elite opinion remains uninformed and apathetic.

Perhaps the primary reason for the imbalance between supporters and opponents is the lack of a compelling domestic justification for U.S. adherence—which follows directly from the stability of existing U.S. democracy and the lack of an incentive to further stabilize the status quo against radical threats. At the very least, it is much easier for the opposition to convince U.S. citizens that the CRC threatens their home and family life than for supporters to clarify common misconceptions about the rights of children. But, in addition, public support for strengthening the rights of children in the United States is weak. Many of the most important child advocacy groups, such as the Children's Defense Fund, perhaps the most prominent such group, focuses primarily on the direct provision of services to children rather than lobbying for rights—and have therefore been criticized for placing a low priority on ratification of the CRC. The absence of any such justification in the case of the United States undermines support for the convention. One point on which advocates and opponents agree is that the United States already has a stable constitution and effective judicial system that guarantees extensive rights for both adults and children. For this reason, and because the United States does not face serious institutionalized violations of children's civil and political rights, the CRC seems to be of no immediate concern to most Americans. This situation, which stands in stark contrast to that prevailing in many countries where more systemic abuse of children exists, means that there is little compelling domestic justification for ratification. According to one leading activist, partisan Democrats simply do not care enough about the issue to move it up on the agenda.

Even so, passionate opposition from a small minority might have been overcome were it not for the decentralized nature of U.S. political institutions. We have seen that as recently as 1994 a majority of senators supported similar treaties, yet the Constitution requires a two-thirds vote—unrealistic without a far larger Democratic majority—as well as strong executive support. Moreover, the legislation was bottled up in the Senate Foreign Relations Committee by the committee's chairman, Senator Jesse Helms, whose power was magnified by the decentralized system of Senate committees with powerful chairs. Helms kept the convention off the Senate agenda—thereby also holding up other human rights treaties, such as CEDAW.

The Consequences of U.S. Unilateralism

Should we care about the failure of the United States to ratify international human rights treaties? Does the ambivalent unilateralism of U.S. human rights policy make any real difference?[55] Nearly all legal academics, NGOs, and politicians who comment on U.S. human rights policy assert that U.S. unilateralism has had a negative impact on the nation's foreign and human rights policies, as well as on the international enforcement of human rights.[56] Yet the available evidence from the sources most often cited—Senate hearings, legal articles, and the most important books on U.S. human rights policy—casts a skeptical light on such assertions. Activists, officials, scholars, and journalists have so far offered very little hard evidence to support the widespread claim that the failure of the United States to ratify human rights treaties has had a negative effect on U.S. international interests or ideals. If any such effects exist, they are certainly very subtle.[57] Of course the lack of evidence cannot decisively disconfirm a claim, absent a structured and comprehensive inquiry. The most responsible conclusion is, therefore, simply that there is little evidence that U.S. ratification (or nonratification) of multilateral treaties has any effect on the realization of U.S. foreign policy goals or the promotion of global human rights. The argument that domestic rights would be enforced more thoroughly is more plausible. This is not to rule out the possibility that evidence for a stronger international impact of U.S. policy might exist, but until it is made available, any claims about the external implications of U.S. human rights policy must be viewed as at best speculative, if not misleading.

Does U.S. Unilateralism Undermine
Global Multilateral Human Rights Regimes?

It is often argued that U.S. nonparticipation undermines international human rights institutions, as well as the global human rights movement. As Patricia Derian asserted before the Senate in 1979: "Ratification by the United States significantly will enhance the legitimacy and acceptance of these standards. It will encourage other countries to join those that have already accepted the treaties. And, in countries where human rights generally are not respected, it will aid citizens in raising human rights issues."[58]

Deputy Secretary of State Warren Christopher went even further, arguing that human rights policy is "a way of taking the ideological initiative, instead of merely reacting." President Carter himself added that it "might possibly reverse the tide that has been going against democracies in the past." Many similar quotations could be cited, since drawing a direct link between U.S. behavior and the effectiveness of international norms has, of course, a powerful rhetorical appeal.

Yet little evidence suggests a close link between U.S. behavior and international norms, let alone domestic democratization. Everywhere in the world, human rights norms have spread without much attention to U.S. domestic policy. Under the European Convention on Human Rights, the Europeans have established the most effective formal system for supranational judicial review of human rights claims, based in Strasbourg, without U.S. participation. In the wake of the "third wave" of democratization in Eastern Europe, East Asia, and Latin America, government after government moved ahead toward more active domestic and international human rights policies without paying much attention to U.S. domestic practice. Indeed, emerging democracies in the Western Hemisphere are following Europe's lead in ratifying and accepting compulsory jurisdiction of a regional human rights court, while ignoring U.S. unwillingness to ratify the American Convention on Human Rights, let alone accept jurisdiction of a supranational court. One might argue with equal plausibility that the pride of Latin American democracies in full adherence to the American Convention on Human Rights is *strengthened* by the unwillingness of the United States, Canada, Mexico, and the stable democracies in the anglophone Caribbean to adhere. Likewise, 191 countries have ratified the CRC in record time without waiting to see what the United States would do. There is little evidence that Rwandan, Serbian, or Iraqi leaders would have been more humane if the United States had submitted to more multilateral human rights commitments. The human rights movement has firmly embedded itself in public opinion and NGO networks, in the United States as well as elsewhere, despite the dubious legal status of international norms in the United States. In sum, the consequences of U.S. nonadherence to global norms, while signaling a weakening in theory, is probably of little import in practice.

Does Unilateralism Undermine the Legitimacy and
Efficacy of U.S. Foreign and International Human Rights Policies?

One common argument for multilateral commitments is that human rights ideology is required to legitimate U.S. foreign policy, in particular, U.S. international human rights policy. The idea underlying such arguments is that full adherence to multilateral treaties is in "the national interest."[59]

The international promotion of human rights, we often read, expresses core U.S. values; indeed, public opinion demands it.[60] This tendency is independent of partisan attachment. Patrick Anderson, Carter's chief speechwriter during the 1976 campaign, observed that "liberals liked human rights because it involved political freedom and getting liberals out of jail in dictatorships, and conservatives liked it because it involved criticisms of Russia."[61] Hence advocates of a human rights policy, liberal and conservative, tend to agree, in the words of Jeanne Kirkpatrick (a trenchant critic of Jimmy Carter's human rights policy), not only that "human rights [should] play a central role in U.S. foreign policy," but also that "no U.S. foreign policy can possibly succeed that does not accord them a central role."[62] The Reagan administration, which began with outright opposition to any human rights policy, except that aimed at the Soviet Union, ended up adopting many human rights policies and exploiting human rights rhetoric.[63]

Some maintain that support for multilateral human rights enforcement buys presidents political capital with which to promote other foreign policy goals—a tactic employed by Woodrow Wilson and Franklin Roosevelt, respectively, to justify the entry of the United States into the two world wars.[64] Sandy Vogelgesang summarizes the case advanced by the Carter administration in the 1970s:

> Failure to deal actively with the causes and effects of the growing global problem of human rights may only compound the problem. . . . For example, past American disregard for racial discrimination in southern Africa accounts for much of the mounting tension and bloodshed there now. Failure to use U.S. influence to turn the tides of either totalitarianism or authoritarianism may mean increasing isolation for the Untied States in the world community. Failure to dissociate the United States from oppressive regimes may hurt the U.S., politically and economically, when and if foreign leaders more respectful of human rights come to power. Finally, indifference to expressed American values does violence to Americans' view of themselves and saps domestic support for U.S. foreign policy.[65]

Looking back on this period, Elizabeth Drew observed that "one of the (at least privately) acknowledged points of speaking out on human rights in the Soviet Union was to give the President 'running room' on the right in the United States so that he could get approval of a SALT (2) agreement."[66]

More focused criticisms are directed at U.S. human rights policy itself. A genuine commitment to multilateralism is often seen as a necessary element in an effective human rights policy. A Senate Foreign Relations Committee report in 1979 concluded that "in view of the leading role that the United States plays in the international struggle for human rights, the absence of U.S. ratification of the Covenant is conspicuous and, in the view of many, hypocritical. The Committee believes that ratification will remove doubts about the seriousness of the U.S. commitment to human rights and strengthen the impact of U.S. efforts in the human rights field."[67]

Such arguments recur constantly in debates in the United States.[68] Most such critiques of U.S. policy equate domestic adherence to international norms with commitment to human rights policy.

Yet the United States enjoys many of the benefits of an active human rights policy through its active unilateral policy and support for the formation of new human rights institutions. These go a considerable distance to balance the United States' occasional absence or rhetorical embarrassment.[69] The United States is in the enviable position of having a unilateral policy that is effective, salient, and legitimate. Thus it remains unclear how much domestic enforcement adds to the effectiveness or legitimacy of U.S. policy.

Since the Carter administration, U.S. unilateral human rights policy appears to have had a considerable impact on global perceptions, despite the country's failure to ratify multilateral treaties. Vogelgesang reports that "from the moment Latin Americans, Africans, and Asians started looking at President Carter as a politician interested in human rights, the United States Embassy ceased being seen by thousands of Third World liberals as a headquarters for conservative maneuvers; it became identified with the nation it represents."[70] In the mid-1970s, and again in response to Reagan administration policies in the mid-1980s, a Democratic Congress, led by a Democratic House of Representatives, passed important legislation to link U.S. foreign policy spending to human rights. Recent U.S. human rights enforcement efforts in Haiti, Guatemala, Kosovo, the Philippines, China, and elsewhere—often conducted in collaboration with global or regional bodies—seems unimpaired by the apparent U.S. hypocrisy.

Some stress, more plausibly, that by failing to ratify treaties the United States forgoes its formal right to participate in shaping the evolution of international norms and procedures in the longer term. To the extent that the United States has specific views on the definition of rights, the means of enforcement, and the strength of the regime, this undermines U.S. interests. As Warren Christopher argued in 1979 Senate hearings: "Ratification also would give the United States an additional forum in which to pursue the advancement of human rights."[71] Before ratifying the ICCPR, for example, the United States could neither vote for members of its Human Rights Committee, nor have its citizens either serve on the committee or petition it. In May 2001, the United States failed to be reelected to the fifty-three-member UN Human Rights Commission in Geneva—according to Philip Alston "the single most important United Nations organ in the human rights field."[72] The United States had held a seat continuously since the commission was established in 1947. Many human rights activists attributed this rebuff to the poor U.S. voting record on human rights issues.[73]

Even where the United States is present, some policymakers maintain, the embarrassment of nonratification undermines U.S. influence. Charles Yost, former U.S. ambassador to the UN, testified in 1979:

> There are, in my judgment, few failures or omissions on our part which have done more to undermine American credibility internationally than this one [not ratifying the International Bill of Rights]. Whenever an American delegate at an international conference, or an American Ambassador . . . raises a question of human rights, as we have in these times many occasions to do, the response public or private, is very likely to be this: If you attach so much importance to human rights, why have you not even ratified the United Nations' conventions and covenants on this subject? . . . Here is a case where our credibility is very seriously questioned, but where we can reestablish it quickly by a simple act of ratification.[74]

Arthur Goldberg, a former Supreme Court justice and ambassador to the UN, testified that the failure to ratify treaties undermined U.S. efforts in the Helsinki process.[75] Such claims are widespread.[76]

It is possible U.S. human rights policy might be slightly more influential if it welcomed formal international human rights commitments, but the overall evidence strongly suggests that the difference is not nearly as great as critics assert. There are few, if any, examples of situations in which the failure of the United States to adhere to multilateral treaties appears to have triggered any significant and undesirable institutional or normative evolution against U.S. interests. One reason is that the United States exerts considerable influence in a number of multilateral forums to which it does not formally belong—in part through an active, flexible executive branch policy. The United States was actively involved in promoting a number of treaties—notably the Helsinki process, the American Convention, the CRC, and the ICC—that it subsequently declined to ratify. The United States is represented on the UN Economic and Social Committee and thereby helps supervise the implementation of the Socio-Economic Covenant, which it has not ratified.[77] Even though the United States has not ratified the American Convention, U.S. nationals serve on its commission and the U.S. government has conducted an active and effective diplomacy to promote its enforcement and to employ it in specific cases.[78] Finally, there is little evidence of a long-term evolution in the international human rights system away from the norms that the United States favors. To be sure, other nations have rebuffed some U.S. proposals, most recently in the ICC negotiations. Yet in most other negotiations, notably those over the CRC, as we have seen, the United States has been quite successful at promoting its views.

Does U.S. Unilateralism Alter the
Bundle of Rights Assured to U.S. Citizens?

The most plausible case for the impact of U.S. unilateralism rests primarily on the consequences for enforcement of human rights norms with regard to U.S. citizens at home and U.S. servicemen abroad. This is hardly surprising, given that this has been the primary focus of domestic debate.

Surely threats to service personnel abroad, no matter how unlikely they are to be realized, helps explain why the United States has been particularly resistant to two important treaties—namely, the Genocide Convention and the statute of the ICC. Each could potentially influence U.S. military personnel. As a normative matter, one might respond that U.S. soldiers should indeed be subject to more stringent punishment for war crimes or genocide. Peter Malanczuk cites the case of Lieutenant William Calley, whose sentence was swiftly commuted by President Richard Nixon and whose associates were never charged.[79] But as a matter of practical politics, one cannot deny the extreme political risk any U.S. politician would face by increasing, even modestly, the risk that U.S. soldiers would face such jeopardy.[80]

What of treaties concerned with civilian activities? Some argue that human rights treaties, if fully applied in the United States, would have significant domestic implications. Jack Goldsmith has observed that the ICCPR "if proposed as a federal statute . . . would be the most ambitious domestic human rights law ever introduced, touching on topics regulated by the Bill of Rights, the Reconstruction Amendments, dozens of civil and political rights statutes, and numerous state tort laws."[81] Differences in wording between current U.S. protections and ICCPR analogues "would lead to litigation in every circumstance where the terms differed."[82]

Is such a reform of U.S. domestic civil rights law desirable? Members of the organized human rights movement answer affirmatively. They point to the inadequacies of U.S. human rights protections in areas such as immigration, discrimination, police behavior, and the death penalty, not least as applied to juveniles.[83] Even critics concede that consistent domestic application of the norms in a document such as the ICCPR "would bring relief to what some view as human rights abuses."[84] Ultimately, as we have seen, the opinion of Americans on this question will probably depend on their ideological and partisan commitments.

Academic critics advance two arguments against such domestic application or incorporation. First, restatement and reinterpretation of fundamental rights would create massive disruption. Goldsmith argues that

> a domesticated ICCPR would generate enormous litigation and uncertainty, potentially changing domestic civil rights law in manifold ways. Human rights protections in the United States are not remotely so deficient as to

warrant these costs. Although there is much debate around the edges of domestic civil and political rights law, there is broad consensus about the appropriate content and scope of this law ... built up slowly over the past century. It is the product of years of judicial interpretation of domestic statutory and constitutional law, various democratic practices, lengthy and varied experimentation, and a great deal of practical local experience. Domestic incorporation of the ICCPR would threaten to upset this balance. It would constitute a massive, largely standardless delegation to federal courts to rethink the content and scope of nearly every aspect of domestic human rights law.[85]

Second, adherence to international norms is unlikely to increase the domestic legitimacy of human rights protection. Goldsmith continues:

It is wrong to conclude, as many do, that [a practice like the death penalty for juveniles] is morally indefensible simply because it is prohibited by most other nations. The United States has a well-established and hugely successful system for sorting out the moral conundrum [involving] a complicated dialogue between democratic processes and courts. . . . This process produces results that are viewed, on the whole, as legitimate within the United States. This is no small achievement in a pluralistic democracy. There is certainly no reason whatsoever to think that a more legitimate consensus would be reached through domestication of the ICCPR. . . . In a flourishing constitutional democracy with a powerful tradition of domestic human rights protection, such issues should not be decided by international norms and institutions.[86]

Whether one agrees with Goldsmith, his analysis surely establishes that the potential impact of human rights treaties on U.S. domestic policy is both significant and politically controversial. It seems reasonable to assume that if the United States had been willing to apply international norms, the civil rights movement in the United States would have advanced further. On issues like the death penalty and socioeconomic rights, full acceptance of international human rights instruments—particularly if they were made self-executing and therefore could be litigated in U.S. courts—could strengthen domestic protection for a range of legal rights over the long term, just as liberals hope and conservatives fear. This appears to be the least speculative and most significant consequence of the idiosyncratic U.S. attitude toward multilateral human rights norms.

Conclusion

It is appropriate to conclude on this point. We have seen that U.S. reticence to implement international human rights treaties is not merely a function of "cultural relativism" in the United States. To the contrary, such reticence is linked to deeply embedded characteristics of the U.S. polity—the stability and decentralization of its political institutions, the conservatism of its political spectrum, and its superpower status. This analysis of human rights policy here could usefully be generalized. The underlying predictions are as follows:

1. The more unilateral power and influence a country wields in a given area of human rights, the less likely it will be to support full compliance with multilateral norms.
2. The more salient the concerns about overall domestic political stability, the more likely a country will act multilaterally to "lock in" those rights.
3. The further the substantive human rights practices of a country are from the international consensus position, the more likely it will act unilaterally.
4. The greater the number of domestic veto points in the process of ratifying international legal commitments (as compared with unilateral action), the more likely a country will act unilaterally rather than multilaterally.

These four claims deserve more rigorous testing across specific human rights issues and across nations. More subtly, this analysis suggests that international consequences—a more peaceful and humanitarian world—tend to be secondary, even in an international policy area such as human rights. U.S. citizens in their own democracy, not beleaguered peoples suffering under dictatorships, are the true beneficiaries or victims, which depends on one's own political perspective, of U.S. unilateralism.

Notes

I gratefully acknowledge the research assistance of Aron Fischer, Christopher Strawn, and Jonathan Cracraft; detailed suggestions from Diane Orentlicher, Anne-Marie Slaughter, and Henry Steiner; as well as use of an unpublished paper by Hema Magge. I am grateful to the Weatherhead Center for International Affairs at Harvard University for research support.

1. For useful overviews, see Forsythe, "The United States, the United Nations, and Human Rights"; and Evans, *U.S. Hegemony and the Project of Universal Human Rights*.

2. Henkin, "US Ratification of Human Rights Conventions: The Ghost of Senator Bricker."

3. *Human Rights Violations in the United States*, p. 2.

4. Letter from the Lawyer's Committee on Human Rights to Senator Claiborne Pell, March 2, 1992, published in *Human Rights Law Journal* 14:3-4, p. 129; Evans, *U.S. Hegemony and the Project of Universal Human Rights*, p. 189.

5. Statement of Patricia Derian, assistant secretary, Bureau of Human Rights and Humanitarian Affairs, Department of State, in U.S. Senate Committee on Foreign Relations, *International Human Rights Treaties: Hearings Before the Committee on*

Foreign Relations, p. 33. In the same Senate hearings, Morton H. Sklar, chairman of the U.S. Helsinki Watch Committee, asserted that, absent ratification of formal treaties, "our efforts abroad to achieve human rights and a greater commitment to the principles of freedom and democracy and human dignity will be very severely damaged." This view is echoed by many major legal scholars. Statement of Morton H. Sklar, Chairman, Washington, D.C. Office of the Helsinki Watch Committee for the United States, in U.S. Senate Committee on Foreign Relations, *International Human Rights Treaties,* p. 261. See, for example, van der Vyver, "Universality and Relativity of Human Rights: American Relativism"; Henkin, "US Ratification"; Malanczuk, "The International Criminal Court and Landmines;" Hannum and Fischer, *Ratification of the International Covenants on Human Rights,* pp. 285–289.

6. Van der Vyver, "Universality and Relativity," p. 65.

7. Forsythe, "The United States," pp. 269, 282.

8. Kaufman, *Human Rights,* p. 45. Natalie Kaufman argues that Southern racism and Cold War McCarthyism merged in the early 1950s and set the rhetorical mold for subsequent debates.

9. This critique also assumes, without proof, that commitment to multilateralism is the most efficient means to promote global human rights.

10. For realist views, see Smith, "The Politics of Dispute Resolution Design"; Gilpin, *War and Change in World* Politics; Waltz, *Theory of International Politics,* p. 200.

11. We therefore expect great powers to demand advantageous provisions and special exceptions. See Smith, "Politics of Dispute Resolution."

12. See Humphrey, *Human Rights and the United Nations: A Great Adventure,* p. 12. More generally, see Evans, *U.S. Hegemony and the Project of Universal Human Rights.* For a contrary view, see Moravcsik, "The Origins of International Human Rights Regimes."

13. Reservations are unilateral means to clarify or restrict the scope of a treaty; they have legal standing if they do not contravene the explicit scope and purpose of the treaty—a quality itself open to dispute and adjudication.

14. Regional powers, notably Brazil and Mexico in the Western Hemisphere, have made particularly extensive use of reservations to defend their discretion in the face of multilateral commitments.

15. The most powerful postwar movement in opposition to human rights treaties, the effort in the early 1950s to pass a Constitutional amendment (the Bricker Amendment) limiting the domestic enforceability of human rights treaties, came within one senatorial vote of passage. See Kaufman, *Human Rights,* p. 34. The Bricker Amendment was a response to a real, if modest, trend in U.S. jurisprudence during the 1940s and 1950s toward the enforcement of international standards.

16. Keck and Sikkink, *Activists Beyond Borders*; Risse, Sikkink, and Ropp, *The Power of Human Rights;* Klotz, *Norms in International Relations.*

17. Smith, *America's Mission;* Doyle, "Kant, Liberal Legacies, and Foreign Affairs."

18. On liberal theory generally, see Moravcsik, "Taking Preferences Seriously." On its application to human rights, see Moravcsik, "Origins of International Human Rights Regimes."

19. In international affairs, the goal of an international commitment is to lock in a certain policy outcome, either in *other* countries (the classic prisoner's dilemma) or at home. Since human rights regimes restructure the relationship between a state and its citizens more than the relationship between states, we would expect the motivation to "self-bind" to be stronger than the motive to bind others. On self-binding, see Goldstein, "International Law and Domestic Institutions"; Putnam, "Diplomacy and Domestic Politics;" Moravcsik, *Why the European Community Strengthens the State.*

20. Recent research has uncovered similar patterns in the inter-American and UN human rights systems, as well as many other international organizations, where transitional democracies, notably in Latin America, have consistently taken the lead. Moravcsik, "Origins of International Human Rights Regimes." The result is that established democracies tend to ally with nondemocracies in opposition to effective multilateral enforcement.

21. Such arguments might be termed "ideational liberal" or "liberal constructivist." Moravcsik, "Taking Preferences Seriously."

22. Goldsmith, "Should International Human Rights Law Trump US Domestic Law?"; Jeremy Rabkin, "Is EU Policy Eroding the Sovereignty of Non-Member States?" For a response, see Moravcsik, "Conservative Idealism and International Institutions."

23. Bloomfield, "From Ideology to Program to Policy," p. 11.

24. One might also mention religion. To a greater degree than is found in other advanced industrial democracies, U.S. conservatives are closely allied to a highly organized and influential Protestant religious right. Such groups play an important role in U.S. politics. The views of this group—suspicion of a secular state, skepticism of public (or any organized) education, support for the death penalty, powerful anticommunism, and earlier support for racial segregation—find little parallel in other countries. In many postwar industrial countries, to be sure, right-wing parties have maintained close links to the Catholic Church, but these have also tended to be "catch-all" parties with a broad appeal.

25. Kaufman, *Human Rights,* p. 37.

26. Harry Berger, who represented the National Economic Council, complained that, under the convention, "the slightest reference to a member of a minority race or religion—such as a newspaper article identifying a man under arrest as a Negro—might be deemed a punishable act." Kaufman, *Human Rights,* pp. 43–44.

27. One member of the ABA committee stated: "I leave to your imagination as to what would happen in . . . municipal law if subversive elements should teach minorities that the field of civil rights and laws had been removed to the field of international law." Kaufman, *Human Rights,* p. 46.

28. Kaufman, *Human Rights,* p. 56.

29. *Human Rights Violations in the United States,* pp. 5–8.

30. Commentators have long recognized that the United States is the only advanced industrial country without a significant socialist movement or labor party. For an analytical overview of this phenomenon, see Lipset, "American Exceptionalism Reaffirmed."

31. Although some have linked this tendency in the 1950s to McCarthyism, opposition to socioeconomic rights has long outlived this era. Cf. Kaufman, *Human Rights,* pp. 12–14.

32. Frank Holman, cited in Kaufman, *Human Rights,* p. 17. On the debate within the ABA, see also pp. 25–28.

33. An article in the *ABA Journal* called the Covenants a program for "extreme egalitarianism." Eleanor Roosevelt herself, a key influence on the drafting of the Universal Declaration and a tireless advocate of U.S. ratification of the UN Covenant on Civil and Political Rights, believed that the Covenant on Economic, Social and Cultural Rights had "not the slightest chance" of ratification. Kaufman, *Human Rights,* pp. 69–70, 72, 19, 64ff. Economic libertarianism has remained an important, if declining, element of the rhetoric among conservative opponents to multilateral treaties.

34. In contrast to the way this issue is often presented, this central cleavage does not primarily divide isolationists and internationalists. Major opponents of international enforcement of human rights—from Henry Cabot Lodge, John Bricker, and Henry Kissinger to Jesse Helms—have not been isolationist.

35. *Human Rights Violations in the United States,* pp. 5–8. The last of these, religious rights, might appear to be a concern of Republicans, but in fact the report calls exclusively for aggressive judicial enforcement of the Religious Freedom Restoration Act, a piece of legislation passed by a Democratic Congress and signed by President Clinton in late 1993. See p. 165ff.

36. This record does not appear to be a spurious correlation driven by background conditions. Democrats commanded a majority of at least 55 votes only 50 percent of the time (14 sessions out of 28). So the fact that all human rights treaties passed during those sessions is striking. More broadly, the Senate contained a Democratic majority for 19 sessions and a Republican majority for 9 sessions. Each of the two parties commanded the presidency for roughly equal periods since 1947.

37. Note that the pattern of submission and ratification does not follow from the (somewhat exogenous) timing of negotiation and signature, since those presidents who submitted the treaties were not typically the same presidents who signed the respective agreements.

38. Kaufman, *Human Rights,* passim. See also, for example, U.S. Senate Committee on Foreign Relations, *International Human Rights Treaties;* U.S. Senate Committee on Foreign Relations, *International Covenant on Civil and Political Rights.*

39. Magge, "Vocal Opposition and Fragmented Support: The U.S. Failure to Ratify the UN Convention on the Rights of the Child," n.p.

40. In three cases Republican presidents—Eisenhower with the Supplementary Slavery Convention and the Convention on the Political Rights of Women, and Bush with the Rights of the Child—were unable or unwilling to block the negotiation of international human rights treaties, even though they made no subsequent effort to secure ratification of them. Indeed, until the recent treaty establishing the ICC, no U.S. government appears to have voted in an international forum against a human rights treaty that passed—although U.S. negotiators have attempted to water down a number of provisions. This suggests that centrist presidents (and even a conservative like Ronald Reagan) and advocates of human rights treaties alike labor under tight political constraints imposed by decentralized U.S. political institutions.

41. In addition, opposition to application of human rights treaties has remained surprisingly strong even as the issues that initially gave rise to it—the role of a liberal federal judiciary, support for segregation, and socioeconomic rights—have become less controversial.

42. Putnam, "Diplomacy and Domestic Politics." See also Martin, *Democratic Commitments.*

43. Kaufman, *Human Rights,* p. 37–38.

44. Cited in Magge, "Vocal Opposition and Fragmented Support: The US Failure to Ratify the U.N. Convention on the Rights of the Child."

45. Forsythe, "The United States," pp. 271-272; Vogelgesang, *American Dream.*

46. Kaufman, *Human Rights,* p. 45.

47. Ibid., pp. 10–12.

48. George Finch, cited in Kaufman, *Human Rights,* p. 54.

49. Kaufman, *Human Rights,* pp. 52–53.

50. For primary research and analysis of the CRC, I would like to acknowledge Magge, "Vocal Opposition."

51. Cited in Magge, "Vocal Opposition."

52. Some opposition appears to reflect traditional conservative hostility toward human rights treaties in general, as well as a belief that other countries may aim to exploit loopholes, whereas the United States tends to examine all existing federal and state laws closely to assure compliance.

53. The Family Research Council sets forth more concrete criticisms of the explicit rights promulgated in articles 12–16 of the CRC. Article 12 (freedom of opinion), they argue, might allow children to air their grievances against their parents in a legal forum. Article 13 (freedom of expression) might permit children to view "objectionable or immoral materials, often disseminated in schools" despite the disapproval of parents. Article 14 (freedom of religion) might forbid parents from sending their children to church if the latter did not want to attend. Article 15 (freedom of association) might prohibit parents from preventing their children from associating with harmful company. Article 16 (protection of privacy) might legalize abortion without parental consent and homosexual conduct in the home.

54. Magge adds: "Another initial obstacle was Article 38, which stated that governments should assure that children under the age of 15 are not involved in hostilities. Many NGOs and governments urged an optional protocol raising the age limit to 18. The Department of Defense opposed this provision, because the US military accepts 17-year-old volunteers with parental permission. . . . In January 2000, the US agreed to sign the optional protocol and change the domestic age limit to 18, though with a clause specifically excluding voluntary recruitment. Though this had little policy impact, it was the first time the US agreed to change a domestic practice specifically in order to meet an international human rights standard."

55. On the charge of hypocrisy, see notes 5–7 above.

56. A smaller number of conservatives argue that overzealous human rights enforcement may undermine global human rights policy, U.S. foreign policy, and U.S. domestic policy. See, for example, Goldsmith, "Should International Human Rights Law Trump?"

57. There is similarly little evidence for the counterclaim that U.S. adherence to human rights treaties would significantly undermine either global human rights promotion or other U.S. foreign policy goals.

58. Patricia Derian, cited in U.S. Senate, *International Human Rights Treaties,* p. 33.

59. Hannum and Fischer, eds. *United States Ratification,* pp. 285–289.

60. Muravchik, *The Uncertain Crusade,* 1986, p. 3. Forsythe, *United States and Human Rights,* p. 22. Much of this literature is overtly hortatory. "[P]romoting respect for human rights abroad helps dissociate the United States from oppressive governments. Americans feel better and hold their heads higher in the international community when the United States avoids direct or indirect responsibility for the odious practices of other governments." Vogelgesang, *American Dream, Global Nightmare,* p. 84.

61. Vogelgesang, *American Dream,* p. 79.

62. Joshua Muravchik, another neoconservative critic of Carter, adds that "in order for the United States to act in the world with a degree of national unity and with a sense of conviction, our policy must be felt to be grounded in those principles." Muravchik, *Uncertain Crusade,* p. 221.

63. Jacoby, "The Reagan Turnaround on Human Rights."

64. Evans, *U.S. Hegemony,* p. 51.

65. Vogelgesang, *American Dream,* p. 253.

66. SALT refers to the Strategic Arms Limitation Talks. Muravchik, *Uncertain Crusade,* p. 18.

67. Senate Foreign Relations Committee report, cited in Cerna, "The United States and the American Convention on Human Rights," p. 100.

68. See notes 6–8 above.

69. Jacoby, "The Reagan Turnaround on Human Rights," p. 1066.

70. Vogelgesang, *American Dream,* p. 81.

71. Warren Christopher, cited in U.S. Congress, *International Human Rights Treaties*, p. 20. Senate Foreign Relations Committee report, cited in Cerna, "The United States and the American Convention on Human Rights," p. 100.

72. Alston, "The Commission on Human Rights," p. 126.

73. According to BBC News Online, "Joanna Weschler, the UN representative of Human Rights Watch, told Reuters news agency that many countries on the Economic and Social Council, whose members elect the commission, resented the poor US voting record on issues like land mines and the availability of AIDS drugs." BBC News Online, "US Thrown off UN Human Rights Body," Thursday, 3 May, 2001. Kenneth Roth, Executive Director of Human Rights Watch, noted that the U.S. delegate on the commission had cast one of the only votes against a declaration of the right to food (Speech at Harvard Law School, May 4, 2001).

74. Yost also notes: "Our refusal to join in the international implementation of the principles we so loudly and frequently proclaim cannot help but give the impression that we do not practice what we preach, that we have something to hide, that we are afraid to allow outsiders even to inquire whether we practice racial discrimination or violate other basic human rights." Statement of the Hon. Charles Yost, former U.S. ambassador to the United Nations, in U.S. Senate, *International Human Rights Treaties*, pp. 4–5.

75. "[It] has been a great problem for the United States and a great embarrassment. . . . [We] insist upon implementation by the Soviet Union and the countries of the East of the human rights provisions of the Helsinki Accords. Our capability, our ability, and our credibility to do so was greatly impaired at Belgrade and will be greatly impaired at Madrid in 1980 by the failure of our country to ratify the human rights treaties which are now before you." Arthur Goldberg, cited in U.S. Senate, *International Human Rights Treaties*, pp. 10-11.

76. In the same hearings, John Carey from the Helsinki Watch Committee echoed this view with regard to the Soviet Union as did Prof. Thomas Buergenthal, University of Texas Law School, in regard to the OAS. U.S. Senate, *International Human Rights Treaties*, pp. 258, 329.

77. Forsythe, "The United States," p. 265. In the 1980s, the ECOSOC's supervisory role was assumed by a group of nonnational experts.

78. Interview with Juan Mendez, University of Notre Dame, November, 2000.

79. Malanczuk, "International Criminal Court," p. 82.

80. The United States has also often been concerned with the definition of "aggression" in such documents, which might lead to a international embarrassment. Malanczuk, "International Criminal Court," p. 83.

81. Goldsmith, "Should International Human Rights Law Trump?," p. 332.

82. Ibid. For example, Goldsmith asks, "Would its guarantee of 'effective' in addition to 'equal' protection change domestic anti-discrimination law? Would its 'protection against discrimination on *any* ground,' including '*status*' extend to discrimination on the basis of homosexuality? Age? Weight? Beauty? Intelligence?"

83. Amnesty International, *United States of America*, p. 334.

84. Goldsmith, "Should International Human Rights Law Trump?," p. 335.

85. Ibid., p. 332.

86. Ibid., p. 335.

15

Ambivalent Multilateralism and the Emerging Backlash: The IMF and WTO

Kimberly Ann Elliott and Gary Clyde Hufbauer

[T]he big question is whether the historian who looks at this history [of economic institution-building] twenty-five years from now—which will be close to the year 2000—will see the twenty-five years since Bretton Woods as part of a historic march toward trade and economic integration or as but a brief interlude between eras of trade restriction and economic nationalism.
—Ambassador Richard Gardner (1969, xciv)

Looking back today, the verdict on the question above would have to be a positive one. Neither trade disputes nor financial crises have been relegated to the dustbin of history. But they have been contained and their worst effects mitigated. Above all, the world economy has avoided the beggar-thy-neighbor policies that deepened the Great Depression and contributed to World War II. And economic integration has not just continued but accelerated. Between 1980 and 1998, merchandise imports grew from $2.0 trillion to $5.5 trillion per year (a growth factor of 2.7). Over the same period, international bank lending expanded from $0.8 trillion to $5.5 trillion annually (a factor of 6.9). Daily foreign exchange transactions grew from $60 billion (1983) to $1.5 trillion (a factor of 25).[1]

Efforts by the United States and Britain to create multilateral economic institutions began during World War II. The IMF and International Bank for Reconstruction and Development (the centerpiece of what became the World Bank Group) were successfully launched soon after the end of the war. Although the treaty establishing the third leg, the International Trade Organization (ITO), failed to gain approval in the U.S. Senate, its conceptual core, GATT, was implemented by the United States as an executive agreement. In broad terms, GATT was born to liberalize, the IMF was born to stabilize, and the World Bank was born to develop. And, if flourishing trade and capital flows are the measure of achievement, both GATT and the IMF have succeeded on a tremendous scale.

In stark contrast to the successes of these economic institutions, the UN was often hamstrung for its first forty-five years by the divisions of the

Cold War and the blocking veto available to all five permanent members of the Security Council. Although U.S. policymakers exploited a few rare opportunities for action permitted by the UN during these decades, notably during the Soviet Union's self-imposed absence at the outset of the Korean War, the United States seldom conceded that UN membership might entail constraints on U.S. foreign policy.

This uneven commitment to multilateralism was also apparent in the realm of economic sanctions, which U.S. policymakers used as they saw fit, and almost always unilaterally. With the end of the Cold War and with declining U.S. leverage in an increasingly integrated world economy, U.S. sanctions have acquired a less unilateral flavor.[2] But U.S. policymakers, particularly in Congress, have yet to recognize the ever-increasing constraints on U.S. unilateralism. Moreover, they still view multilateralism primarily in opportunistic terms, choosing between unilateral and multilateral approaches to foreign policy problems on the basis of a tactical analysis of what best serves their immediate interests in the situation at hand.

The differences are less stark than this comparison suggests, however, since even in the economic arena the U.S. commitment to multilateralism was never absolute. As noted, the ITO was stillborn, and the Nixon administration unilaterally rewrote the rules governing the international financial system when they no longer served U.S. interests.

Moreover, although the benefits are usually greater, economic integration also imposes costs, and challenges to traditionally multilateral approaches to economic policy are growing. In spring 2000, domestic opponents from both the left and right sought to prevent China's full integration into the WTO, trying to block congressional approval of "permanent normal trade relations" with China.[3] Similar coalitions of convenience, uniting traditional adversaries from both ends of the U.S. political spectrum, advocate the abolition or drastic pruning of the functions of the IMF and World Bank. Finding ways to promote multilateral solutions, while respecting the diversity and political autonomy of sovereign nations, will be a major challenge for U.S. policymakers in the years to come.

Money and the IMF

Founded at Bretton Woods, New Hampshire, in July 1944, the International Monetary Fund was constructed to avert a postwar repetition of the beggar-thy-neighbor policies of the 1930s, including competitive currency depreciation and debt default. After the mid-1970s, when the major industrialized countries moved to a system of flexible exchange rates, the IMF's focus shifted to preventing debt defaults in developing countries. In return for lending when the private sector would not, however, the IMF required countries to accept an increasingly lengthy list of market-oriented reform conditions. The IMF's changing role has generated considerable controversy, both from those who oppose its involvement in large "bail-out" packages and from those who believe IMF conditionality worsens poverty.

From Bretton Woods to the Smithsonian

The chief intellectual protagonists at Bretton Woods were Britain's John Maynard Keynes and the United States' Harry Dexter White.[4] The two sharply disagreed over the desirable scope of fund resources, with Keynes wanting more and White wanting less,[5] and over the proposed global monetary unit, with Keynes advocating a medium of exchange ("bancor"), while White endorsed only a unit of account ("unitas"). Underlying these technical disputes was a deeper difference over the burden of adjustment between deficit and surplus countries.[6]

Core rules. Although they disagreed over many elements, Keynes and White were in accord on several central propositions. First and foremost, the IMF would be controlled by the industrial powers. At Bretton Woods, the founders designed a system of weighted voting, very unlike the one-nation, one-vote procedures of the UN General Assembly or GATT. At the fund's inception, the United States, with an initial weighted vote (or quota) exceeding 20 percent, was the sole country possessing effective veto power over major fund decisions, which required an 80 percent weighted vote. Moreover, the industrial powers together held a majority of the IMF's votes, or quotas. Since a country's access to fund resources was directly related to the size of its quota, the implicit focus of the IMF was to be monetary relations between the industrial powers. To further cement U.S. financial hegemony, the fund was located in Washington, D.C., close to the U.S. Treasury.

The architects of the Bretton Woods blueprint firmly believed that postwar monetary stability depended on a regime of fixed exchange rates. This required a high degree of cooperation among countries, including a common set of rules. Members would declare the "par value" of their currencies in terms of gold—initially set relative to a dollar value of $35 per troy ounce—and agree not to change these values without the prior consent of the IMF. Current account convertibility, to facilitate trade, was also a paramount objective. To ensure fixed exchange rates, however, the negotiators at Bretton Woods agreed that capital controls were essential. In other words, capital account *in*convertibility was permitted and indeed welcomed to quell harmful private speculation in exchange markets.

Tension between the rules. The core rules of the IMF were contained in the fund's Articles of Agreement, negotiated between the United States and its European partners. The fund's priorities and the application of the rules continued to be contentious, however. By agreeing to article VIII, members agreed to renounce multiple exchange rates and exchange controls for current account transactions after a postwar transition period of unspecified length. The United States expected the major trading countries to accept these obligations fairly soon. They did not. Prior to 1961, only the United States and Canada, among the major industrial powers, had implemented article VIII.[7]

Meanwhile, starting with the British pound sterling devaluation of 1947, and continuing with a series of exchange rate crises in the 1950s, one major industrial country after another devalued its exchange rates. The United States opposed European devaluation as a regrettable departure from the fixed exchange rate system, believing that higher taxes, tighter control of public expenditures, and greater discipline on union wage claims were the preferable policy responses.[8]

Despite tactical differences, during the 1950s and 1960s the U.S. vision of world monetary affairs dovetailed with the views of Western Europe, Canada, and Japan. Basically, the IMF was supposed to be the stern uncle for countries that faced balance of payments crises.[9] In these crises, the fund expressed not only U.S. policy views but also the views of the major powers not then in difficulty.

Pressures on the system. Differences between the United States and other industrial countries began to sharpen in the late 1960s, and these disagreements increasingly concerned the basic design of the system, not merely the priority of conflicting rules. During the sterling crisis of 1966–1967, the United States opposed sterling devaluation in part because it feared pressure would spill over against the dollar. For the same reason, France stood to one side when the central banks prepared to rescue the Bank of England. Under President Charles de Gaulle, during the 1960s, France complained that the United States enjoyed a free ride in the postwar monetary system. If sterling devaluation unhorsed the mighty U.S. dollar, so much the better.[10]

Sterling devaluation was not the undoing of the dollar, but the combined costs of expensive Great Society programs and the Vietnam War were another matter.[11] By the late 1960s, the U.S. economy was growing rapidly but inflation was also rising. The U.S. trade surplus was shrinking, and policymakers began to worry about a "dollar overhang" and a run on U.S. gold reserves.

For the IMF, the first consequence of these pressures on its most powerful member was that the United States reconsidered its earlier opposition to an IMF currency. It accepted the creation of a special drawing right (SDR), allocated to fund members in proportion to their quotas. The United States hoped that foreign central banks would satisfy their reserve needs through periodic allocations of SDRs, instead of acquiring more gold from Fort Knox. Europeans, then flush with reserves, were less enthusiastic about creating a new kind of money, and President de Gaulle publicly expressed his disdain. The result was tortuous negotiations, and finally creation of the SDR in 1969, via the first amendment to the Articles of the Fund. The first and second SDR allocations, made in 1970 and 1971, together totaled only $6.4 billion. As a price of accepting the SDR, the Europeans insisted on "veto parity" with the United States. This was accomplished by raising the required voting majority for major fund decisions from 80 to 85 percent, a threshold that could be met only with European support.[12]

The United States Rewrites the Rules: The Nixon Shocks and the Smithsonian Accord

Despite an array of small corrective measures (including the SDR), the U.S. balance of payments continued to deteriorate and the Nixon administration turned sharply unilateral. In 1971, the United States experienced a current account deficit for the first time since 1959: a modest $1.4 billion, made much worse by capital outflows of $11.7 billion. Speculation against the dollar became intense. Rather than accept the advice that it had so freely dispensed to other countries—raise taxes and cut public expenditures—in August 1971, President Nixon closed the gold window and imposed a 10 percent surcharge on imports.

The immediate aftermath of Nixon's shock measures was an appreciation of Canadian, European, and Japanese currencies.[13] The Smithsonian Accord of December 1971 ratified what had already happened by permitting fund members a limited degree of currency flexibility around their declared par values (margins of 2.25 percent were generally accepted). The Smithsonian Accord also permitted dollar devaluation to $38 per ounce of gold, and a general revaluation of the other major currencies. The second amendment to the fund articles, passed in 1976, formally replaced the era of fixed-but-adjustable exchange rates with flexible rates.

A New Mission—Macroeconomic Rectitude

With the second amendment, the IMF's central mission of maintaining exchange rate stability became a matter of history. Even before the Nixon shock of 1971, the fund was essentially a bystander in the sterling crisis of 1966–1967 and the French franc-German mark crisis of 1968. These events dramatically changed the character of multilateralism in the international financial system because the industrial countries were no longer constrained by IMF rules.[14] The fund had become too small, both in bureaucratic weight and financial resources, to mold the fiscal and monetary policies of industrial countries.

The IMF needed a new mission, and the United States was happy to oblige. Within a decade the United States, with the support of other industrial powers, had turned the Fund into the nanny for macroeconomic rectitude in emerging markets. Institutionally, the fund was predisposed to play this role. After all, lower inflation and smaller fiscal deficits were the standard cures for balance of payments deficits in the era of fixed exchange rates. In the post-Smithsonian era, the same medicines were applied to the external economic problems of developing countries. There were, however, important differences. Whereas before 1971, countries in trouble were urged *not* to devalue their currencies, after 1971 they were strongly urged *to* devalue. The embrace of flexible exchange rates in turn led to a more skeptical view of capital controls, which were no longer needed to maintain fixed rates.

In the post-Smithsonian world, the IMF's mission was no longer centered on applying agreed rules to industrial countries but on applying a new set of rules, informally amended from time to time, to countries with very little presence on the world stage. The power disparity between creditor and debtor countries conveyed by the fund's weighted voting system, together with the power disparity between the IMF and "clients" facing a financial crisis, laid the groundwork for one of the backlashes now striking the multilateral world economy.

What made the fund's gospel compelling to its new (and relatively weak) "clients" was the frequent eruption of financial shocks. Between 1970 and 1998, IMF members experienced sixty-four banking crises and seventy-nine currency crises (many of them overlapping).[15] In response, the IMF engaged in at least thirty-five country programs, and fund staff worked with the U.S. Treasury to enunciate a common line. In the process, the fund became the world's financial crisis manager, and every crisis became an opportunity to reconfigure the policies of emerging countries through a highly structured ritual now known as "conditionality."[16]

The IMF's new mission grew legs in 1982, when the third-world debt crisis hit Mexico and a long list of other developing countries.[17] The crisis was rooted in excessive sovereign debt to large international banks. Western ideology merged with a pressing need to bail out the large (mainly U.S.) banks. Without IMF assistance, some of these troubled countries might have defaulted, putting important banks in dire straits. The macroeconomic targets imposed on borrowers in the debt crisis came to be known as the "Washington consensus."[18] The ingredients were simple: monetary austerity, fiscal austerity, and a flexible exchange rate. Only the serving sizes were changed to reflect individual circumstances.[19]

The Mission Creeps

In the 1990s, the IMF's agenda was ambitiously expanded beyond the familiar macroeconomic prescriptions of the Washington consensus. Although the debt crisis of the 1980s had passed, growth in developing countries (apart from East Asia) was unsatisfactory, and the fund's agenda, shaped by the United States, now turned to "structural reform" and a controversial list of free-market conditions. The end of the Cold War was a significant background factor. No longer did Washington need to balance its economic advice to developing countries against the strategic realities of great power rivalry. No longer did Washington feel obliged to reach agreement on economic matters with its allies in Europe and Japan. Meanwhile, evidence was accumulating that developing countries grew faster if they not only followed the path of macroeconomic rectitude, but also embraced features of a market economy. "Structural reforms" were thus added to the IMF agenda.

In a sense, such mission creep was a natural course for the IMF. Each bone of the economy is connected to every other bone, directly and indirectly. For example, the public budget is obviously a matter of concern when a country runs into economic problems. From there it is only a small step to an IMF critique of revenue sources (e.g., poor income tax collection, low electricity rates) and the disposition of public expenditure (e.g., rice and gasoline subsidies, military outlays).

While mission creep is a natural bureaucratic tendency, the direction of creep depends on political forces. The particular, structural reforms espoused by the IMF coincided with economic precepts far more popular in the United States and Britain than in Continental Europe, Japan, or Canada. The standard package of recommendations—which came to be known as "Anglo-Saxon capitalism"—included the following:[20]

- Liberalizing trade
- Liberalizing finance (e.g., banks, stock markets)
- Removing barriers to foreign direct investment
- Reforming the tax structure (broaden the base, reduce the rates)
- Cutting public subsidies
- Privatizing public corporations
- Deregulating the economy
- Protecting property rights

This package of reforms has sparked a backlash from a variety of directions in recent years. First, it obviously imposes substantial—and unwelcome—costs on powerful political constituencies in client countries that previously benefited from public subsidies and protection from competition. In addition, the breadth and depth of the fund's intervention in domestic policy areas has inevitably triggered a nationalist backlash in many countries. The development model has also been opposed by a variety of NGOs that assert that it ignores environmental and equity issues. Finally, U.S. efforts to control the size and tenor of the IMF's response in recent crises provoked a negative reaction from other donor countries.

The Mexican crisis of 1994–1995. The 1994–1995 Mexican peso crisis was, in a sense, a throwback.[21] It was rooted in the same macroeconomic policy errors that had caused the earlier debt crisis: a semipegged exchange rate, inflation much higher than in the United States, a large current-account deficit, and extensive short-term dollar borrowing. In addition, the banking system was riddled with poor management and bad loans.

But there was an important difference between Mexico in 1994–1995 and crisis countries during the 1980s. During the presidency of Carlos Salinas de Gortari, Mexico became a poster country for British–U.S. capitalism. Having unilaterally liberalized its trade, Mexico then championed NAFTA, protected intellectual property, and welcomed foreign investment. The United States, which feared a surge in illegal immigration if the Mexican economy crashed, chose to support Mexico on a grand scale.

At the end of January 1995, after the U.S. Congress had refused to approve new funds, the U.S. Treasury cobbled together a controversial rescue package with a nominal value of $51 billion from multilateral and existing bilateral sources. In the words of Michel Camdessus, the IMF's managing director, the fund's share of the package, at $17.8 billion, was "the largest ever approved for a member country, both in absolute amount and in relation to the country's quota [700 percent] in the Fund."[22] From the standpoint of European industrial powers, IMF drawings on this scale amounted to a private U.S. raid on the fund piggy bank. In effect, the United States was bending the normal financial crisis rules—that IMF loans not exceed 300 percent of quota—for its own domestic purposes. In a rare show of discord, several European executive directors abstained in the vote on the Mexican loan.

This crisis also hinted of the backlashes to come. To finance the U.S. share of the package, the Clinton administration drew on the exchange stabilization fund (ESF). Although this step did not require congressional approval, it sparked considerable opposition from congressional Republicans. Besides protesting the unprecedented size of the ESF loan, these critics questioned the principle of using public funds to bail out private investors.[23] This objection was shared by many Mexican citizens who suffered job losses and sharp increases in consumer goods prices, while investors and bankers emerged relatively unscathed.

The Asian crisis of 1997–1998. A different mix of volatile components ignited the crisis that began in Thailand in 1997 and then spread to the rest of Asia.[24] Unlike Mexico in 1994, Asian current account deficits were not outlandish (Thailand was an exception), and inflation rates were low. Asian governments were not big short-term borrowers. Like Mexico, however, most Asian countries were operating semipegged exchange rates, and their banking systems were riddled with poor loans and bad management. Moreover, to a huge extent, Asian private banks and corporations borrowed short-term dollars at low interest rates to make long-term local investments at supposedly higher yields.

In the ensuing crisis, plunging Asian exchange rates and stock markets destroyed more than 50 percent of precrisis share values. Interest rate spreads on sovereign debt reached astonishing levels of 15 to 20 percentage points above the U.S. Treasury bill rate. Real gross domestic product levels fell by 4 to 8 percent. Compared with Asia, Russia's fall was harder still, while Brazil experienced a milder crisis. In both cases, the United States advocated larger loans and softer conditions than other donor countries wanted. All told, official rescue packages reached a headline total of $181 billion for five affected countries (Thailand, Indonesia, South Korea, Russia, and Brazil) between 1997 and 1999. IMF loans amounted to roughly 500 percent of the Thailand and Indonesian quotas, and an astonishing 1,900 percent of the South Korean quota.[25]

The Asian crisis was not, however, remarkable only for the sheer scale of official support. Four other features were almost as controversial. First, the "letters of intent" signed by countries negotiating IMF loans were drenched with detailed conditions showing an "Anglo-Saxon" capitalist bias. In great detail, crisis countries were asked to slash their subsidies, end their local monopolies, reform their tax systems, liberalize their financial systems, and more.[26] While the United States was the most insistent, other industrial powers likewise used the Asia crisis as an occasion to settle old disputes. Japan, for example, inserted language in IMF loan conditions addressing South Korean trade barriers of particular Japanese interest.

Second, even though private banks and investors lost a lot of money in the crises ($350 billion, according to Cline),[27] many observers argued that they should have lost a great deal more. Third, while the Asian crisis was relatively short (compared with the debt crisis of the 1980s), it inflicted a lot of pain. Eminent critics complained that the fund should not have automatically relied on the standard medicines of fiscal and monetary austerity.[28] Instead, it should have tried unorthodox combinations such as fiscal expansion, monetary contraction, and capital controls. Fourth, and finally, in the midst of the Asia crisis, at the World Bank–IMF meetings held in Hong Kong in November 1997, the United States went out of its way to squelch a Japanese initiative to launch an "Asian Monetary Fund."

The fund staff worked in very close cooperation with the U.S. Treasury in designing the most controversial features of the IMF's programs in Asia, Russia, and Brazil. The long professional association between the then deputy secretary of the treasury, Larry Summers and the first deputy managing director of the IMF, Stanley Fischer, epitomized IMF-Treasury cooperation. On substance, U.S. officials and IMF staff both viewed the Asian crisis as an opportunity to exploit unprecedented leverage to force long-sought changes in Asian economic policies. Other donor countries shared this view to some degree, but Europe and Japan, as well as several affected countries, would have welcomed less severe, or at least different, conditionality. Some affected countries would have liked the fund's blessing for capital controls and debt relief.

The crises that swept through East Asia, Russia, and Brazil have now passed, but the backlash against the IMF has yet to play out. The United States, more than any other country, orchestrated the fund's policies during the crises; accordingly, critics of the fund indirectly blame U.S. policies. Thus, the financial crises of the 1990s have again reshaped the battle over the future of the IMF. The battlefield today has two major axes: (1) What is the fund's post-Asian mission? (2) Who will run the post-Asian show? Both axes converge on the U.S. role in a multilateral setting.

Battling over the Future of the IMF Mission

In the wake of the Asian crisis, many voices have urged the IMF to alter its mission statement.[29] These suggestions have ranged from "do nothing" (i.e., go out of business) to "do more." The principal variants and their advocates are summarized below.

A smaller fund. A camp based mainly in the United States, but well outside the executive branch, contends that the IMF has outlived its usefulness. This camp has both right and left wings, and both agree that the fund's mission should be sharply curtailed, if not abolished, but for very different reasons. On the left, the activist group "Fifty Years is Enough" was lobbying for abolition of the fund long before the Asian financial crisis. This group believes that IMF conditionality is antidemocratic and antipoor because of the focus on macroeconomic austerity and laissez-faire Anglo-Saxon capitalism.

The politically conservative argument for curtailing the IMF rests on fear of moral hazard and faith in private markets. Two former treasury secretaries, George Schultz and William Simon, together with former Citibank President Walter Wriston, wrote an influential op-ed piece in the *Wall Street Journal* (February 3, 1998) that pointedly asked, "Who Needs the IMF?" Along with other critics,[30] they accuse the IMF of rescuing governments, corporations, and banks from their own bad policies and decisions, thereby rewarding mismanagement. Consequently, creditors and debtors take less prudent risks than they otherwise would; wealth is redistributed from innocent taxpayers to culpable (and usually wealthy and politically connected) shareholders; and the fund undermines rather than reinforces the process of market reform. The editorial voice of the *Wall Street Journal* also recommended abolishing the IMF once the Asian crisis was past.[31]

The Meltzer Commission, established at congressional insistence in 1999, did not call for the IMF to be abolished, but it did recommend changes that would sharply curtail the use of fund resources, including extending loans only to countries that prequalify for such credits, by a record of good policy behavior, prior to the crisis at hand.[32] Penalty interest rates would also be applied, and borrowings would be strictly for the short term.

Outside the United States, the views of the Meltzer Commission have few adherents. Still, the commission's influential congressional supporters could gain ground *if* other proposals for the mission and management of the IMF erode U.S. influence over the fund. In such a scenario, members of Congress would presumably ask why the United States should support a "wayward" IMF—any more than it supports a wayward UN. In such an environment, enthusiasm for curtailing the fund's mission and resources might spread. After all, in the very midst of the Asian crisis, President Clinton and Treasury Secretary Robert Rubin had to lobby the Congress very hard to enlarge the fund's resources through a quota increase.

A larger fund. A totally different approach is advocated by many developing countries, especially those that have not prospered in the past two decades. These countries argue that they are too often the victims of adverse economic forces beyond their control, such as natural disasters, fluctuations in commodity prices, herding and contagion in capital markets, and sheer distance from important economic centers. These countries demand a new international net that combines both safety and support.

In response to these demands, the fund developed eight "special facilities," designed to provide IMF assistance, with low conditionality, to cope with particular forms of external misfortune (e.g., low commodity prices, high oil prices). In practice, these special facilities have been used to convert short-term IMF loans into medium- and long-term assistance (sometimes up to 20 years)—encroaching on the development mission of the World Bank, and ultimately provoking the wrath of the Meltzer Commission. Indeed, on this point the legislatures in Europe, Canada, the United States, and Japan agree: they will not tolerate the back-door provision of truly large-scale development assistance through the fund.[33]

A back-to-basics fund. In the Asian crisis, the IMF's advice and conditions extended to a long list of microeconomic policies. Critics argued heatedly that these conditions had little relevance to the crises at hand and intruded too far into unrelated functions of domestic policy.[34] The fund's new managing director, Horst Köhler, appears sympathetic to the back-to-basics agenda. This agenda, as it is being implemented by the G-7 finance ministers and IMF, has three major components:[35]

- Closer surveillance of emerging market economies and financial markets
- A limited amount of short-term lending to countries in crisis, accompanied by a modest degree of penalty interest rates

- Loans conditioned on standard macroeconomic targets (exchange rate management, fiscal position, monetary policy) and a short agenda of microeconomic requirements

While the back-to-basics agenda has public adherents in high places, including in the U.S. Treasury and the finance ministries of other industrial countries,[36] the true test will come in individual cases, not broad policy statements. Managing Director Köhler has directed IMF staff to take a parsimonious approach to conditionality.[37] But the problem is not just the fund staff; it is mainly the industrial countries.

In the wake of the Asia crisis, advocates for various reforms have come to appreciate the power of detailed conditionality. The genie is out of the lamp. Reform advocates inside and outside finance ministries know that the key document is the "letter of intent." In a severe crisis, the hapless president or finance minister of a beleaguered country will sign almost anything. This message is not lost on environmental, labor, and other NGO constituencies for various social causes. Nor is it lost on the World Bank, the regional development banks, trade ministers, foreign ministers, members of Congress, and business groups. Indeed, in October 2000, the United States and the fund were said to be pressuring Pakistan to abandon its nuclear and missile programs and do more to fight terrorism in the Middle East as conditions of rescheduling $40 billion of debt.[38] Likewise, at the insistence of member countries of the Organization for Economic Cooperation and Development (OECD), banks that facilitate money laundering and official tolerance of tax evasion could soon be added to the IMF list of unacceptable behavior.

But the continued proliferation of detailed and controversial conditions risks further undermining support for the IMF's increasingly fuzzy mission. Perhaps the best hope is a bargain in which various constituencies endorse a back-to-basics agenda that curtails their own priorities in exchange for curtailing those of others.

Another unresolved issue is whether and how to limit the size and duration of fund loans. It is one thing to impose strict limits on countries that are small, distant and nonstrategic. But what happens when the next crisis emerges in Turkey, Ukraine, Argentina, South Korea, or China? Judging from the first few loans under Köhler's tenure (to Turkey and Argentina), the IMF will continue to extend credit well beyond the "normal" level of 300 percent of quota. What happens when this practice runs up against the limits of fund resources? That brings us to the issue of "private sector involvement."

Private-sector involvement. Cutting across prescriptions for redesigning the IMF is the question of private responsibility. To varying degrees, elements of each of the above three camps embrace the idea of increased private sector "buy-in" in resolving crises. The "smaller fund" camp would essentially force unwise private investors to take a bigger hit by limiting the amount of liquidity provided by public funds. Likewise, developing countries in the "larger fund" camp would obviously seek to reduce their postcrisis debt burden as much as possible, by sharing pain with the private sector. In contrast, U.S. officials who are closest to the "back-to-basics" camp are also the most hesitant about mandating private-sector involvement, since U.S. investors and money managers are among the largest beneficiaries of open global capital markets. The question of the role of the private sector is thus another issue that potentially pits the United States against other donor countries, many client countries, and a variety of civil society groups.

Behind ideological differences are the hard realities of modern capital markets. Reasonable projections of capital flows to emerging markets (shown in Table 15.1) suggest that private capital will totally dominate official resources, and it seems most unlikely that the expansion of IMF resources over the next three decades will permit the fund to cope with future crises in the traditional way (see Table 15.2). This reality in turn raises the issue of "private-sector involvement."[39] This euphemism, also known as PSI, means that private banks and investors should take additional risks and/or more losses when financial crises strike emerging markets. Advocates of PSI typically see evidence of herding and panic behavior among investors, particularly among financial institutions. Accordingly, they assign private capital a high degree of culpability for financial shocks, and they believe that the fund should give its blessing, not its condemnation, to three unorthodox remedies: capital controls, repayment standstills, and debt write-downs (or fresh loans).[40]

Prior to the Asian crisis, the IMF was busy trying to revise its Articles of Agreement to eliminate capital account inconvertibility—the foundation of capital controls. There is a growing body of evidence that supports the long-term merits of freer capital movements, but there are important differences over the details and timing, and the fund's policy emphasis has shifted in the wake of the Asia crisis. The fund now admonishes emerging countries to *sequence* financial liberalization, beginning with stronger and better regulated banks, before opening fully to capital account convertibility.[41] Others go further in advocating a role for capital controls, but while these ideas may from time to time gain a following in individual countries, they stand little chance of broad acceptance, being opposed by private financial institutions, the industrial powers, and the finance ministries of most emerging markets.

More promising are standstills, debt write-downs, and forced loans in the event of a crisis. The idea behind these proposals is to give the crisis country breathing room to rearrange its affairs and, if necessary, restructure its debt.[42] Private creditors would be handed an unpleasant menu: accept delayed repayment; write down part of the debt; or put up fresh money. Until the Asian crisis, "moral hazard" arguments usually kept such choices

Table 15.1   Total Foreign Capital Stock in Emerging Markets ($ billions and percent of GDP)

	1970	1980	1990	2000a	2010b	2020b	2030b	1970	1980	1990	2000a	2010b	2020b	2030b
	($ billions at current prices)				*($ billions at 2000 prices)*			*(percent of GDP of emerging markets)*						
Foreign capital stock in emerging markets	176	770	2,164	4,937	7,300	12,700	21,800	22.1	26.3	45.6	72.6	73.0	84.7	99.1
Long- and medium-term debt stockc	60	457	1,203	2,192	2,000	2,500	3,000	7.5	15.6	25.3	32.2	20.0	16.7	13.6
Official	33	182	630	977				4.1	6.2	13.3	14.4			
Private	28	275	573	1,215				3.5	9.4	12.1	17.9			
Share of official debt (percent)	54%	40%	52%	45%										
Share of private debt (percent)	46%	60%	48%	55%										
Short-term debt stock	50d	147	241	352	400	500	600	6.3	5.0	5.1	5.2	4.0	3.3	2.7
Portfolio investment stock	10e	60e	364	959	2,000	4,000	7,500	1.3	2.0	7.7	14.1	20.0	26.7	34.1
FDI inward stock	56f	106	356	1,434	2,900	5,700	10,700	7.0	3.6	7.5	21.1	30.0	39.0	49.0
								(percent of GDP of G-10)						
Foreign capital stock in emerging markets relative to G-10 GDP								8.8	10.9	14.4	23.3	28.1	36.3	49.5
Long- and medium-term debt stockc								3.0	6.4	8.0	10.3	7.7	7.1	6.8
Official								1.6	2.6	4.2	4.6			
Private								1.4	3.9	3.8	5.7			
Short-term debt stock								2.5	2.1	1.6	1.7	1.5	1.4	1.4
Portfolio investment stock								0.5	0.8	2.4	4.5	7.7	11.4	17.0
FDI inward stock								2.8	1.5	2.4	6.8	11.2	16.3	24.3

(continues)

Table 15.1 Cont.

	1970	1980	1990	2000ᵃ	2010ᵇ	2020ᵇ	2030ᵇ
Memorandum							
GDP of emerging markets[g]	797	2,927	4,747	6,798	10,000	15,000	22,000
GDP of G-10[g]	1,999	7,093	14,997	21,208	26,000	35,000	44,000

Sources: Adapted from Wendy Dobson, and Gary Hufbauer, assisted by Hyun Koo Cho, 2001. *World Capital Markets: Challenge to the G-10.* Washington DC: Institute for International Economics, forthcoming 2001. IMF, *International Capital Markets,* September 1999. United Nations, *World Investment Report,* 1995, 1997. The World Bank, *Global Development Finance,* 1998, 1999, 2000. IMF, *Results of the 1997 Coordinated Portfolio Investment Survey,* 1999.

Notes: a. For the year 2000, figures are extrapolated from the flow figures in IMF, *International Capital Markets* (1999). For short-term debt stock, net bank loans (flow) for 2000 are added to the 1999 stock figure to obtain the 2000 figure.

b. Calculated on the basis of net-net flow (minus interest payments and profit remittances) projections. We assume that net-net capital inflows are divided equally between additions to long- and medium-term debt stock and additions to FDI stock. Cumulating net-net flows to obtain projected debt stock and FDI stock understates the stock figures. The reason is that our procedure subtracts interest payments and profits from the new additions to capital stock.

c. The private figures include portfolio investment, and much of that represents portfolio debt.

d. Short-term debt stock for all emerging markets is arbitrarily estimated at $50 billion in 1970, reflecting the surge in short-term petro-dollar loans during 1970s, especially to Latin America. The total figure was then apportioned between regions according to its share in 1980.

e. Figures are arbitrarily assumed by authors.

f. FDI stock figures for 1970 are estimated by subtracting average inflows of FDI to each region.

g. GDP figures are evaluated at market exchange rates.

Table 15.2 IMF Resources Relative to Financial Magnitudes in Emerging Markets

	1970	1980	1990	1999	2010	2020	2030
		($ billions at current prices)			*($ billions at 2000 prices)*		
IMF Quotas							
Path A (Emerging market import growth path)	28	76	130	289	600[a]	1300[a]	2800[a]
Path B (G-10 GDP growth path)	28	76	130	289	400[b]	520[b]	660[b]
Fund credit extended[c]	3	14	33	79			
Net IMF Resources[d]	25	62	96	210			
Aggregate imports of emerging markets	82	606	918	1728	4000[e]	8700[e]	18800[e]
Total reserves of emerging markets	21	179	350	1044	3000[f]	6000[f]	11000[f]
GDP of emerging markets	797	2927	4747	6521	10000[g]	15000[g]	22000[g]
GDP of G-10	1999	7093	14997	20187	26000[h]	35000[h]	44000[h]
Long- and medium-term debt and FDI stock in emerging markets	116	563	1559	3202	6300	11900	21900
				(percentages)			
IMF Quotas under path A as percent of :							
Aggregate imports of emerging markets	34.7	12.5	14.1	16.7	15.0[a]	15.0[a]	15.0[a]
Total reserves of emerging markets	137.7	42.5	37.0	27.6	20.0	21.7	25.5
GDP of emerging markets	3.6	2.6	2.7	4.9	6.0	8.7	12.7
GDP of G-10	1.4	1.1	0.9	1.4	2.3	3.7	6.4
Long- and medium-term debt and FDI stock in emerging markets	24.5	13.5	8.3	9.0	9.5	10.9	12.8

(continues)

Table 15.2 Cont.

	1970	1980	1990	1999	2010	2020	2030
				(percentages)			
IMF Quotas under path B as percent of :							
Aggregate imports of emerging markets	34.7	12.5	14.1	16.7	10.0	6.0	3.5
Total reserves of emerging markets	137.7	42.5	37.0	27.6	13.3	8.7	6.0
GDP of emerging markets	3.6	2.6	2.7	4.9	4.0	3.5	3.0
GDP of G-10	1.4	1.1	0.9	1.4	1.5b	1.5b	1.5b
Long- and medium-term debt and FDI stock in emerging markets	24.5	13.5	8.3	9.0	6.3	4.4	3.0

Sources: Adapted from Wendy Dobson, and Gary Hufbauer, assisted by Hyun Koo Cho, 2001. *World Capital Markets: Challenge to the G-10*, Washington DC: Institute for International Economics, forthcoming 2001. IMF, *International Financial Statistics*, Yearbook 1998. IMF, *International Financial Statistics*, February 2000. IMF, *World Economic Outlook*, October 2000. The World Bank, *Global Development Finance*, 1998; 1999. United Nations, *World Investment Report*, 1995; 1997.

Notes: Emerging markets represent the rest of the world other than 23 industrialized countries: US, Canada, Australia, Japan, New Zealand, Austria, Belgium, Denmark, Finland, France, Germany, Greece, Iceland, Ireland, Italy, Luxembourg, Netherlands, Norway, Portugal, Spain, Sweden, Switzerland, UK.

a. On Path A, the IMF quotas are assumed to expand so that they bear a constant relation of 15 percent of the aggregate imports of emerging markets through 2030 (see note d).

b. On Path B, the IMF quotas are assumed to expand so that they bear a constant relation of 1.5 percent of the GDP of G-10.

c. Total Fund Credit and Loans Outstanding (calculated as outstanding purchases of local currencies plus outstanding loans).

d. Available resources of the IMF (calculated as IMF quotas less Fund credit extended).

e. The annual growth rate in the 1990s (about 8 percent in real terms) was applied to calculate the figures.

f. Total reserves are assumed to increase from about 20 percent of real GDP in 2000, to 30 percent in 2010, 40 percent in 2020, and 50 percent in 2030.

g. GDP in emerging markets is projected to grow at 4.0 percent per year in real terms.

h. GDP in the G-10 countries is projected to grow at 2.5 percent per year in real terms.

off the official agenda: it was feared that countries would get into a bad cycle of over-borrowing, pursuing bad policies, and then stiffing foreign creditors.[43] This unhappy cycle would dry up private capital flows or make them too expensive, thereby slowing growth in developing countries.

Against these arguments is the recognition that, when a crisis hits, creditors have little incentive to restructure or provide new loans as long as official money is on the table. The IMF becomes the unintended lender of first resort.[44] An even more persuasive argument for standstills is that they recognize the dominant role of private capital and the shrinking relative magnitude of official resources.

For this reason, the IMF is edging toward a new policy of "*only* lend into arrears" instead of "*never* lend into arrears." Under this policy, the fund would make new loans to a crisis country only if payments to private creditors were delayed. While this notion is gaining official acceptance, it is not popular with financial institutions, and U.S. officials have not yet agreed that forced PSI should become a general rule. The United States prefers a case-by-case approach, whereas other industrial powers advocate a set of rules enunciating the requisite extent of PSI in particular circumstances. Among other things, such rules would erode U.S. leverage when crisis strikes. Moreover, the issue of PSI rules threatens to put the main supporters of the IMF—private banks and more recently money managers—at odds with the institution, eroding a fundamental source of support.

Post-Asian Governance

The fund faces not a single backlash but rather conflicting backlashes from different quarters. The U.S. commitment to participate in the international financial system on a multilateral basis lies at the center of these multiple conflicts. So long as there is no major financial shock, the U.S. Treasury and the IMF can balance forces opposing U.S. multilateralism and preserve the status quo. The next major crisis, however, could cripple the institution and dramatically alter the U.S. role in fund affairs. In an extreme scenario, Congress might force the U.S. Treasury's hand and distance the United States from the fund. More likely, the United States and the IMF will reluctantly bow to pressure for new regional monetary institutions, rather than genuine multilateral governance of the fund itself.

Our fund or no fund. Some members of the U.S. Congress already contend that the IMF (like the UN) does not sufficiently reflect U.S. values and priorities. For the moment, these are mainly conservative Republican legislators. But it is easy to see how this view could gain adherents. Liberals, anxious to graft a social agenda onto the fund's mission, could join such a coalition. Private banks and money managers, angered by excessive fund "bullying" on PSI issues, are also potential recruits. While they would not put the choice so starkly, the rallying cry of this camp might be expressed as "Our fund or no fund." The ultimate weapon would be to withhold U.S. resources from the IMF.

More power to the borrowers. Many fund members think the industrial powers (especially the United States) have too big a say in fund affairs. These objections were crystallized in the succession battle following the departure of Michel Camdessus as the IMF's managing director. Some members objected to the unwritten deal that gave the post to Europe (and Europe gave Germany "its turn"), while others resented that only the United States (working behind the scenes) had the power to veto the first German nominee, Caio Koch-Weser. After Koch-Weser's name was withdrawn in the second round, the borrowing countries rebeled at the clubby selection process, nominating Stanley Fischer. In the end, of course, great-power politics prevailed, and Germany's second nominee, Horst Köhler, was named to the post of managing director.

This episode fueled the long debate over weighted voting rights (quotas) in the IMF. From time to time, quotas have been adjusted to reflect the rising economic power of countries such as China and Japan, while the United States, Britain, and other industrial powers have relinquished part of their quotas. But this is a grudging and laborious process. As a group, the industrial powers are not about to hand the fund to borrowing nations. To the extent that pressures to share power are accommodated, even at the margin, disenchantment is likely to grow in the "our fund or no fund" camp.

A new fund? Since the governance of the old fund is essentially frozen, the larger emerging market countries (like China, India, Brazil, and South Africa) are beginning to think about the creation of new monetary institutions in which they would have a greater say. Precedents exist in the regional development banks (the Inter-American Bank, the Asian Development Bank, the African Development Bank, and the European Bank for Reconstruction and Development), which were created to enhance regional voices relative to the World Bank. The United States has less influence over the regional banks, either by virtue of a non-U.S. president, or less voting power, or both.

The most active proposal is for an Asian Monetary Fund (AMF) that would not be under the influence of Washington. Japan floated the idea for an AMF in July 1997, only to see it quickly squelched by the United States, the EU, and the IMF. The adverse reaction was partly colored by the fear, in the midst of the Asian crisis, that the AMF would undermine the fund's conditionality standards. But U.S. and European concerns that an AMF would dilute their influence in Asia were also at play. The AMF is now being revived in calmer financial circumstances.[45] The first step would appear to be a series of swap lines between regional central banks, perhaps totaling $100 billion. While the U.S. Treasury and European finance ministries have not been as openly hostile this time around, they will likely work behind the scenes to sabotage an Asian rival to the IMF. One could anticipate roughly the same quiet antagonism to regional monetary arrangements in Latin America (centered on Brazil) or Africa (centered on South Africa). When the next major financial crisis strikes, however, it may well prove impossible for the United States and the IMF to block the creation of regional monetary funds. Affected countries will almost certainly complain about IMF conditions that are too stiff and inadequate fund loans; congressional critics in the United States will oppose large bailout packages. A plausible reconciliation between these forces is the creation or activation of regional monetary arrangements.

The Consequences of Ambivalent Multilateralism in the Financial System

The multilateral rules of the international financial system have changed fundamentally over the past fifty years and could be on the verge of another shift. The IMF, along with GATT, was created to encourage cooperation among industrialized countries and to avoid beggar-thy-neighbor policies of the type that plagued the 1930s. By the 1980s, however, the IMF had little or no influence over the economic policies of the developed countries. Instead, it was promulgating a different and far broader set of U.S.-inspired policies to less developed countries that had little or no role in developing these rules.

Initially at Bretton Woods, the major powers subscribed to a common set of inconsistent rules. In the 1950s and 1960s, they resolved their differences by unilaterally embracing the rules and exceptions they found most agreeable.[46] In the 1970s, when the tensions created by these inconsistencies could no longer be contained, the United States reneged. The Smithsonian episode in August 1971 was U.S. unilateralism at its worst, or its best—depending on one's view of flexible exchange rates. Our own view is that the intellectual case for abandoning fixed exchange rates had been amply demonstrated years before the Smithsonian Accord. But the rules could not be changed until they pinched the United States itself. When that happened the United States broke enough crockery to force a fundamental redesign. On this reading of history the lessons are simple and direct. Systemic faults will be corrected neither because academic commentators point out fundamental flaws, nor because the flaws inconvenience secondary powers. But they will be corrected when the flaws seriously disadvantage a major power.

Over the past two decades, the major problem facing the international financial system has been the periodic eruption of financial crises in developing countries that are large enough to have global implications. These recurring crises and the fund's responses to them have again forced fundamental rethinking of the IMF's role. And, once again, the United States is at the center of controversies over both the mission and the management of the fund. Unlike the early 1970s, however, the United States no longer has the power to unilaterally determine the future of the system.

GATT, WTO, and Trade

The international financial institutions created at Bretton Woods in 1944 were up and running by 1945, but negotiations on the trade leg of the postwar international economic system lagged. By the time the Havana Charter creating the ITO was agreed in 1948, the Cold War was intensifying, the early postwar enthusiasm for multilateral institution building had faded, and both the Congress and the Truman administration were more concerned with passing the Marshall Plan to provide reconstruction assistance to Europe.

In this environment, the ITO treaty failed to attract congressional support and U.S. negotiators had to fall back on GATT, which governed trade relations for the next fifty years. GATT was intended to be a "provisional agreement" among "contracting parties" to promote multilateral trade liberalization only until the broader and more institutionalized ITO was established. Adding to its tenuous legal status, U.S. negotiators in the 1950s insisted that GATT rules permit agricultural quotas; they also exempted textiles and clothing from normal GATT disciplines. Yet, despite the rocky start, the GATT was more successful in achieving its goals of lowering tariffs and spurring trade growth than the IMF was in promoting economic stability through a system of fixed exchange rates.

Over time, however, the weaknesses and limitations of GATT became more apparent and frustrations grew, particularly in the United States. In 1995, after more than seven years of negotiation, GATT was replaced by the WTO, which is both broader in scope and more institutionalized than GATT (though not as broad in its reach as the ITO would have been). The irony is that this far stronger multilateral institution likely would not have been created if not for a dose of "aggressive unilateralism" in U.S. trade policy in the 1980s. U.S. negotiators successfully used unilateral trade threats to pressure trading partners to strengthen the multilateral rules governing trade. In exchange for new rules in areas that it cared about and a stronger dispute settlement process to enforce those rules, the United States, perhaps without fully realizing it, agreed to tight limits on its ability to act unilaterally on trade matters. The question now is whether U.S. negotiators went too far—and whether multilateralists can overcome the backlash against the WTO from both right and left.

The ITO and GATT

Like those on the IMF, the negotiations to remake the international trade system after World War II initially involved just the United States and Britain. The two parties agreed on the need to reduce trade barriers and to create an international organization to resolve disputes, but they differed sharply on the relationship between trade and employment policies, the use of quantitative restrictions in balance of payments crises, and the relative importance of nondiscrimination. A top priority for U.S. negotiators was to eliminate British imperial preferences and promote nondiscriminatory trade; British negotiators were most concerned with ensuring that trade liberalization did not undermine the achievement of full employment, and they would concede on imperial preferences only in return for substantial, across-the-board tariff cuts. Both countries agreed on the principle of eliminating quantitative restrictions, but differed on the scope of permissible exceptions.[47]

In resolving these issues, both British and U.S. negotiators faced domestic political constraints. U.S. negotiators tried to find solutions that could be ratified at home, in part, by accommodating existing domestic law and practice, which meant working within the strictures of the Reciprocal Trade Agreements Act (RTAA). Designed to avoid repetition of the logrolling that had resulted in the highly protectionist Smoot-Hawley Tariff Act of 1930, the RTAA delegated limited authority to the president to negotiate tariff reductions bilaterally on a product-by-product basis. These cuts would then be generalized through the "most-favored-nation" clause of these agreements, which requires that a tariff cut granted to one trading partner be extended to all other countries with which the United States has trade agreements.

The RTAA, passed by a Democratic Congress and signed into law by President Franklin D. Roosevelt in 1934, was repeatedly renewed for the next dozen years. But passage of the RTAA had been opposed by the Republican Party, which captured the Congress in 1946 just as the ITO negotiations were getting serious. Because the ITO negotiations were taking longer than expected, Truman administration trade negotiators adopted a parallel, "multilateral-bilateral" track for immediate tariff reductions and proposed creation of GATT as a temporary framework for negotiating reductions in trade barriers until the ITO was completed.[48] Although trade negotiations would still need to be bilateral, according to the RTAA, Washington sought to broaden the scope of tariff cuts by bringing a number of countries together in one place at one time. The initial GATT agreement was signed by twenty-three nations in Geneva in 1947.

The following year in Havana, trade partners agreed to a draft ITO charter that reflected both British concerns that trade policy not conflict with full employment goals and the insistence of nonindustrialized countries that the new trade rules not impede their development efforts. The charter also allowed Britain to maintain imperial preferences, at least for a time. Finally, to avoid antagonizing Congress, U.S. negotiators obtained an exception for agricultural quotas in exchange for the balance-of-payments exception to the use of quotas Britain had sought.

The U.S. business community, which had pushed hard to include rules protecting foreign investment as well as liberalizing trade, objected that the ITO was a step backward. The terms of the ITO charter preserved imperial preferences, allowed developing countries to regulate inward investment, contained many exceptions, and was viewed by U.S. business as too heavy-handed in regulating other areas, such as employment policy. With opposition from Republicans, whose constituents were primarily domestically oriented businesses and farmers; with no support from internationally oriented sectors; and with less than total enthusiasm from the Truman administration, the ITO was "dead on arrival."[49]

GATT survived, however, because, in the words of Helen Milner, "it required much less of an adjustment of U.S. policies in return for, or anticipation of, the adjustment of other states' policies than the ITO would have required."[50] GATT incorporated the commercial chapter of the ITO, while omitting broader rules on "industrial stabilization," commodity agreements, investment, full employment, and "fair labor standards." The Truman administration took the view that GATT (unlike the ITO) did not need to be submitted to Congress for ratification, since its provisions could be implemented with existing RTAA authority and, moreover, were being "provisional applied" by contracting parties rather than formally adopted as treaty commitments. U.S. negotiators also tried to ensure that the language of Article XI of the GATT, which restricted quotas, was consistent with U.S. agricultural laws, but subsequent congressional amendments reiterated the primacy of U.S. law should the latter conflict with GATT. In 1954, U.S. negotiators asked for and received a formal waiver from GATT rules for U.S. agricultural programs—a move the United States would soon come to regret.[51]

Thus, GATT was more acceptable than the ITO because it required little substantive change in U.S. policy. But the ITO's demise should not be taken as a blanket rejection of multilateralism. The U.S. business community, for example, opposed the ITO on the grounds that the organization's substantive rules embodied the wrong sort of multilateralism. Poor timing also played a role. By 1949–1950, when the Havana Charter was under consideration, the Cold War was in full gear and the Marshall Plan received higher priority in the Truman administration's plans. Moreover, some ITO provisions, such as those dealing with state trading, coupled with the backlash against the State Department following the Alger Hiss case, led some anticommunist Republicans to view the proposed organization as a hindrance rather than a help in the Cold War. The Truman administration, fearing backsliding on trade, eventually came to view GATT as an acceptable alternative to the ITO.[52]

Finally, although it did not formally recognize GATT until the 1960s, Congress reaffirmed the general U.S. commitment to multilateralism by continuing to renew the president's authority to reach trade agreements under the RTAA, permitting the United States to take part in five GATT tariff-cutting negotiations between 1947 and 1961.[53] In the Trade Expansion Act of 1962 (which authorized U.S. participation in the Kennedy Round of multilateral trade negotiations), Congress was finally persuaded to move away from the product-by-product tariff-cutting approach of the past and toward a "formula approach" that authorized broader across-the-board percentage cuts in tariffs.[54] The Kennedy Round was also the first to try to address the growing problem of nontariff barriers (NTBs). The NTB efforts were not very successful in the end because the U.S. Congress rejected the agreement on antidumping rules and refused to eliminate the "American selling price" method of determining import values, an expression of ambivalence toward multilateral rules perceived as impinging on U.S. sovereignty.[55]

Increasing Frustrations and the Turn to "Aggressive Unilateralism"

By the 1980s, seven rounds of GATT negotiations had reduced weighted average tariffs in the main industrialized countries from 35 percent in 1945 to less than 5 percent.[56] Despite this success, dissatisfaction with GATT's gaps in coverage and institutional weaknesses was growing, particularly in the United States. During the 1980s, these strains were exacerbated by macroeconomic policies that led to an overvalued dollar and burgeoning U.S. trade deficits. These trends strengthened perceptions in Congress and among key constituencies that the United States was more open to imports than other countries, that the "playing field" resulting from thirty years of GATT negotiations was not level, and that unilateral U.S. action was both necessary and appropriate.

The first source of disillusionment with existing GATT rules was the limited coverage of non-tariff barriers, which were becoming more visible and were offsetting, to some degree, the effects of tariff cuts. Many U.S. policymakers believed, with some justification, that other countries relied more heavily on NTBs and other industrial policies than did the United States.[57] A second source of growing frustration was GATT's limited sectoral coverage. When GATT was founded, services trade (other than transportation and tourism) was practically nonexistent, foreign investment was a tiny fraction of what it would become, and intellectual property was a much less important component of most products. Washington hoped to incorporate these new sectors into global trade rules and, although the United States was primarily responsible for limiting GATT's role in agricultural trade, it now sought to restrain and roll back foreign restrictions on agricultural imports.

Accordingly, U.S. negotiators tried to push the limits of the existing GATT rules on subsidies and other NTBs. Given the original emphasis in GATT on informality and negotiation, a premium was placed on consensus in decisionmaking and the negotiated resolution of disputes.[58] Under GATT procedures, there were no deadlines, and countries subjected to complaints could both block adoption of a dispute settlement panel's report and block multilateral authorization for the complaining party to retaliate. Over the years—mainly because of U.S. pressure—the process became more legalistic, with an emphasis on adjudicating disputes based on the rules rather than negotiating mutually acceptable solutions. Opposition to the legalistic approach, combined with the inherent vagueness of some GATT rules, led to increasing pressure on the dispute settlement process.[59]

These tensions were exacerbated by the macroeconomic choices made by the Reagan administration when it entered office in 1981. The combination of expansionary fiscal policy and tight monetary policy yielded large budget deficits and high interest rates, which "crowded in" capital from abroad and put upward pressure on the value of the dollar. At its peak in 1985, the trade-weighted value of the dollar was 50 percent higher than it had been in 1979–1980. The sharp appreciation of the dollar caused the U.S. trade deficit to explode, more than doubling from $28 billion in 1979 to $67 billion in 1983 and almost doubling again in 1984 to $112 billion. U.S. merchandise exports did not regain their 1981 level until 1987.[60]

The Reagan administration's initial response to this trade deficit was both unilateral and multilateral. President Reagan provided ad hoc import protection to a few import-competing industries—including automobiles in 1981, steel in 1982 and 1984, and Harley-Davidson motorcycles in 1983. At the same time, Reagan strongly urged his counterparts at the G-7 economic summit in July 1981 to hold a GATT ministerial meeting the following year to discuss an agenda for the next trade round. But the administration was not willing to tackle the underlying sources of the trade imbalance, depicting the overvalued dollar as a sign of renewed U.S. economic strength.[61] And, in 1982, the administration's attempt at a multilateral initiative was rebuffed by trading partners unwilling to launch a new GATT negotiating round in the midst of a severe recession.

By 1985, U.S. foreign economic policy had shifted nearly 180 degrees. The administration, under new Treasury Secretary James Baker, now sought cooperation from Europe and Japan to engineer a soft landing for the dollar, while U.S. Trade Representative (USTR) Clayton Yeutter turned trade policy more sharply unilateral, though not exclusively so. Yeutter finally convinced the Europeans and Japan to begin planning for a new round of multilateral trade negotiations and, dropping long-standing U.S. opposition to preferential trade arrangements, negotiated a free-trade agreement with Israel in 1985 and launched trade talks with Canada in 1986. J. David Richardson dubbed this new U.S. trade strategy "contingent multilateralism . . . multilateralism where possible, minilateralism where necessary."[62]

The administration remained concerned about the continuing pressures for import protection, however, and it tried to deflect them in the short run with "aggressively unilateral" market-opening negotiations, using section

301 of the Trade Act of 1974 (as amended). The strategy was unilateral in two ways. First, section 301 authorized the USTR's office to determine whether a foreign trade practice was "unfair," even in the absence of a GATT ruling of noncompliance or in areas not covered by any international agreement. Second, if the USTR determined that a foreign trade practice placed "unreasonable" or "unjustifiable" burdens on U.S. commerce, section 301 authorized the USTR to retaliate against exports from the offending country. Thus, U.S. negotiators in these cases typically demanded that the trading partner unilaterally liberalize without any reciprocal concessions from the United States.

Backed by threats to close the U.S. market, negotiators pried open Japanese markets for semiconductors, supercomputers, cigarettes, and beef; Korean markets for insurance, wine, and beef; and tried, less successfully, to stem the erosion of U.S. farmers' market share in the European Community. Contrary to the fears of free-trade critics, aggressive unilateralism opened some markets, generally on a nondiscriminatory basis (that is, for all exporters, not just Americans), and it rarely resulted in increased trade protection. While the United States made greater use of retaliatory threats, these were seldom actually implemented, and not a single case triggered a spiraling tit-for-tat trade war as feared. Thomas Bayard and Kimberly Ann Elliott,[63] who examined ninety-one section 301 cases between 1975 and 1993, found that the United States retaliated in only fifteen, and only three triggered a counterretaliatory response (twice by the European Community and once by Canada).

The Reagan administration launched its aggressively unilateral section 301 policy in September 1985. A year later, a new multilateral trade negotiation was launched in Punta del Este, Uruguay. As desired by U.S. negotiators, the agenda for the round included the new areas of services and intellectual property, as well as a negotiating group on institutional reforms to explore ways to strengthen rule enforcement. When the Uruguay Round concluded at the end of 1993, the old GATT was incorporated in a new WTO. The WTO also encompassed a new General Agreement on Trade in Services, a detailed agreement of rules on the protection of "trade-related intellectual property" (TRIPs), and a more binding dispute settlement understanding (DSU). Except in agriculture, which was now covered by trading rules but not liberalized to a significant extent,[64] a mix of unilateral demands and multilateral negotiation contributed to broad achievement of U.S. trade policy objectives.

Consequences:
From Aggressive Unilateralism to Assertive Multilateralism

The U.S. strategy of aggressive unilateralism in the 1980s and early 1990s elicited harsh criticism from both its targets and certain academics, who objected that the United States had set itself up as judge, jury, and executioner.[65]

They warned that the strategy would close rather than open markets, undermine core GATT principles, and ultimately weaken the international trading regime. Defenders of U.S. policy argued that inaction was a greater threat to the GATT-based trade system than were U.S. pressures to reform it.

In practice, U.S. trade threats altered the incentives facing the United States' trading partners, leading many of the latter to embrace stronger multilateral rules as a way to constrain U.S. unilateralism. In this case, unilateralism was not necessarily inimical to maintenance of the multilateral system. Of course, even the most benign hegemon ultimately seeks to advance its own interests, and the latter may not always be in congruence with broader definitions of global welfare. Still, the 1980s experience suggests it is sometimes necessary to break crockery to move the system forward. If the constraints on unilateral action are too strong, forward movement may stall. Indeed, recent experience suggests that increasing constraints on national action, combined with the expanding scope of multilateral trade rules, risks creating a backlash from a variety of directions against encroachments on national sovereignty.

Responding to the critics of aggressive unilateralism, Robert Hudec advanced an intellectual rationale for "justified disobedience," arguing that it is permissible to depart from multilateral rules when the system is verging on collapse, as GATT seemed to be in the mid-1980s.[66] Similarly, Abram and Antonia Chayes, noting that rule enforcement is not costless, suggest that a country might justifiably choose to "pay the costs of additional enforcement," as the United States arguably did with section 301, because it feared that "the tipping point [toward regime collapse] is close, so that enhanced compliance would be necessary for regime preservation."[67]

Building on these analyses, Bayard and Elliott argue that the U.S. trade strategy during the 1980s and early 1990s was intended to be broadly supportive of the multilateral trade regime. Although mercantilist gains in U.S. exports were clearly one objective of "aggressive unilateralism," U.S. negotiators generally tried to operate within the spirit of GATT rules, if not the letter. Washington was most likely to threaten or impose retaliatory trade sanctions in areas not yet covered by GATT rules, such as services or intellectual property protection, or after the United States had invoked GATT dispute settlement procedures and either received a panel ruling in its favor or had been confronted with what Hudec calls "general legal breakdown."[68] U.S. trade threats, as well as a new receptivity to regional negotiations with Canada and Mexico, were also designed to encourage trading partners to initiate multilateral trade negotiations, to expand the agenda of those negotiations into previously unregulated areas (like services and intellectual property rights), and to strengthen the dispute settlement process.

Critics rejected these "altruistic" justifications for aggressive unilateralism. The economist Jagdish Bhagwati, for example, argued that such a willful disregard of GATT rules would breed cynicism and undermine the long-term sustainability of the system by replacing "the rule of law by the law of the jungle."[69] The obvious problem in evaluating these arguments is that the counterfactual cannot be observed: we cannot know what might have happened to the trading system in the absence of aggressive unilateralism. Still, here is what we do know:

- Congress did not pass sector-specific protectionist legislation.
- The Uruguay Round was launched in September 1986 with an expanded agenda.
- The round was successfully concluded, albeit three years later than planned, and the resulting agreement created a new, stronger WTO that expanded coverage to agriculture, services, and intellectual property.

The causal linkages may still be in dispute, but one thing is not. An aggressively unilateral U.S. trade policy did not destroy the multilateral trade system or even prevent it from becoming stronger.

At the same time, as the critics feared, the United States was not always a "benign hegemon." The most prominent example is the TRIPs agreement creating rules and enforcement measures to protect intellectual property. Under pressure from IP-reliant industries, Congress expanded section 301 in the 1984 Trade Act to include insufficient protection of intellectual property as an "unreasonable" trade practice and, in the 1988 Trade Act, created a "special 301" procedure to force the USTR to give greater priority to IP issues. U.S. negotiators carefully targeted "special 301" cases against countries that opposed inclusion of IP rules in the Uruguay Round. Ultimately, this pressure led developing countries to acquiesce in the TRIPs agreement, in the hope that multilateral rules would provide protection from U.S. unilateral threats and sanctions.

But the TRIPs agreement differs from traditional trade-liberalizing agreements that benefit all adherents, albeit not equally. Middle-income industrializing countries that are also beginning to develop indigenous IP industries will benefit from adopting stronger IP protections. For very poor countries that have yet to develop IP industries, however, the main effect of the agreement will be to transfer income in the form of royalties from poor countries to richer ones, particularly the United States.[70] Thus, the agreement has important distributive effects and it is difficult to say whether the net effect is a gain or loss for global welfare.

Unexpected Constraints and the
Backlash Against Assertive Multilateralism

The "basic dilemma . . . at the heart of international institutional agreements," which John Ikenberry discusses in Chapter 5 of this volume, can be seen clearly in the new WTO. In the Uruguay Round agreements creating the WTO, the United States was willing to accept far more binding constraints on U.S. unilateralism because it received, in return, commitments from its trading partners to lock in policy changes it wanted in agriculture, liberalization of services trade, and protection of intellectual property. But increasingly, some Americans are questioning whether the bargain struck was a good one.

For one thing, an assertive multilateral trade policy, unlike aggressive unilateralism, is available to all members of the WTO, and the United States since 1995 has frequently found itself the target of complaints under the new DSU. In addition, although U.S. negotiators wanted a stronger dispute settlement system to emerge from the Uruguay Round, they seem not to have fully anticipated just how tight the constraints on U.S. action would be. Moreover, EU recalcitrance in implementing panel rulings against it has raised questions about the benefits of that allegedly more powerful system.

The common theme linking the most vociferous critics of the WTO is that the negotiating agenda reaches too far behind national borders and is going too far in restricting U.S. policy autonomy in regulatory areas previously regarded as primarily domestic. As a result of successful WTO complaints, U.S. policymakers either will or already have had to modify U.S. laws or regulations relating to clean air, the preservation of sea turtles, tax policy, and the provision of relief to import-competing firms. These rulings have stimulated opposition from environmentalists and consumer groups concerned about food safety. They have also disturbed congressional representatives from both parties who are concerned about the excessive reach of WTO dispute settlement panels in a number of recent cases involving U.S. laws that provide temporary import relief for U.S. industries ranging from steel to semiconductors and agricultural products.

In sum, the tensions between unilateralism and multilateralism in U.S. approaches to the global trade regime are increasing and the constraints on U.S. freedom of action both at home and abroad are generating backlash from a variety of sources. But the backlash is not always against multilateralism per se. Rather, as with the IMF, some critics want the WTO to do less and some want it to do more.

On the right wing of the U.S. political spectrum, generalized opposition to multilateralism, and a renewed embrace of isolationist or unilateralist tendencies, has become more prominent since the end of the Cold War. On the left, views are more complicated because there is typically more openness to global governance in general. But environmental activists object to WTO encroachments on food safety and other environmental policies, including European restrictions on genetically modified agricultural products and the use of hormones in beef, as well U.S. regulation of gasoline cleanliness. Many of these groups, joined by unions and human rights activists, also resent limitations on the use of trade sanctions to enforce

U.S. priorities globally. Some groups want the WTO to incorporate enforceable labor and environmental standards and, in the absence of that, many groups think the United States should have the latitude to take action unilaterally in support of these standards. In the words of Lori Wallach, a prominent WTO critic, governments should "fix it, or nix it."

In addition to rising opposition to the WTO from the right and left, many traditional import-competing industries are disturbed by recent WTO panel rulings that are perceived as overreaching in their interpretation of antidumping, escape clause, and other statutory provisions authorizing import relief under certain conditions. In previous decades, complaints usually targeted particular import restrictions and rulings required only that the restriction in question be lifted or modified. Recently, however, complaints and rulings have argued that underlying U.S. trade laws or the regulations implementing them are out of step with international rules and must be changed, raising sovereignty issues more directly. Moreover, because some of these laws protect U.S. industries against allegedly "unfair" imports, concerns about the reach of the WTO are spreading to relative trade moderates in the Congress and even to some in the business community.

Some export constituencies are dissatisfied because U.S. negotiators cannot pursue mercantilist or other market-opening objectives as aggressively as before. An early and prominent example was a 1994–1995 trade dispute in which Japan reversed its traditional posture and refused to accept U.S. demands for a "managed trade" solution to alleged barriers against U.S. exports of automobiles and their parts. When U.S. negotiators threatened to retaliate against Japanese exports using section 301, the Japanese made clear they would challenge U.S. sanctions under the WTO's strengthened dispute settlement provisions. The U.S. negotiators backed down.

In the automobile case, multilateral rules arguably performed as intended, disciplining an unjustified attempt by U.S. negotiators to bully a relatively weaker trading partner. But such market-opening initiatives have been important in the past in offsetting opposition from import-competing industries and maintaining support for a liberal U.S. trade policy. The failure of the EU to comply with WTO rulings against it on beef and bananas has also led to disappointment with WTO procedures and has generated support for more aggressive unilateral action, such as the passage of legislation last year requiring "carousel retaliation" against recalcitrant trading partners.[71]

In addition, U.S. negotiators have found themselves with reduced leverage when trying to respond to constituent demands to expand trade rules into new areas, such as worker rights or banning tariffs on e-commerce. Whatever one thinks of particular issues like worker rights, there is a systemic issue involved because the United States has traditionally been the key leader in pushing the trading system forward. That role could be compromised by constraints on its ability to use its market as an incentive to get others to negotiate.[72]

Thus, both WTO rules and the lack of consistent domestic support have reduced the leverage available to U.S. negotiators to launch a new round of multilateral trade negotiations. One means of dealing with backlash, which appears to have been reflected in the Clinton administration's cautious approach to agenda setting at the 1999 WTO meeting in Seattle, is to scale back ambitious plans for the further expansion of the rules. But the WTO is also being squeezed from the other direction. Although many opponents of globalization are disturbed by what they view as undue intervention by international institutions in domestic U.S. matters, others want the WTO to permit U.S. economic leverage as a means of protecting the global environment and promoting respect for worker rights around the world. Some activists want the WTO to embrace their agenda as a multilateral norm. In lieu of that, they believe that vigorous U.S. unilateralism may be the best means to achieve their goals and they are willing to sacrifice multilateralism if need be.

But these demands are vehemently opposed by developing countries, which are increasingly disillusioned with a trade system that they view as skewed in favor of rich, developed countries. President Clinton's embrace of the worker rights agenda in comments at the beginning of the Seattle meeting stimulated a harsh reaction from developing countries and was one factor in the failure to reach agreement on an agenda for a new WTO round. If, in addition to increasing tensions at the international level, U.S. exporters come to believe that international rules no longer are working well, and import-competing industries loudly oppose panel rulings, the perceived value of the WTO bargain could be dangerously eroded.

Conclusions and Implications

The U.S. embrace of multilateralism has perhaps been stronger in the economic area than any other. In planning for the post-World War II world, Secretary of State Cordell Hull and his negotiating team clearly viewed international cooperation and nondiscrimination as central principles of the international economic system they hoped to build. But the U.S. embrace of multilateralism was never unconditional, and U.S. negotiators have naturally sought to control the agenda and the levers of power within the international economic system. As a result of an approach that mixes pragmatism with idealism, U.S. behavior in international economic institutions varies both over time and across issue areas.

A telling difference in official U.S. attitudes toward the multilateral economic institutions is the preference for rules to govern trade relations and for discretion in the operation of the IMF, at least since the Smithsonian Accord of 1971. In the trade system, U.S. negotiators have persistently pushed to expand the scope of the rules and to make them clearer and more enforceable. Indeed, U.S. negotiators may have pushed legalization of the system too far during the Uruguay Round, and the WTO may allow member governments too little discretion in answering serious political challenges to free trade. Many loopholes for responding to domestic protectionist pressures were tightened or closed, and WTO rules are now more binding. Those developments, combined with inevitable uncertainty about the economic and political implications of trade agreements, could make governments more reluctant to sign on to still tighter rules in the future.[73]

The U.S. approach to the IMF has been quite different, at least since the fund turned its attention to developing countries. Because weighted voting gives the U.S. voice disproportionate influence, and because flexibility is viewed as a benefit not a cost, U.S. officials have preferred discretion to rules in the fund. They have exploited the flexibility available under IMF procedures to bend the rules to help out friends, such as Mobutu during the Cold War and Mexico and Brazil in the 1990s. When the traditional rules no longer appeared suitable to resolve the 1980s debt crisis, U.S. officials came up with a plan permitting a portion of debts to be written off, something that was previously unthinkable. In the current debate over the future of the IMF, U.S. officials are pushing a case-by-case approach to PSI, as opposed to the general set of rules preferred by others.

Its power inevitably gives the United States a relatively greater say in shaping whatever multilateral institutions it joins. The United States has also always been willing to break crockery if the rules squeeze key U.S. interests too tightly or if U.S. policymakers decide that the institution needs reform. The cases analyzed here suggest that unilateralism is not necessarily "bad." At times, institutional modernization and reform may be needed but unobtainable without breaking existing rules or altering a structure of incentives that favors the status quo. The flipside of this observation is that multilateral rules and institutions are not, per se, "good." They may become outdated or obsolete, or they may result from coercion rather than negotiation and, therefore, reflect narrow rather than multilateral interests.

But multilateral cooperation in the economic sphere clearly has served U.S. interests quite well over the past fifty-odd years, and the heavy-handed use of U.S. power to push a predominantly national agenda risks serious backlash among other members. In the IMF, the backlash is expressed in efforts to change the fund's management structure to reduce U.S. influence or, if that is impossible, to create alternative regional institutions in which the United States has little or no voice. In the WTO, the backlash against aggressive unilateralism has led to the creation of more expansive and more binding rules, which many countries, including the United States and those of the EU, find uncomfortable. In both cases the credibility and therefore the effectiveness of the institutions are potentially at risk.

Mission "creep" in both the IMF and the WTO is also generating a serious backlash among domestic constituencies in the United States and elsewhere. Historically, steps to lower tariffs have always been opposed by the domestic industries directly affected but have been relatively uncontroversial among the wider populace. As international trade rules reach ever farther behind national borders, however, a greater number of actors—environmentalists, consumer groups concerned about food safety, and unions threatened by capital mobility—have begun to engage in the debate over trade policy. Some of these groups, along with others concerned about human rights and poverty, have also challenged the legitimacy of the laissez-faire economic model guiding IMF conditionality. Many also object to the opaque process by which multilateral rules are made, raising questions about the transparency and accountability of institutions like the IMF and WTO.

Entering the twenty-first century, increasing economic integration and technological change mean that globalization's effects touch more people every day and are more visible to everyone. Likewise, the rules governing international economic relations have more visible and tangible effects on people everywhere. These trends raise a number of challenges for the multilateral economic institutions. Among the most important are

- building a consensus on the evolution of the WTO and the IMF (expansion, contraction, or back to basics?); and
- finding a way to accommodate the public's demand to be heard, at both the domestic and international levels, without giving each group a veto that will bring the whole system to a screeching halt.

Meeting these challenges will require U.S. policymakers to rely more on persuasion than power.

Notes

Gary Hufbauer would like to thank the Smith Richardson Foundation for its support of his work on international capital markets and financial crises. The authors would also like to thank Hyun Koo Cho for research assistance.
1. Data are from IMF (various issues), Bank for International Settlements (various years), and Preeg, *The Trade Deficit, the Dollar, and the U.S. National Interest,* p. 18.

2. Hufbauer, Schott, and Elliott, *Economic Sanctions Reconsidered.*

3. Hufbauer and Rosen, "American Access to China's Market."

4. Keynes in fact advocated concepts that crystallized into the IMF; White modified Keynes's vision, but in addition provided the intellectual basis for the International Bank for Reconstruction and Development (the World Bank). See Solomon, *The International Monetary System,* and Lastra, "The International Monetary Fund in Historical Perspective."

5. As Lord Keynes put their differences, Americans were afraid that his version of the fund would make the United States the "milch cow of the world"; see Keynes, "The International Clearing Union," p. 365.

6. Lastra, "The International Monetary Fund in Historical Perspective," p. 513. The United States wanted to force deficit countries to do the heavy lifting of economic adjustment, whereas Britain believed that the surplus country should also

carry a substantial part of the adjustment burden. This fundamental difference, of course, reflected the expectation that the postwar United States would be a surplus country, while Britain would be a deficit country.

7. Notably, article VIII was only accepted widely when a "dollar surplus" emerged in the late 1950s and early 1960s and acute observers began to write of a "dollar in crisis"; see Harris, *The Dollar in Crisis*.

8. For its part, the United States disappointed Europe by keeping a short leash on IMF resources. Loans were extended in each balance of payments crisis, but they were relatively small. During the 1950s, the Marshall Plan and the International Bank for Reconstruction and Development (IBRD) provided far more resources to Europe and Japan than the fund.

9. In dispensing advice, the fund had three prescriptions in its medicine bag. The pleasant prescription (rationed by the United States) was short-term fund loans at very low interest rates. The unpleasant prescription (dispensed freely by the United States) was to cut public expenditures and raise taxes. The ambiguous prescription, welcomed by some ailing countries, resisted by others, and usually opposed by the United States, was to devalue the exchange rate.

10. Ironically, France, not the United States, was the next victim. In 1968, riots in Paris forced a realignment of the German mark and the French franc. Solomon, *The International Monetary System,* chs. 5 and 9.

11. Ibid., chs. 6 and 7.

12. Ibid., ch. 8 and pp. 389–390.

13. Ibid., ch. 12.

14. IMF article IV requires senior economic officials in all member countries to meet annually with IMF staff members to hear its appraisal of economic policy. At these meetings the industrial country officials generally listen politely and then carry on policy as usual. Within the past two years, for example, Japan ignored IMF advice on cleaning up its banking mess, and the United States ignored IMF advice to raise interest rates further.

15. Goldstein, Kaminsky and Reinhart, *Assessing Financial Vulnerability.*

16. The fund recognizes that countries sometimes get into trouble through no fault of their own. Currently, it has eight low-conditionality facilities to help members cope with unexpected problems, such as natural disasters, shifting international markets—for example, a sudden drop in the price of exported commodities or a sudden rise in the price of imported petroleum—or pure financial contagion from a distressed neighbor. The industrial countries, however, prefer a tight rein on use of these facilities.

17. Solomon, *Money on the Move,* ch. 5.

18. Williamson, *The Political Economy of Policy Reform.*

19. Eventually it became apparent that standard medicine was not curing the debt crisis. Countries could not pay their obligations and economic bad times persisted. Along the way, the old truism became more apparent: if you owe your banker $1 million and can't pay, you have a problem; if you owe your banker $1 billion and can't pay, your banker has a problem. Faced with these realities, the U.S. Treasury devised a new kind of traded instrument, the so-called Brady bond. Brady bonds entailed a partial write-down of sovereign debt (about a third, on average), and enabled banks (if they wished) to sell out their positions on the secondary market (see Cline, *International Debt Reexamined*).

20. A semantic point needs to be made. While some proponents of the "Washington consensus" all along included these *micro*economic components in the policy package, the term "Washington consensus" came to be identified with the core *macro*economic prescriptions. The number of detailed microeconomic conditions

imposed during the Asian financial crisis highlighted the IMF's embrace of what has come to be identified as "Anglo-Saxon capitalism."

21. Leiderman and Thorne, "Mexico's 1994 Financial Crisis and Its Aftermath: Is the Worst Over?"

22. Solomon, *Money on the Move,* p. 124 and ch. 5.

23. Henning, *The Exchange Stabilization Fund: Slush Money or War Chest?*

24. Goldstein, *The Asian Financial Crisis.*

25. De Gregorio et al., *An Independent and Accountable IMF.*

26. Feldstein, "Refocusing the IMF"; Goldstein, "IMF Structural Programs."

27. Cline, "The Management of Financial Crises."

28. See, for example, Krugman, "Saving Asia: It's Time to Get Radical"; and Stiglitz, "Reforming the Global Economic Architecture."

29. Among the many studies and essays must be listed Eichengreen, *Toward a New International Financial Architecture;* De Gregorio et al., *An Independent and Accountable IMF;* Council on Foreign Relations, *Safeguarding Prosperity in a Global Financial System;* Summers, "International Financial Crises: Causes, Prevention, and Cures"; Meltzer Commission, *Report of the International Financial Institution Advisory Commission;* Overseas Development Council, *The Future Role of the IMF in Development;* and Williamson, "The Role of the IMF."

30. See Meltzer, "Asian Problems and the IMF"; and Calomiris, "Blueprint for a New Financial Architecture."

31. April 6, 1998.

32. Like other aspects of the larger debate on financial architecture, the criteria offered for prequalification reflect differing concerns about moral hazard. In its report, the Meltzer Commission majority insisted that countries should permit foreign bank entry; they should have well-capitalized banks with a degree of subordinated debt; and they should publish the maturity structure of sovereign debt. Meltzer Commission, *Report of the International Financial Institution Advisory Commission.* De Gregorio et al., *An Independent and Accountable IMF,* would require collective action clauses in bond covenants. The Council on Foreign Relations, *Safeguarding Prosperity in a Global Financial System,* recommends adoption of the Basel Core Principles of Banking Supervision.

33. Indeed, the proposal to write off the debts of the poorest nations, the so-called highly indebted poor countries (HIPC) initiative, ran into difficulty in the U.S. Senate because it was not sufficiently linked to measures that would take the fund out of the aid-granting business. See letter from Senators Jesse Helms and Phil Gramm (Republican-Texas) to Secretary of the Treasury Larry Summers, dated September 12, 2000.

34. According to Goldstein, "IMF Structural Programs," the number of conditions specified in "letters of intent" submitted by crisis countries to the fund numbered about fifty. The all-star case was the Indonesia bailout with 140 conditions. For other critiques, see Feldstein, "Refocusing the IMF"; Williamson, "The Role of the IMF;" and Goldstein, "Strengthening the International Financial Architecture."

35. See Goldstein, "Strengthening the International Financial Architecture," for details.

36. Williamson, "The Role of the IMF"; Goldstein "Strengthening the International Financial Architecture."

37. Goldstein, "IMF Structural Programs."

38. *IMF Morning Press,* 27 October 2000.

39. Roubini, "Bail-In, Burden-Sharing, Private Sector Involvement (PSI)," in "Crisis Resolution and Constructive Engagement of the Private Sector."

40. Soros, *The Crisis of Global Capitalism,* goes so far as to declare that the capitalist system is endangered by the kind of international market maneuvers that

made him rich. For a range of proposals on private sector involvement, see Goldstein, *The Asian Financial Crisis*; Persaud, "Sending the Herd Off the Cliff;" and Roubini, "Bail-In, Burden-Sharing, Private Sector Involvement (PSI)."

41. Johnston and Sundarajan, *Sequencing Financial Sector Reforms.*

42. The case for a payments standstill has been advanced by Miller and Zhang, "Sovereign Liquidity Crisis," among others. Differing scholars, such as Eichengreen and Ruehl, "The Bail-In Problem: Systematic Goals, Ad Hoc Means," have argued for collective action clauses in loan agreements.

43. The biggest "forced choice" prior to the Asian crisis was the use of Brady bonds to resolve the third world debt crisis of the 1980s; see Cline, *International Debt Reexamined.*

44. Knight, Schembri, and Powell, "Reforming the Global Financial Architecture."

45. Bergsten, "Towards a Tripartite World."

46. As discussed earlier, The United States sought convertible currencies and fixed exchange rates. It urged other governments to cut public expenditure and raise taxes in times of balance of payments distress. The Europeans instead resorted to transition rules (current account *in*convertibility) and exceptional provisions (devaluing the par value of their currencies). In response, the United States kept a lid on the size of IMF loans.

47. Milner, *Interests, Institutions, and Information,* pp. 143–144.

48. Aaronson, *Trade and the American Dream,* pp. 62–63.

49. Ibid, ch. 8.

50. Milner, *Interests, Institutions, and Information,* p. 137.

51. Jackson, *World Trade and the Law of GATT,* pp. 733–737.

52. Aaronson, *Trade and the American Dream,* ch. 8; Odell, *Negotiating the World Economy,* ch. 8.

53. Gardner, *Sterling-Dollar Diplomacy,* p. xxxiv.

54. Sensitive products were specifically exempted from formula tariff cuts, not only in the Kennedy Round but also in subsequent GATT-WTO negotiations.

55. The American selling price was a customs valuation system that sharply raised the effective tariff rate for products to which it applied (mainly chemicals and rubber footwear).

56. Low, *Trading Free,* p. 70.

57. Ibid., pp. 74–76, presents data showing that from 1960 through 1988 both Japan and the EU spent a higher proportion of national income on subsidies—much higher in the case of the EU. Low also presents data showing that a much higher proportion of Japan's imports are subject to "hard-core" nontariff barriers than those of either the United States or the EU.

58. For a fuller discussion, see Jackson, *The World Trading System.*

59. Detailed data compiled by Robert Hudec show that the number of GATT complaints filed more than tripled, from 32 in the 1970s to 115 in the 1980s. Also, of the 40 cases in the 1980s in which violations were found, 7 resulted in no satisfaction for the plaintiff, up from none in the previous three decades, despite the validity of the complaints. Hudec, *Enforcing International Trade Law,* pp. 287, 290.

60. Council of Economic Advisers, *Economic Report of the President.*

61. Destler and Henning, *Dollar Politics,* p. 26.

62. Richardson, *U.S. Trade Policy in the 1980s,* pp. 21–22.

63. Bayard and Elliott, *Reciprocity and Retaliation in U.S. Trade Policy,* p. 67.

64. Josling, "Agricultural Trade Policy: Completing the Reform."

65. Bhagwati and Patrick, *Aggressive Unilateralism.*

66. Hudec, "Thinking About the New Section 301: Beyond Good and Evil."

67. Chayes and Chayes, "On Compliance," pp. 202–203.

68. Bayard and Elliott, *Reciprocity and Retaliation in U.S. Trade Policy,* pp. 69–71.

69. Bhagwati, "Aggressive Unilateralism: An Overview," pp. 30–33, 36.

70. Maskus, *Intellectual Property Rights in the Global Economy,* ch. 6.

71. The provision, which has been protested by the EU and other trading partners, requires the president to rotate the list of items against which retaliatory tariffs are imposed if the targeted country does not comply with a WTO panel ruling against it within a given amount of time.

72. Oye, *Economic Discrimination and Political Exchange.* For detailed discussion of issues related to the linking of trade and labor standards, see Elliott, "International Labor Standards and Trade"; Elliott, "Getting Beyond No . . . ! Promoting Worker Rights and Trade"; and "The ILO and Enforcement of Core Labor Standards."

73. Goldstein and Martin, "Legalization, Trade Liberalization, and Domestic Politics."

16

Climate Change:
Unilateralism, Realism, and
Two-Level Games

Harold K. Jacobson

FROM THE TIME THAT INTERNATIONAL CONCERN ABOUT ENVIRONMENTAL issues first emerged in the late 1960s and through the 1980s, the United States played a leading role in seeking multilateral solutions. Broad concern for the environment developed in the United States in the late 1960s and reached a peak with the first Earth Day in 1970.[1] In the 1960s the United States passed landmark environmental legislation dealing with water and air. This legislation was capped by the adoption in 1969 of the National Environmental Protection Act. During the 1970s, the United States adopted further legislation, including laws dealing with endangered species and the preservation of the country's cultural and natural heritage.

During the 1970s, led by Russell Train, the administration of President Richard M. Nixon took several international initiatives to protect and enhance the environment. U.S. scholars and policymakers were acutely aware of the intractability of what are termed "commons" problems.[2] They understood that many environmental problems could be solved only by collective action involving all of the largest and most populous states and perhaps even all states. In this period, as soon as U.S. legislation designed to protect and enhance the environment was in place, the United States typically proposed that multilateral treaties be negotiated to achieve the same objectives on a global scale. International efforts to preserve and enhance the environment were seen as essential complements to domestic efforts. Among other motivations, the United States did not want U.S. industry to be at a competitive disadvantage because of domestic environmental regulations.

United States leadership in seeking multilateral solutions to environmental problems continued through the 1980s, though there were exceptions. Washington was notably reluctant to respond to Canadian requests for joint action to limit acid depositions, or in more common terms, acid rain. There was scientific uncertainty about the effects of acid rain and, more important, concern about the potentially significant costs of its mitigation. The United States did not reach an agreement with Canada until 1989, enacting legislation to deal with acid rain the following year in an amended Clean Air Act.[3]

Efforts to protect the ozone layer provided the best example of continued U.S. leadership in seeking multilateral solutions to environmental problems. U.S. scientists were the first to discover the possibility that chlorofluorocarbons might damage the stratospheric ozone layer.[4] The U.S. government took the lead in developing broad international scientific agreement that this finding was correct.[5] Then the United States, during the Reagan administration, led negotiations to create the 1985 Vienna Convention, the framework treaty dealing with substances that deplete the stratospheric ozone layer, and the 1987 Montreal Protocol, which committed the parties to phase out the production and consumption of chlorofluorocarbons.

Viewed against this history of constructive leadership of multilateral approaches to protect the global environment, United States policy during the 1990s with respect to climate change appeared to signify a change in course. In the 1990s, the United States was often at odds with other countries, including its closest allies. Does this appearance represent reality? Did the U.S. government shift from multilateralism to unilateralism in dealing with global environmental issues? Did it reject multilateralism? Or did the U.S. ability to affect the outcomes of multilateral negotiations diminish? Did the nature of multilateral outcomes change? Or was it simply that efforts to deal with climate change raised different issues from those involved in earlier international efforts to protect and enhance the environment? To the extent that the United States did move away from multilateralism, what is the explanation? How did the two-level game that a U.S. president must inevitably play affect the process?[6] A U.S. president must simultaneously negotiate with the international partners to an agreement and with the Senate, which according to the Constitution must give its advice and consent to the ratification of any treaty, and with domestic constituents, whose compliance would be essential for a treaty to be effective. The debate about global efforts to mitigate climate change, particularly the Kyoto Protocol, is at the center of these issues.

The Kyoto Protocol

On December 10, 1997, the Third Session of the Conference of the Parties (COP III) of the UN Framework Convention on Climate Change (UN-FCCC) completed the Kyoto Protocol. The Kyoto Protocol would require the developed, or in the technical language of the protocol, "Annex I," countries to reduce their overall greenhouse gas (GHG) emissions "by at least five percent below their 1990 levels in the commitment period 2008 to 2012."[7] Environmental activists, many NGOs, the EU, and the governments of many states had long sought limitations on GHG.

Immediately after COP III adopted the Kyoto Protocol, Republican Senator Chuck Hagel of Nebraska, a congressional observer at the conference, announced in a press conference: "There is no way, if the President signs this, that the vote in the United States Senate will even be close. We will kill this bill." John Kerry, a Democratic Senator from Massachusetts who was also an observer at the conference, said in an interview that the protocol was "not ratifiable" in his judgment.[8]

The United States signed the Kyoto Protocol during COP IV, which met in Buenos Aires in November 1998, but President Clinton did not submit the protocol to the Senate for its advice and consent to ratification. The Kyoto Protocol was an issue in the 2000 presidential election. Vice-President Al Gore, the Democratic Party candidate, argued that the protocol should be ratified, while his Republican rival, Governor George W. Bush of Texas, maintained that it should not be ratified in its present form. President Clinton did not submit the Kyoto Protocol to the Senate before his term of office ended, and President George W. Bush indicated that he would not submit it.

During the election campaign, in response to a question about climate change posed by *Science* (the official publication of the American Association for the Advancement of Science), George W. Bush said that as president he would "work for a comprehensive, fair, and effective agreement—one that harnesses the power of the marketplace and encourages international efforts to develop the technologies to reduce greenhouse gas emissions." He said that he believed that market-based mechanisms would work to mitigate climate change. He said that he supported "investing in technologies that rely on clean, abundant, renewable energy sources, as well as the development of cleaner cars and cleaner burning fuels and alternative sources of fuel and new fuel alternatives."[9]

In the years following COP III, environmental activists, many NGOs, the EU, and the governments of some other states pushed for ratification of the Kyoto Protocol. Some spoke of going ahead without the United States, arguing that it would eventually have to follow. How successful this strategy could be was questionable. Since the protocol cannot enter into effect until it has been ratified by 55 states, including those that accounted for fifty-five percent of carbon dioxide emissions by the Annex I countries in 1990, failure by the United States and one other major country (such as the Russian Federation) to become parties to the protocol would prevent the treaty from coming into force. U.S. emissions accounted for more than a third of the 1990 totals for Annex I countries.

Whether the Kyoto Protocol, with or without modifications, ever comes into force, the international debate about it reflected a longstanding disagreement between the United States and other countries about how best to deal collectively with the problem of climate change. To some extent, these disagreements about the form multilateralism should take extended beyond climate change to other environmental issues.

Overview of the Case

The United States has long disagreed with environmental activists, many NGOs, and several other countries about limiting GHG emissions. This disagreement first drew public attention in June 1988, when Canada organized a nongovernmental conference in Toronto on "The Changing Atmosphere: Implications for Global Security." The gathering called for a 20 percent cut in global carbon emissions from 1988 levels by 2005, and an eventual 50 percent cut.[10] Although Vice-President George Bush, then a Republican presidential candidate, pledged that as president he would use the "White House effect" to counter the greenhouse effect, neither he nor the Reagan administration showed any willingness to accept targets for emissions reductions.

In contrast to this reluctance to accept specified quantitative emissions limitations, in November 1988 the United States instigated the creation of an Intergovernmental Panel on Climate Change (IPCC), under the auspices of the UN Environment Program and the World Meteorological Organization. The purpose of the IPCC is to assess periodically the state of scientific knowledge relevant for national and international policy about climate change and to make public the results of its assessments. U.S. scientists played prominent and important roles in the IPCC, and the United States has provided a substantial portion of the funds to support the panel.

The IPCC's first assessment, released in 1990, provided the scientific basis for the negotiation of the UNFCCC.[11] The report concluded that there was a natural greenhouse effect that "already keeps the Earth warmer than it would otherwise be" and that "emissions resulting from human activities were substantially increasing the atmospheric concentration of the greenhouse gases."[12] It further concluded that if emissions continued as projected under a "business as usual scenario," the rate of increase of global mean temperature would be 0.3 degrees Celsius per decade, resulting in a likely increase of 3.0 degrees Celsius before the end of the twenty-first century. It also projected an average rate of global mean sea level rise of about 6 centimeters per decade.

IPCC's second assessment, released in 1995, provided the scientific basis for the negotiation of the Kyoto Protocol. The IPCC's assessments reaffirmed the scientific consensus that the greenhouse effect was real and that anthropogenic (or human-created) factors were contributing to climate change. The report of IPCC's Working Group II contained a detailed assessment of the impacts of climate change and the potentialities and costs of measures to adapt to or attempt to mitigate climate change.[13] Robert T. Watson, Marufu Zinyowera, and Richard H. Moss were the editors of the report. Dr. Watson was a senior official in the Office of Science and Technology Policy in the Executive Office of the President of the United States. Dr. Moss, an employee of the Battelle Pacific Northwest Laboratory, headed the Technical Support Unit of the Working Group. The report identified potentially serious changes, "including an increase in some regions in the incidence of extreme high-temperature events, floods and droughts, with resultant consequences for fires, pest outbreaks, and ecosystem composition, structure, and functioning, including primary production."[14] It also concluded that "human health, terrestrial and aquatic ecological systems, and socioeconomic systems (e.g. agriculture, forestry, fisheries, water resources) are all vital to human development and well-being and are all sensitive to changes in climate."[15] U.S. scientists, both in the private sector and in official government positions, were clearly part of the consensus that the potential consequences of climate change were sufficiently serious to merit action.

The United States had earlier played a major role in the creation in 1979 of the World Climate Research Program (WCRP) and, subsequently, in the development of WCRP's program. The U.S. government had also been instrumental in the formation of the broader International Geosphere-Biosphere Programme in 1986. The United States had thus acknowledged well before the 1988 Toronto Conference that climate change was a potential problem of enormous significance, and it had sought to gain better understanding of the problem through research.

After George Bush became president in January 1989, the United States stepped up its own research on global change broadly and climate change specifically. The United States launched a Global Change Research Program in 1989, formalizing this in 1990 in the Global Change Research Act. In 1991 President Bush elevated the Environmental Protection Agency (EPA), which President Nixon had created by executive order in 1970, to cabinet rank, thus increasing its status in intergovernment affairs. But, while the United States increased its own research activities and supported increased international research, it approached the Second World Climate Conference in 1990 cautiously. The United States refused to announce an emissions limitation target at the conference, even though some states did.

The Bush administration played a major part in drafting the UNFCCC, a process that started shortly after the Second World Climate Conference. President Bush, however, let it be known that he would not attend the 1992 UN Conference on Environment and Development in Rio de Janeiro, where the convention would be adopted, if that convention contained emissions reduction targets. By contrast, Canada, the European Community, several other countries, and numerous NGOs pushed hard for including targets in the treaty.

Eventually, the negotiators accepted the U.S. position with varying degrees of reluctance and criticism. According to article 2 of the UNFCCC, the ultimate objective of the convention is the "stabilization of greenhouse gas concentrations in the atmosphere at a level that would prevent dangerous anthropogenic interference with the climate system." Significantly the objective of the treaty refers to atmospheric concentrations, not emissions. Article 4, paragraph 2, of the UNFCCC merely commits the developed country parties to the convention to accept the aim of reducing their GHG emissions to 1990 levels by the year 2000. More precise limitations were left to subsequent negotiations.

The United States ratified the UNFCCC on October 15, 1992. During the debate on ratification, the Democrats, who were in control of the Senate, argued that the United States should have gone even further and agreed to emissions limitations. Only three states, Mauritius, the Seychelles, and the Marshall Islands, became parties to the UNFCCC before the United States did. The European Economic Community (EEC—the EU is a party to the treaty under the legal authority embodied in the treaty establishing the EEC) did not become a party to the treaty until December 21, 1993, and several of its member states became parties even later.

Environmental issues were not prominent features in the 1992 presidential election campaign, but Governor Bill Clinton of Arkansas, the Democratic candidate, argued that his administration would be more pro-environment than a second Bush administration. Clinton's running mate, vice-presidential candidate Al Gore, proclaimed his strong concern for environmental issues in his book *Earth in the Balance,* which was published that year.[16] He made a forceful argument in the book that action had to be taken to stop global warming.

Even before the UNFCCC entered into force on March 21, 1994, pressures had begun for the negotiation of GHG emissions limitation targets. These pressures mounted, and the first Conference of the Parties in Berlin in the spring of 1995 adopted the Berlin Mandate. Among other things, the Berlin Mandate specified that negotiations should be launched to establish quantified limitation and reduction objectives for the Annex I countries, targets that should be met within specified time frames.

At the second Conference of the Parties in Geneva in July 1996, Tim Wirth, U.S. Undersecretary of State for Global Affairs, called for negotiations on an agreement to set "a realistic, verifiable and binding medium-term emissions target."[17] This marked the first time that any major state party to the UNFCCC had called for quantified emission limitations to be made binding. Wirth's statement and the positions that the United States pursued helped to energize and shape the negotiations.

Many issues were involved in the negotiations that resulted in the Kyoto Protocol. Participants discussed and debated which GHGs would be included in the emissions limitations, the time frame for achieving the limitations, the quantified nature of the limitations, whether "sinks" that absorb GHG emissions would be counted, and whether flexible mechanisms for achieving limitations would be allowed. The U.S. position prevailed in most of these issues, except that of the level of quantified emissions limitations.

President Clinton initially directed the U.S. delegation to the Kyoto conference to agree only to stabilize GHG emissions at 1990 levels by 2008 to 2012. Subsequently, Vice-President Gore, who joined the U.S. delegation in the last days of COP III and spoke to a plenary session, personally intervened to obtain the president's authorization for U.S. agreement to lower its limitation to 93 percent of its 1990 level.

The EU and several other states—including those in the Association of Small Island States, composed of countries that would be inundated by the sea-level rise caused by climate change—insisted that the protocol contain a stronger commitment from Annex I countries that went beyond stabilizing GHG emissions at 1990s levels. It was widely reported in the media that COP III would fail unless the United States agreed to reduce its emissions below 1990 levels. The shift in the U.S. position was carefully scripted. It was a very visible effort to prevent the failure of COP III. In addition, it pleased environmental groups who were an important component of Vice-President Gore's core supporters and would play an important role in his presidential election bid.

Another major issue—the participation of developing countries—was not officially on the agenda at Kyoto, but it certainly was on the minds of many of the participants and observers. The UNFCCC creates differential obligations for developed (Annex I) countries and developing (non-Annex I) countries. The first principle of the UNFCCC is that "the Parties should protect the climate system for the benefit of present and future generations of humankind, on the basis of equity and in accordance with their common but differentiated responsibilities and respective capabilities."[18] Under Article 2, Annex I countries are required to adopt policies and take measures to limit GHG emissions. Developing country parties are required only to conduct inventories of their emissions by sources and removals by sinks and to communicate these to the secretariat. The Berlin Mandate specified that the Kyoto negotiations should focus on establishing limitations for Annex I countries.

The principal rationale contained in the UNFCCC for requiring the developed countries to initiate the process of limiting GHG emissions is that the developed countries have historically been the largest emitters. In addition, compared with the GHG emissions of developed countries, the emissions of developing countries are generally low on a per capita basis. The UNFCCC acknowledges that economic development must occur in non-Annex I countries and that this will result in increased GHG emissions. In containing differential obligations for developed and developing countries, the UNFCC follows the model created by both the 1985 Vienna Convention for Protection of the Ozone Layer and the 1987 Montreal Protocol.

Many commentators in the United States and elsewhere felt that developing countries needed to do more than the UNFCCC required of them. Before the start of COP III, on July 25, 1997, the Senate by a vote of 95 to 0 adopted a resolution cosponsored by Senators Robert Byrd (Democrat-West Virginia) and Chuck Hagel.[19] The resolution stated that the United States would not agree to a treaty limiting U.S. GHG emissions unless limitations were also applied to developing countries. The resolution also specified that an agreement should not result in serious harm to the U.S. economy.

The resolution would require the president, when submitting any treaty on climate change to the Senate, to accompany the treaty with two documents. One should give a detailed explanation of any domestic legislation or regulations that would be required to implement the agreement. The other should give a detailed analysis of the economic and financial costs that would be incurred by the United States in implementing the agreement.

Critics in the Senate, joined by representatives of industry and labor, argued that unless developing countries were included in the emission limitation requirement, the United States and other developed countries would be at an economic disadvantage. Some opponents of the protocol argued that it would encourage industry to move from industrialized to developing countries. Many pointed out that within the near future, GHG emissions from developing countries would exceed those from developed countries. They argued that it was essential for developing countries to accept some form of emissions limitations; otherwise the effects of decreased emissions by the industrialized countries would be nullified by the increased emissions of developing countries.

During the debate on the Byrd-Hagel resolution, senators insisted that they did not desire to limit economic growth in developing countries and they implied that they understood that the GHG emissions of developing countries would increase.[20] But they wanted these increases to be controlled.

The Clinton administration was caught off guard by the Byrd-Hagel resolution. It did not learn of the resolution until shortly before it was to be considered by the Senate. At that point its lobbyists could only urge that the language of the resolution be softened; they could not prevent the resolution's adoption. The situation was complicated by the fact that Byrd is a prominent Democrat and the administration had to rely on Hagel, a moderate Republican, for support on a number of issues. The production of coal is an important component of the economy of Senator Byrd's state, West Virginia. Agriculture is the most important economic activity in Nebraska, Senator Hagel's state. The mechanized agriculture practiced in Nebraska is very sensitive to fuel prices.

At the Kyoto conference, Vice-President Gore promised that the Clinton administration would not submit the Kyoto Protocol to the Senate until "key" developing countries had agreed to participate in some form in the effort to limit GHG emissions. Before President Clinton signed the Kyoto Protocol, Argentina and Kazakhstan agreed to accept voluntary limitations on their GHG emissions. This did not assuage senatorial concern, however. Senators were principally concerned about the large developing countries such as Brazil, China, India, and Indonesia.

The lack of developing-country participation was not the only reason that the Senate voiced objections to the Kyoto Protocol. Many senators felt that the United States could not achieve the 7 percent reduction from 1990 levels of GHG emissions without seriously harming the U.S. economy. By the end of 1999, U.S. GHG emissions were about 13 percent above 1990 levels, and they were projected to be 26 percent above 1990 levels by 2010. For the United States to meet the Kyoto target, it would have to reduce its emissions by about 30 percent from the projected level for 2010.

The Global Climate Coalition has been the principal industry group lobbying against the Kyoto Protocol. Founded in 1989, and based in Washington, D.C., as of 2001 it represented over 6 million businesses and industries in virtually all sectors of the U.S. economy. The Global Climate Coalition acknowledges that climate change is a serious long-term problem. Nevertheless, it has consistently taken the position that the targets and timetables called for under the Kyoto Protocol are unrealistic and "are not achievable without severely harming the U.S. economy and all American families, workers, seniors and children."[21] Although the Clinton administration strongly disputed this charge, the coalition fought the adoption of the Kyoto Protocol and has continued to lobby against its ratification.

Willingness to become a party to the Kyoto Protocol was only one area in which the United States diverged from many other countries on environmental issues during the 1990s. The Bush administration, for example, refused to sign the Convention on Biological Diversity, the other major convention completed at the UN Conference on Environment and Development in Rio de Janeiro in 1992, and which came into force on December 29, 1993. As of 2000 there were 177 parties to the convention. Although President Clinton signed the treaty on June 4, 1993, by the end of his second term in January 2001, he had not submitted it to the Senate for its advice on and consent to ratification. Similarly, the United States has parted ways with its allies and most other countries in refusing to ratify the 1982 Convention on the Law of the Sea (amended 1994), which contains environmental protection provisions. In both of these cases, the United States played an active and frequently a leading role in the negotiation of the conventions, and it was only after certain provisions had been written into the conventions that U.S. opposition developed.

In broad historical context these cases are exceptional. As mentioned above, starting before the UN Conference on the Human Environment in 1972, the United States has generally been an active participant and most often a leader in multilateral efforts to protect the environment.[22] The nation played a major role in drafting most international environmental accords, which have often been fashioned after domestic U.S. legislation. The United States is a party to the overwhelming majority of these accords, and it has played a leading role in seeking to promote compliance with them. And despite its reluctance about emissions limitations and the Kyoto Protocol, the United States was a leader in climate change research and negotiations throughout the 1990s.

Assessment of Causes

Given the broad historical record of U.S. participation and leadership in multilateral efforts to protect the environment, why was the United States unwilling to ratify the 1997 Kyoto Protocol, the 1992 Convention on Biological Diversity, and the 1982 Convention on the Law of the Sea? Did this unwillingness reflect a basic shift in U.S. policy or a broad change in the fit between U.S. objectives and the outcomes of multilateral processes? Or was it the result of factors that are specific to the issues involved, particularly climate change?

To some extent climate change is a special case. Several factors relating to the problem create particular difficulties for the United States. To begin with, U.S. emissions of GHG have long been greater than those of any other state. On a per capita basis, U.S. GHG emissions in the 1990s exceeded those of any major country; only Australia's and Canada's came close. This has made the United States an inviting target for environmental activists and NGOs because the level of its GHG emissions has seemed immoral to many.

U.S. emissions have been so high and have been growing since the Rio Conference in 1992 for several reasons. The size of the United States and the distances that Americans travel domestically are factors, as is the country's climate. (These same factors help explain why Australia and Canada also have high per capita emissions.)

Geography aside, as a general proposition GHG emissions are a product of a country's population multiplied by its level of development, modified by the country's energy efficiency. During the 1990s, the U.S. population and economy grew more rapidly than those of the EU countries or Japan, and this was a factor in increasing U.S. emissions.

The high level of U.S. GHG emissions is also the result of individual preferences and public policies. Residential patterns in the United States, which emphasize single-family housing on relatively large plots of land, limit the use of public transport. Partly because of its historic role as a petroleum producer, the United States is addicted to inexpensive energy, especially cheap gasoline. American consumers have a strong aversion to increasing taxes on petroleum or other carbon-based sources of energy. When the Clinton administration took office, it sought to enact a "BTU tax" (for British thermal unit, a standard measure of energy) on the energy content of fuels. This would have raised the price of petroleum, electricity, and other forms of energy. Opposition in the Senate, which at the time was controlled by the Democratic Party, killed the proposal, but the administration was able to get Congress to enact a gasoline tax of 4.3 cents per gallon. This tax was attacked by Republicans and was repealed in 1996. The price of petroleum remains much lower in the United States than in Western Europe and Japan, where governments have been able to enact high taxes. Finally, the strength of the antinuclear movement in the United States limits U.S. reliance on nuclear power as a source of non GHG-producing energy.

Whatever the proportion of geography, population and economic growth, individual preferences, and public policy in determining the high level of U.S. GHG emissions, it is clear that limiting such emissions poses formidable difficulties for the United States. Not all countries face the same difficulties. The EU's GHG emissions in the aggregate actually fell during the first half of the 1990s, largely due to significant declines in the emissions of Germany and Britain. Germany's emissions fell because of the collapse of the economy of the former East Germany, and Britain's because of the conversion from coal-powered to natural gas–powered electricity production. By 2000, however, the EU's aggregate emissions were approximately at the level that they had been in 1990.[23]

Similarly, the emissions of all of the former communist countries declined in the 1990s because of the collapse of their economies. Compared with the United States, the EU and the economies in transition also all had significantly lower (even declining) population growth rates.

Another factor responsible for the divergent attitudes between the United States and other countries toward the Kyoto Protocol is the U.S. position regarding treaties. Simply put, the United States will not ratify treaties unless it feels that it can comply with them. In the United States private parties can sue the government, seeking an injunction to force it to comply with a treaty that has been ratified and consequently has become the law of the land. Few other countries allow this. Given the strength of environmental activism and environmental NGOs in the United States, there would be a strong possibility of legal action that would be brought to force the government to comply with the Kyoto Protocol if the United States were a party but not in compliance.

Many other countries, including some members of the EU, sign and ratify treaties that contain commitments that their governments know they will have difficulty fulfilling; these commitments are regarded as targets that they will seek to achieve rather than obligations that they will have to fulfill. This difference in approaches to treaty obligations explains why Undersecretary of State Wirth insisted that the negotiators working within the framework of the Berlin Mandate create "realistic, verifiable, and binding" targets; the U.S. goal was to make all parties take emissions limitations as seriously as the United States would have to. The U.S. government is serious about prohibiting free riding by countries that take their obligations less seriously, particularly in treaties with the potential economic significance of the UNFCCC and the Kyoto Protocol.

Among the Annex I countries, the United States arguably possesses the least regulated economy. Many U.S. senators and other government officials have been concerned that efforts to deal with climate change would involve substantial governmental regulation of the national economy. Accordingly, in the negotiations that led to the protocol, U.S. negotiators fought against European efforts to insert treaty provisions for uniform policies and measures, such as a requirement that appliances have a certain level of energy efficiency. It is also why the United States fought to include "flexible mechanisms" and the possibility of getting credit for "sinks," such as forests that absorb carbon dioxide, into the protocol.

The United States was successful on both counts. The Kyoto Protocol does not include requirements for policies and measures and it does include three flexible mechanisms and the possibility of getting credit for sinks. One flexible mechanism is emission trading, which permits Annex I countries to trade emission allowances. If the United States had difficulty meeting its required limitations, for example, it would be allowed to purchase emission allowances from a state that had lower emissions than its limitation. The Russian Federation was expected to be the major country most likely to be in a position to sell emission allowances because of the collapse of its economy. Joint implementation is another flexible mechanism, allowing countries to share credit for cooperative initiatives. For example, if the United States engaged in a project to increase the sinks through reforestation in the Russian Federation, as it is doing on a pilot basis, the United States and Russia could share the credit for the increased sink. The third flexible mechanism is the clean development mechanism. This would allow Annex I countries that engage in projects in non-Annex I countries that reduce prospective emissions to share the credit for this reduction. For example, if a U.S. firm builds an electrical power plant in Mexico that produced fewer emissions than one built by Mexicans, both countries could share the credit for the difference between the actual and projected emissions.

Estimating the costs for any country's fulfilling the Kyoto Protocol's emissions limitation commitments is extremely difficult. The estimated costs depend on multiple assumptions about population and economic growth, technological change, evolving preferences, and how much credit will be allowed under the flexible mechanisms.[24] It is clear that the costs for the United States would be substantially higher without flexible mechanisms and credit for sinks. One economist said that without flexible mechanisms "the United States could only meet its obligations under the Kyoto protocol if it suffered three successive major economic recessions." The United States has argued that countries should be able to completely fulfill their commitments by using flexible mechanisms and sinks. The EU and its member countries have sought to limit the use of such mechanisms.

Disagreement on this issue was the major factor causing the collapse of negotiations at the Sixth Conference of the Parties in The Hague in November 2000. The Clinton administration offered a compromise that would limit the amount of a country's required emissions reduction that could be offset by flexible mechanisms and sinks. Although the EU's negotiator, John Prescott, Great Britain's environment minister, accepted the proposal, other

EU member countries met to discuss it and rejected it. The French environment minister, Dominique Voynet, was adamantly opposed. Meanwhile, the Clinton administration had repeatedly assured the American public that if the United States were permitted to use flexible mechanisms and sinks, the cost of fulfilling its Kyoto obligations would be minimal.

Whatever arrangements are ultimately worked out about the use of flexible mechanisms and sinks, long-term efforts to reduce GHG emissions will have serious consequences for the United States, involving most if not all aspects of its economy. Even if the effort were focused only on carbon dioxide emissions, which account for the largest share of GHG emissions, the effects on the U.S. economy would be enormous because of the heavy dependence of the transport and energy sectors on burning fossil fuels.

The economic consequences of dealing with climate change stand in sharp contrast to the task of controlling substances that deplete the ozone layer. Such substances—principally chlorofluorocarbons—now account for only a small segment of the U.S. economy. By the time the United States had taken the lead in seeking a multilateral agreement to phase out the production and consumption of chlorofluorocarbons, U.S. manufacturers had discovered substitutes for them. By contrast, as of 2001, there are no reasonably priced substitutes for the internal combustion engines that continue to power cars in the United States. There are also no reasonably priced substitutes for the carbon dioxide–emitting methods by which the United States produces energy, other than nuclear energy, which is of course politically controversial. Thus the economic consequences of attempting to deal with climate change are serious.

Differences in political systems also help explain the divergences between the position of the United States on climate change issues and the positions of other countries. The U.S. Constitution requires that the Senate give its advice on and consent to ratification of any international treaty by a two-thirds majority vote. This establishes a requirement for domestic consensus that is substantially higher than that required in other countries. The separation of power between the executive and legislative branches in the United States invites a struggle for the control of policy, a situation that does not occur in a parliamentary system where the executive can rely on its parliamentary majority to approve its proposals.

Within the executive branch itself, international environmental policy is shaped by the contributions of multiple agencies and departments, which go well beyond the State Department and the EPA. The Council of Economic Advisers, Office of Management and Budget, and Agriculture, Commerce, Interior, and Treasury departments all play a more important role in the formulation of policies on climate change than do their counterpart ministries and departments in Japan and EU member countries. Consequently, the United States has paid a great deal more attention to the potential economic costs of emissions limitations than have other countries, with extensive government and private efforts in the United States to estimate these costs.

Political dynamics in the United States also differ from those in the EU and Japan. For several reasons, including electoral laws, green parties can be potent political forces in a number of European countries. The Green Party is less important in the United States, however, where electoral laws favor a two-party system. In the United States, moreover, significant segments of industry and labor have objected to emissions limitation broadly and to the Kyoto Protocol specifically, whereas industry and labor have not been as vocally opposed to the protocol in Europe and Japan.

Some of the general factors that have affected U.S. policy on climate change are also important in explaining U.S. policy toward the Convention on Biological Diversity and the Law of the Sea, as well as other, nonenvironmental, issues. This is the case with respect to the peculiarities of the U.S. political system, especially the requirement that two-thirds of the senators approve the ratification of treaties and the caution about agreeing to treaties unless U.S. compliance can be assured.

The United States has objected to particular provisions of the Convention on Biodiversity and the Law of the Sea. In both cases, the treaties contained elements of the redistributive ideology prevalent in the UN General Assembly in the 1970s and early 1980s, when countries of the global South demanded the creation of a new international economic order (NIEO). For example, the United States objected to provisions in the Convention on Biological Diversity requiring that the results and benefits of research on biotechnology be shared with the countries from which the genetic resources were obtained. Likewise, the United States objected to provisions of the Convention on the Law of the Sea mandating the sharing of benefits from deep-sea mining with developing countries, as well as provisions for amending parts of the convention that implied that amendments could become binding even on parties that did not accept them. The United States further objected to the efforts by proponents of the NIEO to create mechanisms for the automatic and unconditional transfer of resources to developing countries.

There was a contradiction, in a way, between U.S. policy on climate change and its policy on biological diversity and the law of the sea: flexible mechanisms in the Kyoto Protocol could result in a transfer of resources to developing countries. These transfers, however, would be shaped more by market forces than by decisions of international institutions. Such an outcome would be consistent with the general U.S. preference for market-based solutions to problems involving the global commons.

Consequences

The consequences of the Senate's hostility toward the Kyoto Protocol are hard to estimate. As of late 2000, environmental activists, environmental

NGOs, and other states party to the UNFCCC continued to hope that the United States would eventually ratify the protocol, and they devoted substantial efforts to trying to bring this about. Since most of these efforts through the year 2000 were directed primarily at the Clinton administration, it was not clear how they would affect the Senate, where obstacles to ratification are impressive. As indicated by the unanimous vote on the Byrd-Hagel resolution, there is widespread opposition in the Senate to the approach taken in the Kyoto Protocol. Nor was it clear what impact the pressures of environmental activists and NGOs and other governments will have on the new Bush administration.

Developments in the private sector could have a larger impact on senatorial opinion and the Bush administration than pressure from other governments and NGOs. In the spring of 2000, Ford, Daimler-Chrysler, and General Motors all withdrew from the Global Climate Coalition, the principal industry-labor lobbying group that strongly opposes the Kyoto Protocol. British Petroleum, Dow Chemicals, Shell Oil, and Texaco have also left the group. The withdrawal of these major firms has weakened the Global Climate Coalition and spurred it to alter its strategy and tactics. Some business leaders have concluded that a shift from burning fossil fuels to other sources is inevitable and that there are advantages to leading rather than resisting the shift. Over time the Senate might respond to pressure from U.S. businesses.

Nevertheless, it seems unlikely that the United States will ever ratify the protocol without some modification to it. There were, after all, modifications to the Law of the Sea Convention, as parties to the convention adopted understandings about the deep-sea mining provisions that were intended to assuage U.S. concerns. Similarly, the parties to the Convention on Biological Diversity have sought to reassure the United States on intellectual property and patent concerns. In neither of the two cases, however, has the modification strategy produced U.S. ratification. Modest changes to the Kyoto Protocol, such as extending the timeframe for compliance, probably will not sway senatorial opposition, either.

The parties to the Convention on Biodiversity and the Law of the Sea have proceeded without the United States. Secretariats have been established and conferences have been held. Budgets established for the operations mandated by these conventions rested on the assumption that the United States would participate, and at a substantial level, but the U.S. failure to ratify the conventions forced revision of the budgets and necessitated increased contributions by all parties, particularly developed countries.

The Cartagena Protocol on Biosafety, which was completed in January 2000, was the first protocol to be negotiated under the Convention on Biological Diversity. The United States, as a signatory to the convention, participated in the negotiations on the protocol. Despite its participation, however, it was unable to block the inclusion of treaty provisions to which it objected. Whether the United States would have been in a stronger position had it been a party to the convention is impossible to know. It could be argued that other countries should have been especially sensitive to U.S. views in the hope of inducing the United States to join the convention. On the other hand, other countries might have felt that since the United States was unlikely to ratify the convention, its views might as well be ignored.

In the case of the Convention on Biodiversity and the Law of the Sea, the position of other countries vis-à-vis the United States is somewhat different than in the case of climate change. The United States' capacity in biotechnology is incredibly strong, but it is not unique. Developing countries are the largest source of genetic materials, increasing their leverage. Moreover, U.S. vessels traverse straits, territorial seas, and exclusive economic zones controlled by many countries. In other words, other countries control assets that are important to the United States, and they have power to shape the terms on which they interact with the United States. At the same time, the United States could benefit from both conventions without being a party to them. In the case of the Law of the Sea, the United States has declared that the parts of the convention that it likes have become customary international law. The United States has announced that it will adhere to these norms and it expects other countries to do likewise. Similarly, the 177 state parties to the Convention on Biological Diversity have committed themselves to taking steps to preserve biological diversity. Because of its scientific and financial resources, the United States can benefit from the genetic resources that are preserved, even though it is not a party to the convention.

Climate change poses more daunting collective action problems. For climate change to be addressed successfully, the largest emitter of GHG must be part of the effort. The United States has enormous scientific and technical capacities that are relevant to addressing the problems involved with climate change. Other countries need the United States to take part. Finally, the United States is vulnerable to climate change, and climate change in other parts of the world could have serious implications for the United States. In short, the United States has strong self-interest in doing something about climate change.

Policy Lessons and Recommendations

What can be learned from this case? The U.S. position has regularly diverged from that of many countries, including the member states of the EU and Japan. Despite this, the United States played a leading role in the negotiation of the UNFCCC, and other countries ultimately accepted (if grudgingly) the U.S. position that the convention should not contain binding emissions limitations. The United States was one of the first states to ratify the UNFCCC, and it played a leading role in the negotiation of the Kyoto Protocol, during which many of its positions were accepted. In the end, though, the protocol drew strong opposition in the Senate, and as of January 2001, it seemed unlikely that the protocol would ever be ratified.

Several questions can be asked. The most fundamental is whether any protocol could have been negotiated that the Senate would have ratified. There are many questions within this question, and some related to the international negotiations. Could U.S. negotiators have held firm and blocked the inclusion of provisions that drew Senate fire? The shift in the U.S. target for limiting U.S. emissions by 2008 to 2012 from 1990 levels to 93 percent of 1990 levels was particularly troubling to many in the Senate. Could more have been done to obtain commitments from developing countries as demanded by the Byrd-Hagel resolution? Another set of questions concerns domestic U.S. political processes. Could the Clinton administration have done more to persuade the Senate to take a favorable attitude to the Kyoto Protocol? Could the Clinton administration have done more to mobilize popular support for efforts to limit GHG emissions and thus for the protocol? In other words, could the two-level game have been played differently and more effectively?

Although these questions cannot be answered definitively, there are facts that are relevant to thinking about plausible answers. In the 1990s, participants in international conferences in a variety of fields insisted on including in treaties provisions to which the United States had strong objections. Representatives of NGOs, who were increasingly numerous at international conferences, frequently urged the conferees to include such provisions. Often these NGO representatives were U.S. citizens, who were in effect using an international forum to try to obtain objectives they were unable to obtain in the domestic arena. In the end, however, such provisions were included in treaties only if approved by official government delegations, so that governments, rather than NGOs, must take responsibility for the conventions that resulted. NGOs may have nudged governments but they did not determine their policies. After the end of the Cold War, countries may have become more willing to oppose the United States than they were when security issues structured international relations more. Moreover, as the overwhelming strength of the United States became increasingly apparent in the 1990s, many countries became worried about and resentful of U.S. hegemony. Treaty negotiations provided an outlet for expressing this resentment.

It may be that in these negotiations the Clinton administration sometimes created the impression that it too preferred the outcome sought by the NGOs and other, more supportive governments. Sometimes, as in Kyoto, the United States did give in to pressures at conferences. Resisting pressures to insert provisions that the United States found objectionable had become harder in the 1990s because these pressures had grown more intense. Still, with respect to climate change, the Clinton administration's resistance was less wholehearted than that of some of its predecessors.

With respect to the domestic level of the two-level game, the Clinton administration was unable to work effectively with Congress on climate change issues. In 1993 and 1994 the Democratic Party controlled both the House of Representatives and the Senate, but despite this seemingly favorable situation, the administration was unsuccessful in its efforts to enact a BTU tax. The Clinton administration also periodically submitted climate change action plans to Congress. These plans generally sought to obtain emissions reductions through voluntary programs that would encourage changes in behavior through the provision of incentives and government-sponsored research that would stimulate innovations by the private sector. Congress, however, remained reluctant to enact the proposed tax incentives and refused to appropriate the level of funds the administration sought for research on alternative sources of energy. Then in 1994, the relationship between the administration and Congress deteriorated after the Republicans gained control of both houses.

The Byrd-Hagel resolution was a bipartisan attempt to tie the administration's hands in the negotiations leading up to COP III and the drafting of the Kyoto Protocol. Because the resolution was adopted unanimously, it was a clear warning to the administration, and because the administration was not aware of the resolution until late in the game, its own lobbyists could not block the resolution's adoption. Perhaps the administration may even have thought that the resolution would strengthen its position in the negotiations: the administration appears to have thought that it could get developing countries to make some sort of commitments. But it did not succeed sufficiently to persuade the Senate.

The Clinton administration's failure to forge a bipartisan coalition to deal with climate change and other issues resembled Woodrow Wilson's failure to work with the Republican-controlled Senate to secure the ratification of the Covenant of the League of Nations. In sharp contrast, President Franklin D. Roosevelt worked extensively with Senator Arthur Vandenberg and other Republicans to ensure that the Senate would give its advice and consent to the ratification of the UN Charter.[25] This bipartisanship continued through the first decades of the post–World War II era. Because the Senate must give its advice and consent to the ratification of treaties by a two-thirds majority vote, bipartisan collaboration is essential in efforts to create international law. And never in U.S. history has the president's party controlled two-thirds of the seats in the Senate.

The Clinton administration did not mount a large-scale effort to mobilize public support for serious action to deal with climate change. Neither the president, nor the vice-president, nor other high officials discussed the issue sufficiently in major speeches, the administration having other priorities. Public support for strong action might not have changed senatorial opinion, but public support could have countered some of the highly vocal opposition to the steps envisaged in the Kyoto Protocol.

Whatever the answers to these broad questions about the dynamics during the decade of the 1990s of the two-level game on climate change, the

United States is likely to continue to play a major role in the efforts to deal with climate change. U.S. interests are at stake, the nation is a major contributor to the problem, and U.S. scientific, technological, and economic resources are essential to efforts to mitigate climate change. But the prospects for successful international environmental action to deal with climate change do not necessarily need to be seen as bleak. Because GHG emissions stay in the atmosphere for so long, climate change is a long-term problem. Given that the global population is likely to continue increasing at least through the first half of the twenty-first century and that people and governments throughout the world will seek continued economic growth, GHG emissions can be expected to increase at least through the early decades of the new century. The key issue is the rate of this increase.

If the rate of increase in these emissions are not slowed, the consequences might be unimaginably serious, but whether the slowdown begins in 2000 or 2005 (or even later) will probably not make a great deal of difference to the bio-geo-physical processes involved. What is important is that the international community starts to address the issue. Slowing down global warming will be complicated, and it could be costly: almost all aspects of modern economic life are involved.

The international community has started to address the issue. The UNFCCC is a carefully drafted and sophisticated instrument, and the Kyoto Protocol contains innovative strategies that might reduce the rate of increase in GHG emissions at minimal costs. But joint implementation, the clean development mechanism, and (to a lesser extent) emissions trading are untried mechanisms. As parties to the UNFCCC await the Kyoto Protocol's coming into effect, they have an opportunity to do pilot projects testing these devices.

Konrad von Moltke has observed that international cooperation has often continued and flourished even when conventions negotiated to provide the framework for such cooperation never came into effect.[26] The treaty signed in 1948 to establish the ITO is a case in point. It never came into effect because the U.S. Senate refused to give its advice and consent to ratification. But commercial cooperation nevertheless flourished under the auspices of GATT. Eventually, a proper international governmental organization, the WTO, was established.

All indications are that international cooperation to deal with climate change is moving ahead rapidly and will continue to progress whether or not the Kyoto Protocol is ratified.

Notes

1. For a good account of the history of international actions to deal with environmental issues see Brenton, *The Greening of Machiavelli.*
2. Harding, "The Tragedy of the Commons."

3. See Schmandt, Clarkson, and Roderick, eds., *Acid Rain and Friendly Neighbors: The Policy Dispute Between Canada and the United States.*

4. Molina and Rowland, "Stratospheric Sink for Chlorofluoromethanes."

5. See Benedick, *Ozone Diplomacy.*

6. See Evans, Jacobson, and Putnam, eds., *Double-Edged Diplomacy: International Bargaining and Domestic Politics.*

7. Kyoto Protocol, article 3.1

8. *New York Times,* December 12, 1997.

9. *Science,* vol. 290, p. 269.

10. Brenton, *The Greening of Machiavelli,* p. 166.

11. Houghton, Jenkins, and Ephraums, *Climate Change: The IPCC Scientific Assessment.*

12. Ibid., p. xi.

13. Watson, Zinyowera, and Moss., eds., *Climate Change 1995: Impacts, Adaptations and Mitigation of Climate Change: Scientific-Technical Analyses.*

14. Ibid., p. 3.

15. Ibid., p. 4.

16. Gore, *Earth in the Balance.*

17. Grubb, Vrolijik, and Brack, *The Kyoto Protocol,* p. 54.

18. UNFCCC, article 3 (1).

19. Senate Resolution 105-98.

20. Harris, "International Norms of Responsibility and U.S. Climate Change Policy," pp. 231–235.

21. Global Climate Coalition, "21st Century Climate Agenda."

22. See Brenton, *The Greening of Machiavelli;* Benedick, *Ozone Diplomacy.*

23. Gummer and Moreland, *The European Union & Global Climate Change.*

24. See chapter 5, "Environmental and Economic Implications of the Kyoto Commitments," pp. 155–195, in Grubb with Vrolijk and Brack, *The Kyoto Protocol;* and Weyant, *An Introduction to the Economics of Climate Change.*

25. Hoopes and Brinkley, *FDR and the Creation of the UN.*

26. Introductory comments, Dartmouth Workshop on the Effectiveness of the Climate Regime, January 13–16, 2000.

PART 4

THE FUTURE
OF MULTILATERAL
COOPERATION

17

Multilateralism as a Matter of Fact: U.S. Leadership and the Management of the International Public Sector

Shepard Forman

Multilateral arrangements increasingly will be called upon . . . to deal with growing transnational problems. . . . And when international cooperation—or international governance—comes up short, the United States and other developed countries will have to broker solutions among a wide array of international players—including governments at all levels, multinational corporations, and nonprofit organizations.
—*Global Trends 2015*[1]

Multilateralism for a Global Age

The twentieth century ushered in an era of multilateralism, a historic reckoning of the nation state with a growing number of transnational economic, social and security issues, and increased interstate interdependence. During the past hundred years, and especially since World War II, sovereign countries acceded to thousands of bilateral and multilateral treaties and established layers of global and regional organizations to monitor these agreements and to fulfill their goals. By the beginning of this new century, over two thousand multilateral agreements had been negotiated and more than 1,800 intergovernmental bodies were operating at various levels of vitality.[2]

For much of the past half-century, the United States has been a leader in this evolution toward a more open, cooperative world. With its might and influence at a historical zenith at the end of World War II, the United States helped to create innovative intergovernment forums for international action at both the global and regional levels—from the UN and the Bretton Woods institutions to the NATO alliance. Much of this effort was designed to foster the economic growth and political stability that underpin international peace. The broad pattern of U.S. policy, however, also set in motion a development of profound global importance: the gradual emergence of a substantial international public sector that today affects virtually every aspect of international affairs and domestic well-being around the globe.[3]

Policymakers and the general public are only beginning to appreciate the dimensions and implications of this international public sector. Its composition is heterogeneous and evolving. It consists today of a broad array of institutions and actors that set the legal and normative framework for the conduct of international affairs and also provide a range of goods and services on which people around the world—and in the United States—have come to depend. These institutions range from larger global organizations that are household names, such as the UN and the World Bank, to small, somewhat obscure regional organizations consisting of just a few member countries, such as the West African Health Community. Together with a rapidly growing number of nongovernment and private-sector organizations, they provide the frameworks and processes for functional international cooperation in diverse fields, ranging from peace and security to trade and finance, environmental management, human rights, education, law enforcement, health, science and technology, and the use of the "global commons."

Some of these goods and services are the product of binding international treaties; others are obligations implied by less formal international norms; and still others reflect mere aspirations. Some of them, such as those provided by international postal agreements or the International Meteorological Organization, are by and large simply taken for granted, since they serve rather technical ends and proceed in fairly neutral contexts. Others, such as peacekeeping and humanitarian assistance, are highly politicized and often contested. In all cases national interest calculations intervene, either in claims to sovereignty or in anticipated gains and losses in the global bargain that these arrangements represent. Yet, the sector persists, expands, and diversifies, and it requires serious attention if it is to respond effectively to the growing global needs and opportunities that no single nation, not even the world's most powerful, can attend to on its own.

Most treatments of the international public sector focus either on defining the nature of international public goods and services—that is, identifying those activities that qualify for the label[4]—or on assessing the structure and performance of the international organizations tasked with providing these goods—that is, examining their capacity to deliver.[5] Other analysts argue that such institutions have the capacity to transform the very nature of international relations, that is, to change the rules of the game being played by states and, increasingly, nonstate actors.[6] More recent studies have begun to consider whether these public goods are most effectively provided at the national, regional, or global level[7] and what roles the private sector should play in their delivery.[8]

Remarkably, there has been little discussion about the structure and function of the international public sector within the broader domestic debates about U.S. foreign policy, especially as regards the challenges and global responsibilities the United States will face in the twenty-first century.

Yet, the architecture designed to govern the multiple spheres of international cooperation is undergoing considerable pressure in globalization's wake, at once decentralizing as responsibility devolves from global to regional and subregional organizations,[9] and privatizing as nonstate actors increase their interest and influence in international affairs. Because of its unprecedented economic, political, and military presence, U.S. interests and reach cut across the range of international issue areas, thereby placing this country in an excellent position—perhaps even stronger than in the aftermath of World War II—to play a decisive leadership role in helping to shape these developments.

There are both material and normative reasons for the United States to be involved in shaping the new global architecture. The transnational character of global threats and their volatile and unpredictable nature, as Edward Luck writes in Chapter 2 of this book, "compels an unprecedented degree of multilateral cooperation." Financial crises, extreme poverty, environmental degradation, infectious disease, and regional conflicts, no matter how distant, can all have a direct affect on our shores. The terrorist attacks of September 2001 underlined the nation's vulnerability to global threats and its profound interest in and need for international capacities to respond to them. As Stewart Patrick notes,

> For all its overwhelming power, the United States cannot by itself stem the proliferation of weapons of mass destruction, preserve regional stability, enforce international law and human rights standards, maintain an open and nondiscriminatory trading system, ensure the stability and liquidity of global financial markets, protect the "global commons," stop global warming, stem transnational trafficking in narcotics, thwart organized crime syndicates, slow global population growth, regulate immigration flows, respond to humanitarian catastrophes, stem pandemics, or promote sustainable development.[10]

Multilateralism is no longer a choice. It is a matter of necessity, and of fact.[11] It exists in the thousands of conventions and treaties that nation-states have signed, in the institutions that have been established to implement and monitor these agreements, and in the international courts and tribunals that resolve disputes arising among their members.[12] In its institutional guise, multilateralism provides access to countries that would on their own hardly be players on the world stage, while constraining arbitrary or coercive action by the most powerful. Multilateral institutions provide the legal and normative framework and legitimacy for transnational action. They permit coordination and encourage cost sharing; and they limit outriding by those who would prefer not to follow the rules of the game, as well as free riding by those who would rely on the beneficence or self-interest of others.

Multilateralism, as Ruth Wedgwood states in Chapter 7, also flourishes outside the readily visible institutional framework of global and regional organizations. It takes the form of diverse collaborative arrangements, such as the Group of 77 or the G-8, informal mechanisms for promoting policy objectives among "like-minded" states, and in the "coalitions of the willing" on which much of peacekeeping has come to depend. Increasingly, it manifests itself through the kinds of public-private partnerships that Wolfgang Reinicke identifies as functionally based public-policy networks.[13] Furthermore, it exists in the growing expectations of individuals and NGOs around the globe that have come to believe that the "international system" has an obligation—and should have the capacity—to respond to a range of needs that individual governments can no longer meet.

As a strategy for pursuing national interests, multilateral cooperation has a certain short-term utilitarian value, providing legitimacy to the actions of single states or even saving money by exploiting economies of scale and reducing duplication of effort. Considered in the medium to longer term, however, in this age of accelerated globalization, multilateralism offers the most effective means to realize common goals and contain common threats.

For the most part, the United States has recognized the functional benefits of such cooperation. As John Ikenberry notes in Chapter 5, although the United States was "profoundly ambivalent about agreeing to operate within rule-based multilateral institutions," it nevertheless used these systematically "as tools of grand strategy and world-order building. Indeed, no country has championed multilateral institutions more than the United States or used them more effectively in the advancement of long-term national interests," which Ikenberry identifies as ensuring a predictable and favorable international operating environment.

Yet, a number of changes have occurred in the international operating environment in recent years that have diminished support for an important set of global institutions, both among their member states and among important constituent groups, significantly in the United States itself. Two of these changes merit particular consideration. First, the number of sovereign states has increased significantly as a result of decolonization and the breakup of the Soviet Union. These new states place increasing demands on international organizations to meet an ever-widening set of expectations for goods and services. They also dramatically increase the membership of multilateral organizations and seek to alter their decisionmaking procedures in ways that would countermand weighted voting in the financial institutions and the use of the veto in the UN Security Council. While the new nations' intention is to share in the authority that previously rested with a few key states, their assertiveness has also blocked some peacekeeping and humanitarian assistance programs they deem "interventionist," and tried U.S. patience in these organizations in the process.[14]

At the same time, the failure of global multilateral organizations to meet the demands made upon them by many of their member states—coupled with the desire of weaker states to control the international agenda in smaller, more proximal institutions—has led to the establishment of a large number of regional and sub-regional organizations that are increasingly active in peacekeeping, humanitarian assistance, and other activities. Regional organizations and the principle of subsidiarity (attending to problems closer to their source) are envisioned in the UN Charter, but the effective relationship between these layers of organizations is still being worked out. Moreover, the number and effectiveness of these organizations vary considerably across regions and by sector.[15]

We nonetheless may be heading toward an interregnum in the trend toward globalism, a period in which regionalism and subregionalism will be the organizing principle for multilateral action. Across the board, in areas as diverse as economic development, humanitarian assistance, peacekeeping, and even the management of financial crises, a discussion is proceeding rather quickly—and without sufficient consideration of its ramifications—about the devolution of responsibility from global to regional and subregional organizations. This devolution is being driven in large part by cost-containment and burden-sharing imperatives, and it is occurring on a case-by-case basis in response to particular crises rather than as part of a deliberate strategy.[16]

A second major change in the international operating environment is the growing number of nonstate actors and the effective advocacy roles they have come to play. As Princeton Lyman describes in Chapter 3, we now face a world in which nonstate actors, including transnational corporations, NGOs, and civil society movements, have become major players in the global marketplace.[17] This private sector, including both its profit-making and not-for-profit components, accounts for a vast number of the international transactions that drive globalization and interdependence, even while the intergovernment organizations and mechanisms established to manage such transactions continue to be dominated by states.

This disjunction, between largely closed, state-driven intergovernment organizations and the openness of Internet-driven advocacy groups, is dramatically changing the foreign policy landscape. Multilateral organizations now find themselves caught between the coveted principle of state sovereignty and the permeability that globalization brings to their members' borders. An increasing number of the multilateral responses to conflicts in recent years have their roots in the advocacy of these transnational humanitarian, human rights, and environmental activists, who call international attention to events previously considered to be within the sole purview of the nation-state. A handful of extreme activists even advocate closing down the international financial institutions, which they contend are incapable of effective reform. But most observers—including many concerned with growing inequities between rich and poor, and between those with access to opportunity and those without it—accept the fact that multilateral institutions are a necessary and permanent part of the international landscape.

Less visible, but no less important than these advocacy efforts, is the degree to which privatization now marks significant areas of U.S. foreign policy. Today, more than 30,000 international and community-based NGOs operate programs around the world. In the fields of economic development and humanitarian assistance alone, more than 4,000 Northern-based NGOs disburse $3 billion in foreign aid. Approximately 60 percent of U.S. foreign disaster assistance is programmed through NGOs.[18] Privatization of international affairs has taken an even more dramatic turn, however, with the direct funding of international activities by private individuals, as in the case of Ted Turner's $1 billion gift to the UN, Bill Gates's support of the International AIDS Vaccine Initiative, and George Soros's extensive assistance to transitional countries in Eastern Europe and Central Asia.[19]

As several of the chapters in this book point out, the growing presence of these private actors in international affairs is transforming the domestic and international context in which the United States formulates and carries out its foreign policy. The capacity of these NGOs to influence U.S. public-policy debates is evident in the recent mobilization efforts to establish an ICC, to ban landmines, and to reprogram the WTO and Bretton Woods institutions to cope with the detrimental effects of globalization. Loosely organized as transnational movements, they are placing increased performance demands on intergovernment organizations and, as we saw with the Clinton administration's response to the global backlash protests in Seattle, they are setting a reform agenda that is having some effect on the ways in which these organizations set their policies and programs. Of course, their influence is felt in diverse ways. As Bartram Brown points out in Chapter 13, the United States formulated its positions on the ICC as much in reaction to NGO initiatives as in response to other countries' demands. Similarly, it appears that the Department of Defense may have opposed the landmines ban not solely on the basis of weapons requirements, but also out of a concern that activist NGOs and citizen groups might set a precedent for the way decisions are made on strategic armaments.

The Need for Leadership

The United States has responded in a variety of ways to the challenges and opportunities posed by globalization and increased interstate interdependence, engaging in multilateral cooperation both selectively and instrumentally. As Patrick observes:

> American policymakers tend to pursue a combination of mulilateral and unilateral strategies within each issue area, and they often engage in "forum shopping," choosing among informal coalitions, regional entities, and the UN to secure a venue that will maximize United States control and

minimize United States obligations and potential culpability in the event of failure.[20]

A variety of explanations, from selectivity to ambivalence, have been used to account for the alternative choices the United States has made between unilateral and multilateral approaches to foreign policy. No consistent pattern seems to emerge from the sector-by-sector analysis in this volume, other than a short-term public-policy time horizon and a general unwillingness of the United States to subject itself to the constraints imposed by intergovernment organizations. As Kimberly Ann Elliott and Gary Hufbauer point out in Chapter 15, for example, the United States approaches international economic policy on the basis of a tactical analysis of immediate interest, sometimes short-circuiting the overall benefits it can derive from multilateral organizations. The United States, they write, wanted to lower trade barriers while protecting its own economic interest. Thus, it took the lead in promoting the ill-fated ITO and the GATT, but worked to limit their institutional capacity to constrain U.S. behavior. For Luck, questions of legitimacy as well as performance contribute to U.S. discomfort with multilateral organizations. The United States, he notes, "remains, at best, discriminating in its approach to multilateralism," evidencing a reluctance to provide wholesale support to multilateral organizations that may not meet the legitimacy criteria demanded by the U.S. government and public.[21]

Although they sometimes disagree about whether U.S. behavior reflects an underlying national ambivalence or a deliberately instrumental approach to multilateral frameworks, each of the authors in this volume identifies a problematic record of "ad hocism" in recent U.S. foreign policy.[22] For most of them, the failure of the United States to play a consistent leadership role in managing the process of multilateral formation, that is, in setting the pattern for the behavior of states and in shaping the changing global architecture, comes at some cost.[23] While some short-term benefits might accrue to acting alone, the failure to engage multilaterally has a corrosive effect on the United States' reputation and leadership; diminishes its capacity to negotiate favorable outcomes in particular issue areas; and undercuts its ability to mobilize the support of other states for its longer-term public-policy objectives. For example, Elliott and Hufbauer point out that the United States occasionally pressured the IMF during the Cold War to apply loose conditions on loans to such allies as Zaire and Indonesia, to long-term detriment as we have seen. And Sewell notes that the reversals and oscillations in Clinton administration policy toward UN peacekeeping left the UN with weakened capacity and unable to respond effectively to demands that the United States continues to make on the organization. Likewise, Michael Mastanduno argues that "the [U.S.] use of extraterritorial sanctions deflects attention from the objectionable behavior of an appropriate target—a Soviet Union that invades its neighbors, an Iran that exports terrorism, a Cuba that abuses its population—and turns attention [instead] to the unacceptable behavior of the U.S."

The costs of unilateral action emerge with particular clarity in the area of arms control. According to Thomas Graham and Damien LaVera, the U.S. failure to ratify the CTBT has grave policy implications for bringing India, Pakistan, Israel, and other actual or potential members of the nuclear club into the NPT, as well as for ensuring the indefinite extension of the NPT. Moreover, they point out, refusal to ratify the CTBT limits U.S. efforts to strengthen the verification safeguards that could prevent conversion of nuclear capabilities from peaceful to nuclear weapons use.[24]

In the field of chemical weapons, Amy Smithson contends, the Clinton administration and Congress together squandered an opportunity to achieve a CWC treaty with strong monitoring and verification procedures—and thereby reduce the likelihood that U.S. troops might someday be exposed to chemical weapons. Despite widespread support from the U.S. chemical industry, the intelligence community, the Pentagon (including the Joint Chiefs of Staff), and the general public, the president withdrew the CWC from congressional ratification in the face of strong election-year Republican opposition. Although the administration reintroduced the convention for ratification at the eleventh hour (to make certain that it did not go into effect without U.S. participation), it acquiesced to restrictive congressional exemptions on monitoring, offshore analysis of chemical samples, and declaration of facilities using materials that might pose a proliferation threat. The result of U.S. behavior, according to Smithson, was a substantially weakened treaty whose lack of integrity encouraged copycat exemptions by other signatories and a severely curtailed likelihood of negotiating an effective verification protocol in the Biological Weapons Convention.

In each of these instances, the U.S. decision to abrogate its principles and to forfeit objectives in the longer term for short-term gains antagonized allies and jeopardized the respect traditionally enjoyed by the United States. The imposition of extraterritorial sanctions provides a case in point. As Mastanduno argues, such measures diminish not only the reputation of U.S. companies as reliable trading partners, but also the worthiness of the United States itself as a global leader. Similarly, Smithson argues that the diminished status of the U.S. delegation in the CWC negotiations enabled the treaty's governing bodies to approve policies detrimental to the convention's long-term vitality. And, Brown adds, "the vote taken at the end of the Rome ICC Conference may come to symbolize declining U.S. leadership in multilateral affairs. Caught on the short end of a 120–7 vote in favor of the ICC Statute, the U.S. was also one of only two democracies to vote against it."

Recent U.S. policy is nowhere more damaging to its reputation and its espoused goals than in its decisions over the past decade to opt out of the development and embrace of new international laws and norms, despite its longstanding recognition of their centrality to global order and progress. By seeming to back away from its values and insisting on exceptions to the principle of equal justice, the United States has compromised its credibility and that of international law itself. In Chapter 13, Brown catalogues the reactive and even obstructionist U.S. posture during the negotiations leading to the establishment of the ICC, arguing that this stance limited the country's ability to negotiate effectively for a court that the United States did much to promote.[25]

While the United States may have some legitimate concerns regarding certain provisions of the ICC, it isolated itself in the course of the negotiations, thereby forfeiting whatever influence it might otherwise have wielded among the eventual signatories. Arm-twisting and threats to retaliate again other states at the Rome Conference almost certainly diminished U.S. standing among its allies. Moreover, by asserting the primacy of "family values" while standing essentially alone in opposition to the Convention on the Rights of the Child, the United States only added to a widely held perception abroad that its claims to exceptionalism are self-indulgent, reflecting either a double standard or just plain old hypocrisy.[26]

Recent events, moreover, demonstrated that the United States is increasingly unable to block multilateral initiatives simply by opting out. As Harold Jacobson points out, both the Law of the Sea Convention and the Convention on Biodiversity proceeded without the United States, as did the Convention to Ban Land Mines, preventing the United States from including valid modifications. Although the United States remained party to the negotiations in several cases, its influence was limited by what others perceived as obstructionist or self-interested behavior. As such instances make evident, the greatest cost to selective and ambivalent U.S. multilateralism is likely to be the failure to achieve the broad goals the United States has long promoted, be they protecting the environment, promoting international law and human rights, limiting proliferation of weapons of mass destruction, safeguarding cyberspace, or deterring terrorism.

This is not to argue that unilateralism and multilateralism can be easily equated with "bad" and "good," respectively. Rather, it is a claim that there are tangible consequences associated with the choice of one over the other. As Luck has noted elsewhere, "To make a multilateral system work in one's favor requires paying at least lip service to some of the favorite programs of other states. . . . Multilateralism is a process of quid pro quos, of trade-offs that are the substance of compromise and consensus."[27] Discussing the impact of U.S. policy toward peacekeeping, Sarah Sewell comments that "the renaissance in UN peace operations reflects realities about the give and take of international politics, of the need to meet needs of other national communities in one instance, in order to advance U.S. interests in other areas." This lack of compromise has its price, as William Wallace points out in describing the European reaction to U.S. unilateralism:

The rejection of multilateral institutions as vehicles through which to exert U.S. leadership by many within Congress, [and] the frequent demands by administration officials that allies follow the United States' choice of direction . . . have given impetus to Western European initiatives to increase their autonomy in foreign policy and defense. Western European governments expect the United States to offer them partnership, based on authority and persuasion, not unilateral exercises of power or veto.

In certain circumstances, of course, there may be good reasons for the United States to act alone, for example in the area of national defense, or in the promotion and preservation of underlying national values that may be under threat. In a number of cases, as several authors in this volume argue, the United States has actually claimed a general commitment to multilateralism as a motive for acting alone, basing its argument on the fact that unilateralism can sometimes help to preserve a broader set of values or instruments that require the singular action of an "exceptional" power. Such is the case that Elliott and Huffbauer make for U.S. efforts to secure the multilateral trade system and that Moravcsik argues with regard to human rights.[28] Ruth Wedgwood takes this one step further, suggesting that unilateral action in self-defense against armed aggression enjoys a multilateral sanction in the UN charter, thus providing a higher order rationale for the United States to act alone.

At the same time, as Wedgwood points out, "military action is a singular case for testing the advantages of multilateral and unilateral decision-making." Based on asymmetry of military power and economic means, the United States may calculate that it has the capacity to act alone and that acting in concert with others may not provide "a proportionate return." Yet, both the Gulf War and Kosovo demonstrate the need to act in concert with others, for reasons of logistics, legitimacy, and cost. Utilizing the UN in the one instance and not in the other may reflect a practical response to the inability of the UN Security Council to act in the face of likely vetoes, but it ultimately undermines the authority of the UN itself, making it a less likely venue for collective action in the future. As Sewell notes, by neglecting UN peacekeeping, the United States passed up an opportunity to help the UN expand its legitimacy and effectiveness in promoting international peace and security. Sewell argues strongly that the Clinton administration's neglect of UN peacekeeping has been self-defeating and counterproductive, undercutting the U.S. ability "to accomplish its often stated objectives of increasing international security, burden sharing, and reducing demands upon U.S. military forces."

As tempting as it may be to blame the Clinton administration for reversals in policy toward the UN and other international organizations during the 1990s, executive branch leadership is not the sole determinant of the balance between unilateral and multilateral approaches in U.S. foreign policy. Arguably, the on-again, off-again stance of the United States toward

UN peace operations is best explained by executive-congressional dynamics. As Sewall notes, the administration perceived support for UN peace operations as a way to limit U.S. military involvement overseas, whereas influential voices in Congress saw UN peacekeeping as a potential expansion of U.S. military commitments. What began as a traditional congressional–executive branch disagreement on war powers soon escalated into a divisive partisan debate about the deployment of U.S. troops under UN command and, in the end, about support for the UN itself.

Congress often has a critical impact on the nature of the country's global engagement. Mastanduno notes that the imposition of extraterritorial sanctions usually emanates from Capitol Hill, forcing the administration to engage in a problematic balancing act—complying with legislated requirements while finding safety valves to limit economic and diplomatic damage with U.S. trading partners. Congress has also constrained U.S. cooperation on environmental matters. Although President Clinton ultimately signed the Convention on Biodiversity, he failed to submit it to Congress for ratification, acknowledging that it stood little chance of passing. Congress, supported by the Pentagon, was also the major source of opposition to other multilateral initiatives, including the ICC and the universal ban on the use of landmines. Perhaps the most costly outcome was in the Senate's refusal to ratify the CTBT, which President Clinton had signed with a particularly rhetorical flourish, calling it "the longest-sought and hardest-fought prize in the history of arms control."

Most often, Congress exercises its authority over the conduct of U.S. foreign policy through its control of the national budget and international expenditures. Nowhere has this control been more visible than in the highly problematic relations between the United States and the UN over the past decade, as reported by Margaret Karns and Karen Mingst in Chapter 11. Despite the enormous benefits that it has derived from membership in the UN,[29] the United States, by first delaying and then withholding its assessed contributions during the 1990s, exacerbated a financial crisis that brought the UN near collapse. The UN membership recently agreed to meet congressional demands for limits on U.S. assessments, resulting in the release of a substantial portion of the arrears. The dispute, however, has taken its toll on U.S. standing within the organization and on the world body's capacity to perform, thereby threatening to reignite the negative commentary that sparked withholdings in the first instance.[30]

While each of these examples points to serious consequences in the way the United States engages the world, the problem is exacerbated in the aggregate, resulting in a lost opportunity to ensure the predictable and favorable international operating environment that Ikenberry cites as essential to the national interest. Although the press has focused overwhelmingly on U.S. arrears to the UN, the United States was in arrears throughout the 1990s to virtually every multilateral organization to which it belongs. The list includes the World Bank, the IMF, WTO, IAEA, the Inter-Parliamentary Union, and many other intergovernment organizations that would seem to fit well with U.S. foreign policy objectives.[31] While the prevailing explanation for this pecuniary behavior is that the United States uses its power of the purse to exact reforms within the UN Secretariat and the Bretton Woods institutions, the extent of arrears to most every international organization seems to indicate that something more insidious is going on. It may well be that the publicity surrounding the arrears to the UN provides a smoke screen for a few members of Congress who would deny U.S. participation in any and all multilateral organizations that appear to bind the country to the will and interests of others. At the very least, it would suggest that the United States would do well to review its participatory and fiscal responsibilities within the broader international public sector per se, rather than focusing, as it currently does, on narrow reforms within a handful of intergovernment organizations.

Considering its unprecedented power and influence in economic, military and cultural affairs, as well as its global interests, the United States should be exercising far greater leadership in promoting international law and multilateral responses to global problems than it has in the recent past. It should engage these tasks with the same sort of imagination and sense of purpose that it brought to bear in creating the UN and the Bretton Woods institutions. Given the demands of the present global environment and the likelihood that these will only intensify in the future, the United States should rededicate itself to multilateralism, albeit a new kind of multilateralism that is informed by an appreciation of the evolving transnational phenomena that are part and parcel of the process of today's globalization. This new, constructive multilateralism would include increased reliance on regional, subregional, and national mechanisms; greater openness and transparency; and an integral involvement of civil society institutions to ensure a more effective utilization of resources and set of outcomes.

Shaping the International Public Sector

In its recent publication, *Global Trends 2015: A Dialogue About the Future With Nongovernmental Experts* (December 2000), the National Intelligence Council[32] describes a set of trends and uncertainties that argue persuasively for greater multilateral action in the very near future. As the report makes clear,

> States will continue to be the dominant players on the world stage, but governments will have less and less control over flows of information, technology, diseases, migrants, arms, and financial transactions, whether licit or illicit, across their borders. Nonstate actors ranging from business firms to nonprofit organizations will play increasingly larger roles in both national and international affairs. The quality of governance, both nationally and

internationally, will substantially determine how well states and societies cope with these global forces.[33]

Neither unachievable appeals for "world government" nor more modest exhortations to cooperate for the "common good" are likely to provide the basis for the effective governance that globalization demands. Nor is the United States likely to move forward in developing more effective responses to the collective action problems the world now faces if it finds itself stuck in an endless foreign policy debate over the wisdom of unilateral versus multilateral approaches, or what constitutes the "national interest." There may well be instances when the national interest calls for unitary action, but there will increasingly be others, as described throughout this book and this chapter, in which the national interest is coterminous with the global common good. If it is to be prepared for these inevitabilities, the United States needs to develop a far more coherent and systematic policy approach to the management and financing of the international public sector.

Because of its commanding presence across the globe, the United States should take the lead in crafting a more productive response to the transnational demands of globalization. It should set in motion a deliberative process with domestic and international partners to examine in a holistic way the vast array of institutions and functions that now constitute the international public sector; to determine those that are essential; and to figure out how to advance with key public and private-sector partners on the provision of those public goods that truly require broad-based multilateral cooperation. A critical part of this inquiry would be to ascertain how and where essential international public goods can best be provided, and the most cost-effective ways to pay for them. This will entail a systematic examination of existing multilateral organizations and what in fact they do deliver. It also will require further experimentation with new hybrid organizations that share interest and responsibilities in particular issue areas, such as the Global Environmental Facility that is co-managed by the United Nations Environment Program, the United Nations Development Program, and the World Bank. And, it will demand innovative responses such as the public-private policy networks that are now emerging to assume many of the functions previously reserved to intergovernment organizations.[34]

There will inevitably be differences of opinion and interest concerning what constitutes a public good, who is entitled to it, and how the burdens should be apportioned in producing and providing it. There is also divided opinion on whether it is best to continue the struggle to reform the existing set of intergovernment organizations or to experiment further with new mechanisms that will incorporate the best of public and private capacities. Finding answers to these questions—and agreement on effective solutions to the global problems that now reach across every country's borders—will require a more open and inclusive dialogue among governments, corporations, international civil servants, NGOs, and other members of civil society.[35]

The United States should be a leading proponent of such dialogues, encouraging creative discussion on the shape and scope of the international public sector. The national interest dictates that the United States be not only attentive to the changes that are occurring in the international operating environment, but that it help to mold the responses to them. That will require the United States to work closely with both traditional allies and a range of other states, with regional and subregional organizations, and with the nonstate actors now active in international affairs, including NGOs, transnational social movements, and multinational corporations.

Guiding the Processes of Devolution and Privatization

This new dialogue will need to address the processes of decentralization/ devolution and privatization described earlier in this chapter. Dissatisfaction with global multilateral organizations has resulted in weakened political and financial support for them, resulting in a devolution of responsibility to regional and subregional organizations. Many of these regional organizations are asserting their authority over activities that affect their member states. Such decentralization requires the United States to deal both with a larger number of members in existing global institutions as well as with a far larger and more diverse set of institutional actors on the world stage. How the United States chooses to deal with these changes will greatly affect the efficacy of multilateralism as well as matters of equity and universality in the distribution of global goods.

As the foregoing chapters have made clear, it is no longer possible for the United States to control the agenda, either in the current global institutions or in closed negotiations among a small number of powerful players, like the G-8. Rather, future multilateralism will need to rely on more open and inclusive frameworks. As *Global Trends 2015* notes, the United States will have to heed the advice not only of a few powerful states like Russia and China but also of other emerging players, such as India, Mexico, and Brazil. These countries are demanding more of a voice in the international system, and the United States will need increasingly to rely on them, not as clients but as partners seeking common solutions to common problems. As Jacobson points out in Chapter 16, developing countries' demands for shared benefits, say from research in biotechnology, will increase and possibly be even more effective in the future. And the interests of these countries in achieving quid pro quos in Kyoto-like protocols and negotiations at the WTO and other intergovernment venues will become more difficult to dismiss, especially as the United States grows to rely on them for, among other things, genetic source material, access to territorial waters and sea lanes, and markets for U.S. exports.

The United States also will need to work with other industrialized countries and better endowed countries in each region to ensure that regional and subregional organizations have the resources they need to adequately meet the responsibilities they are increasingly being asked (or desire) to assume. Otherwise, divergences and inequities are likely to increase in the provision of international public goods and services between rich regions and poor ones, with potentially calamitous social consequences. To avoid these regional inequities, the major countries will need to formulate a new approach to development assistance that goes beyond current bilateral modalities to include far greater coordination between and among national aid agencies, the various UN development and humanitarian assistance agencies, the international financial institutions, including the regional development banks, and nonstate actors, both commercial and voluntary.[36] Most important, it also means applying the subsidiarity principle in a way that truly vests responsibility and accountability in those regional and subregional actors, including the recipients themselves, that are closer to the problems being addressed and able to deal with their cross-border implications.[37] Nothing short of a radical reformulation of the concept and practice of overseas development assistance will reverse the tide of diminishing international public assistance expenditures.

The United States and partners in the industrialized world also will need to demonstrate real leadership by way of example. The inherent dangers and risks of subregionalism, especially the commingling of economic integration and security mandates in troubled parts of the developing world, demand a reassertion of universal principles and values and strict adherence to international law. That will require a reaffirmation of the relationship between the UN, as the auspices of standard setting and lawmaking, and regional and subregional organizations, as the purveyors of goods and services.[38] If the United States is really intent on ensuring sustainable peace and development, it will need to take a close look at the evolving global architecture and think hard about how to build its future on the twin pillars of universal principles and international law.

The role of private actors is critical in this regard.[39] As noted above, the 1990s were marked by an increasing privatization of international affairs. This takes the form of contracting NGO services by national governments and intergovernment organizations, as well as through efforts to extend traditional corporate philanthropy and new ideas about corporate social responsibility into formal public-private partnerships for the provision of international public goods and services.[40] Both the UN and the World Bank now have fledgling corporate programs intended to induce financial contributions, to develop partnerships for the delivery of goods and services, or, in the case of the Global Compact launched two years ago by the UN secretary-general at the World Economic Forum, to encourage business and industry to promote human rights, labor standards, and environmental concerns in their for-profit activities. As important as these efforts are, they have not been accompanied as yet by any sharing of authority for agenda setting or policymaking.

NGOs and other civil society actors are clamoring to extend democratic principles to the conduct of international affairs and, particularly, to the decisionmaking chambers of multilateral organizations. Since calls to establish citizen bodies within the UN and other multilateral agencies are unlikely to be accommodated by those state-based organizations anytime soon, other, more collaborative channels will have to be developed. The NGO forums that ran parallel to the UN conferences that occurred throughout the 1990s represent one such modality, although access to them was limited and they tended to be dominated by a few wealthier and Western-based NGOs.[41] The recent invitations to a few humanitarian, peace, and HIV/AIDS organizations to speak before the Security Council advance the process further, but are too limited in frequency and represent opportunities for a few well-chosen NGOs to present their viewpoints rather than a broader opening for participation in decisionmaking. The aforementioned public-private policy networks may well present the most effective means to date to involve nongovernmental actors more directly in the formulation and implementation of international public policy. The United States, true to its democratic and pluralist ideals, should work with other democratic states to make the conduct of international affairs more open and accountable, to ensure that interactions between policymakers and the public are more than testy encounters, and to develop modalities of "global governance" that extend beyond the passive consent of the governed to include their active participation.

Changing the Political Dynamic in the United States

Adjusting current patterns of U.S. behavior in international affairs is no simple task. It will require a reconsideration of the nation's current understandings of the connections between domestic and foreign policy and a greater appreciation of the interrelationship between national welfare and the global common good. It also will require attention to four key elements in the shaping of U.S. foreign policy.

- Congress will need to pay more systematic attention than it currently does to the interactive nature of international and domestic affairs and the need for a more coherent public policy approach to international public sector activities.
- The large number of federal agencies now involved in diverse aspects of international affairs will need to be better prepared to engage globally and to coordinate and synchronize their policies.
- Congress will need to appropriate adequate resources for international programs specifically designed to meet the needs being posed by globalization.

- The public will need to be better informed about the impact of glob-alization and the workings of the international public sector. While the media, NGOs, and educational institutions have an important role to play in this regard, the ultimate success of any such effort at public education will depend on presidential and congressional leadership.

Engaging Congress in bipartisan dialogue. A great deal has been written about a decline in internationalism in Congress since the end of the Cold War. The conventional image is of a legislature that is concerned with do-mestic instead of foreign policy priorities, that dismisses foreign opinion, and that maintains a fundamental belief in the supremacy and singular ca-pacity of the United States. Yet, as the response to several recent financial crises demonstrates, many members of Congress understand the effects of accelerated globalization and the ways in which they affect the well-being of their constituents. While they may harbor doubts about the efficacy of current international organizations, they realize the limits of U.S. capacity to act alone and, hence, the need for multilateral responses to global prob-lems. To bring along more reluctant members, advocates of constructive U.S. multilateralism will need to work hard to counter the vociferous mi-nority that floods congressional offices with anti-multilateral and even iso-lationist views. These advocates will need to demonstrate to the doubters exactly how and in what precise ways transnational challenges and multi-lateral activities impinge on the interest of their constituents and how a more effective and accountable international public sector will be able to respond to these challenges.

As several of the case studies in this book make clear, it is important to raise these issues early and continually with members of Congress and their staffs. Too often, anticipation of a congressional rejection has led to eleventh-hour attempts to get a bill passed or a treaty ratified. Yet, as the prolonged dialogue on UN dues demonstrates, an open, interactive process can have payoff (literally) in the end. And it is far better to concentrate the debate on the substance of the issue at hand than on insidious riders, such as the antiabortion measure attached to the international affairs budget bill.

Congressional leadership is essential to close the gap between current foreign policy formulations and the demands of globalization. Members of Congress would do well to better inform themselves about the array of in-stitutions, actors, goods, and services that make up the international public sector, the costs involved in providing them, and the ways in which sector performance can and should be improved. A bipartisan commission or con-gressional hearings to study and make recommendations on the U.S. role in the international public sector would be a good beginning.

Coordinating federal agencies. Princeton Lyman describes in Chapter 3 both the limited institutional capacity of the State Department to deal with multilateral issues and the changing composition of the official foreign policy establishment that now engages multiple government agencies. As Jacobson shows in Chapter 16, U.S. foreign policy on climate change involves inputs from Congress, the Council of Economic Advisors; the Office of Management and Budget; the Agriculture, Commerce, Interior, and Treasury departments; and the undersecretary of state for global affairs. At least four bilateral agencies share overlapping and duplicative development assistance mandates—USAID, the Peace Corps, the InterAmerican Foundation, and the African Development Foundation—in addition to the various cabinet agencies that deal with international development issues.[42] In a number of instances, as Lyman notes, domestic agencies, such as the Drug Enforcement Agency and the FBI, supercede State Department and NSC authority in the conduct of overseas operations.

Clearly, as Lyman states, a government so organized is ill structured to meet the needs that globalization lays at its doorstep. He argues that new organizational and funding arrangements are needed to overcome competing agency mandates and agendas and accommodate the changing nature of the United States' (and others') global interests. For starters, the State Department needs to encourage its staff to work more collaboratively with counterparts in other agencies who have more technical expertise on cross-cutting agenda items such as trade and labor, trade and environment, health and environment, and conflict and development. The Department of State's office dealing with international organizations also should to be primed to interact more closely with other government agencies such as the NSC, Department of Defense, and CIA, each of which have offices dealing with global issues. Recent coordination experiments, such as President Clinton's special advisor on AIDS or the national economic advisor's role in coordinating debt relief policy, need to be examined for the institutional lessons they provide. In the longer run, however, as Lyman notes, a more fundamental reordering of White House coordination will be required to meet the challenges of globalization in this new century.

Providing sufficient funds. If the United States is to exercise its full leadership potential in international affairs, it will need to improve on its current arrangements for funding multilateral activities. To begin, Congress will have to loosen the budgetary constraints it imposes on the State Department to ensure it sufficient funding to maintain its operations abroad, including essential safeguards for our embassies and their personnel. Second, the activities covered in the international affairs section of the federal budget, the so-called 150 functions, need to be adequately financed. Many of these expenditures—especially those for national security, economic development, international crime control, democracy and human rights promotion, humanitarian assistance, and management of the environment, population, and health—are the first line of defense against the deleterious affects of globalization. Yet, at present, only one penny out of every federal government dollar spent goes for international affairs, and nearly 70 percent of that is for our own overseas operations.[43] Putting domestic agencies in charge of the management and financing of foreign programs could alleviate these problems, as Lyman notes, by activating domestic constituencies in support of international activities and by overriding some of the negative attitudes in Congress toward multilateral organizations. Third, to strengthen U.S. leadership in multilateral organizations, Congress needs to wipe out and not repeat the arrears that mar U.S. standing and reduce institutional effectiveness. And the United States needs to refrain from using the payment of dues and zero-growth assumptions to force multilateral agencies to adopt cost-cutting bureaucratic reforms that may run counter to the goals it would have these organizations meet.

As noted earlier, the singular focus on arrears to the UN has diverted attention from a larger question regarding international public finance that the United States needs to address. There are no reliable cost estimates on international public sector expenditures, but globally they account for less than $300 billion per year, or approximately 1 percent of the estimated $30 trillion in world output. The United States continues to be the largest financer of international goods and services, whether in net official development assistance, in its 50 percent share of global AIDS funding, or in its financial support for landmine removal—this latter in compensation for the official opposition to the convention to ban the use of mines. This level of generosity notwithstanding, U.S. expenditures for international affairs remain a fraction of its actual annual public outlays and only about one-fifteenth of the percentage of the federal budget that the American public believes we are spending on international programs.

This gap between expectation and fact would suggest that it should be possible to build domestic support for an increased foreign affairs budget, either within the State Department or, as Lyman suggests, by expanding the budgets of domestic agencies engaged in international programming. This latter alternative would, of course, require congressional committees that currently see their mandates largely in domestic terms to recognize areas of intersecting domestic and international interests and approve funding for offshore activities. There is a danger, of course, that foreign affairs budgets split among multiple agencies could result in further fragmentation of international policymaking and exacerbate divergences between the political interests that dominate at the State Department and the more technical interests of other agencies. Moreover, cost sharing under budgetary constraints is never an easy sell. The Department of Defense has already demonstrated its reluctance to dip into its own budget in order to share the costs of UN peacekeeping with the Department of State. The United States has, in fact, been more successful in inducing its allies to share in the costs of the Gulf War and the Kosovo mission, indicating that a generalized collective-action strategy for burden sharing might be developed more easily with partners around the globe than with domestic agencies. In this regard, a careful accounting of the current expenditures in the international public sector might suggest ways to ensure a more effective use of available resources while alternative forms of financing—a young and controversial approach—are pursued.[44]

Building a public constituency. As Ed Luck has noted,

> At a time of great change in the world, it should come as no surprise that Americans are uncertain about the nature and scope of their global interests. Prevalent notions of interdependence, global markets, and humanity without borders coexist uneasily with a wariness of distant entanglements, a reluctance to serve as the world's police officer, and a preoccupation with domestic economic and social concerns. . . . Ambivalence may be the natural reaction to the ambiguities of a transition period in world politics, but it provides a shaky foundation for global leadership.[45]

Implicit in Luck's comment is the notion that global leadership must begin at home. The United States has struggled to find a rationale to underpin a global strategy since the end of the Cold War when the "common enemy" basis for U.S. engagement gave way to more diffuse notions of a "new world order" and, subsequently, the spread of liberal democracy and open markets abroad. Neither of these organizing principles, however, seems to have caught the imagination of an American public that is understandably more concerned with the tangible impacts of globalization on their lives than with the abstractions of foreign policy.

While poll after poll demonstrates that a substantial majority of the public endorses a global role for the United States, there is considerable skepticism about the particular institutions and programs through which this role is exercised. Steven Kull demonstrates, for example, that an overwhelming proportion of the American public supports U.S. participation in the UN, even though they have reservations about how the world body performs. And Lyman points out that despite strong moral underpinnings for U.S. engagement abroad, there is considerable uncertainty among the American public over the best way to conduct peacekeeping, manage the environment, or mitigate the detrimental effects of globalization abroad. Moreover, while some U.S. citizens harbor concerns about infringements on the nation's sovereignty through the domestic application of international law, immigration, or the potential displacement effect of low-paid jobs abroad, still more endorse global action through multilateral means for the legitimacy and burden sharing that they provide.

While these occasionally conflicting attitudes may appear paradoxical, they also suggest that U.S. public opinion is nuanced and pragmatic and that the public would be receptive to an informed debate about the changing nature of international affairs, particularly as regards the relationship between domestic and international issues. Insulating U.S. citizens from the facts of globalization will not afford them immunity. Nor will the campaign rhetoric, combative punditry, and seeking of political scapegoats of the kind that so damaged the UN over recent years inform the public about how the interaction between domestic and international issues affects their daily lives and how it can be better managed. Rather, the media need to help inform the public about connections between events abroad and impacts at home, whether in the areas of health, environment, employment, or public safety. Politicians and the public alike need to understand the role of the international public sector in providing a range of international goods and services that help to regulate and order international commerce, transportation, and the health and welfare of people around the world. While this process of enlightenment can and should be undertaken by private groups dedicated to public advocacy, there will be no substitute for leadership from Congress and from the White House to mobilize public support for effective multilateral engagement just as the country has done in other critical moments of the nation's history.

Notes

I am grateful to Charles Graybow, Maurizio Iacopetta, Abby Stoddard, Leona Shluger Forman, and Jacob Forman for their careful reading, fact checking, and content suggestions on this chapter. Barnett Rubin, Stewart Patrick, William Luers, and Princeton Lyman made excellent substantive and editorial suggestions.

1. National Intelligence Council, *Global Trends 2015*, p. 13.

2. Union of International Associations, *Yearbook of International Organizations, 2000–2001*, p. 2406. Calculations by the Center on International Cooperation, at New York University, suggest that the United States is signatory to about 7 percent of the intergovernment bodies and to more than 5,000 conventions and treaties, including bilateral agreements. Over 500 conventions and treaties are deposited with the UN secretary-general. United Nations, *Millennium Summit Multilateral Treaty Framework*. To put this in perspective, the number of intergovernment organizations is more than ten times the number of countries in the world, and about half the number of companies listed on the New York Stock Exchange.

3. The Center on International Cooperation has identified twenty-six areas of multilateral cooperation, which it groups into seven major sectors: economic development; economic and political cooperation; social development; international law; security; science, technology, and communications; and the environment. This public sector consists of some 1,800 intergovernmental organizations, at least 200 of them operating at the regional level; tens of thousands of international civil servants; and equal numbers of private voluntary agencies and their staffs. The center estimates that the annual expenditures of international organizations amount to approximately $300 billion (excluding loan disbursements). Moreover, the OECD's Development Assistance Committee disbursed roughly $40 billion in bilateral aid in 1998, according to the organization. Therefore, the center estimates that at least $300 billion are spent annually for the international public sector.

4. Kaul, Grunberg, and Stern, *Global Public Goods*.

5. Forman and Patrick, eds., *Good Intentions.*

6. See Kahler, "Multilateralism with Small and Large Numbers"; Keohane, *After Hegemony;* Keohane, *International Institutions and State Power;* Ruggie, *Constructing the World Polity;* and Ruggie, "Multilateralism: The Anatomy of an Institution."

7. Kaul, Grunberg, and Stern, eds., *Global Public Goods;* Kanbur and Sandler with Morrison, *The Future of Development Assistance.*

8. Reinicke, *Global Public Policy.*

9. The process of devolution is occurring differentially across the world's regions, most aggressively in Europe and Africa where there has been a multiplication of regional and subregional organizations, as well as across sectors. It is most evident in peacekeeping, but has begun to occur in the fields of humanitarian assistance, human rights, environmental management, and international crime control, and has been broached as a modality for dealing with financial crises. It is also reflected in debates on regional trade associations as "building blocks" or "stumbling blocks" on the way to global markets.

10. Patrick, "America's Retreat from Multilateral Engagement," p. 439.

11. Concluding his introductory essay to the landmark volume, *Multilateralism Matters,* John Ruggie sounds an optimistic note about the durability and adaptability of multilateral institutions, which he roots in the shared principles of expectation and reciprocity that order relations and guide conduct among states. Chiding his academic colleagues for their failure to take note of the importance of institutions and the forms that they assume, he notes (p. 35), "Above all else, policymakers groping for alternatives amid rapid change, hoping to grasp the flow of events and channel it in desirable directions, do not deal in generic choices; theirs are palpably concrete."

12. The Project on International Courts and Tribunals has identified fifteen operating international courts and tribunals. For a full description of these bodies, their jurisdictions, operating budgets, staffs, and decisions, see *www.pict-pcti.org*

13. The Global Public Policy Web site, *www.globalpublicpolicy.net,* describes a diverse number of these public private collaboratives, including the World Commission on Dams, Global Networks for Democracy Promotion, and Jubilee 2000. Our own center has proposed the creation of a Strategic Recovery Facility that would have at hand the expertise and financial resources necessary for reconstructing war-torn societies, economies, and polities. See Forman, Patrick, and Salomons, "Recovering From Conflict: Strategy For An International Response."

14. A recent example can be found in the debates surrounding the *Report of the Panel on United Nations Peace Operations,* the so-called Brahimi Report, which was endorsed by the Security Council with much prodding from the permanent representative of the United States, Richard Holbrooke, but seriously eviscerated by the General Assembly.

15. Regional organizations are most developed in Europe. They have proliferated in Africa, and are present in significant numbers in Latin America and the Caribbean. Their absence is most notable in Asia. See Graybow, Iacopetta, and O'Brien, "A Geographically Based Introduction to Regional Intergovernmental Organizations."

16. The United States has undertaken training and capacity-building activities with a number of regional and subregional organizations, primarily in Africa, but it has done so in an ad hoc and one-off basis, rather than as part of a broader international public policy for developing and sharing responsibility with these organizations.

17. Florini, ed., *The Third Force;* Mathews, "Delinquent Diplomacy," *Washington Post,* March 10, 1997.

18. Forman and Stoddard, "International Assistance."

19. It is interesting to note that these three most visible players are all U.S. citizens with global commercial interests. Moreover, to meet the estimated $300 billion estimated annual costs of the international public sector would require three thousand gifts of the size of Ted Turner's!

20. Patrick, "America's Retreat from Multilateral Engagement," p. 433.

21. Luck enumerates these criteria: (1) a sense of fairness in their processes and consistency with U.S. values; (2) accountability and adherence to democratic principles; (3) compatibility with notions of U.S. exceptionalism; (4) capacity to produce results; and (5) the degree to which they preserve or undermine national sovereignty.

22. The one exception is Moravcsik, who argues that "little current available evidence . . . supports the speculative claim that the U.S. failure to ratify multilateral treaties has undermined U.S. foreign policy, U.S. human rights policy, or global enforcement of human rights. The primary influence of U.S. unilateralism is instead on American citizens at home, who might otherwise be able to plead a broader range of rights before U.S. courts."

23. Although actual cost is nearly impossible to estimate, the U.S. failure to act decisively and early in support of some multilateral arrangements might actually raise the real costs of action over the longer term. Climate change is one case in point. What will be the consequences, for example, if greenhouse gases are allowed to increase over the next decade for want of sufficient U.S. leadership to achieve multilateral agreement and action? While scientific agreement on this subject has not been reached, there is sufficient evidence to suggest that containment costs will increase as the effects of emissions aggregate. The same sort of cost calculation might be made in other fields, such as nonproliferation, making it advisable to conduct a careful accounting of the differential costs and benefits of U.S. behavior in particular issue areas and across the international public sector as a whole, both over the short and long term. For a discussion of the costs of disaggregated humanitarian assistance, see Forman, "Underwriting Humanitarian Assistance."

24. As three former secretaries of defense state in an op-ed piece in the *New York Times,* "There are advantages to the United States in our international relations in ratifying the test ban treaty. The treaty is an important element of the global nonproliferation regime and crucial to American leadership of those efforts." Brown, Laird and Perry, "Ratify, but Review," *New York Times,* January 7, 2001.

25. International law in general, and the ICC in particular, represent particular challenges to conceptions of U.S. sovereignty and the preeminence of U.S. law. Yet, the ICC would seem to represent the fulfillment of U.S. aspirations for a more effective international rule of law regime than the current case-by-case, ad hoc arrangements appear to provide.

26. The United States actually stood with the failed state of Somalia as the only two countries to not sign the Convention.

27. Luck, "The United Nations, Multilateralism and U.S. Interests," p. 31.

28. Moravcsik argues further that for a powerful state like the United States more is to be achieved through unilateral or bilateral approaches than through the demands that multilateral arrangements would make on its autonomy of action or legal sovereignty.

29. Council on Foreign Relations, "American National Interests and the United Nations."

30. See Luers, "Choosing Engagement."

31. Mathews, "Delinquent Diplomacy"; U.S. Department of State, "Advance Appropriations Arrears Request," September 30, 1997.

32. The National Intelligence Council is a research arm of the CIA, composed of a chairman, a vice-chairman, and twelve intelligence officers. It is tasked with coordinating the mid- and long-term strategic analysis of the intelligence community, a group of thirteen U.S. government intelligence agencies and organizations.

33. National Intelligence Council, *Global Trends 2015*, p. 8.

34. See Reinicke, *Global Public Policy.* Also, visit the Web site of the Centre for Global Studies, University of Victoria at *http://www.globalcentres.org*

35. UNAIDS is the only UN organization in which NGOs sit on the executive board. The participating NGOs are selected by regional NGO bodies and rotate every few years. The Gates Foundation is represented on the WHO vaccine program board, and both the Ford and Rockefeller foundations are members of the International Agriculture Research Centers chaired by the World Bank.

36. Lancaster, "Redesigning Foreign Aid," p. 80. The coordination efforts should be pressed within the OECD's Development Assistance Committee.

37. Kanbur and Sandler, *The Future of Development Assistance,* p. 2.

38. There is something to be said for returning the UN Secretariat to its original mission as a forum for setting international norms, laws, and standards, leaving its operational aspirations to its specialized agencies and their private sector partners. Regarding current weakness of the UN and the need to fortify it, see Luers, "Choosing Engagement."

39. Slaughter, "The Real New World Order."

40. Austin, *The Collaboration Challenge;* Levy, *Give and Take.*

41. These NGO forums—on the environment, population and development, social development, human rights, women rights, and human habitats—did a great deal to establish nonstate actors as serious players in international affairs that were often able, either as members of country delegations or through extensive lobbying, to advocate for progressive ideas and programs.

42. Lancaster, "Redesigning Foreign Aid," p. 82.

43. See *http://www.codeal.org/2001/html;* Gardner, "The One Percent Solution."

44. The Center on International Cooperation is currently mapping public expenditures and sources of financing across the range of international public sector activities. While the field of international public finance is relatively new and there is little support for most international taxing schemes, alternative means for ensuring predictable sources of international public financing are being developed. See, for example, Mendez, *International Public Finance.*

45. In Luck, "The United Nations, Multilateralism and U.S. Interests," p. 27.

Acronyms and Abbreviations

ABA	American Bar Association
ABM	Anti-Ballistic Missile (treaty)
ACABQ	Advisory Committee on Administrative and Budgetary Questions (UN)
ACLU	American Civil Liberties Union
AFL-CIO	American Federation of Labor–Congress of Industrial Organizations
AIDS	Acquired Immune Deficiency Syndrome
AMF	Asian Monetary Fund
APEC	Asia-Pacific Economic Cooperation (forum)
ASEAN	Association of Southeast Asian Nations
ATIF	Americans Talk Issues Foundation
BTU	British Thermal Unit
BWC	Biological and Toxin Weapons Convention
CD	Geneva Conference on Disarmament
CEDAW	Convention on the Elimination of All Forms of Discrimination Against Women
CIC	Center on International Cooperation
CICC	Coalition for an International Criminal Court
CoCom	Coordinating Committee for Multilateral Export Controls
COP	Conference of the Parties (climate change)
CPC	Committee for Program and Coordination (UN)
CRC	Convention on the Rights of the Child
CTBT	Comprehensive Nuclear Test Ban Treaty
CWC	Chemical Weapons Convention
DOD	Department of Defense
DOE	Department of Energy
DPKO	Department of Peacekeeping Operations (UN)
DSU	Dispute Settlement Understanding (WTO)
ECHR	European Convention on Human Rights

ECOWAS	Economic Community of West African States
EEC	European Economic Community
EPA	Environmental Protection Agency
ESF	Exchange Stabilization Fund
EU	European Union
FAO	Food and Agriculture Organization
FBI	Federal Bureau of Investigation
FTAA	Free Trade Area for the Americas
FY	Fiscal year
GAO	General Accounting Office
GATT	General Agreement on Tariffs and Trade
GDP	Gross Domestic Product
G-7	Group of Seven
G-8	Group of Eight
GHG	greenhouse gas
GNP	Gross National Product
HHS	Health and Human Services (Department of)
HIPC	Highly Indebted Poor Countries (initiative)
HIV/AIDS	Human Immunodeficiency Virus
IAEA	International Atomic Energy Agency
ICBM	intercontinental ballistic missile
ICC	International Criminal Court
ICCPR	International Covenant on Civil and Political Rights
ICTR	International Criminal Tribunal for Rwanda
ICTY	International Criminal Tribunal for the Former Yugoslavia
IFIs	International financial institutions
ILO	International Labor Organization
ILSA	Iran-Libya Sanctions Act
IMF	International Monetary Fund
INF	Intermediate-Range Nuclear Forces (treaty)
INS	Immigration and Naturalization Service
IPCC	Intergovernmental Panel on Climate Change
IRA	Irish Republican Army
ITO	International Trade Organization
KFOR	Kosovo Force
MAD	mutually assured destruction
NAC	North Atlantic Council
NAFTA	North American Free Trade Agreement
NATO	North Atlantic Treaty Organization
NGO	Nongovernmental organization
NIEO	new international economic order
NIH	National Institutes of Health
NMD	National Missile Defense
NPT	Nuclear Non-Proliferation Treaty

NSC	National Security Council
NSD	National Security Directive
NTBs	non-tariff barriers
OAS	Organization of American States
OAU	Organization of African Unity
OECD	Organization for Economic Cooperation and Development
OMB	Office of Management and Budget
OPCW	Organization for the Prohibition of Chemical Weapons
OSCE	Organization for Security and Cooperation in Europe
PDD	Presidential Decision Directive
PIPA	Program on International Policy Attitudes
PNET	Peaceful Nuclear Explosions Treaty
PRD	Policy Review Document
PSI	private-sector involvement
RTAA	Reciprocal Trade Agreements Act
SALT	Strategic Arms Limitation Talks (I, II)
SDR	Special Drawing Right
SEATO	Southeast Asian Treaty Organization
START	Strategic Arms Reduction Treaty
TRIPs	trade-related intellectual property agreements
TTBT	Threshold Test Ban Treaty
UN	United Nations
UNESCO	United Nations Educational, Scientific, and Cultural Organization
UNFCCC	United Nations Framework Convention on Climate Change
UNHCR	United Nations High Commission for Refugees
UNICEF	United Nations Children's Fund
UNOSOM	United Nations Operation in Somalia
UNPROFOR	United Nations Protection Force (Bosnia-Herzegovina)
UNSCOM	United Nations Special Commission on Iraq
USAID	United States Agency for International Development
USDA	United States Department of Agriculture
USTR	United States Trade Representative
WCRP	World Climate Research Program
WHO	World Health Organization
WMD	weapons of mass destruction
WTO	World Trade Organization

Bibliography

Aaronson, Susan Ariel. *Trade and the American Dream: A Social History of Postwar Trade Policy* (Lexington: University of Kentucky Press, 1996).

Abbott, Kenneth W. "Defining the Extraterritorial Reach of U.S. Export Controls: Congress as Catalyst," *Cornell International Law Journal* 17 (Winter 1984): 79–158.

Aggarwal, Vinod K. "Comparing Regional Cooperation Efforts in the Asia-Pacific and North America," in Andrew Mack and John Ravenhill, eds., *Pacific Cooperation: Building Economic and Security Regimes in the Asia-Pacific Region* (Boulder, CO: Westview Press, 1995).

Aita, Judy. "U.S. Supports Stronger UN Peacekeeping Operations," USIA No. 247189 (October 10, 1992).

Albright, Madeleine K. "The United States and the United Nations: Confrontation or Consensus?" (Address to the Council on Foreign Relations, Washington, DC, January 26, 1995), *U.S. Department of State Dispatch* 6, 6 (February 6, 1995).

Alden, Chris. "From Neglect to 'Virtual Engagement': The United States and Its New Paradigm for Africa," *African Affairs,* 396 (July 2000): 355–371.

Alibek, Ken, with Stephen Handelman. *Biohazard.* (New York: Random House. 1999).

Allard, Kenneth. *Somalia: Lessons Learned* (Washington, DC: National Defense University Press, Institute for National Strategic Studies, 1995).

Alston, Philip, "The Commission on Human Rights," in Philip Alston, ed., *The United Nations and Human Rights: A Critical Appraisal* (Oxford: Oxford University Press, 1992).

Amnesty International. *United States of America: Rights for All—Amnesty International's Recommendations to the United States Government to Address Human Rights Violations in the USA* (New York: Amnesty International, 1998).

Anderson, Kenneth. "The Ottawa Convention Banning Landmines, the Role of International Non-Governmental Organizations and the Idea of International Civil Society," *European Journal of International Law* 11, 1 (2000): 91–120.

Andreani, Gilles. "The Disarray of U.S. Non-Proliferation Policy," *Survival* 41, 4 (Winter 1999–2000): 42–61.

Arms Control and Disarmament Agreements: Texts and Histories of the Negotiations. (Washington, DC: U.S. Arms Control and Disarmament Agency, U.S. Department of State, 1996).

Arthur, Admiral Stanley R. (USN, Ret.) et al. Letter to William J. Clinton, April 3, 1997.

Austin, James E. *The Collaboration Challenge: How Nonprofits and Businesses Succeed through Strategic Alliances* (San Francisco: Jossey-Bass, 2000).

Baker, James A., III. *The Politics of Diplomacy: Revolution, War and Peace, 1989–1992* (New York: G. P. Putnam and Sons, 1995).

Baldwin, David A. *Economic Statecraft* (Princeton, NJ: Princeton University Press, 1985).

———. "Evaluating Economic Sanctions," *International Security* 23, 2 (Fall 1998): 189–195.

Bales, Susan Nall. "Communicating Global Interdependence," memo commissioned by the Frameworks Institute for the Global Interdependence Initiative of the Aspen Institute, August 2000.

Bank for International Settlements. *Central Bank Survey of Foreign Exchange Activity* (Basle, Switzerland: Bank for International Settlements, April 1999).

Barnett, Michael N. "Bringing in the New World Order: Liberalism, Legitimacy, and the United Nations," *World Politics* 49, 4 (July 1997): 526–551.

———. "The Limits of Peacekeeping, Spheres of Influence, and the Future of the United Nations," in Joseph Lepgold and Thomas G. Weiss, eds., *Collective Conflict Management and Changing World Politics* (Albany: State University of New York Press, 1998).

Barnett, Michael N., and Martha Finnemore. "The Politics, Power, and Pathologies of International Organizations," *International Organization* 53, 4 (Autumn 1999): 699–732.

Bassiouni, M. Cherif. "From Versailles to Rwanda in Seventy-Five Years: The Need to Establish a Permanent International Criminal Court," *Harvard Human Rights Journal* 10, 11 (1997): 11–62.

Bayard, Thomas O. and Kimberly Ann Elliott. *Reciprocity and Retaliation in U.S. Trade Policy* (Washington, DC: Institute for International Economics, 1994).

"Bechtel's Cargoscan to Support INF Verification," *Defense News* 4, 16 (April 17, 1989): 35.

Beetham, David. *The Legitimation of Power* (Atlantic Highlands, NJ: Humanities Press International, 1991).

Bell, Coral. "American Ascendancy and the Pretense of Concert," *The National Interest* 57 (Fall 1999): 9–64.

Bell, Daniel. "The 'Hegelian Secret': Civil Society and American Exceptionalism," in Byron Shafer, ed., *Is America Different? A New Look at American Exceptionalism* (Oxford: Clarendon Press, 1991).

Benedick, Richard Elliot. *Ozone Diplomacy: New Directions in Safeguarding the Planet* (Cambridge, MA: Harvard University Press, 1991).

Berdal, Mats R. "Fateful Encounter: the United States and UN Peacekeeping," *Survival* 36, 1 (spring 1994): 30–50.

Berger, Samuel K. "American Foreign Policy for the Global Age," *Foreign Affairs* 79, 6 (November/December 2000): 22–39.

Berger, Samuel R. "American Power: Hegemony, Isolationism or Engagement," remarks to the Council on Foreign Relations, October 21, 1999, available online at *http://www.whitehouse.gov/WH/EOP/NSC/html/speeches/19991021.html* and at *www.foreignrelations.org/public/pubs/SbergerPrepRemarks.html*

Bergsten, C. Fred. "Towards a Tripartite World," *The Economist*, July 15, 2000.

Berman, Harold, and John Garson. "U.S. Export Controls—Past, Present, and Future," *Columbia Law Review* 67, 5 (1967): 791–890.

Bhagwati, Jagdish. "Aggressive Unilateralism: An Overview," in Bhagwati and Patrick, *Aggressive Unilateralism: America's 301 Trade Policy and the World Trading System* (Ann Arbor: University of Michigan Press, 1990).

———. *The World Trading System at Risk* (New York: Harvester Wheatsheaf, 1991).

Bhagwati, Jagdish, and Hugh T. Patrick, eds. *Aggressive Unilateralism: America's 301 Trade Policy and the World Trading System* (Ann Arbor: University of Michigan Press, 1990).

Blechman, Barry. "Emerging from the Intervention Dilemma," in Chester A. Crocker and Fen Osler Hampson, eds., *Managing Global Chaos: Sources of and Responses to International Conflict* (Washington, DC: U.S. Institute of Peace, 1996).

Bloomfield, Lincoln. "From Ideology to Program to Policy: Tracking the Carter Human Rights Policy," *Journal of Policy Analysis and Management* 2, 1 (1982): 1–12.

Bolton, John. "Should We Take Global Governance Seriously?" Paper presented at the American Enterprise Institute conference, "Trends in Global Governance: Do They Threaten American Sovereignty?" Washington, DC, April 4–5, 2000.

Bosco, David L. "Sovereign Myopia," *The American Prospect* 41 (November/ December 1998): 24–27.

Boutros-Ghali, Boutros. *Unvanquished: A U.N.–U.S. Saga* (New York: Random House, 1999).

Bowden, Mark. *Black Hawk Down* (New York: Atlantic Monthly Press, 1999).

Brenton, Tony. *The Greening of Machiavelli: The Evolution of International Environmental Politics* (London: Earthscan, 1994).

Brierly, J. *The Law of Nations: An Introduction to the International Law of Peace*, 6th ed. (Oxford: Oxford University Press, 1963).

Brilmayer, Lea. *American Hegemony: Political Morality in a One-Superpower World* (New Haven, CT: Yale University Press, 1994).

Brinkley, Douglas. "The Clinton Doctrine," *Foreign Policy* 106 (Spring 1997) 111–127.

Brown, Marjorie Ann. *United Nations Peacekeeping: Issues for Congress*, CRS Issue Brief IB90103, Congressional Research Service, January 12, 2001.

Brownlie, Ian. *Principles of Public International Law*, 2nd ed. (Oxford: Oxford University Press, 1973).

Buchanan, Patrick J. *The Great Betrayal: How American Sovereignty and Social Justice Are Being Sacrificed to the Gods of the Global Economy* (Boston: Little, Brown, 1998).

Budget of the United States Government: Fiscal Year 2001 (Washington, DC: U.S. Government Printing Office, 2000).

Burley, Anne-Marie. "Regulating the World: Multilateralism, International Law, and the Projection of the New Deal Regulatory State," in John Gerard Ruggie, ed., *Multilateralism Matters: The Theory and Praxis of an Institutional Form* (New York: Columbia University Press, 1993).

Bush, George. *The President's News Conference on the Persian Gulf Conflict*, January 18, 1991. Public papers, George Bush Presidential Library, *http:// bushlibrary.tamu.edu/papers/1991/91011800.html*

———. *Address to the United Nations General Assembly in New York City*, September 21, 1992. Public papers, George Bush Presidential Library, *http:// bushlibrary.tamu.edu/papers/1992/92092100.html*

———. *Remarks to the United Nations Security Council in New York City*, January 31, 1992. Public papers, George Bush Presidential Library, *http://bushlibrary. tamu.edu/papers/1992/92013100.html*

Bush, George, and Brent Scowcroft. *A World Transformed* (New York: Alfred A. Knopf, 1998).

Buzan, Barry, and Gerald Segal. "Rethinking East Asian Security," *Survival* 36 (Summer 1994).

Cahill, Kevin. *Trade Wars: The High Technology Scandal of the 1980s* (London: W. H. Allen, 1986).

Calomiris, Charles W. "Blueprint for a New Financial Architecture," photocopy (New York: Columbia University, 1998).

Canada, Department of Foreign Affairs and International Trade. "Government Introduces Legislation to Counter U.S. Helms-Burton Act," 1996.

Caporaso, James A. "International Relations Theory and Multilateralism: The Search for Foundations," in John Gerard Ruggie, ed., *Multilateralism Matters: The Theory and Praxis of an Institutional Form* (New York: Columbia University Press, 1993).

Caron, David D. "The Legitimacy of the Collective Authority of the Security Council," *The American Journal of International Law* 87 (1993).

Carpenter, Will D. "How Industry Came to Support the CWC," *OPCW Synthesis, Year in Review 2000*, 48–50.

Carter, Ralph. "Congress and Post–Cold War US Foreign Policy, in James M. Scott, *After the End: Making Foreign Policy in the Post-Cold War World* (Durham, NC: Duke University Press, 1998).

Center on Policy Attitudes. "Americans on Federal Budget Priorities," October 3, 2000.

Center for Security Policy. "Why the Senate Must *Not* Approve the Chemical Weapons Convention." Decision Brief 96-D 45, May 9, 1996.

———. "How Can the 'World's Greatest Deliberative Body' Deliberate on the C.W.C. Unless the Administration Answers the Mail?" Decision Brief 96-D 80, August 26, 1996.

———. "What the World Does *Not* Need Is Any More of Clinton's Non-Proliferation *Non*-Achievements." Decision Brief 96-P81, September 9, 1996.

———. "Republicans' Senate Leadership Offers Constructive Alternative to Fatally Flawed Chemical Weapons Convention." Decision Brief 97-D 43, March 21, 1997.

Cerna, Christina. "The United States and the American Convention on Human Rights: Prospects and Problems of Ratification," in David P. Forsythe, ed., *The United States and Human Rights: Looking Inward and Outward* (Lincoln: University of Nebraska Press, 2000).

Certain Expenses of the United Nations 1962 I.C.J. 151.

Chalmers, Malcolm. *Sharing Security: The Political Economy of Burdensharing* (London: MacMillan, 2000).

Chayes, Abram. *The Cuban Missile Crisis* (New York: Oxford University Press, 1974).

Chayes, Abram, and Antonia H. Chayes. "On Compliance," *International Organization* 47, 2 (Spring 1993): 175–205.

Chemical Manufacturers Association and the Business Executives for National Security. "Making Americans Safer: The Case for the Chemical Weapons Convention (CWC)." Pamphlet, spring 1996 and spring 1997.

"Chemical Weapon Destruction in Russia: Political, Legal and Technical Aspects," in John Hart and Cynthia D. Miller, eds., *Chemical & Biological Warfare Studies* 17, Stockholm International Peace Research Institute (Oxford: Oxford University Press, 1998).

Chinkin, Christine. "The State that Acts Alone: Bully, Good Samaritan, or Iconoclast?" *European Journal of International Law* 11, 3 (2000): 31–41.

Claude, Inis L., Jr. "Collective Legitimacy as a Political Function of the United Nations," *International Organization* 20, 3 (Summer 1966): 367–379.

Clawson, Patrick. "Iran," in Richard N. Haass, ed., *Economic Sanctions and American Diplomacy* (New York: Council on Foreign Relations, 1998).

Cleveland, Harlan van Buren. *The Atlantic Idea and its European Rivals* (Washington, DC: The Brookings Institution, 1966).

Cline, William R. 1995. *International Debt Reexamined* (Washington, DC: Institute for International Economics).

———. "The Management of Financial Crises," preliminary draft (Washington, DC: Institute for International Finance, June 2000).

Clinton, William. "President William J. Clinton Delivers Remarks to the UN General Assembly," Federal Document Clearing House, September 21, 1999.

———. Statement by the president on the Comprehensive Test Ban Treaty, Lyon, France, June 28, 1996.

———. Remarks by the president in address to the 51st General Assembly of the United Nations, New York, September 24, 1996.

Committee on International Security and Arms Control of the National Academy of Sciences. *Nuclear Arms Control Background and Issues* (Washington, DC: National Academy Press, 1985).

Conference on Disarmament. Document 500 (Geneva: Chemical Weapons Ad Hoc Committee, April 13, 1984).

Congressional Budget Office National Security Division. *Costs of Operations*, January 24, 2001.

Cooper, Andrew Fenton, Richard A. Higgott, and Kim Richard Nossal. "Bound to Follow? Leadership and Followership in the Gulf Crisis," *Political Science Quarterly* 106, 3 (1991): 391–410.

Council of Economic Advisers. *Economic Report of the President* (Washington, DC: U.S. Government Printing Office, 1994).

Council on Foreign Relations. *Safeguarding Prosperity in a Global Financial System: The Future International Financial Architecture.* Task Force Report. (New York and Washington, DC: Council on Foreign Relations and Institute for International Economics, 1999).

———. "American National Interests and the United Nations: Statement and Report of an Independent Task Force" (New York: Council on Foreign Relations, 1996).

Cowhey, Peter. "Elect Locally—Order Globally: Domestic Politics and Multilateral Cooperation," in John Gerard Ruggie, ed., *Multilateralism Matter: The Theory and Praxis of an Institutional Form* (New York: Columbia University Press, 1993).

Crone, Donald. "Does Hegemony Matter? The Reorganization of the Pacific Political Economy," *World Politics* 45 (July 1993): 501–525.

Crozier, Michael. *The Bureaucratic Phenomenon* (Chicago: University of Chicago Press, 1964).

Daalder, Ivo H. "Knowing When to Say No: The Development of U.S. Policy for Peacekeeping," in William J. Durch, ed., *UN Peacekeeping, American Politics, and the Uncivil Wars of the 1990s* (Basingstoke: Macmillan, 1997).

Daalder, Ivo, James M. Goldgeier, and James M. Lindsay. "Deploying NMD: Not Whether, but How," *Survival* 42, 1 (Spring 2000): 6–28.

Dallek, Robert. *The American Style of Foreign Policy: Cultural Politics and Foreign Affairs* (New York: Alfred A. Knopf, 1983).

De Gregorio, Jose, Barry Eichengreen, Takatoshi Ito, and Charles Wyplosz. *An Independent and Accountable IMF.* Geneva Reports on the World Economy (Geneva: International Center for Monetary and Banking Studies and Center for Economic Policy Research, 1999).

Deibel, Terry L. *Clinton and Congress,* The Foreign Policy Association, Headline Series, 321 (Fall 2000).

Den Boer, Monica, and William Wallace. "Justice and Home Affairs," in Helen Wallace and William Wallace, eds., *Policy-Making in the European Union*, 4th ed. (Oxford: Oxford University Press, 2000).

Department of Defense. *Dictionary of Military and Associated Terms* (Washington, DC: GPO, 2000).

———. *Joint Pub 3-07.3 Joint Tactics, Techniques and Procedures for Peace Operations* (Washington, DC: U.S. Government Printing Office, 1999).

Department of State, Bureau of International Organization Affairs. *The Clinton Administration's Policy on Reforming Multilateral Peace Operations* (Washington, DC: U.S. Government Printing Office, 1994).

Destler, I. M., and C. Randall Henning. *Dollar Politics: Exchange Rate Policymaking in the United States* (Washington, DC: Institute for International Economics, 1989).

Dimoff, Steven A. "U.N. Arrears: 106th Congress Picks Up Where Last Left Off," *The Interdependent* 25, 1 (Spring 1999): 9–10.

———. "Congress and President in Tug-of-War over U.N. Arrears," *The Interdependent* 25, 3 (Fall 1999): 5–6.

Dinstein, Yoram. *War, Aggression, and Self-Defence*, 2nd ed. (Cambridge: Cambridge University Press, 1994).

Divine, Robert. *Second Chance: The Triumph of Liberal Internationalism in America During World War II* (New York: Atheneum, 1967).

Dole, Robert. "Shaping America's Global Future," *Foreign Policy* 98 (Spring 1995): 29–43.

Doyle, Michael W. "Kant, Liberal Legacies, and Foreign Affairs," *Philosophy & Public Affairs* 12, 3 and 4 (Summer and Fall 1983): 205–235, 323–353.

Dunne, Michael. "US Foreign Policy in the Twentieth Century: from World Power to Global Hegemony," *International Affairs* 76, 1 (January 2000): 25–40.

Durch, William J., ed. *The Evolution of UN Peacekeeping: Case Studies and Comparative Analysis* (New York: St. Martin's Press, 1993).

Editors. "Think Again: Clinton's Foreign Policy," *Foreign Policy* 121 (November/ December 2000): 18–29.

Eichengreen, Barry. *Toward a New International Financial Architecture* (Washington, DC: Institute for International Economics, 1999).

Eichengreen, Barry, and Christof Ruehl. "The Bail-In Problem: Systematic Goals, Ad Hoc Means," Discussion Paper 2427 (London: Centre for Economic Policy Research, 2000).

Ellicott, John. "Extraterritorial Trade Controls—Law, Policy, and Business," in Martha L. Landwehr, ed., *Private Investors Abroad—Problems and Solutions in International Business, 1983* (New York: Matthew Bender, 1983).

Elliott, Kimberly Ann. "The Sanctions Glass: Half-Full or Completely Empty?" *International Security* 23, 1 (Summer 1998): 50–65.

———. "International Labor Standards and Trade: What Should be Done?" in Jeffrey J. Schott, ed., *Launching New Global Trade Talks: An Action Agenda*, Special Report 12 (Washington, DC: Institute for International Economics, 1998).

———. "Getting Beyond No . . . ! Promoting Worker Rights and Trade." In Jeffrey J. Schott, ed., *The WTO After Seattle* (Washington, DC: Institute for International Economics, 2000).

———. "The ILO and Enforcement of Core Labor Standards." Policy Brief Number 00-6 (Washington, DC: Institute for International Economics, 2000).

Ely, John Hart. *War and Responsibility: Constitutional Lessons of Vietnam and Its Aftermath* (Princeton, NJ: Princeton University Press, 1993).

Evans, Peter B., Harold K. Jacobson, and Robert D. Putnam, eds. *Double-Edged Diplomacy: International Bargaining and Domestic Politics* (Berkeley, CA: University of California Press, 1993).

Evans, Tony. *U.S. Hegemony and the Project of Universal Human Rights* (London: Macmillan, 1996).

Feldstein, Martin. "Refocusing the IMF," *Foreign Affairs* 77, 2 (March/April 1998): 2–33.

Fetter, Steve, and Thomas Garwin. "Tags," in Richard Kokoski and Sergey Koulik, eds., *Verification of Conventional Arms Control in Europe: Technological Constraints and Opportunities* (Boulder, CO: Westview Press, 1990).

Fitchett, Joseph. "West Exasperated by a Failed Intervention," *Tocqueville Connection* 16 (May 2000).

Fields, James M., and Howard Schuman. "Public Beliefs About the Beliefs of the Public," *Public Opinion Quarterly* 40 (1976): 427–448.

Florini, Ann M., ed. *The Third Force: The Rise of Transnational Civil Society* (Tokyo and Washington, DC: The Japan Center for International Exchange and the Carnegie Endowment for International Peace, 2000).

Foot, Rosemary. "Pacific Asia: The Development of Regional Dialogue," in Louise Fawcett and Andrew Hurrell, eds., *Regionalism in World Politic: Regional Organization and International Order* (Oxford: Oxford University Press, 1995).

Forman, Shepard, ed. *Diagnosing America: Anthropology and Public Engagement* (Ann Arbor: University of Michigan Press, 1994).

───. "Underwriting Humanitarian Assistance: Mobilizing Resources for Effective Action," in Kevin M. Cahill, ed., *A Framework for Survival: Health, Human Rights, and Humanitarian Assistance in Conflicts and Disasters* (New York: Basic Books and the Council on Foreign Relations, 1999).

Forman, Shepard, and Stewart Patrick, eds. *Good Intentions: Pledges of Aid for Post-Conflict Recovery* (Boulder, CO: Lynne Rienner Publishers, 2000).

Forman, Shepard, Stewart Patrick, and Dirk Salomons. 2000. "Recovering From Conflict: Strategy for An International Response," *Paying for Essentials: A Policy Paper Series* (New York: Center on International Cooperation).

Forman, Shepard, and Abby Stoddard. "International Assistance," in Lester Salamon, ed., *The State of America's Non-Profit Sector* (Bloomington: Indiana University Press, forthcoming).

Forsythe, David P. "The United States, the United Nations, and Human Rights," in Margaret Karns and Karen Mingst, eds., *The United States and Multilateral Institutions: Patterns of Changing Instrumentality and Interest* (Winchester: Unwin Hyman, 1990).

───, ed. *The United States and Human Rights: Looking Inward and Outward* (Lincoln: University of Nebraska Press, 2000).

Franck, Thomas M. *Fairness in International Law and Institutions* (Oxford: Clarendon Press, 1995).

Galtung, Johann. "On the Effects of International Economic Sanctions," *World Politics* 19, 3 (1967): 378–416.

Gardner, Lloyd C. *A Covenant with Power: American and World Order from Wilson to Reagan* (New York: Oxford University Press, 1984).

Gardner, Richard N. *Sterling-Dollar Diplomacy: The Origins and the Prospects of Our International Economic Order,* expanded ed. (New York: McGraw-Hill, 1969).

───. "The Comeback of Liberal Internationalism," *Washington Quarterly* 13, 3 (Summer 1990): 23–39.

————. "The One Percent Solution: Shirking the Cost of World Leadership," *Foreign Affairs* 79, 4 (July/August 2000): 2–11.

Gedmin, Jeffrey. "Our European Problem," *Weekly Standard* 5, 38, (June 19, 2000): 13.

Gee, John. "Implementing the CWC: Experiences After One Year of Entry into Force." Speech to the Friedrich Ebert Foundation, Bonn, May 7, 1998.

George, Alexander, and Timothy J. McKeown. "Case Studies and Theories of Organizational Decision-Making," *Advances in Information Processing in Organizations* 2 (1985): 21–58.

Gershman, Carl. "The United Nations and the New World Order," *Journal of Democracy* 4, 3 (July 1993): 5–16.

Gholz, Eugene, Daryl G. Press, and Harvey M. Sapolsky. "Come Home America: The Strategy of Restraint in the Face of Temptation," *International Security* 21, 4 (Spring 1997): 5–48.

Gilpin, Robert. *War and Change in International Politics* (New York: Cambridge University Press, 1981).

Global Climate Coalition. "21st Century Climate Action Agenda," *http://www.globalclimate.org/Policy_00_0301.htm*

Goethals, G. R. "Fabricating and Ignoring Social Reality: Self-Serving Estimates of Consensus," in C. P. Herman and M. P. Zanna, eds., *Relative Deprivation and Social Comparison: The Ontario Symposium on Social Cognition* 4 (Hillsdale, NJ: Lawrence Earlbaum Associates, 1986).

Goldsmith, Jack. "Should International Human Rights Law Trump US Domestic Law?" *Chicago Journal of International Law* 1, 2 (Fall 2000): 327–339.

Goldstein, Judith. "International Law and Domestic Institutions: Reconciling North American 'Unfair' Trade Laws," *International Organization* 50, no 4 (Summer 1996): 541–564.

Goldstein, Judith, and Lisa L. Martin. "Legalization, Trade Liberalization, and Domestic Politics: A Cautionary Note," *International Organization* 54, 3 (Summer 2000): 603–632.

Goldstein, Morris. *The Asian Financial Crisis: Causes, Cures, and Systemic Implications.* Policy Analyses in International Economics 55 (Washington, DC: Institute for International Economics, 1998).

————. "Strengthening the International Financial Architecture: Where Do We Stand?" Policy Brief Number 00-8 (Washington, DC: Institute for International Economics, 2000).

————. "IMF Structural Programs," National Bureau of Economic Research, Conference on Economic and Financial Crises in Emerging Market Economies, October 19–21, 2000, Woodstock, VT.

Goldstein, Morris, Graciela L. Kaminsky, and Carmen M. Reinhart. *Assessing Financial Vulnerability: An Early Warning System for Emerging Markets* (Washington, DC: Institute for International Economics, 2000).

Goodrich, Leland M. *Korea: A Study of U.S. Policy in the United Nations* (Westport, CT: Greenwood Press, 1956).

Gopinath, Deepak. "Who's the Boss," *Institutional Investor* 33, 9 (September 1999): 89–94.

Gore, Albert, Jr. *Earth in the Balance: Ecology and the Human Spirit* (Boston: Houghton Mifflin, 1992).

Gorman, Hubert J. "The Discovery of Pluralistic Ignorance," *Journal of the History of the Behavioral Sciences* 22 (1986): 333–347.

Gramna International. "U.S. Companies Launch Campaign Against Helms-Burton Act," April 29, 1997.

Graybow, Charles, Mauricio Iacopetta, and David O'Brien. "A Geographically Based Introduction to Regional Intergovernmental Organizations." Center on International Cooperation working paper available at *http//:www.cic.nyu.edu/ publications*

Greenburg, Lawrence. *Unilateral and Coalition Operations in the 1965 Dominican Republic Intervention* (Washington, DC: U.S. Army Center for Military History, 1987).

Gregg, Robert W. *About Face? The United States and the United Nations* (Boulder, CO: Lynne Rienner Publishers, 1993).

Grieco, Joseph M. "Systemic Sources of Variation in Regional Institutionalization in Western Europe, East Asia, and the Americas," in Edward Mansfield and Helen Milner, eds., *The Political Economy of Regionalism* (New York: Columbia University Press, 1997).

———. "Realism and Regionalism: American Power and German and Japanese Institutional Strategies During and After the Cold War," in Ethan B. Kapstein and Michael Mastanduno, eds., *Unipolar Politics: Realism and State Strategies After the Cold War* (New York: Columbia University Press, 1999).

Grosser, Alfred, *The Atlantic Alliance* (London: Macmillan, 1970).

Grubb, Michael, with Christiaan Vrolijk and Duncan Brack. *The Kyoto Protocol: A Guide and Assessment* (London: Royal Institute of International Affairs, 1999).

Guay, Terrence. "Local Government and Global Politics: The Implications of Massachusetts' Burma Law," *Political Science Quarterly* 115, 3 (Fall 2000): 353–376.

Gummer, John, and Robert Moreland. *The European Union & Global Climate Change* (Washington, DC: Pew Center on Global Climate Change, 2000).

Haass, Richard N. "Using Force: Lessons and Choices," in Chester A. Crocker and Fen Osler Hampson, eds., *Managing Global Chaos: Sources of and Responses to International Conflict* (Washington, DC: U.S. Institute of Peace, 1996).

———. "Sanctioning Madness," *Foreign Affairs* 76, 6 (November/December 1997): 74–85.

———. *The Reluctant Sheriff: The United States after the Cold War* (New York: Council on Foreign Relations, 1997).

———, ed. *Economic Sanctions and American Diplomacy* (New York: Council on Foreign Relations, 1998).

———. "What to Do with American Primacy," *Foreign Affairs* 78, 5 (September/ October 1999): pp. 37–49

Hamilton, Alexander. *Pacificus I*, in Harold Syrett, ed., *The Papers of Alexander Hamilton* (New York: Columbia University Press, 1979).

Hannum, U. S. Hurst, and Dana Fischer, eds. *Ratification of the International Covenants on Human Rights* (Washington, DC: The American Society of International Law, 1993).

Harahan, Joseph R. *On-Site Inspections Under the INF Treaty* (Washington, DC: U.S. Department of Defense, On-Site Inspection Agency, 1993).

Harding, Garret. "The Tragedy of the Commons," *Science* 162 (1968): 1243–1248.

Harper, John Lamberton. *American Visions of Europe* (New York: Cambridge University Press, 1996).

Harris, Paul G. "International Norms of Responsibility and U.S. Climate Change Policy," in Paul G. Harris, ed., *Climate Change and American Foreign Policy* (New York: St. Martin's Press, 2000).

Harris, Seymour E., ed. *The Dollar in Crisis* (New York: Harcourt, Brace and World, 1961).

Hartmann, Frederick H., ed. *Basic Documents of International Relations* (1951).

Hartz, Louis. *The Liberal Tradition in America: An Interpretation of American Political Thought Since the Revolution* (New York: Harcourt, Brace and World, 1955).

Hathaway, James C. "America, Defender of Democratic Legitimacy?" *European Journal of International Law* 11, 1 (2000): 121–133.

Headquarters, Department of the Army. *FM 100-23 Peace Operations* (Washington, DC: Training and Doctrine Command, 1994).

Heisbourg, François. "Perceptions of the US Abroad," *Survival* 41, 4 (Winter 1999–2000): 5–15.

Helms, Senator Jesse. "Testimony January 20, 2000, Jesse Helms Senator Senate Foreign Relations Helms Address to Security Council," Federal Document Clearing House, January 20, 2000.

———. "Saving the U.N.: A Challenge to the Next Secretary-General," *Foreign Affairs* 75, 5 (September/October 1996): 2–7.

"Helms Declares U.N. Criminal Court 'Dead-on-Arrival' in Senate Without U.S. Veto," Congressional Press Releases, March 26, 1998.

Henkin, Louis. "US Ratification of Human Rights Conventions: The Ghost of Senator Bricker," *American Journal of International Law* 89 (1995): 341–349.

Henning, C. Randall. "The Exchange Stabilization Fund: Slush Money or War Chest?" *Policy Analyses in International Economics* 57 (Washington, DC: Institute for International Economics, May 1999).

Hillen, John. "Forced Isolation," *National Review* 50, 5 (March 23, 1998).

Hirsch, John and Robert Oakley. *Somalia & Operation Restore Hope: Reflections on Peacemaking & Peacekeeping* (Washington, DC: U.S. Institute of Peace Press, 1995).

Hirsh, Michael. "The Fall Guy: Washington's Self-Defeating Assault on the U.N.," *Foreign Affairs* (November/December 1999): 2–8.

Hoffmann, Stanley. "An American Social Science: International Relations," *Daedalus* 106, 3 (1977): 41–60.

Holloway, Steven. "U.S. Unilateralism at the UN: Why Great Powers Do Not Make Great Multilateralists," *Global Governance* 6, 3 (July–Sept. 2000): 361–381.

Holsti, Ole R. "Public Opinion and U.S. Foreign Policy after the Cold War," in James M. Scott, ed., *After the End: Making U.S. Foreign Policy in the Post–Cold War World* (Durham, NC: Duke University Press, 1998).

Holsti, Ole R., and James N. Rosenau. "Internationalism: Intact or in Trouble?" in Eugene R. Wittkopf and Christopher M. Jones, ed., *The Future of American Foreign Policy,* third edition (New York: Bedford/St. Martin's, 1999).

Holt, Victoria K. *Briefing Book on Peacekeeping: The US Role in United Nations Peace Operations* (Washington, DC: Council for a Livable World, 1994).

Hook, Steven W. "The White House, Congress, and the Paralysis of the U.S. State Department after the Cold War," in James M. Scott, *After the End: Making Foreign Policy in the Post–Cold War World* (Durham, NC: Duke University Press, 1998).

Hoopes, Townsend, and Douglas Brinkley. *FDR and the Creation of the U.N.* (New Haven, CT: Yale University Press, 1997).

Horowitz, Janice M., et al. "Winners & Losers: Seizing The Moment," *Time,* May 5, 1997.

Houghton, J. T., G. J. Jenkins, and J. J. Ephraums, eds. *Climate Change: The IPCC Scientific Assessment* (Cambridge: Cambridge University Press, 1990).

House of Lords. *Dealing with the Third Pillar: the Government's Perspective,* 15th Report from the House of Lords Select Committee on the European Union, Session 1997–1998 (London: Stationery Office, 1998).

Howard, Sean. "News Review," *Disarmament Diplomacy* 45 (April 2000).

Hudec, Robert E. "Thinking About the New Section 301: Beyond Good and Evil," in Jagdish Bhagwati and Hugh T. Patrick, eds., *Aggressive Unilateralism: America's 301 Trade Policy and the World Trading System* (Ann Arbor: University of Michigan Press, 1990).

———. *Enforcing International Trade Law* (Salem, NH: Butterworth Legal Publishers, 1993).

Hufbauer, Gary Clyde, and Daniel H. Rosen. "American Access to China's Market: The Congressional Vote on PNTR." Policy Brief Number 00-3 (Washington, DC: Institute for International Economics 2000).

Hufbauer, Gary Clyde, and Jeffrey Schott, with Kimberly Ann Elliott. *Economic Sanctions Reconsidered: History and Current Policy* (Washington, DC: Institute for International Economics, 1985).

Hufbauer, Gary Clyde, Jeffrey J. Schott, and Kimberly Ann Elliott. *Economic Sanctions Reconsidered*, 3rd ed. (Washington, DC: Institute for International Economics, 2001).

Hughes, Thomas. "The Twilight of Internationalism," *Foreign Policy* 64 (Winter 1985/1986).

Human Rights Violations in the United States: A Report on US Compliance with the International Covenant on Civil and Political Rights (New York: Human Rights Watch and the American Civil Liberties Union, 1993).

Huntington, Samuel. "The Lonely Superpower," *Foreign Affairs* 78, 2 (March/April 1999): 35–49.

Hurd, Ian. "Legitimacy and Authority in International Politics," *International Organization* 53, 2 (Spring 1999): 379–408.

Hurrell, Andrew. "Regionalism in Theoretical Perspective," in Louise Fawcett and Andrew Hurrell, eds., *Regionalism in World Politics: Regional Organization and International Order* (Oxford: Oxford University Press, 1995).

Ikenberry, G. John. "Constitutional Politics in International Relations," *European Review of International Relations* 4, 2 (June 1998): 147–177.

———. "Institutions, Strategic Restraint, and the Persistence of American Postwar Order," *International Security* 23, 3 (Winter 1998/1999): 43–78.

———. *After Victory: Institutions, Strategic Restraint, and the Rebuilding of Order After Major War* (Princeton, NJ: Princeton University Press, 2000).

Ikenberry, G. John, and Charles A. Kupchan. "Socialization and Hegemonic Power," *International Organization* 44, 4 (June 1990): 283–315.

Instructions for the Government of Armies of the United States in the Field, prepared by Francis Lieber, LL.D., Originally Issued as General Orders 100, Adjutant General's Office, April 24, 1863 (Washington, DC: U.S. Government Printing Office, 1898).

International Atomic Energy Agency Annual Report, "Number of States Having Significant Nuclear Activities at the End of 1997, 1998 and 1999," Table A13, on-line on October 21, 2000 at *http://www.iaea.org/worldatom/Documents/Anrep/Anrep99/table_a13.pdf*

International Criminal Tribunal for the Former Yugoslavia. *Final Report to the Prosecutor by the Committee Established to Review the NATO Bombing Campaign Against the Federal Republic of Yugoslavia*, June 8, 2000, 39 I.L.M. 1257 (2000).

International Institute of Strategic Studies, *The Military Balance* (1999).

Ivanov, Igor. "The Missile-Defense Mistake: Undermining Strategic Stability and the ABM Treaty," *Foreign Affairs* 79, 5 (September/October 2000): 15–20.

Jackson, John. *World Trade and the Law of GATT* (New York: The Bobbs-Merrill Company, 1969).

———. *The World Trading System* (Cambridge, MA: MIT Press, 1989).

Jacoby, Tamar. "The Reagan Turnaround on Human Rights," *Foreign Affairs* 64, 4 (Spring 1986): 1066–1086.

Jentleson, Bruce. *Pipeline Politics: The Complex Political Economy of East-West Energy Trade* (Ithaca, NY: Cornell University Press, 1986).

———. "Who, Why, What, and How: Debates Over Post–Cold War Military Intervention," in Robert J. Lieber, ed., *Eagle Adrift: American Foreign Policy at the End of the Century* (New York: Longman, 1997).

———. *American Foreign Policy: The Dynamics of Choice in the Twenty-First Century* (New York: W. W. Norton, 2000).

Jervis, Robert. "Realism, Neoliberalism, and Cooperation: Understanding the Debate," *International Security* 24, 1 (Summer 1999): 42–63.

Johansen, Robert C. "U.S. Policy Toward U.N. Peacekeeping: Addressing the Dissonance Between National Interests and Human Interests." Paper prepared for the International Studies Association, 41st Annual Convention, Los Angeles, CA, March 14–18, 2000.

Johnston, R. Barry, and V. Sundarajan. *Sequencing Financial Sector Reforms: Country Experience and Issues* (Washington, DC: International Monetary Fund, 1999).

Josling, Timothy. "Agricultural Trade Policy: Completing the Reform," in Jeffrey J. Schott, ed., *Launching New Global Trade Talks: An Action Agenda.* Special Report 12 (Washington, DC: Institute for International Economics, 1998).

Kagan, Robert. "The Benevolent Empire," *Foreign Policy* 111 (Summer 1998): 24–35.

Kahler, Miles. "The United States and the International Monetary Fund: Declining Influence or Declining Interest?" in Margaret Karns and Karen Mingst, eds., *The United States and Multilateral Institutions: Patterns of Changing Instrumentality and Interest* (Winchester: Unwin Hyman, 1990).

———. "Multilateralism with Small and Large Numbers." *International Organization* 46, 3 (Summer 1992): 681–708.

———. "Inventing International Relations: International Relations Theory After 1945," in Michael Doyle and G. John Ikenberry, eds., *New Thinking in International Relations Theory* (Boulder, CO: Westview Press, 1997).

Kahn, Joseph. "Clinton Shift on Trade: 'Wake-Up Call,'" *New York Times,* January 21, 2000.

Kanbur, Ravi, and Todd Sandler with Kevin M. Morrison. *The Future of Development Assistance: Common Pools and International Public Goods* (Washington, DC: Overseas Development Council, 1999).

Karns, Margaret P., and Karen A. Mingst. "Continuity and Change in U.S.-IGO Relationships: A Comparative Analysis with Implications for the Future of Multilateralism in U.S. Foreign Policy," in Margaret P. Karns and Karen A. Mingst, eds., *The United States and Multilateral Institutions: Patterns of Changing Instrumentality and Influence* (Boston: Unwin Hyman, 1990).

Karns, Margaret P., and Karen A. Mingst. "The United States and Multilateral Institutions: A Framework for Analysis," in Karns and Mingst, eds., *The United States and Multilateral Institutions: Patterns of Changing Instrumentality and Influence* (Boston: Unwin Hyman, 1990).

Karns, Margaret P., and Karen A. Mingst. "The Past as Prologue: The United States and the Future of the UN System," in Chadwick F. Alger, Gene M. Lyons, and John E. Trent, eds., *The United Nations System: The Policies of Member States* (Tokyo: United Nations University Press, 1995).

Katzenstein, Peter J. "Regionalism in Comparative Perspective," *Cooperation and Conflict* 31 (June 1996): 123–159

_____. "The Cultural Foundations of Murakami's Polymorphic Liberalism," in Kozo Yamamura, ed., *A Vision of a New Liberalism? Critical Essays on Murakami's Anticlassical Analysis* (Stanford, CA: Stanford University Press, 1997).

Kaufman, Natalie Hevener, and David Whiteman. "Opposition to Human Rights Treaties in the United States Senate: The Legacy of the Bricker Amendment," *Human Rights Quarterly* 10 (1988): 309–337.

Kaul, Inge, Isabelle Grunberg, and Marc A. Stern. *Global Public Goods: International Cooperation in the 21st Century* (New York: Oxford University Press, 1999).

Kaufman, Natalie Hevener. *Human Rights Treaties and the Senate: A History of Opposition* (Chapel Hill: University of North Carolina Press, 1990).

Keck, Margaret, and Kathryn Sikkink. *Activists Beyond Borders: Transnational Advocacy Networks in International Politics* (Ithaca, NY: Cornell University Press, 1999).

Keohane, Robert O. *After Hegemony: Cooperation and Discord in the World Political Economy* (Princeton, NJ: Princeton University Press, 1984).

_____. *International Institutions and State Power: Essays in International Relations Theory* (Boulder, CO: Westview Press, 1989).

Keynes, John Maynard (Lord). "The International Clearing Union." Speech delivered to the House of Lords, May 18, 1943. Reprinted in Seymour E. Harris, ed., *The New Economics* (New York: Knopf, 1947).

Kingsbury, Benedict. "Sovereignty and Inequality," in Andrew Hurrell and Ngaire Woods, eds., *Inequality, Globalization, and World Politics* (Oxford: Oxford University Press, 1999).

Kitfield, James. "Episodic Interest," *National Journal* 32, 1 (January 1, 2000): 29.

Kitfield, James, and Steve Hirsch. "In Holbrooke's View, 'We Have a Stake'," *National Journal* 32, 36 (September 2, 2000): 27–30.

Klein, Edith, and EDK Associates. *Becoming Global Citizens: How Americans View the World at the Beginning of the 21st Century* (Boston: Oxfam America, May 2000).

Klotz, Audie, *Norms in International Relations: The Struggle Against Apartheid* (Ithaca, NY: Cornell University Press, 1995).

Knight, Malcolm, Lawrence Schembri, and James Powell. "Reforming the Global Financial Architecture: Just Tinkering Around the Edges?" Paper for Bank of England Conference, May 5–6, 2000.

Knock, Thomas J. *To End All Wars: Woodrow Wilson and the Quest for a New World Order* (New York: Oxford University Press, 1992).

Koh, Harold H. "Transnational Public Law Litigation," *Yale Law Journal* 100, no 3 (1991): 2347–2401.

Kohut, Andrew. "Washington Leaders Wary of Public Opinion" (Washington, DC: Pew Center for People and the Press, April 17, 1998).

Krasner, Stephen D. *Sovereignty: Organized Hypocrisy* (Princeton, NJ: Princeton University Press, 1999).

Krauthammer, Charles, "The Unipolar Moment," *Foreign Affairs* 70, 1 (1990–1991): 23–33.

_____. "A World Imagined: The Flawed Premises of Liberal Foreign Policy," *The New Republic*, March 15, 1999.

Krepon, Michael, and Dan Caldwell, eds. *The Politics of Treaty Ratification* (New York: St. Martin's Press, 1991).

Kristol, William, and Robert Kagan. "Toward a Neo-Reaganite Foreign Policy," *Foreign Affairs* 75, 4 (July/August 1996): 18–32.

Krugman, Paul. "Saving Asia: It's Time to Get Radical," *Fortune*, September 7, 1998.

Kull, Steven. *The Foreign Policy Gap* (College Park, MD: The Center for International Security Studies at the University of Maryland, October 1997).

Kull, Steven, and I. M. Destler. *Misreading the Public: The Myth of a New Isolationism* (Washington, DC: Brookings Institution Press, 1999).

Lake, Anthony. "From Containment to Enlargement," *Vital Speeches of the Day* 60 (October 15, 1993).

———. "Confronting Backlash States," *Foreign Affairs* 73, 2 (March/April 1994): 45–55.

Lake, David A. *Entangling Relations: American Foreign Policy in Its Century* (Princeton, NJ: Princeton University Press, 1999).

Lancaster, Carol. *Transforming Foreign Aid: United States Assistance in the 21st Century* (Washington, DC: Institute for International Economics, August 2000).

———. "Redesigning Foreign Aid," *Foreign Affairs* 79, 5 (September/October 2000): 74–88.

Lane, Charles. "Changing Iran: Germany's New Ostpolitik," *Foreign Affairs* 74, 6 (November/December 1995): 77–89.

Lastra, Rosa Maria. "The International Monetary Fund in Historical Perspective," *Journal of International Economic Law* 3, 3 (September 2000): 507–523.

Laurenti, Jeffrey. "The United Nations and International Security: Dilemmas and Agendas for American Engagement." Prepared for Bipartisan Dialogue on America's National Interests in Multilateral Engagement, James A. Baker III Institute for Public Policy, Rice University, Houston, Texas, April 10, 2000.

LaVera, Damien J. "History and Summary of the CTBT," in Jack Mendelsohn, ed., *White Paper on the Comprehensive Test Ban Treaty* (Washington, DC: Lawyers Alliance for World Security, Fall 2000).

Lecce, D. J. "International Law Regarding Pro-Democratic Intervention: A Study of the Dominican Republic and Haiti," *Naval Law Review* 45 (1998).

Leiderman, Leonardo, and Alfredo E. Thorne. "The 1994 Mexican Financial Crisis and Its Aftermath: What Are the Main Lessons?" in Guillermo A. Calvo, Morris Goldstein, and Eduard Hochreiter, eds., *Private Capital Flows to Emerging Markets after the Mexican Crisis* (Washington, DC: Institute for International Economics and Austrian National Bank, 1996).

Levy, Reynold. *Give and Take: A Candid Account of Coporate Philanthropy* (Cambridge, MA: Harvard Business School Press, 1999).

Levitt, Jeremy. "Humanitarian Intervention by Regional Actors in International Conflicts, and the Cases of ECOWAS in Liberia and Sierra Leone," *Temple International & Comparative Law Journal* 12 (1998).

Lindley-French, Julian. *Leading Alone or Acting Together? The Transatlantic Security Agenda for the Next US Presidency*. Occasional Paper 20, WEU Institute for Security Studies, September 2000.

———. "Why America Needs Europe," Newsletter of the WEU Institute of Security Studies, Paris, October 2000.

Lindsay, James M. "End of an Era: Congress and Foreign Policy after the Cold War," in Eugene R. Wittkopf and James M. McCormick, eds., *The Domestic Sources of American Foreign Policy: Insights and Evidence* (New York: Rowman & Littlefield, 1999).

———. "The New Apathy: How an Uninterested Public is Reshaping Foreign Policy," *Foreign Affairs* 79, 5 (September/October 2000): 2–8.

Lipset, Seymour Martin. "American Exceptionalism Reaffirmed," in Byron Shafer, ed., *Is America Different? A New Look at American Exceptionalism* (Oxford: Clarendon Press, 1991).

Litwak, Robert. S. *Rogue States and U.S. Foreign Policy* (Washington, DC: Woodrow Wilson Center Press, 2000).

Lobel, Jules, and Michael Ratner. "Bypassing the Security Council: Ambiguous Authorizations to Use Force, Ceasefires and the Iraqi Inspection Regime," *American Journal of International Law* 93 (1999).

Losman, Donald. *International Economic Sanctions: The Cases of Cuba, Rhodesia, and Israel* (Albuquerque: University of New Mexico Press, 1979).

Low, Patrick. *Trading Free: The GATT and US Trade Policy* (New York: Twentieth Century Fund, 1993).

Lowenthal, Abraham F. *The Dominican Intervention* (Baltimore: Johns Hopkins University Press, 1972).

Lowi, Theodore. "Making Democracy Safe for the World," in James Rosenau, ed., *Domestic Sources of Foreign Policy* (New York: Free Press, 1969).

Luck, Edward C. "The United Nations, Multilateralism and U.S. Interests." In Charles William Maynes and Richard S. Williamson, eds., *U.S. Foreign Policy and the United Nations System* (New York and London: W. W. Norton, 1996).

―――. *Mixed Messages: American Politics and International Organization, 1919–1999* (Washington, DC: Brookings Institution Press, 1999).

―――. "American Exceptionalism and International Organization: Lessons from the 1990s," in Rosemary Foot, Neil MacFarlane, and Michael Mastanduno, eds., *The US and Multilateral Organizations* (Oxford: Oxford University Press, forthcoming).

Luck, Edward, and Peter Fromuth. "Anti-Americanism at the United Nations: Perception or Reality?," in Alvin Z. Rubinstein and Donald E. Smith, eds., *Anti-Americanism in the Third World: Implications for U.S. Foreign Policy* (New York: Praeger, 1985).

Luers, William H. "Choosing Engagement: Uniting the U.N. with U.S. Interests," *Foreign Affairs* 79, 5 (September/October 2000): 9–14.

Lyman, Princeton N. "Saving the UN Security Council—A Challenge for the United States," *Max Planck Yearbook of United Nations Law* 4 (2000): 127–146.

McDougal, Walter A. *Promised Land, Crusader State: The American Encounter with the World Since 1776* (New York: Houghton Mifflin, 1997).

MacKinnon, Michael G. *The Evolution of US Peacekeeping Policy Under Clinton: A Fairweather Friend?* (London: Frank Cass Publishers, 2000).

Magge, Hema, "Vocal Opposition and Fragmented Support: The US Failure to Ratify the U.N. Convention on the Rights of the Child." Unpublished paper, Harvard University, May 2000.

"Major Breakthroughs at Eleventh Session of the OPCW's Executive Council." Press Release 021/98. (The Hague: Organization for the Prohibition of Chemical Weapons, September 8, 1998).

Malanzcuk, Peter. "The International Criminal Court and Landmines: What Are the Consequences of Leaving the US Behind?" *European Journal of International Law* 11, 1 (2000): 77–90.

Mallaby, Sebastian. "The Irrelevant Election," *Foreign Policy* 120 (September–October 2000): 74–80.

Martin, Lisa. *Coercive Cooperation* (Princeton, NJ: Princeton University Press, 1992).

―――. "The Rational State Choice of Multilateralism," in John Ruggie, ed., *Multilateralism Matters: The Theory and Praxis of an Institutional Form* (New York: Columbia University Press, 1993).

―――. *Democratic Commitments: Legislatures and International Co-operation* (Princeton, NJ: Princeton University Press, 2000).

Maskus, Keith E. *Intellectual Property Rights in the Global Economy* (Washington, DC: Institute for International Economics, 2000).

Mastanduno, Michael. "Economic Statecraft, Interdependence, and National Security: Agendas for Research," *Security Studies* 9, 1, 2 (Autumn 1999/Winter 2000), pp. 288–316.

———. "Trade as a Strategic Weapon," *International Organization* (1988).

———. *Economic Containment: CoCom and the Politics of East-West Trade* (Ithaca, NY: Cornell University Press, 1992).

———. "Preserving the Unipolar Moment: Realist Theories and U.S. Grand Strategy after the Cold War," in Ethan B. Kapstein and Michael Mastanduno, eds., *Unipolar Politics: Realism and State Strategies After the Cold War* (New York: Columbia University Press, 1999).

Mathews, Jessica. "Power Shift," *Foreign Affairs* 76, 1 (January–February 1997): 50–66.

Maynes, Charles William. "America's Fading Commitments," *World Policy Journal* 16, 2 (Summer 1999): 11–22.

———. "America's Fading Commitments to the World," in Martha Honey and Tom Barry, eds., *Global Focus: U.S. Foreign Policy at the Turn of the Millenium* (New York: St. Martin's Press, 2000).

Meltzer, Alan. "Asian Problems and the IMF." Testimony before the Joint Economic Committee of the U.S. Congress, February 24, 1998.

Meltzer Commission. *Report of the International Financial Institution Advisory Commission* (Washington, DC: March 2000).

Mendelsohn, Catherine R. *Arms Control and Disarmament: The U.S. Commitment* (Washington, DC: U.S. Information Agency, 1997).

Mendez, Ruben P. *International Public Finance: A New Perspective on Global Relations* (New York: Oxford University Press, 1992).

Meselson, Matthew, et al. "The Sverdlovsk Anthrax Outbreak of 1979," *Science* 266, 5188 (November 18, 1994): 1202–1208.

Miller, Marcus, and Lei Zhang. "Sovereign Liquidity Crisis: The Strategic Case for a Payments Standstill." Working Paper 99-9 (Washington, DC: Institute for International Economics, 1999).

Milner, Helen. *Interests, Institutions, and Information: Domestic Politics and International Relations* (Princeton, NJ: Princeton University Press, 1997).

Mingst, Karen A., and Margaret P. Karns. *The United Nations in The Post–Cold War Era*, 2nd ed. (Boulder, CO: Westview Press, 2000).

Mitrany, David. *The Progress of International Government* (New Haven, CT: Yale University Press, 1933).

———. "The Functional Approach to International Organization," *International Affairs* 24 (July 1948): 350–363.

Moe, Terry M. "Political Institutions: The Neglected Side of the Story," *Journal of Law, Economics, and Organization* 6 (Special Issue 1990): 213–254.

Molina, Mario J., and F. Sherwood Rowland. "Stratospheric Sink for Chlorofluoromethanes: Chlorine Atomic Catalyzed Destruction of Ozone," *Nature* 249 (1974): 810–812.

Moravcsik, Andrew. *Why the European Community Strengthens the State: International Cooperation and Domestic Politics.* Center for European Studies Working Paper Series 52 (Cambridge, MA: Harvard University, 1994).

———. "Taking Preferences Seriously: A Liberal Theory of International Politics," *International Organization* 51, 4 (Autumn 1997): 513–553.

———. "The Origins of International Human Rights Regimes: Democratic Delegation in Postwar Europe," *International Organization* 54, 2 (Spring 2000): 217–252.

———. "Conservative Idealism and International Institutions," *Chicago Journal of International Law* 1, 2 (Fall 2000): pp. 291–314.

Muravchik, Joshua. *The Uncertain Crusade: Jimmy Carter and the Dilemmas of Human Rights Policy* (Lanham, MD: Hamilton Press, 1986).

Murphy, John F. "Force and Arms," in O. Schacter and C. C. Joyner, eds., *United Nations Legal Order* (Cambridge: Cambridge University Press, 1995).

Murphy, Sean D. "Contemporary Practice of the United States Relating to International Law," *The American Journal of International Law* 94 (April 2000): 348–354.

Naim, Moises. "Lori's War," *Foreign Policy* 119 (Spring 2000): 34–52.

National Intelligence Council. *Global Trends 2015: A Dialogue About the Future with Nongovernmental Experts* (Washington, DC: Central Intelligence Agency, 2000).

National Research Council, Office of International Affairs. *The Pervasive Role of Science, Technology, and Health in Foreign Policy* (Washington DC, National Academy Press, 1999).

Neustadt, Richard E. *Presidential Power: The Politics of Leadership,* rev. ed. (Free Press, 1990).

Neville-Jones, Pauline. "Dayton, IFOR and Alliance Relations," *Survival* 38, 4 (Winter 1996–7): 45–65.

Oakley, Robert B. "Using the United Nations to Advance U.S. Interests," in Ted Galen Carpenter, ed., *Delusions of Grandeur* (Washington, DC: Cato Institute, 1997).

Oakley, Robert, and John Hirsch. *Somalia and Operation Restore Hope* (Washington, DC: U.S. Institute for Peace, 1995).

Odell, John S. *Negotiating the World Economy* (Ithaca, NY: Cornell University Press, 2000).

Office of Richard G. Lugar. "Lugar Criticizes Anti-Chemical Weapons Treaty Campaign: Senator Refutes Flawed, Misleading Foreign Relations Committee Press Release." Media Release, February 3, 1997.

Office of the Secretary of State Resources, Plans and Policy, U.S. Department of State. *Congressional Budget Justification for Foreign Operations, Fiscal Year 2001,* March 15, 2000. Full text available at *http://www.state.gov/www/budget/fy2001/fn150/forops_full/150fy01_fo_global-prog.html*

Olonisakin, Funmi. *Reinventing Peacekeeping in Africa: Conceptual and Legal Issues in ECOMOG Operations* (London: Kluwer Law International, 2000).

Olson, Kyle. "Disarmament and the Chemical Industry," in Brad Roberts, ed., *Chemical Disarmament and U.S. Security* (Boulder, CO: Westview Press, 1992).

OPCW Annual Report 1999 (The Hague: Organization for the Prohibition of Chemical Weapons, 2000).

Ornstein, Norman J., and Shirley Edler. *Interest Groups, Lobbying and Policy-Making* (Washington, DC: Congressional Quarterly Press, 1978).

Overseas Development Council. *The Future Role of the IMF in Development.* ODC Task Force Report. (Washington, DC: Overseas Development Council, 2000).

Oye, Kenneth A. *Economic Discrimination and Political Exchange.* (Princeton, NJ: Princeton University Press, 1992).

Pape, Robert A. "Why Economic Sanctions Do Not Work," *International Security* 22, 2 (Fall 1997): 90–136.

Pastor, Robert A. "The United States: Divided by a Revolutionary Vision," in Robert A. Pastor, ed., *A Century's Journey: How the Great Powers Shaped the World* (New York: Basic Books, 1999).

Patrick, Stewart. "America's Retreat from Multilateral Engagement," *Current History* (December 2000): 430–439.

"Pay Up and Play the Game," *The Economist* 352, 8146 (September 18, 1999): 20.

"Peace-keeping Guidelines Set Out by Security Council," *UN Chronicle* 31, 3 (September 1994): 54.

Perroy, Alain. "The Contribution of the Chemical Industry to the Chemical Weapons Convention." *OPCW Synthesis, Year in Review 2000* (2000): 38–39.

Persaud, Avinash D. "Sending the Herd Off the Cliff: The Disturbing Interaction between Herding and Market-Sensitive Risk Management Practices." First prize, Essay Competition in Honor of Jacques de Larosière (Washington, DC: Institute of International Finance, 2000).

Petersen, Keith S. "The Uses of the Uniting for Peace Resolution since 1950," *International Organization* 13 (1959).

Powlick, Philip J. "The Sources of Public Opinion for American Foreign Policy Officials," *International Studies Quarterly* 39, 4 (December 1995): 427–451.

Preeg, Ernest H. *The Trade Deficit, the Dollar, and the U.S. National Interest* (Indianapolis: Hudson Institute, 2000).

"Presidential Forum: Gore and Bush offer their Views on Science," *Science,* 290 (October 13, 2000): 262–269.

Purcell, Susan Kaufman. "Cuba," in Richard N. Haass, ed., *Economic Sanctions and American Diplomacy* (New York: Council on Foreign Relations, 1998).

Putnam, Robert D. "Diplomacy and Domestic Politics," *International Organization* 42, 3 (Summer 1988): 427–461.

Rabkin, Jeremy. "International Law vs. the American Constitution—Something's Got to Give," *The National Interest* 55 (Spring 1999): 30–41.

———. "Is EU Policy Eroding the Sovereignty of Non-Member States?" *Chicago Journal of International Law* 1, 2 (Fall 2000): 273–290.

Reilly, John E. "Americans and the World: A Survey at Century's End," *Foreign Policy* 114 (Spring 1999): 97–114.

Reinicke, Wolfgang. *Global Public Policy: Governing Without Government?* (Washington, DC: Brookings Institution Press, 1997).

Reisman, W. Michael. "The United States and International Institutions," *Survival* 41, 4 (Winter 1999–2000): 62–80.

———. "Unilateral Action and the Transformations of the World Constitutive Process: The Special Problem of Humanitarian Intervention," *European Journal of International Law* 11, 1 (2000): 3–18.

"Remarks on Signing the Treaty Eliminating Intermediate-Range and Short-Range Nuclear Missiles." *Weekly Compilations of Presidential Documents* 23 (December 8, 1987): 1458.

Rice, Condoleezza. "Campaign 2000—Promoting the National Interest," *Foreign Affairs* 79, 1 (January/February 2000): 45–62.

Richardson, J. David. *U.S. Trade Policy in the 1980s: Turns—and Roads Not Taken.* NBER Working Paper 3725 (Cambridge, MA: National Bureau of Economic Research, 1991).

Rieff, David. "A New Hierarchy of Values and Interests," *World Policy Journal* 16, 3 (Fall 1999): 28–34.

Rimmington, Anthony. "From Military to Industrial Complex? The Conversion of Biological Weapons Facilities in the Russian Federation." *Contemporary Security Policy* 17, 1 (April 1996): 80–112.

Risse, Thomas, Kathryn Sikkink, and Steven Ropp, eds. *The Power of Human Rights: International Norms and Domestic Change* (Cambridge: Cambridge University Press, 1999).

Rodman, Peter W. "The World's Resentment: Anti-Americanism as a Global Phenomenon," *The National Interest* 60 (Summer 2000): 33–41.

Rose, Gideon. "Libya," in Richard N. Haass, ed., *Economic Sanctions and American Diplomacy* (New York: Council on Foreign Relations, 1998).

Rosenau, James, *Along the Domestic-Foreign Frontier* (Cambridge: Cambridge University Press, 1997).

Rosenthal, Douglas E., and William M. Knighton. *National Laws and International Commerce: The Problem of Extraterritoriality.* Chatham House Papers 17, The Royal Institute of International Affairs (London: Routledge and Kegan Paul, 1982).

Rosner, Jeremy D. *The New Tug of War: Congress, the Executive Branch, and National Security* (Washington, DC: Carnegie Endowment for International Peace, 1995).

Roubini, Nouriel. "Bail-In, Burden-Sharing, Private Sector Involvement (PSI) in Crisis Resolution and Constructive Engagement of the Private Sector." Photocopy, Stern School of Business, New York University, September 2000.

Roy, Olivier, Steven Simon, and Daniel Benjamin. "America and the New Terrorism: An Exchange," *Survival* 42, 2 (Summer 2000): 156–161.

Rueckert, George. *Global Double Zero: The INF Treaty from Its Origins to Implementation* (Westport, CT: Greenwood Press, 1993).

Ruggie, John Gerard. "Multilateralism: The Anatomy of an Institution," in John Gerard Ruggie, ed., *Multilateralism Matters: The Theory and Praxis of an Institutional Form* (New York: Columbia University Press, 1993).

———. *Winning the Peace: America and World Order in the New Era* (New York: Columbia University Press, 1996).

———. *Constructing the World Polity: Essays on International Institutionalization* (London and New York: Routledge, 1998)

Russell, Ruth B. *A History of the United Nations Charter: The Role of the United States 1940–1945* (Washington, DC: The Brookings Institution, 1958).

Russett, Bruce. "Ten Balances for Weighing UN Reform Proposals," in Bruce Russett, ed., *The Once and Future Security Council* (New York: St. Martin's Press, 1997).

Scheffer, David J. "Developments at the Rome Treaty Conference." Statement by the ambassador at large for war crimes issues and head of the U.S. delegation to the UN Diplomatic Conference on the Establishment of a Permanent International Criminal Court before the Senate Foreign Relations Committee (*"Scheffer Statement to the Senate"*), Washington, DC; July 23, 1998, Department of State Dispatch, August 1998.

———. "Atrocities Prevention: Lessons from Rwanda." Speech at the Conference on Atrocities Prevention and Response at the United States Holocaust Memorial Museum, October 29, 1999. Full text available at *http://www.usinfo.state.gov/topical/pol/usandun/schef29.htm*

Schiff, Benjamin N. "Dominance Without Hegemony: U.S. Relations with the International Atomic Energy Agency," in Margaret P. Karns and Karen A. Mingst, eds., *The United States and Multilateral Institutions: Patterns of Changing Instrumentality and Influence* (Boston: Unwin Hyman, 1990).

Schiffer, Robert L., and Selma, eds. *Looking Outward: Years of Crisis at the United Nations* (New York: Harper & Row, 1963).

Schlesinger, Arthur, Jr. "America and the World: Isolationism Resurgent?" Louis Nizer Lecture on Public Policy, Carnegie Council on Ethics and International Affairs, New York, December 6, 1995.

Schmandt, Jurgen, Judith Clarkson, and Hilliard Roderick, eds. *Acid Rain and Friendly Neighbors: The Policy Dispute Between Canada and the United States* (Durham, NC: Duke University Press, rev. ed. 1988).

Schweller, Randall L., and David Priess. "A Tale of Two Realisms: Expanding the Institutions Debate," *Mershon International Studies Review* 41 (1997): 1–32.

"Secretary of State Madeleine Albright Discusses Her Visit to Ohio to Get Support from American People for Military Action Against Iraq," NBC News Transcripts, *The Today Show,* February 19, 1998.

Serafino, Nina. *Peacekeeping: Issues of U.S. Military Involvement,* CRS Issue Brief IB94040, Congressional Research Service, January 17, 2001.

Shalikashvili, General John M. (USA, Ret.). *Findings and Recommendations Concerning the Comprehensive Nuclear Test Ban Treaty.* Report of the Special Advisor to the President and the Secretary of State for the Comprehensive Test Ban Treaty, January 2001.

Shambaugh, George E. *States, Firms, and Power: Successful Sanctions in United States Foreign Policy* (Albany: State University of New York Press, 2000).

Shamir, Jacob, and Michael Shamir, "Pluralistic Ignorance Across Issues and Over Time: Information Cues and Biases," *Public Opinion Quarterly* 61, 2 (Summer 1997): 227–260.

Shultz, George P. *Turmoil and Triumph: My Years as Secretary of State* (New York: Charles Scribner's Sons, 1993).

Simma, Bruno, ed. *The Charter of the United Nations: A Commentary* (Oxford: Oxford University Press, 1994).

Slaughter, Anne-Marie. "The Real New World Order," *Foreign Affairs* 76, 5 (September/October 1997): 183–197.

Sloan, Stanley R. "The US Role in a New World Order: Prospects for George Bush's Global Vision" (Washington, DC: Congressional Research Service, March 29, 1991).

———. *The United States and European Defence.* Chaillot Paper 39 (Paris: WEU Institute for Security Studies, 2000).

Sloan, Stanley, Mary Locke, and Casimir Yost. *The Foreign Policy Struggle: Congress and the President in the 1990s and Beyond* (Washington, DC: Georgetown University, Institute for the Study of Diplomacy, Edmund A. Walsh School of Foreign Service, 2000).

Smith, Courtney B. "The United States in the United Nations: A New Opportunity?" Paper presented at the Thirteenth Annual Meeting of the Academic Council on the United Nations System, Oslo, June 16–June 18, 2000.

Smith, James McCall. "The Politics of Dispute Resolution Design: Explaining Legalism in Regional Trade Pacts," *International Organization* 54, 1 (Autumn 2000): 137–180.

Smith, Senator Howard A. *Congressional Record,* 79th Congress, 1st Session, July 27, 1945, pt. 6, p. 8033.

Smith, Tony. *America's Mission: The United States and the Worldwide Struggle for Democracy in the Twentieth Century* (Princeton, NJ: Princeton University Press, 1994).

Smithson, Amy E. "Chemical Inspectors: On the Outside Looking In?" *Bulletin of the Atomic Scientists* 47, 8 (October 1991): 22–25.

———. "Chemical Weapons: The End of the Beginning," *Bulletin of the Atomic Scientists* 48, 8 (October 1992): 36–40.

———. "Tottering Toward a Treaty," *Bulletin of the Atomic Scientists* 48, 6 (July/August 1992): 9–11.

———. "Dateline Washington, DC: Clinton Fumbles the CWC," *Foreign Policy* 99 (Summer 1995): 169–182.

Smouts, Marie-Claude. "International Organizations and Inequality Among States," *International Social Science Journal,* 47, 2 (June 1995): 229–240.

Snidal, Duncan. "IGOs, Regimes, and Cooperation: Challenges for International Relations Theory," in Margaret P. Karns and Karen A. Mingst, eds., *The United*

States and Multilateral Institutions: Patterns of Changing Instrumentality and Influence (Boston: Unwin Hyman, 1990).

Sokolsky, Joel J. "Great Ideals and Uneasy Compromises: The United States Approach to Peacekeeping," *International Journal* vol, (Spring 1995): pp.

Solomon, Robert. *The International Monetary System* (New York: Harper & Row, 1982).

———. *Money on the Move: The Revolution in International Finance Since 1980* (Princeton, NJ: Princeton University Press, 1999).

Soros, George. *The Crisis of Global Capitalism* (New York: Public Affairs, 1998).

Spiro, Peter J. "The New Sovereigntists: American Exceptionalism and Its False Prophets," *Foreign Affairs* 79, 6 (November/December 2000): 9–15.

Speth, James Gustave. "The Plight of the World's Poor," *Foreign Affairs* 78, 3 (May/June 1999): 13–17.

Spring, Baker. "The Chemical Weapons Convention: A Bad Deal for America." The Heritage Foundation, Committee Brief No. 25, April 15, 1996.

———. "Ratifying the Chemical Weapons Convention: American Business Will Pay the Price," The Heritage Foundation, *F.Y.I,* 111 (July 18, 1996).

Statement of Senator Jesse Helms Hearing on the United Nations International Criminal Court, Federal Document Clearing House, Congressional Testimony, July 23, 1998.

Steel, Ronald. *Temptations of a Superpower* (Cambridge, MA: Harvard University Press, 1995).

Stein, Eric. *Thoughts from a Bridge: A Retrospective on New Europe and American Federalism* (Ann Arbor: University of Michigan Press, 2000).

Stiglitz, Joseph E. "Reforming the Global Economic Architecture: Lessons from Recent Crisis," *Journal of Finance* 54, no 4 (August 1999): 1508–1521.

Sterling-Folker, Jennifer. "Between a Rock and a Hard Place: Assertive Multilateralism and Post-Cold War US Foreign Policy Making," in James M. Scott, *After the End: Making Foreign Policy in the Post–Cold War World* (Durham, NC: Duke University Press, 1998).

Stromseth, Jen E. "Rethinking War Powers: Congress, the President, and the United Nations," 81 *Georgetown Law Journal* (1993).

Summers, Lawrence H. "International Financial Crises: Causes, Prevention, and Cures," *American Economic Review: AEA Papers and Proceedings* 90 (May 2000): 1–16.

Temperley, H. W., ed. *A History of the Peace Conference of Paris,* vol. I (London: Oxford University Press, 1920.

Tetlock, Philip E., and Aaron Belkin. *Counterfactual Thought Experiments in World Politics: Logical, Methodological, and Psychological Perspectives.* (Princeton, NJ: Princeton University Press, 1996).

The Chemical Weapons Convention. US Senate. 104th Congress, 2nd session, Executive Report 104-33 (Washington, DC: U.S. Government Printing Office, 1996): 241–352.

"The Chemical Weapons Convention, Constitutionality, and Unwarranted Fears" (issue brief) (Washington, DC: The Henry L. Stimson Center, February 3, 1997).

"The CWC Critics' Case Against Articles X and XI: Nonsense" (issue brief) (Washington, DC: The Henry L. Stimson Center. April 17, 1997).

Thiessen, Mark A., and Mark Leonard. "When Worlds Collide" (debate), *Foreign Policy* (March/April 2001): 64–74.

Thorne, Christopher. "American Political Culture and the End of the Cold War," *Journal of American Studies* 26, 3 (1992): 303–330.

Tonelson, Alan. "What is the National Interest?" *The Atlantic* 268, 1 (July 1991): 35–52.

Towell, Pat. "Aspiring NATO Newcomers Face Long Road to Integration," *Congressional Quarterly,* February 7, 1998.

Traub, James. "Holbrooke's Campaign," *The New York Times Magazine,* March 26, 2000.

Treverton, Gregory. *The Dollar Drain and American Forces in Germany* (Athens: Ohio University Press, 1978).

Tucker, Robert W. "Alone or With Others," *Foreign Affairs* 78, 6 (November/ December 1999): 15–20.

Union of International Associations. *Yearbook of International Organizations, 2000–2001* (Brussels: Union of International Associations, 2000).

UN General Assembly, Special Committee on Peace-keeping Operations. A/AC. 121/PV.15 (August 16, 1965), pp. 6, 7, 8–10, 12.

UN Security Council. *Report by the Secretary-General on the Activities of the Special Commission Established by the Secretary-General Pursuant to Paragraph 9(b) of Resolution 687 (1991).* Document S/1996/848 (New York: United Nations, June 21, 1993).

United Nations. *An Agenda for Peace: Preventive Diplomacy, Peacemaking and Peacekeeping,* A/47/277–S/24111, 17 June 1992. Full text available at *http:// www.un.org/Docs/SG/agpeace.html*

———. *Millennium Summit Multilateral Treaty Framework: An Invitation to Universal Participation* (New York: United Nations, 2000).

———. "Report of the Panel on United Nations Peace Operations," A/55/305, S/2000/809, 2000. Full text available at *http://www.un.org/peace/reports/ peace_operations/*

———. *Report of the Panel on United Nations Peace Operations* (the Brahimi Report), A/55/305-S/2000/809, August 2000.

U.S. Department of Health and Human Services. "Global Strategy: A Healthy World and a Healthy America" (draft document) (Washington, DC: December 2000).

U.S. Department of State. "Advance Appropriations Arrears Request," September 30, 1997.

U.S. General Accounting Office. *Report to the Chairman, Committee on International Relations, House of Representatives, United Nations: Status of US Contributions and Arrears,* GAO/NSIAD-99-187 (Washington, 1999).

———. *Briefing Report to the Chairman, Committee on International Affairs, House of Representatives, United Nations: Cost of Peacekeeping Is Likely to Exceed Current Estimates,* GAO/NSIAD-00-228BR (Washington, DC: 2000).

———. *United Nations Financial Issues and U.S. Arrears,* appendix 4, comments from the Department of State. 1998.

———. *United Nations Reform Initiatives Have Strengthened Operations, but Overall Objectives Have Not Yet Been Achieved* (GAO/NSIAD-OO-150), May 2000.

U.S. House of Representatives. *U.S. Policy in the United Nations: Hearings and Markup Before the House Committee On Foreign Affairs and its Subcommittee On Human Rights and International Organizations, and on International Operations,* 99th Cong., 1st Session, 58 (1985).

U.S. House Commerce, Justice, State, and Judiciary Subcommittee of the Appropriations Committee. *State Department Fiscal Year 1993 Funding Proposal,* 103rd Congress, 3 March 1992.

U.S. House International Security, International Organizations and Human Rights Subcommittee of the Foreign Affairs Committee. *US Participation in UN Peacekeeping Missions,* 103rd Congress, June 24, 1993.

U.S. Senate. Senator Robert Byrd(D-WV), "Carnage in Somalia," 103rd Congress, 1st session, *Congressional Record* (October 4, 1993), vol. 139, 132, S12876.

U.S. Senate Committee on Armed Services. *Military Implications of the Chemical Weapons Convention.* 103rd Congress, 2nd session, S.Hrg. 103-835 (Washington, DC: U.S. Government Printing Office. 1994).

————. *U.S. Military Operations in Somalia,* Hearings, May 12, 1994, 103rd Congress, 2nd session (U.S. Government Printing Office, 1994).

U.S. Senate Committee on Foreign Relations. *International Human Rights Treaties: Hearings Before the Committee on Foreign Relations,* 96th Congress, 1st Session on Ex. C, D, E, and F, 95-2—Four Treaties Relating to Human Rights, November 14, 15, 16, and 19, 1979 (1980).

————. *Chemical Weapons Convention Hearings.* 103rd Congress, 2nd session, S.Hrg. 103-869. (Washington, DC: U.S. Government Printing Office, 1984).

————. *International Covenant on Civil and Political Rights: Hearing Before the Committee on Foreign Relations,* 102nd Congress, 1st Session, November 21, 1991 (1992).

————. *United Nations Reforms,* 107th Congress, January 9, 2001.

Van der Vyver, J. D. "Universality and Relativity of Human Rights: American Relativism," *Buffalo Human Rights Law Review* (1998): 64–66.

Van Eekelen, Wim. *Debating European Security: 1948–1998* (The Hague: SDU Publishers, 1998).

Vogelgesang, Sandy. *American Dream, Global Nightmare: The Dilemma of U.S. Human Rights Policy* (New York: W. W. Norton, 1980).

"Votkinsk Portal Monitoring System: System Description" (Albuquerque, NM: Sandia National Laboratories, June 16, 1989).

Wallace, William. "From the Atlantic to the Bug, from the Arctic to the Tigris? The Transformation of the EU and NATO," *International Affairs* 76, 3 (July 2000): 475–494.

————. "Issue Linkage Among Atlantic Governments," *International Affairs* (April 1976): 163–179.

Wallace, William, and Jan Zielonka. "Misunderstanding Europe," *Foreign Affairs* 77, 6 (November–December 1998): 65–79.

Walt, Stephen. "Two Cheers for Clinton's Legacy," *Foreign Affairs* 79, 2 (March/April 2000): 63–79.

Waltz, Kenneth N. *Theory of International Politics* (Reading, MA: Addison-Wesley, 1979).

Watson, Robert T., Marufu C. Zinyowera, Richard H. Moss, and David J. Dokken. *Climate Change 1995: Impacts, Adaptations and Mitigation of Climate Change: Scientific-Technical Analyses: Contribution of Working Group II to the Second Assessment Report of the Intergovernmental Panel on Climate Change* (Cambridge: Cambridge University Press, 1996).

Weber, Steve. "Shaping the Postwar Balance of Power: Multilateralism in NATO," in John Ruggie, ed., *Multilateralism Matters: The Theory and Praxis of an Institutional Form* (New York: Columbia University Press, 1993).

Wedgwood, Ruth. "Fiddling in Rome: America and the International Criminal Court," *Foreign Affairs* 77, 6 (November/December 1998): 20–24.

———. "Courting Disaster: The US Takes a Stand," *Foreign Service Journal* 77, 3 (March 2000): 34–41.

———. "NATO's Campaign in Yugoslavia," *American Journal of International Law* 93 (1999).

———. "The Enforcement of Security Council Resolution 687: The Threat of Force Against Iraq's Weapons of Mass Destruction," *American Journal of International Law* 92 (1998).

———. "Responding to Terrorism: The Strikes Against bin Laden," *Yale Journal of International Law* 24 (1999).

Weller, Mark. "The US, Iraq, and the Use of Force in a Unipolar World," *Survival* 41, 4 (Winter 1999–2000), 81–100.

Weyant, John. *An Introduction to the Economics of Climate Change* (Washington, DC: Pew Center on Climate Change, 2000).

White House. "The President's News Conference," October 14, 1993, *Weekly Compilation of Presidential Documents* 29, 39 (1993): 2068.

———. "Remarks of President Clinton to the 48th Session of the United Nations General Assembly in New York City," 27 September 1993, *Weekly Compilation of Presidential Documents* 29, 39 (1993): 1901.

———. *A National Security Strategy of Engagement and Enlargement* (Washington, DC: The White House, February 1995).

White House Office of the Press Secretary. *International Education Policy* (Oklahoma City: April 19, 2000).

———. "Press Briefing by National Security Advisor Tony Lake and Director for Strategic Plans and Policy General Wesley Clark." 5 May 1994: *http://www.pub.whitehouse.gov/uri-res/I2R?urn:pdi://oma.eop.gov.us/1994/5/5/6.text.1*

Williams, Phil. "Multilateralism: Critique and Appraisal," in Michael Brenner, ed., *Multilateralism and Western Strategy* (London: St. Martins, 1995).

Williams, Stacy. "Billion Dollar Donations: Should the United Nations Look a Gift Horse in the Mouth?" *The Georgia Journal of International and Comparative Law* 27, 2 (Spring 1999): 425–455.

Williamson, John, ed. *The Political Economy of Policy Reform* (Washington, DC: Institute for International Economics, 1994).

———. "The Role of the IMF: A Guide to the Reports." Policy Brief 00-5 (Washington, DC: Institute for International Economics, 2000).

Wippman, David. "Enforcing the Peace: ECOWAS and the Liberian Civil War," in L. Damrosch, ed., *Enforcing Restraint: Collective Intervention in Internal Conflicts* (Washington: Brookings Institution, 1993).

Woods, Ngaire. "Order, Globalization, and Inequality in World Politics," in Andrew Hurrell and Ngaire Woods, eds., *Inequality, Globalization, and World Politics* (Oxford: Oxford University Press, 1999).

World Trade Organization. "10 Benefits of the WTO Trading System," *http://www.wto.org*

Yates, Lawrence A. *Power Pack: Intervention in the Dominican Republic, 1965–1966* (Ft. Leavenworth, KS: U.S. Army Command and Staff College, Combat Studies Institute, 1988).

Zeman, Laurinda. *Making Peace while Staying Ready for War: The Challenges of U.S. Military Participation in Peace Operations.* CBO Paper, Congressional Budget Office, December 1999.

Zilinskas, Raymond A. "Iraq's Biological Weapons: The Past as Future?" *Journal of the American Medical Association* 278, 5 (August 6, 1997): 418–421.

Zoellick, Robert. "Congress and the Making of US Foreign Policy," *Survival* 41, 4 (Winter 1999–2000): 20–41.

———. "Campaign 2000—A Republican Foreign Policy," *Foreign Affairs* 79, 1 (January-Spring 2000): 63–78.

Zoller, Elizabeth. "The 'Corporate Will' of the United Nations and the Rights of the Minority," *American Journal of International Law* 81, 3 (July 1987): 610–634.

The Contributors

Bartram Brown is professor of law at the Chicago-Kent College of Law of the Illinois Institute of Technology. He is author of *The United States and the Politicization of the World Bank: Issues of International Law and Policy;* his many other works include "Primacy or Complementarity: Reconciling the Jurisdiction of National Courts and International Criminal Tribunals," *Yale Journal of International Law,* and "Humanitarian Intervention at a Crossroads," *William & Mary Law Review.*

Kimberly Ann Elliot is research fellow at the Institute for International Economics and adjunct professor at the School of Advanced International Studies, Johns Hopkins University. Her recent publications include *Can International Labor Standards Improve Under Globalization?; Economic Sanctions Reconsidered; Corruption and the Global Economy*; and *Reciprocity and Retaliation in US Trade Policy.*

Shepard Forman is founder and director of the Center on International Cooperation at New York University. Dr. Forman was previously director of the Ford Foundation's Human Rights and Governance and International Affairs programs. He is the author of *The Brazilian Peasantry;* editor of *Diagnosing America: Anthropology and Public Engagement;* and coeditor (with Stewart Patrick) of *Good Intentions: Pledges of Aid for Post-Conflict Recovery* and (with Romita Ghosh) *Promoting Reproductive Health: Investing in Health for Development.*

Thomas Graham Jr. is president of the Lawyers Alliance for World Security. He served as the special representative of the president for arms control, non-proliferation, and disarmament with the rank of ambassador from 1994 to 1997, leading U.S. government efforts to achieve a permanent Nuclear Non-Proliferation Treaty. He was acting director of the U.S. Arms Control and Disarmament Agency from 1993 to 1994 and was ACDA general counsel for fourteen years.

Gary Clyde Hufbauer is Reginald Jones senior fellow at the Institute for International Economics. Previously he was Marcus Wallenberg professor of international financial diplomacy at Georgetown University and Maurice Greenberg chair at the Council on Foreign Relations. He has coauthored *World Capital Markets: Challenge to the G-10* and *Economic Sanctions Reconsidered.*

G. John Ikenberry is the Peter F. Krogh professor of global justice at Georgetown University, with an appointment in both the Edmund A. Walsh School of Foreign Service and the Government Department. He is the author of *After Victory: Institutions, Strategic Restraint, and the Rebuilding of Order after Major Wars;* editor of *American Unipolarity and the Future of the Balance of Power;* and coeditor of U.S. *Democracy Promotion: Impulses, Strategies, and Impacts.*

Harold K. Jacobson was Jesse Siddal Reeves professor of political science and Senior Research Scientist at the Center for Political Studies at the University of Michigan. Dr. Jacobson wrote widely on the origins, functioning, activities, and consequences of international institutions. He was coeditor of *Engaging Countries: Strengthening Compliance with International Environmental Accords* and *Double-Edged Diplomacy: International Bargaining and Domestic Politics.*

Margaret P. Karns is professor of political science at the University of Dayton. She has written on peacekeeping, global governance, and ad hoc multilateral diplomacy. With Karen Mingst, she is coeditor of *The United States and Multilateral Institutions: Patterns of Instrumentality and Influence,* and coauthor of *The United Nations in the Post–Cold War Era* and *Networks of International Organizations: The Politics and Processes of Global Governance.*

Steven Kull is director of the Program on International Policy Attitudes at the University of Maryland. As a political psychologist who studies public attitudes on international issues, he regularly briefs government officials in the United States and abroad. His most recent book (coauthored with I. M. Destler) is *Misreading the Public: The Myth of a New Isolationism.*

Damien J. LaVera is senior programs and communications director for the Lawyers Alliance for World Security. Mr. LaVera previously worked in the Office of General John M. Shalikashvili, special advisor to the president and secretary of state for the Comprehensive Test Ban Treaty at the U.S. Department of State. He has written a wide variety of nuclear nonproliferation-related issues.

Edward C. Luck is director of the Center on International Organizations and Institutions and professor at the School of International and Public

Affairs at Columbia University. Formerly, he was executive director of the Center for the Study of International Organization at the NYU School of Law and the Woodrow Wilson School of Princeton University. A past president of the United Nations Association of the U.S.A., he is author of *Mixed Messages: American Politics and International Organization 1919–1999*.

Princeton N. Lyman is executive director of the Global Interdependence Initiative at the Aspen Institute. He served in the U.S. government as assistant secretary of state for international organization affairs, and ambassador to Nigeria and to South Africa. He has directed the project America's National Interests in Multilateral Engagement: A Bipartisan Dialogue for the Overseas Development Council, and published articles on UN Security Council reform, peacekeeping, U.S. foreign policy, international health, Africa, and Asia.

Michael Mastanduno is professor of government at Dartmouth College. Dr. Mastanduno is author of "Economic Statecraft, Interdependence, and National Security," in *Security Studies,* "Preserving the Unipolar Moment: US Grand Strategy after the Cold War," in *International Security,* and *Economic Containment: CoCom and the Politics of East-West Trade.* He edited *Unipolar Politics: Realism and State Strategies After the Cold War.*

Karen A. Mingst is professor in the Department of Political Science at the University of Kentucky (Lexington). She wrote *Essentials of International Relations* and *Politics and the African Development Bank.* She is the co-author of *The United Nations in the Post-Cold War World* and coeditor of *The United States and Multilateral Institutions; Teaching International Affairs with Cases;* and *Essential Readings in World Politics.*

Andrew Moravcsik is professor of government and director of the European Union Center at Harvard University. He wrote *The Choice for Europe* and, as head of a Council on Foreign Relations project, edited *Centralization or Fragmentation?* His research covers regional integration, international human rights, and international relations theory.

Stewart Patrick is research associate at the Center on International Cooperation at New York University, where he is also adjunct professor of political science. An international affairs fellow of the Council on Foreign Relations for 2001/2002, he is the coeditor of *Good Intentions: Pledges of Aid for Post-Conflict Recovery.*

Sarah B. Sewall is program director at the Carr Center for Human Rights Policy at Harvard's Kennedy School of Government and adjunct lecturer at the Kennedy School. From 1993 to 1996 she served as deputy assistant secretary of defense for peacekeeping. She is coeditor of *The United States* *and the International Criminal Court: National Security and International Law.*

Amy E. Smithson is senior associate and director of the Chemical and Biological Weapons Nonproliferation Project at the Henry L. Stimson Center. Dr. Smithson coedited *Open Skies, Arms Control, and Cooperative Security.*

William Wallace (Lord Wallace of Saltaire) is professor of international relations at the London School of Economics and former Walter F. Hallstein fellow of St. Antony's College, Oxford. As a member of the House of Lords, Dr. Wallace speaks for the Liberal Democratic Party on foreign affairs and defense. He wrote *The Transformation of Western Europe* and is coeditor of *Policy-Making in the European Union* and *Regional Integration: The West European Experience.*

Ruth Wedgwood is professor of law at Yale University, senior fellow at the Council on Foreign Relations, and a member of the secretary of state's advisory committee on international law. In 2001–2002, she will be the Edward Burling Professor of International Law and Diplomacy at the Johns Hopkins School of Advanced International Studies. She is author of *The Use of Force in International Affairs* and editor of a symposium on "State Reconstruction After Civil Conflict."

Index

About the Book

WHEN SHOULD THE UNITED STATES COOPERATE WITH OTHERS IN CONFRONTING global problems? Why is the United States often ambivalent about multilateral cooperation? What are the costs of acting alone? These are some of the timely questions addressed in this examination of the role of multilateralism in U.S. foreign policy.

The authors isolate a number of factors that help to explain U.S. reluctance to commit to multilateral cooperation. They then analyze recent policy in specific areas—e.g., the use of force, peacekeeping, arms control, human rights, the United Nations, sanctions, international trade, environmental protection—probing the causes and consequences of U.S. decisions to act alone or opt out of multilateral initiatives. A concluding chapter underscores the point that increasingly pressing transnational problems may require the U.S. to reform its policymaking structures and to reconsider longstanding assumptions about national sovereignty and freedom of action.

Stewart Patrick is research associate at the Center on International Cooperation (CIC) at New York University. He is coeditor (with Shepard Forman) of *Good Intentions: Pledges of Aid for Postconflict Recovery*. **Shepard Forman** is founder and director of CIC. Previously, he was director of the Ford Foundation's Human Rights and Governance and International Affairs programs. His publications include *Diagnosing America: Anthropology and Public Engagement*.